The SAGE Handbook of

Transport Studies

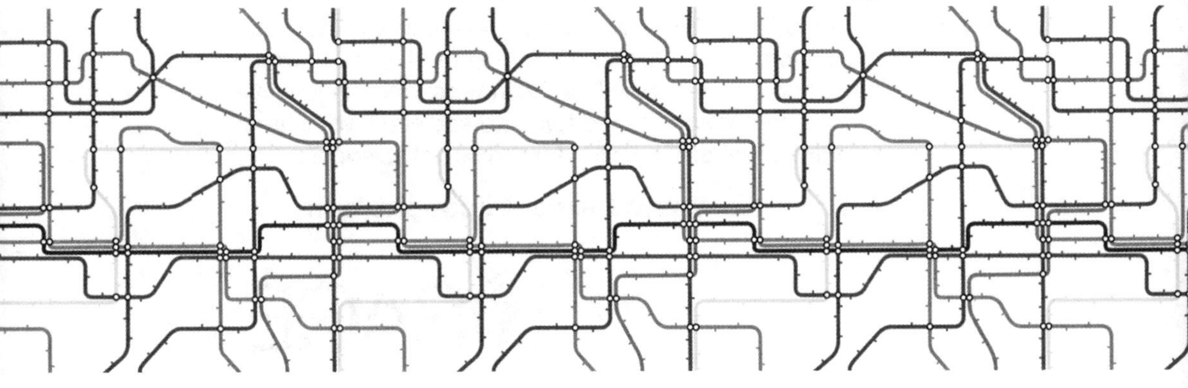

The SAGE Handbook of

Transport Studies

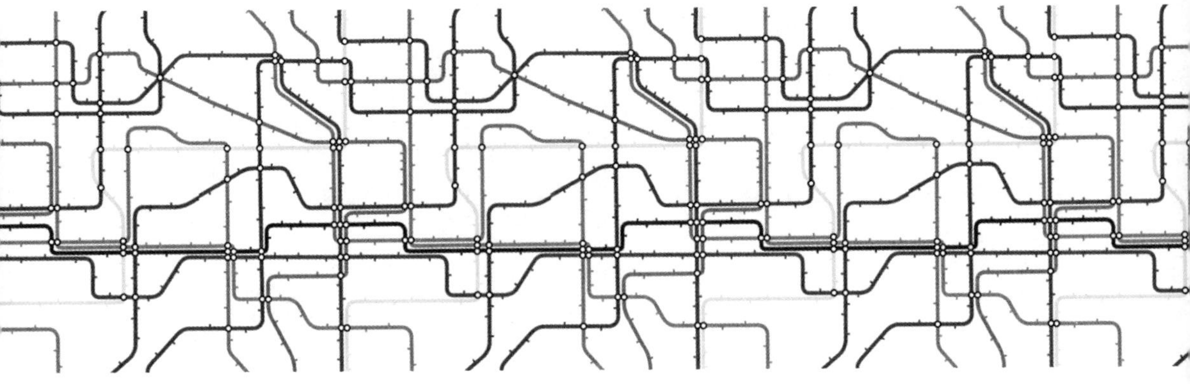

Edited by
Jean-Paul Rodrigue,
Theo Notteboom
and Jon Shaw

Los Angeles | London | New Delhi
Singapore | Washington DC

Los Angeles | London | New Delhi
Singapore | Washington DC

SAGE Publications Ltd
1 Oliver's Yard
55 City Road
London EC1Y 1SP

SAGE Publications Inc.
2455 Teller Road
Thousand Oaks, California 91320

SAGE Publications India Pvt Ltd
B 1/I 1 Mohan Cooperative Industrial Area
Mathura Road
New Delhi 110 044

SAGE Publications Asia-Pacific Pte Ltd
3 Church Street
#10-04 Samsung Hub
Singapore 049483

Editor: Robert Rojek
Editorial assistant: Alana Clogan
Production editor: Katherine Haw
Project manager: Jill Birch
Copyeditor: Jill Birch
Proofreader: David Hemsley
Indexer: Gary Birch
Marketing manager: Michael Ainsley
Cover design: Wendy Scott
Typeset by: C&M Digitals (P) Ltd, Chennai, India
Printed by: Henry Ling Limited at the Dorset Press, Dorchester, DT1 1HD

First published 2013

Library of Congress Control Number: 2012945287

British Library Cataloguing in Publication data

A catalogue record for this book is available from the British Library

ISBN 978-1-84920-789-8

Contents

List of Contributors

William P. Anderson, University of Windsor, Canada – Dr Anderson received his doctorate in geography from Boston University in 1984 and acts as Ontario Research Chair in Cross-Border Transportation Policy, Founding Director of the Cross-Border Transportation Centre and Professor in the Department of Political Science at the University of Windsor. His main research interests are in transportation studies, international trade and business, Canada–US economic integration, energy and environmental studies, and urban and regional economic analysis.

Hugh Annett, Bristol City Council and NHS Bristol, England – Dr Annett is the Joint Director of Public Health for Bristol City Council and NHS Bristol. He is responsible for public health policy in Bristol, ensuring a coordinated approach between health and local government, and for driving improvement in the health of the population. Dr Annett is a Visiting Professor at the University of the West of England, Research Fellow at the School of Social and Community Medicine, University of Bristol and a NHS representative on the NICE Appeal Committee. Dr Annett has lived and worked in various regions of the world and maintains his engagement with global health issues through teaching, research and consultancy.

Christopher Berridge, The Open University, England – Dr Berridge is a Chartered Engineer (C.Eng.) and member of the Institution of Engineering and Technology (MIET). His PhD, investigating the design of the distribution system for hydrogen-powered vehicles, was awarded in Autumn 2010. Chris's specific research interests are the costs, efficiency and environmental issues associated with the development of hydrogen supply infrastructure that will be needed for any future hydrogen-based economy for vehicle fuel.

Michiel C.J. Bliemer, University of Sydney, Australia – Michiel holds a Chair in Transport and Logistics Network Modeling at the Institute for Transport and Logistics Studies. In the past 10 years, he has published over 200 scientific articles in peer-reviewed journals, books and conference proceedings, and is an active member of the network modelling and survey methods committees at the Transportation Research Board (USA), the innovative methods committee at ETC (Europe), and the scientific board of the DTA conference. His recent research has focused on experimental designs for stated choice surveys, which in cooperation with colleagues has led to the Ngene software for generating experimental designs.

John T. Bowen, Jr, Central Washington University, USA – Dr Bowen joined CWU in 2008 after 10 years teaching at the University of Wisconsin-Oshkosh. A native of New England, John graduated with a BA from Dartmouth College in 1988 and a PhD from the University of Kentucky in 1993. Apart from his work in academia, Dr Bowen was a cargo marketing executive at Singapore Airlines' headquarters in Singapore for three years in the 1990s. As an economic geographer and a transportation geographer, his particular areas of expertise include the airline industry, the aircraft industry and Southeast Asia.

Lee Chapman, University of Birmingham, England – a Senior Lecturer in the School of Geography, Earth and Environmental Sciences, Dr Chapman has research interests related to the impact of weather and climate on the built environment. Current areas of particular interest are urban climatology and infrastructure meteorology with a focus on adapting transport and energy networks to cope with increasing levels of urban heat. His latest book *Transport and Climate Change* was published in 2012, and he remains actively involved in consultancy work with a range of industrial partners.

Claude Comtois, Université de Montréal, Canada – Dr Comtois is professor of geography at Montreal University. He is affiliated with the Research Centre on Enterprise Networks, Logistics and Transportation of Montreal University. He has extensive experience as transport project director for the Canadian International Development Agency in China. His teaching and research are centred on transport systems with an emphasis on shipping and ports. He is the author or the co-author of over 100 scientific publications and 250 communications. He currently supervises projects on the competitiveness of port systems, on environmental changes and the resilience of transport infrastructures, and on the development of logistics platforms.

Matthew Cook, The Open University, England – Dr Cook is a Lecturer in Design and Innovation. He joined the Open University in October 2009 after previously working at Cranfield University as lecturer in Economic Geography and Planning and in UK local government as a spatial planner and cartographer. Matthew's research interests are in design, innovation and transformation to sustainable development. His research focuses on spatiality and power associated with these topics; as such, he draws upon and makes connections between literature of several related fields including science and technology studies, innovation studies, urban studies and spatial planning.

Laetitia Dablanc – Dr Dablanc is Director of Research at the French Institute of Science and Technology for Transport, Development and Networks (IFSTTAR). Her areas of research are freight transportation, freight and the environment, urban freight and logistics, rail freight, freight transport policies. She is a member of the steering committee of the World Conference on Transport Research Society and a member of the Urban Freight Committee of the Transportation Research Board (USA). She received a PhD in transportation planning from Ecole des Ponts-ParisTech, and a Master's degree in city and regional planning from Cornell University. She was initially trained in policy analysis and economics at Science Po Paris. She is currently working on logistics sprawl issues and freight transportation planning in US and European mega regions. For that, Laetitia was a visiting scholar at the Georgia Institute of Technology (2010–2011) and the University of Southern California/METRANS (2011–2012).

Adrian Davis, FFPH, NHS Bristol, England – Adrian Davis investigates the relationships between road transport and health. A founder member of the Transport and Health Study Group in 1988, Adrian has been a consultant to WHO Europe, the UK Department of Health, and other public bodies. He has a first degree in history and sociology, and a PhD in inter-sectoral collaboration on transport and health. He is a Visiting Professor at the University of the West of England.

Iain Docherty, University of Glasgow, Scotland – Professor Docherty is Head of the Department of Management at the University of Glasgow. His research and teaching address the interconnecting issues of public management, institutional change and regional competitiveness. He has authored and edited six books on transport issues and held a number of advisory roles including Non-Executive Director of Transport Scotland. He also served as a member of the UK Commission for Integrated Transport's Expert Academic Panel.

César Ducruet, Université Paris 1 Panthéon-Sorbonne, France – since 2009 Dr Ducruet has worked as a Research Fellow for the French National Centre for Scientific Research (CNRS) in the Géographie-Cités research unit. His research interests include transport networks, territorial integration and spatial analysis, from the perspective of urban-port development and maritime networks. He gives regular lectures in Asia and Europe, and is currently involved in several research projects on port cities and maritime networks such as ESPON-TIGER and Marie Curie ERG (Europe), OECD (expert) and CNRS-PE/PS (France).

Antoine Frémont, Université de Paris-Est, France – Dr Frémont is a Director of Research at the French Institute of Science and Technology for Transport, Development and Networks (IFSTTAR). He is an economic geographer and graduated from Le Havre University (PhD, 1996) and Paris Panthéon-Sorbonne University (Accreditation to Supervise Research, 2005). His main research interest is researching the role of shipping lines in globalization: the organization of their maritime networks, their involvement in inland services and their role in the logistics chain. He currently holds the position of project manager for territorial planning at Reseau Ferre de France, the French railway infrastructure manager.

David Gillen, University of British Columbia, Canada – Professor Gillen graduated in 1975 from the University of Toronto with a PhD in Economics. He currently holds the positions of YVR Professor of Transportation Policy in the Sauder School of Business and Director of the Centre for Transportation Studies. In addition he is a Research Economist at the Institute of Transportation Studies at the University of California, Berkeley. Professor Gillen has published over 100 books, technical reports, journal papers, conference presentations and other articles in various areas of transportation economics, including airline competition and industry structure, airport economics and noise externalities, and transportation policy in Canada and the United States.

Markus Hesse, University of Luxembourg, Luxembourg – Professor Hesse is an urban and economic geographer, with an academic background in spatial planning and in human geography. His research interests are clustered around urban and regional development; economic networks, mobilities and flows; metropolitan governance, policy and planning; and discourse analysis. Areas of empirical investigation include metropolitan regions in Western Europe and North America. Professor Hesse is an elected member of the Academy of Spatial Research and Regional Planning (ARL) in Germany; a board member of BIVEC-GIBET, the Benelux Association of Transport Researchers; and active as an expert for organizations such as OECD and others.

Pushkin Kachroo, University of Nevada, Las Vegas, USA – a Professor in the Department of Electrical and Computer Engineering and Director of the Transportation Research Center, Pushkin's research interests in areas such as Artificial Intelligence, signal processing and filtering, and software and systems engineering have direct transport systems and transportronics applications. He is currently involved in numerous research endeavors, including on incident management and I-15 project analysis.

Rob Konings, Delft University of Technology, The Netherlands – Dr Konings is senior researcher at OTB Research Institute of Delft University of Technology. He is an economist with specialization in spatial and transport economics. He has been involved in many different research projects regarding passenger and freight transport. His main research expertise is freight transport with a focus on intermodal transport and related topics. In recent years he has extended his working field to sustainability issues regarding transport systems, including the analysis and evaluation of innovations in transport systems.

Ekki Kreutzberger, Delft University of Technology, The Netherlands – after studying at the Technical Universities of Karlsruhe, Delft and Berlin, Dr Kreutzberger has worked in numerous fields including urban and regional planning, the evaluation of European development projects, industrial sector analysis, regional housing programming, national income distribution statistics, strategic and tactical traffic policy development, freight networks and nodes, intermodal rail transport, and the bundling of flows. Since 1989 he has been affiliated with the OTB Research Institute at the Technical University of Delft. He has initiated and coordinated the R&D projects TERMINET and Twin hub network (currently running) and contributed to LIIIFT and Havenspoor Rotterdam.

Per-Anders Langendahl, The Open University, England – Per-Anders is a PhD research student in the Design and Innovation Group. He was educated at the Swedish University for Agricultural Sciences (SLU) and Cranfield University, where he obtained an MSc in Environmental Management for Business. Per-Anders joined the Open University in October 2009 to complete his PhD project, entitled 'An ethnographic study of an environmental innovation journey in a firm from the UK food and farming sector'.

Karen Lucas, University of Oxford, England – Dr Lucas is a Senior Research Fellow in the Transport Studies Unit. Karen has established an international reputation for her research into the role of transport in social exclusion and has presented and published extensively on this topic. In 2002, she was seconded to the UK Government's Social Exclusion Unit (SEU) to act as a policy advisor on their study of transport and social exclusion, and has subsequently worked with the Department for Transport to develop guidance for the implementation of accessibility planning.

Igor Lugo, National Autonomous University of Mexico, Mexico – a Research Professor at the Regional Center for Multidisciplinary Research (CRIM), Dr Lugo's interests are in urban and regional economics industrial organization, transport networks, complex systems, spatial econometrics and geomatics. Recent projects in France and Mexico have involved the study of the evolution of cities based on nonlinear systems applying agent-based models; the analysis of road and port networks using graph theory and complex networks; and the assessment of production spillover effects using a vector-based cellular automata model.

Danny MacKinnon – Professor MacKinnon is based in the Centre for Urban and Regional Development Studies (CURDS) and the School of Geography, Politics and Sociology, Newcastle University, England. He is also an Editor of *Urban Studies*. His main research interests are in regional economic development, governance and devolution. He publishes regularly on these topics and has had a pivotal involvement in major research projects assessing all three issues in relation to transport policy and provision. He has authored and edited four books, including the acclaimed textbook *An Introduction to Economic Geography* (with Andrew Cumbers).

Bryan Matthews, University of Leeds, England – Bryan is a Senior Research Fellow at the Institute for Transport Studies working on transport research and consultancy projects that encompass pricing and regulation, accessibility and inclusion, travel behavior, and investment appraisal. Clients include the European Commission, the British Disability Rights Commission, the European Conference of Ministers of Transport, the Community of European Railways and the UK Department for Transport.

Patricia L. Mokhtarian, University of California Davis, USA – Dr Mokhtarian is Professor of Civil and Environmental Engineering, the Associate Director for Education of the Institute of Transportation Studies, and Chair of the Interdisciplinary Graduate Program in Transportation Technology and Policy. She specializes in the application of quantitative methods to the study of travel behavior, authoring or co-authoring more than 160 refereed journal articles, technical reports and other publications. One of her key research interests has been the impact of telecommunications technology on travel behavior.

Chris Nash, University of Leeds, England – Professor Nash works in the Institute of Transport Studies and has acted as advisor to many bodies, including the European Commission High Level Group on Transport Infrastructure Charging, the European Union Committee of the House of Lords, the Transport Committee of the House of Commons and the Railways Group of the European Conference of Ministers of Transport. He is a member of the Editorial Board of the *Journal of Transport Policy and Economics* (of which he is a former editor), the *South African Journal of Transportation and Supply Chain Management*, the *International Journal of Transport Economics* and the *International Journal of Green Economics*.

Theo Notteboom, University of Antwerp, Belgium – Professor Notteboom is President of the Institute of Transport & Maritime Management Antwerp (ITMMA). He also holds a part-time Professorship in Maritime Transport at the Antwerp Maritime Academy as well as visiting positions at Dalian Maritime University in China and the World Maritime University in Sweden. He currently is President of the International Association of Maritime Economists (IAME) and chairman of the Board of Directors of Belgian Institute of Transport Organizers (BITO). He has received six awards for his academic work from organizations such as the International Association of Ports and Harbors and is a fellow of the Belgian Royal Academy of Overseas Sciences.

Kaan Özbay, Rutgers University, USA – Professor Özbay is the founding director of the Rutgers Intelligent Transportation Systems (RITS) laboratory. His research interest in transportation includes modeling and deployment of incident and emergency management operations, real-time control techniques for traffic, and field evaluation of advanced ITS technology applications. Professor Özbay is the recipient of the prestigious National Science Foundation (NSF) CAREER award, and since 1994 has been the Principal Investigator and/or Co-Principal Investigator of 71 projects valued at more than $10,500,000 by, among others, the National Science Foundation and the US Department of Transport.

Stephen Potter, The Open University, England – as Professor of Transport Strategy, Stephen undertakes work on the design processes involved for the diffusion of cleaner transport technologies, cleaner vehicle technologies (including participation in the Milton Keynes electric vehicle project) and sustainable travel behavior. This also includes work on specific topics such as travel plans and the design of transport environmental taxation. He is also engaged in studies of other sustainable design issues.

Jean-Paul Rodrigue, Hofstra University, USA – Dr Rodrigue received a PhD in Transport Geography from the Université de Montréal in 1994 and has been a Professor at Hofstra University since 1999. Dr Rodrigue's research interests mainly cover the fields of transportation and economics as they relate to logistics and global freight distribution. Areas of interest involve North America, Latin America and the Caribbean, and East and Southeast Asia.

Specific topics on which he has published extensively cover maritime transport systems and logistics, global supply chains and production networks, and gateways and transport corridors.

Tim Ryley, Loughborough University, England – Dr Ryley is a Senior Lecturer in Transport Studies within the Transport Studies Group, in the School of Civil and Building Engineering. He has over 17 years of transport research experience, with expertise in travel behaviour analysis, and transport and climate change issues, across a range of transport applications. Dr Ryley has recently been the principal investigator on two multi-disciplinary EPSRC projects concerning airport surface access and demand responsive transport. His edited book, *Transport and Climate Change*, was published in 2012.

Jon Shaw, Plymouth University, England – Professor Shaw holds a chair in Transport Geography and is Director of the Centre for Sustainable Transport. He has particular research interests in issues of transport governance and policy, and the intersection of transport geography and the new mobilities paradigm. He has authored and/or edited eight books within the general area of transport geography, and has served as Associate Editor of the *Journal of Transport Geography* and Chair of the Transport Geography Research Group. He has held a number of advisory positions, including that of Specialist Adviser to the UK House of Commons' Transport Committee.

Neveen Shlayan, University of Nevada Las Vegas, USA – Dr Shlayan holds an Assistant Research Professorship sponsored by National Security Technologies. She was formerly a Researcher at the Singapore-MIT Alliance for Research and Technology and at the Transportation Research Center at UNLV. Among other things, she has worked on various aspects of modeling and analysis of transport networks, real-time data processing, simulation and software development.

Brian Slack, Concordia University, Canada – Professor Slack's research focus is on container shipping, notably the relationships between container shipping networks and logistics and the ability of intermediate hubs to attract logistics activities. He also has an interest in bulk shipping. Recently, he has been working on projects for Transport Canada on developing performance indicators for Canadian bulk terminals, and on assessing the implications for Canadian bulk ports of the rapid upscaling in ship sizes in the world fleet.

Gil Tal, University of California Davis, USA – a post-doctoral researcher in the Plug-in, Hybrid & Electric Vehicle Research Center of the Institute of Transportation Studies, Dr Tal's work focuses on travel behavior and the implementation of travel behavior related policies. He is currently examining the spatial and temporal demand for Electric Vehicles and Electric Vehicle charging infrastructure. Gil holds a PhD in transportation technology and policy from UC Davis, and was formerly a post-doctoral researcher with the Center for Global Metropolitan Studies and the University of California Transportation Center at UC Berkeley.

Lóránt A. Tavasszy, Delft University of Technology, The Netherlands – Dr Tavasszy is Endowed Professor of Freight Transport and Logistics. He is also a senior consultant in Mobility and Logistics at TNO in Delft, focusing on innovative solutions for freight transport and issues such as accessibility and urban quality of life. He lectures on the subject of freight transport modeling and leads the research program on sustainable accessibility for freight transport within the Randstad, funded by the NWO.

Veronique Van Acker, Ghent University, Belgium – Veronique is a post-doctoral researcher in the Geography Department. Her work focuses on the interaction between the built environment and travel behavior, taking into account subjective influences such as lifestyles and attitudes. She holds a PhD in Geography from Ghent University. Her PhD was awarded with the Eric Pas Dissertation Prize 2010 by the International Association for Travel Behavior Research (IATBR).

Frank Witlox, Ghent University, Belgium – Frank Witlox is Professor of Economic Geography in the Department of Geography, where he teaches a range of topics including Transport Geography, Economic Geography, Spatial Modeling Techniques, and Transport, Logistics and Space. He is also a Visiting Professor at ITMMA (Institute of Transport and Maritime Management Antwerp) where he teaches Warehouse and Hinterland Distribution Management, and an Associate Director of GaWC (Globalization and World Cities, Loughborough University). Since 2010 he has been the Director of the Doctoral School of Natural Sciences (UGent). His research focuses on transport economics and geography, (city) logistics, world cities and globalization, and land use change/development.

Acknowledgements

Pulling together a book such as this requires a great deal of effort from many people, and we are indebted to all who have helped in the endeavor. We would first and foremost like to thank our fellow contributors for providing sharp and incisive reviews of their subject areas, which combine to provide a wide-ranging overview of key issues and debates in the field of transport studies. This has made our job as editors much easier than we had a right to expect. We are also extremely grateful to Tim Absalom, Shaun Lewin and especially Jamie Quinn, of Plymouth University's GeoMapping Unit, for providing the very high quality artwork contained within the book. We are sure you'll agree this significantly enhances the book's presentation. Thanks to Clive Charlton for some characteristically insightful advice, and, finally, to all at Sage, particularly Robert Rojek and Alana Clogan, who have given us very valuable support and shown considerable patience and understanding as we assembled the final manuscript.

Introduction

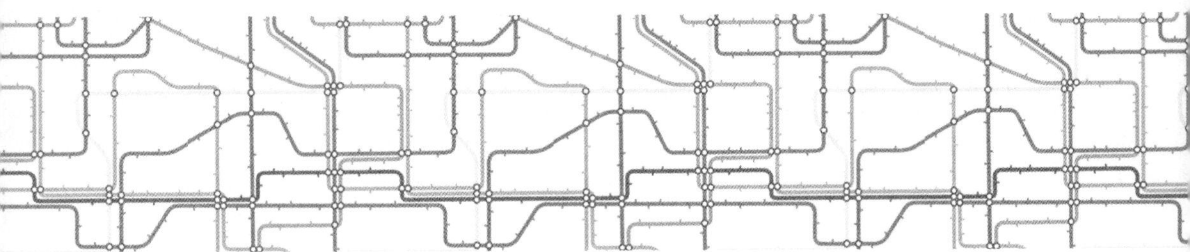

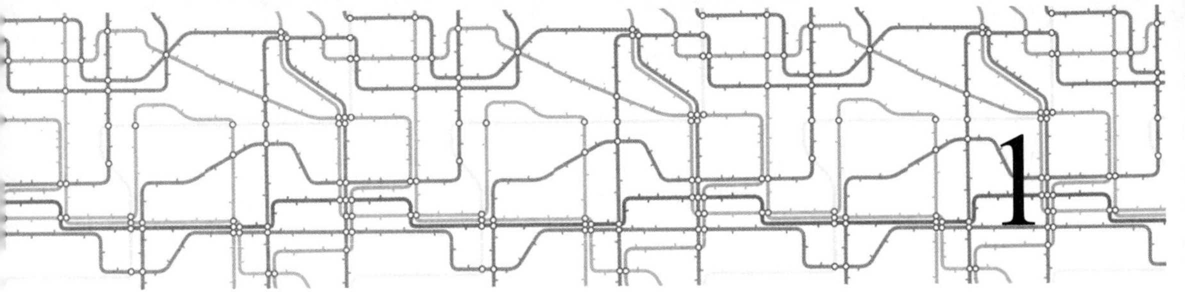

1

The Handbook of Transport Studies

Jean-Paul Rodrigue,
Theo Notteboom and Jon Shaw

TRANSPORTATION: A SCIENCE OR A FIELD OF APPLICATION?

This book is about transportation. It is common to state that transportation is not a science but a field of application. While such a statement may give the impression that transportation is not an endeavor serious enough to require its own formal discipline, the reality is rather the opposite. Transportation is so complex, multifaceted and extensive that no single scientific discipline would be able to encompass its role, functions and operations. Trying to define a science of transportation would probably end up being counterproductive, as it would seek to provide finality to a field that is constantly evolving as economic, technological and social conditions change.

The multidisciplinary character of transportation can be seen as both a weakness and as a strength. It is a weakness in the sense that it is unlikely that a consensus will ever be reached, outside generalities, about what transportation truly involves as a field of investigation. Different issues arise as important depending on whether one looks at transportation from an engineering, economic, operations research, sociological, environmental or geographical standpoint. For an engineer, transportation is composed of modes and infrastructure, from road pavement to container cranes. This infrastructure must be built, operated and maintained. For an economist, transportation could relate to commercial opportunities and the impacts of transport costs on flows and the price of products and services. For a sociologist, transportation could relate to mobility levels according to income, gender and socio-economic status. Indeed, the now well established "mobilities paradigm" in the social sciences demonstrates the very wide range of sociocultural concerns now commonly researched in the field of transportation (see Cresswell, 2006; Sheller and Urry, 2006; and the *Handbook of Mobilities* edited by Adey et al., 2013).

Transportation studies' multidisciplinarity is also a strength in that it has conveyed a long tradition of using perspectives and methodologies borrowed from various disciplines where they are relevant and useful. Pragmatism often prevails in transportation as the goal is commonly to improve the capacity and performance of various transportation systems such as highways, transit systems, maritime shipping and logistics. Conflicts of ideology are less common, although by no means absent; the field of transport policy can be subject to controversy around issues such as modal choice and approach, type of ownership, regulation level, governance, investment priorities and level of expected impact.

Nevertheless, from this range of perspectives and methodologies we can identify a series of elements, characteristics and methods that might be regarded as core to transport studies. Our aim is not to provide a detailed exposition of each of these, but rather to introduce them as a framework to help understand the themes that develop in relation to the various *transport systems* described and explained throughout the book.

What are transport systems?

In the context that the fields of application in transport studies cannot be effectively reconciled under some "unifying theory", a good start is to consider transportation as a system. This immediately implies complexity and interrelations between different elements, and three such elements are:

- *Transportation nodes.* Transportation primarily links locations, often referred to as nodes. They serve as access points to a transport system or as transshipment/intermediary locations within a transport network. This function is mainly serviced by transport terminals where flows originate, end or are being transshipped from one mode to another.
- *Transportation networks.* This relates to the spatial structure and organization of transport infrastructures and terminals supporting and shaping movements.
- *Transportation demand.* This considers the demand for transport services as well as the modes used to support movements. Once this demand is realized, it is expressed as interactions that flow through a transport network.

It is instructive to note here a number of conceptual characteristics of transport systems and their inter-related elements drawn from complexity science, as recognized by the OECD (2009). Key among these are:

- *Adaptability.* This is a standard characteristic that is best reflected by the concept of competition where transport firms adapt to their competitors and to other socioeconomic changes (which lead to changes in demand).
- *Self-organization.* Individuals' choice of modes and routing within a transport network is the outcome of the consideration of all the respective advantages/disadvantages of modes and terminals. Supply chain management is also illustrative of self-organization as sourcing and distribution strategies change to reflect complex changes in input and distribution costs.
- *Non-linearity.* This refers to the fact that transport systems' operation is not stable and uniform but subject to sudden perturbations. These in turn may be thought of as rhythmic or non-rhythmic. Peak hour congestion on a road or railway system is a good example of a rhythmic non-linear characteristic, as it is reasonably predictable but each degree of additional congestion results in exponential delays. Non-rhythmic disruptions, such as a serious road accident or the shutting down of an airport hub because of a snow storm or a volcanic eruption, will trigger significant but potentially unexpected disruptions through the whole network. Transport systems thus need to be designed with issues of capacity and resilience firmly in mind.
- *Attractors.* These represent the stable components of the transport system that have a long-term influence on the nature and extent of both the system itself and the flows within. Land use is a particularly stable component of spatial interactions since its characteristics are slow to change. The same applies to transport terminals that are long-term locations in the convergence of flows.
- *Phase transition.* Although a considerable degree of long-term stability in any given transport system may be expected, certain developments or tipping points may trigger notable changes in its properties. Technological (or technical) innovations have in the past involved paradigm shifts

for transportation systems – for instance, containerization generated entirely new flow patterns, modes and terminals, as did the advent of commercial aviation – but other issues such as those related to peak oil are also likely to be highly significant in triggering a phase transition in 21st century transport systems. Phase transitions are themselves non-linear and can often be system-specific, although this is not to say that 'spillover' effects will not be observable, such as the impact of fast-moving information and communications technology development on the operation of automobile and public transport systems.

How do we study transport systems?

Transportation planning and analysis are interdisciplinary by nature, involving among others, civil engineers, economists, urban planners and geographers. Each discipline has developed methodologies dealing with its respective array of problems. Because transportation is an infrastructure-intensive activity, engineering has been the dominant approach to transportation studies, but any number of issues from globalization, through the setting of extended supply chains, to economic development and social exclusion require methods related to management science, operations research, economics and finance, sociology and anthropology as well as from other perspectives. Two common traits of transportation studies, regardless of disciplinary affiliation, are a heavy reliance on empirical data and the intensive use of data analytic techniques, ranging from simple descriptive measures to more complex modeling structures.

Transportation studies is not restricted to methods developed with transportation in mind, but to whatever is relevant to a specific problem – as we said, transport studies has a leaning towards pragmatism. In fact, many methods that were initially developed for other problems have widespread use in transportation studies. These include methods used to collect primary data, such as questionnaires and interviews. Some analytical techniques are straightforward to implement and interpret, such as graphs, tables and maps. Others are more complex, such as inferential statistics like the t-test, analysis of variance, regression and chi-square, and logit and probit models. Increasingly, transportation studies are concerned with impacts and public policy issues. They rely more on qualitative information such as policy statements, rules and regulations. Various types of impacts are considered, including economic (e.g. community development), social (e.g. access to services), environmental (e.g. air or water pollution) and health (e.g. road accidents). The broad fields of environmental impact assessment, risk assessment and policy analysis are relevant to these issues.

CONTEMPORARY TRANSPORTATION SYSTEMS

Driving forces

The era following World War II has seen a considerable growth in transport demand related to individual (passengers) as well as freight mobility. This growth is jointly the result of larger quantities of passengers and freight being moved, but also the longer distances over which they are carried. Recent trends underline an ongoing process of mobility growth, which has led to the multiplication of the number of journeys involving a wide variety of modes that service transport demands.

Despite the high capital and operational costs of modes such as ships and planes, costs per unit transported have dropped significantly over the last decades. This has made it possible to overcome larger distances and further exploit the comparative advantages of the global economy. As a result, despite the lower costs, the share of transport activities in the economy has remained relatively constant in time.

These trends have obviously extended the requirements for transport infrastructure both quantitatively (capacity) and qualitatively (performance/reliability). This has made transportation more dependent on finance as it represents a substantial sector of capital accumulation. Roads, harbors, airports, telecommunication facilities and pipelines have expanded considerably to service new areas and add capacity to existing networks. Transportation infrastructures are thus a major component of land use, notably in developed countries.

A global perspective

The structure of the global land transport network is a function of the density and intensity of economic activities as well as efforts made to access inland resources (Figure 1.1). It is important to underline that while at the global level road and rail networks appear to be integrated and interconnected, this is far from being the case. Road networks are designed to service local and regional flows and fewer corridors are used for long-distance trade. Most rail networks are national with limited international services with the exception of Europe and North America. Still, different loading gauges remain impediments to the realization of a true pan-European rail network. The North American rail network is integrated but different segments are owned by different carriers.

Container ports are reflective of the world's commercial geography particularly since they dominantly handle finished goods and parts. The world's most important ports were North American (e.g. New York) and Western European (e.g. Rotterdam). Containerization completely changed the world's commercial geography with the emergence of new major port locations reflecting changes in the global geography of production and consumption (Figure 1.2). This geography indicates a high level of traffic concentration around large port facilities, notably Pacific Asian ports along the Tokyo to Singapore corridor. As export-oriented economic development strategies took shape, the number of containers handled in Pacific Asian, notably Chinese, ports surged.

There is also an evolving geography of container ports where there is a specialization between container ports acting as gateways and container ports acting as intermediate hubs. Gateway ports command access to large manufacturing or market regions, and Hong Kong, Los Angeles and Rotterdam are notable examples. Intermediate hub ports (or offshore hubs) act as intermediary locations where containers are transshipped between different segments of the global maritime

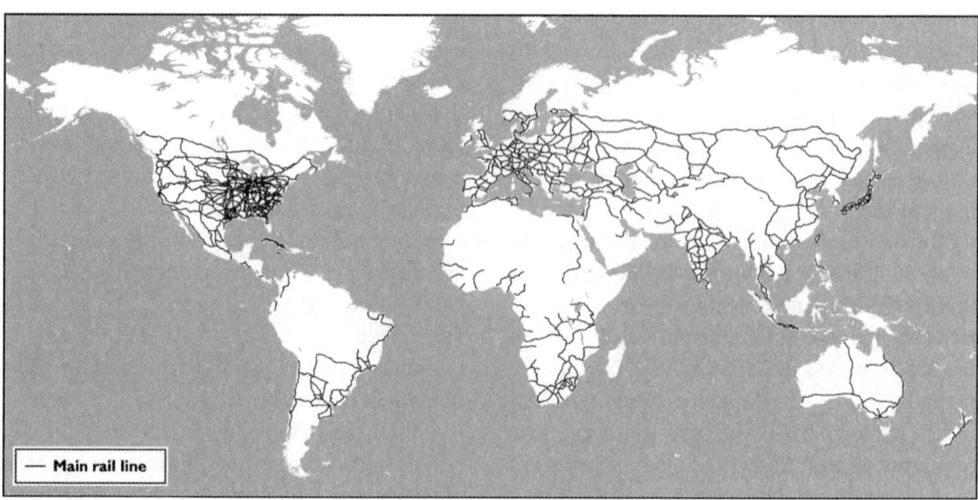

Figure 1.1 The world's main rail networks

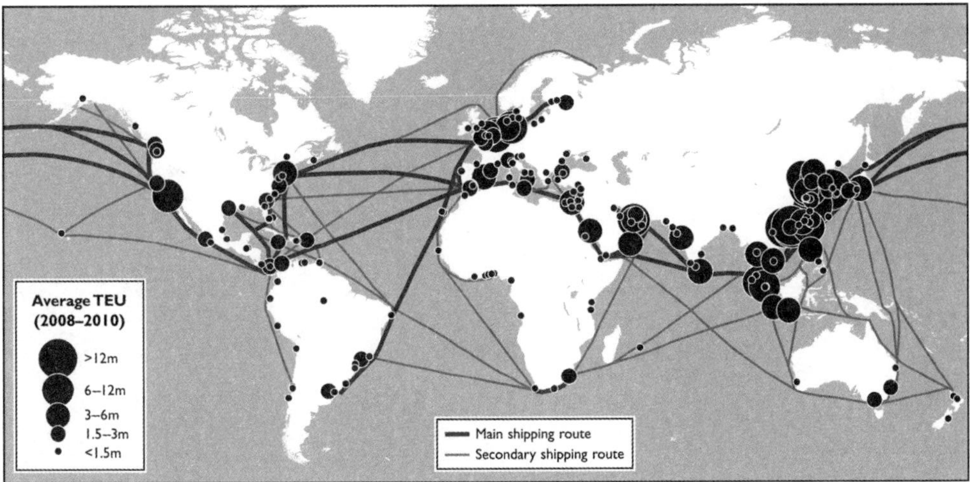

Figure 1.2 The world's major container ports, 2008–10

transport system in a manner similar to hubs in air transportation. Singapore and Dubai are among the most prominent transshipment hubs, each servicing a specific transshipment market.

The most important airports enjoy either centrality within one of the world's foremost city-regions, intermediacy between key markets, or both. There are three major concentrations of airports where the world's air traffic is articulated: Eastern North America, Western Europe and Japan (Figure 1.3). The key airports of these concentrations, or rather the main airport cities since they have more than one airport, are New York, London and Tokyo. They correspond to the world's most prominent cities and the most important financial centers, and have developed to host a series of related activities such as distribution centers, just-in-time manufacturers,

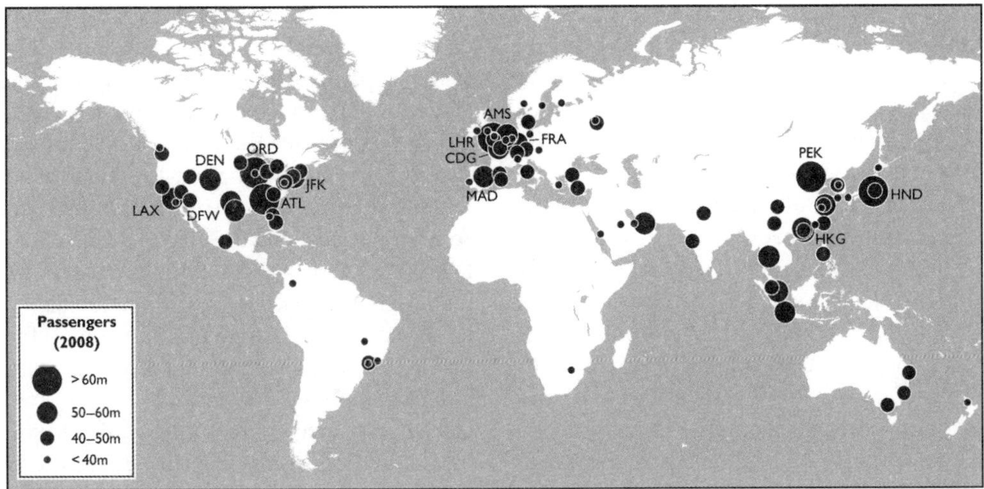

Figure 1.3 Passenger traffic at the world's largest airports, 2008

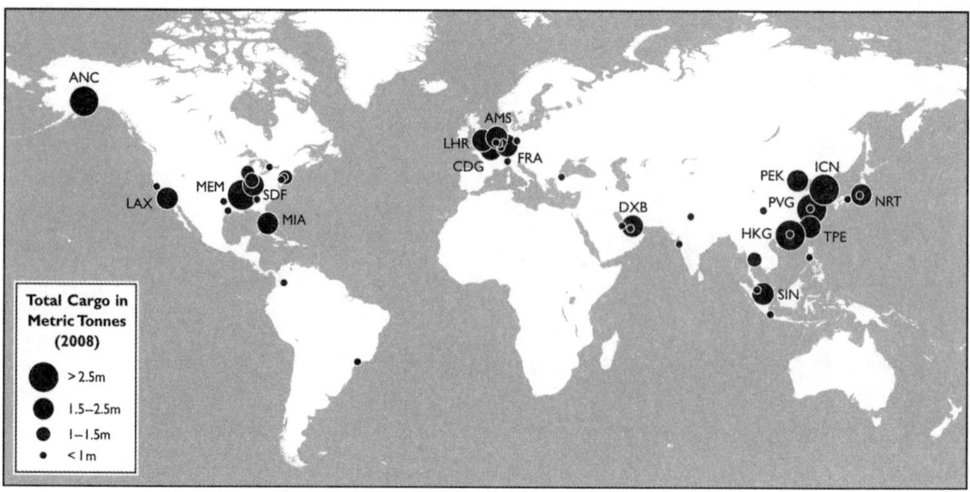

Figure 1.4 Freight traffic at the world's largest airports, 2008

office parks, hotels, restaurants, and convention centers. While there is a direct relationship between the level of air passenger traffic and the primacy of a city in the world urban system, as in the case of the geography of container ports change results from both the emergence of new cities of global prominence and the rapid development of intermediate hubs such as Dubai.

The level of freight activity at airports tends to be different than from that of passenger, especially in the United States (Figure 1.4). The Midwest being the demographic and economic centroid of the United States, many airfreight forwarders have located their hubs at airports such as Memphis (Federal Express) and Louisville (UPS) that generate little passenger traffic. The importance of Pacific Asian airports is linked with the specific role of the region in the global economy, especially in relation to electronics. Since these products tend to have a high value-to-weight ratio, air transport is particularly suitable for their shipping to North American and Western European markets. Because long-distance cargo planes have had less range than passenger planes, two airports have traditionally played a notable intermediate role: Anchorage (Pacific Asia – North America traffic) and Dubai (Pacific Asia – Western Europe traffic).

The development of fiber optic transmission technology provided a substantial impetus in the setting of a global telecommunications network since it permitted significantly higher bandwidth and less signal degradation. Throughputs of hundreds of gigabytes of information per second became possible. The first transatlantic fiber optic cable (TAT-8) was laid in 1988 and over the years fiber optic cables were laid across the world, connecting economies and societies increasingly dependent on telecommunications (Figure 1.5). The internet could not have existed otherwise. While initial submarine cables were laid on a point-to-point basis, technical advances permitted branching so that one cable could service a sequence of hubs (e.g. Africa and Latin America). The global network is designed for redundancy as several cables are laid in parallel for major connections (transatlantic and transpacific), implying that a failure in one cable can be mitigated by rerouting traffic to the others. In recent years, Pacific Asia has seen significant submarine cable laying activities, in support of its economic development.

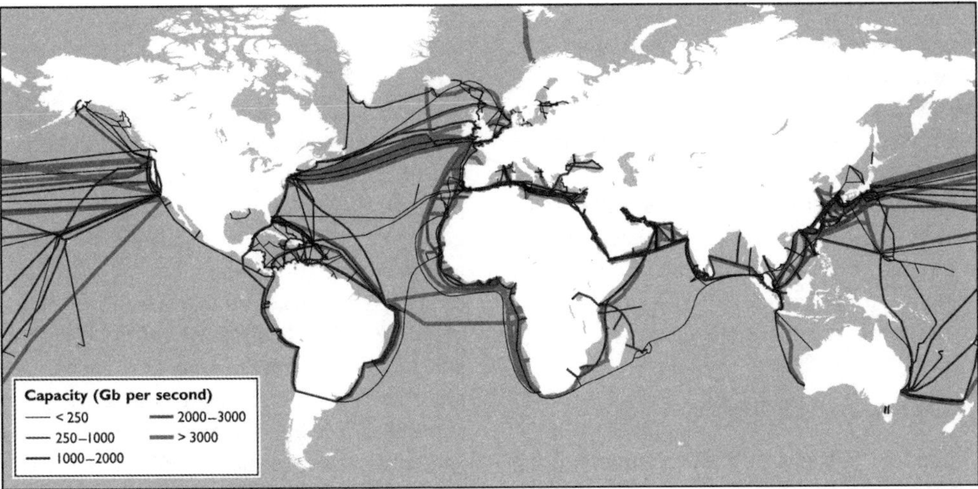

Figure 1.5 Global submarine cable network

Source: dataset encoded by Greg Mahlknecht, http://www.cablemap.info

A LOOK AT THE FUTURE

Transportation studies, by offering a broad perspective over the existing pattern and process of transportation systems, also offers ways to glimpse at future developments. Casting back over transport developments since the industrial revolution underlines that each mode, due to its geographical and technical specificities, has been characterized by different technologies and different rates of innovation and diffusion. A transport innovation can thus be an additive force where a new technology expands or makes an existing mode more efficient and competitive. It can also be a destructive force when a new technology marks the obsolescence and the demise of an existing mode. Still, in many cases an older technology will endure because of its wide level of adoption, utilization and accumulated capital investment. This is commonly known as path dependency. Vested interests in an existing mode – a good current example being the car – may also delay or impede an innovation (see Geels et al., 2012).

Historically, technological innovation is linked with faster and more efficient transport systems. This process implied a space–time convergence where a greater amount of space could be exchanged with a lesser amount of time. But one of the pitfalls in discussing future trends resides in looking at the future simply as an extrapolation of the past. It is often assumed that the future will involve a technology that already exists, but simply operating an extended scale beyond what is currently possible. This can be seen as an incremental change bias. The parameters of such an extrapolation commonly involve a greater speed, mass availability, a higher capacity and/or a better accessibility, all of which imply similar or lower costs.

The prediction of future outcomes generally considers what is within the realm of forecasting and scenario building. Forecasting tries to evaluate near-term outcomes by considering that parameters do not change much, while scenario building tries to assess a series of possible outcomes based upon expected fluctuation in parameters. A common failure of such predictions is their lack of capacity to anticipate paradigm shifts brought about by new technologies as well as economic and social conditions. But then care should also be taken not to assume the massive diffusion of any game-changing new technology over a very short period of time (the so-called "silver bullet effect"). This rarely takes place as most innovations go through a cycle of introduction, adoption, growth, peak and then obsolescence, which can take several years, if not decades. Even in the telecommunications sector, which accounts for the fastest diffusion levels, the adoption of a technology tends to take place over a period of about ten years.

Some speculations

Since the introduction of commercial jet planes, high-speed train networks and the container in the late 1960s, no significant technological change has impacted passengers and freight transport systems, at least from a paradigm shift perspective. The early 21st century is an era of car and truck dependency, which tends to constrain the development of alternative modes of transportation, as most of the technical improvements aim at insuring the dominance of oil as a source of energy. With concerns about oil reserves, however, there is strong evidence that the end of the dominance of the internal combustion engine is approaching. Energy prices are expected to remain high (and indeed continue to rise) in relation to their 1990–2000 price range, and trigger the most important technological transition in transportation since the automobile. In such an environment several transport technologies look promising.

Automated/intelligent transport systems refer to the development of a set of information and communication technologies (ICTs) to improve the speed, efficiency, safety and reliability of movements. These systems could involve the improvement of existing modes, such as automated highway systems or the better provision of information to drivers, or the creation of new types of nodes and transshipment systems in public transit and freight transportation (e.g. automated terminals). The goal of such initiatives is mainly to use existing infrastructures more efficiently through information technologies, and many gains still remain to be achieved through the better management of existing infrastructures and vehicles.

There is also a range of alternative technologies, modes and fuels that could replace but more likely complement existing modes, particularly for the transportation of passengers. One technology is maglev, short for magnetic levitation, which has the advantage of having no friction (except air friction), enabling operational speeds of 500–600 km per hour to be reached (higher speeds are possible if the train circulates in a low pressure tube). On the other side of the mobility spectrum urban transportation shows some potential for a more effective use of alternative modes, particularly in car-dependent cities and this for passengers and freight transportation alike. For instance, various public transit schemes such as light rail systems, on-demand transit vehicles, not forgetting the bicycle, may help support urban mobility.

Alternative fuels mainly concern existing modes but the sources of fuel and/or the engine technology are modified. For instance, hybrid vehicles involve the use of two types of motor technologies, commonly an internal combustion engine and an electric motor. In simple terms, braking is used to recharge a battery, which then can be used to power the electric motor. Although gasoline appears to be the most prevalent fuel choice for hybrid engines, diesel has a high potential since it can also be made from coal or organic fuels. Diesel can thus be a fuel part of a lower petroleum dependency energy strategy. Hybrid engines have often been perceived as a transitional technology to cope with higher energy prices. There is also a possibility in this regard of greater reliance on biofuels as an additive (and possibly a supplement) to petroleum, but their impacts on food production must be carefully assessed.

More far-reaching in terms of energy transition are fuel cells, which involve an electric generator using the catalytic conversion of hydrogen and oxygen. The electricity generated can be used for many purposes, such as supplying an electric motor. Current technological prospects do not foresee high output fuel cells, indicating they are applicable only to light vehicles, notably cars, or to small power systems. Nevertheless, fuel cells represent a low environmental impact alternative to generate energy if the hydrogen can be generated in a sustainable manner. Additional challenges in the use of fuel cells involve hydrogen storage (especially in a vehicle) as well as establishing a distribution system to supply the consumers.

Still, anticipating future transport trends is difficult. Technological change has historically created paradigm shifts and is likely to do so again in the future, but not necessarily in ways or with consequences that we might currently expect. There is an expectation for change, because existing transport systems are highly beneficial but at the same time beset with externalities such as congestion, pollution and CO_2 emissions. But congestion and pollution have proved resilient problems – one of the major concerns in London in the late 19th century was that by the mid-20th century the amount of horse manure generated by transport activities would become unmanageable – and the emergence of transport's role in promoting climate change reminds us how, alongside benefits, technologically-driven shifts in a transport system can result in consequences every bit as (or more) harmful as those they originally resolved.

HANDBOOK OVERVIEW

In what follows we have assembled a range of contributions on a range of topics from renowned international experts. Together the chapters speak to the main issues in contemporary transportation studies by developing our brief introductory discussion. We would be the first to say that the coverage of the book is not exhaustive in the sense of seeking to address the detail of every flow or movement pattern, or of every operational or policy area. Such an approach would require an encyclopedia. But in reading this handbook you should gain a solid understanding of the principal features, characteristics and consequences of transport systems as they have developed around the world, in relation to the movement of both freight and passengers. Further reading can be found in the references section to each chapter, and as already mentioned the *Handbook of Mobilities* (Adey et al., 2013) provides a thoroughgoing exposition of this related paradigm.

We have divided the chapters into six sections. The first two of these, *Transport in the global world* and *Transport in regions and localities* recognize the nature, extent and functionality of transport systems across and between different scales. The remaining sections – *Transport, economy and society*; *Transport policy*; *Transport networks and models*; and *Transport and the environment* – reflect numerous ways in which transport systems and activities are fundamentally connected with broader imperatives and, as such, how and why they are planned and managed.

At the broadest scale, the configuration and operational characteristics of *Transport in the global world* are related to the division of production by multinational corporations. The main expression of this is a global network of gateways and hubs that command access to vast production and consumption markets (Chapter 2). As such, transportation and transport policy are truly international issues requiring concerted efforts of trans-border cooperation and coordination (Chapter 3), even more so in recent years as heightened safety and security concerns have forced the adaptation of transport actors. Major changes in international transportation have taken place in recent decades, key among which has been the adoption of containerized freight shipment, and the related integration of several modes into a continuous chain, known as intermodal transportation, has led to very significant productivity improvements (Chapter 4). While for long-distance passenger movements, air transportation has grown to be the main service provider (Chapter 5), this domination can be challenged in some regional markets by high-speed rail. Maritime transportation (Chapter 6) is the dominant mode for long-distance freight movements but air freight has been very successful at establishing niche services mainly for high-value goods.

In *regions and localities*, a very specific but highly important type of mobility concerns urban areas where large numbers of passengers and significant amounts of freight are moving over short distances. This brings sharply into focus the relationship between transport and urban land use (Chapter 7) and the important field of city logistics (Chapter 8). The siting and setting of airport terminals (Chapter 9) is inevitably interlinked with the effective functioning of the transport system of any urban area and, indeed, logistics – the comprehensive management of transportation – has been responsible for many improvements in the reliability and performance of transportation systems. The emergence of supply chain management underlines a growing integration of production, distribution, transportation and retailing in a streamlined system, which has been linked to specific forms of agglomeration such as logistics zones (Chapter 10). Such zones are served by a variety of inland terminals that underpin intermodal transport development (Chapter 11) and often act as load centers for their respective markets.

Transportation has obvious links with the *economy and society*. It is an economic activity on its own as well as a support for other activities; it is largely but by no means completely a derived demand. Transport markets (Chapter 12) employ labor, necessitate investments in infrastructure and confer a level of accessibility to resources and markets. There is a clear consensus that transport and economic development (Chapter 13) are interrelated, but what is less clear is the nature and extent of this relation, such as the growing divergence between transportation and economic growth. Transport is also crucial in underpinning a wide range of societal functions by enabling people to access goods and services. Of course, mobility is only one aspect of accessibility – information and communications technologies (ICTs) offer a new form of accessibility to goods and services and it is clear that the impacts of ICTs on travel behavior (Chapter 14) have been many and varied. In part this is because transport enables people to maintain face-to-face social networks and, through these, build and maintain social capital. People who are unable to access goods, services and social networks/capital can be regarded as socially excluded (Chapter 15).

Governments and various agencies have a significant role in the scope, operation and regulation of the transportation sector within and between their jurisdictions. Through a variety of *transport policy* instruments (Chapter 16) they can intervene in ownership, sometimes taking direct control through nationalization or, conversely, favoring an environment where the private sector is the main actor. Historically, transportation has been a highly regulated industry but recent decades have mainly been characterized by a push toward deregulation, with competition and the new market entry becoming more prevalent. This has had notable impacts on pricing and subsidy (Chapter 17). A further key policy concern is the influence of transport systems on the health of society (Chapter 18). In addition to direct effects such as accidents and the impacts of transport-related pollutants, the increased reliance on mechanized transport, especially the private car, is resulting in potentially harmful long-term health consequences.

Transport planning aims to evaluate the consequences of socioeconomic trends on transport systems as well as seeking to determine what potential consequences, positive or negative, may result from changes in existing transport infrastructures. We have already noted that Chapter 7 focuses on the relationship between transportation and land use, but here our focus is on *transport networks* and the *models* that can be used to simulate the behavior of transport systems. Modeling techniques related to transport flow, distribution and allocation (Chapter 19) and to the structure and dynamics of transport networks (Chapter 20) are examined, as are locational transport models (Chapter 21) and ways in which incident and emergency traffic management can be modeled and addressed (Chapter 22).

Of increasing importance in the context of policy approaches taking cognizance of concerns about climate change, is the relationship between *transport and the environment.* Transportation systems are commonly significant contributors to a variety of environmental externalities, and the transportation sector is a large consumer of energy – particularly petroleum – so the dynamics of transport and energy use (Chapter 23) are intrinsically linked. From global climate change to local noise, the environmental impacts of transportation are complex and difficult to mitigate (Chapter 24). Finally, since production, transportation and distribution are embedded, it is in the supply chain that many environmental benefits can be realized either directly, such as reverse distribution, or indirectly through energy efficiency; this is the realm of green logistics (Chapter 25). Even if sustainable transportation is ultimately an evasive goal, it has become a conceptual and ideological framework to which transport planning, policy and management are increasingly responsive.

REFERENCES

Adey, P., Bissell, D., Hannam, K., Merriman, P. and Sheller, M. (eds) (2013) *The Routledge Handbook of Mobilities*. Routledge, London.

Cresswell, T. (2006) *On the move: mobility in the western world*. Routledge, New York.

Geels, F., Kemp, R., Lyons, G. and Dudley, G. (eds) (2012) *Automobility in transition? A socio-technical analysis*. Routledge, London.

OECD (2009) "Applications of Complexity Science for Public Policy: New Tools for Finding Unanticipated Consequences and Unrealized Opportunities", Global Science Forum.

Sheller, M. and Urry, J. (2006) "The new mobilities paradigm." *Environment and Planning A*, 38, 207–26.

SECTION 1

Transport in the Global World

2

Transport and Globalization

Jean-Paul Rodrigue

TRADE AND THE GLOBAL ECONOMY

The emergence of interdependencies

In a global economy, no nation is self-sufficient. Each is involved at different levels in trade to sell what it produces, to acquire what it lacks and also to produce more efficiently in some economic sectors than its trade partners. As supported by conventional economic theory, trade promotes economic efficiency by providing a wider variety of goods, often at lower costs, notably because of specialization, economies of scale and the related comparative advantages (Porter, 1990; Feenstra, 2004). The globalization of production is concomitant to the globalization of trade as one cannot function without the other. Even though international trade took place centuries before the modern era, as ancient trade routes such as the Silk Road can testify, trade has occurred at an ever-increasing scale over the last 600 years to play an even more active part in the economic life of nations and regions (Braudel, 1982; Bernstein, 2008; Bairoch and Kozul-Wright, 1996). This process has been facilitated by significant technical changes in the transport sector (Gilbert and Perl, 2008). The scale, volume and efficiency of international trade have all continued to increase since the 1970s. As such, space/time convergence was an ongoing process that implied a wider market coverage could be accessed with a lower amount of time. It has become increasingly possible to trade between parts of the world that previously had limited access to international transportation systems. Further, the division and the fragmentation of production that went along with these processes also expanded trade. Trade thus contributes to lower manufacturing costs.

Without international trade, few nations could maintain an adequate standard of living. With only domestic resources being available, each country could only produce a limited number of products and shortages would be prevalent. Global trade allows for an enormous variety of resources – from Persian

Gulf oil, Brazilian coffee to Chinese labor – to be made more widely accessible. It also facilitates the distribution of many different manufactured goods that are produced in different parts of the world to what can be labeled as the global market. Wealth becomes increasingly derived through the regional specialization of economic activities. This way, production costs are lowered, productivity rises and surpluses are generated, which can be transferred or traded for commodities that would be too expensive to produce domestically or would simply not be available. As a result, international trade decreases the overall costs of production worldwide. Consumers can buy more goods from the wages they earn, and standards of living should, in theory, increase. International trade is also subject to much contention since it can at times be a disruptive economic and social force as it changes the conditions through which wealth is distributed within a national economy, particularly due to changes in prices and wages.

The flows of globalization

International trade consequently demonstrates the extent of globalization with increased spatial interdependencies between elements of the global economy and their level of integration. These interdependencies imply numerous relationships where flows of capital, goods, raw materials and services are established between regions of the world. There are three main types of flows in a global economy (Table 2.1):

- Freight (trade). Concerns flows taking place to satisfy material demands ranging from raw materials to finished goods. This is mainly assumed by maritime shipping, which is supported by port infrastructures acting as the main gateways of this flow system, but airports play an important role in the trade of high-value goods.
- Passengers (migration). The flows of people taking place for a variety of reasons, most of them related to tourism, with air transportation being the dominant mode supporting such flows. The global air transport system can handle about four million passengers per day.
- Information (telecommunications). The complex and extensive flows of information used for communication, power exchanges (e.g. an online order) and symbolic exchanges (e.g. education). Information flows can take both physical (e.g. parcels) and non-physical forms, which are dominantly articulated by a network of global cities.

Emergence of the global trade system

The emergence of the global trade system can mainly be articulated within three major phases. The first phase concerns a conventional perspective on international trade that prevailed until the 1970s where factors of production were much less mobile. Particularly, there was a limited level of mobility of raw materials, parts and finished products in a setting which was fairly regulated with impediments such as tariffs, quotas and limitations to foreign ownership (Bernstein, 2008). Trade mainly concerned a range of specific products, namely commodities (and very few

Table 2.1 The flows of globalization

	Trade	Migration	Telecommunication
Nature	Flows of physical goods	Flows of people	Flows of information
Types	Raw materials, energy, food, parts and consumption goods	Permanent, temporary (migrant workers), tourism, business transactions	Communication, power exchanges, symbolic exchanges
Medium	Transport modes and terminals (freight)	Transport modes and terminals (passengers)	Transport modes and terminals (postal), telecommunication systems
Main gateways	Ports	Airports	Global cities
Speed	Low to average	Slow to fast	Instantaneous
Capacity	Very large	Large	Almost unlimited

services), that were not readily available in regional economies. Due to regulations, protectionism and fairly high transportation costs, trade remained limited and delayed by inefficient freight distribution. In this context, trade was more an exercise to cope with scarcity than to promote economic efficiency.

From the 1980s, the mobility of factors of production, particularly capital, became possible, which permitted the setting of the second phase (Baldwin and Martin, 1999). The legal and physical environment in which international trade was taking place incited a better realization of the comparative advantages of specific locations (e.g. Daniels, Radebaugh and Sullivan, 2010). Concomitantly, regional trade agreements emerged and the global trade framework was strengthened from a legal and transactional standpoint (GATT/WTO). In addition, containerization provided the capabilities to support more complex and long-distance trade flows, as did the growing air traffic. Due to high production (legacy) costs in old industrial regions, activities that were labor intensive were gradually relocated to lower-cost locations. The process began as a national one, then went to nearby countries when possible and afterwards became a truly global phenomenon. Thus, foreign direct investments surged, particularly towards new manufacturing regions as multinational corporations became increasingly flexible in the global positioning of their assets.

The third phase marks the setting of global value chains with international trade now including a wide variety of services that were previously fixed to regional markets and a surge in the mobility of the factors of production. Since these trends are well established, the priority is now shifting to the geographical and functional integration of production, distribution and consumption with the emergence of global production networks (Dicken, 2007). Complex networks involving flows of information, commodities, parts and finished goods have been set, which in turn demands a high level of command of logistics and freight distribution. In such an environment, powerful actors have emerged that are not directly involved in the function of production and retailing, but mainly taking the responsibility of managing the web of flows.

The global economic system is thus characterized by a growing level of integrated services, finance, retail, manufacturing and nonetheless distribution, which in turn is mainly the outcome of improved transport and logistics, a more efficient exploitation of regional comparative advantages and a transactional environment supportive of the legal and financial complexities of global trade.

Trade surge

As of the beginning of the 21st century, the flows of globalization have been shaped by three salient trends. The first is an ongoing growth of international trade, both in absolute terms and in relation to global national income. Since the late 1970s the value of international trade has grown by a factor of 16 times if measured in current dollars (Figure 2.1). The second is a higher relative growth of trade in Pacific Asia as many economies developed an export-oriented development strategy that has been associated with imbalances in commercial relations. The third is the growing role of multinational corporations as vectors for international trade, particularly in terms of the share of international trade taking place within corporations.

Global trade has grown both in absolute and relative terms, especially after 1990 when global exports surged in the wake of rapid industrialization in developing countries, particularly China. The value of global exports first exceeded US$1 trillion in 1977, and by 2008 more than 16 trillion current US dollars of merchandises were exported. During the same time period, the share of the world GDP accounted by merchandise trade, imports and exports combined, surged from 18% to 52%. This trend is correlated with a growth in international transportation. Yet, this fast growth is skewed by the international

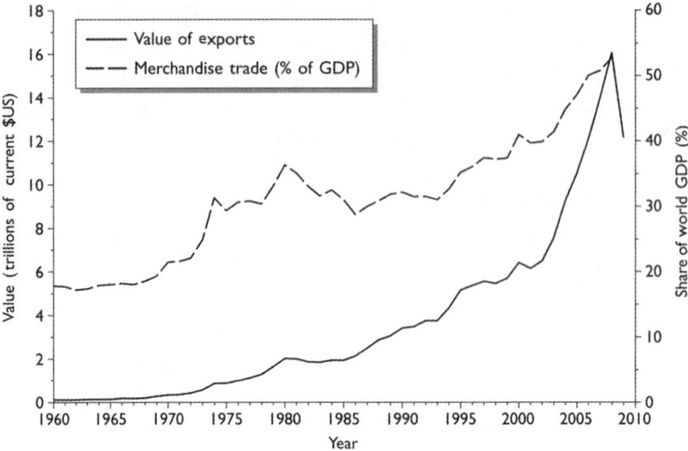

Figure 2.1 World merchandise trade, 1960–2010

Source: WTO

division of production where parts can be traded several times before an assembled good is ready for final consumption.

The growth of exports is indicative of a diffusion cycle where globalization may have reached maturity, particularly in light of the acceleration phase that took place after 2001. This process cannot go on indefinitely as growth in trade was also accompanied by a surge in trade imbalances. The financial crisis of 2008–2009 was accompanied by a significant decline of global merchandise trade, close to 25% in just one year. The main factor behind this decline was a drop in the consumption of durable goods (e.g. furniture, appliances, cars) since consumers are able to postpone these type of purchases if they are uncertain about the future.

Trade imbalances

An overview of the world's largest exporters and importers underlines that international trade reflects market size but is also characterized by acute imbalances (Figure 2.2). The United States, Germany, China and Japan are the world's largest importers and consequently the world's largest economies. In recent years Germany overtook the traditional position of the world's largest exporter held by United States over the last 50 years. The integration of China within the global economy has been accompanied by a growing level of participation in trade both in absolute and relative terms, improving the rank of China from the seventh largest exporter in 2000, to the third largest in 2005 and finally to the largest in 2008, supplanting the United States and Germany.

With respect to trade imbalances, some countries, notably the United States and the United Kingdom, have significant trade deficits which are reflected in their balance of payments. This aspect is dominantly linked with service and technology-oriented economies that have experienced a relocation of labor-intensive production activities to lower-cost locations. They are highly dependent on the efficient distribution of goods and commodities. Conversely, countries having a positive trade balance tend to be export-oriented with a level of dependency on international markets. Germany, Japan, South Korea and China are among the most notable examples. China has a positive trade balance, but most of this surplus concerns the United States. It maintains a negative trade balance with many of its partners, especially resources providers (e.g. Australia).

Acute trade imbalances cannot be maintained indefinitely without a readjustment. The surge in international trade, particularly

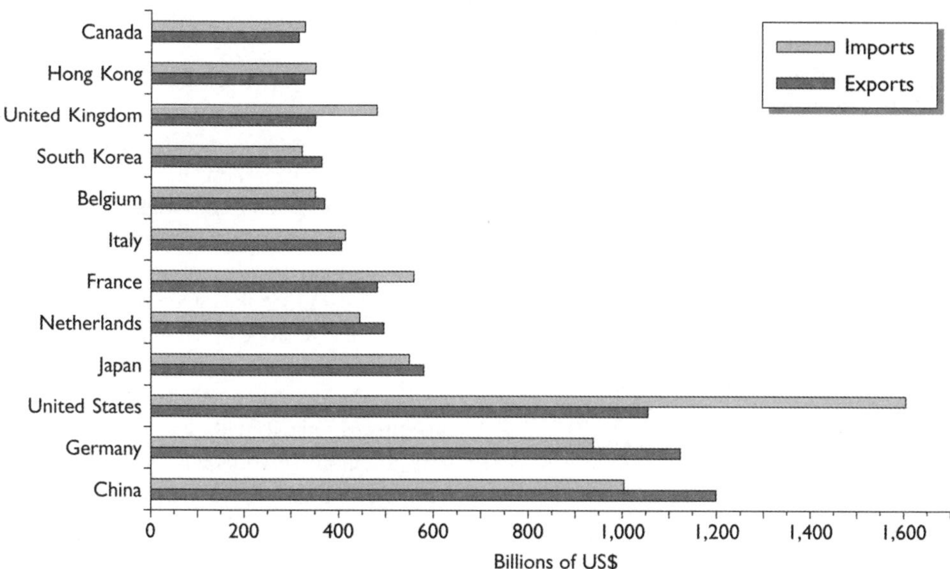

Figure 2.2 The world's 12 largest exporters and importers, 2009
Source: WTO

after 2002, was linked with a phase of asset inflation (i.e. the real estate bubble), particularly in the United States and several European countries (e.g. United Kingdom, Spain) coupled with heavy borrowing using these assets as collateral. A share of this debt was used for the purpose of consumption of imported goods, which turned out to be unsustainable. Over the coming years, global trade will be significantly readjusted to better reflect production and consumption capabilities.

TRADE FACILITATION

Trade costs

The volume of exchanged goods and services between nations is taking a growing share of the generation of wealth, mainly by offering economic growth opportunities in new regions and by reducing the costs of a wide array of manufacturing goods. By 2007, international trade surpassed 50% of global GDP for the first time, a twofold increase in its share since 1950 (see Figure 2.1). The facilitation of trade involves seeing how the procedures regulating the international movements of goods can be improved. It depends on the reduction of the general costs of trade, which considers transaction, tariff, transport and time costs, often labeled as the "Four Ts" of international trade:

- Transaction costs. The costs related to the economic exchange behind trade. It can include the gathering of information, negotiating, and enforcing contracts, letters of credit and transactions, including monetary exchange if a transaction takes place in another currency. Transactions taking place within a corporation are commonly lower than for transactions taking place between corporations. Still, with e-commerce they have declined substantially.
- Tariff and non-tariff costs. Levies imposed by governments on a realized trade flow. They can involve a direct monetary cost according to the product being traded (e.g. agricultural goods, finished goods, petroleum, etc.) or standards to be abided by for a product to be allowed entry into a foreign market. A variety of multilateral and bilateral arrangements have reduced tariffs and internationally recognized standards (e.g. ISO) have marginalized non-tariff barriers.
- Transport costs. The full costs of shipping goods from the point of production to the point of consumption. Containerization, intermodal transportation and economies of scale have reduced transport costs significantly.

- Time costs. The delays related to the lag between an order and the moment it is received by the purchaser. Long-distance international trade is often related with time delays that can be compounded by customs inspection delays (Hummels, 2001). Supply chain management strategies are able to mitigate effectively time constraints, namely through the inventory in transit concept.

Facilitation framework

Thus, the ability to compete in a global economy is dependent on the transport system as well as a trade facilitation framework, with activities including:

- Distribution-based. A multimodal and intermodal freight transport system composed of modes, infrastructures and terminals that spans across the globe. It ensures a physical capacity to support trade.
- Regulation-based. Customs procedures, tariffs, regulations and handling of documentation. They ensure that trade flows abide to the rules and regulations of the jurisdictions they cross.
- Transaction-based. Banking, finance, legal and insurance activities where accounts can be settled and risk mitigated. They ensure that the sellers of goods and services receive an agreed upon compensation and that the purchasers have a legal recourse if the outcome of the transaction is judged unsatisfactory or is insured if a partial or full loss incurs.

The quality, cost and efficiency of these services influence the trading environment as well as the overall costs linked with the international trade of goods (Lakshmanan et al., 2001). Many factors have been conductive to trade facilitation in recent decades, including integration processes, standardization, production systems, transport efficiency and transactional efficiency.

Integration processes

Processes of integration have resulted in the emergence of economic blocks and the decrease of tariffs at a global scale through agreements, as regulatory regimes were harmonized. One straightforward measure of integration relates to custom delays, which can be a significant trade impediment since it adds uncertainty in supply chain management. The higher the level of economic integration, the more likely the concerned elements are to trade. International trade has consequently been facilitated by a set of factors linked with growing levels of economic integration, the outcome of processes such as the European Union or the North American Free Trade Agreement (Brooks, 2008). The transactional capacity is consequently facilitated with the development of transportation networks and the adjustment of trade flows that follows increased integration. Integration processes have also taken place at the local scale with the creation of free trade zones where an area is given a different governance structure in order to promote trade, particularly export-oriented activities. In this case, the integration process is not uniform as only a portion of a territory is involved. China is a salient example of the far-reaching impacts of the setting of special economic zones.

Standardization concerns the setting of a common and ubiquitous frame of reference over information and physical flows. Standards facilitate trade since those abiding by them benefit from reliable, interoperable and compatible goods and services, which often results in lower production, distribution and maintenance costs. Measurement units were among the first globally accepted standards (the metric system) and the development of information technologies eventually led to common operating and telecommunication systems. It is, however, the container that is considered to be the most significant international standard for trade facilitation. By offering a load unit that can be handled by any mode and terminal with the proper equipment, access to international trade is improved.

Production systems have become more flexible and embedded. It is effectively productive to maintain a network of geographically diversified inputs, which favors the exchange of commodities, parts and services. Information technologies have played a role by facilitating transactions and the management of complex business operations. Foreign direct investments are commonly linked with the globalization of production as corporations invest abroad in search of lower production costs and new markets. China is a leading example of such a process, which went on par with a growing availability of goods and services that can be traded on the global market.

Transport efficiency has increased significantly because of innovations and improvements in the modes and infrastructures in terms of their capacity and throughput. Ports are particularly important in such a context since they are gateways to international trade through maritime shipping networks. As a result, the transferability of commodities, parts and finished goods has improved. Decreasing transport costs does more than increasing trade; it can also help change the location of economic activities. Yet, transborder transportation issues remain to be better addressed in terms of capacity, efficiency and security (Brooks, 2008).

Finally, the financial sector also plays a significant role in integrating global trade, namely by providing credit for international commercial transactions. For instance, a letter of credit may be issued based upon an export contract. An exporter can thus receive a payment guarantee from a bank until its customer finalizes the transaction upon delivery. This is particularly important since the delivery of international trade transactions can take several weeks due to the long distances involved. During the transfer, it is also common that the cargo is insured against the event of damage, theft or delays, a function supported by insurance companies. Also, global financial systems permit the conversion of currencies according to exchange rates that are commonly set by market forces, while some currencies, such as the Chinese Yuan, are set by policy. Monetary policy can thus be a tool, albeit a contentious one, used to influence trade.

GLOBAL TRADE FLOWS

Geographical and functional shifts

Global trade flows have recently shifted with many developing countries having a growing participation in international trade. The nature of what can be considered international trade has also changed, particularly with the emergence of global value chains. This trend obviously reflects the strategies of multinational corporations positioning their manufacturing assets in order to lower costs and maximize new market opportunities, while maintaining the cohesion of their supply chains and the freight distribution systems that support them. In addition, another emerging trade flow concerns the imports of resources from developing countries, namely energy, commodities and agricultural products, which diverge from the conventional role of developing countries as exporters of resources.

The dominant factor behind the growth in international trade has been an increasing share of manufacturing activities taking place in developing countries with manufacturers seeking low-cost locations for many stages of the supply chain. The evolution of international trade thus has a concordance with the evolution of production. There are, however, significant fluctuations in international trade that are linked with economic cycles of growth and recession, and fluctuations in the price of raw materials, as well as disruptive geopolitical and financial events (Figure 2.3). The international division of production has been accompanied by growing flows of manufactured goods, which take a growing share of international trade. There are relatively fewer bulk liquids (such as oil) and more dry bulk and general cargo being traded.

While growth rates of the world GDP and merchandise production have a very high level of concordance, total merchandise trade is subject to significant fluctuations. Periods of decline are all corresponding to recessions, such as 1981–1982, the Asian Financial crisis

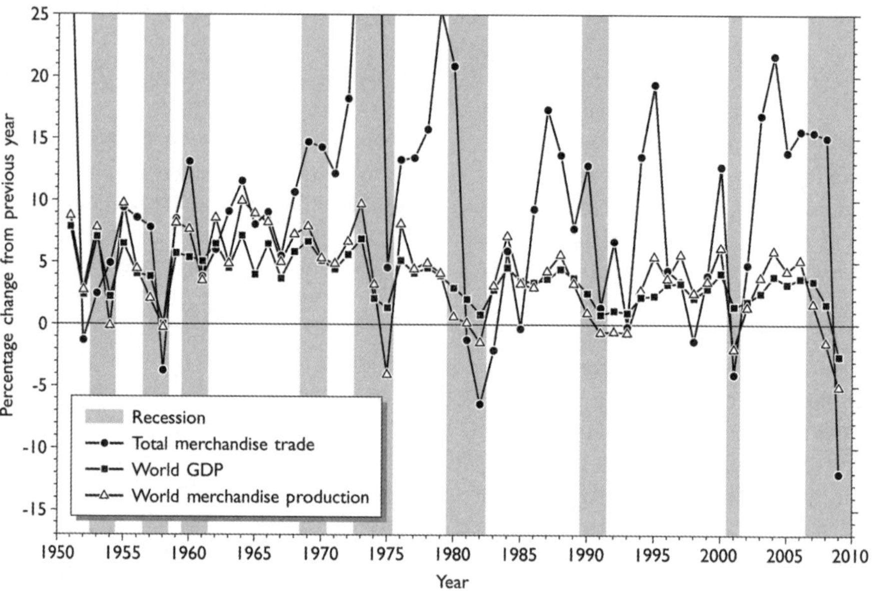

Figure 2.3 Changes in the value of the world's merchandise trade, production and GDP, 1950–2009 (in %)

Source: WTO

of 1997, the recession of 2001 and the financial crisis of 2008–2009. Commodity price fluctuations, particularly agricultural products and minerals (fossil fuels), are the factors contributing the most to changes in merchandise trade. The level of association between trade and production is much lower, particularly in recent years as many manufacturing activities were relocated to lower-cost locations. Thus, without additional demand, the relocation of a factory from one part of the world to another can be considered as a zero sum game from a production standpoint, but from a trade standpoint it results in additional flows. However, relocation commonly results in lower costs, which are likely to trigger additional demand.

A growing divergence is noted and which took place in three phases. Until the 1970s, the growth of trade, GDP and production was quite similar, underlining that globalization was still in its early stages and mostly involving finished goods and raw materials. The first significant divergence took place in the 1970s and was mainly related with the first two oil shocks that resulted in significantly higher energy prices and the corresponding surge in the value of total merchandise trade. This divergence was therefore driven by commodity prices. The second divergence took place after 1985 and was mainly linked with the emergence of an international division of production with the setting of manufacturing activities in developing countries. This divergence was driven by the setting of global production networks and supply chains. Once globalization reaches maturity, implying modest growth levels in trade, it is quite possible that commodity prices will again become the main factor of divergence between trade and economic output.

The triad

The geography of international trade still reveals the dominance of a small number of countries, mainly in North America, Europe and East Asia, which are commonly referred to as the triad. The United States, Germany and Japan account for about a third of

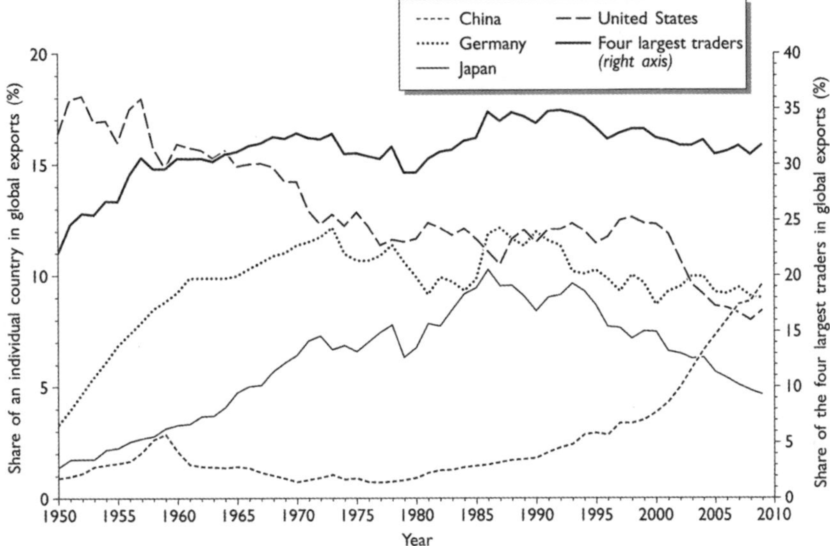

Figure 2.4 Share of world goods exports, leading exporters, 1950–2010

Source: WTO

all global trade, but this supremacy is being seriously challenged by emerging economies (Figure 2.4). Those geographical and economic changes are also reflected over trans-oceanic trade, with Trans-Pacific trade growing faster than Trans-Atlantic trade.

The first decade of the 21st century has seen a significant shift in the share of global trade of the leading exporters (United States, Japan, Germany and China more recently). The enduring trend involving the relative decline of American exports has accelerated to the point that Germany became the world's leading exporter in 2003, a role which was overtaken by China in 2009. Japan's share has been declining for about 25 years as it became an expensive location for manufacturing. There is thus a convergence and an enduring stability of the share of the world's four leading exporters, hovering around 30% of total exports. However, it must be considered that many American, Japanese and Korean corporations have relocated some of their production facilities to China, so a share of Chinese exports are embedded within supply chains essentially controlled by foreign interests.

Neo-mercantilism

Neo-mercantilism is reflective of global trade flows as several countries have been actively pursuing export-oriented economic development policies using infrastructure development, subsidies and exchange rates as tools. This strategy has been followed by developing economies, particularly in Pacific Asia, and resulted in growing physical and capital flow imbalances in international trade. This is particularly reflective in the American container trade structure, which is highly imbalanced and has acute differences in the composition of imports and exports. Still, these imbalances must be looked at with caution as products are composed of parts manufactured in several countries, with assembly often taking place in a low-cost location. In international trade statistics, this location assumes the full value of a finished good imported elsewhere even though it may have only contributed to a small share of the total added value. Electronic devices are illustrative of this issue (Figure 2.5).

The iPhone, a cellular phone marketed by Apple Computers, reflects well a product

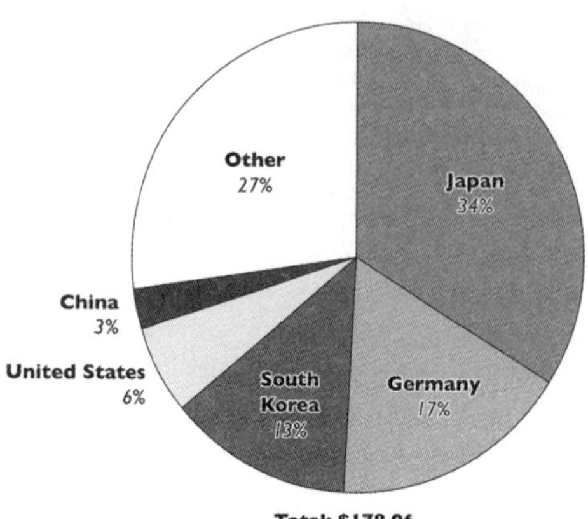

Figure 2.5 Value of iPhone 3G components and labor, 2009

Source: Xing and Detert, 2010

having an international division of production with parts and assembly taking place in several countries. It also represents well the difficulties of correctly assessing international trade balances in such a context. Since the final assembly of the iPhone takes place in China, if it is imported in the United States, its entire wholesale value (US$178.96 in this case) is attributed as a trade deficit with China. In reality, only about 3% of the wholesale value takes place in China, with the bulk of it concerning Japan (mostly for flash memory and tactile screen). In this case, the product exaggerates the true extent of trade imbalances since the country of origin accounts for a small share of the total added value of the good.

Regionalization has been one of the dominant features of global trade as the bulk of international trade has a regional connotation, promoted by proximity and the establishment of economic blocs such as NAFTA and the European Union. The closer economic entities are, the more likely they are to trade, which explains that the most intense trade relations are within Western Europe and North America. A similar, but more recent trend has also emerged in Asia, particularly between Japan, China, Korea and Taiwan.

INTERNATIONAL TRANSPORTATION

Physically enabling global trade

The growth of the amount of freight being traded as well as a great variety of origins and destinations promotes the importance of international transportation as a fundamental element supporting the global economy (CEMT, 2005). Economic development in Pacific Asia, and in China in particular, has been the dominant factor behind the growth of international transportation in recent years. Since the trading distances involved are often considerable, this has resulted in increasing demands on the maritime shipping industry and on port activities. As its industrial and manufacturing activities develop, China is importing growing quantities of raw materials and energy and exporting growing quantities of manufactured goods. The outcome has been a surge in demands for long-distance international transportation. The ports in the Pearl River delta in Guangdong province now handle almost as many containers as all the ports in the United States combined.

International transportation systems have been under increasing pressures to support additional demands in freight volume and the distance at which this freight is being carried. This could not have occurred without considerable technical improvements permitting the transport of larger quantities of passengers and freight, more quickly and more efficiently. Few other technical improvements than containerization have contributed to this growing mobility of freight. Since containers and their intermodal transport systems improve the efficiency of global distribution, a growing share of general cargo moving globally is containerized.

Consequently, transportation is often referred to as an enabling factor that is not necessarily the cause of international trade, but as a condition without which globalization could not have occurred. A common development problem is the inability of international transportation infrastructures to support flows, undermining access to the global market and the benefits that can be derived from international trade.

Transport chains

International trade requires distribution infrastructures that can support trade between several partners. Three components of international transportation facilitate trade:

- Transportation infrastructure. Concerns physical infrastructures such as terminals, vehicles and networks. Efficiencies or deficiencies in transport infrastructures will either promote or inhibit international trade.
- Transportation services. Concerns the complex set of services involved in the international circulation of passengers and freight. It includes activities such as distribution, logistics, finance, insurance and marketing.
- Transactional environment. Concerns the complex legal, political, financial and cultural setting in which international transport systems operate. It includes aspects such as exchange rates, regulations, quotas and tariffs, but also consumer preferences.

About half of all global trade takes place between locations more than 3,000 km apart. Because of this geography, most international freight movements involve several modes since it is impossible to have a physical continuity in freight flows. Transport chains must thus be established to service these flows, which reinforces the importance of intermodal transportation modes and terminals at strategic locations (Figure 2.6).

International trade is based on the notion of exchange, which involves what is being traded, the partners involved and the transactional environment within which trade takes place, namely custom procedures (tariff and non-tariff barriers). Commonly, international trade is seen as a series of commercial transactions between trade partners that tracks the value of what is being traded as well as the concerned nature of goods (such as standard international trade classification). Its extent, either in value or volume, is an abstract expression of the quantity of goods being exchanged as they do not represent the actual physical flows supporting trade.

The physical realization of international trade requires a transport chain which is a series of logistical activities that organize modes and terminals, such as railway, maritime and road transportation systems, and thus the continuity along the supply chain

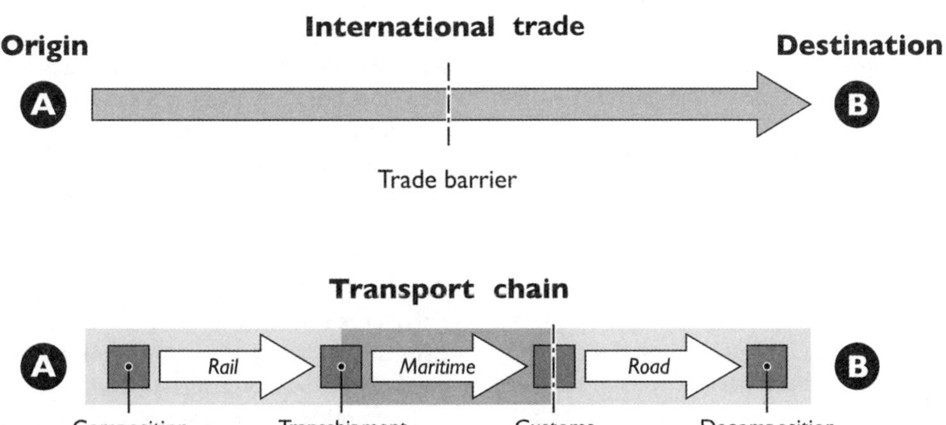

Figure 2.6 International trade, transportation chains and flows

through a set of stages, the most common being:

- The first stage in the transport chain is composition where loads are assembled at the origin, often on pallets and/or containers. Composition is an important process as it tries to achieve economies of scale over a transport chain by providing larger and easier to handle load units.
- The cargo being traded then moves along the transport chain using a transport mode, commonly rail or road, to reach a terminal where it is transshipped on an international transport mode (port or airport depending on the nature of what is being transported). Additional economies of scale become possible as several load units can be consolidated into a single large shipment, such as a loaded containership.
- Once cargo enters another country through a gateway (point of entry), customs inspection takes place as the cargo is transshipped over the inland transport system. Custom procedures and delays are among the most constraining factors in global freight distribution.
- The final stage of the transport chain, decomposition, takes place in proximity of the final destination. Loads are broken down into units corresponding to effective demand (orders).

In the operational reality of modes and terminals, international trade is a series of physical flows that may not necessarily use the most direct path, but the path of least resistance. The existence of inland corridors where economies of scale are more effective shapes the structure of freight flows as well as the selection of the port of exit. On the maritime side, transshipments hubs have become fundamental intermediary locations helping consolidate maritime flows and connecting different maritime systems of circulation. In such a setting, the container has become the fundamental element facilitating transfers between modes and supporting international trade flows. Distribution centers play an important role in physical flows since they can act as a buffer helping reconcile the temporal and spatial requirements of demand.

International transport modes

The importance of maritime transportation in global freight trade is unmistakable, particularly in terms of tonnage as it handles about 90% of the global trade. Thus, globalization is the realm of maritime shipping, with containerized shipping at the forefront of the process. The global maritime transport system is composed of a series of major gateways granting access to major production and consumption regions. Between those gateways are major hubs acting as points of interconnection and transshipment between systems of maritime circulation.

Although in terms tonnage air transportation carries an insignificant amount of freight (0.2% of total tonnage) compared with maritime transportation, its importance in terms of the total value is much more significant: 15% of the value of global trade. International air freight is about 70 times more valuable than its maritime counterpart and about 30 times more valuable than freight carried overland, which is linked with the types of goods it transports (e.g. electronics). The location of freight airports correspond to high-technology manufacturing clusters as well as intermediary locations where freight planes are refueled and/or cargo is transshipped.

The global system of freight circulation is articulated by major gateway regions (or gateway systems), often composed of a cluster of ports and airports within a metropolitan area. This does not mean that ports and airports are functionally integrated, but that the region they service is a major load center serviced by a variety of globally-oriented supply chains. Put together, the 39 largest gateway regions account for 90% of the containerized and air freight traffic. This underlines their fundamental importance in the transshipment of the world's trade and as intermediary (or final) locations within global supply chains (O'Connor, 2010).

The world's largest gateway region is the Hong Kong–Shenzhen freight cluster, accounts for 14.8% of the containerized and air freight traffic. If this cluster is expanded to include the Pearl River Delta (with Guangzhou), then its share reaches 16.7%. For Europe, the Rhine/Scheldt delta (from Amsterdam to Brussels) accounts for 7.5% of the global containerized and air freight volume. The most important North American gateway system is the Los Angeles/Long Beach system. Some of the gateways are dominantly hubs transshipping freight from one system of circulation to the other, such as Singapore, Colombo or Dubai.

Road and railway modes tend to occupy a more marginal portion of international transportation since they are above all modes for national or regional transport services. Their importance is focused on their role in the "first and last miles" of global distribution. Freight is mainly brought to port and airport terminals by trucking or rail. There are, however, notable exceptions in the role of overland transportation in international trade. A substantial share of the NAFTA trade between Canada, United States and Mexico is supported by trucking, as well as a large share of the Western European trade. In spite of this, these exchanges are a priori regional by definition, although intermodal transportation confers a more complex setting in the interpretation of these flows.

CONCLUSION

Many challenges are impacting future developments in international trade and transportation, mostly in terms of demographic, energy and environmental issues (Klare, 2001). While the global population and its derived demand will continue to grow and reach around 9 billion by 2050, the aging of the population, particularly in developed countries, will transform consumption patterns as a growing share of the population shifts from wealth producing (working and saving) to wealth consuming (selling saved assets). The demographic dividend in terms of peak share of working age population that many countries benefited from, particularly China, will recede (Bloom et al., 2003).

As both maritime and air freight transportation depend on petroleum, the expected scarcity of this fossil fuel will impose a rationalization of international trade and its underlying supply chains. Environmental issues have also become more salient with the growing tendency of the public sector to regulate components of international transportation that are judged to have negative externalities. Also, international trade enables several countries to mask their energy consumption and pollutant emissions by importing goods that are produced elsewhere and where environmental externalities are generated. Thus, international trade has permitted a shift in the international division of production, but also a division between the generation of environmental externalities and the consumption of the goods related to these externalities.

REFERENCES

Bairoch, P. and R. Kozul-Wright (1996) *Globalization Myths: Some Historical Reflections on Integration, Industrialization and Growth in the World Economy*, UNCTAD Discussion Paper No. 113.

Baldwin, R.E. and P. Martin (1999) *Two Waves of Globalisation: Superficial Similarities, Fundamental Differences*, NBER Working Paper No. 6904.

Bernstein, W.J. (2008) *A Splendid Exchange: How Trade Shaped the World*, New York: Atlantic Monthly Press.

Bloom, D.E., D. Canning and J. Sevilla (2003) *The Demographic Dividend: A New Perspective on the Economic Consequences of Population Change*, Population Matters Monograph MR-1274, Santa Monica: RAND Corporation.

Braudel, F. (1982) *The Wheels of Commerce: Civilization and Capitalism 15th–18th Century, Vol. II*, New York: Harper & Row.

Brooks, M. (2008) *North American Freight Transportation: The Road to Security and Prosperity*, Cheltenham, UK: Edward Elgar.

CEMT (2005) *Transport and International Trade*, Conclusions of Round Table 131.

Daniels, J.D., L.H. Radebaugh and D. Sullivan (2010) *International Business: Environments and Operations*, 13th Edition, New York: Prentice Hall.

Dicken, P. (2007) *Global Shift: Mapping the Changing Contours of the World Economy*, 5th Edition, London: Sage Publications.

Feenstra, R. (2004) *Advanced International Trade: Theory and Evidence*, Princeton, NJ: Princeton University Press.
Gilbert, R. and A. Perl (2008) *Transport Revolutions: Moving People and Freight without Oil*, London: Earthscan.
Hummels, D. (2001) *Time as a Trade Barrier*, GTAP Working Paper No. 18.
Klare, M.T. (2001) *Resource Wars: The New Landscape of Global Conflict*, New York: Henry Holt and Company.
Lakshmanan, T.J. et al. (2001) *Integration of Transport and Trade Facilitation: Selected Regional Case Studies*, Washington, DC: World Bank.
O'Connor, K. (2010) "Global City Regions and the Location of Logistics Activity", *Journal of Transport Geography*, Vol. 18, No. 3, pp. 354–362.
Porter M.E. (1990) *The Competitive Advantage of Nations*, London: Macmillan.
World Trade Organization (2010) *International Trade Statistics 2010*, Geneva: WTO.
Xing, Y. and N. Detert (2010) *How the iPhone Widens the United States Trade Deficit with the People's Republic of China*, ADBI Working Paper 257, Tokyo: Asian Development Bank Institute.

3

Transborder Transportation

William P. Anderson

INTRODUCTION

Globalization generally implies ever increasing flows of people and goods across international borders. Thus, an ever increasing proportion of personal and freight transportation operations must cope with borders as impediments to movement. At a time when tariff barriers are falling and technologies for identification and surveillance are proliferating, this might seem to be no great problem, as borders are more easily crossed than in the past. However, concerns with issues of international terrorism and illegal immigration have led some states to ever more scrutiny at their borders. Thus, crossing borders remains one of the greatest challenges in global transportation for both passengers and freight.

The purpose of this chapter is to review issues surrounding this challenge. Its focus will be on crossing land borders, which for our purpose may be defined as crossing borders by road and rail mode, but significant attention is also given to cross-border air and marine transportation. While both personal and freight transportation are considered, the emphasis is on freight. Many of the ideas introduced in this chapter will be illustrated with reference to the Canada–US border, which clears most of the international goods movement in the world's largest bilateral trade relationship.

The chapter is organized as follows. The next section provides a review of terminology and concepts related to borders and cross-border transportation. This is followed by a section that defines and reviews the major border functions: customs, immigration and security. Subsequent sections review the cost of border crossing, technological and institutional innovations to improve the efficiency of border functions and the provision of transportation services across borders.

BOUNDARIES AND BORDERS

While most people have an intuitive notion of what a border is, a precise definition of geographical concepts is helpful. First, a *boundary* is an abstract line separating the territories over which two states have sovereignty. Since the boundary is a legal entity, its precise location must be determined in a treaty between the two states. This means that for a state to have precisely defined territory, it must have boundary treaties with all contiguous states. Even where such treaties exist, the boundary may be delineated on paper but not demarcated on the ground, which means its exact location cannot be found without surveying.

The *border* is a more broadly defined geographical entity, comprising elements of the natural and built environment that define the boundary and control passage across it. Sometimes the distinction between the boundary and the border is one of precision; for example, one might say that a river defines the border between two countries, while the boundary is a precise line located somewhere in the river. For our purposes the main point is that the border includes a set of things that facilitate (roads, bridges, ferries), prevent (fences, military installations), monitor (cameras, motion detectors) and control (border crossing facilities) movement across the boundary. Another useful geographical notion is the *border region*, which is an area whose economy and daily life is highly influenced by its proximity to the border (Baud and Van Schendel, 1997).

The precise delineation of boundaries is relatively new in human history. Before the availability of surveying and cartographical technologies, impediments to travel such as mountain ranges, water bodies or even things as broad as forests and deserts were used to separate the territories of political entities. In Europe, the 1648 Peace of Westphalia gave rise to a more territorially-based notion of the sovereign state, creating an imperative for the delineation and demarcation of boundaries and the establishment of border facilities. The colonial expansion of European states in the 17th, 18th and 19th centuries led to the creation of many international boundaries that endure to this day, despite the fact that they were often drawn arbitrarily. As recently as the late 19th century, European powers delineated boundaries on the map of Africa without surveys on the ground and without regard to the economy or culture of African people. Until the second half of the 20th century, international boundaries were subject to change arising from diplomatic agreements and military conflict. In the years following World War II, an international consensus arose around the *territorial integrity norm*, a principle that in order to prevent armed conflict, existing boundaries should be treated as unchangeable (Zacher, 2001). While this has led to the preservation of colonial era boundaries that have retarded economic and cultural development in Africa, the frequency of wars over territory has declined. This does not mean that the political map has remained unchanged. The disintegration of states including the Soviet Union and Yugoslavia into multiple smaller states has created new international boundaries within pre-existing boundaries.

The late 20th century also saw the opening of a period of new definitions and disputes regarding marine boundaries. While this is a far too complicated topic to treat in any detail here, some basic definitions are important. Traditionally, each coastal state claimed sovereignty over a *territorial sea* within a relatively short distance of its coastline. Fishing disputes in the 1970s led some states to claim a much larger marine territory. In 1982, the Third United Nations Convention on the Law of the Sea set a number of territorial definitions that have been broadly adopted. Full sovereignty is extended to a territorial sea extending 12 nautical miles (about 19 kilometers) from the coast. In addition, control over marine resources is extended to an *exclusive economic zone* (EEZ) extending 200 nautical miles (370 kilometers) beyond the territorial sea (Figure 3.1). Not surprisingly, this has led to a proliferation of disputes since the EEZs of two or more states frequently overlap – especially where states claim sovereignty to small islands. From a transportation perspective, an important distinction is that vessels of other states have

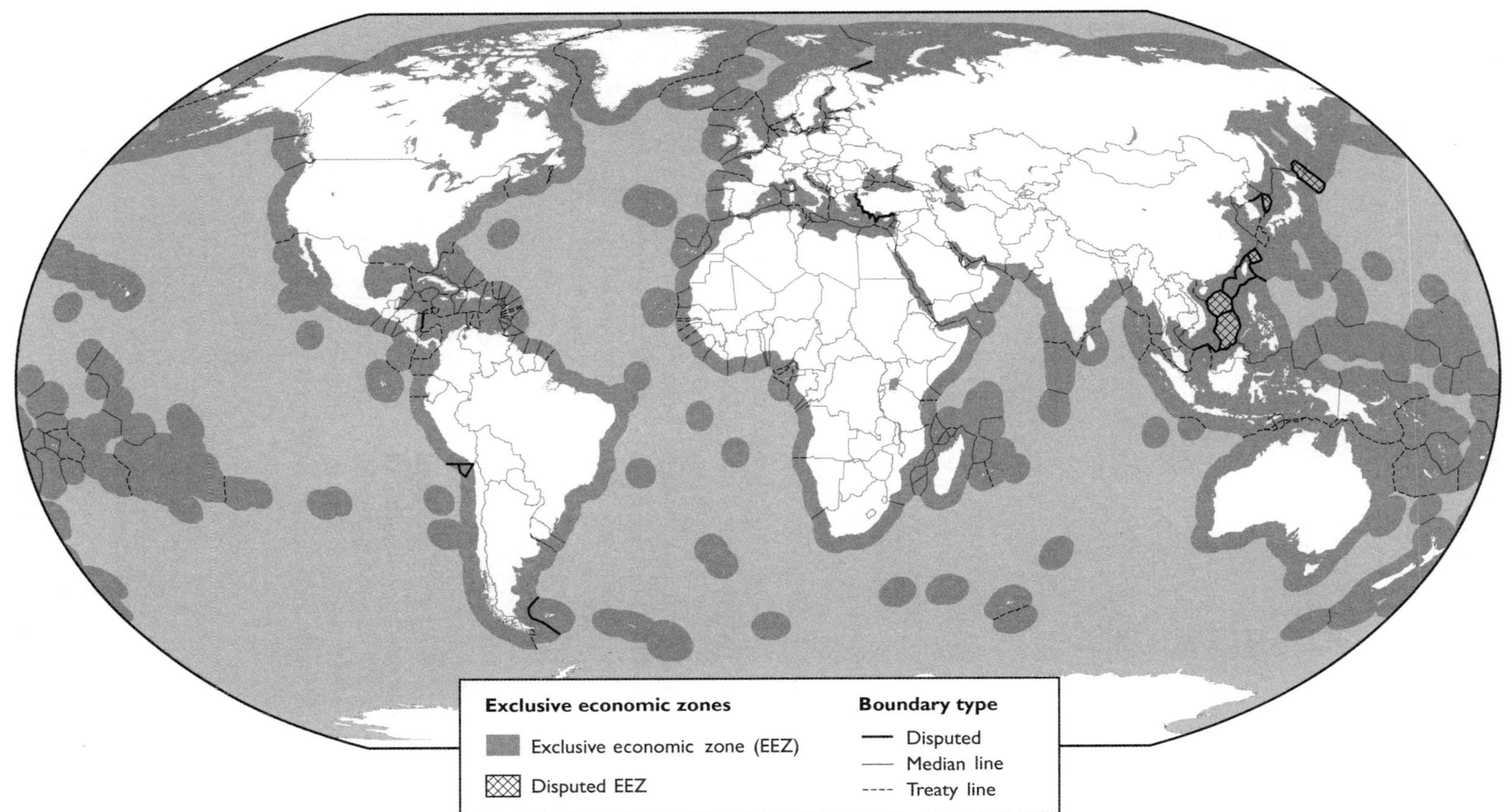

Figure 3.1 Global exclusive economic zones

Source: http://people.hofstra.edu/geotrans/eng/ch5en/conc5en/EEZ.html

freedom of navigation and flight within the EEZ. While they also have the more restricted right to "innocent passage" through the territorial sea, the coastal state has much greater authority over foreign vessels in that zone.

While boundaries have become more clearly delineated and immutable, it might appear that borders – or more specifically border functions – are declining in importance. At one time, the most important border function was defense. Since territory increasingly defined the state, defending territory was critical to preserving sovereignty. To some extent, the territorial integrity norm has reduced the importance of border defense. But changes in the technology of warfare that undermine the importance and even the possibility of defending lines on the ground have also reduced the defensive function of borders. After defense, the main functions of borders are customs and immigration control. With the reduction of tariffs and the application of information and communications technology to both customs and immigration, one might expect that borders as impediments to the movement of goods and people would be a matter of declining importance. Yet we are a long way from a "borderless world," and in some places such as North America border impediments have actually increased in recent years.

This is due in part to the emergence of what Andreas (2003) calls *clandestine transnational actors* (CTA) as a principal concern of border officials. CTAs are non-state actors who seek to cross borders for illegal purposes, including illegal immigrants, smugglers of contraband goods such as drugs and weapons, and terrorists. The attacks of September 11, 2001 had a transformative effect on the emphasis placed on the interdiction of terrorists as they cross international borders, especially to the United States. As I will discuss further below, the new emphasis on CTAs has at least partially offset technological and institutional developments that should make cross-border movement of people and goods easier.

The actual placement of boundaries and borders often depends on accidents of history and geography. For a country that is an island (Iceland) or archipelago (Japan), there are no land borders. For landlocked countries like Switzerland, Botswana and Laos, there are only land borders. "Land" border is often a misnomer since a river or lake often constitutes the border. While rivers provide natural lines on the map that are often made use of in boundary negotiations, they are problematic borders for a couple of reasons. First, river valleys have historically been regions of dense cultivation and settlement. Using rivers as borders often splits such regions leading to economic and cultural disruptions. (For example, the choice of the Congo River as a border by European colonialists in the 19th century divided its valley into what are now the independent states of The Republic of the Congo and The Democratic Republic of the Congo.) Second, for a river that is an important transportation artery, its use as a border implies that ships travelling on it will be able to make frequent stops without the delays and costs of border clearance on only one side of the river.

Borders also have the effect of creating bottlenecks in transportation networks. Figure 3.2 shows a hypothetical transportation network that is bisected by a border. Since the facilities needed for border inspections are expensive to build and maintain, there are usually only a few (in this case two) crossings, creating a few links that are subject to congestion and making the whole network vulnerable to the disruption of those links. Naturally this problem is exacerbated when a river forms the border because each crossing requires bridge, tunnel or ferry infrastructure. For this reason, the goal of complete elimination of border facilities (discussed below) can also lead to more highly connected transportation networks.

From the perspective of law enforcement and national security, borders play a special role as *lines of interdiction* and *zones of enhanced scrutiny*. "Interdiction" is a military term that refers to destroying, weakening or delaying your enemy *en route* to the battle ground. This type of strategy may also

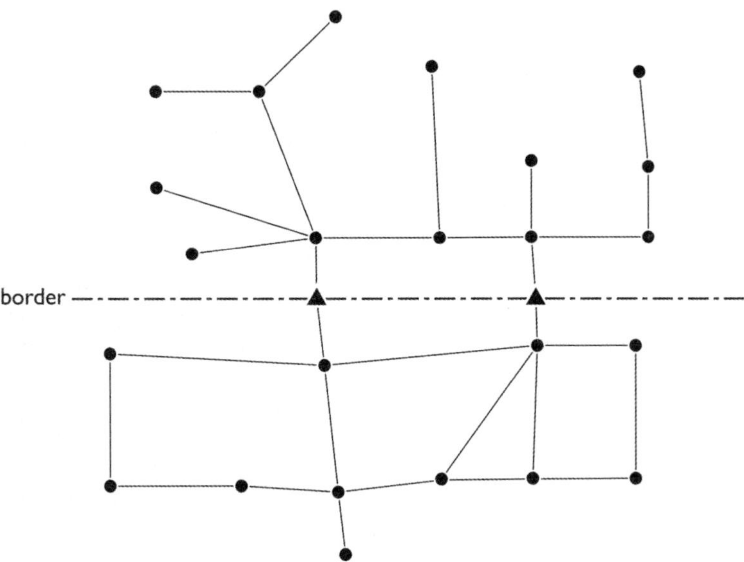

Figure 3.2 The effect of a border on a transportation network

apply in law enforcement, as in the case of interrupting the flow of drugs on its way to its ultimate point of consumption. Of course, the interdiction applies equally to preventing terrorist acts, since stopping a suicide bomber is more difficult once he has arrived at his intended target. In such contexts, borders are natural lines of interdiction. This is true not only because some criminal and terrorist activities involve movement of people and goods from outside the national territory, but also because borders are zones within which law enforcement and security agencies are free to apply a higher level of scrutiny than elsewhere. For example, in most Western countries a police officer cannot stop you on the street without cause and ask where you have been, where you are going or what you plan to do there, nor can he or she search your person or your vehicle. But a border official can do all of these things. In essence, borders are places where the relationship between the state and the individual is different than elsewhere and many civil rights are suspended. This applies not only to foreign nationals crossing into a country but also to citizens of that country returning after a trip abroad. While this generally makes us uncomfortable, it would be impossible for border agencies to carry out immigration, customs and security functions were this not the case.

BORDER FUNCTIONS

Border functions are actions that government agencies do to ensure that no goods or people pass into their territories illegally. There is a fundamental difference in how these functions are applied to goods and people who are transported by road or rail transportation as opposed to marine and air transportation. In the case of road and rail, paperwork, investigation and (if necessary) interdictions normally occur at the border itself. For marine and air transportation, these functions are carried out at terminal facilities (ports and airports) that may be located deep within national territory. Thus not all "border functions" occur on the border. This does not mean, however, that national boundaries are irrelevant to marine and air transportation, since ships and planes come under the authority of the state in question as soon as they pass into its territorial sea or air space.

Border agencies are government organizations that carry out border functions. At many borders, more than one agency is involved, including those responsible for customs, immigration, agricultural inspection, vehicle inspection, security, etc. At many borders there is also a military presence. Naturally, fragmentation of institutional responsibilities can lead to delays and confusion if their activities are not closely coordinated. There has been a tendency in recent years to consolidate responsibility for border functions under a common umbrella agency. For example, employees of separate agencies for customs, immigration, agricultural inspection, border patrol and a few others were combined into US Customs and Border Protection (CBP), an agency of the newly created Department of Homeland Security. While the impetus for this reorganization was the heightened concern over the terrorist threat, the consolidation of these functions makes it possible for a single office to carry out a broader range of functions. Other countries, including Canada (Canadian Border Service Agency) and the United Kingdom (UK Border Agency), have made similar consolidations in recent years.

Customs

Customs duties are government charges on imports or exports as they cross the border. (The word "*tariff*," which technically means a schedule of duties, is generally used to mean the rate at which the customs duty is charged.) Duties may be either specific, meaning that the tariff is defined on a per-unit basis, or *ad valorem*, which means that it is set as a percentage of the good's value. While duties may be charged on either imports or exports, import duties are much more common, because they can be used as a way of protecting domestic industries against foreign competitors.

Each country has a customs agency whose duty it is to collect all required customs duties and to ensure that all other laws related to goods coming across the border are enforced. In order to assess customs duties, the customs agency generally requires information on three characteristics of the goods:

1 *Goods classification*: Since customs duties are often targeted so as to protect particular industries or even particular firms, most countries have tariff rates that vary significantly across different types of goods. Before the duty is assessed, therefore, the goods must be assigned according to a detailed classification system. Most countries use the Harmonized System developed by the World Customs Organization.
2 *Goods valuation*: Duties charged on an *ad valorem* basis require an accurate statement of their value. Customs agencies are especially suspicious of attempts to reduce payments by underreporting the value of goods. Valuation practices also vary across countries; for example some countries' tariff rates are applied to a value that includes insurance and freight while others are charged only on the factory gate value.
3 *Country of origin*: Duties may also vary according to the country of origin. This is especially true for members of trade blocs in which goods originating from other bloc members are charged lower or zero duties. Determining the country of origin of goods with components produced in various countries is a complex task, requiring extensive paperwork.

Collection of duties is not the only responsibility of customs agencies. Some countries impose quotas, under which a maximum annual quantity of a particular type of good can be imported from each country of origin. National standards for quality or design may also be applied to imports, so for example certain garments may only be imported if it can be certified that they are made from fire retardant materials. Evidence of inspections may also be required, especially on agricultural commodities. Things like quotas, standards and inspections are often referred to as *non-tariff barriers* and may be an even greater impediment to cross-border trade than duties.

Generally the onus is on the importer to provide all the necessary information so that duties may be accurately assessed and other national laws regarding imports may be applied. Given the complexity of this task, the great majority of importers employ certified customs brokers to manage the reporting and payment of duties. (See David and Steward, 2008, chapter 16 for more information on customs procedures.)

One can imagine the delays that occur when all of this information has to be reported and assessed at the border. It is not very long ago that truck drivers had to bring information regarding their loads to the offices of customs brokers located in close proximity to the border, who in turn would generate the necessary paperwork to get the truck cleared through customs. In fact, this type of process is still found at border crossings in many developing countries. In the developed world, information is now exchanged electronically among importers, carriers and customs brokers, as well as submitted electronically to customs agencies, making the process of customs clearance much faster.

Interdiction of contraband is a law enforcement function that is generally the responsibility of customs agencies. Contraband refers to goods that may not be legally transported across the border such as drugs and weapons. Drug interdictions are among the most highly publicized activities of border agencies.

Immigration

The immigration border function ensures that no one enters the national territory illegally. The term "immigration" is misleading here because the great majority of people who pass under the scrutiny of immigration authorities are only entering temporarily for business, tourism, family visits and similar short-term purposes. While the principal focus of most immigration authorities has been the prevention of illegal immigrants, the interdiction of terrorists has now emerged as a high-priority goal.

Immigration officers must examine two types of travel documents: passports and visas. The passport is a document issued by the holder's country to confirm his or her identity and citizenship. Despite some shortcomings, the passport has become the universally accepted standard for identification at borders (Salter, 2004). The visa is a document issued by the country the person wants to enter defining the period and circumstances under which he or she may remain there. Some countries have visa waiver programs for countries whose citizens are considered less of a threat, allowing them to enter with only a passport. In the US, people eligible for visa waiver coming from countries other than Canada must register under the Electronic System for Travel Authorization (ESTA) several days prior to presenting themselves for entry.

Visas may in some cases be obtained upon arrival at the country, but more often they must be obtained in advance through the embassy or consulate offices of the country that issues them. Visas are defined for different purposes such as transit, tourism, education, business and temporary work.

The level of scrutiny on people entering the United States was ramped up significantly with the introduction of the US-VISIT program (Visitor and Immigration Status Indicator Technology), which required biometric information of people entering the country so that it can be checked against databases of terrorists and other known criminals. Originally only required for those that require visas, US-VISIT has now been extended to all non-US citizens, with the exception of Canadians.

While immigration functions are mostly relevant for personal transportation, they have significant implications for freight, since every truck driver, train crew member and other freight worker is subject to immigration scrutiny. In some cases it is necessary to change drivers and crews as trucks and trains cross the border in order to comply with rules about foreign workers.

Security

Border security refers to measures taken by a national government to prevent people and goods from illegally passing into its territory. As such, it is not really distinct from customs and immigration. However, the increased emphasis on security expressed by border agencies in recent years reflects a shift in emphasis from preventing illegal crossing intended for economic gain to preventing crossings by people intent on causing direct harm to the nation and its people – most notably members of non-state terrorist entities. While border agencies have always been concerned with the movement of terrorist agents and their weapons, these concerns have become more highly emphasized in the aftermath of the attacks of September 11, 2001 (Kaufmann, 2007). This is especially true in the US, as indicated by the following statement of priorities:

> CBP is one of the Department of Homeland Security's largest and most complex components, with a priority mission of keeping terrorists and their weapons out of the U.S. It also has a responsibility for securing and facilitating trade and travel while enforcing hundreds of U.S. regulations, including immigration and drug laws.[1]

This statement supports Andreas' (2003) argument that the emphasis on the border has shifted to the interdiction of clandestine transnational actors. It is also supports the often repeated dictum that security "trumps" trade when it comes to US border policy. This does not mean, however, that a completely separate set of border functions is required to enforce security. After all, the basic processes employed in customs and immigration functions contribute to security objectives. Investigations are made to ensure that no container or vehicle is carrying goods other than those that have been reported and that no traveler is crossing the border other than for the legitimate purpose that he or she claims.

The shift in emphasis, however, calls for an intensification of scrutiny. Most border agencies would be content to know that they discover a very large proportion, say 95%, of falsely reported customs declarations or smuggled drugs and handguns. The costs of achieving higher rates would probably exceed the benefits. When it comes to terrorists and their weapons, it may be that no failure rate is regarded as acceptable. This is true for both practical and political reasons. While the failure to stop one illegal immigrant will have little aggregate economic impact, the failure to stop one terrorist, or one small shipment containing a bomb or contaminant, could have catastrophic consequences. Also, terrorist acts have greater political impact than trade issues or even illegal drug shipments. As a result, proposed solutions that come out of the political sphere, such as 100% inspection of containers, may carry more force than the recommendations of transportation security experts. Especially in North America, there have been numerous calls for border policies that strike a balance between the goals of security against terrorism and the facilitation of trade (Kirgin and Matthieson, 2008; Sands, 2009), but the priority of security over economic benefit remains a predominant political theme.

International organizations have introduced a number of standards to upgrade security at transportation facilities. Noteworthy among these is the International Maritime Organization's International Ship and Port Facility Security (ISPS) Code, which came into force in 2004 and has been signed onto by most significant trading nations. The ISPS Code enhances security by requiring: (1) enhanced control over who has access to port facilities, (2) monitoring of port activities using surveillance cameras and enhanced record keeping, and (3) improved communications systems to more quickly spread information about a real or suspected threat (David and Steward, 2008, chapter 15).

The World Customs Organization (WCO) has also played a major role in upgrading freight security. While the ISPS deals mostly with port facilities, the WCO SAFE (Security and Facilitation in a Global Environment) addresses the individual shipment. Its underlying logic is that it is far better to focus inspection on high-risk shipments, and that the risk of a particular shipment can be assessed on the basis of information in its customs documents. Thus the customs and security functions need to be highly integrated. The main mechanism in SAFE is the transfer of customs information to officials in the destination country *before* it leaves the port of origin. This allows officials in the destination country to identify high risk consignments in advance and request that they be inspected by customs officials in the port of origin before they are loaded onto a ship, plane or other vehicle (WCO, 2007).

The International Civil Aviation Organization (ICAO), an agency of the United Nations that establishes standards and procedures for non-military aviation, has undertaken a number of security initiatives. The Universal Security Audit Programme assesses the capability of national governments in maintaining international standards of aviation security and provides support for upgrading those that fall short. It has also been responsible for establishing international standards for passports through its Machine Readable Travel Documents Programme.

Some countries, most notably the United States, have introduced their own security measures that go well beyond those of international institutions. For example, under the US Trade Act of 2002, cargo information for all shipments to the United States must be conveyed electronically to CBP in advance of presentation at the border or port of entry. The required lead time varies by mode: 24 hours for marine, 4 hours for air, 2 hours for rail and 1 for truck. Other new requirements on persons travelling into the US affect truck drivers and train crews as well as business and pleasure travelers. For example, the US Visit program subjects people other than Canadian citizens to registration with border officials and possible fingerprinting. The Western Hemisphere Travel Initiative now requires all people entering the US to carry passports (Canadians were previously exempt from the passport requirement).

BORDER COSTS

Dealing with the requirement of customs, immigration and security and the delays that occur at border checkpoints implies a significant cost of moving goods and people across the border. The cost of delays depends not only on the average delay time, but also on the variability of that time (Anderson and Coates, 2010). For goods moving in Just-In-Time (JIT) supply chains, late delivery of a component could result in shutting down a production facility, so extraordinary steps need to be taken to cope with this uncertainty. This is typically addressed by either building buffer times into shipping schedules or holding buffer inventories on the opposite side of the borders, both of which are costly strategies (Cudmore, 2006; Anderson, 2009). Adding buffer times results in extra labor costs and reduced equipment cycles while buffer inventories have significant holding costs. In cases where manufacturing supply chains are integrated across the border, such as in the US and Canadian automotive industries, these costs are multiplied as the same component may cross the border several times (Center for Automotive Research, 2002).

A good way to think of border costs is as the difference between the cost of moving a shipment or person a given distance with and without a border along the route – in other words, moving domestically *vs.* moving internationally. For example, a factory faced with the choice of sourcing an input from two suppliers will make its decision based on the delivered price, which in the case of the domestic supplier will include transportation costs and in the case of the cross-border supplier will include both conventional transportation costs and all the costs of crossing the border. Thus, while many border costs such as preparing customs documents or running background checks on drivers do not fall under the conventional definition of transportation costs, their ultimate effects are the same as increments to transportation costs.

In this example we can define the delivered price of the domestic supplier as

$$p_d = \overline{p}_d + t_d$$

where $\overline{p}_d$ is the mill (factory gate) price of the domestic supplier and t_d is its transportation cost. The comparable delivered price for the cross-border supplier is

$$p_c = \bar{p}_c + t_c + b_c$$

where b_c is the cost of crossing the border. If the two suppliers are equivalent in terms of quality and reliability and if $t_d = t_c$, then the factory will only source from the cross-border supplier if

$$\bar{p}_d - \bar{p}_c > b_c$$

Thus, the cross-border supplier can only win the business if its mill price is lower than that of the domestic supplier by a sufficient amount to offset the border cost. This implies a cost to the cross-border supplier because it must be willing to accept a lower per unit revenue than the domestics supplier. It also implies a potential cost to the factory because in those cases where $\bar{p}_d - \bar{p}_c > 0$ but $\bar{p}_d - \bar{p}_c < b_c$ it is not able to take advantage of whatever cost or efficiency advantages allow the cross-border supplier to sell the input at a lower price.

Note that the border cost has the same effect as a customs duty – in fact if there is a non-zero duty it should be included in b_c. We can therefore define the border costs as a tariff rate equivalent r_c, such that

$$p_c = (\bar{p}_c + t_c)(1 + r_c)$$

$$r_c = \frac{b_c}{(\bar{p}_c + t_c)}$$

There have been a number of attempts to measure the border effect as expressed by r_c. Most have used an econometric approach whereby trade flows among domestic jurisdictions are compared with trade flows among international jurisdictions (for example, trade flows between pairs of US states are compared with flows between states and Canadian provinces) and after controlling for other factors such as distances and relative wages, the differences are attributed to border costs (McCallum, 1995; Helliwell, 1997; Brown and Anderson, 2002; Anderson and Wincoop, 2003). These studies generate high estimates of tariff equivalent in the range of 0.2 to 0.5 or even greater. However, since they undoubtedly reflect a host of influences such as historical patterns, cultural differences, differences in preferences and within-firm transfers they grossly overestimate the type of border costs we have in mind here. A more focused econometric approach is to test whether the increased security regime that came into place after September 11, 2001 increased border costs sufficiently to have an impact on trade flows. Two studies of this type come to opposite conclusions, with Burt (2007) finding no impact and Globerman and Storer (2009) finding a significant negative effect on Canadian exports to the US.

The alternative method is to make a detailed accounting of actual expenditures on both border delays and compliance with all legal border requirements. Since this is an arduous task there are few such studies. Taylor, Robideaux and Jackson (2004) conducted such a study for border crossings between the US and Canada. Their general finding was that overall border costs represent a tariff equivalent of about 2.7%, but that this value is 4% for truck freight. Table 3.1 summarizes their midrange annual cost estimates, separated into those that are attributable to delays and uncertainty in crossing times and "general" border costs that include the administrative costs of customs and all other border programs and duties paid. The last category is substantial (about \$1.6 billion) because despite the fact that the US and Canada are part of the NAFTA free trade zone, they are not part of a customs union, so duties are required for goods originating outside the NAFTA zone. Of the costs borne by carriers, the largest category is delay due to the referral of a small proportion of loads to secondary inspection for examination that may involve scanning or complete unpacking. The major delay and uncertainty cost borne by manufacturers is due to losses when lower cost sourcing options are foregone because of high and uncertain crossing times. The largest single

Table 3.1 Summary of Canada–US border crossing costs

Delay and uncertainty cost	US$m	% of total
Carrier		
Primary delays	324.2	3.1%
Secondary delays	755.4	7.3%
Excess plan time	416.4	4.0%
Reduced cycles/other	120.7	1.2%
Driver documentation/fax	250.7	2.4%
Carrier subtotal	1,867.4	18.1%
Manufacturer		
Lost sourcing benefits	1,530.0	14.9%
Extra inventory carrying	458.0	4.4%
Manufacturer subtotal	1,988.0	19.3%
Personal traveler	159.0	1.5%
Total delay and uncertainty		
Related cost	4,014.4	39.0%
General border costs		
Carrier	350.0	3.4%
Manufacturer	5,358.0	52.1%
Federal Staff	571.5	5.6%
General subtotal	6,279.5	61.0%
Total border cost	10,293.9	100.0%

Source: Taylor et al., 2004, midrange estimates

cost category, accounting for over 50% of total border costs, is the "general" cost to manufacturers, which is principally the cost of customs compliance.

The above-average tariff equivalent cost for trucking implies that rail, which is the other major freight mode for Canada–US trade, must have lower border costs. There is a number of reasons for this. For one thing, the management of information in the rail industry is more highly centralized, which makes it easier to comply with requirements such advanced conveyance of manifests. Since rail is less labor intensive than trucking, there are fewer personnel to pass through immigration. Also rail lends itself to the application of scanning technologies more easily. At most Canada–US crossings intermodal trains are subjected to 100% VACIS scanning (see below) without causing major, unpredictable delay.

TECHNOLOGICAL AND INSTITUTIONAL INNOVATIONS

There is a variety of strategies available for reducing delays and costs associated with border crossing. Some involve new technologies, some involve institutional innovations and many involve both. We can differentiate these strategies into two main types: those that increase the speed and efficiency of functions occurring at the border and those that shift traditional border functions to other locations.

Naturally the simplest way to speed procedures at the border is to increase the staffing of border agencies so that more vehicles, shipments and individuals can be inspected simultaneously. Increased staffing is sometimes limited in the short run by available infrastructure such as too few inspection lanes or too little space for secondary inspection. Expanding this infrastructure is often constrained by an inadequately large footprint at border facilities, so the construction of bigger and better inspection plazas is often needed before staff can be increased substantially. Since the busiest border crossings are often in built-up urban areas, such expansion is often a challenge.

Another way to increase the rate of inspection is to use technology that allows inspections to occur more quickly. Two technologies have been particularly effective in this regard. The Radio Frequency Identification (RFID) technology makes it possible to automatically transfer information about the traveler, vehicle or load to the inspection agent as it approaches the inspection station. RFID chips included in passports and other travel documents are recognized by a sensor as soon as coming within a few meters of the inspection line and the information on the document is electronically transferred. As a result the inspector has access to security and other databases on his or her screen before the vehicle or person arrives.

In those cases where some physical inspection of a shipment is required, opening and unpacking the truck or container can often be replaced by scanning with a Vehicle And Cargo Inspection System (VACIS) that uses gamma rays to allow general identification of contents. Unpacking is still sometimes necessary, as the VACIS image is not precise enough to distinguish between similar types of loads. But the VACIS image can tell if the load is of a different type than reported on official documents (for example, metal rather than soft goods), if the container has contents when it is reported empty, or if it contains stowaways.

Of course, increasing the rate of throughput from inspection plazas is of little use if the capacity of infrastructure leading up to them is inadequate. In such cases, only construction of new roads, bridges, tunnels, ports, airports, etc. can speed up the rate of clearance. However, at most facilities – especially land border facilities – it is the inspection process rather than the capacity of transportation infrastructure that leads to delay.

As already noted, there is a large number of complex functions that need to be executed in order to ensure that goods and people enter the national territory legally. Given that most of these functions must take place at the point of border inspection, it is not surprising that borders create bottlenecks. A natural approach to speeding up movement through border is to shift as many as possible of those functions to another place and an earlier time. This is essentially the rationale for requiring advanced electronic conveyance of manifests. The information in those documents is fed into risk assessment software and in some cases reviewed by human agents to determine whether the load should be cleared for entry or whether secondary inspection is warranted. If the manifest information were not presented until the shipment arrived at the border, clearance would be delayed while its risks were assessed on the spot. With advanced conveyance, the determination is made in advance so that those trucks or containers that are deemed to pose a risk can be separated and all others can be released more quickly.

Taking this general approach a step further are *trusted traveler* and *trusted shipper* programs. While advanced conveyance prescreens loads on a case-by-case basis, these programs provide more permanent forms of pre-qualification. In the case of trusted traveler programs, an individual submits to a background check and an interview with border officials. If he or she is deemed to be of low risk, a card is issued that allows the bearer to use special expedited lanes in the inspection area. (Examples are the US–Canada and US–Mexico NEXUS cards.) *Trusted shipper* programs are similar in spirit but somewhat more complicated. Shippers such as manufacturers who regularly sell across the border and carriers that specialize in cross-border goods movement are unlikely to intentionally harbor terrorists or move contraband across the border. The main risk is that their staff may be infiltrated by criminal groups or that illegal goods may be surreptitiously placed onto their vehicles. Thus, even regular cross-border shipments cannot be treated at low risk unless it can be verified that a high level of supply-chain security has been maintained. Programs such as the US Customs–Trade Partnership Against Terrorism (C–TPAT) and the Canadian Partnership in Protection (PIP) invite various supply-chain partners (shippers, carriers, owner-operators, customs brokers, third party logistics providers, etc.) to become certified by adopting high security standards and submitting to regular inspections of not only their vehicles but also their terminal facilities and personnel. If every supply chain partner associated with a particular shipment is C–TPAT certified, it can be cleared into the US using the accelerated FAST (Free and Secure Trade) lane. Similarly, if all partners are PIP certified the shipment can use a FAST lane entering Canada.

While the advantages of becoming eligible for the FAST lane seem obvious, several years into the program it is still the case that most cross-border shipments are not eligible. Part of the reason is that gaining C–TPAT and PIP certification is expensive, as it generally requires major upgrades to security systems, running security checks on employees and changes to facilities such as the installation of secured gates to truck yards and the construction of fences to separate areas for truck storage and employee parking. There are significant scale economies involved in making such improvements, so the cost per shipment is generally too high for small carriers. The payoff to accelerated clearance is greatest for firms carrying high value goods in JIT supply chains, since it helps avoid the carrying cost of buffer inventory. Not surprisingly, the automotive industry with its large firms, high value shipments and lean supply chains has the highest penetration of C–TPAT and PIP certification. A major problem with trusted shipper programs is that shipments that are eligible for rapid clearance often have to wait in the same queue with ineligible shipments – such as when a single lane for trucks leads across a long bridge before separate lanes are available for eligible trucks. (This is the situation at the Ambassador Bridge between in the Windsor–Detroit corridor, the busiest land crossing for freight between Canada and the US; see Anderson, 2010.)

ELIMINATION OF BORDERS

Given the economic friction caused by movement across borders, the complete elimination of border functions is an often cited objective. But as Andreas (2003) and others have observed, the hoped for transition to a borderless world has been thwarted by the rise of terrorism, human smuggling and other threats. In some places borders have actually become more impermeable in recent years. This does not, however, rule out the possibility that some borders between closely associated states can be eliminated. Especially within regional trade blocs, it may be possible to harmonize policies sufficiently so that border functions become unnecessary, making it possible to dismantle the normal border apparatus.

The most prominent example of this is the *Schengen Area*, a set of states within which international passage is no longer subject to border inspections. Named for a town in Luxembourg where a 1985 treaty was signed committing states to work toward the elimination of border functions, the Schengen Area now includes most of the states of the European Union and three non-EU states: Iceland, Norway and Switzerland. (It is not yet completely implemented in three EU states: Bulgaria, Romania and Cyprus.) This does not mean that states in the Schengen Area have opened their borders to the rest of the world. Rather, all border functions have been transferred to *perimeter borders* separating Schengen states from non-Schengen states (Anderson, 2000). Thus, the idea of eliminating some borders based on the Schengen model is often called the *perimeter approach*.

The keys to the perimeter approach are policy harmonization and mutual trust regarding enforcement. The necessity of border functions arises because of inconsistency in policies of the bordering states. For example, if the visa requirements of two states were identical, and if each state trusted the other to adequately enforce those requirements on people entering its territory from third countries, it would not be necessary to check identifications at the border because anyone who made legal entry into one state would be eligible for legal entry into the other. For the movement of goods, common policies on external tariff, product standards, agricultural policy, health inspection and a range of other issues would be needed to completely eliminate the need for border checks.

It has become common to conflate the notions shifting functions away from the border and the perimeter approach, but there is a fundamental difference between them. In the former case functions are shifted to different places and times where they can be executed more efficiently than at the border, while in the latter they are eliminated entirely. For example, under a true perimeter approach trucks that cross boundaries would not be subjected to any greater security requirements than those that provide only domestic service. Thus programs like C–TPAT, PIP and FAST would not be needed.

The institutional vehicle for implementing the perimeter approach would be some form of regional trade bloc or other regional organization of states. Given the example of the European Union, there has been an ongoing discussion of the possibility for eliminating border checks in the NAFTA area, or at least between the United States and Canada (Noble, 2005). The practicality of such a plan is limited by the impediments to establishing sufficient harmonization and trust under the type of free trade relationship that exists in North America.

Regional trade blocs can generally be placed in the following four categories based on their level of integration:

- *Free trade area*: a set of states among which tariffs and non-tariff barriers have been eliminated.
- *Customs union*: a free trade area in which all states agree to a common external tariff, so that customs functions for movement among the states can be eliminated.
- *Common market*: a customs union within which there is free movement of capital and labor. Free trade in services is also generally implied.
- *Political union*: a common market where the member states have agreed to harmonize or jointly determine policies that lie outside the traditional definition of trade policy, including labor, health, agricultural, transportation, environmental and foreign policies. It is also linked with a common currency.

The European Union is the only major trade bloc that has progressed to the state of political union and is therefore the most capable of the level of policy harmonization required by the perimeter approach. By contrast, NAFTA is not even a customs union. Even if a customs union could be established, the issue of immigration from Mexico to the United States makes it extremely unlikely that a NAFTA common market would be achieved. The prospects may be better for the US and Canada, but the absence of any supranational institution such as the European Commission means that negotiations would be complex and lengthy, especially on issues where there are significant policy differences such as firearms and visa requirements.

This does not suggest that the elimination of border checks is not a worthy goal, but it is unlikely to be achieved soon. Also, while a comprehensive application of the perimeter approach may not be possible in the short term, the strategy of policy harmonization to eliminate border functions might be applied in specific areas such as agricultural and food safety. While such an approach cannot make the border disappear, it should make the border run more smoothly by reducing the number of border functions.

CROSS-BORDER TRANSPORTATION SERVICES

Unless all goods are unloaded and transferred at the border, cross-border freight movement involves some trade in transportation services. For example, if an American trucking company moves a consignment from a US origin to a Canadian destination it is providing transportation services in a foreign country as soon as it crosses the border. This brings up two types of problems. The first is compliance with technical standards for transportation operators, which may vary between the two states. The second is cabotage restrictions that limit the ability of transportation providers to sell their services in a foreign country.

The classic problem of technical standards is when national rail systems have inconsistent track gauges, making it impossible to link networks across borders. While most gauge inconsistencies have been resolved with adoption of the standard gauge (1435 mm), some still exist, for example between countries of the former Soviet Union that use the 1520 mm Russian gauge and neighboring EU countries using standard gauge.

A more current problem, especially in North America, is inconsistency in truck size and weight (TSW) standards. Most of the trade within NAFTA is in goods moved by trucks, but the three countries have widely varying

TSW standards, with Mexico and Canada both allowing higher gross weights and having more liberal regulations on long combination vehicles (LCVs) than the United States. To complicate matters further, Canadian provinces and US states have their own TSW regulations, leading to 66 different regulatory regimes within the NAFTA area (Mercier, 2007). This presents carriers with the choice between making cargo swaps between trucks with different configurations or operating with the lowest common denominator configuration that will be legal in all jurisdictions – generally a single semi-trailer truck carrying no more than 36,288 kg (80,000 pounds).

Cabotage refers to the provision of transportation service between two points within the same country by a foreign firm. Cabotage is restricted under NAFTA in the sense that a Canadian truck could move loads from a Canadian origin to US destination or from US origin to a Canadian destination, but not between a US origin and US destination since it would be considered as cabotage. The problem with cabotage restrictions is that they lead to frequent empty back hauls, especially at crossings where cross-border flows are imbalanced. For example, a recent survey of trucks crossing the Canada–US border at Blaine Washington found that more than half of trucks delivering goods from the US to Canada came back empty (Goodchild and Klein, 2010). Cabotage restrictions reflect the fact that NAFTA does not extend to free trade in transportation services. In the case of the European Union, cabotage restrictions have been lifted but only after many years of negotiation and legal challenge (Lakshmanan et al., 2000).

CONCLUDING COMMENTS

Despite trade liberalization, new technologies for communication and surveillance, and improved border procedures, crossing borders remains one of the principal challenges in global transportation. Increased concern about the movements of terrorists and other clandestine transnational actors has led to a new regime of enhanced scrutiny that has offset many of the institutional and technological changes that once promised to make borders irrelevant. While the threat of international terrorism is very real, the intensification of scrutiny is reinforced by public opinion that is more aware of the benefits of security than of the benefits of trade. Especially in the United States, the strategy of interdiction takes priority over trade facilitation.

While the Schengen Area provides an example of how some borders can be completely eliminated by means of policy harmonization, the institutional context in which Schengen developed is not present in many other places. The elimination of borders by means of a perimeter strategy is therefore a long-term objective at best in most regions. In the short term, more incremental steps of the type described above are needed to mitigate the enormous friction on global trade created by international borders.

Finally, there is a set of critical and complex issues that this chapter has not addressed. Nearly all technological and institutional innovations that make it possible to speed up security functions at borders have implications in terms of privacy and rights. Risk assessment requires databases of detailed personal and commercial information. Can the secrecy of these databases be guaranteed? Might sensitive information be conveyed inappropriately via an RFID chip? A perfectly innocent person or firm may be identified as high risk because others with similar profiles have committed violations in the past. While this probably cannot be helped, it presents the danger that such an assessment might circulate beyond its intended sphere leading to possible economic losses and even violations of civil rights. One might argue that a person or firm wanting to avoid such possibilities should simply refrain from crossing borders, but how realistic and how equitable is this in the globalized society? These questions may have been put to the side in the scramble to make borders function in the intensified security regime of the past decade, but they are likely to become more pressing in the future.

NOTE

1 http://www.cbp.gov/xp/cgov/about/

REFERENCES

Anderson, J.E. and E. Van Wincoop (2003) Gravity with Gravitas: A Solution to the Border Puzzle, *American Economic Review*, Vol. 93, No. 1, pp. 170–192.

Anderson, M. (2000) The Transformation of Border Controls: A European Precedent?, in P. Andreas and T. Snyder (eds.) *The Wall Around the West: State Borders and Immigration Controls in North America and Europe*, Rowman & Littlefield, Lanham, MD.

Anderson, W.P. (2009) Cross-border Supply Chains in the Post 9/11 Security Environment, The Impact of Volatility on Canada's Supply Chains and Transportation, *Proceedings of the 44th Annual Conference of the Canadian Transportation Research Forum*, pp. 471–484.

Anderson, W.P. (2010) Strategies for Increasing the Use of the FAST Program at Canada–US Border Crossings, *Proceedings: Seminar on Canada–US Border Management Policy Issues*, April 12, 2010, Border Policy Research Institute, Western Washington University.

Anderson, W.P. and A. Coates (2010) Delays and Uncertainty in Freight Movements: the Canada–US Border Crossings, Transportation Logistics Trends and Policies: Successes and Failures, *Proceedings of the 45th Annual Conference of the Canadian Transportation Research Forum*, pp. 129–143.

Andreas, P. (2003) Redrawing the Line: Borders and Security in the 21st Century, *International Security*, Vol. 28, No. 2, pp. 78–111.

Baud, M. and W. Van Schendel (1997) Toward a comparative history of borderlands, *Journal of World History*, Vol. 8, No. 2, pp. 211–242.

Brown, M. and W.P. Anderson (2002) Spatial Markets and the Potential for Integration Among Canadian and American Regions, *Papers in Regional Science*, Vol. 81, No.1, pp. 99–120.

Burt, M. (2007) *Tighter Border Security and its Effect on Canadian Exports*, Conference Board of Canada, International Trade and Investment Centre, Ottawa.

Center for Automotive Research (2002) *Estimating the New Automotive Value Chain*, Sustainability and Economics Development Strategies Group, Ann Arbor, MI.

Cudmore, E. (2006) Just In Time Inventory Systems and Uncertain Border Wait Times, unpublished document, University of Waterloo.

David, P. and R. Steward (2008) *International Logistics: The Management of International Trade Operations*, Third Edition, Cengage Learning, Mason, OH.

Globerman, S. and P. Storer (2009) Border Security and Canadian Exports to the United States: Evidence and Policy Implications, *Canadian Public Policy*, Vol. 35, No. 2, pp. 171–186.

Goodchild, A. and M. Klein (2010) Near Border Operational and Logistical Efficiency: Implications for Policy Makers, *Proceedings: Seminar on Canada–US Border Management Policy Issues*, April 12, 2010, Border Policy Research Institute, Western Washington University.

Helliwell, J.F. (1997) National Borders, Trade and Migration, *Pacific Economic Review*, Vol. 2, No. 3, pp. 165–185.

Lakshmanan, T.R., U. Subramanian, W.P. Anderson and F. Leautier (2000) *Integration of Transport and Trade Facilitation*, The World Bank, Washington, DC.

Kaufmann, D. (2007) Does security trump trade?, *Law and Business Review of the Americas*, Vol. 13, No. 3, pp. 619–642.

Kirgin, M. and B. Matthieson (2008) *A New Bridge for Old Allies*, Canadian International Council, Ottawa.

McCallum, J. (1995) National Borders Matter, *American Economic Review*, Vol. 85, No. 3, pp. 615–623.

Mercier, T.J. (2007) Bringing Harmony to North America's Truck Size and Weight Regulations, *Journal of Transportation Law, Logistics and Policy*, Vol. 74, No. 1, pp. 55–85.

Noble, J. (2005) Fortress America or Fortress North America?, *Law and Business Review of the Americas*, Vol. 13, No. 3, pp. 619–642.

Salter, M.B. (2004) Passports, Mobility and Security: How Smart Can the Border Be?, *International Studies Perspectives*, Vol. 5, pp. 71–91.

Sands, C. (2009) *Toward a New Frontier: Improving the US–Canadian Border*, Brookings Institution, Washington, DC.

Taylor, J., D.R. Robideaux and G.C. Jackson (2004) U.S.–Canada Transportation and Logistics: Border Impacts and Costs, Causes and Possible Solutions, *Transportation Journal*, Vol. 43, No. 4, pp.5–21.

World Customs Organization (2007) WCO SAFE Framework of Standards, http://www.wcoomd.org/files/1.%20Public%20files/PDFandDocuments/SAFE%20Framework_EN_2007_for_publication.pdf

Zacher, M.W. (2001) The Territorial Integrity Norm: International Boundaries and the Use of Force, *International Organization*, Vol. 55, No. 2, pp. 215–220.

4

Containerization and Intermodal Transportation

Antoine Frémont

INTRODUCTION

In half a century, containerization – the use of standardized large containers, unopened in transit between shipper and consignee, transferable from one type of transport to another – has reshaped international shipping, linking previously independent transport modes. Scheduled ocean lines formerly carried cargo between seaports only; once unloaded onto docks, freight was reloaded and moved inland via trucks, trains, barges or a combination of means known as "multimodal" or "combined transport". (The latter term applies to shipping via several modes, but with a minimized trucking segment.) Standardized containers and handling equipment gradually replaced that segmented system with one that integrates all transport steps and modes – ships, trucks, railroad cars, barges. (Another mode, shipping via airplanes, offers a faster alternative for high-margin goods.) This containerized freight shipping system is referred to as "intermodal". Intermodal transport systems link far-flung factories, supplying them with components and parts and conveying finished goods to distribution centres near large metropolitan areas. It is safe to say, in fact, that globalization could not have taken its present form without containerized international freight shipping.

Originally a simple technical innovation, the container has gone on to drive much broader changes. From the beginning, scheduled-lines shipping companies, freight brokers and handlers suspected containers might revolutionize their industry. They eventually retooled ocean cargo systems to fit the intermodal systems and supply chains sought by manufacturers and distributors. This chapter describes the opportunities containerization created, showing how this "box" led the shipping industry to create a new international transport system. It emphasizes containerization's effects on intermodal freight networks and the pivotal role of seaports within them.

TECHNICAL AND ORGANIZATIONAL PROGRESS

Handling productivity gains

Originating in the 1950s with Malcolm McLean in the United States (Levinson, 2006), containerization is a simple idea, based on moving freight in high-capacity standardized containers. These units fit onto 53-foot-long freight trucks, and their structure allows them to be stacked seven high in ships' cargo holds. A twist-lock mechanism facilitates handling and stowage. Containerization's popularity quickly led to standardized container sizes, definitively set by the ISO (International Standards Organization) in 1974. As easy to handle and stow as basic boxes, specialized container types include open top, flat rack, refrigerated and tank formats. Containerization rests on standardized load sizes, containers, shipping vehicles and container ships that can carry an infinite variety of freight, from textiles or electronics to waste paper for recycling.

With containers, portside handling achieves very high levels of productivity. While traditional cargo ships spent about 60% of their time in port, no cargo handling would take place during four-fifths of each docking period. A 21 January 1965 article in the *Financial Times* claimed the Matson Line could unload a specially-equipped 6,500-tonne ship in 850 man-hours instead of the 11,000 man-hours needed for a traditional vessel of the same size, reducing dockworkers' handling time by 90% and the length of port calls by 80%. Cranes, lifts and transtainers (which transfer containers from sea-going vessels onto either trucks or rail wagons) can move several thousand tonnes of freight within ten hours or so. Those few hours added to the time needed to enter port, dock and perform other manoeuvres means that a container ship remains in port for only twenty hours or so in all – a spectacular gain in handling productivity, and one that underpins containers' success.

Table 4.1 Increases in the size of world's fully cellular container fleet

	Average ship size	Average number of new buildings delivered per year	Largest container ship in world fleet (TEU)
1991	1,362	1,819	4,428
2000	1,824	2,841	7,060
2008	2,653	3,452	14,000

Source: Drewry, 2009

Vessel size and economies of scale

A second major consequence of containerization lies in increasing ship sizes to reduce slot costs and increase loading rates. Economies of scale prove the surest way for shipowners to reduce their costs in a competitive industry. On a per-unit-shipped basis, ocean freight's share of a product's total cost has decreased since the 1960s, and remains marginal. This is a remarkable statistic: it reflects the five generations of successively larger container ships that have emerged during that period. The decisive step occurred at the end of the 1980s, when shipowners began to order "post-Panamax" vessels, too large to traverse the Panama Canal. Its locks can only accommodate 32-metre (5,000-TEU capacity[1]) or smaller ships, at least until an expansion is completed in 2015 (Charlier, 2000). The largest container ships measure nearly 400 metres, draw 16 metres of water when fully loaded, and have a more than 12,000-TEU capacity (Table 4.1). The economic crisis beginning in 2008 abruptly halted the evolution towards ever-larger ships. But in December 2010, the world's leading shipping company, Maersk Line, ordered a series of record-breaking 18,000-TEU container ships from a South Korean shipyard. These ocean carriers will be longer and wider than anything ever built before, and require a new generation of cranes that can stretch across 22 rows of containers. The carriers follow a revolutionary design, with new propulsion systems and other advanced technology, meant to greatly reduce slot costs and carbon dioxide emissions.

Intermodal transport: Port-to-port, door-to-door logistics

The intermodal container allows door-to-door supply chains. Unloading at a port terminal is but one step in the journey from exporter to importer. Segmented shipping has given way to a variety of modes, selected not only for their intrinsic advantages but for their relative contributions to the chain. Each mode keeps its identity and importance, but its role is determined by the shipping system's objectives (Hayuth, 1992). Large-volume shipping via rail and waterways can maintain economies of scale, but these modes must surmount high fixed costs and dependence on infrastructure. They are cost-effective for short-distance, regular, large-volume shipments, and especially advantageous for long distances. Conversely, trucking offers the most flexibility relative to demand, and usually boasts a well-developed and interlinked network, difficult to beat for short distances. Frequency and regularity provide two other key features of intermodal shipping: ocean carrier services often run weekly, with multiple companies serving the same route. The frequency of inland rail and waterway services depends on volume; trucking, on the other hand, adapts to demand constantly. Door-to-door transport follows production or distribution logistics that run from supplier to customer, with production driven by demand.

Containerized door-to-door transport systems lend themselves especially well to managing extended freight flows, due to their frequency, regularity and reliability. "Full Container Load" (FCL) containers take on complete loads from one consignor; their numbers can be increased or decreased depending on quantities and destination. Containerization also allows regular shipping of small lots, by grouping freight from different sources into a single container; this is known as a "Less Than Container Load" (LCL), a shipment type that provides work and profits for freight forwarders. Heaver (2002a) lists the potential advantages of this type of logistics integration for a container operator. For a shipping line, demand from one client for a certain activity may support another. Just as airlines build hotels to fill their planes, carriers may provide logistics services to fill up their containers and secure a more extensive customer base. They may find opportunities to reduce transaction costs between chain components by internalizing them and controlling the entire supply chain; this provides greater transparency.

Other synergies arise from shared information systems, which can expand carrier services from simply managing container flows to managing goods. Lastly, logistics integration enables greater business diversification, thus providing better protection against demand and price fluctuations in any one segment of the supply chain. These reasons show why individual ocean carrier companies (such as Maersk Line) now control many distribution functions that formerly remained separate. With an increasing level of functional integration, many intermediate steps in the transport system have disappeared. However, vertical integration of the supply chain also opens up competition between various stakeholders seeking to control it (Figure 4.1).

Hub-and-spoke networks and "fewer-but-bigger" strategies

Increased ship size requires larger freight flows, since economies of scale depend on higher cargo load factors. This means freight flows must concentrate along a few major shipping routes. Starting in the 1980s, the hub-and-spoke system – developed by airlines for express courier services – began spreading to ocean carriers. Hub-and-spoke networks offer all possible linkages, organizing traffic in a star shape around a geographic centre with connections to other destinations. At these "transshipment" ports, large "mother ships" transfer containers to smaller vessels that connect with local service routes; this process is known as "feedering" and the number of containers handled by a transshipment port is

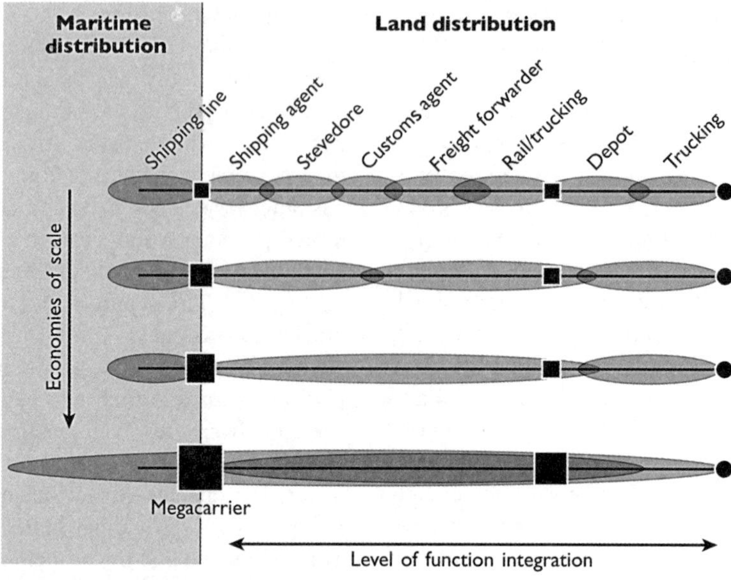

Figure 4.1 Transport system integration
Source: Notteboom and Rodrigue, 2005

its "throughput". Carriers developed transshipment ports – critical nodes in maritime networks – to increase efficiency.

In Figure 4.2, the number of connections declines from ten in a fully interconnected network (Figure 4.2a) to four in a pure hub-and-spoke model (Figure 4.2b); large freight units become necessary for the latter to reach economies of scale. In real life, an intermediate solution occurs: most often structured as a hub, it also offers direct (point-to-point) services, depending on market demand.

Hubs relay freight to those secondary markets where traffic flows do not justify opening direct intercontinental routes. A powerful freight consolidation tool, the hub also multiplies the number of possible destinations; smaller markets can be served by a single supplementary physical link, e.g. by a small feeder ship. Hub-and-spoke systems follow a global, integrated market logic rather than a segmented one.

The example in Figure 4.3 shows how a single origin/destination matrix and a number of transported containers can provide several shipping combinations. Our hypothetical case links two continents with a flow of exports from cities and ports of origin (CO, PO) towards ports and cities of arrival (PA, CA). The exported volumes are proportional to the scale of the cities and the ports, as measured e.g. by their economic importance or population size. The first configuration (Figure 4.3a) involves a direct land link between the ports and the cities of origin or destination and two ocean carrier services; it can occur for two reasons. One arises from the early days of containerization, when ships' capacity remained limited and shipping volumes might justify two services. The other arises if CO3 and PO3 generate a demand for shipping large enough to justify a dedicated ocean carrier service. The second configuration (Figure 4.3b) shows an increase in the size of container ships, which may occur when the export zone achieves economic and political integration; this in turn allows rationalization of the network, merging two ocean carrier services into one and creating economies of scale for the maritime leg of the trip.

The third configuration (Figure 4.3c) shows the network as structured by one or more very high-capacity ocean carrier services, calling

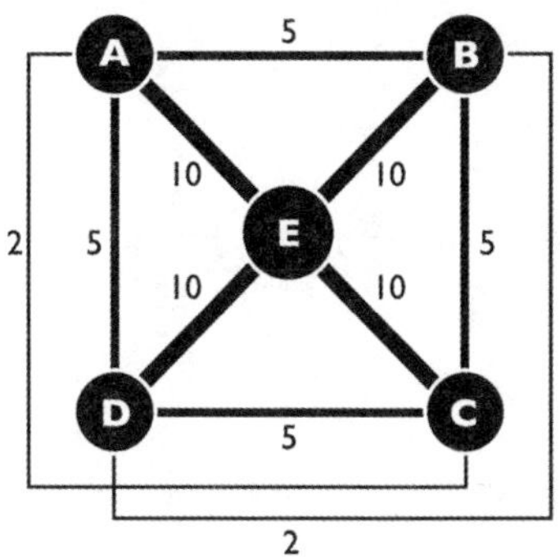

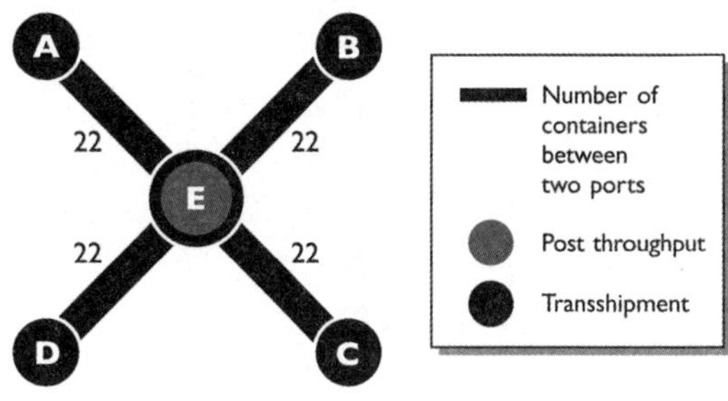

Figure 4.2 Hub-and-spoke network

only at the largest ports. Two feeder services link them with secondary ports. Unit freight trains on the import side create a direct and cost-competitive link between PA3 and inland destinations. PA3's hinterland is no longer restricted to CA3, but enlarges considerably. The number of containers handled in PO3 and PA3 significantly increases as a result of feedering transshipments. These sites act as maritime and terrestrial hubs and as transshipment and hinterland ports. In (Figure 4.3d) exports depend on a maritime transshipment hub (TH) located near the region of origin and on major East–West ocean traffic flows. This maritime hub means that very large mother ships need not deviate from their round-the-world routes (Zohil and Prijon, 1999; Ashar, 2000, 2002). All of the containers are handled twice in this model. The transshipment hub has no inland link; it is a purely maritime harbour whose success entirely rests on the intermediacy of its location (Fleming and Hayuth, 1994). By setting up direct high-capacity links with an inland centre (IC), PA3 has strengthened its hold on the extended and consolidated hinterland, as well as its role as a hinterland port.

These four theoretical configurations are not mutually exclusive. They can be combined, depending on the shipping lines' objectives and – above all – according to the market situation. The first two solutions would provide shippers with the shortest transit times and the greatest market accessibility. However, the hub solution lengthens transit times, increases the number of transshipment steps, and requires high coordination between the regular shipping lines that call at the port. The carrier's choice of hinterland ports or transshipment hubs critically affects shipping performance. The hub genuinely acts as the network's nerve centre; it may offer greater flexibility, but its extended system remains vulnerable to disruptions along the transport chain.

Transshipped containers represent an ever-increasing share of worldwide port traffic, rising from 17% in 1990 to 28% in 2008 (Drewry Shipping Consultants, 2009) – reflecting the success of hub-and-spoke systems. Within intermodal networks, one should distinguish three types of ports: those with hinterland connections, transshipment ports, and those that offer facilities for both. The expansion of these intermodal networks requires information systems that can track containers and freight in real time, bill various service combinations, and process customs operations. Containerization thus relies on the rapid development of information and communication technologies.

GEOGRAPHY OF CONTAINERIZATION AND INTERMODAL TRANSPORTATION

In addition to transforming the maritime and port industries, containerization and intermodal

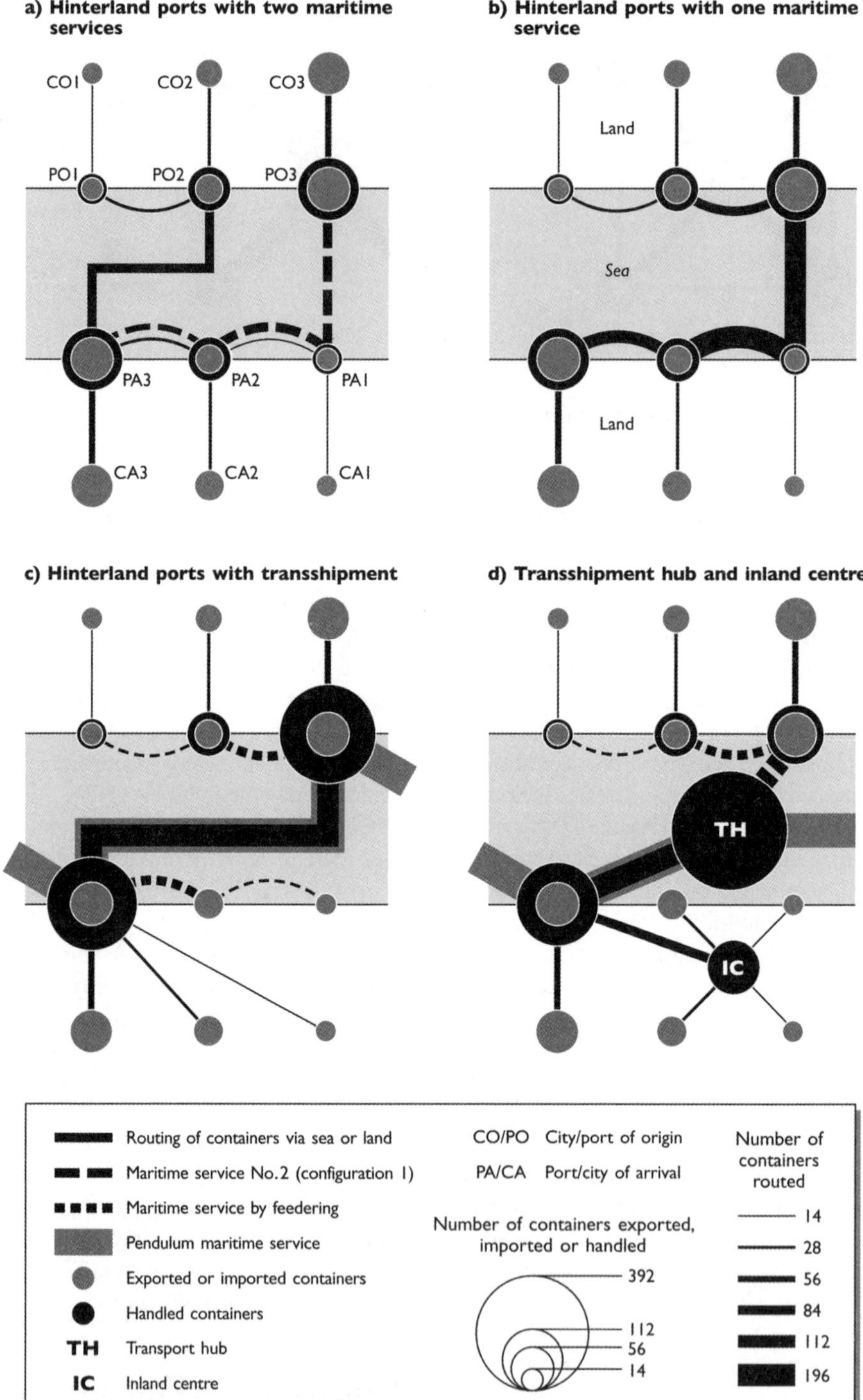

Figure 4.3 Maritime and inland port configurations

freight transport have had an enormous effect on the world's economy. In fact, their broadening of international trade makes them key factors in globalization, changing the hierarchy of ports worldwide and favouring the development of global intermodal shippers and servicers.

The snowball effect

International trade growth since the Second World War would not have been possible without containerization, at least not at current levels. The very idea of large-scale, diverse manufacturing centres several thousand miles from intermediate or final markets remained inconceivable, as long as ocean shipping proved unreliable, slow and expensive. By removing those constraints, containerization has provided the backbone of world trade and globalization. Since the 1970s, it has grown 8% to 10% per year: the world's ports handled more than 500 million TEUs of freight in 2008, up from 88 million in 1990, 39 million in 1980 and a little over 4 million in 1970. The share of general cargo in total ocean freight cargoes rose to 40% in 2008, versus less than 30% at the beginning of the 1970s. An estimated 80% of general cargo is now containerized. In 2010, the capacity of the world's fleet of container ships exceeded 13 million TEUs, compared to 0.5 TEUs in 1990 (UNCTAD, 2010).

In 2009, a 12% decline in international trade – unprecedented in the post-war period – provoked a severe crisis in containerized ocean shipping. Port container traffic dropped more than 10%; orders for new ships abruptly stopped in autumn 2008; nearly 10% of the container ship fleet went into mothballs by spring 2009; ocean shipping rates tumbled on all routes, and shipping companies suffered financial losses (Containerisation International, 2010). While shipping companies undergo cyclical crises due to oversupply, the recession that started in 2008 proved especially brutal. However, international trade once again made strong gains in 2010. These events provoke two questions: has the period of uninterrupted high growth since the 1970s now ended? Is containerization entering a more mature period with lower growth rates? The answers depend in large part on the evolution of international trade – both its future geography and its modes of integration.

The Asian ocean cargo axis

Eighty percent of all containers circulate between three economic centres: North America, Europe and East Asia, with the last-named now acting as the prime mover of ocean shipping. The growth of Asian economies has rested on containerization as an essential tool. According to Global Insight, four of the five largest container-exporting nations are Asian: China, Japan, Taiwan and South Korea, with the United States holding second place overall. In 2009, East Asian ports handled more than half of the world's containers, up from less than 25% in 1980 (Figure 4.4). The region boasts six of the world's largest ports and 12 of the top 20, compared to seven in 1980 and only one in 1970 (ISL, 2010). Asia is structured along a North–South maritime axis that runs from a group of Japanese ports – Tokyo–Yokohama, Nagoya, Osaka–Kobe – to Singapore, including the port of Busan in South Korea, the Chinese ports on the Yangtze River and Pearl River Delta, and the port of Kaohsiung, Taiwan (Figure 4.5).

This maritime axis has gradually developed since the 1970s, in tandem with the region's national economies. The so-called "Asian Dragon" ports emerged in the 1980s: Hong Kong, Singapore, Kaohsiung and Busan, their importance notably due to transshipment traffic. Since the 1990s, China has been the centre of growth: its ports visibly joined the Asian maritime axis in the 2000s, handling more than 100 million TEUs in 2008, up from 1.5 million in 1990 and only a few thousand in 1980. China's share of

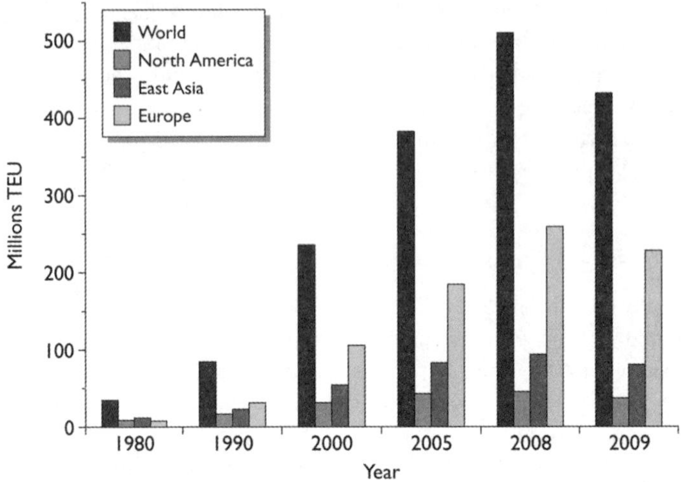

Figure 4.4 Maritime container traffic increases since 1980, by region (millions TEU)

Source: based on CI-OnLine

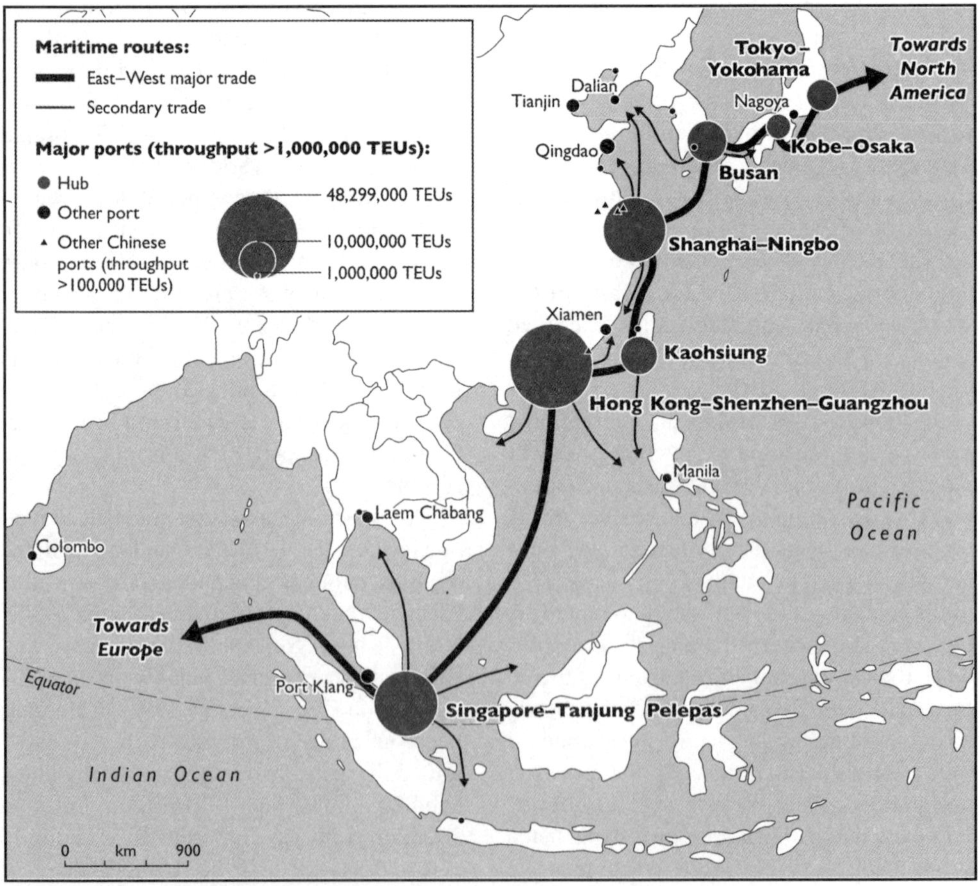

Figure 4.5 Asia's maritime routes, 2010

Source: A. Frémont and L. Vacher, 2011, Université Paris-Est, IFSTTAR, SPLOTT

Asian ocean freight handling has risen to 50%. Three large port regions concentrate most of China's external trade: the northern ports around the Bohai Gulf, i.e. Dalian, Quinhuangdao, Tianjin and Qingdao; the Yangtze River Delta ports, Shanghai and Ningbo; and the Pearl River Delta ports, Hong Kong, Shenzhen and Guangzhou. The latter two port regions are the world's largest, achieving a throughput of 30 million and 50 million TEUs respectively. Between the Shanghai–Ningbo pair and the Pearl River Delta, China's Xiamen port stands opposite Taiwan's Kaohsiung. Intra-Asian container traffic further increases the importance of this cargo axis: it accounted for 50 million TEUs in 2008, or nearly 30% of the world's container trade, making the intra-Asian market the largest in the world (Drewry Shipping Consultants, 2010).

East Asia: the centre of a worldwide maritime highway

The Trans-Pacific shipping route runs east from the heart of Asia to the United States or west towards Europe via the Indian peninsula and Suez Canal. The Asian cargo trade axis forms one segment of a cargo-shipping artery that circumnavigates the globe, linking the world's three main economic centres. Since the 1980s, the North Atlantic route has been reduced to a side road along this shipping freeway. Container traffic reflects the asymmetric and enormous international trade imbalance: many ships leave Europe and North America with empty cargo containers! Since the 1990s, the percentage of empty containers handled in the world's ports has remained at more than 20% (Drewry Shipping Consultants, 2010).

Along this East–West freight freeway, transshipment ports sprout on each side of the Panama Canal – from the Suez to Gibraltar at Algeciras and Gioia Tauro in the Mediterranean and, from the Red Sea to Singapore, at Dubai, Colombo in Sri Lanka and Port Klang in Malaysia. These transshipment ports play a vital role in organizing North–South traffic: buoyed by the overall growth in the containerized system, their importance increases in absolute value even as their share of world cargo traffic – about 20% – has remained constant since the 1980s.

On a global scale, two major land-based intermodal systems extend the maritime networks: the North American railroad system and the Rhine River waterway system. The former continues the Trans-Pacific route. It originated in the 1980s with a simple technological innovation: container double-stacking on railroad flatbeds. Trains' carrying capacity doubled for a marginal additional cost, making rail freight competitive with trucking; some American trains can carry up to 400 TEUs of double-stacked containers. Historically, freight railroads follow an East–West axis, and are owned by several companies; they play a key role in bringing containers from Asia inland (Figure 4.6). A limited number of inland freight terminals, regularly linked by shuttle trains from seaports, allows freight traffic to spread out across the continent; trucks then carry the containerized cargo up to about 500 km to inland warehouses, where it is unloaded and sorted for distribution to its final destinations. Chicago is the most important rail link by far, serving as the hub for the entire continent.

In Europe, the Rhine River forms the main inland shipping axis, running 800 km from Rotterdam to Basel. It traverses the economic heart of Europe, including Germany's Rhine Valley, the second largest exporter in the world. More than two million containers flow along the Rhine, including one million between Rotterdam and Antwerp alone. In accordance with the Vienna International Congress of 1815 and the Mannheim Convention in 1864, the Rhine and its tributaries form an international free-trade zone, without customs taxes at the borders or fuel taxes. This gives the river a sizeable advantage over roadways. Containerized freight services shuttle between the ports of Rotterdam and Antwerp, along the Middle Rhine to the Saar–Rhine–Main region, and along the Upper

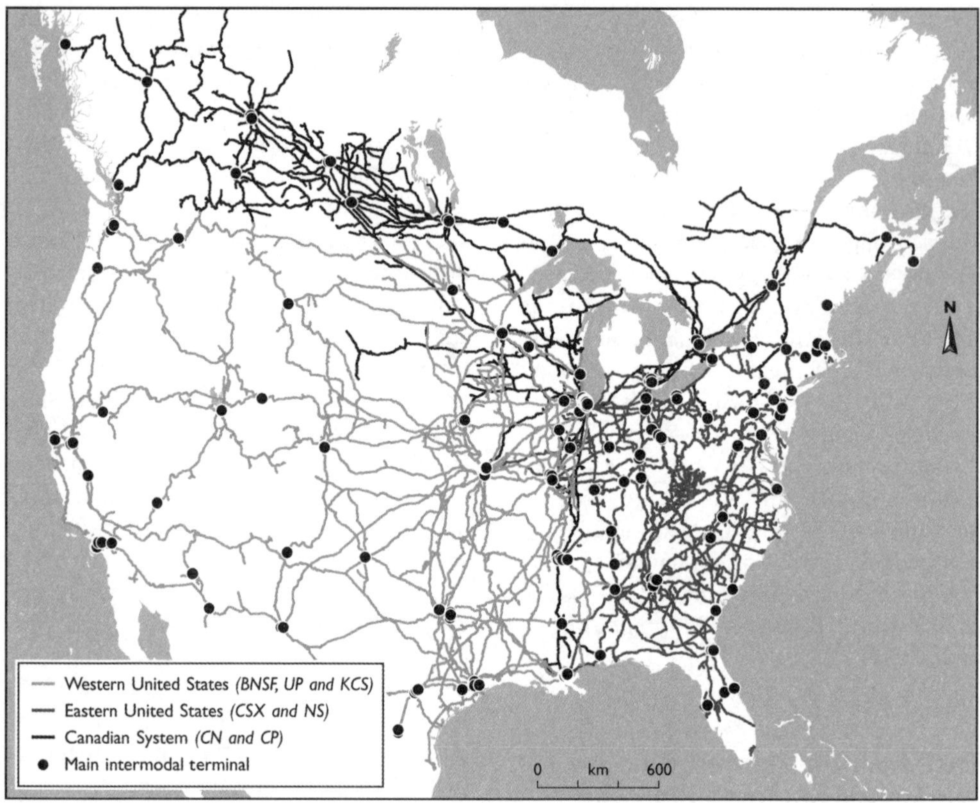

Figure 4.6 North American rail system

Source: Rodrigue and Notteboom, 2009a

Rhine at Karlsruhe to Basel. On the Lower and Middle Rhine, convoys can transport up to 500 TEUs, while the Upper Rhine's capacity is limited to 192 TEUs. Between Rotterdam and the Upper Rhine, river freight rates run 30% less than trucking rates. Rail freight services, from ports in northern Europe to inland destinations without waterway access, complete the intermodal service, carrying up to 80 TEUs. These rail links play an important role in the German ports of Bremerhaven and Hamburg, which lack the river connections Rotterdam and Antwerp possess (Debrie and Gouvernal, 2006).

In East Asia, economic development has primarily taken place along the coasts, with vast industrial zones bordering the major ports. Given the short distances involved, pre- and post-shipment deliveries depend on trucking rather than rail. However, as China's interior develops, Chinese ports will increasingly face the challenge of serving a distant hinterland. The Yangtze River already serves as a major river freight axis, running from the port of Shanghai to some major cities in central China, notably Nanjing and Wuhan.

Global intermodal transport companies

Three main types of companies control intermodal transport: shipping lines, cargo handlers and forwarding agents/logistics providers. Without a doubt, containerization has favoured the industry's horizontal integration and consolidation. In 1980, the top 20 shipping lines accounted for 45% of the world's container traffic capacity. In 2000, their share had risen to 52%, and to 82% by 2007. During the same period, the top five operators' share rose from 17% to 24% and then to 43%. Since 2000, the industry's consolidation has accelerated sharply. A system of global alliances that has combined Asian shipping lines also warrants mention. Through mergers and acquisitions or alliances, shipping lines aim at global maritime networks, capable of providing high-frequency, high-capacity services to the world's three main economic centres: East Asia, North America and Europe.

Similarly, since the end of the 1990s, a few terminal operators have dominated the market. They have developed worldwide terminal networks, always targeting the three main centres of the world's economy. They may operate terminals exclusively, act as subsidiaries of shipping lines, or even remain integrated within a shipping line's business. Such global cargo handlers' share of in-port handling operations was only 18% in 1996. Ten years later, it was 70%; investment programmes now underway should further reinforce the trend (Drewry Shipping Consultants, 2010).

Lastly, a few major freight forwarders/logistics providers have made their presence felt on a global scale (Table 4.2). They offer their clients worldwide services via their vast networks of agencies. More often than not, these service networks arise through buyouts of local firms, triggering vast consolidation of the sector. Their activities range from express courier delivery to complete management of a shipper's supply chain. Originally, their business centred on freight forwarding. Unlike shipping lines and cargo handlers, their activities are knowledge- rather than capital-intensive.

SEAPORTS' INTEGRATION INTO INTERMODAL FREIGHT TRANSPORT SYSTEMS

The richness of its hinterland and access to the ocean determines a seaport's traffic volume. Access depends on the level of the port's draught, its location relative to major ocean routes and its freight handling quality. Pure transhipment ports rely solely on their ocean access. However, beyond this single criterion, port rankings – based on high to low volumes – reflect a port's level of integration in intermodal transport systems. Integration depends on three key factors: the port's attractiveness for global operators, the existence of intermodal transport corridors that allow deep hinterland penetration and the local territory's acceptance and support of the port's system.

The landlord port model and its consequences

Since the 1970s, the "landlord" port model has gradually come to dominate the port industry worldwide, replacing the "tool" or operating port model (Debrie, Gouvernal and Slack, 2007). With a landlord port, the public port authority – whether municipal (Antwerp, Rotterdam, Los Angeles, New York), regional (Hamburg) or national (South Korea, France) – retains policing functions and land and infrastructure ownership, e.g. access channels, harbours and wharves. It leases or rents the port on a 20–30 years' basis to a terminal operator specialized in cargo handling, most often a stevedoring company. In contrast to a tool port, a landlord port authority does not own the port's cargo-handling equipment or provide longshoremen; rather, the terminal operator invests in cargo-handling equipment (cranes, forklifts, etc.) and labour. The "service" port represents a completely different configuration: the port authority and operator are one – usually a privatized entity – and provide all port infrastructure and services.

The dominant landlord port model results from the convergence of several factors, notably containerization and its capital investment requirements. Starting in the 1970s, ports became starved for public funds, and saw their revenues plummet with a reduction in cargo ship traffic, especially

Table 4.2 Leading intermodal operators

The top five shipping lines		
Name	**Nationality**	**% of the world fleet capacity (2010)**
Maersk	Denmark	14.5
MSC	Switzerland	11.9
CMA-CGM	France	7.9
Hapag-Lloyd	Germany	4.3
Evergreen	Taiwan	4.2
The three major alliances		
Name	**Partners**	**% of the world fleet capacity (2009)**
CKHY	COSCON, K-Line, Yang Ming, Hanjin	12.1
Grand Alliance	Hapag Lloyd, NYK, MISC, OOCL	11.3
The New World Alliance	APL, Hyundai, MOL	8.9
The top five terminal operators		
Name	**Nationality**	**% of TEU throughput of world ports (2007)**
Hutchison Port Holdings	Hong Kong	13.3
APM Terminals	Denmark	12.1
PSA	Singapore	11.0
DPW	Dubai	8.7
Cosco	China	5.5
The top five freight forwarders		
Name	**Nationality**	**Turnover ($ billion) (2007)**
DHL	Switzerland	38.3
Kuehne & Nagel	Switzerland	19.1
Schenker	Germany	20.5
UPS	United States	8.0
Panalpina	Switzerland	7.6

Source: based on Alphaliner, K Line Annual report 2009, Drewry Shipping Consultants 2010, Global logistics and supply chain strategies, May 2007

oil tankers; port authorities therefore turned to private investors. At the same time, the United States initiated deregulation, soon taken up by the United Kingdom and then the rest of the world; this encouraged the rise of international public- and private-sector intermodal providers, especially scheduled-lines shipowners and terminal operators (Strubbe, 2002).

These evolutions led to two port configuration types. The first features a seaport that juxtaposes several terminals, not necessarily directly linked; a different operator runs each terminal, controlling its own supply chain. The second features a concept known as the terminalization of port competition (Slack, 2007), where one or several operators attempt to establish a network of controlled terminals in a multi-port gateway region. Such forms of "coopetition", i.e. competition and cooperation, occur only where ports are densely implanted. They require close

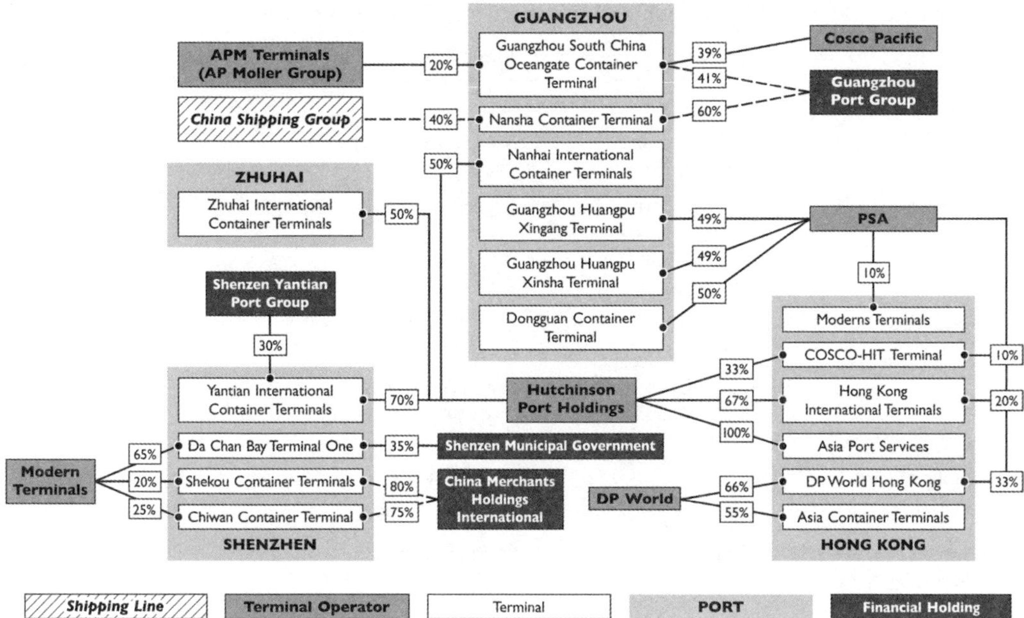

Figure 4.7 Inter-firm relationships in the Pearl River Delta's main container ports, 2010

Source: Notteboom and Rodrigue, 2010

geographic proximity between ports, as in northern Europe or the Pearl River Delta (Figure 4.7). Stevedoring companies from Hong Kong have invested heavily in China's Shenzhen Province, particularly the Hutchinson Group in the Port of Yantian. The Pearl River Delta provides an example of a network of container terminals dominated by a few operators (Wang and Olivier, 2007). This raises a question: Should we talk about competition between Hong Kong and Shenzhen or more about *de facto* cooperation between private operators?

Inter-port competition and inland corridors

A closer look at transport configurations and port stakeholders may begin to address this question. A port cannot become a "load centre", or major terminal centre for all container cargo in the port region, without well-organized terminals to attract shipping companies and their ocean carriers (Hayuth, 1992; Heaver, 2002b; Panayides and Cullinane, 2002; Robinson, 2002; Notteboom, 2004). It must also provide access to the hinterland. The usual model is a transport corridor connecting seaport gateways to inland distribution systems, which in turn can reach widely dispersed interior regions. High freight throughput volumes are achieved by using intermodal "combined" railroad-plus-roadway or waterway-plus-road transport. Ever-increasing port traffic challenges trucking's dominance of hinterland freight services because of cost, congestion, competitiveness and growing environmental constraints – even for short-haul distances where, until recently, trucking held the advantage.

It is worth noting in this connection, that, despite the different benefits they stand to gain, port stakeholders have all tended to promote combined transport. These stakeholders cover three basic types: (1) economic agents, e.g. shippers and shipping lines, freight forwarders and handlers, who are directly

Table 4.3 The benefits of combined transport for different stakeholders

	Costs	Traffic flow	The environment
Economic agents			
Shippers	Reducing inland transport prices	Need for reliable transport chains	Showing interest in/ factoring in sustainable development
Shipping lines	Competing with other transport organizers to attract freight from shippers	Offering reliable supply chains	Anticipating a possible inclusion of environmental costs in transport costs
Forwarders		Offering reliable supply chains	
Freight handlers	Same as above if the freight handler is also a transport organizer (as in Hamburg)	Reliability of maritime terminal operations	
Public officials			
Port management	Inter-port competition	Inter-port competition	Promoting sustainable development
National, regional and municipal governments	Economic development and jobs	Regional planning	
Public opinion	Same as above	Low tolerance for negative environmental impacts NIMBY syndrome	

Source: Frémont and Franc, 2009

involved in organizing transport operations; (2) public officials, primarily port authorities and managers along with municipal, regional and national decision-making bodies; and (3) community groups whose concerns are most often expressed through the media or lobbyists, in particular environmental groups representing the public interest. All three groups concern themselves, to a greater or lesser degree, with cost, congestion and environmental constraints, and find the combined model the preferred solution to date. We will conclude this analysis by examining how each concern affects the different stakeholders.

Intermodal costs form an increasing part of total door-to-door transport cost. Therefore, even if the organizational complexity of combined intermodal transport is greater than trucking alone, its higher overall volumes reduce costs on the inland transport leg (Table 4.3). Consequently, inland transport costs primarily concern economic agents because of their direct impact on operations. For shippers, the result may be lower supply-chain costs. It is also obviously in the interest of shipping organizers, e.g. shipping lines or freight forwarders, to provide clients with services that cost less. Shipowning companies organize efficient combined transport services to attract cargo volumes and fill vessels rather than to increase profits on the inland leg (Franc and Van den Horst, 2010). In addition, with the emergence of global trade imbalances (Rodrigue and Notteboom, 2009b), the repositioning of empty containers has become a key challenge for shipping lines that own or lease containers.

Promoting combined transport is also in the interests of port officials: it can extend the port's hinterland (and thereby enable it to compete with neighbouring port hinterlands) and preserve its customer base from competing ports along the same maritime gateway. The neighbouring port responds by also promoting combined transport to protect its market. Public opinion is sensitive to these arguments, since preserving or increasing port activity has a commensurate effect on local jobs.

Even if port traffic volumes tended to drop in 2009's economic slowdown, most large ports have experienced strong increases in container traffic for many years. Therefore, the risk arises that these large ports will suffer congestion and that some of their traffic will be transferred to less congested secondary ports, in what is known as the peripheral port challenge (Hayuth, 1981). By offering diversified transport modes and higher volumes than are possible by roads alone, combined transport is one way to improve traffic volumes between a port and its hinterland (ECMT, 2006b). The issue of traffic flow is thus decisive for port managers and for public officials, since part of a port's competitiveness depends upon it. Dependable combined transport can equally serve shippers' interests and ensure service reliability.

Finally, inland transport is the only major sector of the economy responsible for an ever-increasing percentage of total CO_2 emissions (ECMT, 2006a). On average, waterways are more energy-efficient per tonne transported than rail, by a factor of 2 to 1; rail is more energy-efficient than road transport, by a factor of 2.6 to 1 (ECMT, 2006b). Public officials must address these environmental problems. Strong support comes from national governments, but local interests also exert pressure to reduce the environmental harm caused by economic activities, particularly transportation. Such factors provide significant political and social impetus in favour of combined transport.

CONCLUSION

With globalization, containerization's theoretical potential has been realized on an unparalleled scale. The interaction between containerization, container operators and globalization has led to worldwide intermodal supply chains. Each participant's role in the supply chain has changed, from the location of ports, to maritime and inland shipping routes, to the integration of ports within and between other modes. While the ocean segment of intermodal transport dominates intercontinental trade, use of intermodal shipping remains limited for purely land-based trade. For example, inside North America or Europe, trucking's great flexibility allows it to dominate freight shipping. However, increasing energy costs and environmental constraints should intensify the search for inland freight transport solutions. New possibilities arise with improved articulations between various supply chains over long-, medium- and short-haul distances. Mastering and implementing these supply chains poses a major challenge; while already a dominant concern in the shipping industry, intermodal freight transport has yet to reach its maturity.

NOTE

1 TEU or "Twenty-feet Equivalent Units" is a measurement that quantifies the number of containers based on one 20-foot container: one TEU equals one 20-foot container; one 40-foot container equals two TEUs.

REFERENCES

Ashar, A. (2000) 2020 vision, *Containerisation International*, January, pp. 35–39.

Ashar, A. (2002) Revolution now, *Containerisation International*, January, pp. 56–59.

Containerisation International (2010) Building bridges, *Containerisation International*, 1 June 2010.

Charlier, J. (2000) De la norme panamax à l'essor des over panamax, *Acta Geographica*, no. 121, pp. 102–111.

Debrie, J. and Gouvernal, E. (2006) Intermodal rail in Western Europe: actors and services in a new regulatory environment, *Growth and Change*, vol. 37, no. 3, pp. 444–459.

Debrie, J., Gouvernal, E. and Slack, B. (2007) Port devolution revisited: the case of regional ports and the role of lower tier governments, *Journal of Transport Geography*, vol. 15, no. 6, pp. 455–464.

Drewry Shipping Consultants (2009) *Container Market 2009/10*, Annual Review and Forecast, London, 215 pp.

Drewry Shipping Consultants (2010) *Global Container Terminal Operators 2010*, Annual Review and Forecast, London, 128 pp.

European Conference of Ministers of Transport (2006a) *Inland Waterways and Environmental Protection*. Paris: OECD.

European Conference of Ministers of Transport (2006b) *Strengthening Inland Waterway Transport. Pan-European Co-operation for Progress*. Paris: OECD.

Fleming, D.K. and Hayuth, Y. (1994) Spatial characteristics of transportation hubs: centrality and intermediacy, *Journal of Transport Geography*, vol. 2, pp. 3–18.

Franc, P. and Van Den Horst, M. (2010) Understanding hinterland service integration by shipping lines and terminal operators: a theoretical and empirical analysis, *Journal of Transport Geography*, vol. 18, no. 4, pp. 557–566.

Frémont, A., Franc, P. and Slack, B. (2009) Inland barge services and container transport: the case of the ports of Le Havre and Marseille in the European context, *Cybergéo: European Journal of Geography* [On Line], Espace, Société, Territoire, document 437, URL: http://www.cybergeo.eu/index21743.html.

Hayuth, Y. (1981) Containerization and the Load Center Concept, *Economic Geography*, vol. 57, no. 2, pp. 160–176.

Hayuth, Y. (1992) Multimodal freight transport, in B. Hoyle and R. Knowles (eds), *Modern Transport Geography*. London: Belhaven, pp. 200–214.

Heaver, T.D. (2002a) The evolving roles of shipping lines in international logistics, *International Journal of Maritime Economics*, no. 4, pp. 210–230.

Heaver, T.D. (2002b) Supply chain and logistics management, in C. Th. Grammenos (ed.), *The Handbook of Maritime Economics and Business*. London, Hong Kong: LLP Professional Publishing, pp. 375–396.

Institute of Shipping Economics and Logistics (ISL) (2010) *Shipping Statistics Yearbook 2010*, Bremen.

Levinson, M. (2006) *The Box. How the Shipping Container Made the World Smaller and the World Economy Bigger*. Princeton, NJ and Oxford: Princeton University Press.

Notteboom, T. (2004) A carrier's perspective on container network configuration at sea and on land, *Journal of International Logistics and Trade*, vol. 1, no. 2, pp. 65–87.

Notteboom, T. and Rodrigue, J.-P. (2005) Port regionalization: towards a new phase in port development, *Maritime Policy and Management*, vol. 32, no. 3, pp. 297–313.

Notteboom, T. and Rodrigue, J.-P. (2010) Foreland-based regionalization: integrating intermediate hubs with port hinterlands, *Research in Transportation Economics*, vol. 27, pp. 19–29.

Panayides, P.M. and Cullinane, K. (2002) Competitive advantage in liner shipping: a review and research agenda, *International Journal of Maritime Economics*, no. 4, pp. 189–209.

Rodrigue, J.-P. and Notteboom, Th. (2009a) The terminalization of supply chains: reassessing the role of terminals in port/hinterland logistical relationships, *Maritime Policy and Management*, vol. 36, no. 2, pp. 165–183.

Rodrigue, J.-P and Notteboom, Th. (2009b) The geography of containerization: half a century of revolution, adaptation and diffusion, *Geojournal*, vol. 74, no. 1, pp. 1–5.

Robinson, R. (2002) Ports as elements in value-driven chain systems: the new paradigm, *Maritime Policy and Management*, vol. 29, no. 3, pp. 241–255.

Slack, B. (2007) The terminalisation of seaports, in J. Wang, D. Olivier, T. Notteboom and B. Slack (eds), *Ports, Cities, and Global Supply Chains*. Aldershot, UK: Ashgate, pp. 41–50.

Strubbe, J. (2002) Government, port policy and social welfare, in M. Huybrechts, H. Meersman, E. Van de Voorde, E. Van Hooydonk, A. Verbeke and W. Winkelmans (eds), *Port Competitiveness*. Antwerp: De Boeck, pp. 3–6.

United Nations Conference on Trade and Development (UNCTAD) (2010) *Review of Maritime Transport*, United Nations Publication, 213 pp.

Wang, J.J. and Olivier, D. (2007) Hong Kong and Shenzhen: the Nexus in South China, in K. Cullinane and S. Dong-Wook (eds), *Asian Container Ports*. New York: Palgrave Macmillan, pp. 198–212.

Zohil, J. and Prijon, M. (1999) The MED Rule: the interdependence of container throughput and transhipment volumes in the Mediterranean ports, *Maritime Policy and Management*, vol. 26, no. 2, pp. 175–193.

5

Global Air Transportation

John T. Bowen, Jr

AVIATION IN THE INTERSTICES OF EVERYDAY LIFE

On April 14, 2010, Eyjafjallajokull, an ice-covered volcano in southern Iceland erupted in what was, by geologic standards, a moderate-sized event. Yet because of its effects upon commercial aviation, the 2010 blast in Iceland was heard round the world. Fear that ash from the volcano would damage aircraft engines and cause mid-flight power losses compelled European authorities to suspend operations at scores of airports beneath the spreading ash cloud, including such pivotal centers as London-Heathrow, Paris-Charles de Gaulle, and Frankfurt. By the time airspace over Europe began to be reopened on April 21, more than 95,000 flights had been canceled and at least nine million travelers had been stranded (Clark, 2010), forced to postpone or forgo business trips, seaside holidays, visits to friends or relatives, or journeys home. The unprecedented interruption also grounded vast volumes of cargo with effects that rippled throughout the world. The Kenyan flower industry, critically dependent upon airborne exports to Europe, seized up. Sushi chefs in Japan and across the world had to pirouette from their usual dependence on Norwegian salmon to fishing grounds half a world away in New Zealand. Nissan curtailed production at factories in Mississippi and Tennessee due to a lack of pneumatic sensors from Ireland (Gross, 2010).

The Eyjafjallajokull crisis showed the extraordinary reach of air transportation. The cataclysm of that April was unusual but the everyday dependence upon aviation is not. On a typical day in 2010, about 750,000 people – approximately the population of Cracow, Raleigh, or Tunis – were airborne on commercial flights at any given moment (see Bowen, 2010: p. 2 for estimation methodology). The growth of both air passenger and air cargo traffic has been stunning, notwithstanding a significant downturn in 2009 (Figure 5.1).

As air traffic has grown, flight has been woven ever more abundantly – even flamboyantly – into the fabric of everyday

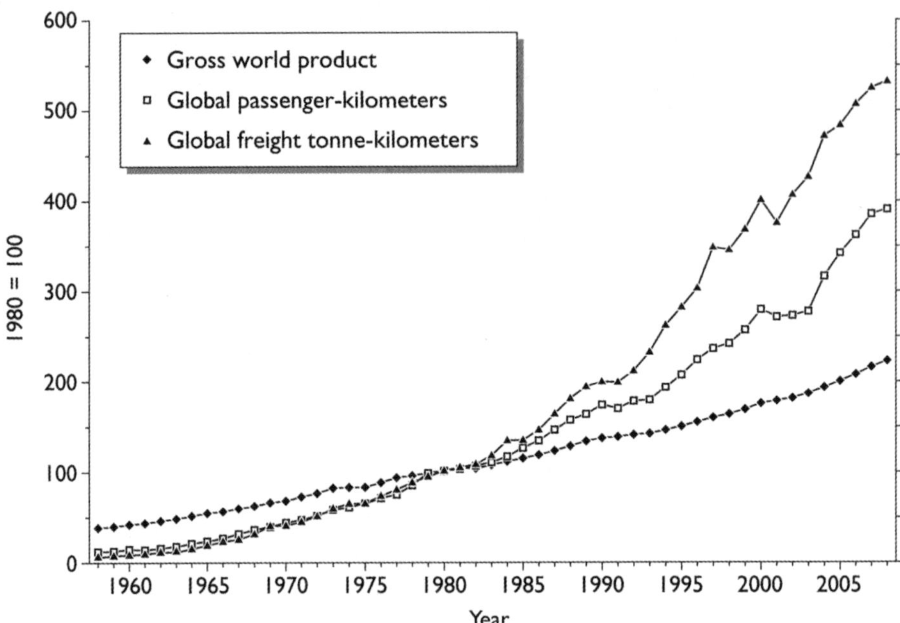

Figure 5.1 Growth of air traffic, 1959–2009

Sources: ICAO, 1998, and various ICAO Journal reports and ICAO press releases

life. Something of the increasing pervasiveness of air travel is suggested by a study of passengers on Aer Lingus and Ryanair in Ireland and Malaysia Airlines and AirAsia in Malaysia (O'Connell and Williams, 2005). Business travelers comprised a minority on all four carriers, but because they pay typically higher fares they are highly sought after by most airlines (Figure 5.2). More interesting, however, were the non-business travel purposes, which dominated all four samples – especially for AirAsia. Visiting friends and relatives was the single most important reason for travel on three of the four sample airlines. Aviation is a "key enabler of social distanciation" (Adey et al., 2007), partly culpable for the increased distances that separate people from those they care for but also a mechanism for overcoming those distances, at least occasionally. About 10 percent of the respondents in all four samples were traveling for a weekend break; and, incredibly, another 10 percent or so in three of the samples were flying for "sports" and a few percent on each of the Malaysian carriers were on shopping trips. The diversity of purposes suggests how far "aeromobility" – that is, the routinization of air travel (Adey et al., 2007) – has worked its way into these two societies. The same process has unfolded across most other developed countries and a growing number of developing countries.

Something similar can be observed in air cargo flows. Once, air freight was primarily relied upon for emergency shipments; but in many industries reliance upon air transportation is now taken for granted. The expansion of e-commerce is one factor that has driven air freight flows. Customers who are able to buy things quickly on the internet want them delivered quickly, too; and e-commerce tends to foster smaller, more frequent shipments – characteristics amenable to air freight (Lasserre, 2004). FedEx was labeled the "Airline of the Internet" long ago (Lappin, 1996), but other carriers have profited from the proliferation of e-commerce, too. Second, the emphasis on speed and reliability in supply chain management has encouraged emphasis on faster modes, including air transportation (Hesse and Rodrigue, 2004). Third,

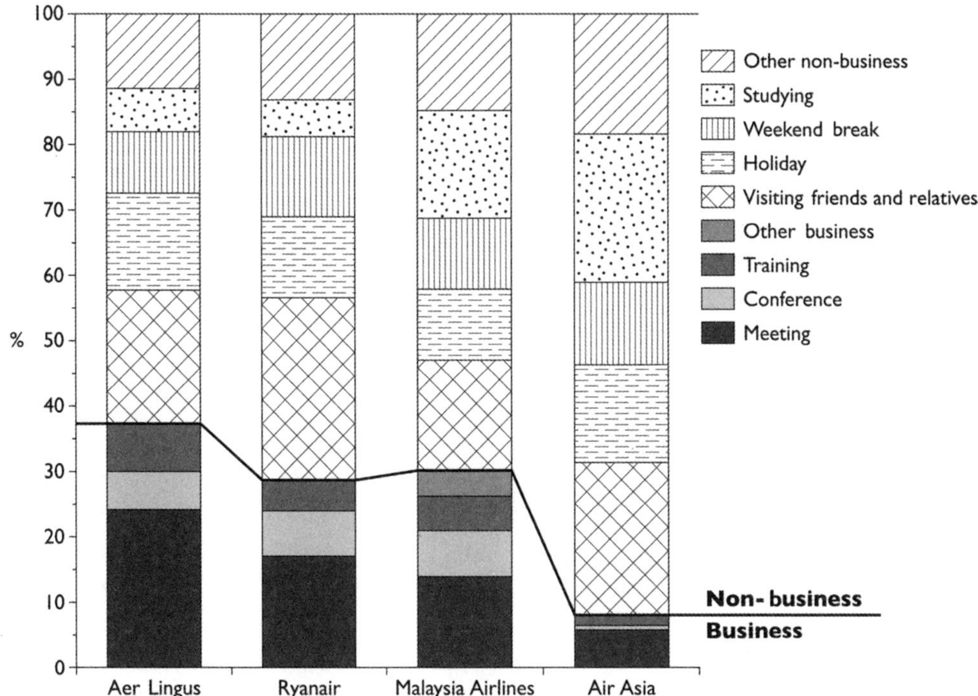

Figure 5.2 Travel purposes for passengers on four airlines

Note: travelers on Aer Lingus and Ryanair were surveyed at two airports in Ireland. Malaysia Airlines and AirAsia travelers were surveyed at Kuala Lumpur International Airport. The total sample size was 528.

Source: derived from O'Connell and Williams, 2005

higher value-to-weight ratios make air freight affordable for more goods. For an Apple iPad, for instance, the cost of air freight from a Chinese manufacturing plant to global markets is very small in relation to the product's retail value. Finally, increased incomes, much as they are a stimulant for air passenger traffic also promote air freight traffic. The boom in perishable and exotics air freight (Vega, 2008), for instance, has made possible "permanent global summertime" for affluent consumers in mid- and high-latitude countries.

The imbalance in airborne perishables flows between the global North and South hints at the broader unevenness in air transportation flows. It should come as no surprise that the most heavily trafficked routes are mainly within or between North America, Western Europe, and Asia-Pacific (Table 5.1). And yet the shifts in the rankings of the top city-pairs suggest that some parts of the developing world have begun to catch up with the "aeromobility" of the West. Furthermore, aviation is not just a reflection of development patterns but also a tool for changing them. Air cargo services, for instance, have a significant effect upon economic growth (Ying et al., 2008). Similarly, a variety of studies have documented the development impact of air passenger services, especially international flights (e.g. Button and Taylor, 2000).

The purpose of this chapter is to synthesize previous research to better understand the dynamism and significance of air transportation. The next section provides an overview of the development of aviation technology, which has been the main catalyst for the remarkable growth of air traffic over the past century. The third section examines air transport liberalization, beginning with domestic

Table 5.1 City-pairs ranked by air passenger capacity, 2008

	International			Domestic		
2008 Rank	City-pair	Weekly scheduled seats per week	1998 Rank	City-pair	Weekly scheduled seats per week	1998 Rank
1	Hong Kong–Taipei	180,070	1	Sapporo–Tokyo	216,919	2
2	Dublin–London	121,666	3	Osaka–Tokyo	199,230	11
3	London–New York	119,604	2	Rio de Janeiro–Sao Paulo	185,795	4
4	Seoul–Tokyo	96,688	19	Fukuoka–Tokyo	181,502	3
5	Amsterdam–London	83,732	4	Melbourne–Sydney	173,794	5
6	Jakarta–Singapore	78,368	8	Jeju–Seoul	170,009	23
7	Bangkok–Hong Kong	76,383	6	Beijing–Shanghai	164,838	43
8	Madrid–Paris	72,600	33	Cape Town–Johannesburg	127,462	18
9	Bangkok–Singapore	70,993	9	Barcelona–Madrid	123,296	15
10	Hong Kong–Singapore	61,435	12	Milan–Rome	122,491	12

Note: the figures shown are the sum of capacity in both directions for each city-pair

Source: author's analysis of OAG, 1998 and OAG, 2008

deregulation in the US and culminating with the recent removal of many restrictions on transatlantic aviation. The fourth section details the three main kinds of airlines that ply the world's airways: full service network carriers (FSNCs), low-cost carriers (LCCs), and cargo carriers. Finally, the last section looks to the future. Just over a century after the Wright Brothers' flight, aviation faces formidable challenges that will persist and grow long after the dust from Eyjafjallajokull settles. And yet, the forces propelling aviation skyward are strong and spreading.

AVIATION TECHNOLOGY, TIME, AND SPACE

The massive growth of passenger traffic and freight traffic over the last half-century is attributable to the lifting of two kinds of restraints: the technological and the political. Technologically, commercial aircraft have improved most in their efficiency. The two newest large commercial aircraft are likely to perpetuate that trend. Both the Airbus A380, which made its commercial debut in 2007, and the Boeing 787, which did so four years later, are premised on lowering the cost of air transportation, though they do so in different ways and are targeted at different markets (Table 5.2).

Whatever their impact, the A380 and 787 will likely pale by comparison with the early jetliners – especially the Boeing 707 and Douglas DC-8. Early jet travel seemed to dramatically "shrink" the world (Berkvist, 1961). As with other transport innovations, the pattern of time–space convergence fostered by advances in jet aviation has been uneven as favored places have been drawn closer to one another faster than less important centers (Knowles, 2006). To capture this idea metaphorically, L'Hostis (2009) suggests that rather than thinking of the world as shrinking, we should envision a world that has "shriveled" like a ripening fruit – that is, one whose surface area is smaller but also crumpled so that the raised surfaces such as London and Mumbai are drawn closer to one another but are separated by dimples of relatively poor accessibility.

Interestingly, jet aircraft reached a speed plateau early on. The Boeing 787, for instance, has a design cruise speed nearly identical to that of the Boeing 707. The speed stasis was predicted in a remarkably prescient article by Morrison (1984). Writing in the wake of the

Table 5.2 Specifications for selected airliners

	Boeing 707-100	Boeing 737-100	Boeing 747-100	Airbus A320	Boeing 777-200	Airbus A380	Boeing 787-8
Length (m)	44	29	71	38	64	73	57
Wingspan (m)	40	28	60	34	61	80	60
Typical passenger load	132	85	366	150	301	525	225
Cruising speed (kph)	915	850	895	875	895	950	905
Normal maximum range (km)	5,230	2,850	9,815	5,560	14,260	15,195	15,000
Date of first airline service	1958	1968	1970	1988	1995	2007	2011
First passenger airline	Pan Am	Lufthansa	Pan Am	Air France	United	Singapore	ANA
First passenger route	New York–Gander–Paris	Munich–Frankfurt	New York–London	Paris–Frankfurt	Washington–London	Singapore–Sydney	Tokyo–Hong Kong

Source: Bowen, 2010

oil crises of the 1970s and 1980s, Morrison predicted that the economics of aircraft design were such that high fuel prices would favor aircraft with lower cruising speeds, wider wingspans, and higher development costs (as airlines trade higher capital costs for lower operating costs). He has been proven generally correct on all three counts. A prominent decades-long trend in aircraft design *not* predicted by Morrison has been the significant lengthening of aircraft ranges, an important means of saving time without increasing cruising speeds and of better tying together an increasingly globalized economy.

The Boeing 787, for instance, has a range of about 15,000 kilometers, enough to link most city-pairs on earth nonstop. The 787 is designed to use up to 20 percent less fuel than similar-sized aircraft through the use of lightweight composite materials, new engines, and improved aerodynamics. With a typical seating capacity of 210–250 passengers for the most popular version, the airliner is premised on future fragmentation of travel among more city-pairs, involving many so-called hub-bypass routes (Mason, 2007). Nonstop services linking city-pairs such as Tampa Bay–London and New York–Pisa over the Atlantic are furthering time–space convergence even if jet cruising speeds are flat.

Fragmentation is one reason why the average aircraft size in most markets has been flat or even fallen in recent decades despite increased traffic volumes (Swan, 2007). Other downward influences on aircraft size include passenger preference for higher frequency service and the cost advantages associated with quicker airport turnarounds by smaller aircraft. The tendency of airlines to accommodate traffic growth with increased frequencies rather than larger airplanes has important implications for airport congestion, infrastructure costs, and perhaps environmental externalities – though the link between air pollution and aircraft size is complex (Givoni and Rietveld, 2009).

The preference for higher frequency service is one reason why the four-engine Airbus A380, the largest ever commercial passenger airplane with typical seating for just over 500 passengers, has not sold especially well – notwithstanding the stunning cumulative orders for 90 by Emirates (accounting for nearly 40 percent of all A380 orders). But the A380 is more a complement to rather than a substitute for smaller jets (King, 2007). Like the Boeing 787, the A380 has also been sold on its efficiency (achieved in this case partly through economies of scale). After three years of service, the A380 has been deployed mainly on the kinds of routes for which it was designed: long-range sectors between major hubs (Figure 5.3). Emirates' use of the "Superjumbos" is, in its own way,

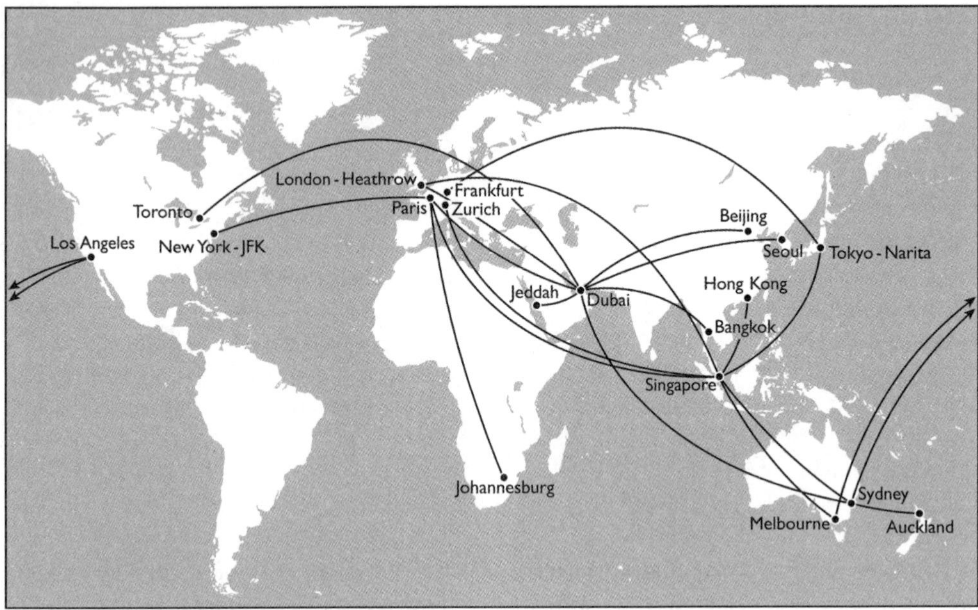

Figure 5.3 Airbus A380 routes, mid-2010

Note: all regularly scheduled A380 routes are shown

Sources: corporate websites of A380 operators Air France, Emirates, Lufthansa, Qantas, and Singapore Airlines

an endorsement of the hub-bypass strategy in that the carrier has marketed its geographic position as making possible one-stop service between any two cities on earth (Vespermann et al., 2008). No other carrier – save perhaps what *The Economist* (2010) labels fellow Middle Eastern "super-connecting" airlines (Eithad Airways and Qatar Airways) – could offer one-stop service among city-pairs as diverse as Manchester–Auckland, Dakar–Beijing, and New York–Lahore (with at least one leg of each of these Emirates connections potentially on board an A380 in 2010).

AVIATION POLICY AND COMPETITION IN THE AIRLINE INDUSTRY

It is fair to say that liberalization, which comprises privatization and deregulation, has had a greater effect on air transportation than any technological change (though the advent of the internet might be a contender) over the past quarter century. The decades of heavy state involvement in the industry, including state-owned airlines in most markets other than the US and government regulation of fares, entry, and exit almost everywhere, were justified by the economic, military, and nation-building value of the infant industry and by the belief that the economics of the industry made free competition unsustainable. Later, regulatory capture (rent-seeking) by airlines and their unionized workforces helped perpetuate the strictures even after – at least in markets such as the US – air transportation matured. Over time regulation had the effect of stifling competition and decoupling prices from costs so that in some markets (e.g. long-haul domestic sectors in the US) fares were set at too high a level, and in others (e.g. domestic markets in much of the developing world) fares were set too low to recover costs.

The deregulation of domestic air transportation

The tide began to shift against regulation in the 1970s due in part to a difficult economic environment and a favorable political one. High inflation made the potential cost-savings of deregulation and privatization more pressing, and the election of more strongly free-market-oriented governments in the US, Britain, and some other countries put in power leaders more than willing to relax the yoke of government control. Yet as Elizabeth Bailey (2008: 1) has observed, "Air passenger deregulation was driven in no small measure by purveyors of ideas." In the 1960s and 1970s, economists had offered evidence that unregulated intra-state carriers offered lower fares than interstate carriers did in comparable markets and did so profitably and that regulation encouraged interstate carriers to provide overly frequent services at load factors that would be otherwise unsustainable. The weight of such evidence added momentum to the push for reform.

Airline deregulation in the US

The watershed 1978 US Airline Deregulation Act (ADA) rapidly reduced the US government's power to control domestic market entry and exit, service levels, and fares, though the state retained important roles in ensuring safety, subsidizing service to small communities, limiting monopolies, and allocating slots at four chronically congested airports. The effects of American airline deregulation have been discussed and debated at length (e.g., Goetz and Sutton, 1997; Borenstein and Rose, 2007). On the positive side of the ledger, air fares (and air freight rates) have generally declined; fares in 2005 were an estimated 30 percent lower than they would have been had regulation continued (Borenstein and Rose, 2007).

Yet the welfare gains from deregulation have been unevenly distributed. After deregulation, fares – adjusted for stage length – became much more variable among domestic routes and among passengers. The increased variability in fares among routes reflects differences in: (1) the degree to which individual carriers dominate a market, such as on routes involving one or two "fortress hubs" (Goetz, 2002); and (2) the presence of low-cost carriers. In particular, the "Southwest effect", meaning the downward pressure on fares exerted by Southwest Airlines, has been amply documented (Vowles, 2001; Morrison, 2001; Goolsbee and Syverson, 2007). The increased variability in fares among passengers is due to quite different causes, including price discrimination in the increasingly sophisticated yield management systems developed after deregulation and more recently in internet-based bidding systems.

The performance of US airlines has also become more highly variable under deregulation (Borenstein and Rose, 2007). The fluctuations in the industry's financial performance are attributable to relatively elastic demand combined with labor costs that are inflexible over the short term and unpredictable, exogenously determined fuel costs. The first decade of the 21st century was especially brutal; the US airline industry lost $56 billion between 2000 and 2009 (measured in real 2009 dollars) and was only profitable in three of those 10 years. In fact the losses in the decade were greater than the cumulative real operating profits of the industry since the dawn of the Jet Age (analysis of ATA, 2010).

The airlines' financial losses have been echoed in massive job losses. Between 2000 and 2010, the combined employment of all US passenger airlines fell by 20 percent (BTS, 2010). Unsurprisingly, the shedding of jobs has been imbalanced between legacy carriers (i.e. those that were interstate carriers before deregulation) and new entrants. United Airlines, for instance, cut more than half of its workforce during the decade, with the job losses concentrated between 2002 and 2006 when the carrier was in bankruptcy protection. The losses have extended beyond the airlines' active workforces. In 1995, for instance, a bankrupt United Airlines terminated four severely underfunded defined benefit pension programs and turned over its obligations to the Pension Benefit Guarantee Corporation, an agency of the US government (Bowen, 2010). Like other carriers that have gone through the same process, United emerged from bankruptcy leaner and better able to better fend off the challenge posed by new entrants, with the benefits ultimately redounding to passengers and air cargo shippers. Indeed, one could argue that airline deregulation generally has shifted wealth from legacy airline shareholders, employees, and retirees to frequent flyers.

The diffusion of deregulation

Despite its mixed results, US airline deregulation had something of a demonstration effect globally. For instance, Hooper (1998) notes that advocates of Australian airline deregulation drew upon the US experience in arguing for reforms there. Overall, the evidence from Australia and elsewhere suggests outcomes broadly similar to those in the US, including the loss of market share by incumbents to new entrants, increased productivity, and wider gyrations in financial performance (Quiggin, 1997; Barrett, 2006).

Airline deregulation outside the US has differed, however, in that it has often been partial, halting, or reversible. In Asia, for instance, the state has continued to intervene quite aggressively in the market after deregulation – partly because of the perceived centrality of aviation to national economic development. China, by virtue of its size and growth, is a particularly important case. There, the domestic market was gradually and partially deregulated beginning in 1978 and especially after 1997. Yet the contemporary structure of the Chinese industry, particularly its dominance by Air China, China Southern Airlines, and China Eastern Airlines, is the result of a government-orchestrated consolidation in 2002 (Shaw et al., 2009).

In China and much of the rest of the world, privatization has accompanied deregulation. Deregulation in Canada began in 1984 and the partial privatization of Air Canada followed not long behind in 1988. In Australia, domestic aviation was deregulated in 1990 and Qantas was partially privatized in 1995. And in Japan, privatization of the flag carrier came first: Japan Airlines was fully privatized in stages between 1985 and 1987, and then the domestic market was deregulated in 1988. Although the three cited flag carriers have performed unevenly since privatization, several studies have found that privatized airlines generally perform better than public sector airlines (Al-Jazzaf, 1999; Ng and Seabright, 2001; Backx et al., 2002).

Privatization has been substantially more difficult in some emerging markets. In India, for instance, diverse social obligations (e.g. routes to the country's impoverished northeast), a high cost structure, and a national government reluctant to relinquish control of air transportation to foreign investors have together stymied repeated efforts to privatize Air India (Hooper, 1998). Still, new entrants in the deregulated Indian domestic market and in many other countries with struggling state-owned carriers have injected new dynamism in the market. Jet Airways and Air Sahara are two among the bevy of new entrants – some of which have attracted substantial foreign direct investment – that have rapidly captured market share in India (Findlay and Goldstein, 2004).

The deregulation of international air transportation

Measured in seats per week, most air transport capacity is operated over domestic routes; yet the trend is towards an increasingly international airline industry. Between 1998 and 2008, for instance, the domestic share of seats on all scheduled flights globally fell from 69.6 percent to 61.8 percent (author's analysis of OAG, 1998 and OAG, 2008). The internationalization of air transportation is unsurprising given the globalization of economic activity – including tourism, larger immigrant and guest worker movements, and most fundamentally the falling cost of distance. More specifically, internationalization has been fostered by (and has encouraged) the spread of deregulation at the international level. The benefits to travelers and shippers have been substantial (Piermartini and Rousuvá, 2008).

The most liberalized international routes are those operated under the provisions of Open Skies bilateral air service agreements (ASAs). These mandate minimal governmental controls on designation, capacity, fares, and code-sharing and other forms of marketing cooperation. Over the past two decades, the US has signed Open Skies agreements with nearly 100 countries. But perhaps the most significant Open Skies agreement involving the US was not negotiated with another country but rather with the European Union. Signed in 2007, the agreement was unprecedented both in its scope and its break with a half century of almost exclusively country-to-country negotiations. It is important to note, however, that the agreement was just the first stage of negotiations and that the survival of the 2007 reforms is dependent upon progress in second stage negotiations, including easing restrictions on foreign investment in airlines.

The 2007 agreement came after more than a decade of an increasingly multilateral approach to air services liberalization in the European Union and in some nearby countries which form the European Common Aviation Area (Graham, 1995). The shift from national to supranational regulation (or more precisely deregulation) of European aviation is one factor supporting predictions of increasing domination of European aviation by three mega-carriers: Air France/KLM, Lufthansa Group (Lufthansa, Austrian, bmi, and Swiss), and British Airways/Iberia (Cento, 2009).

NETWORKS, COSTS, AND CUSTOMERS: AIRLINE STRATEGIES IN A LIBERALIZED MARKET

In July 2010, the chief executive officer of Ryanair, Michael O'Leary, announced that the carrier was investigating the feasibility of "vertical seats" in order to squeeze more passengers on board its jets and thereby lower its fares. O'Leary claimed to be in discussions with Boeing, but seasoned observers of the airline and its CEO quickly pronounced the scheme yet another O'Leary publicity stunt. Ryanair and other low-cost carriers (LCCs) have attracted a lot of attention and not just for gimmicks; the LCCs' impact upon air transportation has been genuine and substantial. Yet two other kinds of airlines are actually more important in carrying traffic: full-service network carriers (FSNCs) move most passengers and together the FSNCs and all-cargo carriers such as FedEx and Cargolux move most air freight. All three kinds of airlines are discussed in this section.

Networked fortunes: an industry of global mega-carriers?

Airline networks can take a variety of forms, but in the literature it is common to contrast two forms: the hub-and-spoke network and the point-to-point network (Cento, 2009). Hubbing delivers significant benefits to carriers, including economies of scope and density. In June 2010, for instance, FSNC Qatar Airways added Buenos Aires and São Paolo to its network and thereby gained a presence in dozens of markets (e.g. Mumbai–São Paolo, Buenos Aires–Shanghai) connected via its Doha hub, illustrating economies of scope. And by combining passengers (and cargo) from multiple inbound flights onto its Doha–São Paulo–Buenos Aires service, Qatar Airways also realizes economies of density – meaning it is able to offer more frequent service (offering travelers and shippers greater convenience) and/or use larger equipment, which typically have lower per passenger costs (Sorenson, 1991).

Over time, many airlines have sought to build larger networks in order to harness greater scope, density, and scale economies (the latter are realized, for instance, through negotiating power in equipment purchases). Capturing those advantages has been a driving force behind the waves of mergers that have washed over the airline industry, including the recent mega-mergers between Delta and Northwest and between United and Continental. Outside the US, horizontal integration has also been quite common as liberalization has spread. Since 2000, the largest airline mergers, ranked by the size of the smaller of the two airlines involved as measured by passenger-kilometers performed in the year preceding the merger (author's research of various sources), have included:

1. United Airlines-Continental Air Lines (2010)
2. Delta Air Lines-Northwest Airlines (2008)
3. Air France-KLM (2003)
4. British Airways-Iberia (2010)
5. American-TWA (2001)
6. US Airways-America West Airlines (2005)
7. Air Canada-Canadian Airlines International (2000)
8. Lufthansa Group-Swiss (2005)
9. Air Berlin-LTU (2007)
10. Lufthansa-Austrian Airlines (2009)
11. Japan Airlines-Japan Air System (2002)
12. China Eastern Airlines-Shanghai Airlines (2009)
13. Gol-Varig (2007)
14. Lufthansa-bmi (2009)
15. Air India-Indian Airlines (2007)

Interestingly, five of the top fifteen mergers – all of them in Europe – were cross-border mergers. Europe is suited to cross-border mergers due to the abundance of closely spaced national flag carriers and hubs that emerged during the industry's infancy. The Air France-KLM merger, for instance, combined two airlines with hubs just 430 kilometers apart and with significant duplication in the their networks (e.g. both served Manila in 2003; only KLM did in 2010). The merger of Air France and KLM drew Europe's other major carriers down the same path. BA recently consummated a deal with Iberia, and Lufthansa has consolidated its position at the heart of Europe with a bevy of smaller mergers (Flottau, 2009). In the past, such mergers would have been prevented by the nationality clauses written into most bilateral ASAs requiring, for instance, that an airline using international traffic rights granted to Austria be a majority Austrian-owned airline. In Europe's multilateral liberalized market, however, nationality clauses have lost their force.

In the longer term, the further globalization of air travel and liberalization of air transportation may lead to one or more intercontinental airline mergers. In the meantime, however, most of the world's major carriers are already tied together through one of three main strategic alliances: the Star Alliance, oneworld, and SkyTeam (Figure 5.4). Alliances involve coordinated marketing, schedules meshing, and code-sharing (e.g. marketing United Airlines flight 6631 from Milwaukee to Chicago as Lufthansa flight 5673). In some sectors, the alliances have been granted antitrust immunity (ATI), permitting higher levels of fare and capacity coordination, including in some cases "metal neutrality" – meaning the participants pool revenue and costs such that they are indifferent to which alliance member's airplanes actually carry the traffic. Delta, Northwest, Air France, and KLM were granted "metal neutrality" ATI on most transatlantic routes in 2008 (Keiner et al., 2009).

From a theoretical perspective, alliance membership is an attractive alternative to merging, particularly in view of antitrust constraints on the former (Fan et al., 2001). Further, given some realistic assumptions, membership in an alliance must deliver fewer cost synergies than a merger in order to be profitable (Barla and Constantatos, 2006). Travelers have generally benefitted, too (Morrish and Hamilton, 2002). A study by Brueckner (2003) found that alliance membership, code-sharing, and antitrust immunity would lead to a 27 percent reduction in interline fares. For passengers on Star Alliance carriers, such savings amounted to $80 million in 1999 – when the alliance was substantially smaller than it is today. The growth of the Star Alliance and of oneworld and SkyTeam since then validates the conclusion of Fan et al. (2001) that of six possible scenarios for the industry's future structure the one most likely to come to fruition was further dominance by several major alliances.

Low-cost carriers: a revolution in the making?

It is instructive that of the 10 most downloaded articles published in the *Journal of Air Transport Management*, eight concern low-cost

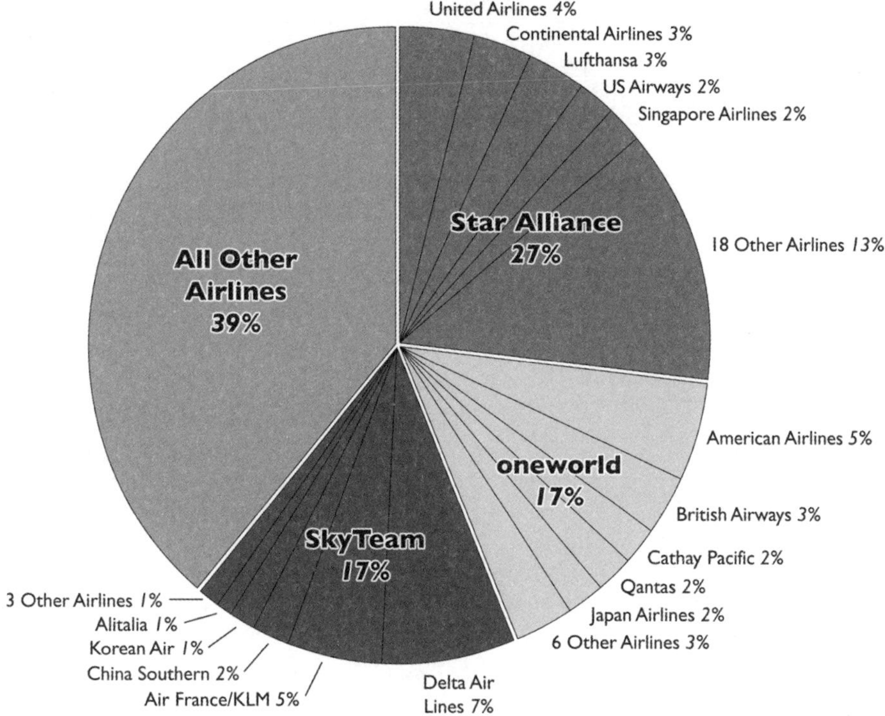

Figure 5.4 Major airline alliances traffic, 2009

Note: figures shown are each carrier's share of global revenue passenger-kilometers

Source: derived from *Air Transport World*, 2010b

carriers (LCCs). The attention given to LCCs seems incommensurate with their significance on the ground and in the air. In the US, they accounted for 30 percent of domestic revenue passenger-kilometers (RPKs) in 2009 and – in an increasingly global industry – just 3 percent of international RPKs performed by American carriers (analysis of BTS, 2010). In Europe, their collective share of traffic is even smaller – just 18 percent in 2004 (Dobruszkes, 2006). In Asia-Pacific, they carry about 15 percent of traffic (Kaur, 2010). Globally, the 10 largest passenger airlines include just one LCC (Table 5.3).

There *are* some markets where LCCs are substantially more important. In Europe, they are more important in the UK and Ireland. In Asia, the Philippines' top LCC, Cebu Pacific, had a 51 percent domestic market share in early 2010 (*Business World*, 2010). And in Brazil, four LCCs (Gol, Azul, Webjet, and TRIP) had a combined 53 percent domestic market share (measured in revenue passenger-kilometers), also in early 2010 (Shannon, 2010). But in most developing countries (e.g. China) and even some developed ones (e.g. Japan) and especially on long-haul routes, LCCs are still relatively minor players. The uneven geography of the LCCs' significance reflects in turn unevenness in liberalization, entrepreneurship, market size, and the adequacy of supporting infrastructure including, of course, affordable airport takeoff and landing slots but also widespread internet access (Francis et al., 2006). Those factors came together in Europe in the 1990s such that LCCs accounted for 50 percent of capacity growth between 1995 and 2004 (Dobruszkes, 2006).

The LCCs' cost advantage, which has powered their traffic growth, is rooted in several

Table 5.3 Airlines ranked by passenger traffic, 2009

Rank	Carrier	Type[a]	Traffic (millions of passenger-kilometers)	Alliance	2008 network size[b]	
					D	I
1	Delta Air Lines	F	304,025	SkyTeam	203	108
2	Air France/KLM	F	202,455	SkyTeam	47	191
3	American Airlines	F	196,997	oneworld	151	90
4	United Airlines	F	161,740	Star	173	45
5	Continental Air Lines	F	128,497	Star	145	133
6	Emirates	F	126,331	–	1	87
7	Lufthansa[c]	F	122,991	Star	18	176
8	Southwest Airlines	L	120,042	–	64	0
9	British Airways	F	110,851	oneworld	24	147
10	US Airways	F	93,190	Star	170	48

Notes: a. F = full service network carrier
L = low-cost carrier
b. D = domestic
I = international
c. Excludes Austrian, Swiss, bmi, Brussels Airlines

Sources: *Air Transport World*, 2010b; author's analysis of OAG, 2008

factors (O'Connell and Williams, 2005; Doganis, 2006). First, most budget carriers operate only one or a relative handful of aircraft types, lowering maintenance costs. Second, most LCCs operate a single class of service and use a narrow pitch between seats to achieve a high passenger density. Third, LCCs typically achieve higher daily utilization through the use of narrow-body aircraft and minimal in-flight services to minimize airport turn-around times. Fourth, LCCs have lower labor costs, partly because rapid growth has meant that the average staff tenure is short. LCCs also emphasize greater workforce flexibility (e.g. through outsourced services).

There are important geographic differences between network carriers and LCCs. The latter often operate networks less tightly focused on a hub or hubs, and even when they do exhibit high levels of spatial concentration, they may not have the temporal concentration or through-ticketing that facilitates connections at network carrier hubs (Reynolds-Feighan, 2001). Apart from the cost savings that come with reduced spatial and temporal concentration, Pels (2009) explains the difference in hubbing as a product of the constraints and opportunities of a liberalized market. Under liberalization, network carriers have an incentive to protect their existing hub-and-spoke networks and the scope and density economies therein while at the same time adding new spokes; the mergers and alliances discussed above are two means of achieving these aims. LCCs, conversely, enjoy greater freedom to respond where opportunities are to be found (i.e. "cherry-picking"), including niche markets. The result may be a more interconnected network. As an example, contrast the networks of two Romanian airlines: TAROM, which is the country's flag carrier and a new member of the SkyTeam, and budget carrier Blue Air (Figure 5.5).

Despite the differences between them, the classification of low-cost carriers and network carriers is losing its relevance as the latter cut services and costs and at least some of the former build increasingly extensive, even intercontinental networks (Bowen, 2010). Some network carriers have emulated features of the LCC model. A particularly extreme case is that of Aer Lingus; faced with unremitting

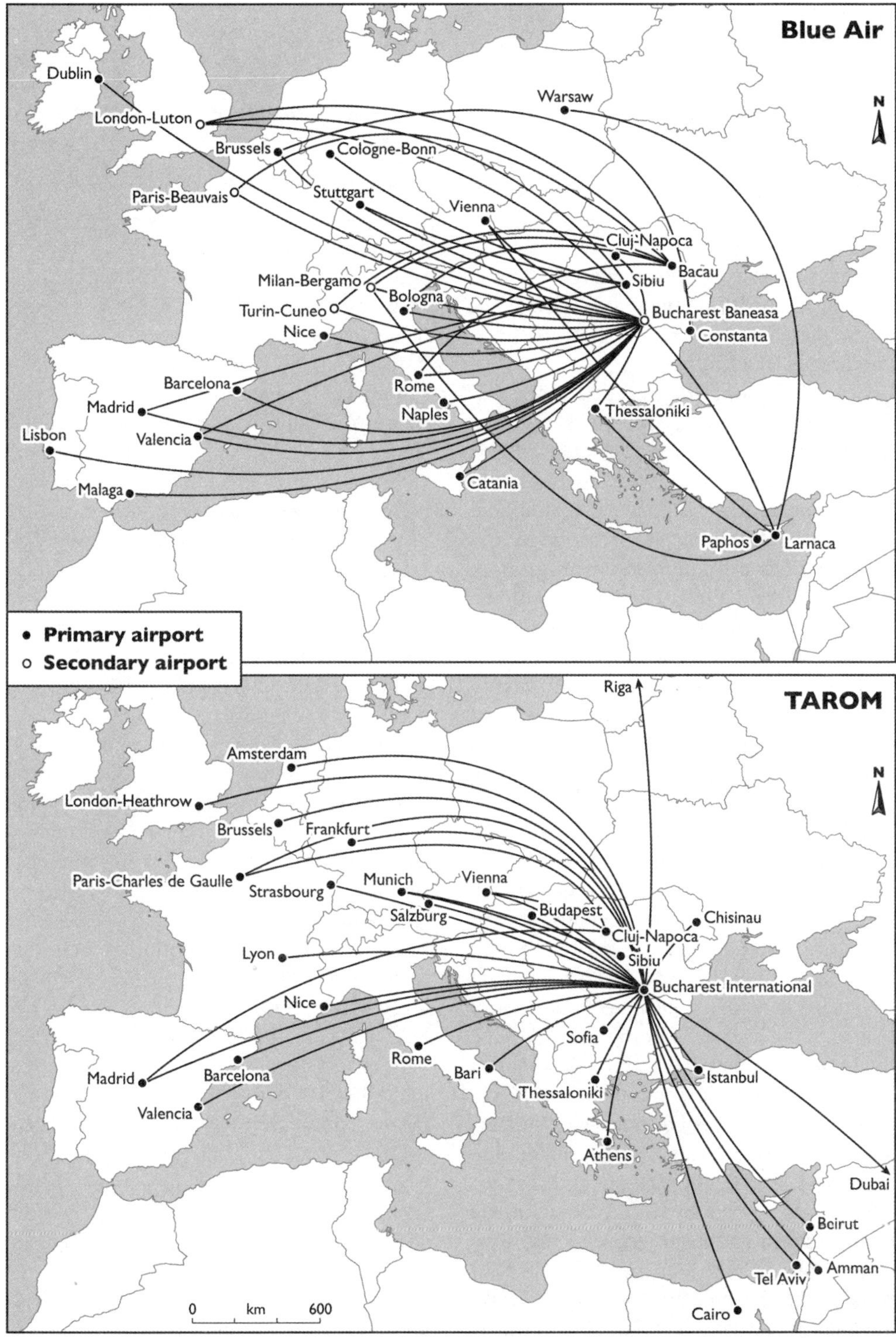

Figure 5.5 Networks of low-cost carrier Blue Air and full service network carrier TAROM, 2010

Source: airline websites

competition by LCCs in its main markets, the Irish flag carrier morphed into a "quasi-LCC" beginning in 2001 (Barrett, 2006; Cento, 2009). At the same time, some LCCs have broken out of the mould. Air Berlin, for instance, serves several long-haul destinations in North America, the Caribbean, southern Africa, and Southeast Asia; and recently agreed to become a member of oneworld. JetBlue, which controls valuable slots at John F. Kennedy International Airport, has marketing alliances with American Airlines, Aer Lingus, and Lufthansa.

Few LCCs conform perfectly to the traditional model of what an LCC should be; a study by Alamdari and Fagan (2005) found that even Southwest Airlines had just 62 percent adherence to that model (for instance, Southwest offers cargo services and has a frequent flyer program in contrast to the model). The airline with the highest score among their sample of 10 carriers was Ryanair at 85 percent. Not coincidentally, Ryanair has been highly profitable and has gone further than most other LCCs in turning air travel into a commodity: a seat – or even standing room – sold solely on price.

The gap in costs per available seat-kilometer for leading LCCs and their network carrier competitors is not as great as in the past but it is still substantial: in 2004, Southwest had a 36 percent cost advantage versus US network carriers, and Ryanair had a 64 percent advantage versus European network carriers (Cento, 2009). Lower costs translate into lower fares, and lower fares stimulate market growth, including in some nonmetropolitan areas neglected by network carriers (Williams and Baláž, 2009; Donzelli, 2010). In the case of Europe specifically, the strengths of the connections forged by LCCs between the region's north and south and east and west spurred one pair of journalists to title their piece on the phenomenon: "Air travel shrinks a continent" (Walker and Ho, 2005). This is hyperbole, of course. Still, the LCCs do comprise an important innovation in the way that aviation works, an innovation as important in some ways as the advent of jet travel two generations earlier.

Separate ways: air cargo carriers

The airline that perhaps most embodies the liberalization and internationalization – even globalization – of aviation is neither a low-cost carrier like Southwest Airlines nor a full service network carrier such as Air France/KLM but FedEx. The carrier's emergence as a household name was made possible by deregulation in the US in the 1970s (Bailey, 2008), and its subsequent globalization, including foreign hubs, would have been impossible without the spread of liberalization. Through acquisitions and organic growth, FedEx has established a presence in most markets worldwide, and not just on international routes: the company performs domestic express services in markets as diverse as Mexico, China, and the United Kingdom. Its fleet of aircraft and ground vehicles has helped to make the verb "FedEx" part of the lexicon in the US and in a growing number of foreign markets (Figure 5.6).

FedEx is an integrator, meaning a company that performs integrated, door-to-door, nearly seamless air and ground transportation. The integrators led the air cargo industry in tying the various links in the typical transport chain together with sophisticated electronic data interchange (EDI) systems. Early and aggressive adoption of EDI conferred one of the integrators' greatest advantages versus traditional cargo carriers. The latter have long been able to move goods very quickly from airport to airport, but the multiplicity of parties involved on the ground meant a slow service overall; the typical conventional transpacific air cargo shipment took 6 to 6.5 days to complete its journey in 2007 (Perrett, 2007). In a world in which speed has become a source of competitive advantage in a growing number of industries, the four main integrators (FedEx, UPS, DHL, and TNT) have become critical service providers for many firms. Indeed, FedEx and UPS carry an estimated 10 percent of US gross domestic product and 3.5 percent of

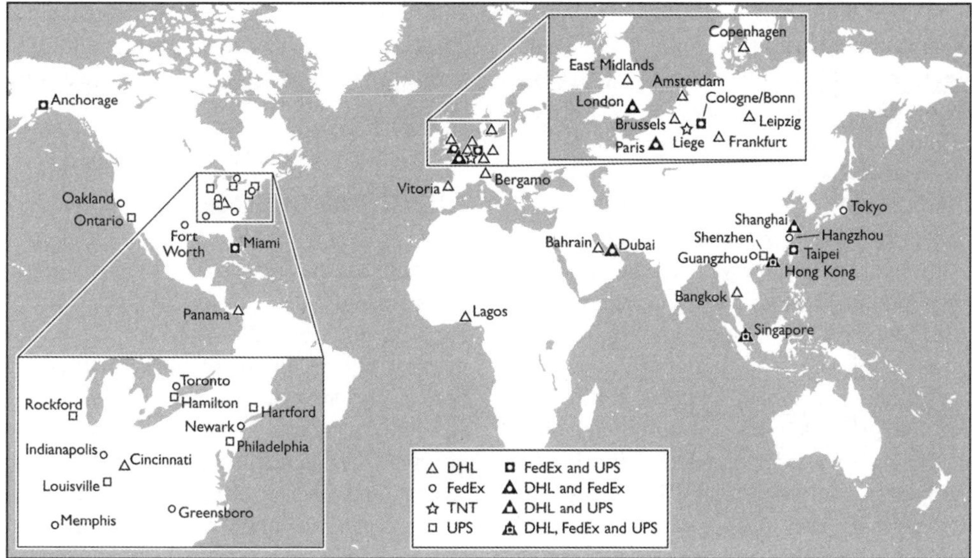

Figure 5.6 Integrator hubs, 2010

Source: corporate websites

global gross domestic product (Levitz, 2010). Despite that importance, very little research has been published on the integrators, due mainly to a lack of data.

Interestingly, most of the world's top 10 freight carriers are not integrators but rather full service network carriers (Table 5.4). While the integrators deal directly with shippers

Table 5.4 Airlines ranked by cargo traffic, 2009

Rank	Carrier	Domicile	Type[a]	Traffic (millions of freight tonne-kilometers)	2010 operating fleet size[b]	
					P	F
1	FedEx	USA	I	14,140	0	329
2	Air France/KLM	France/Neth.	C	11,155	356	6
2	UPS Airlines	USA	I	9,428	0	212
3	Korean Air	S. Korea	C	8,427	102	23
5	Cathay Pacific Airways	China (HK)	C	8,256	96	22
6	Lufthansa	Germany	C	7,425	263	14
7	SIA Cargo	Singapore	C	6,659	108	11
8	Emirates	UAE	C	6,369	138	10
9	China Airlines	Taiwan	C	4,959	46	19
10	Cargolux	Luxembourg	A	4,800	0	13

Notes: a. A = non-integrated all freight airline
C = combination airline
I = integrator
b. Jet and turboprop aircraft only
P = passenger aircraft
F = freighter aircraft

Source: *Air Transport World*, 2010a; *Air Transport World*, 2010b; IATA, 2010

(e.g. manufacturers) and consignees (e.g. retailers), other cargo carriers work in conjunction with freight forwarders (Zhang et al., 2007). The air freight forwarding business, even more than air transportation, has been globalized and is today dominated by a relative handful of firms. The world leaders in 2007 were DHL (based in Germany), DB Schenker (Germany), Kuehne & Nagle (Switzerland), Panalpina (Switzerland), and UPS Supply Chain Solutions (USA); the top five together had a global 35 percent market share (Kuehne & Nagel, 2009). The fact that DHL and UPS rank among the largest freight forwarders attests to the breakdown of conventional classifications in the air cargo industry. DHL, which has stated that it wants to become the "Coca Cola of logistics" (*Business Times*, 2003), is especially versatile.

About 60 percent of air cargo is moved in freighter aircraft, including many freighters operated by combination airlines (carriers that serve both passenger and cargo markets); the remainder is carried in the belly space aboard passenger aircraft (Bowen, 2010). The long-term trend has been for freighters to become more important. Among the attractions of freighters are the spatial and temporal flexibility they offer airlines to organize their operations to best suit the needs of cargo shippers. For example, late-night departures and arrivals work well with just-in-time production systems. Most importantly, freighters can be deployed on routes where there is a mismatch between air passenger and air cargo demand.

Unsurprisingly, freighters are strongly concentrated on routes to, from, and within Asia (Bowen, 2004). The most profitable link in the FedEx network in 2004, for instance, was the daily McDonnell Douglas MD-11F from Shanghai to Memphis (Harney and Roberts, 2004). That airplane had to stop en route at Anchorage to refuel but in 2010 was replaced with nonstop service by one of the carrier's new Boeing 777Fs. The 777F gives Asian shippers two hours of additional manufacturing time to make the cutoff for next-day delivery in the US, shrinking (or shriveling) the Pacific a little bit further (Levitz, 2010).

THE FUTURE OF FLIGHT

Aviation has traveled a long way in the 50 years since the dawn of the Jet Age. What of the next 50 years? As described above, the massive expansion of air transportation has been catalyzed by the removal of technological and political constraints and fueled by rising incomes, the internationalization of economic activity, and the ever-increasing importance of flying as a means of accruing social, cultural, and economic capital (Randles and Mander, 2009). Are future trends in this regard likely to be as favorable?

Technologically, the development of commercial airframes and aircraft engines continues apace. The Boeing 787, a highly innovative and even daring airplane, has been the fastest-selling new jetliner in history (*Economist*, 2009). And new technologies are on the horizon, including the geared turbofan (GTF), an engine design that promises substantial emissions and noise improvements. In the longer term, rising education levels in the developing world are likely to increase the number of aerospace scientists and engineers, helping to perpetuate the long-term trend towards more capable, efficient airplanes. In particular, the shortage of qualified personnel has been a constraint on the Chinese airliner industry; that constraint is likely to ease, with potentially global implications.

Changes in the developing world are also potentially the most significant in terms of the policy environment for air transportation. In Subsaharan Africa, for instance, aviation has been hampered not just by pervasive poverty but also by highly restrictive bilateral agreements. The Yamoussoukro Decision of 1999 committed African leaders to the full liberalization of the region's air services, but there has been little progress in implementing the agreement (Moores, 2010).

Not everyone would be enthusiastic about the rapid growth of aviation in the developing world, however. Air transportation has been singled out as a key and fast-growing contributor to global climate change, one of several environmental issues that will shape the future of flight. Innovations in aircraft, including the wider use of lightweight composites, will ameliorate aviation emissions as will improved air traffic management systems (e.g. Europe's Single Sky program or America's NextGen); but new technologies alone may not be enough to satisfactorily constrain aviation emissions. In Europe, an emissions trading system (ETS) for aviation began operations in 2012, against the strenuous opposition of many in the airline industry – especially growth-minded LCCs (Bowen, 2010). Another environmental issue, noise, could also be a brake upon the airline industry's future. Once again, technological progress has been made in terms of the noise produced by individual aircraft and further improvements are in the offing, but those reductions have been offset by the boom in air traffic (Cidell, 2008).

Perhaps the most obvious constraint on the future of flight is the price and availability of oil. Though various efforts are under way to develop alternative fuels for aviation, for the foreseeable future this mode is likely to rely almost exclusively on oil-derived fuels. The industry's 2008–2009 financial crisis began with the severe run-up of oil prices in 2008, and it remains highly vulnerable to a repeat performance.

Together, these challenges may diminish the advantages that have almost continuously borne air transportation to new heights. Alternative modes that are less energy-intensive, less polluting, and/or less laden with the security concerns that now envelop aviation are likely to capture away some of the traffic that now flies. Further, the speed advantage of air transportation is not as great as it once was. High-speed passenger rail and more efficient containerized freight systems can rival airlines for a growing number of city-pairs. Consider the case of the route between Seoul and Busan. In 1998, it was the 10th busiest air route in the world in terms of scheduled seats per week. By 2008, following the completion of the Korea Train eXpress (KTX) link between the two cities, airline seat capacity had fallen by nearly 40 percent (Author's analysis of OAG, 1998 and OAG, 2008).

And yet, the overall capacity of carriers flying on routes to, from, and within South Korea grew by 33 percent in the 10-year interval. By 2008, the domestic route between Seoul and the Korean resort island of Jeju had moved into the top 10 busiest globally, and many additional international links had been spun from Seoul, with new nonstops to cities such as Atlanta, Munich, Phnom Penh, and Shenzhen. In the story of Korea's air links, there is perhaps a harbinger of things to come elsewhere: air transportation will be different in mid-century, but the global volume of air passengers and air freight will almost certainly be greater.

REFERENCES

Adey, P., L. Budd, and P. Hubbard (2007) "Flying Lessons: Exploring the Social and Cultural Geographies of Global Air Travel", *Progress in Human Geography*, 31 (6): pp. 773–91.

Air Transport World (2010a) "Individual Airline Fleets", July: pp. 95–107.

Air Transport World (2010b) "World Airline Traffic Results 2009", July: pp. 41–9.

Alamdari, F. and S. Fagan (2005) "Impact of the Adherence to the Original Low-Cost Model on the Profitability of Low-Cost Airlines", *Transport Reviews*, 25 (3): pp. 377–92.

Al-Jazzaf, M.I. (1999) "Impact of Privatization on Airlines Performance: An Empirical Analysis", *Journal of Air Transport Management*, 5 (1): pp. 45–52.

ATA [Air Transport Association] (2010) "Annual Results: US airlines" Online. Available at http://www.airlines.org/ (accessed July 25, 2010).

Backx, M., M. Carney, and E. Gedajlovic (2002) "Public, Private and Mixed Ownership and the Performance of International Airlines", *Journal of Air Transport Management*, 8 (4): pp. 213–20.

Bailey, E.E. (2008) "Air Transportation Deregulation", Presentation at the Annual Meeting of the American Economics Association, New Orleans, January 4.

Barla, P. and C. Constantatos (2006) "On the Choice between Strategic Alliance and Merger in the Airline Sector: The Role of Strategic Effects", *Journal of Transport Economics and Policy*, 40 (3): pp. 409–24.

Barrett, S. (2006) "Commercialising a National Airline – The Aer Lingus Case Study", *Journal of Air Transport Management*, 12: pp. 159–67.

Berkvist, R. (1961) "A Shrinking Globe: Jets Transform Oceans into Ponds, Travelers into Demons for Speed", *The New York Times*, April 16: p. 3.

Borenstein, S. and N. Rose (2007) *How Airline Markets Work .... Or Do They? Regulatory Reform in the Airline Industry*, NBER Working Paper 13452.

Bowen, J. (2004) "The Geography of Freighter Aircraft Operations in the Pacific Basin", *Journal of Transport Geography*, 12 (1): pp. 1–11.

Bowen, J. (2010) *The Economic Geography of Air Transportation: Space, Time, and the Freedom of the Sky*, London: Routledge.

Brueckner, J.K. (2003) "The Benefits of Codesharing and Antitrust Immunity for International Passengers, with an Application to the Star Alliance", *Journal of Air Transport Management*, 9 (2): pp. 83–9.

BTS (2010) "Revenue Passenger-Miles (The Number of Passengers and the Distance Flown in Thousands (000)): All U.S. carriers – All airports", Online. Available at http://www.transtats.bts.gov/ (accessed July 18, 2010).

Business World (Manila) (2010) "Cebu Pacific Claims Number 1 Spot from PAL", June 9: p. S7.

Business Times, The (Singapore) (2003) "DHL Brand Unites Merger of DHL, Danzas, Deutsche Post", April 2: p. 16.

Button, K. and S. Taylor (2000) "International Air Transportation and Economic Development", *Journal of Air Transport Management*, 6: pp. 209–22.

Cento, A. (2009) *The Airline Industry: Challenges in the 21st Century*, Heidelberg: Physica-Verlag.

Cidell, J. (2008) "Challenging the Contours: Critical Cartography, Local Knowledge, and the Public", *Environment and Planning A*, 40: pp. 1202–18.

Clark, N. (2010) "UN Strives for Aircraft-Ash Benchmark; Plane-Makers, Airlines, Airports and Experts on Safety Would Set Criteria", *International Herald Tribune*, April 23, p. 4.

Dobruszkes, F. (2006) "An Analysis of European Low Cost Carriers and Their Networks", *Journal of Transport Geography*, 14: pp. 249–64.

Doganis, R. (2006) *The Airline Business*, 2nd edition, New York: Routledge.

Donzelli, M. (2010) "The Effect of Low-Cost Air Transportation on the Local Economy: Evidence from Southern Italy", *Journal of Air Transport Management*, 16 (3): pp. 121–6.

Economist, The (2009) "Upwards and Onwards: Maiden Flights for Boeing and Airbus", December 19: pp. 37–40.

Economist, The (2010) "Rulers of the New Silk Road", June 5: pp. 75–7.

Fan, T., L. Vigeant-Langlois, C. Geissler, B. Bosler, and J. Wilmking (2001) "Evolution of Global Airline Strategic Alliance and Consolidation in the Twenty-First Century", *Journal of Air Transport Management*, 7: pp. 349–60.

Findlay, C. and A. Goldstein (2004) "Liberalization and Foreign Direct Investment in Asian Transport Systems: The Case of Aviation", *Asian Development Review*, 21 (2): pp. 37–65.

Flottau, J. (2009) "Hanging Together", *Aviation Week & Space Technology*, November 30: p. 48.

Francis, G., I. Humphreys, S. Ison, and M. Aicken (2006) "Where Next for Low Cost Airlines? A Spatial and Temporal Comparative Study", *Journal of Transport Geography*, 14: pp. 83–94.

Givoni, M. and P. Rietveld (2009) "Airlines Choice of Aircraft Size – Explanations and Implications", *Transportation Research Part A*, 43: pp. 500–510.

Goetz, A.R. (2002) "Deregulation, Competition, and Antitrust Implications in the US Airline Industry", *Journal of Transport Geography*, 10 (1): pp. 1–19.

Goetz, A.R. and C.J. Sutton (1997) "The Geography of Deregulation in the U.S. Airline Industry", *Annals of the Association of American Geographers*, 87 (2): pp. 228–63.

Goolsbee, A. and C. Syverson (2008) "How Do Incumbents Respond to the Threat of Entry? Evidence from the Major Airlines", *Quarterly Journal of Economics*, 123 (4): pp. 1611–33.

Graham, B. (1995) *Geography and Air Transport*, New York: John Wiley.

Gross, D. (2010) "The Day the Earth Stood Still: With a Huff and a Puff, Mother Nature Grounded the Global Economy – and Pointed Up the Need to Fix Our Fragile System", *Newsweek*, May 3: p. 46.

Harney, A. and D. Roberts (2004) "Midnight in Memphis, New Dawn in China", *Financial Times*, August 9: p. 15.

Hesse, M. and Rodrigue, J.-P. (2004) "The Transport Geography of Logistics and Freight Distribution", *Journal of Transport Geography*, 12: pp. 171–84.

Hooper, P. (1998) "Airline Competition and Deregulation in Developed and Developing Country Contexts – Australia and India", *Journal of Transport Geography*, 6 (2): pp. 105–16.

IATA [International Air Transport Association] (2010) *World Air Transport Statistics,* 54th edition, Montreal.

ICAO [International Civil Aviation Organization] (1998) "1997 Airline Finances Amongst Best in Past 50 Years", press release dated June 16.

Kaur, K. (2010) "Garuda Targets Budget Travelers", *The Straits Times* (Singapore), February 4.

Keiner, R.B., L.B. Halloway, and G.F. Murphy (2009) "Airline Alliances, Antitrust Immunity, and Mergers in the United States", Crowell & Moring legal brief. Online. Available at http://www.crowell.com/ (accessed July 29, 2010).

King, J.C.M. (2007) "The Airbus A380 and Boeing 787: A Role in the Recovery of the Airline Transport Market", *Journal of Air Transport Management*, 13 (1): pp. 16–22.

Knowles, R.D. (2006) "Transport Shaping Space: Differential Collapse in Time-Space", *Journal of Transport Geography*, 14 (6): pp. 407–25.

Kuehne & Nagle (2009) "Analyst Conference – Result 2008", Online. Available at http://www.kn-portal.com/ (accessed July 18, 2010).

Lappin, T. (1996) "The Airline of the Internet", *Wired*, 4 (12), Online. Available at http://www.wired.com (accessed June 24, 2008).

Lasserre, F. (2004) "Logistics and the Internet: Transportation and Location Issues Are Crucial in the Logistics Chain", *Journal of Transport Geography*, 12 (1): pp. 73–84.

Levitz, J. (2010) "FedEx Looks to 777s to Deliver an Edge", *The Wall Street Journal*, July 13: p. B1.

L'Hostis, A. (2009) "The Shriveled USA: Representing Time–Space in the Context of Metropolitanization and the Development of High-Speed Transport", *Journal of Transport Geography*, 17 (6): pp. 433–9.

Mason, K.J. (2007) "Airframe Manufacturers: Which Has a Better View of the Future?", *Journal of Air Transport Management*, 13: pp. 9–15.

Moores, V. (2010) "African Pride", *Airline Business*, 26 (4): pp. 32–6.

Morrish, S.C. and R.T. Hamilton (2002) "Airline Alliances: Who Benefits?", *Journal of Air Transport Management*, 8 (6): pp. 401–407.

Morrison, S.A. (1984) "An Economic Analysis of Aircraft Design", *Journal of Transport Economics and Policy*, 18 (2): pp. 123–43.

Morrison, S.A. (2001) "Actual, Adjacent, and Potential Competition: Estimating the Full Effect of Southwest Airlines", *Journal of Transport Economics and Policy*, 35 (2): pp. 239–56.

Ng, C.K. and P. Seabright (2001) "Competition, Privatization and Productive Efficiency: Evidence from the Airline Industry", *The Economic Journal*, 111: pp. 591–619.

OAG (1998) OAG Max database for April 1998.

OAG (2008) OAG Max database for April 2008.

O'Connell, J.F. and G. Williams (2005) "Passengers' Perceptions of Low Cost Airlines and Full Service Carriers: A Case Study Involving Ryanair, Aer Lingus, Air Asia, and Malaysia Airlines", *Journal of Air Transport Management*, 11: pp. 259–72.

Pels, E. (2009) "Network Competition in the Open Aviation Area", *Journal of Air Transport Management*, 15 (2): pp. 83–9.

Perrett, B. (2007) "Paper Chase", *Aviation Week & Space Technology*, May 7: p. 68.

Piermartini, R. and L. Rousuvá (2008) *Liberalization of Air Transport Services and Passenger Traffic*, World Trade Organization, Economics and Statistics Research Division, Staff Working Paper ESRD-2008-6.

Quiggin, J. (1997) "Evaluating Airline Deregulation in Australia", *The Australian Economic Review*, 30 (1): pp. 45–56.

Randles, S. and S. Mander (2009) "Aviation, Consumption, and the Climate Change Debate: 'Are You Going to Tell Me Off for Flying?'" *Technology Analysis & Strategic Management*, 21 (1): pp. 93–113.

Reynolds-Feighan, A. (2001) "Traffic Distribution in Low-Cost and Full Service Carrier Networks in the US Air Transportation Market", *Journal of Air Transport Management*, 7 (5): pp. 265–75.

Shannon, D. (2010) "Brazil's Carriers Benefit from Growth, Increased Demand", *Aviation Daily*, July 19: p. 4.

Shaw, S.L., F. Lu, J. Chen, and C. Zhou (2009) "China's Airline Consolidation and Its Effects on Domestic Airline Networks and Competition", *Journal of Transport Geography*, 17 (4): pp. 293–305.

Sorenson, N. (1991) "The Impact of Geographic Scale and Traffic Density on Airline Production Costs: The Decline of the No-Frills Airlines", *Economic Geography*, 67 (3): pp. 333–45.

Swan, W. (2007) "Misunderstandings about Airline Growth", *Journal of Air Transport Management*, 13: pp. 3–8.

Vega, H. (2008) "Air Cargo, Trade, and Transportation Costs of Perishables and Exotics from South America", *Journal of Air Transport Management*, 14 (6): pp. 324–8.

Vespermann, J., A. Wald, and R. Gleich (2008) "Aviation Growth in the Middle East: Impacts on Incumbent Players and Potential Strategic Reactions", *Journal of Transport Geography*, 16 (6): pp. 388–94.

Vowles, T.M. (2001) "The 'Southwest Effect' in Multi-Airport Regions", *Journal of Air Transport Management*, 7 (4): pp. 251–8.

Walker, N. and R. Ho (2005) "Air Travel Shrinks a Continent", *South China Morning Post*, May 9: p. 10.

Williams, A.M. and V. Baláž (2009) "Low Cost Carriers, Economies of Flows, and Regional Externalities", *Regional Studies*, 43 (5): pp. 677–91.

Ying, Y.-H., C.-P. Chang, and M.-C. Hsieh (2008) "Air Cargo as an Impetus for Economic Growth through the Channel of Openness: The Case of OECD Countries", *International Journal of Transport Economics*, 35 (1): pp. 31–44.

Zhang, A., C. Lang, Y.V. Hui, and L. Leung (2007) "Intermodal Alliance and Rivalry of Transport Chains: The Air Cargo Market", *Transportation Research E*, 43: pp. 234–46.

6 Maritime Transportation and Seaports

Theo Notteboom

INTRODUCTION

Earth is also called the blue planet since oceans cover about 70% of its surface and separate land masses. Throughout history, maritime transport and seaports have been catalysts of economic development and prosperity. Many empires were largely based on mastering the seas and opening up new trade routes. The importance of travel across land (e.g. the Silk Road) declined in the Middle Ages as transport shifted to the oceans. For example, the Chinese explorer and soldier Zheng had a large fleet at his disposal in the early fifteenth century, not for war purposes but to consolidate trade relations with the Indian subcontinent, the Middle East and parts of Eastern Africa. Spain and Portugal instigated the great discoveries of the fifteenth and sixteenth centuries as they went in search of wealth on other continents. In the eighteenth and nineteenth centuries the colonization of the world hit its peak supported by maritime transport. In the nineteenth century a huge migration started in Europe as people left for North America through seaports by ocean liners.

Maritime transport and seaports that handle cargo and passengers enable interactions between regions and nations. They ensure the security of supply of energy, food and commodities and are key to trade with the rest of the world. For example, almost 90% of the external freight trade of the European Union is seaborne, while about of 40% of intra-EU exchanges in terms of ton-kilometres are carried by short sea shipping along the European coastlines. Overall, the port and maritime industries are an important source of direct and indirect employment and value-added. Yet the maritime industry and seaports face a lot of challenges in terms of the accommodation of anticipated future trade flows and supply chains, market demands (e.g. competition, supply/demand balance, etc.), safety and security, environmental impacts and social aspects (e.g. working conditions).

This chapter deals with maritime transport and seaports as key constituents of the global logistics and transport system. We first discuss segmentation in the shipping and cargo handling markets. In the second part, the chapter unravels contemporary supply chain dynamics and their impact on shipping and ports. A last theme discusses how and under which conditions cargo flows will move globally within a supply chain perspective.

MARKET SEGMENTATION IN MARITIME TRANSPORT AND PORT HANDLING

Freight as a key determinant

Maritime transport and seaports are very much focused on the types of goods being transported and their packaging or transportation form. Products in their original form are seldom suitable for maritime transportation and handling in seaports. In the past, except for gases and some liquids, all products were packaged in such a way that they could be handled by stevedores. This meant a reduction in size and mass of goods. In this basic form of transportation bulk goods, which required the physical capabilities of people, also had to be bundled into 'man loads', using boxes, bags and the like. Weight of the load unit was a very dominant factor in freight transport. Because large amounts of goods were regularly offered for transport, specialized handling tools were developed. Initially this was only possible when moving liquids where equipment for continuous transport (such as pipelines) could be used. Due to the large increase in demand, solutions were also found for the continuous transportation of bulk products such as grain, coal and ores.

Due to the ever-increasing flow of goods it was impossible to continue to effectively use stevedores for break-bulk operations. An increase of the scale of the vessels, which expanded from the late 1960s, meant that the grouping of man loads could no longer be sustained. Logistics became volume-oriented, because it became more important to change the dimensions of transport resources and transport tools. Man loads, which initially were so important, disappeared in ports. This process took place so rapidly that it is referred to as a 'goods explosion'. The man load was incorporated in bulk loads, which could be transported as such. On the other hand man loads were merged into bigger units such as pallets and later into containers. The cargo unit was born. This goods explosion also brought about a revolution in handling techniques and equipment. When dealing with bulk, solutions were initially sought by resizing the grippers of cranes. Conveyor belts soon followed. The continuous gripper was the next step in this evolution. The conveyor and the stacker/reclaimer found an application in the ship's hold, so self-unloading bulk cargo ships became a reality. The rise of the cargo unit, the most important example being the container, and the development of custom cranes led to a sharp reduction in the loading and unloading times. Here too clearly the aim was a bigger scale, which accelerated the loading and unloading process so that the productivity of the port could be improved.

Given the above developments, a modern division into categories of goods is therefore no longer based on the nature of the goods, but on their handling characteristics. A distinction is made between bulk goods and general cargo. Bulk cargo includes liquid bulk (e.g., oil), gases (e.g., LNG) and dry bulk, such as powders (flour, chemicals), grains (cereals, fertilisers) and/or chunks (coal, ores). General cargo is not homogeneous, except in the form of unit shipments in containers, trailers, flats, pallets or preslung. They may also be conventionally packed in bales, barrels, crates and similar, also called 'break bulk', or as heavy units (heavy unit loads) such as machines, transformers, etc. There is also a category of goods in between bulk goods and general cargo. These are semi- or neobulk goods, i.e., not bulk but homogeneous, such as wood, paper rolls, fruit, cars and steel rolls or coils. The appearance is not only important for the handling of goods in seaport terminals. It also determines the requirements in terms of the maritime transport resources to be used.

Table 6.1 Development of international seaborne trade (millions of tons loaded)

	Oil	Main bulks	Other dry cargo	Total
1970	1,442	448	676	2,566
1980	1,871	796	1,037	3,704
1990	1,755	968	1,285	4,008
2000	2,163	1,288	2,533	5,984
2006	2,698	1,836	3,166	7,700
2007	2,747	1,957	3,330	8,034
2008	2,742	2,059	3,428	8,229
2009	2,642	2,094	3,122	7,858
2010	2,752	2,333	3,323	8,408

Source: UNCTAD, 2011

Table 6.1 shows the global international seaborne trade by main commodities. The oil and oil products shipping market represents about 2.7 billion of loaded tons. However, most of the growth came from dry bulk cargoes. The main bulks include iron ore, grain, coal, bauxite/alumina and phosphate. Other dry cargo mainly relates to minor bulks (e.g. minerals and agricultural products), dry container cargo and conventional general cargo. As can be noticed the economic crisis affected growth in world maritime transport. The economic crisis was also felt at the level of port throughput figures, particularly in North America and Europe. For example, the total European port throughput amounted to 4.26 billion tons in 2008, 3.76 billion tons in 2009 and 4.04 billion tons in 2010 (Figure 6.1). Container trade, dry bulk and conventional general cargo were affected the most in 2009.

Tramp shipping vs. liner shipping

Tramp shipping involves irregular shipping services, mainly over nonstandard routes, with no definite schedule. This implies tramp shipping only takes place when cargo is available. The tramp shipping segment of

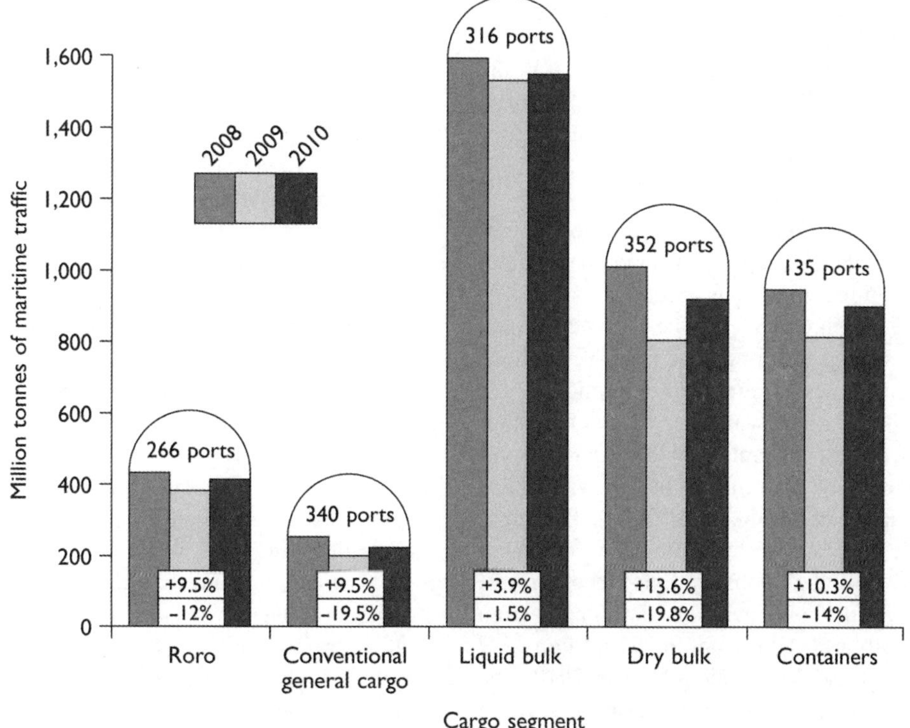

Figure 6.1 Maritime cargo throughput in the European port system (in million metric tonnes)

the market is guided by fixtures of vessels to load any cargo from any port to any port. Liner shipping is based on a set of fixed scheduled services, at regular intervals, between named ports, and offers transport to any goods in the catchment area served by those ports and ready for transit by their sailing dates.

The 'goods explosion' phase ended the era of the versatile multi-deck vessels which transported all sorts of cargo in drums, barrels, bags and other man loads. Instead, the segmentation in the appearance of goods coincided with the rise of specialized ships (e.g. bulk carriers, natural gas carriers, container ships, roll on/roll off (roro) vessels, heavy lift ships, reefer ships, etc.) and the development of distinct shipping markets. The cargo carrying fleets were no longer interchangeable between tramp and liner services. The liner shipping and tramp markets became increasingly separated. This process started in the early 1920s when more sophisticated cargo liners entered the market (e.g. refrigerated holds, tanks, specialized handling gear and roro decks, sometimes even on the same vessel), but saw a strong acceleration in the late 1950s with the growth of a specialized bulk carrier fleet and the beginning of containerization. Scale was not the only important theme but also specialization.

Container liner shipping developed rapidly due to the adoption of standard container sizes in the mid-1960s and the awareness of industry players about the advantages and cost savings resulting from faster vessel turnaround times in ports, the reduction in the level of damages and associated insurance fees, and the integration with inland transport modes such as trucks, barges and trains (Rodrigue and Notteboom, 2009). The large-scale adoption of the container in combination with the globalization process drove worldwide container port throughput from 36 million TEU in 1980 to 237 million TEU in 2000 and 545 million TEU in 2010. The container penetration in world general cargo traffic increased from 21% in 1980 to a rather stable 65% in the past five years (Figure 6.2).

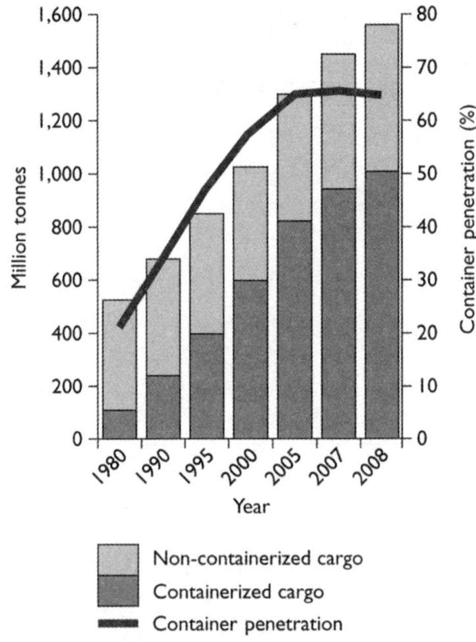

Figure 6.2 World general cargo traffic and container penetration

Source: author's own compilation based on world maritime traffic data

For example, the evolution of the containerization degrees in the ports of the Hamburg–Le Havre range in Europe in Figure 6.3 shows that all large container ports in the range (i.e. Rotterdam, Antwerp, Hamburg, Bremerhaven and Le Havre) have reached containerization degrees above 80%. Since almost all break-bulk cargo that could be containerized (i.e. in terms of dimensions, weights, etc.) has been containerized this substitution process is essentially near to completion in developed economies. It is also rising rapidly in less developed countries.

Despite the existence of separate shipping markets mainly based on the type of goods/commodities involved, the freight rates in these separate markets are surprisingly strongly correlated over time when seen in a multi-year perspective (Randers and Göluke, 2007). Several reasons can be identified. First, the shipping markets are characterized by some common 'market sentiment' as investors and financial institutions (many of which

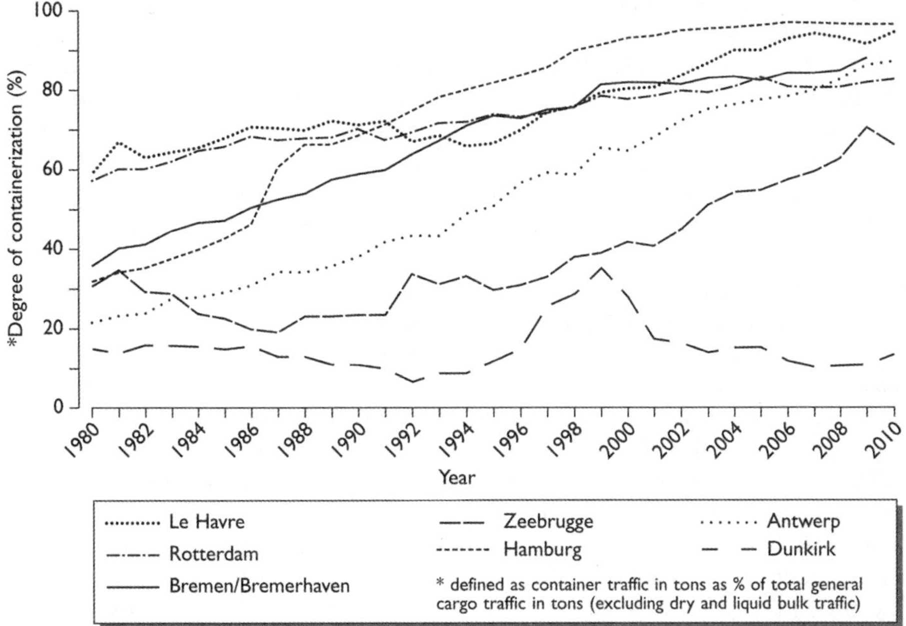

Figure 6.3 Evolution of the containerization degree in seaports of the Le Havre–Hamburg range in Europe (in %)

Source: author's own compilation based on data of respective port authorities

are based in maritime centres such as London, New York or Hong Kong) are to some level undifferentiated as to specific markets or trades. The increasing financialization of the port and shipping markets and the associated changing patterns in risk perception (see Rodrigue et al., 2011) are strengthening this aspect. Second, there is some level of substitutability of cargoes among vessels across routes. For example, reefer containers are competing with reefer ships, and the former are rapidly gaining market share. The world's refrigerated ship fleet is fast shrinking as a new generation of container ships with a large reefer capacity transforms how fruit, meat and other perishable foods move around the globe (Rodrigue and Notteboom, 2011). This process is accelerated by a lack of investments in new reefer vessels: 33% of the fleet is aged above 26 years and only 3% is aged below 5 years. The substitutability between reefer boxes and reefer ships is further illustrated by the sudden market surge in the use of reefer ships in early 2012 for the export of fruit out of South America due to availability problems of reefer containers.

The impact on seaport activities

Given the specialization in and cost evolution of highly sophisticated vessels, reducing (un-) loading times in seaports became imperative. Terminals became larger and intermediate storage was organized in order to ensure that the connection between the maritime vessel and the other modes went smoothly. Bird (1980) captured this reality in the 'anyport model'. Starting from the initial port site with small lateral quays adjacent to the town centre, port expansion is the product of evolving maritime technologies and improvements in cargo handling. Three major steps can be observed in the port development process identified by the 'anyport model': setting, expansion and specialization (Notteboom and Rodrigue, 2005).

The above changes in maritime transport and spatial dimensions of port infrastructures influenced the port–city interface dramatically. Whereas the port was formerly known as a spot of commodities, the modern port evolved to a horizontal cross-section of different supply chains. Due to these trends, the port–city interface evolved. Although every port has its own characteristics (geographical, political, economic and technological), Hoyle (1998) generalized the different stages in the port–city interface and points to an increasing spatial disconnection of city and port. For most established port cities in Europe (London, Antwerp, Rotterdam, Genoa, Naples, Marseille, etc.) the evolution of the port–city interface to a large extent follows the model of Hoyle as these ports were confronted with the search of port companies for deeper (tidal) draft berths and more extensive terminals away from urban areas, thereby abandoning older port areas.

Port activities inevitably have an impact on the environment as a result of land use, environmental effects and congestion. Local public support for further port development is often low. Structural consultation with diverse social groups (the so-called stakeholder relations management; see Notteboom and Winkelmans, 2003) now constitutes a fixed element in port development processes. Ports nowadays provide a significant contribution to the environmental context, among others through the clustering of goods flows into closed and sustainable circuits and by encouraging inland waterway and rail transport as an alternative to road transport.

MARITIME TRANSPORT, SEAPORTS AND SUPPLY CHAINS

Dynamics in supply chains

In recent decades developments in the field of supply chain management have accelerated and resulted in a comprehensive approach to logistics. The handling and organization of goods flows within the product chain are considered in a systematic and integrated manner. Logistics processes and models evolve continuously. The increased competition between logistics players and the growing demands of customers increase costs, making the margins smaller. These changes lead to structural changes in the organization of the supply chain and this in a number of areas. There is an increasing outsourcing of logistics operations, a pressure to evolve towards increased logistics integration by mergers and acquisitions among others, the growing importance of ICT and e-business and a constant pressure to review the configuration of logistics networks.

Many manufacturers outsource logistical tasks such as transport, warehousing and distribution to specialized logistics service providers. The trend towards the outsourcing of logistics activities allows companies to concentrate on their core business and results in significant cost savings. The outsourcing trend is a breeding ground for the growth in services offered by specialist logistics companies, small local operators and even global players. The increasing drive to outsource has led to the emergence of Third Party Logistics (3PLs). Companies choose to restrict the number of partners to which they outsource activities to a minimum in order to save costs and improve their service. Companies thus increasingly opt in favour of a one-stop shop approach: a logistics service provider who can take on all the logistical activities related to specific product chains. This development fueled expansion and consolidation in the logistics market. The logistics service providers will start to offer total solutions by becoming a single focal point for the customer and this through the linking of ICT and logistics services.

International supply chains are increasingly the playing field of global logistics operators such as DHL, Kuehne & Nagel, Geodis, Cevatrans, Sinotrans and many others. Logistic integration leads to a functional blurring of distinctions between logistics and transport. The various parties involved, such as shipping lines, transport operators and logistics service providers, try to penetrate each other's markets. Market demand is the first major driving force behind this vertical integration. More than ever, transport services have to fulfil high requirements in terms of frequency, punctuality, reliability and demand for greater geographical coverage. In addition, shippers are looking for more specialized door-to-door door logistics services, which seek to provide an appropriate reply to highly customer-specific questions. The changed market demand has prompted the various market players to invest in new customer-focused logistics solutions, in consultation with other market players in some cases. Vertical market integration allows a player to differentiate itself from the competition by also offering services in other links of the supply chain. Market players can increase the scale of their core business through horizontal integration, thus being able to assist the customer on a wider geographical scale and/or with greater capacity to meet their demands.

Many players develop a mixed strategy of far-reaching horizontal integration through alliances and mergers/acquisitions, combined with a vertical integration in some areas which are an extension of the core business. This is evidenced in the wave of mergers, acquisitions and strategic alliances in container shipping, cargo handling in ports and logistics services. Strategic alliances in logistics and transport are growing exponentially to form global networks and thus to meet the growing demand for global logistics. The decision-making power in the supply chain thereby resides with a limited number of players.

Good facilities in terms of information and communication technology (ICT) are an increasingly important condition for success to be able to effectively respond to the rapidly changing quality requirements of international business and the authorities. The Internet revolution and the creation of powerful IT systems have had an impact on logistics systems and concepts in many ways. Information systems facilitate the development of 3PL and 4PL and allow for the development and management of complex supply chains and networks. The Internet has already resulted in the creation of a series of virtual markets where buyers and suppliers can find one another. The possibility of online ordering has had a significant impact on the requirements for a distribution system. Information systems have considerably increased transparency within supply chains in three ways. First, thanks to ICT it is now possible to follow cargo using so-called 'tracking and tracing'. Transponders and GPS systems have already become quite customary in the logistics world. The development of RFID (radio frequency identification) technology makes it possible to remotely identify objects or read information. Second, ICT can provide real-time information about events. This information can be used to predict and respond appropriately to possible problems in the supply chain ('event management'). Finally, ICT is important in the context of performance management: it allows the collection of data on all aspects of logistics services and enables the testing of these data against quality requirements as well as contractual obligations with customers. A good example is the reliable delivery of consignments.

The (re)design of logistics and distribution systems gave rise to a substantial reduction of claims in terms of the environmental utilization space (fossil fuels, water, mineral resources, primary production of ecosystems and environmental degradation as a result of pollution). A wave of initiatives in the area of 'green' logistics has ensured that logistics activities are not only more efficient but also less polluting. This, for example, is achieved by avoiding (empty) movements, optimizing the use of transport resources by optimal routing, bundling loads, the use of environmentally-friendly vehicles and engines, redefining distribution networks as a function of environmental objectives, developing 'green' warehouses with a high energy efficiency and sometimes even generating own power from solar panels and windmills.

The rise of intermodal transport and inland terminals

The configuration of rail and barge networks is of crucial importance in accommodating global supply chains and connecting shipping and seaport activities to hinterlands. A certain level of traffic concentration in a seaport system is required in order to allow a virtuous cycle of modal shifts from road haulage to high-volume transport modes. But even port systems with a low degree of concentration have embraced intermodal transport. Extensive cargo concentration on a few trunk lines opens possibilities for economies of scale in inland shuttles, but even more likely for higher frequencies. Smaller ports and new terminals often seek connection to the extensive hinterland networks of the larger ports.

In the last fifteen years, the dynamics in logistics networks have created the right conditions for a large-scale development of freight villages and inland ports. The range of functions presented by inland logistics centres is wide-ranging from simple cargo consolidation to advanced logistics services. Many inland locations with multimodal access have become broader logistics zones. Not only have they assumed a significant number of traditional cargo handling functions and services, but they have also attracted many related services, such as distribution centres, shipping agents, trucking companies, forwarders, container-repair facilities and packing firms. The concept of logistics zones in the hinterland is now well-advanced in Europe: e.g. 'platformes logistiques' in France, the Güterverkehrszentren (GVZ) in Germany, Interporti in Italy, Freight Villages in the UK and the Zonas de Actividades Logisticas (ZAL) in Spain. Logistics zones are usually created within the framework of regional development policies as joint initiatives by firms, intermodal operators, national, regional and/or local authorities, and/or the Chambers of Commerce and, Industry. Quite a few of these logistics zones are competing with seaports as far as the location of distribution facilities and value added logistics (VAL) are concerned. Shortage of industrial premises, high land prices, congestion problems, the inland location of markets and severe environmental restrictions are some of the well-known arguments for companies not to locate in a seaport.

Impact on the shipping market

Today, shipping companies operate in all types of maritime transport. They have adopted the form of international companies, with representation in almost all countries, by agents or other parties. A large number of companies are moving towards vertical and horizontal integration. In terms of horizontal integration, there are various forms of cooperation between shipping lines, irrespective of the effective amalgamation of companies through mergers and acquisitions.

The prevailing form of cooperation in liner shipping is an operational cooperation agreement between shipping companies by sharing ships (vessel sharing agreements), by making available part of the cargo hold to a fellow company (slot charting agreements), to more intense forms of cooperation, such as consortia and alliances, whereby ships are introduced in joint liner services. As a result of the horizontal integration, shipping companies with a huge fleet capacity are created. In 2012, the four biggest container shipping lines (Maersk Line, MSC, CMA CGM and COSCO) controlled approximately 40% of overall container shipping capacity.

The vertical integration of shipping lines manifests itself in different ways. There is a trend towards more liner agents' networks, especially in those ports which play a key role in the liner shipping networks of the shipping company. Shipping companies also seem to be extending the activities of their agents' networks to encompass services typically offered by freight forwarders. By integrating the sales function in the operating system, companies seek to acquire more direct control over the cargo, to reduce the distance to the customer and to attract more cargo to their road and rail transport networks. The direct involvement of shipping companies in hinterland transport is tangible in rail traffic, inland shipping, road transport and coastal shipping. Shipping companies can choose to do everything themselves or to purchase services from third parties. Most container companies continue to use local hauliers. In the railway sector a number of leading container shipping companies provide rail services as part of an integrated marine–land transport system. Large shipping companies make extensive use of so-called common-user-feeders. These are independent local shipping companies which assure contract liner services between major ports (hubs) and smaller ports (the feeder ports) for the large shipping companies.

Shipping companies are increasingly interested in having their own dedicated terminals in strategically located ports within their network, at least if container volumes allow. Either the company seeks to achieve (partial) control over the terminal through full ownership, participation and lease/concession formulas, or the company wants to exercise indirect control over a terminal through specific contractual arrangements with the relevant terminal operator. Finally, shipping companies are increasingly positioning themselves as full-fledged logistics service providers by including a wider range of logistics activities in their services (warehousing, packaging, distribution). The final goal of this strategy is to create a situation whereby the shipping company is the only party doing business with the customer/shipper for the management of the supply chains (one-stop shopping).

The vertical and horizontal integration in the shipping market is due to several factors. First, increased market demand for a more integrated service incites many shipping companies to vertically integrate activities within the supply chains, resulting in door-to-door logistics services. Shipping companies and freight forwarders, for example, are competing for direct access to the shipper. They try to fulfil the requirements in terms of frequency, punctuality and reliability and the demand for greater geographic coverage through vertical and horizontal integration.

Second, in addition to demand, there are also internal motives for shipping companies, which drive them to work with similar or different companies such as the desire to realize economies of scale, gaining access through one's partner to technologies, markets and/or capital, to reduce the entrepreneurial risks and influence the competitive environment.

A third major impetus for such a supply chain strategy in the liner shipping market is also evident on the supply side, namely the desire to formulate an appropriate answer to the fierce competition in the shipping market. Because transport is a derived demand, companies can barely have an influence in the short term on market size. The competition between companies is focused on increasing the mutual market share. Shipping lines have always attached great attention to cost and asset management. Since the 1990s a great deal of attention is devoted to larger, more fuel-efficient vessels. The average vessel size increased from 1,155 TEU in 1987 to 2,618 TEU in 2009 (UNCTAD, 2009). The size of a typical container vessel deployed on the Far East–Europe trade increased from 4,500–5,500 TEU in 2000 to about 8,500 TEU in 2011. Units of close to 15,000 TEU have become recently operational and the announced triple 'E' class of Maersk Line with a unit capacity of 18,000 TEU should start calling at ports in 2014.

The increase in tonnage results in significant economies of scale at sea: the shipping cost per transported container falls dramatically (albeit not proportionally) as shipping capacity increases (Cullinane and Khanna, 1999). At the same time, slow steaming or the reduction in the sailing speed of maritime vessels has become an increasingly common practice in container liner shipping since 2008, as the amount and unit size of available vessel capacity rises and the price of fuel increases (Notteboom and Vernimmen, 2009). Slow steaming has helped to absorb vessel overcapacity during the crisis (more vessels are required to maintain the same service frequency), to save on fuel costs, to restore liner shipping company profitability and to reduce environmental emissions by ships at sea. However, the focus of container carriers on larger vessel sizes and slow steaming did not lead to a more stable market environment. Unpredictable business cycles and the seasonality on some of the major trade lanes (e.g. demand peak just before Chinese New Year) have more than once resulted in unstable cargo guarantees to shipping lines. In June 2011, Maersk Line started the discussion on a new mission for container shipping based on three pillars: (1) on time performance/reliability; (2) ease of business (i.e. avoid complexity, increase transparency); and (3) environmental performance. These three aspects should be considered in a supply chain perspective.

A fourth reason for integration movements in the shipping industry is the cost of land operations, more specifically terminal handling and hinterland transportation. The relative importance of land transport costs in the overall cost structure of a shipping company are on the increase. On the one hand, this is a result of the concentration of freight traffic in just a few ports, meaning that the costs associated with land and maritime transport increase substantially. On the other hand, the share of the costs associated with container transport and land transport in the overall costs of a liner service rise as larger ships are used. The increase in average vessel capacity within the fleet of leading container shipping companies decrease the relative importance of shipping costs in the cost structure and increases the preponderance of port and land transport operations. In addition to this the expected cost savings at the maritime end are reducing, while several savings can still be realized on the land side. The group of shipping companies, which is also undertaking land transport operations, is growing largely because they wish to increase direct control of their container park (specifically in terms of the repositioning of empty containers) and the desire to obtain direct access to shippers by offering door-to-door transport.

Impact on the function and strategies of seaports

Ports constitute nodes in national and intercontinental transport chains. The transport, storage and distribution functions are the raison d'être for seaports. Not all ports have an economically important and vast hinterland. As a result of the growth of transport flows in larger ports, clusters of activities are created. Larger ports enable the use of relatively environmentally efficient transport modes: transport takes place by road, as well as by rail and by barge (and through pipelines for petrochemical products). Many ports assure the transit of goods that are not destined for their own country. The transit function contributes to the realization of scale effects in transport and logistics. As a result the transport costs for import and export flows drop. Because major transport infrastructures and resources per ton transported are usually more environmentally efficient, the environmental impact per ton transported is also reduced as a result.

Many ports also have an important industrial function. Production processes require several inputs: in addition to raw materials and semi-finished products these processes also require efficient transportation facilities, the development and application of new knowledge and good labour relations. Large-scale (petro)chemical industry is often located in seaports: companies have made tremendous investments in refineries and chemical plants in seaport areas. As a result of scaling, clusters of industries related to this activity were created around these plants. The same development is evident in the automotive industry. The diversity, scale and quality of the available facilities (companies, government bodies and institutions) contribute to an attractive business climate for developing existing industries and attracting new business. This results in a self-reinforcing process: increased activity results in more benefits and more benefits result in more activity.

Over the years, the seaport sector has evolved into a fully-fledged economic sector with its own dynamics. In the 1960s and 1970s port areas played a prominent role in attracting the petrochemical and chemical industry. The so-called MIDAs (Maritime Industrial Development Areas) which were created are extremely important economic poles and also have a major logistics and distribution function. As important pillars ports contribute to the economic development of regions. If the seaport industry is neglected, then the superstructure starts to struggle, especially in small open economies.

The recent developments in supply chains are having far-reaching effects on the function and strategy of seaports, as described in the sections below.

Supply chains are the relevant focus in port competition

First, the vertical integration strategies of the market players have blurred the traditional division of tasks within the logistics chain and as such created an environment in which seaports are increasingly competing not as individual places that handle ships but within transport chains or supply chains. The logistics chain has become more than ever the relevant scope for analyzing port competitiveness. It also implies that a port's competitiveness becomes increasingly dependent on external coordination and control by outside actors. As a result, major port clients consider ports merely as a sub-system in the supply chain. Accordingly they concentrate their service packages not on the ports' sea-to-land interface but on the quality and reliability of the entire transport chain. Port choice becomes more a function of network costs. Port selection criteria are related to the entire network in which the port is just one node. The ports that are being chosen are those that will help to minimize the sum of sea, port and inland costs.

Seaports are increasingly confronted with powerful port users

Second, seaports are increasingly confronted with powerful port users as a result of logistics integration and a concentration of power at the port demand side. Seaports increasingly have to deal with large port clients who possess a strong bargaining power vis-à-vis terminal operations and inland transport operations. In the contemporary logistic-restructured port environment it has become more difficult to identify the port customers who really exert power in the logistics chain. The question of who really decides which port to choose, depends primarily on the type of cargo involved, the cargo-generating power of the shipper and the characteristics related to specific trade routes. In some cases market players are port user and port service supplier at the same time (e.g. a shipping line operating a dedicated terminal). While cooperation at the operational level between the actors in the supply chain may have increased, this has not necessarily resulted in increased commitment to a long-term future relationship with the port. The purchasing power of the large intermodal carriers, reinforced by strategic alliances between them, is used to play off one port or group of ports against another. The loyalty of a port client cannot be taken for granted. Ports face the constant risk of losing important clients, not because of deficiencies in port infrastructure or terminal operations, but because the client has rearranged its service networks or has engaged in new partnerships with other carriers.

Need for coordination with other nodes and players

Third, ports are trying to 'anchor' some shippers and carriers who control huge cargo flows and who are in a good position to generate added value for the port region. If a seaport wants to attract or retain some of the megacarriers, it has to position itself as an efficient intermodal hub and distribution service centre acting within extensive transport and communications networks. A port management strategy solely based on the provision of terminal infrastructures does not provide all necessary conditions for capturing important 'footloose' clients on a sustainable basis. In this competitive environment, the ultimate success of a port will depend on the ability to integrate the port effectively into the networks of business relationships that shape supply chains. In other words, the success of a seaport no longer exclusively depends on its internal weaknesses and strengths. It is being more and more determined by the ability of the port community to fully exploit synergies with other transport nodes and other players within the logistics networks of which they are part. To be successful, ports need to think along with the customer, to try to figure out what his/her needs are, not only in the port but throughout the logistics chains and networks. This demands the creation of a platform in which various stakeholders (carriers, shippers, transport operators, labour and government bodies) are working together to identify and address issues affecting logistics performance. Port authorities can be a catalyst in this process, even though their direct impact on cargo flows is limited. The availability of powerful information channels and systems and the capability of having a knowledge transfer among companies are two of the main determinants for the success of economic clusters, and also for the success of logistics zones.

Seaports as habitats for logistics

Fourth, seaports are key constituents of many supply chains. The gateway position of major seaports offers opportunities for the development of value-added logistics (VAL). Seaports are evolving from pure cargo handling centres to a complex of key functions within a logistics system. In cooperation with other parties, involved port authorities can actively stimulate logistics polarization in port areas through the enhancement of flexible labour conditions, smooth customs formalities (in combination with freeport status) and powerful information systems. Warehouses are traditionally located just behind the terminals. At present logistics activities can take place on the terminal itself, in a logistics park where several logistics activities are concentrated or, in the case of industrial subcontracting, on the site of an industrial company. While there is a clear tendency in the container sector to move away from the terminal, in other cargo categories an expansion of logistics on the terminal itself can be witnessed. As such, a mixture of pure stevedoring activities and logistics activities occurs. In the new logistic market environment, the following logistics activities typically find a good habitat in ports: (a) logistics activities resulting in a considerable reduction in the transported volume; (b) logistics activities involving big volumes of bulk cargoes, suitable for inland navigation and rail; (c) logistics activities directly related to companies which have a site in the port area; (d) logistics activities related to cargo that needs flexible storage to create a buffer (products subject to season-dependent fluctuations or irregular supply); and (e) logistics activities with a high dependency on short-sea shipping. Moreover, port areas typically possess a strong competitiveness for distribution centres in a multiple import structure and as a consolidation centre for export cargo.

Strengthening port–hinterland relationships

Fifth, changes in supply chains have paved the way towards stronger port–hinterland relationships. Through port regionalization strategies (see Notteboom and Rodrigue, 2005), the orientation for many ports has tended to shift from a local port city level to a more axial development pattern (i.e. the corridors towards the hinterland). Corridor development enhances the location of logistics sites in seaports and inland ports and along the axes between seaports and inland ports. The interaction between seaports and inland locations leads to the development of a large logistics pool consisting of several logistics zones. This trend towards the geographical concentration of distribution platforms in many cases occurs spontaneously as the result of a slow, market-driven process. But also national, regional and/or local authorities try to direct this process by means of offering financial incentives. The creation of large logistics poles poses new challenges in the relations between seaports and inland ports. A large number of port authorities promote an efficient intermodal system in order to secure cargo under conditions of high competition. This includes, for example, the involvement in the introduction of new shuttle train services to the hinterland, together with the respective national railway companies, rail operators, terminal operators, shipping companies and/or large shippers. The focus by port users on logistics networks is a clear invitation to port managers to consider cooperation with inland ports in the field of traffic management, land issuing, hinterland connections and services, environmental protection and research and development (R&D). In practice, mainly private market players are involved in setting up these types of cooperative networks. But informal programmes of coordination between port authorities and inland ports are now slowly developing. Rotterdam and Antwerp are two European examples:

- The Port of Rotterdam is expanding its involvement with and in (container) handling in the hinterland. This is being done in both the Benelux and Germany by individual companies: ECT (extended gate strategy through European Gateway Services), APMT (also adopted an extended gate strategy), DP World, Van Uden, CMA CGM, NYK, partly in collaboration with the Port of Rotterdam Authority. The Port Authority of Rotterdam has also launched the 'Container Transferium' concept to support further growth of container activity in Rotterdam by transferring cargo to barges.
- The port of Antwerp has developed multiple initiatives concerning its hinterland development. Through its hinterland policy the Port Authority is seeking to raise the proportion of freight sent by barge and rail and to develop multimodal hinterland hubs. Many of the recent initiatives as regards hinterland strategy are integrated in the 'Total Project for a More Competitive Port', which was started in 2009 by the Antwerp Port Authority and Alfaport (the association of port companies). The inland strategy of the port of Antwerp is built around three tiers or geographical layers. Tier 1 encompasses the consolidation of volumes via transferia close to the port (e.g. WCT Meerhout, Beverdonk Container Terminal, TCT Willebroek). Tier 2 focuses on trimodal hinterland hubs in the southwest (LAR Kortrijk/Moeskroen) and southeast (Athus/Liège) of Belgium. At tier 3, we find the hinterland corridors by rail and barge to the south (mainly to France and Spain: Lille/Paris, Hendaye, Lyon, Marseille, Perpignan, Irun, Barcelona, and to Italy/Switzerland: Basel, Milan East and West) and the eastern Lanes (including the Rhine corridor, Germany/Austria/Hungary and the Czech Republic and Poland). The Antwerp Port Authority is also participating in the Beverdonk Container Terminal, situated about 50 km east of the port, and has set up a collaboration agreement with the port of Liège to develop the Trilogiport site in Liège, a new terminal and logistics area located along the Albert Canal. Liège is the third largest inland port in Europe after Duisburg and Paris.

While ports around the world are evolving towards being more proactive players, cooperating indirectly with different players in the hinterland, direct cooperation efforts between seaports and inland locations, in which profits and risks are shared, are less common.

A changing port hierarchy

Sixth, new liner service networks and larger ships force previously non-competing ports into head-on competition. This has led to a new port hierarchy in container port systems. For example, seaports located far away from each other are now to some extent competing. Evidence exists that ports in the Hamburg–Le Havre range in Europe are now competing with UK ports, especially for transshipment traffic. Competition is also growing between the Mediterranean port system and the Hamburg–Le Havre range, as these two different port systems are in a good position to reach the economic and industrial heartland of Europe (Notteboom, 2010). Furthermore, the new requirements related to deep-sea services do not necessarily make the existing large container ports the best locations for setting up hub operations. That is why the position of the large load centres is to some extent threatened by medium-sized ports and new hub terminals. Dynamics in the hinterland can also affect port hierarchy. On the one hand, the formation of inland terminals enables smaller ports in a port system to seek connection to the extensive hinterland networks of the large ports. On the other hand, inland terminals help the large ports to preserve their attractiveness and to fully exploit potential economies of scale. The corridors towards the inland terminal network create the necessary margin for further growth of seaborne container traffic. Inland terminals as such acquire an important satellite function with respect to seaports, as they help to relieve seaport areas from potential congestion.

Strategies of terminal operators in ports

Finally, the logistics developments have also altered the strategies of terminal operators as key players in seaports (Notteboom and Rodrigue, 2012). Increased competitive pressure has prompted stevedores to continuously adapt their strategy. Like shipping companies, terminal operators are increasingly becoming aware of supply chain thinking and how they can try to maximize their share in this market. Terminal operators try to consolidate their position as much as possible by entering alliances/joint ventures with shipping companies and inland terminals to get a grip on the increasingly important hinterland transport. This strategy is mainly aimed at acquiring sufficient critical mass in terms of hinterland volumes by bundling the volumes of different shipping companies, with respect to inland terminals, and thus to generate sufficient import and export flows. Not all stevedores are adopting the same integration strategy. Often the terminal operators achieve good network integration through a better coordination with hinterland modes and other logistics service providers. In some cases a stevedore will start offering additional logistics services through a logistics subsidiary, such as making import cargo customer- or country-specific. The motives underlying the increasing involvement of terminal operators in the hinterland operations relate to reducing costs and retaining cargoes. Besides vertical integration, horizontal concentration movements in the cargo handling market have taken off, especially in the container handling market. The consolidation policy of major (maritime) terminal groups such as Hutchison Port Holding of China, PSA Corporation of Singapore, DP World of Dubai and Eurogate, which was established in 1999 in Germany, has contributed greatly to the expansion of the container handling market. These groups operate terminals all over the world. A number of terminal operators run more than 50 terminals.

MARITIME TRANSPORT, SEAPORTS AND THE ROUTING OF GOODS

The future of maritime transport and seaports is heavily influenced by future trade flows. However, it is also about how and under which conditions these flows will move globally within a supply chain perspective using the available services and infrastructure. In this last section, we discuss key developments in this field.

The changing geography of trade flows

International trade represents a growing share of global output, and growth in trade is expected to outstrip overall growth in output for the foreseeable future. The rising significance of trade is a consequence of the increasing integration of the global economy. Legal and cultural obstacles to trade are diminishing at the same time as the motivation to trade is increasing. Integration is occurring both at the regional level, through initiatives such as NAFTA and the EU Single Market, and at the global level, supported by the continuing evolution of WTO. The last three decades have seen important modifications in international trade flows. The bulk of international trade occurs within economic blocs, especially the European Union and NAFTA. Other significant flows are between Asia/Pacific and North America (especially the United States), between Europe and North America and between Europe and Asia/Pacific. The world economy is increasingly influenced by developing countries and economies in transition. Recently, other regions of the world have

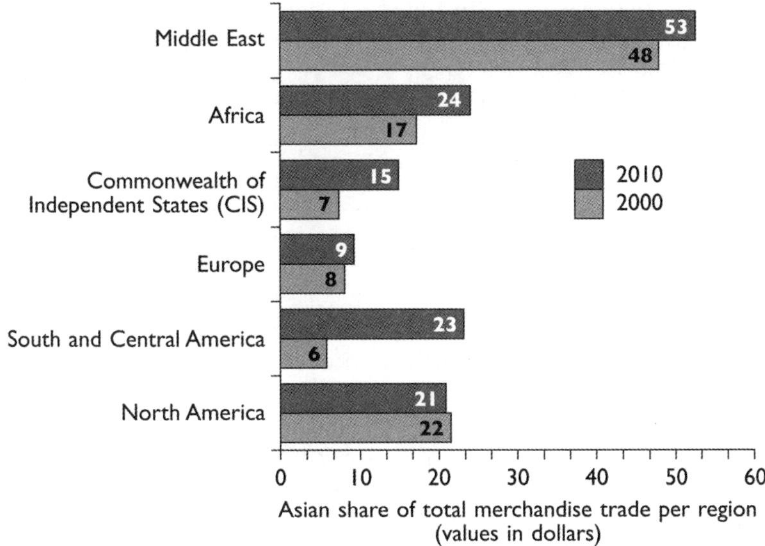

Figure 6.4 The share of Asia in total merchandise trade per region (based on values in dollars)

Source: author's own compilation based on trade data of the World Trade Organisation (WTO)

seen much faster population growth than West Europe. Eventually this will lead to economic areas shifting in the direction of these concentrations of people with an increasing income profile. A prime example is the rise of China. In the last ten years, China posted an annual GDP growth of between 7% and 13%. The changing geography of world trade is illustrated by the growing share of Asian trade (Figure 6.4).

Maritime networks: the transport routes across the oceans

Corridors have become the main arteries of world trade. Strategic points along maritime corridors such as the Panama Canal, Suez Canal, the Straits of Malacca and the Straits of Gibraltar function as important turntables in extensive hub-and-spoke and relay/interlining activities. Many of the world's larger ports can be found near these key locations: e.g. Port Said and Damietta near the Suez Canal, Algeciras and Tanger Med near the Straits of Gibraltar, and Singapore and Tanjung Pelepas near the Straits of Malacca.

The Suez Canal is one of the main canals worldwide and connects the Mediterranean with the Red Sea. In ancient Egypt, people had wondered how to promote trade on the various seas but it was only in 1869 that a modern canal was opened. The canal is 192 km long and links the port city of Port Said to the north with Suez in southern Egypt. The largest container ships pay an amount equivalent to US$700,000 per crossing. On average it takes between 11 and 16 hours to sail through the canal. The transit and use of the Suez Canal is still an important element in trade policy. An estimated 31 million TEU passed through the Suez Canal in 2008 compared to 20 million in 2004 (figures Suez Canal Authority). Nearly 93% of these container flows are related to the Europe–Asia trade routes. The almost monopolistic position of the Suez route on many trade routes is being scrutinized by rising security concerns caused by piracy acts, high Suez Canal charges and an ever-changing geography in world trade patterns. The Cape route could in the long run serve as an alternative to the Suez option on trades between Asia and South America, Asia and West Africa and South America and East Africa. The expected emergence of the Cape route should be seen as the embodiment of a promising development of south–south trade volumes between Asia, Sub-Saharan Africa and South America.

The Panama Canal, which opened in 1914, is also considered one of the key transit routes for ships. Because this canal has a huge influence on the maritime trade routes, it has tremendous strategic value for America. The total length of the channel is 77 km and runs through a hilly region. The structure of the channel can be best described as an amalgamation of (artificial) lakes and water corridors connected to the open sea via three lock complexes. The Panamanian government is building a new set of larger locks so that larger ships can use it. The opening of new larger Panama Canal locks in 2014 (allowing container vessels of up to 14,000 TEU) will open up opportunities for shipping lines to reintroduce equatorial round-the-world container services. This could pull some direct calls away from major port regions such as North Europe and the North American East Coast to transshipment hubs on the maritime beltway of the world.

The containerization wave went hand in hand with a restructuring within the liner shipping services. Containers, as a result of their modular design, are more suited to bundling than bulk (limited number of destinations) or general cargo (more time required to process this). Thanks to a concentration of the calls in some main ports or hubs from where goods could be distributed across a large area, companies were able to use larger ships. Most liner services combine a limited number of main ports in a region (e.g. the Far East) with a number of calls in another region (e.g. Northern Europe). Liner services or 'loops' are like bus services. A typical service between Europe and the Far East will call in seven to ten ports.

The centralization of traffic in a few ports stands a better chance of succeeding if accompanied by significant economies of scale in land transport and if the diseconomies of scale in ports as a result of the deployment of larger vessels remain limited. Container shipping companies do not put all their eggs in one basket. Many strategic alliances between companies provide several services between northern Europe and the Far East or North America, and the scheduled ports of call may vary per service. In some cases, the choice of port of call may even vary depending on the direction of transport. Even shipping companies that have built their own terminals leave other options open. Shipping companies and shipping groups thus are quite flexible. This allows them to meet the needs of their customers in the best possible way and make use of the geographic advantages of each port. In addition, they can also keep up the pressure on freight forwarders.

Although a certain standardization seems evident between the big shipping companies in terms of the nature of the deployed ships and the general configuration of the liner services, there still appears to be a number of substantial differences at the level of the geographic spread of liner services. A number of companies almost unilaterally focus on the important east–west axis. This concentration on routes with heavy traffic flows is also associated with a high traffic concentration in a limited number of ports of call. Other shipping companies (such as Maersk, MSC and CMA CGM) have a network that covers the whole world, although it remains heavily focused on the main routes. This can lead to important 'interlining' flows between deep sea vessels of different sizes that are used for the various east–west and north–south services.

Challenges to maritime transport and seaports for the routing of goods

The efficient cargo routing across the world requires adequate infrastructure and port and shipping operations. We argue that three groups of factors will play an increasingly important role in the performance of shipping services and ports: (a) cost efficiency; (b) reliability, flexibility and resilience; and (c) sustainability.

Efficient cost management

Efficient cost management in shipping and ports requires, among others, efficient asset management. In shipping markets, liner carriers operate regular frequent services around the globe with high fixed costs and massive asset investment. Once the structure is set for a service there is no other choice except to fill it with freight. Demand is volatile due to seasonality effects and trade imbalances on some trade lanes. In periods of vessel overcapacity, carriers struggle for cargo volumes to maintain their market share. They sometimes cut freight rates to low levels just to achieve their marginal cost or get into long-term freight agreements with shippers to secure a stable revenue stream. Asset management and the related service cost structure are the keys to the success of liner companies. Efficient asset management in shipping is not only about achieving lower costs through scale increases in vessel size or a better deployment of the fleet. It is also about the right timing for selling/buying vessels or chartering ships in/out. There are substantial time gaps between taking a decision to invest in or to upgrade any asset and the deployment of such assets. During these time gaps the decision factors may have turned dramatically against the earlier decision creating the core of observed supply/demand imbalances in liner shipping. Also, port operators are challenged to achieve cost efficiency through smart asset management. For example, Notteboom and Rodrigue (2012) demonstrated that the financial results of the global terminal operator industry in 2009 were rather good despite the economic crisis, due to severe cost-control measures, including a revision of investment plans, equipment maintenance schedules and asset deployment strategies.

Flexibility, reliability and resilience

The shipping markets and seaports need to demonstrate ever higher levels of flexibility, reliability and resilience. *Flexibility* mainly relates to the routing options available to the users of shipping and port services and the possibility to make last-minute changes to the routing if desired. For example, production units and distribution centres in the hinterland typically value the flexibility a port system offers in terms of available routing options for import and export cargo. Seaports should therefore develop a greater attention to the benefits offered by the presence of adjacent seaports in terms of the flexibility they offer to customers. Several gateways together can create synergies in reaching out to the hinterland and in offering the best possible maritime connectivity to overseas regions. It is up to the port regions to develop strategies and policies to find adequate answer to the unique combination of network flexibility on the one hand and concentration and bundling of flows on the other. Coordination and collective actions between ports and market players is essential to meet the objective of increasing the share of co-modal solutions and to bundle cargo.

Reliability relates to the need to offer shipping and port services that meet the requirements of users in terms of arrival times and the avoidance of delays. For example, the liner shipping industry overall shows a low schedule integrity with the best performers (i.e. Maersk Line) only reaching about 75% on-time arrivals in ports, meaning that 25% of the ships arrive one day or more late (see Notteboom, 2006 for a discussion on schedule unreliability). The worst performers only reach 40% of on-time arrivals. Ports and ship operators will increasingly have to offer service guarantees in a supply chain setting (foreland–port–hinterland), even in a more volatile business environment. This might require the adoption of new partnership models.

Resilience relates to the need to make shipping and ports less vulnerable to unexpected events such as natural disasters (e.g. earthquake in Japan, flooding in Thailand) or political turmoil (e.g. Arab Spring) to support supply chain resilience.

Sustainability

The need for sustainability is partly linked to higher regulatory and societal requirements. Environmental compliance is required not only in order to ensure community support for port development and shipping activities, but also to attract customers. Hence, big shippers increasingly focus on the carbon footprint associated with the supply chains they manage. In order to implement sustainability in the business processes, many shipping and port-related actors have adopted environmental management systems, sustainability reporting and other environmental measurement and control instruments on top of regulations imposed by organizations such as the International Maritime Organization (IMO – see for instance the MARPOL Convention). For example, the port authorities of Amsterdam, Le Havre, Rotterdam, Antwerp, Hamburg and Bremen in cooperation with International Association of Ports and Harbors (IAPH), set up the Environmental Ship Index. Shipping companies can register their ships for this index on a website. On the basis of the data entered, such as fuel consumption and emissions, each ship is given a score from 0 to 100 (from highly-polluting to emission-free). The ports themselves decide what advantages to offer participating ships, but it mostly comes down to a discount on tonnage dues when calling the port. The Environmental Ship Index is an example of incentive pricing at the level of port dues in view of improving environmental ship standards in ports. The problem remains that the customers are typically not willing to pay for the costs shipping lines, port operators and port authorities make in view of going beyond compliance.

CONCLUSION

Maritime transport and seaports are key constituents of the global logistics and transport system. Both shipping and seaport activities have historically been affected by a 'goods explosion' phase, which resulted in the current level of market segmentation based on commodity types. Still, the different market segments in shipping and port activity are to some extent functionally linked and the markets exert a strong sense of a common market sentiment. Supply chain perspectives and increased logistics integration in the market have dramatically affected port functions, port competition and business models in liner shipping. The increasing role of the hinterland dimension can be put forward as one of the most far-reaching developments heavily affecting the strategies and market dynamics in the shipping and port markets. Cargo flows will move globally within a supply chain perspective and this has extensive implications on (trans)port services and (trans)port infrastructure. This chapter underlined that maritime transport and seaports will have to respond to an increasing need for cost efficiency, reliability, flexibility, resilience and sustainability while accommodating global commodity flows.

REFERENCES

Bird, J. (1980) *Seaports and Seaport Terminals*, Hutchinson University: London

Cullinane, K. and Khanna, M. (1999) 'Economies of scale in large container ships', *Journal of Transport Economics and Policy*, vol. 33, no. 2, pp. 185–208.

Hoyle, B. (1998) 'The redevelopment of derelict port areas', *The Dock & Harbour Authority*, vol. 79, pp. 46–49.

Notteboom, T. (2006) 'The time factor in liner shipping services', *Maritime Economics and Logistics*, vol. 8, no. 1, pp. 19–39.

Notteboom, T. (2010) 'Concentration and the formation of multi-port gateway regions in the European container port system: an update', *Journal of Transport Geography*, vol. 18, no. 4, pp. 567–583.

Notteboom, T. and Rodrigue, J.-P. (2005) 'Port regionalization: towards a new phase in port development', *Maritime Policy and Management*, vol. 32, no. 3, pp. 297–313.

Notteboom, T. and Rodrigue, J.-P. (2012) 'The corporate geography of global container terminal operators', *Maritime Policy and Management*, vol. 39, no. 3, pp. 249–279.

Notteboom, T. and Vernimmen, B. (2009) 'The effect of high fuel costs on liner service configuration in container shipping', *Journal of Transport Geography*, vol. 17, no. 5, pp. 325–337.

Notteboom, T. and Winkelmans, W. (2003) 'Dealing with stakeholders in the port planning process', in: Dullaert, W., Jourquin, B., Polak, J. (eds), *Across the Border: Building Upon a Quarter Century of Transport Research in the Benelux*, De Boeck: Antwerp, pp. 249–265.

Randers J. and Göluke, J. (2007) 'Forecasting turning points in shipping freight rates: lessons from 30 years of practical effort', *System Dynamics Review*, vol. 23, no. 2/3, pp. 253–284.

Rodrigue, J.-P. and Notteboom, T. (2009) 'The geography of containerisation: half a century of revolution, adaptation and diffusion', *Geojournal*, vol. 74, no. 1, pp. 1–5.

Rodrigue, J.-P. and Notteboom, T. (2011) 'Looking inside the box: Evidence from the containerization of commodities and the Cold Chain', *Proceedings of the ECONSHIP 2011 Conference, University of the Aegean*, Chios, 22–24 June 2011.

Rodrigue, J.-P., Notteboom, T. and Pallis, A. (2011) 'The financialization of the port and terminal industry: revisiting risk and embeddedness', *Maritime Policy and Management*, vol. 38, no. 2, pp. 191–213.

UNCTAD (2009) *Review of Maritime Transport*, Geneva: UNCTAD.

UNCTAD (2011) *Review of Maritime Transport*, Geneva: UNCTAD.

SECTION 2

Transport in Regions and Localities

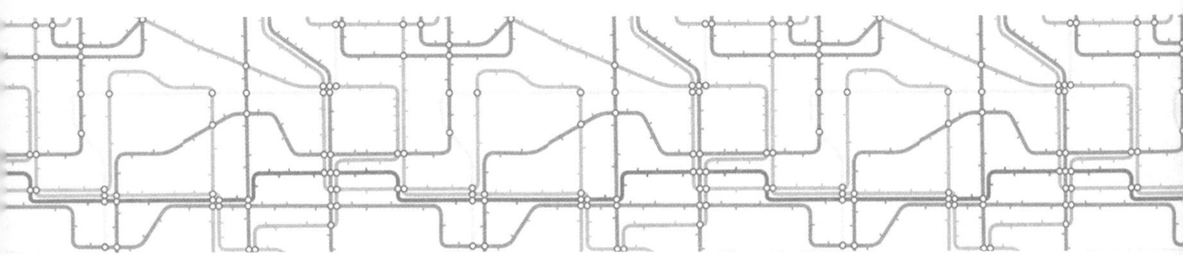

7 Urban Transportation and Land Use

Jean-Paul Rodrigue

URBAN MOBILITY

Forms of urban mobility

Urban transportation is organized in three broad categories of collective, individual and freight transportation (Gwilliam, 2002). In several instances, they are complementary to one another, but sometimes they may be competing for passengers, the usage of available land and transport infrastructures:

- Collective transportation (public transit). The purpose of collective transportation is to provide publicly accessible mobility over specific parts of a city. Its efficiency is based upon transporting large numbers of people and achieving economies of scale (Cervero, 1998). It includes modes such as tramways, buses, trains, subways and ferries.
- Individual transportation. Includes any mode where mobility is the outcome of a personal choice and means such as the automobile, walking, cycling and the motorcycle. The majority of people walk to satisfy their basic mobility, but this number varies according to the city considered. For instance, walking accounts for 88% of all movements inside Tokyo while this figure is only 3% for Los Angeles.
- Freight transportation. As cities are dominant centers of production and consumption, urban activities are accompanied by large movements of freight. These movements are mostly characterized by delivery trucks moving between industries, distribution centers, warehouses and retail activities, as well as from major terminals such as ports, railyards, distribution centers and airports.

Rapid urban development occurring across much of the globe implies increased quantities of passengers and freight moving within urban areas (Carter, 1995; Docherty, Giuliano and Houston, 2008). Movements also tend to involve longer distances, but evidence suggests that commuting times have remained relatively similar through the last hundred years, approximately 1 to 1.2 hours per day (Marchetti, 1994). This means that commuting has gradually shifted to faster transport modes and consequently greater distances could be traveled using the same amount of time. Different transport technologies and infrastructures have been implemented, resulting in a wide variety of urban transport systems around the world.

In the majority of cases, fast urban growth led to a scramble to provide transport infrastructure in an inadequate fashion. Each form of urban mobility, be it walking, the private automobile or urban transit, has a level of suitability to fill mobility needs. In recent years, motorization and the diffusion of personal mobility has been an ongoing trend linked with substantial declines in the share of public transit in urban mobility.

Urban mobilities

Movements are linked to specific urban activities and their land use. Each type of land use involves the generation and attraction of a particular array of movements. This relationship is complex, but is linked to factors such as recurrence, income, urban form, spatial accumulation, level of development and technology (Camagni, Gibelli and Rigamonti, 2002). Urban movements are either obligatory, when they are linked to scheduled activities (such as home-to-work movements), or voluntary, when those generating it are free to decide on their scheduling (such as leisure). The most common types of urban movements are:

- Pendulum movements. These are obligatory movements involving commuting between locations of residence and work. They are highly cyclical since they are predictable and recurring on a regular basis, most of the time a daily occurrence, thus the term pendulum.
- Professional movements. These are movements linked to professional, work-based, activities such as meetings and customer services, dominantly taking place during work hours.
- Personal movements. These are voluntary movements linked to the location of commercial activities, which includes shopping and recreation.
- Touristic movements. Important for cities having historical and recreational features and involve interactions between landmarks and amenities such as hotels and restaurants. They tend to be seasonal in nature or occurring at specific moments. Major sport events such as the World Cup or the Olympics are important generators of urban movements during their occurrence.
- Distribution movements. These are concerned with the distribution of freight to satisfy consumption and manufacturing requirements. They are mostly linked with transport terminals, distribution centers and retail outlets.

The share of the automobile in urban trips varies in relation to location, social status, income, quality of public transit and parking availability. Mass transit is often affordable, but several social groups, such as students, the elderly and the poor are a captive market. There are important variations in mobility according to age, income, gender and disability. Gender and age gaps in mobility are prevalent and have not changed significantly. The peak mobility age is around 40 years when individuals are in their most productive years and fully employed. Gender differences in mobility can be linked to various factors such as vocational differences, income differences as well as a more conventional role assumed by women in several households. Consequently, in some instances modal choice is more a modal constraint linked to economic opportunities.

In central locations, there are generally few transport availability problems because private and public transport facilities are present. However, in locations outside the central core that are accessible only by the automobile, a significant share of the population is isolated if it does not own an automobile. Limited public transit and high automobile ownership costs have created a class of spatially constrained (mobility deprived) people. They do not have access to services in the suburbs, but more importantly to the jobs that are increasingly concentrated in those areas.

THE URBAN FORM

The urban spatial structure

Demographic and mobility growth have been shaped by the capacity and requirements of urban transport infrastructures, such as roads, transit systems or simply walkways. Consequently, there is a wide variety of urban forms, spatial structures and associated urban transportation systems (Kaplan, Wheeler and Holloway, 2009). The urban spatial structure can be categorized by its level of centralization and clustering (Figure 7.1):

- Centralization. Refers to the setting of activities in relation to the whole urban area. A centralized city has a significant share of its activities in its center while a decentralized city does not. Large employers such as financial institutions are the main drivers of centralization.
- Clustering. Refers to the setting of activities in relation to a specific part of the urban area. A cluster of activities is therefore a concentration around a specific focal point, which tend to be transport infrastructures such as a highway interchange, a transit terminal or a smaller town that has been absorbed by the expansion of the metropolis.

Although the four types of urban spatial structures depicted on Figure 7.1 are possible, the two most significant trends that have impacted urban spatial structures have been decentralization, but while maintaining a high level of clustering (Figure 7.1c). This is reflective of a multicentric city.

Interdependent urban functions related to trade, production and telecommunications are associated with a spatial form which varies according to the modes being used. What has not changed much is that cities tend to opt for a grid street pattern. This was the case for many Roman cities built in the 1st century as it was for American cities built in the 20th century. The reasons behind this permanence are relatively simple: a grid pattern jointly optimizes accessibility and available real estate. Obviously, many cities are not organized as a grid. They correspond to older cities, many former fortified towns, as well as cities which grew from a constrained location such as an island or a river junction. Local geographical and historical characteristics remain important influences on the urban form.

In an age of motorization and personal mobility, an increasing number of cities are developing a spatial structure that increases reliance on motorized transportation, particularly the privately owned automobile (Kenworthy et al., 1999; Newman and Kenworthy, 1999). Dispersion, or urban

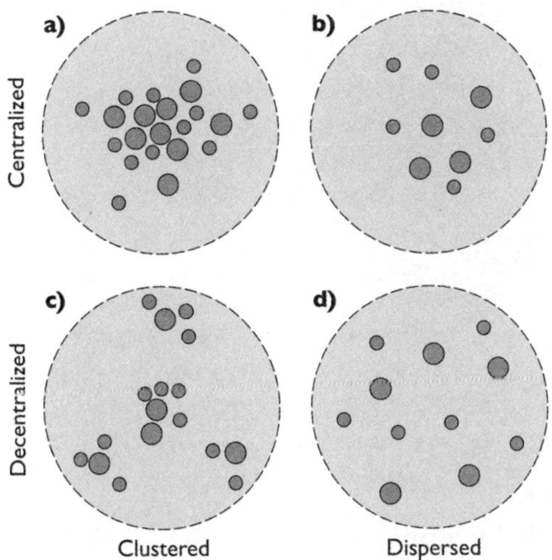

Figure 7.1 A simple typology of urban spatial structures

sprawl, is taking place in many different types of cities, from dense, centralized European metropolises such as Madrid, Paris and London, to rapidly industrializing metropolises such as Seoul, Shanghai and Buenos Aires, to those experiencing recent, fast and uncontrolled urban growth, such as Bombay and Lagos. Recent urban expansion is consequently almost all geared towards the automobile but there are also significant countervailing forces where the concept of sustainability incites a review of the existing urban spatial structure and the relations with existing urban transport modes.

Evolution of the urban spatial structure

Historically, movements within cities tended to be restricted to walking, which made medium and long distance urban linkages rather inefficient and time-consuming. Thus, activity nodes tended to be agglomerated and urban forms compact (Muller, 2004). Many modern cities have inherited an urban form created under such circumstances, even though they are no longer prevailing. The dense urban cores of many European, Japanese and Chinese cities, for example, enable residents to make between one-third and two-thirds of all trips by walking and cycling. At the other end of the spectrum, the dispersed urban forms of most Australian, Canadian and American cities, which were built recently, encourages automobile dependency and are linked with high levels of mobility. Many major cities are also port cities with maritime accessibility playing an enduring role not only for the economic vitality but also in the urban spatial structure with the port district being an important node. Airport terminals

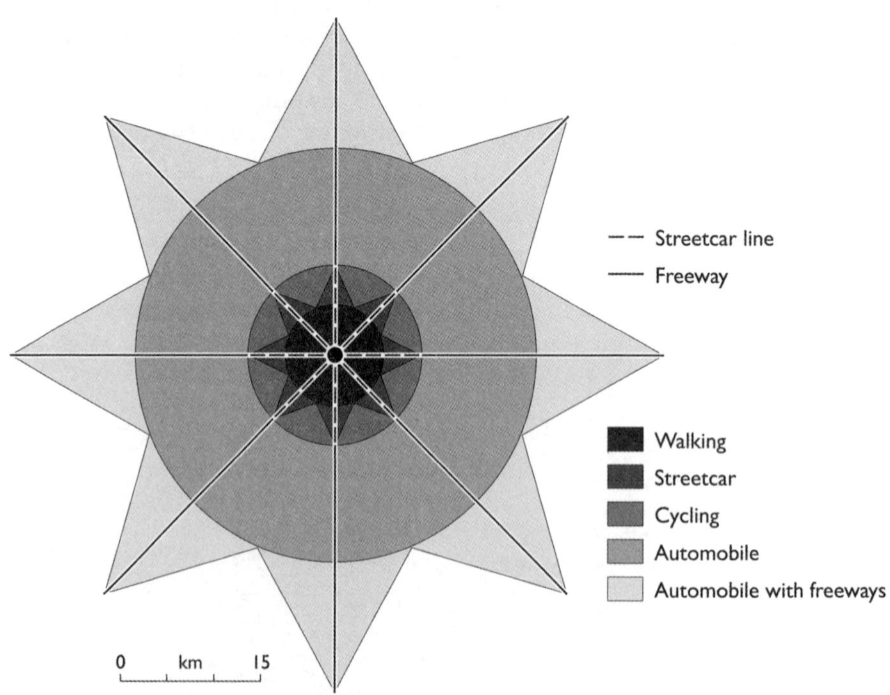

Figure 7.2 One-hour commuting according to different urban transportation modes
Source: Hugill, 1995

have also been playing a growing role in the urban spatial structure as they can be considered as cities within cities. The evolution of transportation has generally led to changes in urban form. The more radical the changes in transport technology have been, the more the alterations on the urban form, with the commuting range for specific modes a proxy of these alterations. Figure 7.2 depicts a theoretical urban form which is the summation of successive transport influences and assumes a uniform friction of distance and a uniform capacity of transport infrastructure.

Among the most fundamental changes in the urban form is the emergence of new clusters expressing new urban activities and new relationships between elements of the urban system. In many cities, the central business district (CBD), once the primary destination of commuters and serviced by public transportation, has been changed by new manufacturing, retailing and management practices. Whereas traditional manufacturing depended on centralized workplaces and transportation, technological and transportation developments rendered modern industry more flexible. In many cases, manufacturing relocated in a suburban setting, if not altogether to entirely new low cost locations offshore. Retail and office activities are also suburbanizing, producing changes in the urban form. Concomitantly, many important transport terminals, namely port facilities and railyards, have emerged in suburban areas following new requirements in modern freight distribution brought in part by containerization. The urban spatial structure shifted from a nodal to a multi-nodal character.

Initially, suburban growth mainly took place adjacent to major road corridors, leaving plots of vacant or farm land in between. Later, intermediate spaces were gradually filled up, more or less coherently. Highways and ring roads, which circled and radiated from cities, favored the development of suburbs and the emergence of important sub-centers that compete with the central business district for the attraction of economic activities. As a result, many new job opportunities have shifted to the suburbs (if not to entirely new locations abroad) and the activity system of cities has been considerably modified. Different parts of a city have different dynamism depending on its spatial pattern. These changes have occurred according to a variety of geographical and historical contexts, notably in North America and Europe as each subsequent phase of urban transportation developments led to different spatial structures. Sometimes, particularly when new modern urban road infrastructures are built, the subsequent changes in the urban form can be significant.

Dispersion and decentralization

Dispersion and decentralization had a substantial impact on contemporary urban forms. Dispersed urban land development patterns have been dominant in North America over the last 50 years, where land is abundant, transportation costs were low, and where the economy became dominated by tertiary and quaternary activities. Under such circumstances, it is not surprising to find that there is a strong relationship between urban density and automobile use. For many cities their built-up areas have grown at a faster rate than their populations. In addition, commuting became relatively inexpensive compared with land costs, so households had an incentive to buy lower-priced housing at the urban periphery. Similar patterns can be found in other cities around the world, but this change is occurring at a slower pace and involving a smaller range.

The decentralization of activities resulted in two opposite effects. First, commuting time has remained relatively stable in duration. Second, commuting increasingly tends to be longer and made by using the automobile rather than by public transit. Most transit and road systems were developed to facilitate suburb-to-city, rather than suburb-to-suburb, commuting. Addressing these changes in the urban spatial structure remains a challenge for urban transit. As a result, suburban highways are often as congested as urban highways.

Globally, people are spending a similar amount of time per day commuting, wherever this takes place in a low or a high mobility setting. Different transport technologies, however, are associated with different travel speeds and capacity. As a result, cities that rely primarily on non-motorized transport tend to be different than auto-dependent cities. Transport technology thus plays a very important role in defining urban form and the spatial pattern of various activities. Still, the evolution of the urban form is path dependent, implying that the current spatial structure is obviously the outcome of past developments, but that those developments were strongly related to local conditions involving the setting, physical constraints and investments in infrastructures and modes.

THE SPATIALITY OF URBAN TRANSPORTATION

Spatial imprint

The amount of urban land allocated to transportation is often correlated with the level of mobility. In the pre-automobile era, about 10% of the urban land was devoted to transportation which were simply roads for a dominantly pedestrian traffic. As the mobility of people and freight increased, a growing share of urban areas was allocated to transport and the infrastructures supporting it. Large variations in the spatial imprint of urban transportation are observed between different cities as well as between different parts of a city, such as between central and peripheral areas. The major components of the spatial imprint of urban transportation are:

- Pedestrian areas. Refer to the amount of space devoted to walking. This space is often shared with roads as sidewalks may use between 10% and 20% of a road's right of way. In central areas, pedestrian areas tend to use a greater share of the right of way and, in some instances, whole areas are reserved for pedestrians. However, in a motorized context, most pedestrian areas are for servicing people's access to transport modes such as parked automobiles.
- Roads and parking areas. Refer to the amount of space devoted to road transportation, which has two states of activity; moving or parked. In a motorized city, on average 30% of the surface is devoted to roads while another 20% is required for off-street parking. This implies for each automobile about two off-street and two on-street parking spaces. In North American cities, roads and parking lots account for between 30% and 60% of the total surface.
- Cycling areas. In a disorganized form, cycling simply shares access to pedestrian and road space. However, many attempts have been made to create spaces specifically for bicycles in urban areas, with reserved lanes and parking facilities. The Netherlands has been particularly proactive over this issue with biking paths part of the urban transport system; 27% of the total amount of commuting is accounted for by cycling.
- Transit systems. Many transit systems, such as buses and tramways, share road space with automobiles, which often impairs their respective efficiency. Attempts to mitigate congestion have resulted in the creation of road lanes reserved to buses either on a permanent or temporary (during rush hour) basis. Other transport systems such as subways and rail have their own infrastructures and, consequently, their own rights of way.
- Transport terminals. Refer to the amount of space devoted to terminal facilities such as ports, airports, transit stations, railyards and distribution centers. Globalization has increased the mobility of people and freight, both in relative and absolute terms, and consequently the amount of urban space required to support those activities. Many major terminals are located in the peripheral areas of cities, which are the only locations where sufficient amounts of land are available.

The spatial importance of each transport mode varies according to a number of factors, density being the most important (Moore and Thorsnes, 1994). If density is considered as a gradient, rings of mobility represent variations in the spatial importance of each mode at providing urban mobility. Further, each transport mode has unique performance and space consumption characteristics. The automobile is the most relevant example. It requires space to move around (roads) but it also spends about 95% of its existence stationary in a parking space. Consequently, a significant amount of urban space must be allocated to accommodate the automobile, especially when it does not move and is thus economically and socially useless. In large urban agglomerations close to all the available street parking space in areas of average density and above is occupied throughout the day. At an aggregate level, measures reveal a significant spatial imprint of road transportation among developed countries. In the United States, more land is thus used by the automobile than for housing. In Western Europe, roads account for between 15% and 20% of the urban surface, while for developing countries this figure is about 10% (6% on average for Chinese cities, but rising rapidly).

The polycentric paradigm

Urbanization involves an increased number of trips in urban areas. Cities have traditionally responded to growth in mobility by expanding the transportation supply, by building new highways and transit lines. In the developed world, that has mainly meant building more roads to accommodate an ever-growing number of vehicles. Several urban spatial structures have accordingly emerged, with the reliance on the automobile being the most important discriminatory factor. The outcome has been the dominance of the polycentric paradigm (Figure 7.3).

The urban spatial structure basically considers the location of different activities as well as their relationships. Core activities are those of the highest order in the urban spatial structure, namely tertiary and quaternary activities involved in management (finance and insurance) and consumption (retailing). Central activities are concerned by production and distribution with activities such as warehousing, manufacturing, wholesaling and transportation. Peripheral activities are dominantly residential or servicing local needs. A central area refers to an agglomeration of core and/or central activities within a specific location. The emergence of a CBD is the result of an historical process, often occurring over several centuries (depending on the age of a city), that has changed the urban form and the location of economic activities.

There are different scales where transportation systems influence the structure of communities, districts and the whole metropolitan area. For instance, one of the most significant impacts of transportation on the

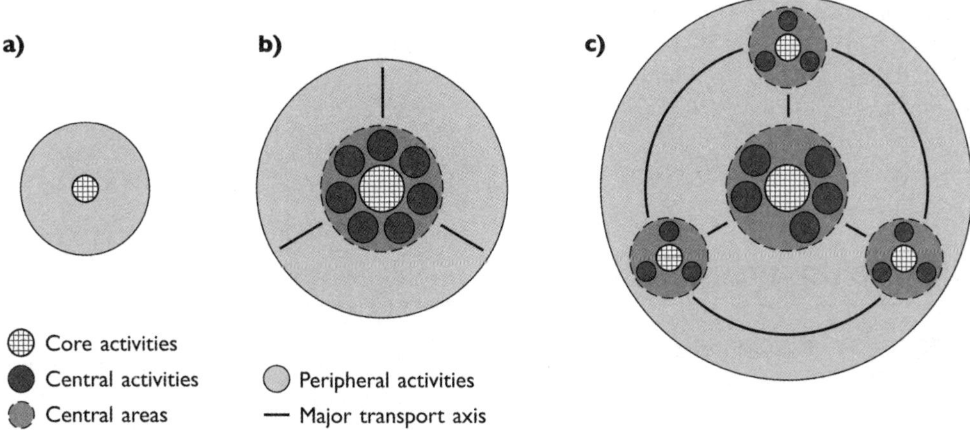

Figure 7.3 Evolution of the spatial structure of a city

urban structure has been the clustering of activities near areas of high accessibility. The impact of transport on the spatial structure is particularly evident in the emergence of suburbia. Although many other factors are important in the development of suburbia, including low land costs, available land (large lots), the environment (clean and quiet), safety, and automobile-oriented services (shopping malls), the spatial imprint of the automobile is dominant. Although it can be argued that roads and the automobile have limited impacts on the extent of urban sprawl itself, they are a required condition for sprawl to take place. While it is difficult to assess in which specific circumstances the first suburbs emerged, suburban developments have occurred in many cities worldwide, although no other places have achieved such a low density and automobile dependency than in North America.

Facing the expansion of urban areas, congestion problems and the increasing importance of inter-urban movements, several ring roads have been built around major cities. They became an important attribute of the spatial structures of cities, notably in North America. Highway interchanges in suburban areas are notable examples of new clusters of urban development. The extension (and the over-extension) of urban areas have created what may be called peri-urban areas. They are located well outside the urban core and the suburbs, but are within reasonable commuting distances; the term "edge cities" has been used to label a cluster of urban development taking place in a suburban settings. While this is particularly salient in settings of high automobile dependency, it is also emerging in developing countries.

THE LAND USE–TRANSPORT SYSTEM

A complex relationship

Urban land use comprises two elements; the nature of land use which relates to which activities are taking place where, and the level of spatial accumulation, which indicates their intensity and concentration. Most economic, social or cultural activities imply a multitude of functions, such as production, consumption and distribution. These functions take place at specific locations and are part of an activity system. Some are routine activities, because they occur regularly and are thus predictable, such as commuting and shopping. Others are institutional activities that tend to be irregular, and are shaped by lifestyle (e.g. sports and leisure) or by special needs (e.g. healthcare). Others are production activities that are related to manufacturing and distribution, whose linkages may be local, regional or global. The behavioral patterns of individuals, institutions and firms have an imprint on land use in terms of their locational choice.

Land use implies a set of relationships with other land uses. For instance, commercial land use involves relationships with its supplier and customers. While relationships with suppliers will dominantly be related with movements of freight, relationships with customers would include movements of people. Thus, a level of accessibility to both systems of circulation must be present. Since each type of land use has its own specific mobility requirements, transportation is a factor of activity location, and is therefore associated intimately with land use. Within the urban system each activity occupies a suitable, but not necessarily optimal location, from which it derives rent.

Transportation and land use interactions mostly consider the retroactive relationships between activities, which are land use related, and accessibility, which is transportation related. These relationships have often been described as a "chicken-and-egg" problem since it is difficult to identify the triggering cause of change; do transportation changes precede land use changes or vice-versa? There is a scale effect at play as large infrastructure projects tend to precede and trigger land use changes while small-scale transportation projects tend to complement the existing land use pattern. Further, the expansion of urban land uses takes place over various circumstances such as infilling (near the city center) or sprawl (far from the city center) and where transportation plays a different role.

Urban transportation aims at supporting transport demands generated by the diversity of urban activities in a diversity of urban contexts. A key for understanding urban entities thus lies in the analysis of patterns and processes of the transport/land use system. This system is highly complex and involves several relationships between the transport system, spatial interactions and land use (Figure 7.4):

- Transport system. Considers the set of transport infrastructures and modes that support urban movements of passengers and freight. It generally expresses the level of accessibility and is composed of infrastructures conferring a level of supply. For instance, traffic assignment models take an existing spatial interaction structure and infer flows within a transportation network. Conceptual flows consequently become a physical reality.
- Spatial interactions. Consider the nature, extent, origins and destinations of the urban movements of passengers and freight. They take into consideration the attributes of the transport system as well as the land use factors that are generating and attracting movements. It assumes the flows between locations are mainly related to a function of spatial impendence, which reflects the friction of the urban space. Many spatial interaction models were developed that rely on distance decay parameters. Another dimension of spatial interactions concerns the modes involved in urban trips, particularly which mode will be used for which trip.
- Land use. Considers the level of spatial accumulation of activities and their associated levels of mobility requirements. There is a wide base of spatial economic models aiming at estimating transport demand, mainly through the generation and attraction of traffic by different land use zones. Land use is commonly linked with demographic and economic attributes.

A conundrum concerns the difficulties of linking a specific mode of transportation with specific land use patterns. While public transit systems tend to be associated with higher densities of residential and commercial activities, particularly focused around transit stations, and highways with lower densities, the multiplicity of modes available in urban areas, including freight distribution, conveys an unclear and complex relationship.

Urban land use models

The relationships between transportation and land use are rich in theoretical representations that have contributed much to regional sciences. Since transportation is a distance-decay altering technology, spatial organization is assumed to be strongly influenced by the concepts of location and distance. Several descriptive and analytical models of urban land use have been developed over time, with increased levels of

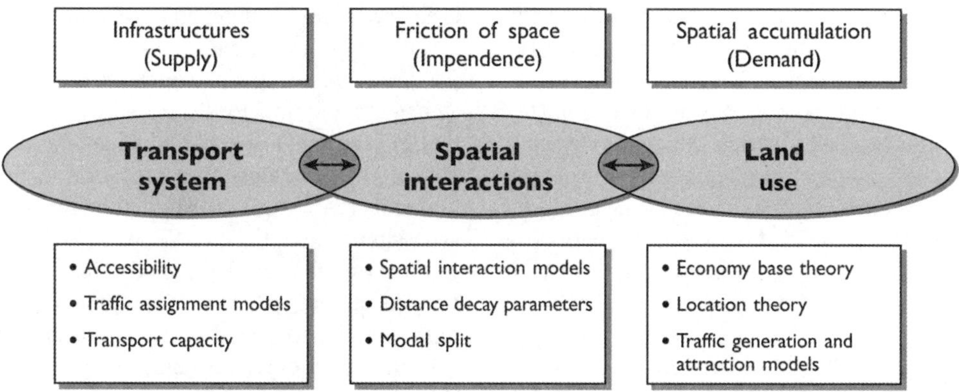

Figure 7.4 The transport/land use system

complexity. All involve some consideration of transport in the explanations of urban land use structures (Carter, 1995; Hanson and Giuliano, 2004). The following is a non-exhaustive categorization.

Central places and concentric land uses

Von Thunen's regional land use model is the oldest representation based on a central place, the market town, and its concentric impacts on surrounding land uses. It was initially developed in the early 19th century (1826) for the analysis of agricultural land use patterns in Germany. It used the concept of economic rent to explain a spatial organization where different agricultural activities are competing for the usage of land. The underlying principles of this model have been the foundation of many others where economic considerations, namely land rent and distance-decay, are incorporated. The core assumption of the model is that agricultural land use is patterned in the form of concentric circles around a market that consumes all the surplus production, which must be transported. Many concordances of this model with reality have been found, notably in North America.

Concentric urban land uses

The Burgess concentric model was among the first attempts to investigate spatial patterns at the urban level (1925). Although the purpose of the model was to analyze social classes, it recognized that transportation and mobility were important factors behind the spatial organization of urban areas. The formal land use representation of this model is derived from commuting distance from the central business district, creating concentric circles. Each circle represents a specific socioeconomic urban landscape. This model is conceptually a direct adaptation of Von Thunen's model to urban land use since it deals with a concentric representation.

Polycentric and zonal land uses

Sector and multiple nuclei land use models were developed to take into account numerous factors overlooked by concentric models, namely the influence of transport axis (Hoyt, 1939) and multiple nuclei (Harris and Ullman, 1945) on land use and growth. Both representations consider the emerging impacts of motorization on the urban spatial structure. Such representations also considered that transportation infrastructures, particularly terminals such as rail stations or ports, occupy specific locations and can be considered as land uses.

Hybrid land uses

Hybrid models are an attempt to include the concentric, sector and nuclei behavior of different processes in explaining urban land use. They are an attempt to integrate the strengths of each approach since none of these appear to provide a completely satisfactory explanation. Thus, hybrid models, such as that developed by Isard (1955), consider the concentric effect of central locations (CBDs and sub-centers) and the radial effect of transport axis, all overlain to form a land use pattern. Also, hybrid representations are suitable to explain the evolution of the urban spatial structure as they combine different spatial impacts of transportation on urban land use, let them be concentric or radial, and this at different points in time (Figure 7.5).

Land use market

Land rent theory was also developed to explain land use as a market where different urban activities are competing for land usage at a location. It is strongly based in the market principle of spatial competition where actors are bidding to secure and maintain their presence at a specific location (Harvey, 1996). The more desirable a location is, the higher its rent value. Transportation, through accessibility and distance-decay, is a strong explanatory factor on the land rent and its impacts on land use. However, conventional representations of land rent leaning on the concentric paradigm are being challenged by structural modifications of contemporary cities.

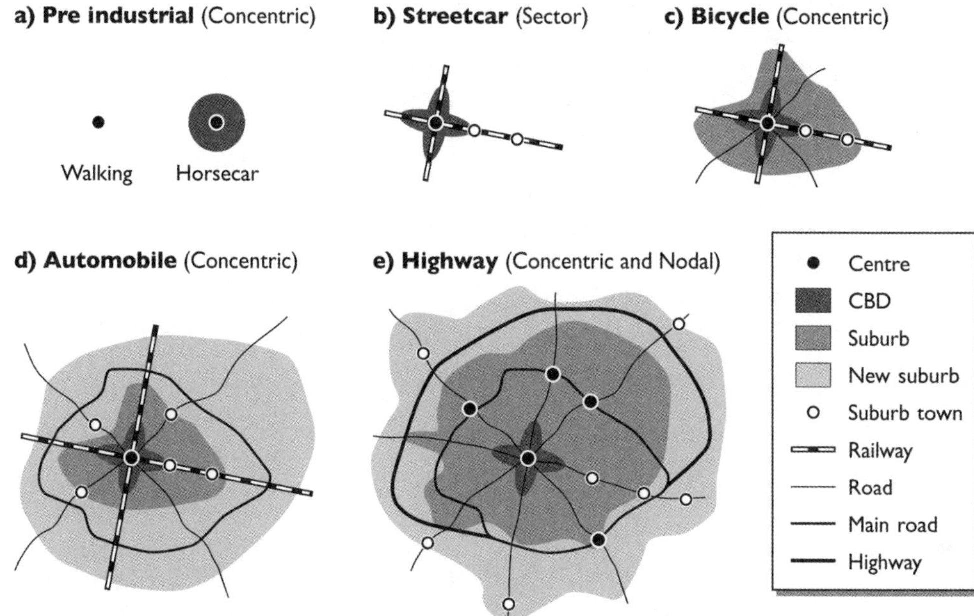

Figure 7.5 Transportation and the constitution of urban landscapes

Source: Taaffe, Gauthier and O'Kelly, 1996

Cellular automata

Dynamic land use representations developed on the principle that space can be represented as a grid where each cell is a discrete land use unit. Cell states thus symbolize land uses and transition rules express the likelihood of a change from one land use state to another. Because cells are symbolically connected and interrelated (e.g. adjacency), models can be used to investigate the dynamics, evolution and self-organization of cellar automata land use systems (White and Engelen, 1993). The cellular approach enables achievement of a high level of spatial detail (resolution) and realism, as well as to link the simulation directly to visible outcomes on the regional spatial structure. They are also readily implementable since Geographic Information Systems are designed to work effectively with grid-based spatial representations.

Cellular automata improves upon most transportation–land use models that are essentially static as they explain land use patterns, but they do not explicitly consider the processes that are creating or changing them.

The applicability and dynamics of land use models is related to issues such as the age, size and the locational setting of a city. For instance, concentric cities are generally older and of smaller size, while polycentric cities are larger and relate to urban development processes that took place more recently. While most of the conceptual approaches related to transportation and land use relationships have been developed using empirical evidence related to North America and Western Europe, this perspective does not necessarily apply to other parts of the world.

Urban dynamics

Both land use and transportation are part of a dynamic system that is subject to external influences. Each component of the system is constantly evolving due to changes in technology, policy, economics, demographics and even culture or values. As a result, the interactions between land use and transportation are played out as the outcome of the many decisions made by residents, businesses and governments. The field of urban dynamics has expanded the scope of conventional land use models, which tended to be descriptive, by trying to consider relationships behind the evolution of the urban spatial structure. This has led to a complex modeling framework including a wide variety of components. Among the concepts supporting urban dynamics representations are retroactions, whereby one component influences others. The changes will influence the initial component back, either positively or negatively.

Urban dynamics try to evaluate the main components initiating or being affected by changes in an urban area. Among the numerous factors in urban dynamics, transportation is of high significance as it is often expected that investments in transportation will have positive economic consequences that may even feedback into future transport investments (Figure 7.6). Transport investments are expected to improve the accessibility of passengers and freight, which in turn will improve the overall performance of a regional economy. Even if strong associations can be identified between transport improvements and economic (and spatial) changes, stating causality is conceptually inaccurate. For this reason alone, understanding urban dynamics remains a complex and uncertain task.

The issue about how to articulate these relations remains, particularly in the current context of interdependency between local, regional and global processes. Globalization has substantially blurred the relationships between transportation and land use as well as its dynamics. The main paradigm is concerned with the point that factors once endogenous to a regional setting become exogenous. Consequently, many economic activities that provide employment and multiplying effects, such as manufacturing, are driven by forces that are global in scope and may have little to do with regional dynamics. For instance, capital investment could come from external sources and the bulk of the output could be bound to international markets. In such a context it would be difficult to explain urban development processes taking place in coastal Chinese cities, or in a region such as the Pearl River Delta, since export-oriented strategies are among the most significant driving forces. Looking at the urban dynamics of such a system from an endogenous perspective would fail to capture driving forces that are dominantly exogenous.

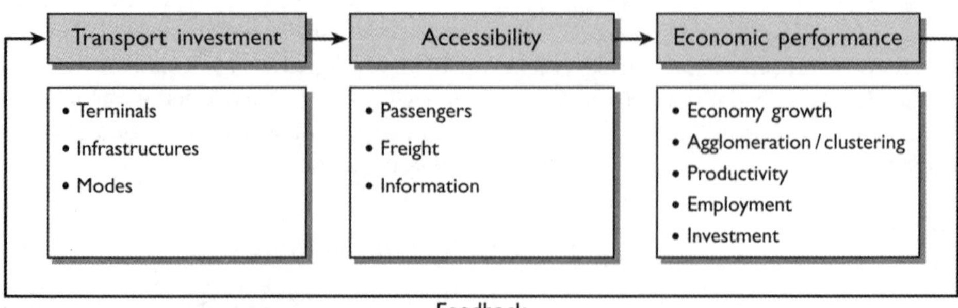

Figure 7.6 Basic urban dynamics

CONCLUSION: CHALLENGES FOR URBAN TRANSPORTATION

Cities are locations having a high level of accumulation and concentration of economic activities and are complex spatial structures that are supported by transport systems. The most important transport problems are often related to urban areas and take place when transport systems, for a variety of reasons, cannot satisfy the numerous requirements of urban mobility. Urban productivity is highly dependent on the efficiency of its transport system to move labor, consumers and freight between multiple origins and destinations. Additionally, important transport terminals such as ports, airports and railyards are located within urban areas, contributing to a specific array of problems. Some problems are ancient, like congestion (which plagued cities such as Rome), while others are new like urban freight distribution or environmental impacts. Among the most notable urban transport problems are:

- Traffic congestion and parking difficulties. Congestion is one of the most prevalent transport problems in large urban agglomerations, usually above a threshold of about 1 million inhabitants (Texas Transportation Institute, 2010). It is particularly linked with motorization and the diffusion of the automobile, which has increased the demand for transport infrastructures. However, the supply of infrastructures has often not been able to keep up with the growth of mobility. Since vehicles spend the majority of the time parked, motorization has expanded the demand for parking space, which has created space consumption problems particularly in central areas; the spatial imprint of parked vehicles is significant.
- Public transport inadequacy. Many public transit systems, or parts of them, are either over or under used. During peak hours, crowdedness creates discomfort for users as the system copes with a temporary surge in demand. Low ridership makes many services financially unsustainable, particularly in suburban areas. In spite of significant subsidies and cross-financing (e.g. tolls) almost every public transit system cannot generate sufficient income to cover its operating and capital costs. While in the past deficits were deemed acceptable because of the essential service public transit was providing for urban mobility, its financial burden is increasingly controversial.
- Difficulties for non-motorized transport. These difficulties are either the outcome of intense traffic, where the mobility of pedestrians, bicycles and vehicles is impaired, but also because of a blatant lack of consideration for pedestrians and bicycles in the physical design of infrastructures and facilities.
- Loss of public space. The majority of roads are publicly owned and free of access. Increased traffic has adverse impacts on public activities which once crowded the streets such as markets, agoras, parades and processions, games, and community interactions. These have gradually disappeared to be replaced by automobiles. In many cases, these activities have shifted to shopping malls, while in other cases they have been abandoned altogether. Traffic flows influence the life and interactions of residents and their usage of street space. More traffic impedes social interactions and street activities (Hart and Parkhurst, 2011). People tend to walk and cycle less when traffic is high.
- Environmental impacts and energy consumption. Pollution, including noise, generated by circulation has become a serious impediment to the quality of life and even the health of urban populations. Further, energy consumption by urban transportation has dramatically increased and so the dependency on petroleum. Yet, peak oil considerations are increasingly linked with peak mobility expectations where high energy prices incite a shift towards more efficient and sustainable forms of urban transportation, namely public transit (Newman and Kenworthy, 2011; UN-HABITAT, 2009).
- Accidents and safety. Growing traffic in urban areas is linked with a growing number of accidents and fatalities, especially in developing countries. Accidents account for a significant share of recurring delays. As traffic increases, people feel less safe to use the streets.
- Land consumption. The territorial imprint of transportation is significant, particularly for the automobile. Between 30% and 60% of a metropolitan area may be devoted to transportation, an outcome of the over-reliance on some forms of urban transportation. Yet, this land consumption also underlines the

strategic importance of transportation in the economic and social welfare of cities.

- Freight distribution. Globalization and the materialization of the economy have resulted in growing quantities of freight moving within cities. As freight traffic commonly shares infrastructures with the circulation of passengers, the mobility of freight in urban areas has become increasingly problematic. City logistics strategies can be established to mitigate the variety of challenges faced by urban freight distribution (Dablanc, 2009).

Many dimensions to the urban transport problem are linked with the dominance of the automobile. There are many alternatives to automobile dependency such as intermodality (combining the advantages of individual and collective transport) or carpooling (strengthened by policy and regulation by the US government). These alternatives can only be partially executed as the automobile remains the prime choice for providing urban mobility and a dominant force shaping urban land use. This has raised issues concerning the sustainability of highly motorized cities and which forms of transportation–land use relations are likely to emerge in the future.

REFERENCES

Camagni, R., M.C. Gibelli and P. Rigamonti (2002) "Urban Mobility and Urban Form: The Social and Environmental Costs of Different Patterns of Urban Expansion", *Ecological Economics*, Vol. 40, pp. 199–216.

Carter, H. (1995) *The Study of Urban Geography*, Fourth Edition, London: Arnold.

Cervero, R. (1998) *The Transit Metropolis: A Global Inquiry*, Washington, DC: Island Press.

Dablanc, L. (2009) *Freight Transport, A Key for the New Urban Economy*. World Bank, Freight Transport for Development: a Policy Toolkit, July.

Docherty, I., G. Giuliano and D. Houston (2008) Connected Cities, in R.D. Knowles, J. Shaw and I. Docherty (eds) *Transport Geographies: Mobilities, Flows and Spaces*, London: Blackwell, pp. 83–101.

Gwilliam, K. (ed.) (2002) *Cities on the Move: A World Bank Urban Transport Strategy Review*, Strategy Paper, Washington, DC: World Bank.

Hanson, S. and G. Giuliano (eds) (2004) *The Geography of Urban Transportation*, Third Edition, New York: The Guilford Press.

Hart, J. and G. Parkhurst (2011) "Driven To Excess: Impacts of Motor Vehicles on the Quality of Life of Residents of Three Streets in Bristol UK", *World Transport Policy and Practice*, Vol. 17, No. 2, pp. 12–30.

Harvey, J. (1996) *Urban Land Economics*, Basingstoke: Macmillan.

Hugill, P. (1995) *World Trade Since 1431*, Baltimore, OH: The Johns Hopkins University Press.

Kaplan, D., J. Wheeler and S. Holloway (2009) *Urban Geography*, Second Edition, New York: Wiley.

Kenworthy J., F. Laube, P. Newman, P. Barter, T. Raad, C. Poboon and B. Guia (1999) *An International Sourcebook of Automobile Dependence in Cities, 1960–1990*, Boulder, CO: University Press of Colorado.

Marchetti, C. (1994) "Anthropological Invariants in Travel Behaviour", *Technical Forecasting and Social Change*, Vol. 47, No. 1, pp. 75–78.

Moore, T. and P. Thorsnes (1994) *The Transportation/Land Use Connection*, Report # 448/449, Washington, DC: American Planning Association.

Muller, P.O. (2004) "Transportation and Urban Form: Stages in the Spatial Evolution of the American Metropolis", in S. Hanson and G. Giuliano (eds) *The Geography of Urban Transportation*, Third Edition, New York: Guilford, pp. 59–84.

Newman, P. and J. Kenworthy (1999) *Sustainability and Cities: Overcoming Automobile Dependence*, Washington, DC: Island Press.

Newman, P. and J. Kenworthy (2011) "'Peak Car Use': Understanding the Demise of Automobile Dependence", *World Transport Policy and Practice*, Vol. 17, No. 2, pp. 31–42.

Taaffe, E.J., H.L. Gauthier and M.E. O'Kelly (1996) *Geography of Transportation*, Upper Saddle River, NJ: Prentice Hall.

Texas Transportation Institute (2010) *The 2010 Annual Mobility Report*, College Station, Texas.

UN-HABITAT (2009) *Planning Sustainable Cities, Global Report on Human Settlements 2009*, United Nations Human Settlements Programme, London: Earthscan.

White R. and G. Engelen (1993) "Cellular automata and fractal urban form: a cellular modelling approach to the evolution of urban land-use patterns", *Environment and Planning A*, Vol. 25, No. 8, pp. 1175–1199.

8

City Logistics

Laetitia Dablanc

INTRODUCTION

City logistics can be defined as any service provision contributing to efficiently managing the movements of goods in cities and providing innovative responses to customer demands. City logistics represents a global organization of physical and informational flows that makes deliveries to urban residents and businesses possible in a manner that promotes the best economic and environmental standards. It includes physical services such as order preparation, transport and deliveries (including home deliveries), short or medium term storage of goods, management of drop-off/pick-up boxes for parcels, return of pallets and empty packages. To ensure a coherent management of these different tasks, city logistics generally requires data processing and information and communication technologies. Because it takes place in cities, which are complex territories governed by multiple layers of regulations, city logistics differs from common logistics operations in that it must be space efficient and must take many policy dimensions into account.

Defined as such, city logistics does not apply well to the way goods deliveries are currently made in cities worldwide. A significant portion of the urban freight and logistics activities remain inefficient and costly (Dablanc, 2007). In cities, the most important logistics activity in terms of costs and the number of staff involved is urban goods transport, which can account for up to a third of the total logistics costs of a shipment. To decrease cost, increase city logistics efficiency and promote environmental sustainability, there has been recently a surge in innovative practices in urban freight and city logistics. They involve important stakeholders such as large transport operators and logistics providers, real estate developers, major retailers, as well as start-up companies. New logistics services have emerged in cities around the world, especially in areas having high levels of commercial activities, such as city centers. Although not yet significant in terms of volume and environmental benefits, these practices provide new directions and a framework for more sustainable city logistics activities.

This chapter is composed of three sections. In the first section, urban freight and city logistics are defined and described. The main issues and challenges are presented, including environmental impact assessment. In the second section, two city logistics initiatives are presented: an urban goods' consolidation center in Yokohama, Japan, and a delivery start-up company using electrically assisted tricycles in Paris, France. The impact and results of these initiatives are described and the role of the different stakeholders is discussed. The third section is dedicated to local and national policies that are currently applied in cities around the world. It provides some evidence for promoting more efficient and sustainable city logistics activities.

ISSUES AND CHALLENGES

What is urban freight? Different cities, different needs, and many specific supply chains

Urban freight presents a remarkable diversity. In a single city, vehicles, delivery times, and the size of shipments differ for each business or customer. When comparing cities worldwide, the diversity of urban freight is even more evident. How can one compare a Yamato employee in a small hybrid multi-temperature truck delivering to homes in Tokyo residential districts, to a farmer transporting homegrown vegetables in a little pushcart to be sold on a street market in La Paz? Nevertheless, both of them have many issues in common since they contribute to the urban economy and the well-being of residents and businesses. A survey of 1,650 Mexico City truck drivers (Lozano Cuevas, 2006) revealed the challenges of urban freight operations that are common to many large cities, especially in developing countries: congestion, lack of loading and unloading space, complex legislation, police corruption, risk of theft, and lack of safety are among the drivers' greatest concerns.

In terms of their basic urban features such as density, demographics, geography, cities throughout the world are very different and that makes their freight transport and logistics activities very diverse. Past characteristics and local circumstances create specific patterns for the urban distribution of goods. For example, Chicago has been preoccupied with maintaining its national and international prominence as a rail freight hub for North America, and is thus concerned about rail freight movements between the numerous rail terminals located within the city. Los Angeles is primarily concerned with air pollution and targets drayage associated with the ports of Long Beach and Los Angeles. Shanghai has become the largest cargo port in the world and its logistics added value is estimated at 13% of its GDP: logistics as a major economic activity is the focus of Shanghai policy-makers. Activities from the three ports of the bay of Tokyo add much lorry traffic to the city of Tokyo's streets and the municipality targets truck congestion in its transport policy. In Mexico City, 42% of the working population works in micro-companies of which half are home-based workshops or street-based, generating very specific patterns of deliveries (OECD, 2004), while the wholesale market in Mexico City (Central de Abastos) generates 52,000 truck trips every day.

Cities in developing countries share some common characteristics that imply specific urban freight issues. In poor countries, rural migration and population growth have led to very rapid urbanization, while the public supply of infrastructure and transport services has lagged behind. A significant proportion of roads is unpaved and poorly maintained. Air pollution has decreased with the gradual phasing out of leaded gasoline and the introduction of regulations on cleaner fuels in many countries, such as India and Mexico. However, diesel trucks remain a major source of particulate matter and nitrous oxide (NOx). Traffic congestion is a significant operational problem for the urban freight system. A major contributor to this congestion is the mixing of transport modes, with slow non-motorized vehicles (including hand or animal pulled carts) merging with faster motorized traffic. Other features of cities in developing countries include a greater use of manual labor for transport and handling. Warehouses and logistic processes are less mechanized than in more developed economies. Also, the recycling of used goods, packages, and cardboard takes specific forms. In developing countries, cities essentially leave a significant share of the recycling of goods to the informal sector. Rag-pickers and scavengers are an important feature of city life. The volumes and financial flows generated by informal waste recycling are important. Urban scenes in developing regions also include street vending. In the poorest cities of Africa or Asia, street vendors literally take over the streets selling everything from fresh fruits to electronics goods. Slums are also part of the city landscape, and have specific characteristics and supply needs. Finally, in some countries such as China, Egypt, and Morocco the deregulation of what was previously a tightly controlled truck market has had wide-reaching effects on urban operations. Co-operatives and small private firms are largely replacing state-controlled trucking companies, expanding freight capacity in cities.

However, it is important to note that in most cities of developing and emerging countries, part of the economy is fully integrated into global economic networks. What best characterizes these cities is their economic dualism: the informal sector operates alongside very advanced industries and services that have logistics behaviors and concerns similar to those in more mature urban economies. Today, the demand for modern logistics services is as strong in São Paulo or Istanbul as it is in Athens or Sydney.

A city is provisioned by hundreds of supply chains (at least 150 were observed in French cities; Routhier et al., 2001), as diverse as, for example, the supply of office products to banks or the delivery of bottles to restaurants and bars. All these supply chains are the result of logistics decisions, which are in turn based on the demands of the production and distribution sectors, themselves dependent on the behavior of economic agents such as households and firms. Each activity (commercial, service, industrial, administrative) taking place in an urban environment can be associated with a specific freight generation profile. Whereas passenger transport can be roughly broken down into a handful of categories (usually by mode and trip purpose), freight transport is extremely fragmented by transport mode, operator type, and goods origin (i.e. long-distance supply chain or local transactions). Vehicles are also very diverse: trucks and vans of all sizes and weights (and various names: in Indonesia, for example, a tuk-tuk or a sudako represents a sort of minibus also used for freight), passenger cars, motorbikes and bicycles, pedestrian push-carts, and more rarely rail and waterborne transport. Genuine urban delivery systems unique to one city can also develop, such as the famous "dabbawallas" in Mumbai, India: 200,000 lunch boxes made at home are delivered each day to businessmen at their workplace through a collection/sorting/delivery system using bicycles, trains, and pedestrian modes of transport (Rai, 2007). In cities, freight can be handled as private carriage (also called "own account," where transport is carried out by manufacturers with their own employees and fleet, or by an independent retailer with his or her own vehicle to supply the store) or by a common carrier (on "third account," i.e. done by a professional carrier). In a typical European city, both categories make an equal number of deliveries. In developing countries, private carriage is more dominant, and includes transport serving the informal sector. In Medan, Indonesia, 90% of local companies surveyed in 2004 owned their own delivery trucks (Kato and Sato, 2006).

Another interesting feature of urban supply chains is that within the same country and within the same economic sector, urban businesses are often supplied in a rather similar manner, whatever the city they are located in. From a logistics point of view, a drugstore (or a bakery, or a bank, or an optician) operates in much the same way whether it is located in a dense and very populated metropolitan area or in a smaller less developed city in another part of the country: supply chains are the results of logistics decisions that are not attached to the specific cities where goods are eventually delivered (Ambrosini et al., 2004). This makes it difficult for local governments to promote a change in the way goods are distributed in their jurisdictions.

A sustained effort in freight data collection and modeling is yet to be accomplished in many cities around the world. Although a lot of progress was made in the last decade, survey methods remain heterogeneous, making it difficult to compare results from one city to another (Ambrosini and Routhier, 2004; Bestufs, 2006). In France, the FRETURB model (Laboratoire d'Economie des Transports, Lyon) has adopted a methodology well suited for urban economies. It describes current urban freight demand and simulates future demand based on policy and economic scenarios. It identifies detailed delivery and pick-up patterns of urban establishments from extensive – but expensive – "Urban Goods Movements" surveys. These surveys revealed a key ratio for French cities: there are as many urban deliveries a week as there are jobs in a metropolitan area (Ambrosini et al., 2004).

Main urban distribution chains

Despite the diversity of urban supply chains and urban freight transport patterns, categories of city logistics exist for which common characteristics in freight and deliveries can be identified:

- *Independent retailing, including the informal sector and local convenience stores.* These sectors together can represent 30% to 40% of all daily deliveries in a city. These local stores are supplied three to ten times a week. Suppliers are diverse, with a predominant use of own-account vans (or bikes and carriages in poorer countries).
- *Chain retailing and commercial centers.* In European cities, large retailing stores with subsidiaries or franchises are increasing their share of urban space at the expense of independent local stores (this transition has already occurred in the US). This changes the way goods are supplied to stores, with less frequent deliveries, a larger share of consolidated shipments, and larger and better-loaded vehicles.
- *Parcel deliveries (less than full truck load) and express services* are one of the fastest growing urban transport businesses. This industry uses large vans or small to medium-sized trucks, and is based on consolidated delivery tours departing from cross-dock terminals. Vehicles from the leading express transport companies (UPS, DHL, TNT, FedEx) are now in most of the world's cities, with some geographic specialization (DHL in European cities, UPS in US cities). This industry was hit by the 2008–2009 world financial and economic crisis, as customers downgraded their demand from express to cheaper services.
- A sub-sector of the parcel transport business is *home deliveries.* The online shopping market represented €200 billion (6% of all retailing) in Europe in 2009 (Center for Retail Research, 2013). Large postal operators dominate these markets, but new players are emerging. Japanese "takkyubins," parcel transport companies that specialize in home deliveries (see below), are a unique feature of Japanese city logistics (Dablanc, 2009a).
- *Building sites* supply chains are a key segment because of the tonnage they generate, which can account for up to 30% of tons carried in cities. Vehicles are generally heavy trucks that do damage to roads. Building sites supply is notoriously inefficient. Multiple suppliers and poorly planned delivery schedules lead to a high number of deliveries, queuing, and general disorder on the sites. Some cities, such as London and Stockholm in Europe, have launched consolidation schemes. The London Construction Consolidation Centre was implemented in 2006 with funds from Transport for London and private investors. A 2007 assessment showed that the scheme achieved a 68% reduction in the number of vehicles and a 75% reduction in CO_2 emissions (Transport for London, 2007).

- *Food markets*, particularly important in developing countries, have extremely diverse supply modes, including bicycles, and hand- or animal-driven carts. Few data exist on the actual volume of freight flows generated. A survey of 300 market vendors in Phnom Penh, Cambodia showed that 87% of market deliveries were made by the vendors themselves, and 13% by transport providers (Ripert, 2006).

Environmental impacts of urban freight

Urban freight is more polluting than long-distance freight transport, because of the average age of the vehicles and the high number of short trips and stops. Detailed impact surveys made in different French cities (LET et al., 2006), correlated by other European cities' surveys (Bestufs, 2006), show that freight transport generates between 20% and 60% (according to the pollutants considered) of local transport-based pollution. Table 8.1 shows the example of Dijon, in France.

Nitrogen oxide (NO_x) and particulate matter (PM) are pollutants for which urban freight transport has a particularly important responsibility. Both pollutants are very harmful to the health of urban residents, and in European cities their concentration tends to stagnate or even increase, contrary to many other urban air pollutants (Dablanc, 2008). In the metropolitan area of Mexico, 71% of the 3,500 tons of PM_{10} generated in 2002 by mobile sources were from freight vehicles (Lozano Cuevas, 2006). Urban freight vehicles also tend to be quite old. In Dublin in 2004, a fourth of all vehicles were manufactured at least a decade beforehand. Only 15% of the vehicles were new (one year or less). In the Milan region, 40% of trucks circulating are more than ten years old (Bestufs, 2006). In poorer countries, fleets are even older. In Mexico City, the average age of trucks and vans is twelve years. The renewal of urban freight vehicles is generally slow (slower than for non-urban road freight traffic), because most transport companies operating in urban areas are very small, competition among operators is acute and profit margins are low: many operators save money by buying used trucks or vans and using them as long as possible.

Greenhouse gas emissions and noise pollution are also among the most severe environmental impacts of freight in cities. Freight represents about one fourth of CO_2 emissions coming from transport activities in European cities. In Dijon, France, 26% of the total road traffic-related consumption of tons equivalent petrol (TEP) comes from freight transport. This represents the equivalent of 67 TEP each day to supply Dijon. It has been estimated that during the morning rush hour in Bordeaux, France, the circulation of freight transport vehicles added five decibels (dB(A)) to the noise from the circulation of private cars (LET et al., 2006).

Table 8.1 Pollutant emissions due to road traffic in Dijon, France

Emissions (kg/hour)	CO_2	NO_x	HC	PM_{10}
All traffic	1,124	312	166	15
Private cars	894	173	122	5
Local freight transport	225	113	41	9
Freight in transit	5	26	3	1
Proportion of local freight in urban transport emissions	20%	36%	25%	60%
Proportion of local freight and freight in transit in urban transport emissions	20%	45%	27%	67%

Source: LET et al., 2006

Another important issue is road safety. Lorries have a low share of accidents in cities but the accidents involving them are more serious. In European cities, about 5% to 10% of fatal accidents involve light commercial trucks and 10% to 15% involve heavy commercial trucks (Bestufs, 2006). In Australian cities, in the 1980s, 13% of fatal crashes involved trucks (Ogden, 1992). In 2005, 2,789 people were killed or seriously injured on London's roads, with 402 of these incidents involving freight vehicles. About 14% of all collisions involving goods vehicles result in serious or fatal injuries, which is higher than for other road users (Transport for London, 2007). The reconciliation of truck traffic with a rapidly increasing bicycle use has been a recent cause of concerns in Paris and London following much-publicized fatal collisions.

The need to provide global logistics services

Logistics services are key assets for metropolitan areas. Cities that do not provide these kinds of services, both quantitatively and qualitatively, may have difficulties in serving businesses already in place and in attracting new companies. In Medan, Indonesia, a city of two million people, logistics services are not developed with most local companies using their own warehouses. Logistics services are quite basic, as companies have only a few channels through which goods can be traded. A low level of confidence in trading explains that there are very few large-scale wholesalers (Kato and Sato, 2006). Shanghai is a notable example of the way efficient logistics services have been introduced (Chin et al., 2007). Large traditional state-owned companies once dominated the market but now make up only 5% of current companies. Private domestic logistics companies (37% of current companies) emerged in the 1980s. They are medium-sized companies, quite efficient but lacking capital. Since the deregulation of transport in 2005 following the entry into the World Trade Organization, two new groups of logistics providers have emerged. Sino-foreign or foreign capital logistics providers represent 11% of current companies, TNT and DHL being the first. And companies affiliated to large manufacturers which became separate profit centers or even independent third party logistics providers represent 47% of logistics companies. These firms make Shanghai one of the most active places for logistics services in Asia, serving both local and global markets.

Logistics sprawl

Logistics sprawl is the spatial deconcentration of logistics facilities in metropolitan areas. Historically, freight transport terminals tended to be close to the city centers, originally favoring a proximity to railway networks and port facilities. Confronted with the severe land pressure as well as with the large urban renewal projects that took place during the 1960s and 1970s, logistics and transport companies began to follow a centrifugal locational pattern (Hesse, 2004; Woudsma et al., 2007; Cidell, 2010). The physical moves were done by small-scale changes in their spatial organization, with the closing of urban terminals and the opening of new ones further away. In Figure 8.1 the relocation of cross-dock facilities for parcel and express transport companies in the Paris region between 1974 and 2010 (Dablanc and Rakotonarivo, 2010) is evident.

The first consequence of terminals' deconcentration is the increase in distances travelled by trucks and vans to service their urban markets where jobs remain more concentrated. This is further reinforced by the general tendency to locate logistic facilities close to arterial road networks while reducing the total number of facilities. Terminals today are larger and each one serves more businesses and households than they used to do. All this leads to more vehicle-miles travelled by trucks and vans in the metropolitan area. Dablanc and Rakotonarivo (2010) have

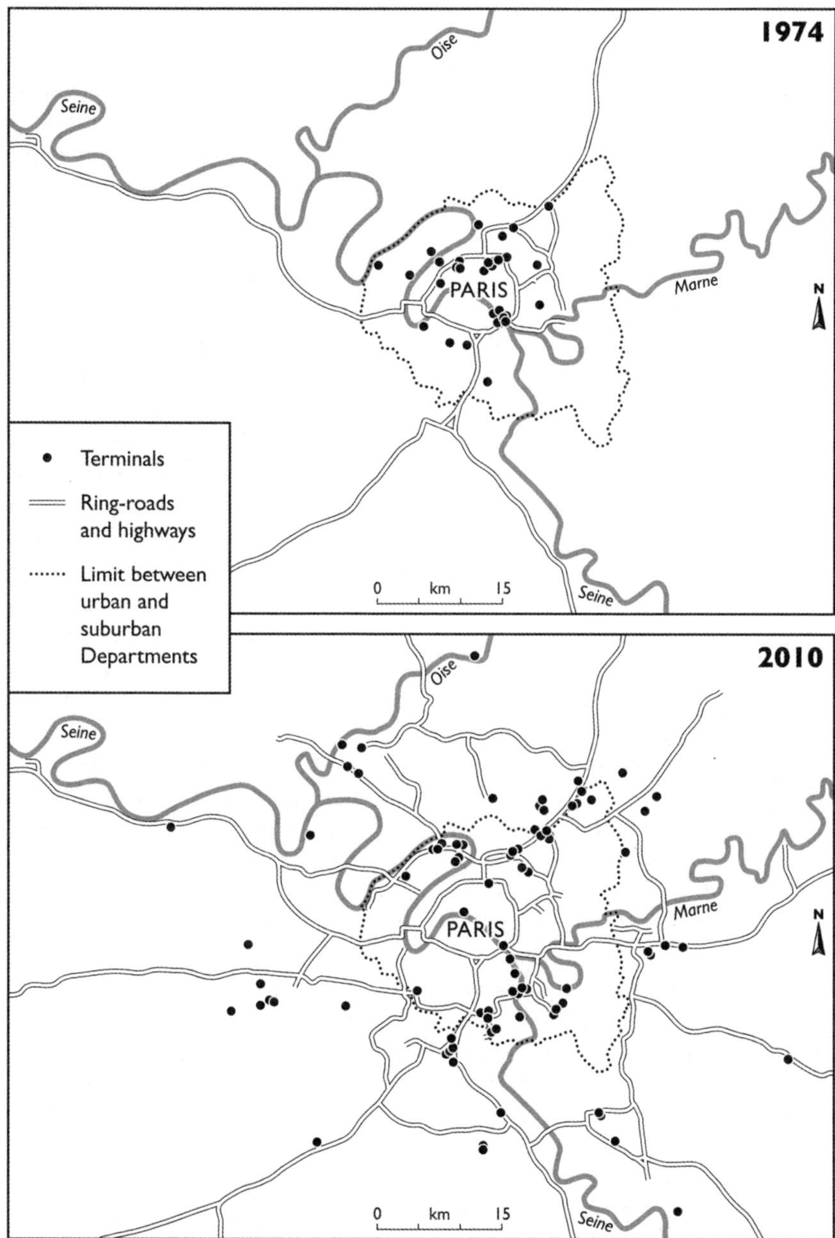

Figure 8.1 Logistics sprawl of parcel transport terminals in the Paris region, 1974 and 2010

Source: D. Andriankaja, IFSTTAR

estimated that on average cross-dock facilities serving the Paris region have moved 12 kilometers away from their barycenter between 1974 and 2010. Meanwhile, customers of parcel and express transport services (shippers and receivers) have moved 2 kilometers away from their barycenter on average. It was estimated that this relative additional distance between cross-dock facilities and their clients has generated 16,350 additional tons of CO_2 in 2010 compared with 1974.

Labor issues and subcontracting

Subcontracting is a common practice in the organization of urban deliveries. It means that the actual delivery of a shipment is made by a different operator from the one formally hired by the shipper. In French cities, 80% to 100% of urban freight operations in express parcel transport are subcontracted to small operators. Illicit practices, such as the hiring of undeclared workers, are a common feature of urban transport outsourcing. Subcontractors' activities are often associated with the use of older vehicles, and with drivers who exceed the authorized driving time, leading to tiredness and a greater frequency of accidents.

Delivery workers are often the least regarded workers in the trucking industry, with low wages and stressful work. Lack of labor and difficulties in recruiting skilled employees have been an enduring feature of many urban transport markets. Worker turnover can be high, leading to difficulties in providing good services, and generating a high level of traffic code infractions. The share of urban deliveries done without a proper contract is high, leading to poor working conditions and insurance problems in case of accidents.

The development of courier services or food home deliveries on motor bikes is associated with difficult working conditions. Drivers are often paid on the number of deliveries they perform every day, leading to risky behaviors such as fast driving and neglecting basic safety rules in order to perform as many deliveries as possible.

CITY LOGISTICS INITIATIVES

The emergence of innovative city logistics services

Innovative city logistics services are logistics activities that specifically respond to new demands from urban businesses and consumers, but this response tends to take place at a slow pace.

Consumer behavior has changed rapidly in recent years. In Europe, Japan, Korea and North America, online shopping has become a mainstream consumers' activity. E-commerce is also increasing in many low- and medium-income countries, especially in large cities. This generates a demand for new logistics and transport services, among them home deliveries or deliveries at the office or in drop-off/pick-up boxes and depots. Companies also have growing demands for new logistics services. Surveys have shown that many inner city retailers are interested in, and willing to pay for, new services such as the rental of storage space, the provision of dedicated areas for the reception of their deliveries out of the stores' premises, and specialized services for the pick up of palettes and empty boxes and packages (from French surveys described in Boudouin, 2006).

In response to these demands, the number of initiatives taken by the logistics sector has been surprisingly low and it is only since the mid 2000s that entrepreneurial initiatives in city logistics can be found in European cities (Dablanc, 2007). Companies such as Shurgard provide urban storage space for shopkeepers. Star's Services, a French transport company with 1,500 truck drivers, has been highly successful by specializing in home deliveries of grocery products to urban households. In Germany, Deutsche Post has installed thousands of "PackStations," or automated locker banks, in cities' public spaces so that e-commerce consignments can be delivered at any time of the day to customers. In Rungis, the largest wholesale market of fresh products of Europe located South of Paris, logisticians have proposed new delivery services to groceries. In other regions of the world, innovative delivery services develop on niche markets (delivery of cooked meals on workplaces in Mumbai, for example). Only in Japanese cities has the development of new transport services matched and even preceded the urban demand. Takkyubins, which are parcel transport companies specializing in home delivery and business to consumer deliveries (B2C), have responded quickly to the evolution of consumer behavior. Yamato invented the concept in 1971 with Sagawa and Nippon Express following through as competitors. The variety of products passing through a takkyubin terminal is much greater than what can be observed in Europe or North America. Letters, general parcels but also frozen goods and voluminous products such as luggage, skis, and golf equipment are processed in the same terminal. The size of their networks, the diversity of their services, their high level of logistics efficiency, and the extensive use of home deliveries by Japanese families make takkyubins stand out as a model, which has not been yet been applied anywhere else in the world (Dablanc, 2009a).

Two case studies: Motomachi and La Petite Reine

Among the various city logistics initiatives around the world (see SUGAR, 2011, for a detailed survey), some stand out even though their implementation was met with difficulties. Two currently running operations, one from Japan and another one from Europe, are presented.

Motomachi urban consolidation center in Yokohama, Japan

Motomachi is a neighborhood of Yokohama in Japan with a retail area covering three pedestrian streets in the city center. The 450 stores market upscale brands. In 2004, a consolidated delivery scheme, Motomachi urban consolidation center (UCC), was implemented and has proved very successful since then (SUGAR, 2011; Figures 8.2 and 8.3). It

Figure 8.2 Motomachi UCC employees unloading a CNG truck

Source: photo L. Dablanc

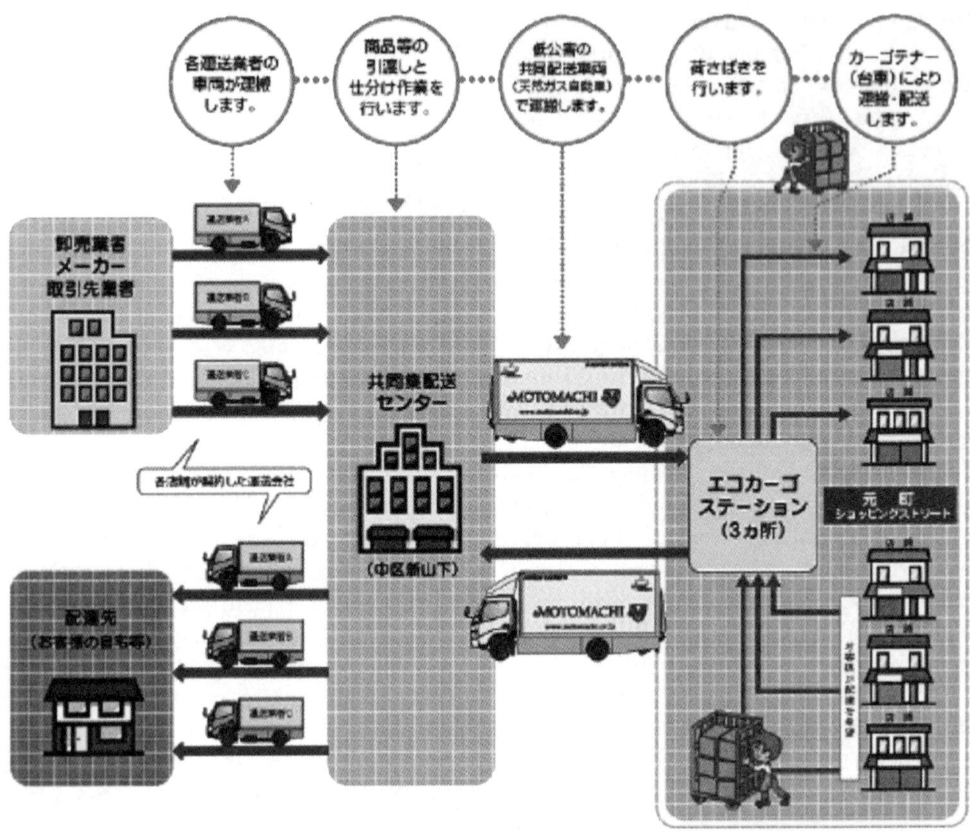

Figure 8.3 The operational scheme of Motomachi UCC

Source: courtesy of Motomachi UCC managers

is managed by a shopkeepers' association and serves most of the stores in the area.

In the 1990s and early 2000s, Motomachi neighborhood was facing problems of congestion, double-parked trucks impeding shop window visibility, and traffic accidents. The municipality applied to the national Pilot Program in Clean Urban Transport, which in turn suggested experimenting with the concept of consolidated logistics. From then, the project for Motomachi UCC required six years of work before implementation. A public/private partnership was created involving residents' associations, the police, the municipality's department of transport and other departments (commerce), environmental organizations, the departmental branch of the main Japanese carriers' organization, and the retailers' associations, which have been the key players in the implementation of the scheme. Motomachi UCC provides a delivery service to all freight carriers that need to deliver to one of the 450 shops affiliated with the association. A consolidation terminal of 330 m^2 is located a few hundred meters away from the retailing area. On an average day, twenty-two truck companies use the facility. Sagawa, one of the most important Japanese parcel and B2C transport companies, represents 60% of all UCC activity. The UCC and its fourteen employees process about 350,000 parcels per year. Three low-emission CNG trucks make delivery rounds from the consolidation center to the shops. The quality of the service has been recognized by shopkeepers and carriers. Initial market surveys had forecasted that 1,800 parcels a day would be delivered by the UCC. Only 1,500 were initially delivered but five years later, with the addition of deliveries to private customers' homes, the UCC has reached its initial targets. The consolidation center has managed to break even financially. The operating budget is ¥55 million (about €412,000), 95% of which comes from the revenue generated by the fees (¥150 or about €1.25 per parcel delivered) paid by the freight carriers using the UCC. A subsidy from the shopkeepers' association covers the remaining operational deficit.

A key element of the decision-making process has been to propose that the UCC be operated by a company not previously distributing goods in Motomachi. The current UCC manager is a freight handling specialist in the port of Yokohama, with no direct stake in the parcel transport business. This made it easier for carriers delivering to Motomachi to accept to transfer their deliveries to the consolidation center.

To a European or North American audience, the absence of accompanying local regulations, such as local ordinances restricting access to trucks with high environmental impacts or large size, is surprising. Truck companies and shopkeepers, once having agreed to participate in the system, now continue to apply its terms. A sign reading "reserved delivery area for truck companies currently delivering goods" is enough to protect the delivery bays from illegal parking.

La Petite Reine tricycle operator in Paris, France

La Petite Reine (the Little Queen, a nickname for bicycles in French) is a delivery company using a new concept of vehicles, the "cargocycle," a tricycle with electrical assistance accommodating a special container in the back (Figure 8.4). La Petite Reine designed the tricycles. The company was created in 2002 in Paris, and today, it delivers one million parcels a year in several European cities

Figure 8.4 A La Petite Reine cargocycle in the streets of Paris

Source: photo L. Dablanc

(Paris, Bordeaux, Rennes, Geneva, Lyon) using 60 cargocycles. La Petite Reine has developed its own cargocycle technology (through its subsidiary company called Lovelo), and it sells its cargocycles to other transport companies or municipalities. Cargocycles can be seen in the streets of many cities, such as in London's Regent St for the deliveries of Office Depot.

La Petite Reine provides last mile parcel delivery services to businesses in urban locations. Originally dedicated to parcel and express transport (La Petite Reine has been a subcontractor for DHL, Chronopost, Coliposte, Adrexo), the company today has diversified its customer base with home deliveries becoming an important activity. La Petite Reine operates home deliveries for the French wine seller Nicolas, for Simply Market, a French grocery and general goods retail chain, and for Leroy-Merlin, a DIY (do-it-yourself) products and services chain of stores. It has recently experimented with a "frigocycle" to deliver Dannon fresh dairy products to small retailers such as bakeries. The use of cargocycles brings great environmental benefits. It has been estimated that La Petite Reine saves 200 tons of CO_2 per year compared to the conventional way (diesel vans and trucks) of delivering an equivalent amount of merchandise. However, there is one drawback with using bicycles to deliver goods in urban areas. Although electrically assisted, cargocycles remain cycles, and their use is considered quite strenuous by employees. Also, the cost of maintenance is higher than expected as the cargocycle is not yet well adapted to the transport of loads. Wheels need to be changed often and this generates an important maintenance cost to the company. Some cost issues have led la Petite Reine to stop operating in Dijon, France in February 2011.

What is most interesting in the La Petite Reine experience is that the company uses small terminals located in inner city locations. A good example is an underground parking facility close to the Louvre museum. This terminal is leased by the municipality of Paris at a low price, in exchange for testing environmentally friendly delivery services. Since 2003, the municipality of Paris has carried out a dedicated program to improve last mile deliveries which includes the implementation of "Urban Logistics Spaces" (ULS), dedicated small transshipment facilities located in the densest areas of Paris. So far (2012), the city has allocated seven logistics spaces of between 250 m^2 to 1,000 m^2, most of them located in underground municipally-owned car parking facilities. Spaces are allocated following a bid for tender: the logistics operator offering the greenest mode of delivery while retaining an economically sustainable organization is preferred. The rent required by the city is set at an affordable level, under market prices. The rent is actually set at the price level of the average rental price of logistics facilities in the region (€60/m^2).

Contrary to other city logistics experiments in Europe, Paris underground Urban Logistics Spaces do not require direct public subsidies. However, they represent an indirect cost for the municipality, as these spaces could generate high car parking fees if they were not used for logistics activities.

POLICIES DESIGNED TO MANAGE URBAN FREIGHT AND CITY LOGISTICS

Involvement in urban freight for the public sector can be manifold and at various levels. Cities are in charge of the urban road network, which is heavily impacted by urban commercial vehicle traffic. Cities are also interested in local economic development, and therefore have to make sure that the provision of goods and logistics services is adequate. Cities control the use of land, including the land necessary for logistics activities (warehouses and terminals), and are in charge of local traffic and parking regulations, including all regulations that relate to delivery vehicles. Finally, cities are concerned with environmental and social issues, which are openly associated with urban freight activities (Anderson et al., 2005).

Despite these many mandates and potential objectives, actual local public policies regarding freight are quite modest. In urban areas, with a growing population but a constrained space, urban freight has little weight over people's transport when choices of development are made. Most cities still view truck traffic as something that should be banned or at least strictly regulated, and few of them consider freight activities as a service they should help organize in a more efficient manner to benefit the local economy. Local policies are generally very parochial and can be conflicting. In the Lyon metropolitan area (France) as many as thirty different rules on trucks' access regulations based on weight and size exist, forcing truck drivers to decide which rules they will comply with, and which ones they will disregard.

Major events such as the Olympics or the World Cup, or major urban development projects such as the implementation of a tramway or a subway system, may provide opportunities to organize a change in urban freight operations citywide. The municipality of Athens imposed a night deliveries regulation during the 2004 Olympics. Afterwards, the measure was discussed for becoming permanent for some categories of vehicles. Similarly, during the 2000 Olympics, Sydney, prohibited deliveries after 8 am.

This section presents what cities are actually engaged in with regards to urban freight. Pros and cons of each policy are discussed.

Institutions involved

Tools involved in the definition of a freight policy can be found at various levels of public authorities:

- Locally: street management, parking policy, building permits, land use, and urban design are defined by municipalities or inter-municipal bodies at a metropolitan scale. Many indirect regulations (environmental and safety regulations on warehouses, for example) have also a direct effect on urban freight.
- Nationally: management of major road networks, vehicle standards and specifications, requirements for professional training, companies' licensing are usually defined by state administrations.
- Depending on each country's organization, intermediate levels of government may have an influence, such as regions (in Australia, there are different truck sizes and weight in each of the six regions of the country) or supranational institutions ("Euro" standards[1] applied to trucks in all member states are defined by the European Union).

Economic tools such as taxes and subsidies are also available at each institutional level. Within one local government, many departments have tools and mandates that can directly or indirectly affect urban freight, such as economic development, commerce, environment, traffic and mobility, infrastructure, planning, and health. These administrations often do not work in a coordinated manner, especially for topics such as freight, which is generally ignored as a potentially transversal policy target.

Truck and van access restrictions

The tool that cities, when confronted with freight activities, use in priority is truck access restriction. These restrictions are based on various criteria (used alone or combined): time windows, weight (total or per axle), size (length, height, surface), noise emission, air pollution, loading factor, and type of goods (hazardous, voluminous). European cities have used this kind of regulation since the Roman Empire. In recent history, the most famous truck ban in Europe is the London Lorry Ban, in place since 1975. Heavy goods vehicles over 18 tons cannot circulate at night and weekends within a delimited area. To the contrary, Paris bans trucks (over $29\,m^2$) during day time. In Tokyo, many neighborhoods are not accessible to trucks over three tons. Like in Paris, all trucks in Seoul have been banned since 1979 from the central areas during working hours (Castro & Kuse, 2005). In São Paulo, to alleviate congestion, access is based on the plate number, with two days per week allowed per vehicle, including freight vehicles. It is common in large Chinese cities to ban trucks above five tons from the city center during peak hours.

Restricting large trucks in cities has also been a popular measure in poorer countries, partly due to road limitations. The policy in Manila is one of the earliest and well-known cases of large truck restrictions as it dates back to 1978. Trucks with a gross weight of more than 4.5 tons cannot travel along eleven primary arterial roads from six in the morning until nine in the evening. Ten other roads are prohibited during peak hours with alternate routes made available to reach the port of Manila (Castro and Kuse, 2005).

Truck access rules based on weight or size policies have several drawbacks. They tend to promote small capacity vehicles (vans, light trucks), which increases total congestion and diminishes the efficiency of freight transport. According to studies quoted by Castro and Kuse (2005), Manila's restrictions have decreased the productivity of trucks (in number of truck trips per day) by 50–60%. In Seoul, light own-account trucks have become popular as a consequence of the truck restriction. A second issue is that regulating truck access requires enforcement and control, meaning a sufficient and well-trained staff, with good communication. In Medan, Indonesia, large-size trucks have been prohibited from entering the central business district since 2004, but interviews with truck drivers revealed that most of them were unaware of the ban (Kato and Sato, 2006).

The most recent trends in access restrictions are environmental standards and road pricing. Both can be combined, as is the case for the London congestion charge. Urban tolls are not specific to commercial vehicles, while many environmental zones or "Low Emission Zones" are. Many European cities today apply truck access restrictions based on environmental criteria. In these regulations, only recent trucks, or fully loaded trucks, are permitted to enter the city center. In Amsterdam (Netherlands) a truck may make deliveries in limited access zones if it meets the following four conditions: it must be less than eight years old, have a maximum length of ten meters, and load or unload at least 80% of its merchandise in the central city. In London, the Low Emission Zone (which is different from the congestion charge zone) prohibits trucks older than the Euro IV standard (trucks manufactured since 2006) to enter the metropolitan area, which is defined as the area surrounded by the M25 highway totalling 1,580 km^2. In Tokyo, since 2003, the most polluting diesel vehicles have been prohibited.

In the case of urban tolls, vehicles are charged for the use of the street space according to the marginal costs they impose on others, including external costs. In the 1970s, when the first tolls appeared, external costs were mostly computed with regards to congestion whereas air pollution today is the most common target of tolls' differentiation policies. Energy consumption and the related CO_2 emissions could well be targets for the future. However, it is not clear how elastic urban freight distribution is in regard to an increase in road use prices. It was underlined that even with substantial charges, operators may not change their organizational patterns. For instance, since the congestion charge was implemented in 2003 in London, the number of vans and lorries in the restricted zone remained stable, while at the same time the number of cars decreased by 30% (Transport for London, 2007). Other cases show an impact. Rotaris et al. (2009) describe the impact of Ecopass in central Milan. Ecopass (replaced in 2012 by a simpler system called AreaC) was a road charging scheme in which the charge varied according to the vehicles' Euro standards. Euro VI and Euro V trucks (trucks manufactured after 2006) did not pay, Euro III trucks (manufactured between 2001 and 2005) had to pay €5 per day, older trucks had to pay €10 per day.

Ecopass was implemented in January 2008 and by March 2008 the number of commercial vehicles for the transport of goods had decreased significantly: before Ecopass, 13,174 commercial vehicles entered the zone daily on average, and with Ecopass the number was reduced to an average of 10,500 (–20%). The authors estimated that over a year, total benefits gained in pollutants' emissions of NOx and PM_{10} attributed to Ecopass were €1.8 million and for CO_2 emissions were equivalent to €0.6 million. Commercial vehicle users gained €2.2 million in time savings and reliability. On the other hand, they lost €5.2 million in toll charges and penalties.

In European and many Asian cities, new enforcement technologies have increased the efficiency of truck access restriction policies. Automatic control systems such as automatic number plate recognition cameras, mobile enforcement, vehicle positioning, and on-board equipment have been introduced in many cities. This highly efficient technology comes at a cost, such as in London where it costs £30,000 per traffic enforcement camera to install and monitor.

Finally, the reduction of noise generated by deliveries and the promotion of night (or early morning/late evening) deliveries are a new target of urban freight policies. According to a survey made in New York City, businesses most likely to change to off peak deliveries are shippers doing their own transport (own account), and receivers open during extended hours such as restaurants (Holguin-Veras, 2010). This does not make a sufficient target group for the promotion of night deliveries, and some cities implement a strong policy combining the promotion of silent equipments and some regulations. In the Netherlands, in twenty-five pilot cities, the national government provided financial help for operators investing in silent delivery equipments, which are vehicles and handling equipment generating noise emissions below 65 dB, for night deliveries at supermarkets. Tests have shown that companies save 30% in delivery cost and 25% in diesel consumption (Goevaers, 2011). This program is now being duplicated in other European cities. The human factor remains a key element for noise abatement. Recent trials done in Paris have shown that the same equipment used by different truck drivers results in very different noise impacts due to personal behaviors. Holguin-Veras (2010) demonstrated that financial incentives to receivers were the most efficient way to ensure a better participation of receivers to night time delivery schemes, but these kinds of policies are costly and may generate competition issues.

Parking policies, provision of delivery spaces

Freight needs dedicated urban spaces, such as loading and unloading areas, be they public or private, on street or off street. Insufficient delivery spaces will transfer delivery operations on traffic lanes or sidewalks, and will lead to congestion and traffic accidents. Delivery personnel must have appropriate pick-up and delivery points with good access. In busy urban areas and city centers, this means that adequate on-street loading and unloading bays must be identified. Providing adequate delivery spaces, therefore, has positive impacts and has been implemented in

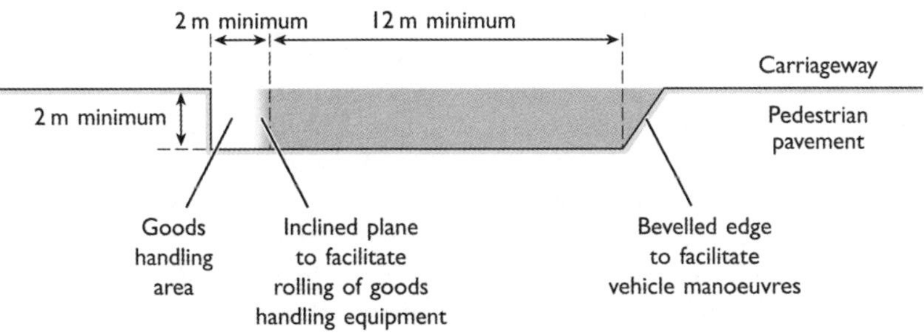

Figure 8.5 Proposed design of an unloading/loading bay

Source: City of Paris, 2005

many cities. A Paris transport department's guideline imposes a minimum of one delivery bay every 100 meters in the city streets. Figure 8.5 shows one specific delivery bay design that uses part of the sidewalk which has had good results in Paris.

Alternative designs exist, such as loading bays positioned at an angle to the curb. Attention must be paid to removing obstacles around the loading bay, such as humps and posts. Obstacles often prevent drivers from operating on-board handling equipment, which makes for more difficult manual work. A sufficient number of loading bays must be provided with a ratio of one delivery area for ten to twelve businesses at street level often seen as appropriate. Other interesting layouts include dedicating entire sections of a parking lane to deliveries during certain time windows. In Koriyama City in Japan, one lane of the roadway has been converted into loading space. In Kashiwa City, a joint parking space for delivery trucks is managed collectively by retailers. And in Nerima (Tokyo), the "pocket loading" system provides loading space that has been secured by converting a part of an existing parking lot into a reserved delivery space (Futumata, 2009). These are part of the Japanese government's Pilot Programs on urban transport, with a strong focus on the management of loading/unloading and parking spaces, both on street and off street. In London and Paris, some bus lanes are shared with delivery vehicles.

In Buenos Aires, Argentina, a global policy on loading/unloading areas was implemented in February 2009, but the number of spots remains limited with only 750 on-street delivery areas laid out in downtown Buenos Aires, much less than in central Paris (10,000) or Barcelona (8,000). Also, the Buenos Aires delivery spaces seem insufficiently dimensioned, as they are limited to a length of 8 meters. Guidelines in Europe favour bigger spaces. In Paris, on-street delivery areas must be at least 10 meters long, to facilitate trucks' manoeuvres and the handling of goods.

Time sharing is a good way to improve the road network and parking capacity. In Seoul in the four "Freight Districts" identified in the metropolitan area, different time windows have been allocated to trucks and passenger cars for on-street parking areas. In Barcelona, Spain, the municipality has created an innovative organization on some of its main boulevards, by devoting the two lateral lanes to traffic during peak hours, deliveries during off peak hours, and residential parking during the night. The city is also renowned for its global policy on freight street management, which has led to interesting results. In the city's largest commercial area (the Ensanche), a dedicated mobility motor squad consisting of 300 agents circulating with a motorbike has been organized to control all on-street parking activities including loading/unloading zones. This has prevented illegal long-term parking and made these zones always available to delivery truck drivers.

Long-term truck parking is a major issue for urban areas. Many trucks need to park during night time before early store opening. These parking areas can also be a place for the transfer of goods into smaller lorries. Few municipalities have set up organized truck parking centers, but in some cities, private truck parking yards have been provided.

Providing logistics parks

Efficient goods distribution is closely related to logistics service provision. Making logistics services available means organizing business opportunities, providing space at affordable prices, and promoting logistics job training. A prevalent global solution is the development of logistics parks (sometimes called freight villages), partly through public investment. Some notable examples include Sogaris, a Paris-based company which built and now operates large logistics parks in the inner suburbs or within city limits of Paris, Lyon and Marseille; the *Güterverkehrszentrum* (GVZ) at the outskirts of most large German cities, and the Italian *interporti*. These logistics parks include common services for all companies located on the site, such as surveillance, catering, fueling, cleaning stations for trucks, overnight truck parking, and night accommodation for drivers. These parks must be accessible by public transport over extended hours, as logistics jobs require unconventional working hours. Environmental standards set or promoted by the municipality should enhance the quality of the buildings and mitigate impacts, through low-noise road pavement, solar panels on roofs, and protection against earthquake exposure. In Japan, twenty-two freight facilities in Tokyo, and fourteen in other cities, have been implemented with the help of the national state in order to solve urban difficulties for truck companies. The Korean government is creating a network of forty logistics hubs located in the major metropolitan areas of the country. The municipality of Seoul is contributing to this policy by setting up freight distribution centers to make urban truck operations more efficient.

Former industrial areas can be used when developing specialized logistics areas. However, necessary remediation efforts (e.g. for the removal of polluted soil) should not be too extensive, as programs for logistics spaces cannot tolerate high land costs.

Land use policies, zoning and building regulations

Land use regulations can serve a local freight policy since many cities impose the building of off-street delivery areas in new commercial or industrial developments. The Tokyo off-street parking ordinance of 2002 compels all department stores, offices or warehouses to provide for loading/unloading facilities when they have a floor area of more than 2,000 m^2. European cities' regulations are generally stricter, as buildings of 400 to 1,000 m^2 are subjected to the off-street loading zone regulations. Barcelona has a very original regulation with the municipal building code of 1998 stating that all new bars and restaurants are required to build a storage area with a minimal size of 5 m^2 within their premises. The rationale behind this rule is that restaurants will not need a daily supply of bottles and beverages if they store sufficient volumes.

Cities should also be careful in avoiding inadequate regulations in their building and planning codes. Access to underground parking, for example, whether in public parks or in private buildings, can be very difficult for commercial vehicles, even small ones, because of height and size limits. The Chicago Downtown Freight Study (January 2008) mentions this as an important problem for truck drivers. The municipality now works on a loading zone plan and inventory, parking violation fines during peak times, and an alley obstruction enforcement campaign.

Space availability is scarce, and has to be used the best way possible. Some municipalities do it by accepting the development of multi-activity buildings, with logistics on street levels and other activities on the upper levels. Some also do it with the development of multi-story warehouses. The logistics developer ProLogis has built seven- to nine-story logistics terminals in downtown Tokyo. These terminals are also common in Hong-Kong where space availability is scarce. The acceptance of such projects is increasingly conditioned to environmental criteria and to a careful attention to the integration of buildings into the existing urban landscape.

Planning strategies taking freight into account are a recent trend in large US metropolitan areas. The Dallas Fort Worth region has set up "freight oriented developments." In the greater Toronto area, "freight supportive land use guidelines" have been defined. The Southern California Association of Governments (SCAG, Los Angeles) has identified "freight-supportive design strategies" in its regional transportation plan (NCHRP, 2007).

Urban Consolidation Centers

Some public authorities promote the development of urban logistics spaces in central areas, such as small terminals located in dense urban areas providing logistics services to neighborhood businesses and residents. These logistics spaces (of about 500 to 2,000 m^2) can be provided directly by public authorities in the real estate they control, such as underground parking garages. A request for proposal can be organized so that operators demonstrating the best practices with regards to environmental, social and economic objectives become users of the facilities at low rental cost (see La Petite Reine above). Urban Consolidation Centers (UCC) are a specific case of urban logistics as they provide a specific service of bundled and coordinated deliveries, often requiring public subsidies. A UCC is a logistics facility located in close proximity to the geographic area that it serves, which is generally a city center but also any kind of dense commercial area, from which consolidated deliveries are carried out within that area, in which a range of other value-added logistics and retail services can be provided (Bestufs, 2007).

Up to 200 such terminals existed in European cities in the 1990s–early 2000s. Due to operating costs, most of them closed down when municipalities could no longer subsidize them. Today, a few UCCs are operating, mostly in medium-size cities: Bristol in the UK, Modena, Padua, and other Italian cities, La Rochelle in France, Motomachi in Japan (see above). These consolidation centers are expensive and the allocation of operating costs is difficult. The Italian case is specifically illustrative with around ten urban consolidation terminals in existence. They are in different stages of implementation, but all share the purpose of protecting historic centers with rich architectural heritage. It should be noted that own-account transport (i.e. shop holders or artisans handling their own supply and delivery) plays an important role in supplying urban business sites in Italy. Likewise, even when third-party transport is used, it is dominated by the *padroncini*, small individual entrepreneurs. These two groups, the self supplied shop owners and the small third-party carriers, have a characteristic in common: quite inefficient operations. They generally do a small number of truck trips per week or less than truckload poorly organized tours.

While urban goods distribution is under-optimized across Europe (Dablanc, 2007), this phenomenon reaches an extreme in Italian cities. Under such conditions, Italian local officials are attempting to impose more efficient freight transport strategies in city centers. Vicenza has prohibited all goods transport to the city center except goods delivered by VELOCE, the municipal UCC. This has generated legal complications, as representatives of large express transport companies litigated against the municipality for breaching fair competition laws (Ville et al., 2010). The example of Parma is also revealing. A 2008 city ordinance creates an accreditation that carriers must obtain if they wish to deliver to the historic center. If they are not accredited, they must use the services of the Urban Consolidation Center called Ecologistics. To receive accreditation, vehicles must meet the Euro III standard (trucks built after 2001), they must be loaded to 70% of capacity (in volume or weight), and they must possess a geo-positioning system that allows tracking.

Consultation policies, private/public partnerships

The urban distribution of goods is organized by private stakeholders (producers, carriers, retailers, final consumers), operating in an environment, the urban space, which is managed by public authorities. In this regard, private/public partnerships, or Freight Forums, represent an option. Consultation processes with private stakeholders provide a better understanding of the constraints and obligations of each party, and allow the development of concerted action programs. In France, when a local transport plan is designed, consultation procedures provide, often for the first time, an opportunity for local authorities and transportation professionals to meet. In June 2006, the city of Paris and the most important carriers' and shippers' associations signed an urban freight transport "Charter," in which they committed to several points which are favorable to the environment, to the drivers' working conditions, and to the productivity of urban delivery activities. In the United Kingdom, in many cities in general and in London in particular, it has been a common practice for years to discuss and negotiate with transport and logistics professional organizations, leading to compromises. For example, the level of the congestion tax assigned to delivery trucks, which was £5 a day at the start of the congestion charging scheme in 2003, was a result of a two-year discussion: truck companies wanted no tax, as no alternative other than road transport was available for goods transport; the municipality wanted commercial vehicles to pay much more than cars because of the severe road damages caused by trucks. At the end, both parties compromised on a fee equal to that paid by private cars.

All stakeholders are not always equally represented in local consultation processes. On the one hand, small operators usually do not have a representative organization (professional syndicate). On the other hand, large transport and logistics companies or their organizations are not willing to participate in local consultations in cities other than in major or capital cities, because of a lack of interest or insufficient staff. Local shopkeepers' organizations tend to find no interest in freight groups. However, consultation processes in urban freight can provide unique collaborative opportunities between private companies that otherwise would not be willing to work together. Consultation processes can lead directly to initiatives such as recognition schemes, which is a certification process that identifies the best urban freight operators. Certification confers privileges on an operator, such as extended delivery hours or the use of designated loading/unloading facilities. It may also provide operators with a competitive advantage when bidding for contracts, as clients are increasingly committed to selecting bidders that offer the best environmental guarantees. An example of such an initiative is the FORS (Freight Operator Recognition Scheme) in London. FORS provides a performance benchmark for the trucking industry (Transport for London, 2007) by certifying operators that comply with a list of efficiency, safety, and environmental impact criteria at bronze, silver and gold levels. It gives certified companies access to data, benchmark information, and training programs for their drivers.

Another incentive-based policy implemented successfully in London is the Delivery and Servicing Plans (DSP) program, a simplifying process of deliveries initiated by a company or hospital or institution. Creating a DSP with an organization allows Transport for London to engage with the customers of freight and let them take the lead in a reduced delivery program. Transport for London's own Palestra building in Southwark (south-east London) reduced the number of deliveries by 20% through a DSP program in 2009–2010.

CONCLUSION

This chapter has examined the significance of city logistics in the context of the supply and demand of urban goods deliveries. City logistics is an innovative response to urban customers' demands for new services such as home deliveries. It also responds to cities' concerns over the environmental impacts of current urban deliveries. By targeting an efficient management of the movement of goods in cities, city logistics initiatives achieve reductions in commercial vehicles-miles traveled and in noise and atmospheric emissions.

Several strategies about how goods are delivered or collected in urban areas were examined. Despite traffic difficulties and costs associated to activities in urban areas, freight operators manage to serve the vast majority of their urban customers, but this often comes at an environmental cost. Goods movements represent 10–15% of all transport in an urban area, but up to a third and even more of the local pollutants related to transport in a city.

They are also responsible for a quarter of transport-related carbon dioxide emissions in urban areas. Another feature of urban freight is its impressive diversity, from one economic sector to another, and across urban areas. This makes it difficult to identify common technologies and strategies which could fit a specific market, such as clean delivery vehicles, tour optimization software, or urban logistics facilities.

Despite those difficulties, a growing number of innovative city logistics initiatives have emerged. The Motomachi urban consolidation center in Japan and the electrically assisted cargocycles of La Petite Reine in Paris are salient examples of these initiatives. They both involve successful partnerships between retailers and carriers in the case of Motomachi and between a freight operator and a municipality in the case of La Petite Reine. Drawing from these experiences and others, opportunities for successful public policies in urban freight and city logistics were discussed in the last part of this chapter. The need for cities to address urban freight with a large spectrum of tools and measures was emphasized, which can be helped by collecting data. Cities need to identify truck and van access regulations that are coherent region-wide and that do not impair the operations of freight companies. They need to integrate freight and logistics into their planning, land use, and transportation strategies by promoting innovative experiments especially when these initiatives come from logistics entrepreneurs faced with difficulties in finding facilities that can accommodate their activities. Cities and upper levels of governments also need to address training and educational issues in order to contribute to better working conditions and a more attractive urban freight and logistics labor market.

ACKNOWLEDGMENTS

This chapter in based in part on research undertaken in 2009 for the World Bank (Dablanc, 2009b) as an element of the "Freight Transport for Development" initiative. I thank the World Bank for permitting the use of this material. Part of this paper was also presented at the January 2010 Transportation Research Board in Washington.

NOTE

1 Euro standards are European Union's requirements defining the limits for exhaust emissions of new vehicles sold in all Member States. Progressively more stringent Euro classes have been defined by successive European Directives. For new diesel trucks, the Euro VI standard is effective since January 2013.

REFERENCES

Ambrosini, C. and J.L. Routhier (2004) Objectives, methods and results of surveys carried out in the field of urban freight transport: an international comparison, *Transport Reviews*, 24(1), pp. 57–77.

Ambrosini, C., D. Patier and J.L. Routhier (2004) Urban freight establishment and tour based surveys for policy oriented modeling, *Procedia – Social and Behavioral Sciences, The Sixth International Conference on City Logistics*, Edited by E. Tanguchi and R.G. Thompson, 2(3), pp. 6013–6026.

Anderson, S., J. Allen and M. Browne (2005) Urban logistics: how can it meet policy makers' sustainability objectives?, *Journal of Transport Geography*, 13(1), pp.71–81.

Bestufs (2006) *Quantification of Urban Freight Transport Effects I*, Prepared for the European Commission. Available from www.bestufs.net/download/BESTUFS_II/key_issuesII/BESTUF_Quantification_of_effects.pdf (retrieved on February 4, 2013).

Bestufs (2007) *Good Practice Guide on Urban Freight*. Prepared for the European Commission. Available from www.bestufs.net/download/BESTUFS_II/good_practice/English_BESTUFS_Guide.pdf (retrieved on February 4, 2013).

Boudouin, D. (2006) *Les espaces logistiques urbains*. Paris, La documentation française, 112pp.

Castro, J.T. and H. Kuse (2005) Impacts of large truck restrictions in freight carrier operations in metro Manila, *Journal of the Eastern Asia Society for Transportation Studies*, 6, pp. 2947–2962.

Centre for Retail Research (2013) *Online Retailing: Britain and Europe 2012*. Available from http://www.

retailresearch.org/onlineretailing.php (retrieved on February 4, 2013).

Chin, F.C., J.H. Bae and G.O. Kim (2007) A Survey on the Logistics Service Providers in Shanghai. Non published, courtesy of the authors.

Cidell, J. (2010) Concentration and decentralisation: the new geography of freight distribution in US metropolitan areas, *Journal of Transport Geography*, 18, pp. 363–371.

City of Paris (2005) *Technical guide to delivery areas for the City of Paris*, First Edition, Paris. Available in English from Paris City Roads & Transport Department.

Dablanc, L. (2007) Goods transport in large European cities: difficult to organize, difficult to modernize, *Transportation Research Part A*, 41, pp. 280–285.

Dablanc, L. (2008) Urban goods movement and air quality, policy and regulation issues in European cities, *Journal of Environmental Law*, 20(2), pp. 245–266.

Dablanc, L. (2009a) Le territoire urbain des konbini et des takkyubin au Japon, *Flux*, 78(4), October–December, pp. 68–70.

Dablanc, L. (2009b) *Freight Transport, A Key for the New Urban Economy*, Report for the World Bank as part of the initiative Freight Transport for Development: a Policy Toolkit, 52p.

Dablanc, L. and D. Rakotonarivo (2010) The impacts of logistic sprawl: how does the location of parcel transport terminals affect the energy efficiency of goods' movements in Paris and what can we do about it? *Procedia – Social and Behavioral Sciences, The Sixth International Conference on City Logistics*, Edited by E. Tanguchi and R. G. Thompson, 2(3), pp. 6087–6096.

Futumata, Y. (2009) City logistics from road policy aspect, *Japanese–French seminar on Urban Freight Transport*, Japan Society of Civil Engineers, Tokyo, Japan, January 20.

Goevaers, R. (2011) PIEK City Logistics Program. Presentation at the *Transportation Research Board 90th Annual Meeting*, Washington, DC, USA, January 26.

Hesse, M. (2004) Land for logistics: locational dynamics, real estate markets and political regulation of regional distribution complexes, *Tijdschrift voor Economische en Sociale Geografie*, (95)2, pp. 162–173.

Holguín-Veras, J. (2010) Approximation model to estimate joint market share in off-hour deliveries, Presentation at the *12th World Conference on Transport Research*, Lisbon, Portugal, July 11–15.

Kato, H. and J. Sato (2006) Urban Freight Transportation analysis in Developing Countries: Case Study in Medan, Indonesia, unpublished.

LET – Aria Technologies – Systems Consult (2006) *Mise en place d'une méthodologie pour un bilan environnemental physique du transport de marchandises en ville, consommation, émissions, qualité de l'air.* ADEME, CERTU co-publishing, Lyon.

Lozano Cuevas, A. (Principal Investigator) (2006) *Estudio integral metropolitano de transporte de carga y medio ambiente para el Valle de México (EIMTC-MAVM)*, Final Report, Universidad Autonoma de México, Comision Ambiental Metropolitana. September.

National Cooperative Highway Research Program (2007) *Guidebook for Integrating Freight into Transportation Planning and Project Selection Processes*, Report 594, Transportation Research Board of the National Academies, 188pp.

Organization for Economic Co-operation and Development (2004) *OECD Territorial Reviews: Mexico City*, Paris, OECD, 149pp.

Ogden K. (1992) *Urban Goods Movement: A Guide to Policy and Planning*, Ashgate, Cambridge University Press.

Rai, S. (2007) In India, Grandma Cooks, They Deliver, *New York Times*, May 29.

Ripert C., (2006) Approvisionner, desservir, transiter, in: Municipalité de Phnom Penh Mairie de Paris, APUR, *Phnom Penh Centre*, Paris, APUR Publishing, 64 pp.

Rotaris, L., R. Danielis, E. Marcucci, J. Massiani (2010) The urban road pricing scheme to curb pollution in Milan, Italy: description, impacts and preliminary cost-benefit analysis assessment, *Transportation Research Part A*, 44(5), pp. 359–375.

Routhier, J.L., E. Ségalou and S. Durand (2001) *Mesurer l'impact du transport de marchandises en ville – le modele Freturb* (version 1), Programme national marchandises en ville DRAST-ADEME, p. 104.

SUGAR project (2011) *City Logistics Best Practices: A Handbook for Authorities*. Prepared for the European Commission, 272pp. Available from www.sugarlogistics.eu/pliki/handbook.pdf (retrieved on February 4, 2013).

Transport for London (2007) *London Freight Plan – sustainable freight distribution: a plan for London*, Mayor of London, Transport for London, October, 104pp.

Ville, S., J. Gonzalez-Feliu and L. Dablanc (2010) The limits of public policy intervention in urban logistics: lessons from Vicenza, Italy, *European Planning Studies*, DOI 10.1080/09654313.2012.722954.

Woudsma, C., J., Jensen, P. Karoglou and H. Maoh (2007) Logistics land use and the city: a spatial–temporal modelling approach, *Transportation Research Part E,* 44, pp. 277–297.

9

The Siting and Setting of Airport Terminals

David Gillen

INTRODUCTION

In 2009 the world's airlines carried approximately 4.7 billion passengers and 79.8 million tonnes of freight. There were 74.1 million aircraft movements and all of this took place at approximately 49,000 airports in the world (Airports Council International Fact Sheet, 2010). Likely ten countries and approximately 100 airports accounted for the bulk, between 40 and 50 percent, of this activity, nonetheless the numbers suggest the airport industry represents a staggering amount of investment, employment and economic activity. While relatively few airports are decommissioned, except perhaps for military airfields, there has been considerable growth in airport infrastructure particularly in Southeast Asia where whole new airports have been built. In Europe a number of former military airfields have been converted to civilian use for scheduled passenger and freight traffic.

Table 9.1 lists the top 50 airports in 2009 ranked by passengers handled while Table 9.2 lists the top 30 airports (2009 data) based on cargo handled; the passenger airports represent 40 percent of total passengers while the cargo airports account for 56 percent of total world air cargo. A few features are noteworthy in comparing the two sets of airports. First, the correlation in rankings is relatively low, which is surprising since over 90 percent of cargo moves in the belly of passenger aircraft. Second, there are airports included in the cargo list which do not even appear on the passenger list. This is due to the large of amount of integrated courier cargo. Cargo operators prefer airports that operate 24 hours a day and which are uncongested.

In this chapter three subject areas of airports and terminals are discussed. First, the issue of ownership and regulation has an impact on airport performance but also on the ability of airports to finance investments in new airside and terminal capacity. Second, the chapter examines differences among airports where terminals can be owned by the airport or the airline or in some cases by a

Table 9.1 World's busiest airports by passenger traffic

Rank	Airport	Location	Passengers
1	Hartsfield-Jackson Atlanta International Airport	Atlanta, Georgia, United States	88,032,086
2	London Heathrow Airport	Hillingdon, Greater London, England, United Kingdom	66,037,578
3	Beijing Capital International Airport	Chaoyang, Beijing, China	65,372,012
4	O'Hare International Airport	Chicago, Illinois, United States	64,158,343
5	Tokyo International Airport	Ōta, Tokyo, Japan	61,903,656
6	Paris Charles de Gaulle Airport	Roissy-en-France, Val d'Oise, Île-de-France, France	57,906,866
7	Los Angeles International Airport	Los Angeles, California, United States	56,520,843
8	Dallas-Fort Worth International Airport	Dallas/Fort Worth, Texas, United States	56,030,457
9	Frankfurt Airport	Flughafen (Frankfurt am Main), Frankfurt, Hessen, Germany	50,932,840
10	Denver International Airport	Denver, Colorado, United States	50,167,485
11	Madrid-Barajas Airport	Madrid, Comunidad de Madrid, Spain	48,250,784
12	John F. Kennedy International Airport	Queens, New York City, New York, United States	45,915,069
13	Hong Kong International Airport	Chek Lap Kok, Hong Kong, China	45,558,807
14	Amsterdam Airport Schiphol	Haarlemmermeer, North Holland, Netherlands	43,570,370
15	Dubai International Airport	Garhoud, Dubai, United Arab Emirates	40,901,752
16	Suvarnabhumi Airport	RachaThewa, Bang Phli, SamutPrakan, Bangkok, Thailand	40,500,224
17	McCarran International Airport	Las Vegas, Nevada, United States	40,469,012
18	George Bush Intercontinental Airport	Houston, Texas, United States	40,007,354
19	Phoenix Sky Harbor International Airport	Phoenix, Arizona, United States	37,824,982
20	San Francisco International Airport	San Mateo County, California, United States	37,338,942
21	Singapore Changi Airport	Changi, East Region, Singapore	37,203,978
22	Soekarno-Hatta International Airport	Cengkareng, Jakarta, Java, Indonesia	37,143,719
23	Guangzhou Baiyun International Airport	Huadu District, Guangzhou, Guangdong, China	37,048,712
24	Charlotte Douglas International Airport	Charlotte, North Carolina, United States	34,536,666
25	Miami International Airport	Miami-Dade County, Florida, United States	33,886,025
26	Leonardo da Vinci Airport	Fiumicino, Rome, Italy	33,723,213
27	Orlando International Airport	Orlando, Florida, United States	33,693,649
28	Sydney Airport	Sydney, New South Wales, Australia	33,451,383

(Continued)

Table 9.1 (Continued)

Rank	Airport	Location	Passengers
29	Newark Liberty International Airport	Newark, New Jersey, United States	33,399,207
30	Munich Airport	Munich, Bavaria, Germany	32,681,067
31	London Gatwick Airport	Crawley, West Sussex, England, United Kingdom	32,398,979
32	Minneapolis-Saint Paul International Airport	Fort Snelling, Minnesota, United States	32,378,599
33	Narita International Airport	Narita, Chiba, Japan	32,135,191
34	Shanghai Pudong International Airport	Pudong, Shanghai, China	32,102,549
35	Detroit Metropolitan Wayne County Airport	Detroit, Michigan, United States	31,357,388
36	Seattle-Tacoma International Airport	Seattle, Washington, United States	31,227,512
37	Philadelphia International Airport	Philadelphia, Pennsylvania, United States	30,669,564
38	Toronto Pearson International Airport	Mississauga, Ontario, Canada	30,368,339
39	Atatürk International Airport	Yesilköy, Istanbul, Turkey	29,854,119
40	Kuala Lumpur International Airport	Sepang, Selangor, Malaysia	29,682,093
41	Seoul Incheon International Airport	Incheon, Republic of Korea	28,677,161
42	Barcelona Airport	Barcelona, Catalonia, Spain	27,301,662
43	Logan International Airport	Boston, Massachusetts, United States	25,512,086
44	Indira Gandhi International Airport	Delhi, India	25,252,814
45	Melbourne Airport	Melbourne, Victoria, Australia	25,248,762
46	Paris-Orly Airport	Orly, France	25,107,693
47	Shanghai Hongqiao International Airport	Changning District, Shanghai, China	25,078,548
48	ChhatrapatiShivaji International Airport	Mumbai, Maharashtra, India	24,804,766
49	Shenzhen Bao'an International Airport	Bao'an District, Shenzhen, Guangdong, China	24,486,406
50	Mexico City International Airport	Mexico City, Mexico	24,243,056
		Total	1,952,054,368

Source: Airports Council International

Table 9.2 World's busiest airports by cargo traffic

Rank	Airport	Location	Total cargo (metric tonnes)
1	Memphis International Airport	Memphis Tennessee, United States	3,697,054
2	Hong Kong International Airport	Chek Lap Kok, Hong Kong, China	3,385,313
3	Shanghai Pudong International Airport	Pudong, Shanghai, China	2,543,394
4	Incheon International Airport	Incheon, South Korea	2,313,001

Rank	Airport	Location	Total cargo (metric tonnes)
5	Paris Charles de Gaulle Airport	Roissy-en-France, Val d'Oise, Île-de-France, France	2,054,515
6	Ted Stevens Achorage Airport	Anchorage Alasak, United States	1,994,629
7	Louisville International	Lousiville Kentucky, United States	1,949,528
8	Dubai International Airport	Garhoud, Dubai, United Arab Emirates	1,927,520
9	Frankfurt Airport	Flughafen (Frankfurt am Main), Frankfurt, Hessen, Germany	1,887,686
10	Narita International Airport	Narita, Chiba, Japan	1,851,972
11	Singapore Changi Airport	Changi, East Region, Singapore	1,660,724
12	Miami International Airport	Miami-Dade County, Florida, United States	1,557,401
13	Los Angeles International Airport	Los Angeles, California, United States	1,509,326
14	Beijing Capital International Airport	Chaoyang, Beijing, China	1,475,649
15	Taiwan TaoyuanIntrnational Airport	Dayuan, Taoyuan, Taiwan, Republic of China	1,358,304
16	London Heathrow Airport	Hillingdon, Greater London, England, United Kingdom	1,349,571
17	Amsterdam Airport Schiphol	Haarlemmermeer, North Holland, Netherlands	1,317,120
18	John F. Kennedy International Airport	Queens, New York City, New York, United States	1,144,894
19	O'Hare International Airport	Chicago, Illinois, United States	1,047,917
20	Suvarnabhumi Airport	RachaThewa, Bang Phli, SamutPrakan, Bangkok, Thailand	1,045,194
21	Guangzhou Baiyun International Airport	Huadu District, Guangzhou, Guangdong, China	955,270
22	Indianapolis International Airport	Indianapolis Indiana, United States	944,805
23	Newark Liberty International Airport	Newark, New Jersey, United States	779,642
24	Tokyo International Airport	Ōta, Tokyo, Japan	779,118
25	Luxemborg-Findel Airport	Fibdel, SandweilerLuxemborg	628,667
26	Kansai international Airport	Izumisano/Sennan/Tajiri Osaka, japan	608,876
27	Shenzhen Bao'an International Airport	Bao'an District, Shenzhen, Guangdong, China	605,469
28	Kuala Lumpour International Airport	Sepang, Selangor, Malaysia	601,620
29	Dallas-Fort Worth International Airport	Dallas/Fort Worth, Texas, United States	578,906
30	ChhatrapatiShivaji International Airport	Mumbai, Maharashtra, India	566,368
		Total	44,119,453

Source: Airports Council International

third party. Third, the chapter examines how different factors can affect terminal design and integration particularly at multiple terminal airports such as London Heathrow, Los Angeles, Chicago O'Hare, Toronto Pearson International and Madrid's Barajas Airport. These factors include dominant home carriers, liberalization of international air service agreements, dominant carrier network design and membership in airline alliances and policies with respect to IT.

AIRPORT GOVERNANCE AND REGULATION: EVOLUTION OVER THE LAST THREE DECADES

In the majority of developed countries around the world, airport ownership, governance and regulation have undergone significant change. Governments have pursued new airport policies, sometimes in conjunction with aviation system reform as in the EU. The shift that occurred across many countries had several common sources. Air traffic was growing at rapid rates and airports needed to invest in capacity. There was a general rethinking of the role government should play in the economy, and airports were considered a place where the private sector could legitimately provide the needed service and investment. The deregulated airline sector was showing significant improvements in productivity and product innovation and many argued that this could be and should be extended to the airport sector. There was a newfound recognition of the relationship between ownership structure, governance and economic performance.

The forces of reform have, for several reasons, been slow to deal with airports. The move to private ownership has been slower than in other industries. In many cases, governments have opted for partial rather than full privatization. In North America, even though there is a long tradition of privately owned utilities and transport industries, there has been a reluctance to move away from public or local ownership of airports. Canada, for example, chose the 'not-for-profit' governance model rather than privatization. The move towards full privatization has been strongest in the UK and later Australia and New Zealand, both countries which formerly relied on the UK model of public enterprise, and which followed the UK with extensive privatization programs. In continental Europe there has been a preference for partial privatization, with the public sector remaining with majority ownership in many cases.

If one differentiates between the degree and mode of the shift of airports out of public ownership, there are at least seven possible ownership/governance structures:

- Government owned/operated (US, Spain, Singapore, Finland, Sweden)
- Government owned, privately operated (US (via contracts), Chile, Hamilton – Canada)
- Independent not-for-profit corporations (Canada)
- Fully private for-profit via IPO (Initial Public Offering) with stock widely held (originally BAA (the British Airport Authority))
- Fully private for-profit via trade sale with share ownership tightly held (Australia, New Zealand)
- Partially private for-profit with private controlling interest (Denmark, Austria, Switzerland)
- Partially private for-profit with government controlling interest (Hamburg, France, China, Japan (Kansai)).

Government-owned/operated airports

The general goal of government-owned and operated airports is to focus on the primary function of the airport and to suppress other sources of commercial value. Often, government-run airports have non-commercial objectives that have included the protection of national carriers or promotion of economic activities and development, with less of a long-term focus with respect to infrastructure investments. For such airports, investments are likely to compete with other government priorities and often there is an observed lack of consistency between aviation policy and the efficient use of airport assets. Airports can also be used for economic and development objectives; many regional airports would fit this class even in places in Europe.

Government owned, privately operated

In the US, (almost all) airports are government owned (locally) but effectively privately operated, with a high degree of contracting out.[1] US airports benefit from Federal grants and interest-free bonds when investment is required, yet they typically exhibit a lack of investment in aeronautical infrastructure, albeit in many cases due to local land use restrictions, zoning laws and political pressure from vocal interest groups. US airports also exhibit some airline participation in the ownership of terminal buildings. The top 50 airports in the US show a significant interest in developing non-aeronautical commercial value, but beyond this there is a high degree of variability across airports (reflecting local government willingness to extend airport operations beyond the primary function).

The US model, particularly of Port Authorities (for example, Port Authorities include New York & New Jersey, Seattle and Boston), has become deep-rooted because of long-term leases signed between airports and airlines giving them in many cases exclusive control of entire terminals or concourses and the right to approve or veto capital spending plans. This type of arrangement made the 'signatory airlines' joint ventures with the airport. For taking this risk, the incumbent airlines were able to control airport expansion and to some degree the ability of competitors to enter some markets.

Independent not-for-profit corporations

This structure is the current regime in Canada, arising from a gradual devolution from government operation that began in the mid-1990s. Canadian airport authorities operate their airports under a 60-year lease agreement (which is extendable), after which time the land and assets revert to the federal government. As not-for-profit entities, Canadian airports have not been subject to direct regulation (of aeronautical charges). There has been a significant amount of infrastructure investment at Canadian airports over the last ten years. However, the types and levels of investment have been subject to some debate concerning the possibility of 'gold plating': extravagant or unnecessary investment that leads to higher charges for airlines and passengers. Canadian airports exhibit varying degrees of focus on complementary non-aviation activities but all of the larger airports utilize passenger facility charges (usually bundled into airfare prices) to help finance investments. An ongoing issue in Canada is the payment of 'ground rent' by airports to the Federal government, which under the current regime amounts to 12 percent of gross revenues for any airport with annual revenues over $250m Cdn. Airports and airlines have argued that the form and level of rent payments had led to inflated aeronautical charges. The Canadian model of airport governance has not been duplicated anywhere else in the world.

Fully private for-profit via IPO

Fully privatized airports have shown both a strong market orientation and a strong customer focus. The BAA, which is currently majority owned by Ferrovial of Spain, is the oldest example of airport privatization implemented via an IPO. BAA, which includes London Heathrow (LHR) and Stansted (STN) plus two airports in Scotland, has exhibited a strong orientation towards complementary retail business and non-complementary business on and off airport land. This is perhaps explained in part by the form of price regulation applied to these airports: a 'single-till' price-cap, under which revenue from all sources (aeronautical and non-aeronautical) is used in deciding how much aeronautical prices can increase. This has led to low (non-market) aeronautical prices at LHR. It has also led to a reduction in service quality and an underinvestment in some assets, mostly terminals.

While these airports have shown a willingness to develop markets and make strategic investments, there is also evidence that links between management and the government have remained strong and that political decision-making plays a direct role in augmenting private commercial interests (for example, the private demand for an additional runway at LHR and the public decision to instead support an additional runway at STN). A recent competition commission report recommended the divestiture of the three main London airports into separate entities, and in December 2009 BAA owner Ferrovial sold Gatwick to Global Infrastructure Partners (who also bought Edinburgh Airport from BAA in 2012).

Fully private for-profit via trade sale

In Australia, airports under Federal ownership were corporatized in the 1980s – which meant that the airports had a more commercial focus, were expected to achieve cost recovery as a group (though there were cross subsidies from large to smaller airports), and their accounts were publicly available. Smaller airports were owned either by the Federal or local governments, and in the 1980s the federal government transferred ownership of smaller airports to local governments.

Airports in Australia were privatized beginning in 1996–97. Brisbane, Melbourne and Perth were privatized first. Sydney airport was privatized in 2002. Airports have been sold to private interests via trade sales in which investment consortia bid to purchase the airports. These consortia typically have included airport management companies and/or infrastructure investment companies (along with pension funds). In Australia, airports were sold under a lease agreement of 50 years plus an automatic extension of 49 years, after which the airports revert to the federal government. Like UK airports, Australian airports have exhibited a strong market focus, but unlike their UK counterparts Australian investors seem to have taken a more long-term investment perspective immediately following the sale and have, according to some, a more unified strategic view of how the airport should develop.

The main three New Zealand airports, Auckland, Wellington and Christchurch, were corporatized in the late 1980s. New Zealand followed a similar model to Australia but governments did have some share ownership; government shareholdings in Auckland and Wellington were sold in part in the late 1990s and the airports now have majority private ownership, with only Auckland being publicly listed. Christchurch remains owned by the local government. After an attempt by the Ontario Teachers' Pension Fund to purchase majority ownership in 2008, the New Zealand Government placed restrictions on who could purchase shares and the amount any one shareholder could hold.

Partially private for-profit with government controlling interest

Athens, Rome and Hamburg are all examples of airports that are for-profit entities where private investors are limited to a minority interest; others include Belfast, Brussels, Budapest, Copenhagen, Dusseldorf and Frankfurt and airports in Argentina, Chile, Colombia and Mexico. Interestingly, the existence of a for-profit (commercial) objective and minority private interest has in general been viewed by the stakeholders as enough to cause a fundamental change in management attitude and orientation towards developing commercial value. It appears that even though government remains the majority shareholder, these airports are able to make decisions and develop strategies that a government-run airport would not. This includes air route development and retail development. (For example, Hamburg Airport reported 20 new routes in 2007 and opened a 7,000 m^2 retail plaza in 2008. It has also had a significant increase in the number of carriers serving the airport including low-cost and charter carriers.) In some cases such airports have pursued strategic investments with carriers and have sought to maximize the relative contribution of non-aviation revenues. The degree and intrusiveness of government intervention via regulation and oversight remains a potential issue.

Partially private for-profit with private controlling interest

Copenhagen airport is an example of an airport that has become a for-profit company with the majority share held by a single private investor (Macquarie Airports). This form of governance has, like those airports with minority private ownership, been successful in bringing a more entrepreneurial and commercial orientation to airport operations and strategy. One potential effect of this form of privatization is the possibility of raising more private capital (investors willing to pay more for a controlling interest) and also the possibility of a more coherent long-term investment orientation. For 'hands-on' investors like Macquarie Airports, majority ownership appears to be a minimum condition for their involvement; however, there may be little *de facto* difference between minority and majority ownership. The reason for this is that governments through regulation and oversight can exert significant influence and constraint on the development of commercial value, whether or not there is a majority ownership.[2] Consequently, in the realm of partial privatization a lot may depend on jurisdiction-dependent government regulations, oversight, larger objectives and transparency in airport management-government relations.

Airport regulation: options and experience from various countries

An airport has two obvious sides to its business: the airside market (passenger airlines and cargo companies as direct customers, and fixed base operators as tenants) and the non-airside market (enplaning and deplaning passengers as direct customers, retail businesses as tenants, and landside tenants). Each side gives rise to a multitude of outputs with peak and off-peak periods in both markets. However, revenues are generally bundled as airside (monies from fees and charges to airlines for runway, apron and terminal use) and non-aviation (monies from retail and commercial activity including land leases).

The perception that airports are monopolies and will exploit their monopoly power has figured into the regulation of charges that airports can levy. This includes charges for airside activities such as landing and passenger terminal fees but also fees for non-aviation activities.[3] The form that this regulation has taken varies from country to country. Essentially there are four types of price regulation: *single-till price regulation* takes the form of a price-cap applied to all revenues deriving from the airport on all commercial activities. Price regulation is by way of a price-cap using the RPI-X formula and the regulatory review periods vary between three to five years.[4] With single-till price regulation, carriers share part of the airports' commercial revenues by paying lower aeronautical charges. *Dual-till price regulation* separates aeronautical functions from non-aeronautical ones. The regulator determines the level of allowed average aeronautical charges by considering aeronautical revenues and costs only. Consequently, the corresponding asset base includes aeronautical assets only. *Rate-of-return* regulation benchmarks the profitability of regulated activities to the average obtained from reference airports or businesses. It sets an allowed return on a defined asset base. *Price monitoring* is currently implemented in Australia and New Zealand. The regulators use a trigger or 'grim strategy' regulation where a light-handed form of regulation is used until the subject firm sets prices or earns profits or reduces quality beyond some point, and thus triggers a long-term commitment to intruding regulation (see Gillen (2011) for a description of potential changes in New Zealand).

The essence of the debate of single versus dual till is the impact it has on airport economic efficiency. The relative merits of dual versus single till essentially rest on two issues. First, do airports have (and exercise) market power in both aviation and non-aviation sectors, and second what represents a 'fair' distribution of the rents? There is significant debate regarding the first question.

The major argument for not including non-aviation revenues under a single till is that they result in perverse incentives when airports are capacity constrained and they may create costs when airports have lots of capacity. When airports are capacity constrained and a single till is in place, as more revenue is made on the non-aeronautical side, aeronautical charges must be lowered to remain under the price-cap. Thus, in the presence of congestion, prices are reduced when economic efficiency dictates that they should be raised. If profit-maximizing airports are not capacity constrained, they have every incentive to stimulate demand (and revenue) via lower prices on the aeronautical side. Thus, in the non-constrained case, single-till price-cap regulation is not necessary. Indeed, in the US, airports voluntarily enter into contracts with airlines to share rents if the signatory airlines agree to share the risks of costs exceeding revenues. There is no regulation requiring this type of agreement. There is the often-cited condition that US airports should not make profits, but that is not the case. Airports must use any revenues in excess of expenses to improve the airport; these funds cannot be diverted to non-airport use.

At an airport without capacity constraints, the incentive is for the airport to lower charges on the airside, due to demand complementarities with non-airside business. Even here the airlines obtain the rents since they do not pass the lower airside fees on to passengers in the form of lower prices, unless the market is highly competitive. This airside pricing is efficient because the marginal cost associated with excess capacity is likely to be below average cost and consequently the efficient outcome is to promote the use of airside capital. Therefore, non-airside rents are used to promote more efficient use of airside capacity. If there are demand side complementarities, the airport would set fees on the airside such that the marginal revenue from an additional operation, which would include both airside and non-airside revenue, is equal to marginal cost. In other words they would fully internalize the externality.

While the comparison of single- and dual-till forms of price-cap regulation favors dual till, there is a strong argument to be made for no price-cap regulation. This is because the implementation of a single regulatory regime will have divergent efficiency and distributional effects across the system given the heterogeneous characteristics (congestion, location-based market power, degree of airline competition) of airports.

In addition, there are two cost-side effects of regulation. First, the determination of allowed capital investment in the rate base distorts incentives for capital, as airports will strategically engage in over-investment. Second, once the regulatory rule is in place, airports have an incentive to minimize costs if the target allowable revenue level is reached. Thus, we would expect over-investment in some infrastructure (gold plating) in order to influence the price-cap and then reductions in operation costs (lowering of service quality) in order to maximize realized profits. In the case of larger national airports in the Canadian system, the airport authorities are formally treated as 'not-for-profit' entities under the corporation act, so that any profits must be reinvested. The resulting incentive structure therefore exacerbates the gold plating problem.

Finally, what is not often considered in the debate on airport regulation is that airports can directly contribute to the degree of airline competition through pricing and capital investment decisions. Therefore policy makers should not only consider the welfare effects of airport regulation in relation to airports and their customers, but also the associated welfare effects on airline competition that result from airport pricing and investment decisions under the various regulatory regimes; for a full discussion of this issue see Zhang and Zhang (2006) and Basso and Zhang (2007).

Aside from efficiency considerations, distributional concerns remain as to which parties will capture the rents arising from geographic location and scarcity of supply. Location rents are essential to allocate limited space efficiently. Currently, at capacity constrained airports, airlines holding property rights to peak-demand slots capture all the rents that could be shared with or allocated to the airport. Under a single-till price-cap, where the tendency is for aeronautical charges to fall, airlines will actually obtain some of the airport's location rents as well. The airlines might argue that they are responsible for generating the non-airside rents and therefore are as deserving of them as the airport. But it is the airport that undertakes the investments and contracts and therefore takes the risk.

Airport regulation in the US

US airport regulation is essentially a cost-of-service form of regulation. This type of regulation is relatively intrusive as the regulator must approve every price change and, in some cases, service decision. While the US has no formal regulator, airports must justify with the carriers and their political masters that airport fees are cost-based. One could also argue that those airports that still adhere to the principles of residual financing behave as if they operate under a single-till form of price-cap regulation.[5] The important difference in the US is that sharing of revenues is voluntary, albeit under governance that requires break-even; the airports are required to set aeronautical fees so as to collect revenues that reflect the costs of providing the service. Thus individual prices are indirectly regulated in the sense that the aggregate of revenues cannot exceed costs. This, however, does not imply cost minimization.

The US form of indirect regulation provides for neither static nor dynamic efficiency; static efficiency is not achieved since fees reflect accounting rather than economic costs. Any excess demands are rationed through a quantity method such as flow control, whereby either flights within a given time or distance from the constrained airport are not allowed to depart until a slot is available for them or arriving aircraft are stacked up waiting their turn to land. Dynamic efficiency refers to innovation in both improved processes and product development. It also ensures that the incumbent airlines appropriate the majority of rents at capacity constrained airports due to slot ownership and fare premiums. Dynamic efficiency is frustrated since there are no price signals that reveal the value of added capacity. Any excess demand reflects a failure to price scarce resources appropriately and the rent due to slots accrues to the carriers that hold the slots. They show up in the form of hub premiums.

Airport regulation in the EU

In the EU, rate-of-return or price-cap regulation is the norm. The best examples are the UK (which regulates the BAA), France, Denmark and Ireland. With rate-of-return regulation (ROR) the key questions are first what constitutes a 'fair' return on capital invested and second, what capital invested should be included in the 'allowed rate base'? This form of regulation is very time-intensive and generally involves lengthy regulatory hearings. As Tretheway (2001) points out, ROR regulation tends to be complex, unresponsive and expensive to administer.

Price-cap regulation, by far the dominant form of regulation in the UK, on the other hand was introduced precisely to overcome the problems associated with rate-of-return regulation. It was designed to lower the overall costs of regulation and to provide the incentives for firms to act in a way that improves economic welfare. Given the information asymmetry between the regulator and the regulated firm, one of the key objectives is to incentivize the firm to reveal its true costs by allowing the firm to keep efficiency gains within the price control period. The next period's prices are adjusted for inflation and the X-factor.

Pure and hybrid price-caps differ in the way in which the X in the price-cap formula is set. A pure price-cap sets X without reference to the costs of the regulated airport but may set it with reference to a broad airport benchmarked cost, while hybrid price-caps set the X with reference to a regulated cost base. Hybrid price-caps provide fewer incentives for cost reductions. For European airports none of the regulators have developed a pure price-capping system. The price-caps at Aéroports de Paris (ADP), Copenhagen and Dublin are based on costs.

At some EU airports, predominantly in Germany, we also observe revenue sharing agreements which often relate the level of charges to the passenger growth over a certain period. The model is that the airline and the airport agree that airside charges will be reduced if the rate of passenger growth is achieved or maintained at some agreed upon level. At two German airports, Frankfurt and Düsseldorf, the revenue sharing agreements are the result of Memorandum of Understanding between the airports and its users. This agreement was legalized as a public contract between the airport and regulator (Klenk, 2004). In case of disagreement the charges would be fixed according to cost-based regulations. These so-called sliding scales can be combined with price-cap regulation as in the case of Hamburg (Gillen and Niemeier, 2008) and Vienna. At Frankfurt airport, for example, both parties agreed that with a projected passenger growth rate of 4 percent, average charges could be increased by 2 percent since 4 percent was deemed to be below the desired target. In the case of a higher growth rate, airlines participate with a 33 percent share in additional revenues. With lower growth rates the airport cannot fully compensate revenue losses through higher charges. Only 33 percent of the loss can be compensated. The agreement results in a sliding scale of airport charges that is related to passenger growth.

Recent new directions for airport regulation in the EU

A proposal on airport charges was approved by the European Parliament on October 23, 2008 and sent to the European Council. It was approved on February 11, 2009. The objective of the Directive is to establish a general framework setting common principles for the levying of airport charges. The Directive imposes new obligations on many airports regarding transparency, consultation, non-discrimination and arbitration, and it opens up a new avenue for airlines to pursue their grievances. This move by the EU sustains its view that airports have market power and will use it. This continental European view differs from what we see in Australia, New Zealand and even the US.

Airport regulation in Australia and New Zealand

Australia and New Zealand have what has been termed 'light-handed' regulation, something unique to these two countries. The major airports in both countries have been privatized since the mid-1990s with the exception of Sydney which was privatized in 2002. With this change in ownership and governance, formal regulation was put in place in Australia and airports were subjected to a price-cap of the RPI-X form. These caps were in place for five years, at which time there would be a review (Forsyth, 2002). It was expected that price-caps would probably be continued. The caps were set by the government and they were administered by the Australian Competition and Consumer Commission (ACCC). In both Australia and New Zealand it was a dual-till system.

In 2001, the Australian Productivity Commission released a report which recommended the end of price-cap regulation for all airports. This move was stimulated in part by the tight control of prices under the price-cap while the airline industry faced turmoil. The result was a poor financial performance for airports. Price-cap regulation seemed to be workable in strong economic conditions but was not flexible with economic downturns and weak airline performance. In 2002, the government announced that it would replace regulation with monitoring for seven major capital city airports, and would not regulate or monitor other airports, a move from formal dual-till price-cap regulation to 'light-handed' regulation. This regulatory form places no immediate constraints on aeronautical charges but monitors prices with a view to 'taking action' if prices are judged to be too high. After its first five years in operation, price monitoring was reviewed in 2007 and renewed for another five years (with some adjustments). Local/municipal relations (land development) and the valuation of airport land and assets (for determining aeronautical charges) have been issues under this system.

New Zealand did not formally regulate its airports after privatization, though it did provide for a review of airport pricing behaviour with the threat of more explicit regulation should this behaviour be unacceptable. The New Zealand approach involved a general provision set out in legislation to enable a review of pricing in industries such as airports. This review could be initiated by the Minister at any time. In 1998, a review of pricing at Auckland, Christchurch and Wellington airports was initiated. The Commerce Commission undertook the review and recommended price regulation of Auckland airport (NZ Commerce Commission, 2002).

A Commerce Act review was undertaken in 2007. The government recommended that Auckland, Wellington and Christchurch (all international airports) be subject to much more stringent, hands-on, price monitoring and even regulation and that it be administered by the New Zealand Commerce Commission. These recommendations have not yet been introduced with legislative changes.

Forsyth (2006) provides an assessment of the light-handed regulatory approach. He notes that it works reasonably well, with prices somewhat above what might be the case under tight regulation but well below monopoly levels. Also, airports seem to be relatively cost efficient, probably because increasing profits from increased efficiency is unlikely to draw the ire of 'light-handed' regulators. In effect the regulator seems willing to allow airports that are efficient to keep some of the gains obtained from being cost efficient. A heavy-handed regulator might have reduced prices so all the cost efficiency gains were passed on to the airline. There are problems with investment incentives as well as with the 'process' of light-handed regulation because it does not provide guidelines by which to judge or sanction the performance of the airports. Forsyth (2006) stresses that cost-based guidelines would result in inefficient cost-plus regulation. Better to establish first the objectives of regulation and then set in place a set of guidelines that provide incentives for efficiency.

Other airport regulatory models

Canada's lack of formal airport regulation stems from the form of governance that resulted when the Federal government devolved the airports beginning in the mid-1990s. The Federal government did not want airports to be privatized mostly because of the lack of worldwide experience with the fully privatized airport model at that time. It was also concerned that the use of revenue bonds by airports to invest in capacity can have a deleterious impact on downstream airline competition. The reason is that airlines provide the bond guarantees and this in turn gives the airlines some power over capacity investment. The Canadian government chose a not-for-profit model which seemed to address all of the concerns the government had in adopting the new airports policy. The policy was evolutionary in starting with four airports (Vancouver, Edmonton, Calgary and Montreal) and subsequently including the remaining Tier 1 airports; Tier 1 airports are those included in the National Airport System.

Fees and charges under the Airport Authority legislation were not regulated or subject to review. Airport Authorities were free to set charges where they wanted and could impose different types of charges as they wished. Because they were established as non-share capital entities they could not go to the capital market for funds for investments. Therefore, all airport authorities levy an airport improvement fee (AIF) as a source of funds for capital investments. The nature of the Canadian model led to a lack of price regulation; first, the not-for-profit model meant all monies must be reinvested and second the lack of access to the broader capital market to fund needed investments meant there was a need for the AIF. Any constraints on the airports' ability to set these fees as needed could potentially jeopardize investments in capacity.

There is relatively little work which has assessed airport regulation in China. A recent study by Zhang and Yen (2007) indicates that seven airports in China have been privatized and are listed on the Chinese stock exchange. These airports include Xiamen, Shanghai, Shenzhen, Beijing, Hainan and Guangzhou – in which Shanghai International Airport Ltd holds both Hongqiao and Pudong airports. They point out that the fundamental role of the IPOs was to improve airport efficiency, not necessarily to raise capital. Market discipline was to be introduced. The evidence was that cost efficiency was low. The economic performance of airports in China is challenged from two opposing forces. Growth in the aviation sector is larger than any other aviation market in the world and more capacity is needed quickly. Therefore cost efficiency is not a priority. On the other hand, the ownership and governance structure of airports are being shifted to more local control, and although the state has influence, local concerns for efficiency place pressure on the airport.

TERMINAL OWNERSHIP AND GATE ALLOCATION

The conventional model of airport governance structure is the airside (runway, taxiway, apron and parking) and terminal assets are owned by one entity. This is in part a holdover from the period when governments built, owned and managed airports but it is also a reflection of a management belief by some that the joint relationship between terminal and airside assets requires single ownership and management. The most common model is certainly single ownership but ownership by airlines and third parties is also evident in some countries. In Australia up until the mid-1990s the airport owned the airside assets but each airline owned and operated its own terminal. Similarly in the US there are numerous examples of airlines owning their own terminals, such as United and American airlines in Chicago, American in Dallas Fort Worth and Delta in Atlanta. It is also possible that an airline could take out a lease, generally long term, for control and operation of a terminal. In some cases government-owned airlines would be given management control over a terminal and could undertake leasehold improvements to suit their business model and network strategy. This was common in Europe with its numerous state-owned carriers including Air France at Charles de Gaulle, Lufthansa at Frankfurt and Iberia in Madrid, but also in Canada with Air Canada (Toronto) and in Asia; Singapore Airlines, Thai Airlines and Japan Airlines in Tokyo, for example. One case of third-party ownership was the building of Terminal 3 in Toronto, Canada at Pearson Airport; the terminal opened in 1991. The Terminal was designed and built by private investors who also managed the terminal. However, under the National Airports Policy, Pearson Airport was transferred into a Local Airport Authority in 1996 and was renamed Greater Toronto Airports Authority (GTAA). Terminal 3 was purchased from the private developers a few years after the GTAA was formed.

Presently there are a variety of terminal ownership/management arrangements across the world. The most important drivers of these arrangements include the move to full or semi privatization of airport infrastructure, the increased liberalization of aviation markets domestically and an increased trend in liberalization in air service agreements which govern international aviation, evolving business models for airlines including network architecture and the evolution of the airport from a public utility to a modern business and enjoying increased non-aviation revenues.

In Europe Lufthansa has a 9.9 percent equity stake in Fraport, the firm which owns and operates Frankfurt Airport. Lufthansa also partnered with Munich Airport to build a second terminal, which is exclusive to Lufthansa and Star Alliance flights. In Singapore and UAE the major airline and prime airport are under common ownership. But joint ownership is not required for airports to work closely with current or former national carriers; this is evident in Netherlands between Schiphol and KLM, in France with Air France and Charles de Gaulle, in Spain between Iberia and Madrid Barajas Airport. In the United States, still the largest aviation market in the world, there are still examples of airlines owning and managing their own terminals such as at Chicago O'Hare Airport and American at Dallas Forth-Worth Airport. There is also the case of British Airways owning and managing Terminal 7 at JFK Airport in New York. However, the more common arrangement is for the airport to own and manage the terminals and provide gate access to airlines under differing contractual conditions.

Gate management and terminal management are linked and the motivation for airlines to control gates is twofold. First, they are able to better coordinate connecting flights and manage schedules and second they are able to foreclose entry to other carriers and additional flights; the first motivation is more important with those carriers that operate a hub and spoke network. With the evolution of the 'airport business', airport managers/owners recognized that non-aviation revenue was a growing and important revenue stream that needed to be developed. They also recognized that they could manage their traffic by marketing their airport and drawing in new carriers and broadening the array of destinations accessible from their airport. A key to developing this strategy was to have control of aircraft bridges and gates; the mechanisms that connected the aircraft to the terminal. Traditionally gates were classified as exclusive use gates which are reserved for a specific carrier (or set of carriers), managed gates which are allocated by the airport on some established basis for a specified length of time and common use gates which anyone can use and are generally allocated by the airport on a short-term basis. Modern airport managers want to control as much of their capital as possible and bridges and gates are not only an important direct revenue source, they are an important component in managing and building passenger traffic at the terminal.

Terminal ownership by an airline is more or less important depending on the airline's business model and route network strategy. After domestic deregulation the hub and spoke system became the dominant form of network structure for the legacy airlines such as United, American, Delta, Northwest, British Airways, Lufthansa, Japan Airlines, Qantas and numerous others. This network strategy had one or more primary hubs and multiple spoke airports and routes would pass passengers through the hub. Such a strategy requires banks of flights arriving from the numerous spoke airports, exchanging passengers and departing. The airport operates with peaking traffic and requires numerous gates and gate allocations that facilitate the passenger and baggage exchange. Owning a terminal allows the airline better control but it may also be that the carrier becomes so large that it dominates the entire airport not just a terminal; for example, Northwest, Delta and Lufthansa.

A second type of airline business model is the low-cost carrier (LCC), or value-based airline; examples include Southwest, Jet Blue, Air Tran, Ryanair, easyJet, WestJet, Virgin Blue, Air Berlin, Whizz and Air-Asia to name a few of many. The LCC has a simple homogeneous product, generally single aircraft type, simple pricing and relatively simple point-to-point network; most or all points served will be connected with one another. With this type of network and business model a simple terminal is all that is required, to keep costs low in keeping with the business strategy and ownership is not an asset. At some airports LCC terminals have been developed; examples include Copenhagen, Schiphol (Amsterdam), Luton (London), Tegel (Berlin),

Frankfurt-Hahn, Changi (Singapore), Kuala-Lumpur (Malaysia). Airports in many cases are transforming to reflect the new economic realities and the increasing demand for low-cost travel. Airlines have responded to this need with the LCC business model and now airports are adapting their business models to accommodate both airlines and budget travelers by building dedicated 'budget' terminals to support the growth of new LCC air services.

Cargo terminals

Cargo, although growing in importance, is still relatively small in comparison to passenger activity. Four important features of air cargo are: approximately 90 percent moves in the hold of passenger aircraft; cargo terminals are generally owned and/or operated by third parties; there are two distinguishable types of air cargo, integrator and general freight; and air cargo markets are governed by the same types of economic regulations that govern passenger markets. The largest air cargo airlines are the integrated couriers FedEx and UPS, while airlines such as Korean Air, Japan Airlines, Lufthansa, Singapore and Cathay Pacific have large dedicated cargo aircraft and operations. For the integrated courier carriers their business strategy requires they have transfer hubs and dedicated terminals for sorting and resorting packages; FedEx at Memphis, UPS at Louisville, for example. Air cargo is stored, sorted, delivered and distributed from terminals and warehouses quite separate from passenger terminals. There are numerous reasons for this including safety and security, the need for trucks to access such terminals and the surrounding access highways and roads, needs for sorting and warehousing the cargo and in some cases treating sensitive cargo such as fresh seafood and flowers. It would also have cargo in bond, areas for animals that are transported and possibly foreign-trade-zones. Modern cargo facilities such as found at Hong Kong Chep Lap Kok Airport, Changi airport in Singapore, Shanghai Pudong International Airport and Paris Charles de Gaulle Airport are sophisticated, highly computerized and will generally adopt newer technologies before the passenger sector. An additional factor is the evolution of logistics and distribution systems where warehouses can be located directly on an airport and orders received can be processed quickly with an overnight or one day delivery.

The fact that the majority of air cargo moves in the belly of passenger aircraft means that freight offloaded from a passenger aircraft must be moved from one area of the airport to another. In Frankfurt, for example, the air cargo terminals are on the opposite side of the field from the passenger terminals and this means all cargo transported in the belly hold of the passenger aircraft must be moved across the airport. This creates costs and complexity in both design as well as management of such transfers.

FACTORS AFFECTING TERMINAL DESIGN AND INTEGRATION

The majority of the world's airports have not changed much if at all since the early 1980s; there are approximately 44,000 airports worldwide with somewhat just over 15,000 in the US. The world transformed to jet aviation in the late 1950s with the introduction of the DC-8 and Boeing 707, both four-engine jet aircraft. This type of aircraft grew as a proportion of the aircraft fleets and this meant runways had to be lengthened. With the introduction of the Boeing 747 in 1970, pressure was placed on expanding and redesigning terminals, gates and bridges. In North America, Europe and Australia and New Zealand, airports have changed for the most part in the number and/or size of terminals, relatively few new runways have been built; a new airport was built in Denver and opened in 1995. In the US and Europe a number of former military bases have been converted to civilian use and are served by scheduled commercial passenger and cargo airlines. New airports are being built in the Middle East and Asia; Thailand, Malaysia, China (several) and Pakistan, for example. There are a number

Table 9.3 Measures of forecast growth in air traffic and aircraft fleet

Growth measures	Asia-Pacific	China	Oceania (Australasia)	North America	Europe	Middle East	Latin America	Africa	C.I.S.	World
GDP growth rate	4.6	7.3	2.7	2.7	1.9	4	4	4.4	3.3	3.2
Traffic growth rate	6.8	7.6	6	3.4	4.4	7.1	6.9	5.5	4.8	5.3
Cargo growth rate	6.8	7.4	6.2	5	5	6.8	6.7	6.1	5.7	5.9
Fleet growth rate	5.6	6.2	4	1.6	2.8	4.8	4.6	2.7	0.6	3.3
Ratio RPK/ GDP growth	1.5	1.1	2.2	1.3	2.3	1.8	1.7	1.3	1.5	1.7
Aircraft fleet size in 2009	4,110	1,570	420	6,590	4,300	950	1,130	660	1,150	18,890
Aircraft fleet size in 2029	12,200	5,180	920	9,000	7,460	2,440	2,770	1,130	1,300	36,300
% Change in fleet	197%	230%	119%	37%	73%	157%	145%	71%	13%	92%

Source: Boeing market outlook

of forces that are driving this growth of terminal expansion in relatively mature aviation markets and wholesale new airports in emerging aviation markets. Table 9.3 provides the forecasts for expected traffic market growth for different regions of the world for the next 20 years. The growth numbers are staggering in some regions but for our interest this traffic growth manifests itself in a huge growth in aircraft fleets; the number of aircraft flying in the world are expected to almost double in the next 20 years. All of these aircraft have to operate to and from airports.

Economic growth and growth of economies

Economic growth is the major driver of aviation activity. Examine a trend growth of revenue passenger kilometers and there is a steady trend up with some minor dips for the energy crises in 1974 and 1978, the Gulf War in early 1990, the attack on New York in 2001 and SARS in 2003. Not all markets are affected equally by these events and markets recover; even the 20 percent decline in passenger traffic in 2009 with the financial crises had been recovered by the end of 2010. Three important forces were at work to accelerate the growth of aviation activity. First, the removal of barriers to trade and the resultant growth in international trade with globalization has stimulated traffic growth particularly in the Asia Pacific markets. Second, the growth of the high technology sector and an increase in trade in services have both been important in growing passenger and freight traffic in most markets. Third has been the growth in international tourism.

Airline business models and alliances

A second force that has driven growth in aviation traffic has been the new airline business models and the evolution of strategic alliances that encompass a majority of the larger scheduled carriers. The development of the low-cost carrier business model was made possible by domestic airline deregulation. The development of the LCC model was important in three respects. First, it lowered prices to serve a segment of the market, which had not been served previously so the aggregate market grew. Second, it put downward pressure on fares generally and traditional legacy airlines were forced to lower their fares as well, and third, it put pressure on legacy carriers to lower their costs that tended to preserve the lower fares. All of this led to a rapid expansion of the market both in terms of making existing markets larger to some degree but more importantly expanding the number of markets served. Ryanair carries more passengers than any other European airline and Southwest carries more passengers than any carrier in the United States.

An important feature of LCC carriers is they tend to serve secondary airports. This is for two reasons. First, the costs are lower and this is consistent with their business model, and second, it reduces head-to-head competition with other major carriers. LCCs have begun in every developed and many developing nations and are responsible for the bulk of the growth in passenger traffic.

Airline alliances first emerged in early 1990s. The underlying forces were the need to circumvent restrictive air service agreements that prevented carriers from serving 'before' and 'beyond' gateway traffic. A passenger flying from Madison Wisconsin to Hamburg Germany would have to fly to an airport with international flights like Dulles Airport in Washington, DC and fly to Frankfurt Germany where they would transfer to a German airline to complete the journey to Hamburg. Strategic alliances were agreements between carriers whereby the passenger could travel from origin to destination in a seamless way. The alliances generally sought anti-trust exemption that meant the carriers involved could discuss pricing, capacity and service levels to better coordinate activities. Despite having some negative features of reducing market competition, the alliances have generated net traffic growth through lower fares and access to a broader range of destinations. There are presently three large alliances: Star Alliance, One World and Sky Team.

Alliances place different pressures on airports since the hub airport(s) of the legacy carriers will also be gateway airports and will become international transfer hubs. Hubbing activity will now involve not one airline but many airlines belonging to the alliance. Alliances have a preference to be collected in one terminal or one sector of a terminal to facilitate passenger transfer. Baggage systems will also have to be designed to facilitate transfer of bags between member carriers.

Aviation liberalization

The growth in traffic resulting from economic growth and the emergence of LCCs would not have been possible without aviation liberalization, with its removal of constraints of pricing, route entry, capacity choice and frequency choice. Airline economic deregulation began in 1978 in the US. Once it became clear what significant economic benefits flowed from this policy change most other developed economies followed suit by deregulating their domestic aviation markets. Now most countries, both developed and developing, have deregulated or substantially liberalized their domestic markets. This has resulted in significant growth in passenger and freight traffic, opening up of many new routes, the expansion of networks to join cities that previously were not connected by air and provided a boon to economic development as service frequencies meant aviation became an effective business tool. This traffic growth meant airports now were facing pressures to expand their runway and terminal capacity and redesign their systems to handle the inflow of passengers. These systems included baggage, check-in, gates and bridges, aircraft parking, apron mobility and aircraft servicing such as fuel and catering.

Liberalization of international aviation markets has been much slower than domestic deregulation. International aviation routes, entry, pricing freedoms and capacity and frequency choice are governed by air service agreements (ASA). Countries negotiate these

ASAs, generally on a bilateral basis but more recently multilateral agreements are becoming more widespread and in the last decade open skies agreements have been introduced. The US, for example, has 92 open skies agreements signed and this provides American travelers or travelers using American carriers with a broad range of competitive services and a high level of connectivity. Included is an open skies agreement with the EU.

There has been a number of liberal regional 'air trade agreements' which have open skies features. Canada signed its first open skies agreement with the US in 1995 and this agreement was re-negotiated and broadened, made even more open, in 2005. Australia and New Zealand have also a liberal accord particularly across the Tasman. The EU has taken additional steps that focus on liberalization within the European Economic Area, although individual member States and the EU have also concluded aviation agreements with countries outside the EU. The emergence of an internal European Community air transport market represented a major achievement in creating a liberal regional market for air services. The three packages of reform introduced over a decade from the mid-1980s gradually removed impediments to the free provision of transport services within the EU. An airline substantially owned and effectively controlled by citizens of a country within the European Economic Area (EEA) can now establish itself anywhere within the EEA and can offer services, including cabotage, within the area. There are no tariff controls (except in exceptional circumstances) and there is a gradual movement to liberalize and introduce effective competition in ancillary services.[6]

In 2008 the EU and US signed an open skies (first stage) agreement which provided significant liberalization for air services and included the entire EEA. In this first stage both the commercial agreement as well as the legal framework for cooperation had to be negotiated. In their second stage the details become stickier and the legal issues thornier: night flight bans in the EU, symmetric traffic rights, foreign ownership and control, US homeland security, EU-style slot coordination and so on. Rising marginal costs and declining incremental benefits are likely to be the outcome.

There are also other, more recent harbingers of freer trade areas in air services such as the MALIAT agreement, signed in 2001, and includes the US, Chile, Singapore, New-Zealand, Brunei, Samoa and Tonga.[7] This development is less extensive than the EU Single Market in air services, but it represents movement forward. The Yamoussoukro Decision reached in July 2000 at the Organization of African Unity meeting in Togo and the 2004 Association of Southeast Asian Nations (ASEAN) roadmap to permit unlimited services between all ten member countries by target dates are also encouraging initial moves towards liberalizing air transport.

Airports as modern businesses

Doganis (1992) used this term to portray the shift that was beginning in the late 1980s with the sale of British Airport Authority in a stock tendering and signaled a change in perspective, attitude and business strategy. The evolution is discussed thoroughly earlier in this chapter. What needs to be explained are the consequences of an institutional shift to create governance structures, which have airports thinking and acting as modern businesses including marketing departments, something unheard of in the 'public utility' days of airports. Regardless of whether the airport is for-profit or not, the modern airport has an incentive to think and act as a modern firm in any industry. Airports receive revenue from many sources and have many customer segments including airlines, passengers, retail suppliers, third-party firms located on the airport (for example, aircraft service firms) to name a few. Airports compete for airline services, new carriers and new routes and seek to have airlines establish a base at their airport. Airports have to market themselves to all of their customer groups.

Table 9.4 Non-aviation revenue proportions, 2009

Region	Percent non-aviation revenue in total
Asia/Pacific	49.6
Europe	47
Caribbean/Latin America	28
North America	53
Total	48.7

Source: Airports Council International

The most recent strategic shift for airports is the focus on non-aviation, primarily retail, revenue as a large and increasing dominant source of revenue. Table 9.4 shows for 2009 the proportion, an average across airports, of the percentage of revenue from non-aviation; it is near 50 percent across regions and it is growing. Airports have transformed themselves and have become a destination of sorts; for example, Dubai (UAE) and Changi (Singapore). Terminal design now must handle significant amounts of retail space and decisions about what and how much retail to place before and after security can vary from market to market. The development of retail strategies has led to a wholesale design change for the interior of terminals particularly in the management of traffic flow from check-in through to security and through to boarding hold areas and gates. This has changed the 'airport experience' and the retail strategy is a component of competitive strategies between long haul connecting hubs such as Schiphol, London Heathrow, Charles de Gaulle and Frankfurt in Europe, Singapore, Hong Kong and Shanghai in Southeast Asia and Vancouver, Seattle, San Francisco on the west coast of North America.

Airports must be cost efficient for competitive reasons and to ensure access to capital. They must undertake investments, which are expensive, long lived and sunk. Unlike an airline an airport's capital is immobile and it therefore faces high risks from airline exit but also from economic downturns and even technological change; for example, fuel-efficient long haul aircraft can fly non-stop between international destinations. Airports have been pursuing different strategies to get and keep their costs down and others trade-off service quality and capacity decisions for lower costs. Many US airports contract out a majority of their work and have relatively few employees; Altlanta, one of the busiest airports in the world, has fewer than 800 airport employees, while Fraport which owns and runs Frankfurt Airport has 50,000 or more employees.

Costs will vary with traffic but also with being hub, handling international traffic, number of terminals, range of airlines serving the airport, proportion of air cargo handled, but also factor prices including land and labour.

CONCLUSION

This chapter has provided a discussion of the forces that shape the design and use of passenger and cargo terminals at airports. When scheduled aviation was in its infancy in the 1920s, airports had few if any terminal buildings and those that were built housed administrative and airline staff. This is a long way from the recent terminals we see in Madrid Barajas Airport, Nagoya Airport (Japan), Toronto Pearson International (Canada), Hong Kong Chep Lap Kok or Beijing Capital International Airport. The most significant change that has occurred has been the shift in governance structure and regulation. This has brought about a significant shift on the strategies pursued by the airport and has shifted the airport from a public utility to a modern business. The change in governance has taken a variety of forms across the world with the share of public ownership varying from 0 to 100 percent.

The chapter also examined the case of airline-terminal ownership and multiple terminals at an airport and why one might observe this; certainly there are numerous cases of each not just across the world but even within the same domestic market as the

US and EU provide examples. Finally, the chapter examined external or exogenous forces that influence airport operations, traffic and management and hence terminal operations. These factors include dominant home carriers, liberalization of international air service agreements, dominant carrier network design and membership in airline alliances and policies with respect to IT.

One important force that is operating and might be considered endogenous is that of airport management themselves. The shift in attitude and approach to running airports and towards a customer service focus was important in pushing for the institutional and governance changes to allow airport management/owners to pursue their own strategies. The airport as a modern business means the organizational structure will not differ dramatically from firms in other industries. There will be a relative shift away from operations towards customer service so engineers will give way to business people who will develop business strategies. In the past airports had a supply-side focus while today operations becomes a tactic used to pursue a strategic direction.

NOTES

1 Midway Airport in Chicago was going to be the only US airport to be privatized and would have been an important experiment to possibly shape future US airport governance. In October 2008, Chicago City Council had approved a 99-year lease to a consortium of companies led by YVR Aviation Services. However, the consortium was not able to obtain financing to fulfill the lease contract. The airport remains in public hands with plans to re-open the bidding for a long-term lease once access to capital funds improves.

2 That being said, Macquarie Airports has divested all airports in which they held minority shares.

3 Airside fees would include landing, terminal, security and emergency/policing fees. Commercial fees are those negotiated for concession and lease agreements.

4 In the RPI-X formula RPI is the retail price index and 'X' is the limiting offset. The value of X is determined by the regulator based on a range of criteria including, for example, whether the industry is high or low productivity, the performance of the firm in the previous regulated period and whether the regulator wishes to incentivize the firm to reduce costs.

5 Residual financing means that at the end of the fiscal year if revenues are less than costs the signatory airlines using the airport are responsible for covering the difference.

6 Having said this, there are what are termed Schengen and non-Schengen countries in the EU. Under the Schengen agreement people and cargo can pass between Schengen countries with no border controls. Of the EU members the UK, Ireland, Romania and Bulgaria are non-Schengen countries. Thus a flight from London, UK to Amsterdam, Netherlands is classified as an international flight.

7 The key features of the Multilateral Agreement are: an open route schedule; open traffic rights including seventh freedom cargo services; open capacity; airline investment provisions which focus on effective control and principal place of business, but protect against flag of convenience carriers; multiple airline designation; third-country code-sharing; and a minimal tariff filing regime.

REFERENCES

Airports Council International (2010) Fact Sheet: Airport Traffic Reports (http://www.aci-na.org/content/airport-traffic-reports).

Basso, L.J. and Zhang, A. (2007) Congestible Facility Rivalry in Vertical Structures, *Journal of Urban Economics* 61, 218–237.

Doganis, Rigas (1992) *The Airport Business*, Routledge, UK.

Forsyth, Peter (2002) Privatization and Regulation of Australian and New Zealand Airports, *Journal of Air Transport Management* 8, 19–28.

Forsyth, Peter (2006) Airport Policy in Australia and New Zealand: Privatization, LightHanded Regulation and Performance, in Clifford Winston and Gines de Rus (eds), *Aviation Infrastructure Performance: A Study in Comparative Political Economy*, Brookings Institution, Washington, DC.

Gillen, David (2011) The Evolution of Airport Ownership and Governance, *Journal of Air Transport Management* 17(1): 3–11.

Gillen, David and Niemeier, Hans Martin (2008) The European Union: The Evolution of Privatization, Regulation and Slot Reform, in Clifford Winston and Gines de Rus (eds), *Aviation Infrastructure Performance: A Study in Comparative Political Economy*, Brookings Institution, Washington, DC.

Klenk, Michael (2004) New Approaches in Airline-Airport relations: The Charges Framework of Frankfurt Airport, in Peter Forsyth, David Gillen, Andreas Knorr, Otto Mayer, Hans Martin Niemeier and David Starkie (eds), *The Economic Regulation of Airports: Recent Developments in Australasia, North America and Europe*, Ashgate Publishers, Aldershot, UK.

New Zealand Commerce Commission (2002) *Final Report: Part IV Inquiry into Airfield Services at Auckland, Wellington and Christchurch International Airports*, NZ Commerce Commission.

Tretheway, Michael (2001) *Airport Ownership, Management & Price Regulation*, submission to the Canada Transportation Act Review Committee.

Zhang, Anming and Yen, Andrew (2007) Airport Policy and Performance in Mainland China, in Clifford Winston and Gines de Rus (eds), *Aviation Infrastructure Performance: A Study in Comparative Political Economy*, Brookings Institution, Washington, DC.

Zhang, Anming and Zhang, Yimin (2006) Airport Capacity and Congestion When Carriers Have Market Power, *Journal of Urban Economics* 60, 229–247.

10

Freight Distribution Centres, Freight Clusters and Logistic Parks

Markus Hesse

INTRODUCTION

The recent transformation of value creation in manufacturing, wholesale and retail and the associated logistics changes have triggered the establishment of new facilities dedicated to the management of freight flows, particularly for the storage, transshipment and consolidation of consignments. As a consequence of the integrated management of supply chains, distribution centres (DCs) and logistics parks have emerged. DCs have not necessarily replaced the traditional warehouse, but they now represent key components of the newly established, increasingly globalized logistics networks and supply chains. Due to their size and their functional requirements, DCs and particularly freight clusters are no longer exclusively placed at core mainport locales (in seaports, close to airports) or within urban areas, following the distribution of population, but have moved towards the more distant hinterland. They have thus contributed to re-arranging the geography of freight distribution significantly.

This chapter presents an overview of distribution centres and freight clusters or logistics parks, by reconstructing the rationale of their development, presenting their main characteristics and discussing their significance both for the logistics system and concerning their geographical environment. The subject matter is twofold: whereas the term DC is used for introducing newly established *single* facilities for the handling of commodities (including related corporate services), the term freight cluster represents commercial areas as the *assemblage* of several DCs, combined with particular infrastructures and the provision of services for a certain number of customers. Different from operating single DCs, which are subject to corporate decision making, commercial areas hosting logistics parks or freight clusters have often been supported or established by urban planning and public policy, in order to make freight operations more efficient and also more acceptable from an environmental point of view. Consequently, this chapter not only focuses on issues such as form, function or transport requirements of DCs and freight clusters; it also emphasizes the broader territorial distribution of freight facilities, problems of urban and regional integration and related challenges for policy and planning. In empirical terms, the chapter mainly focuses on developments taking place in Europe and North America. Given that warehousing, wholesale and freight handling have for long been essentially urban activities which are now being increasingly de-centralized, the chapter finally raises some theoretical questions on the nature of such changes and their consequences for cities and urban regions.

THE RATIONALE FOR THE EMERGENCE OF DISTRIBUTION CENTRES AND LOGISTICS PARKS

Changing markets, technological innovation, driving competition

The recent development of logistics and physical distribution is an outcome of a broad set of economic structural changes and the related corporate strategies. Among these, sectoral shifts including the rise of service economies, the introduction of new information and communication technologies and the emergence of global trade and global production networks are considered most important. These changing framework conditions have triggered a fundamental re-organization of production and distribution of commodities and services, respectively, bringing about an emerging network of global flows and hubs that depend upon efficiently working transport systems and infrastructures (Waters, 2010).

The key term in the analysis and interpretation of modern logistics is supply chain management (SCM): the comprehensive management of value-added processes and interactions including all components and activities that are dedicated to the manufacturing, processing, marketing and finally consumption of commodities (cf. Gattorna, 1990: 8). Different from earlier versions of logistics management, SCM is understood as an integrated approach, in which logistics management and freight distribution are closely interwoven. Initially, the two segments of materials supply and physical distribution had become integrated (Bowersox et al., 1968). Later on, they became part of a broader logistics concept of the firm and the related networks (Handfield and Nichols, 1999). The increasing degree of logistics integration provided by SCM was only possible through the invention and application of the new information and communication technologies. Implementing the principle of flow permitted the reduction of inventories in time-sensitive manufacturing activities and cost-sensitive wholesale and retail operations. Economies of scale were now applied to the whole supply chain, particularly to the function of distribution. Yet applying economies of scale in distribution was also associated with an increasing degree of spatial fragmentation: the more integrated the supply chain became, the more disintegrated were the related activities developing across space and time.

The demand for a new type of facility for goods handling

The changes in market environments and market behaviour as mentioned here have triggered the emergence of a new type of facility: the distribution centre (DC). This happened for different reasons. First, speaking quantitatively, the growth of logistics services in general spurred the demand for more distribution space. Since manufacturing and retail firms have been consolidating or even outsourcing their warehousing activities, additional capacity was required to accommodate growth and consolidation effects. Second, in more qualitative terms, is logistics companies' demand for buffer and organization space, according to the greater magnitude and complexity of freight flows and with respect to the increasing flexibility which customers demand. Third, even supply chain management that is primarily based on electronic front-end operations requires physical infrastructure and distribution. DCs have been invented primarily in retail and wholesale, not only in the core logistics industries. Based on UK data, in 2007 almost 60 per cent of the newly established DCs (> 10,000 m^2) were operated by retail chains, while logistics firms and manufacturers shared the rest, varying between 10 and 20 per cent (McKinnon, 2009: S295).

The new possibilities offered by digital information systems allow for overcoming the traditional barriers between manufacturer, wholesaler, shipper and retailer, with multiple storage, limited information flow and common delays accumulated as inventories in warehouses. Electronic data exchange has enabled the sharing of data among trading partners and thus dramatically improved the ability to predict demand and to manage the chain. Since supply and demand for commodities still tend to fluctuate and are hard to predict, buffers have switched from fixed inventory to information management. As a result, firms are not only able to eliminate costly parts of supply chain organization, but also to reduce inventory and thus avoid capital costs. As the new technologies support the continual movement of products in the supply chain, the need to stack inventory begins to diminish. Consequently, the demand for traditional storage has shrunk significantly. Instead, the timely delivery of consignments in the exact quantity and quality to the point of sale or to the facility where they are being provided for delivery to the customer becomes essential.

Accordingly, the concentration of warehousing and logistics services in one unit instead of several brings about facilities that are increasingly designed as a flow- or throughput-oriented DC, instead of a warehouse holding large, expensive inventories: "The process of centralisation is now at an advanced stage, with many warehousing operations now concentrated at a single location or in premises that have reached their maximum economic size" (McKinnon, 2009: S295). This allows for the utilization of economies of scale and thus contributes to making the business more profitable. Consequently, logistics networks became re-designed and the question of location was reframed. However, once logistics functions are concentrated in selected facilities at strategic

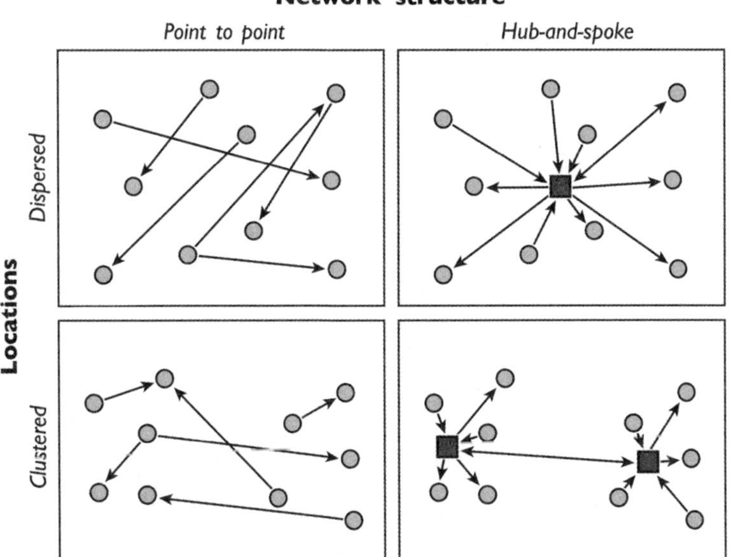

Figure 10.1 Logistics network patterns
Source: Hesse and Rodrigue, 2009

locations, this does not mean that national or regional distribution centres totally vanish. Depending on specific functional needs and modes of organization (e.g. density of customers, traffic conditions), a multi-tier distribution system with regional, national or international DCs may still be required, for instance in the case of cold chain logistics. Distribution is now increasingly planned and operated on the basis of largely stretched networks. Economies of scale in the network configuration lead to a shift towards larger DCs, often serving significant transnational catchments. When the number of facilities for handling goods is decreasing, distribution areas will expand, as a result of the coarsely meshed logistic networks and due to the internationalization of commodity flows (De Ligt and Wever, 1998). The structure of networks has also adapted to fulfil the requirements of an integrated freight transport demand. This includes both direct networks that mainly comprise point-to-point deliveries as well as hub-and-spoke-networks that comprise different hierarchies of connection (Figure 10.1).

CHARACTERISTICS OF DISTRIBUTION CENTRES AND LOGISTICS PARKS

Distribution centres

Referring to a classical definition, a DC represents a "physical facility used to complete the process of product line adjustment in the exchange channel. Primary emphasis is placed upon product flow in contrast to storage" (Bowersox et al., 1968: 246). The basic functions provided in a modern DC comprise receiving, pick operations, storage, value-added activities, shipping, return processing and the associated information management (Strauss-Wieder, 2001: 10). More specifically, one can distinguish between DCs mainly devoted to *turnover* and those primarily designed for *storage*; some DCs may offer both, thus representing a hybrid. Major differences result from specific product requirements of the commodities to be moved and handled, such as pallets/less-than-truckload units, bulk freight, containers, refrigerated goods, etc.

Within the warehouse category, industrial real estate usually identifies five different types: regional, bulk, heavy distribution, refrigerated and rack-supported warehouse (Belmonte, 2004). Distinct from warehousing is the freight forwarding DC, consisting of truck terminals or air cargo. These two types also host the most important function of a DC: the consolidation of incoming freight and its immediate shipping to final destination. This particularly applies to the case of "cross-docking", when incoming consignments will be offloaded, stored on a flat surface and then re-loaded after consolidation. Facilities that are designed to fulfil the "need for speed" resulting from specific market demands are also labelled as *High Throughput Buildings*. Storage is practised with respect to those commodity groups that either will be delivered including delays or that require further processing. The same applies to the newly established fulfilment-centres operated by e-commerce firms (Lasserre, 2004). Most businesses need to keep a certain inventory in-stock, in order to ensure fast delivery times, and like parcel services they use conveyor-belts for the internal movement of items. Depending on throughput volumes and customer density, these firms also use satellite terminals and subordinate warehouses, in order to guarantee high service qualities close to customers. Added value created in a DC is being pursued in post-production/pre-distribution processes, including assembly and customization (labelling, assortment), packaging, ticketing or product return and repair, also reverse logistics. Such activities also take place in so-called "flex-buildings", a hybrid of office, tech/light manufacturing, R&D and distribution uses.

The size of DCs varies considerably. It particularly depends on factors such as throughput volumes, network composition and size of the market area to be served by the DC (Hatton, 1990). With the trend towards concentrated supply-chain functions and thus

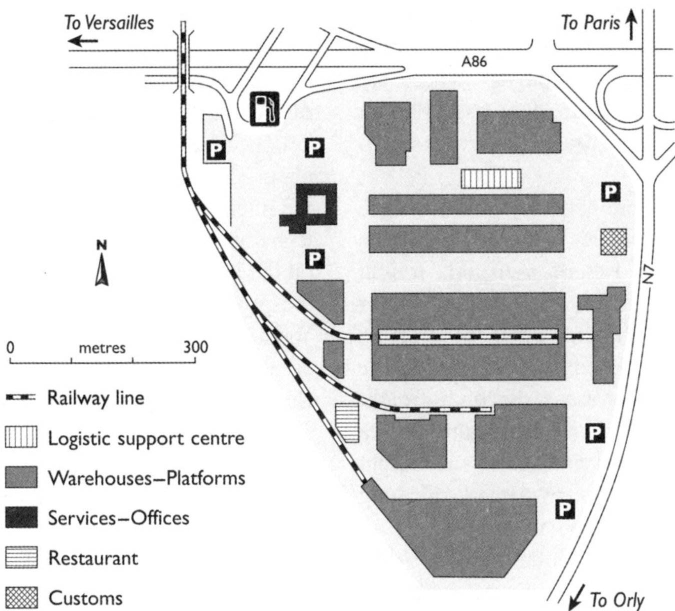

Figure 10.2 Typical layout and internal design of a DC
Source: author's own, adapted from Sogaris

to operating a limited number of DCs, the average size of a facility is steadily increasing, simply following the law of economies of scale. Regional DCs normally have a size of 10,000 m^2, sometimes up to 20,000 m^2. Nationally oriented facilities are likely to exceed that by far. Large-scale DCs can easily achieve a magnitude of 50,000 to 75,000 m^2 or even more. Major North American retail chains such as Wal-Mart or Safeway operate big DCs much beyond the 100,000 m^2-threshold, for serving goods distribution to stores in multiple states. In such case a DC may employ about 1,500 people, and both functional requirements (e.g. traffic accessibility) and the impact on the DC's neighbourhood and environment are significant. In terms of vertical reach, most DCs have in common that they are built out as a single-story facility with a minimum height of 7–8 metres and 10–12 metres maximum. The more important goods turnover in a DC is, the higher is the number of loading docks provided. In order to ensure a high ratio of dock doors to floor area, some DCs obtain a typical U-formed layout. Avoiding columns within the DC or warehouse, providing superflat floors that allow for automated vehicle operations and lighting standards that support energy savings have also become quite common recently (Figure 10.2).

Freight centres and logistics parks

Freight centres, logistics parks or clusters represent specialized commercial areas that resemble agglomerations of DCs, not only including buildings of warehousing, wholesale and freight forwarding firms, but also joint infrastructures for the transshipment of consignments and the transloading of units such as containers. In some cases, they also provide third-party services for vehicle maintenance and repair, gas stations and tyre sales (as offered by truck stops) or even restaurants and hotels. They expand the advantages of single DCs through external economies of agglomeration, implying that the concentration of DCs within the cluster bears the potential to reduce costs substantially.

Some European freight centres are organized as so-called *Europlatforms*, understanding themselves as "freight villages". These are freight centres coordinated by a public or private agent and that are open for all companies involved.

Freight centres are currently built for three reasons: first, they provide large, well-accessible sites for locating freight transport, freight forwarding and warehousing firms, and offer proper operating conditions without affecting sensitive neighbourhoods which is often the case in inner-urban areas. Second, freight centres are supposed to contribute to the transshipment of road haulage to rail freight and waterway operators, particularly for long distance transport, hence multimodal infrastructure is supplied in many cases. Also, concentrating firms allows for bundling freight flows for the final goods supply into denser urban space. The related transport on the "last mile" could thus be done in a more acceptable, sustainable manner, with smaller delivery vans instead of heavy vehicles. Initially, freight centres were also supposed to provide the framework for interfirm co-operation which was considered essential for such "city-logistics". Third, DC-agglomerations coined as "freight clusters" are increasingly conceived as relevant for regional economic development. By locating different firms of the same sector close to each other, certain agglomeration benefits are expected to further mobilize economic impacts such as network building, innovation or job creation.

The size of the freight centres varies as that of DCs does, mainly depending on customers' demand, space available and local framework conditions. Small and medium-sized logistics parks comprise areas of about 20–50 hectares, the bigger ones easily reaching the three-digits scale. Sogaris, the French developer of logistics and warehousing space, operates a freight centre in Rungis, just 7 kilometres south of Paris, with a gross size of about 120 hectares. Sogaris is also developing a new logistics hub on a former military site in Luxembourg-Bettembourg, of about 20 hectares. The *Güterverkehrszentrum* (GVZ) in Bremen, northern Germany, comprises a gross area of about 200 hectares, hosts about 150 firms employing about 8,000 people; the GVZ south of Berlin, Germany, covers an area of about 260 hectares (gross), hosting 55 firms with about 3,650 employees. The *Raritan Center* at the Interstate I-95 in New Jersey (USA) seems to be among the largest planned freight zone on the US East Coast, with a size of 950 hectares, hosting 3,000 tenants which employ about 15,000 people. Not only in such extreme cases, locational requirements are always critical, since freight operations generate a significant amount of lorry traffic which requires sufficient road transport capacity. Freight centres also tend to be problematic in terms of the associated emissions generated by vehicle operations (e.g. air pollution of particulates, carbon dioxide etc.). The sensitivity of urban neigbourhoods against noise emissions generated by heavy goods vehicles is another factor that makes these facilities extremely difficult to be placed in core urban areas.

Intermodality is key to the idea of freight centres, and logically there are many overlaps between the concept of the freight centre or logistics park and that of inland ports (Leitner and Harrison, 2001). In most cases inland ports are staffed with intermodal infrastructure, particularly for connecting the emerging distribution complexes in the hinterland of mainports with rail and barge and also to provide the associated handling infrastructure (Tioga Group, 2006). The provision of intermodality is often critical though, judging from the cost perspective, and realization usually depends on government support and subsidies. This tends to be regular practice at least in Europe, and since the 1990s it may have become more common in the US as well. However, major infrastructure investments will only be efficient once there are a minimum number of customers available, and the freight village or inland port is devoted to ensure a critical mass of potential users on-site.

Freight centres or clusters can be further distinguished depending on the sectors represented by major tenants, particularly regarding wholesale and retail trade on the one hand and transport and logistics on the other hand, although these differences are not indicative concerning the demand for space or traffic generation. Freight centres were also established for quite different reasons, in particular for providing industrial space or for enhancing intermodality. Finally, an important question points to the issue of firm collaboration: do freight centres consist of networks, or do they enable better networking? Concerning the degree of functional integration and interrelation of firms in a freight village, Notteboom and Rodrigue (2009) has distinguished between *logistics zones* as loosely associated firms at the same place, *logistics clusters* staffed with intermodal terminals and fully fledged *logistics poles* that are characterized by strong linkages among the related corporations. An associated term in the French realm is *plate-form logistique multimodal* (Pochet et al., 2000). However, recent discourse in economic geography would probably suggest the term "cluster" to be most appropriate in characterizing a particular set of proximate corporate interrelations. Speaking in more general terms, and independent from labelling, there is some evidence that it is extremely difficult to strategically design and implement DC clusters or freight centres based on industrial linkages provided on-site (cf. on clusters Martin and Sunley, 2003; on logistics industry linkages McCalla et al., 2001). In fact it has become very popular to create added value just by grouping firms of the same sector (or of different sectors, but similar markets) at a given locale, calling this a "logistics cluster" or "logistics region". This, however, often mirrors conventional policy wisdom, rather than clear empirical evidence.

EMPIRICAL EVIDENCE FROM EUROPE AND NORTH AMERICA

Distribution centres and logistics parks in Europe and North America

The setting of large distribution centres, often part of freight centres or clusters, has been a dominant tendency both in Europe and in North America. Against the background of an underlying pressure towards functional concentration and spatial de-concentration, recent trends on both continents are characterized by increasing locational mobility and shifting centres of gravity. When presenting the big picture of locational trends and territorial distribution, it has to be noted that official data revealing these dynamics are scarce, particularly in Europe, where national statistical systems are highly variegated. Due to the lack of specified (four- or five-digit) statistical sources, developments at the macro level can only be described on the basis of real estate market reports and selected research studies on particular regions.

Europe has witnessed rapid changes in logistics and distribution over the last decades, with DCs and freight centres mushrooming in core countries such as Benelux, France, Germany and the UK (Cushman and Wakefield, 2009; JonesLangLaSalle, 2008). McKinnon (2009: S294) notes that warehouse floorspace in the UK has grown between 1998 and 2004 at an average rate of 2.5 per cent, with 40 to 50 new DCs being built each year between 1996 and 2008, the average size doubling from about 10,000 to 20,000 m^2 (ibid.). In addition to the aforementioned changing market conditions and corporate strategies, the European case is quite specific due to significant geopolitical changes, namely the fall of the Wall in 1989, the emergence of the common European market in 1992 and the Eastern enlargement of the EU in 2004. It is also notable that freight markets became deregulated much later than in the US or in the UK, which triggered a certain push on this sector since the 1990s. One immediate consequence of the logistics restructuring is the emergence of "European Distribution Centres (EDC)" – large DCs that are being used for consolidating regional or national warehouses into pan-European centres.

By offering access to a significant part of the European marketplace, core Europe is the preferred location for placing EDCs – most notably Belgium, the Netherlands and north-eastern France. In all these countries national and regional centres have become under pressure as distributors aim at large-scale consolidation. The Netherlands is famous for being most attractive for European logistics, due to excellent accessibility, advanced terminal and transport infrastructure, critical mass of logistics functions and a good business climate. Schiphol Airport and the Port of Rotterdam are among the most important hubs for international freight flows in Europe; accordingly, these regions are densely packed with DCs and freight parks. Based on port regionalization processes towards hinterland areas, the Dutch/German-border region has been the focus of most recent DC-investments. Major population concentrations are also well represented, in particular the Paris, London, Ruhr and Frankfurt regions (Frankfurt being Europe's largest air cargo hub); yet the high degree of urbanization, congestion and high land rent levels in these regions may limit future growth. Flanders in northern Belgium and the Nord-Pas de Calais in northern France also score highly, Flanders particularly due to the Port of Antwerp. The port hosts the largest concentration of warehousing and distribution space in continental Europe, but is also affected by gateway extension into the more remote hinterland. France has been strongly developing as a result of improved connectivity between the British Isles and the continent via the Channel Tunnel. In response, UK distributors have been increasingly in favour of northwest Europe or even more distant locations for placing their DCs (McKinnon, 2009, S297). Following the enlargement of the EU, Germany became geographically central, attracting new DCs mostly at the periphery of large conurbations such as Berlin, Hannover, the eastern Ruhr area, eastern Munich, or the region around Frankfurt/Main airport. A traditional trajectory also reveals the strong position of the port cities of Hamburg and Bremen at the North Sea coast.

In the United States warehousing and storage employment grew between 1998 and 2005 by 383 per cent, being the highest growth rate among all transport subsections, and the number of establishments with more than 250 employees had jumped from 26 total in 1998 to 520 total in 2005, at an average annual growth rate of 52.5 per cent (Bowen, 2008: 363). Bowen investigated goods transportation and distribution locations in the US and the related links to accessibility. He found out that whereas distribution firms still favour metropolitan regions overall, recent growth has definitely taken place at outer suburban and ex-urban areas, with highest growth rates prevalent in non-core city areas of metro regions. Regarding the US situation, Cidell (2010) measured the regional performance of distribution industries between the mid-1980s and the mid-2000s. She identified similar trends compared to Bowen's study, yet emphasizes also deviations from a picture that would simply focus on sub- and ex-urban areas. Her study revealed a number of cases where also core counties encompassed significant growth in the number of warehousing and distribution establishments.

The spatial pattern of this industry's transformation reveals concentration along inland ports emerging in the Midwest, the Pacific Northwest and the Piedmont regions of the East Coast stretching from New Jersey to Alabama (Cidell, 2010). Against the background of a strong correlation between the distribution of population and the number of freight establishments (and given that highway access is almost ubiquitous in US metro areas), railway accessibility turns out to be one important factor in explaining warehousing distribution patterns per capita. Also, a certain Midwest-shift of the industry is related to lower salary levels compared to metros at the East and West coasts, explaining the strong performance of cities such as Memphis (the global hub of the express-distributor Federal Express) or Oklahoma City. The role of Chicago as a prime railway hub and traditional inland gateway city stands out in any regard among the metro areas studied (Cidell, 2010: 367). One of the largest complexes of DCs, freight clusters and new inland hubs has emerged along the Ohio River Valley in the US Midwest, stretching from Ohio and Indiana to Kentucky and Tennessee. Freight forwarders, courier, express and parcel services and also e-commerce providers have been gravitating there and established large, centralized distribution facilities. Industrial real estate markets of cities such as Columbus, Ohio, Indianapolis, Indiana, or Louisville in Kentucky, which hosts the global air freight hub of UPS, have been developing extraordinarily (Belmonte, 2004: 67).

Territorial dynamics: towards a new geography of distribution

This section summarizes the locational trends associated with the emergence of inland DCs that can be observed in Europe and North America. The introduction of integrated supply chain management, the increasing locational mobility of logistics businesses, the related establishment of DCs and the resulting spatial distribution of freight and logistics activities has changed significantly. The places where the new DCs and logistics parks have been built are no longer urban agglomerations from which the customers could be served and where a majority of customers live, but increasingly sub- and ex-urban areas. It is indicative that the once strong attachment of the distribution system to central places of settlement and market areas had already begun fading out in post-war times, as Chinitz (1960) had already observed in the case of the suburbanization of wholesale establishments, warehouses and terminals in the greater New York City/New Jersey area. The more recent technological and organizational changes in supply chain management have transformed location systems further (Waters, 2010). The related sites were no longer functions of production (the place of manufacturing) or consumption (the locale of retail trade), but were placed according to the intrinsic network logic of distribution itself, emphasizing factors such as multiple network hierarchies, intermediate locations, complex routing algorithms, economies of scale (due to the enlarged service areas) etc.

Integrated SCM thus tends to put location decisions in a new context, not only following factors such as time, distance and related costs, but subject to the overall imperative of mobility and accessibility. However, due to the emerging notion of flow, distribution firms and freight centres necessarily locate at those places that offer excellent transport conditions. In the first instance, such locales are commercial and industrial areas with good motorway access, a consequence not only of the door-to-door service level provided by the lorry, but also of almost ubiquitous infrastructure supply and the deregulation of the road transport industry. Moreover, those places come into play that are close to intermodal infrastructure of the rail, barge and air cargo transport modes, particularly in the vicinity of mainports, responding to global trade growth. This trend might be reinforced with the ongoing movement of inland port facilities towards the hinterland of major mainports.

Given the concentration effect that is inherent to DCs and their extraordinary demand for space, cheap land is essential for placing the increasingly large facilities. The same is true for transport access, in light of the high amount of lorry traffic generated by DCs. Such factors seem to be essential at the micro-economic level (Hesse, 2004), both regarding the *turnover* and the *stock-keeping* type of DC, and this applies even more to freight centres or clusters. Consequently, these particular considerations are being taken into account once a site for a DC or a freight centre is sought, against the background of logistics network composition and the size of the markets that have to be served (Daskin and Owen, 1999). Trade-offs between inventory and transport costs are carefully balanced yet essentially clear: locations remote from customers offer cheap land but

Table 10.1 Locational change of placing goods handling in urban areas

	Function	Location	Examples
The city as a marketplace	Traditional place of goods exchange (the city as a location for regional distribution)	Historical urban centres; temporary use of areas for warehousing and transshipment	Marketplaces, traditional locations for urban retail, warehouses
Port cities, inland-port cities	Traditional place of goods exchange (the city as a location for long-distance distribution)	Traditionally at shorelines, large inland waterways, intersections of distant trade-routes	Ports and port-infrastructures, storage buildings, warehouses, magazines
Rail freight terminals	Development of new transshipment points according to the industrial urbanization	Main stations and their backyards, close to the urban core, e.g. in "zones of transition"	Rail terminals and railyards, until recently in all major cities with railway access
Wholesale, freight forwarding	Suburbanization of distribution functions out of the core city (first outward drift)	Urban peripheric locations, close to highway intersections	Transportation intensive land uses (commercial, industrial areas)
"New" centres of distribution at the urban periphery	Spatial anchor or magnet of modern logistics and distribution networks (second outward drift)	Areas at motorway intersections with cheap land and workforce, close to the customers' area (urban markets)	Shopping malls, "big box" commercial areas, industrial DCs and warehouses, almost ubiquitious
Large-scale distribution of/for retail, wholesale, warehousing	Decoupling of distribution from the urban market place (counter-urbanization related drift)	Peripheral regions with cheap land, workforce and motorway access	National HUBs of distribution firms, pan-European DCs, inland ports, e.g. the Ohio River Valley
Interregional mainports	Gateways of the global and international goods flow	Selected sea ports, large freight airports,	The ports of Los Angeles/ Long Beach, Rotterdam, Hamburg, new airfreight hubs in the US Midwest

Source: author's own compilation

trigger rising transport costs; inner urban sites allow for maximum speed and accessibility, but at high cost for site and operations (e.g. labour). Concomitantly, as a majority of core urban areas are characterized by high land rents and critical transport conditions and not least by comparatively higher labour cost and a higher degree of unionized workers, being perceived as typical disadvantages of urban areas, de-concentration seems to be evident for the distribution industries for some time now (Table 10.1).

In summarizing this, locational dynamics of freight distribution are driven by different logics of development: one is directed from the core urban areas towards the urban fringes and beyond, based on what was usually considered the process of industrial suburbanization. It can be explained on the basis of a particular assessment of the benefits and costs of agglomeration, but the process, once initiated, also reveals a more complex picture of subsequent development dynamics, e.g. once DCs evolve into a freight centre (Hesse, 2008: 16ff; 170ff). The second locational dynamic originates from the traditional mainports of goods flows, particularly seaports, inland ports and airports, which are often suffering from space and infrastructure capacity; in this respect, the model of "port-regionalization" (Notteboom and Rodrigue, 2005) is instrumental. Not coincidentally, these two different logics – the city-regional and the large-scale one – often co-evolve and lead to the development of rural areas not too distant from major agglomerations for logistics purposes. Finally, a third locational dynamic is associated with the emergence of new market areas, such as the single European market or the opening of Eastern Europe as a market and a consumer economy. Such macro-economic events have significantly contributed to the re-configuration of logistics networks and triggered the establishment of new DCs and freight clusters.

THE IMPACT OF DISTRIBUTION CENTRES AND LOGISTICS PARKS

Land use and transport

The rising demand for DCs both in terms of size and numbers and the associated establishment of freight centres or clusters raises serious questions regarding socio-economic, environmental and transport related issues. The often large-scale facilities are space consuming entities per se, particularly since this impact increasingly occurs in outer urban areas, predominantly on greenfield sites and quite often without intermodal access. DCs and freight centres require a certain amount of land not only for placing the buildings but also because space is needed for parking vehicles, storing empty containers, water retention basins etc. This applies both to core urban areas and to sub- or ex-urban locations. It is notable that the two major transport modes – road and rail – have developed quite distinctly in terms of land use: Whereas railyards and the related sites that hosted depots, maintenance etc. have been converted until recently to other uses (e.g. housing, services), DCs and freight centres that took over the goods supply in urban regions were in fact pushing land consumption further, both within and beyond urban boundaries.

Due to the lack of data, it is hardly possible to estimate or quantify the amount of land that is being used for distribution purposes on a reliable basis. Most recent studies highlighting freight distribution at all were primarily focusing on either transport volumes or on occupation. Based on data from a government report, McKinnon (2009: S293) reports that in England and Wales about 151 million square metres of warehouse floorspace exist, contributing to a gross total of 23,500 hectares. The London study on logistics land estimated that in 2006 there was about 16 million sqm of warehouse floorspace established covering about 2,800 hectares of warehousing land in London, with an increase of 16 per cent total predicted to take place until 2026 (Mayor of London, 2007). The port city of Hamburg, Germany has investigated the future demand for commercial space suitable for logistics purposes. Between 2005 and 2015, a future demand was estimated at about 17 hectares per year within the city, an additional four hectares per annum in the suburbs and another 19 hectares per annum in the port. Due to the lower productivity of distribution compared to manufacturing, the specific demand for space is also relatively high: a recent study from the (port) city of Bremen found about 27.5 employees per hectare in the big suburban freight centre, compared to more than 85 per hectare in two modern business parks with manufacturing and related services (Senator für Wirtschaft und Häfen, 2008).

In order to reduce the demand for space triggered by DCs and freight centres without exerting a general ban on lorries and warehouses from urban areas, the brownfield or infill-type of DC is increasingly being discussed. An early study on this issue in the New York/New Jersey area found that there is indeed a big potential to convert old industrial sites into freight centres or at least to host single DCs, once certain conditions are met, particularly in terms of cost and functionality (Strauss-Wieder, 2001). A real estate development firm has recently emphasized the importance of infill locations for logistics businesses, concluding that "a property owner having a long-term infill strategy enjoys superior occupancy, rental growth and returns, and supports efficient supply chain operations" (Twist and Binkley, 2010: 1). There were also certain cost savings identified (time, transport cost) associated with an integrated instead of suburban DC-location.

Table 10.2 Lorry traffic generated from commercial land use

	Industrial park land use	Transport related land use	Logistics and distribution land use
Average daily trip rate per hectare	10–12	10–15	40–90
Average daily trip rate per employee	0.6–0.8	2–4	2–9

Source: Bosserhoff 2000, cited Wagner 2010

In addition, the research pointed out that infill locations may also prove to be more sustainable, which reflects the propositions made in the context of *smart growth*-debates.

DCs and freight clusters definitely tend to generate a high amount of traffic, which is an explicit outcome of their role in physical distribution. The more DCs are dedicated to turnover rather than storage, the higher will be the frequency of the lorry traffic on-site. Capacity problems and related conflicts occur locally, due to the mere effect of concentration. Indeed the contribution of DCs, freight centres and terminals to generating freight traffic is significant, compared to other commercial areas or even industrial parks (Table 10.2). Having said that, it is also suggested that functional concentration helps improve the overall transport efficiency and energy impact, particularly by raising load factors or by shifting consignments from road to rail or barge modes, if market allows. However, empirical evidence is scarce, with punctual findings that may not easily be generalized (Kia et al., 2003; Matthews and Hendrickson, 2003).

There are also major interdependencies between land use and transport to be taken into account (Ryan, 1999). It can be assumed that the spatial shift from the old warehouse, often connected with railways, to the new DC or freight centre at greenfield locations necessarily implies a certain modal shift from rail to road. On the other hand, carefully planned locations of new freight centres could contribute to minimizing trip generation to some extent, although again empirical evidence is scarce and sometimes confusingly varied. A study from the Hamburg region reveals that an inner-city freight village, compared to a large suburban freight centre, could reduce the number of daily trips and lorry miles generated (Wagner, 2010). According to this study, trip generation depends more on the composition of the site rather than on the specific location. Torbianelli (2009) suggests that a decentralized network of DCs could contribute to both minimizing congestion at a mainport and to increasing the overall efficiency of the transport system; yet data supporting his assumption are missing. The same applies to Kohn and Brodin (2008) suggesting positive impacts of centralized distribution on carbon dioxide-emissions. In any case trade-offs between the local (traffic probably increasing through central DC) and the regional scales (potential for higher efficiency and intermodality) will be difficult to assess and handle in terms of politics. As new DCs are often situated in larger freight zones or logistics parcs, these locales make them more accessible to modern rail and port container terminals, and they also tend to absorb their impact in a larger context.

Community and the environment

Due to serious externalities and recent growth rates, there is the need for balancing the freight sector with community demands, particularly once it comes to placing new facilities. Key issues that communities have relative to freight operations and facilities include traffic flow and congestion, safety and security, economic development, air quality, noise and vibrations, and land use and value (TRB, 2003). As in many cases, economic growth is assumed by acquiring DCs and freight centres, yet at the same time particular concerns emerge about lorry trip generation and local neighborhood impacts of inner-city DCs. It is

Table 10.3 Community related measures in selected cases of US metropolitan freight projects

Profiled project	Issue areas							Freight types			
	Traffic flow	Safety and security	Economic development	Air quality/ environment	Noise/vibrations	Land use and value	Communications	Rail	Trucking	Air Cargo	Water
FAST Corridor	X	X	X	X			X	X	X		X
Morristown and Erie Railway and Toys 'R' Us Distribution Center	X	X	X		X	X	X	X			
Louisville Quiet Zone		X			X		X	X			
Alameda Corridor	X	X	X	X	X	X	X	X	X		X
Guild's Lake Industrial Sanctuary	X		X		X	X	X	X	X		X
Port of NY/NJ Green Ports Initiative				X	X		X				X
CSX Syracuse Intermodal Terminal	X	X	X		X	X	X	X	X		

Source: author's own after TRB, 2003

no coincidence that related conflicts are important drivers of the suburban drift of DCs and freight centres. Regarding inner-city locales, those areas in the immediate vicinity of ports, railyards or wholesale districts are most critical, as e.g. air pollution tends to be severe (see Hall, 2007, reporting on South Los Angeles). Since such areas are often occupied by relatively disadvantaged households, they deserve special attention. Hence when freight locations have to be kept within the city, it is essential to lower their environmental and social burden and to ensure the acceptability of the site. Related activity (for key strategies see Table 10.3) should be undertaken both by policy and planning and by corporate responsibility policies ("good neighbour").

Local opposition often occurs once new DCs are being built, even in sub- and ex-urban areas. Despite the strong desire of developers and municipalities to realize such projects, particularly in de-industrialized or rural regions, site neighbours, NGOs and the public tend to be critical. Planning requirements, environmental impact assessments etc. are already quite demanding. Depending on size and spatial reach of the DC or on heavy goods vehicle frequencies triggered, such projects can indeed raise intense political conflict. A typical case in this respect represents Wal-Mart, the world's largest retailer. On the one hand, Wal-Mart is known for its extraordinary competitiveness in terms of cutting costs, applying high-technologies and achieving overall agility of its business. It has reached this position particularly through operating a sophisticated distribution system that has been constantly improved since long ago (Bonacic, 2006). On the other hand, the

Table 10.4 Dimensions of environmental building policy according to the LEED® (Leadership in Energy and Environmental Design) Standard

Sustainable Sites (SS)	Materials and Resources (MR)
Water Efficiency (WE)	Indoor Environmental Quality (EQ)
Energy and Atmosphere (EA)	Innovation and Design Process (ID)

Source: author's own after Prologis 2008 Sustainability Report, http://ip.prologis.com

Table 10.5 "Sustainable Sites" application according to the LEED® Standard

Sustainable Sites	Site selection
	Urban Redevelopment
	Brownfield Redevelopment
	Alternative Transportation
	Reduced Site Disturbance
	Stormwater Management
	Landscape & Exterior Design to Reduce Heat Islands
	Light Pollution Reduction

Source: author's own after Prologis 2008 Sustainability Report, http://ip.prologis.com

firm is facing increasing resistance from local groups against store-openings and recently also with respect to their DCs. In September 2009, the City of Merced in Northern California (70,000 inhabitants), has approved plans of Wal-Mart to establish a massive DC on a greenfield site, after three years of appraisal and public debate. The 24/7-operated DC will comprise a floorspace of about 110,000 m^2 on a lot of about 100 hectares, generating 900 additional lorry trips a day. Due to this, community concerns have been raised leading to hundreds of queries from NGOs and local residents, regarding both the unavoidable impacts that are associated with the project and also plenty of issues that were claimed to be subject to mitigation. Since the economic impact of new DCs and freight centres is considered significant (Wal-Mart promises to create about 1,200 jobs in Merced), municipalities are likely to attract these investments, expecting taxes, corporate fees and infrastructure investments.

In response to environmental criticism, ports, logistics and distribution businesses are increasingly aiming at performing in a "green" and responsible manner. To some extent, this ties in with earlier attempts to make distribution more environmentally sound (e.g. by better co-ordination of urban goods flow). However, such policies often leave out the core logistics organization and also the issue of location, since these parts of their business are often considered hard to change, for the sake of competition. One consequence for DC-operators is to increase vehicle efficiency and, particularly, to further improve the building in terms of energy use, waste disposal, materials management etc. Meanwhile certain standards are being developed regarding the latter, e.g. according to the *LEED*®-classification (*Leadership in Energy and Environmental Design*), in order to systemize, control and further develop related measures. The search for "sustainable sites" is among such measures (Tables 10.4 and 10.5). Initiatives such as "green ports" are underway as well, yet the single DC or the road transport based freight centre still appear critical in this respect.

In the foreseeable future, the biggest challenge for the distribution system will be rising energy prices which are currently subject to much speculation about the future of transport in general and the circulation industries in particular. Besides expecting major modal shifts from road and air freight towards rail and shipping modes, an important question is whether higher transport costs may change the rationale of logistics restructuring and the associated trade-off between fixed and variable costs that had favoured centralized DC-networks. It is assumed that a rather moderate re-adjustment of distribution concepts and locations could take place, by adding few links to the network as only one of major possible responses (Sahling, 2010). However, it seems to be evident that rising transport and logistics costs will be the greatest stimulus among any other measures to re-organize the way materials flow and goods are delivered.

Policy responses, institutional settings and policy conflicts

The emergence of DCs and logistics parks is not only driven by market changes and corporate strategies, but also an outcome of policy and politics. Locational assets at the local level are not provided for without public policy and governance, which applies both to DCs and freight centres. Zoning, economic development incentives, infrastructure provision and last but not least a qualified workforce remain important location factors for placing DCs and logistics parks. Given their impact on community and the environment, public agents are committed to balance the costs and benefits of developing industrial land for DCs and freight centres. In this regard it is important to note that infrastructure provision is increasingly becoming subject to private decision making, as policies in the freight realm are primarily driven by business interests anyway. Also new players have emerged on the real estate market highlighting land capitalization and competition, but disregarding urban planning and integration issues and thus changing the planning conditions (Hesse, 2008: 60ff). The related speculative nature of development tends to stimulate further land consumption. As a consequence, policy goals become more difficult to achieve. Competitive dynamics between firms and – particularly – between municipalities do not allow for setting policy or planning standards too strictly.

How could the aforementioned problems be solved? First, there is the need to integrate the demand for land and transport access associated with DCs with local and regional land use plans and building codes. Particular emphasis should be put on the question of whether and where to place a DC or freight centre, how transport access can be ensured and how to deal with the consequences for the environment and community needs. Sensitive land uses have to be buffered against disturbances caused by the 24/7-operation of vehicles, forklifts, dock doors etc. Second, public and private agents should collaborate in order to enhance and further promote activities which may support a more sustainable management of the supply chains. Third, such activities should be framed within a regional distribution concept, answering the question whether such industries are a useful target of the region's economic development, whether the region offers particular advantages for mobilizing competitive potentials, and how all this can be organized within a coherent policy framework at the local, regional and national scales.

THE CITY AS A TERMINAL – REFLECTIONS ON AN ECONOMY ON THE MOVE

The recent development of the logistics and freight distribution business can be characterized by an increasing overall degree of volatility and mobility. This is not only true given the rising number of freight consignments, containers and vessels being moved across the globe, but can also be applied to highly dynamic locational trends and the changing territorial attachment of the logistics firms. The movement of DCs and freight clusters to places far beyond the urban fringes and in the hinterland of major gateways does not only bring about a new "logistics landscape" (cf. Waldheim and Berger, 2008; see also Figure 10.3). It also raises the question of how far these new settings may shape the interrelation between the city and freight distribution and logistics in general (cf. Hesse, 2008: 13ff). Given the mere empirical situation, the historical link between urbanization and accessibility is of course still at work: the functionality of logistics – in a broad understanding of the term – is still considered a prime location factor for cities in the changing framework of the network economy or network society: "Cities and urban regions become, in a sense, staging

Figure 10.3 Example of the new logistics landscape, Northern California DCs
Source: author's own, September 2001

posts in the perpetual flux of infrastructure mediated flow, movement and exchange" (Graham, 2002). The new role of services or the demand for "agile" manufacturing might not be accomplished without efficient logistics and infrastructure, as does the increasing interregional trade. The benefits of agglomeration obviously still provide an appropriate framework for bundling dispersed economic functions.

However, there is an emerging notion of "flow" in contemporary urban and geographical thinking, both in a metaphorical and in a literal sense, emphasized in a number of contributions that reassert both the role of networks and flows and a changing understanding of cities. Related contemporary interpretations of urban places as economic spaces have gone far beyond the meaning of the city as a mere concentration of people, jobs or added value. As Amin and Thrift (2002) have put it, cities are increasingly considered being a part of a large-scale economic network, rather than a spatial fix in the world of flows:

> Instead of conceiving cities as either bounded or punctured economic entities, we see them as assemblages of more or less distanciated economic relations with different intensities at different locations. Economic activity is now irremediably distributed. Even when economic activity seems to be spatially clustered, a close examination will reveal that the clusters rely on a multiplicity of sites, institutions and connections, which do not just stretch beyond these clusters, but actually constitute them. (Amin and Thrift, 2002: 52)

Consequently, the authors "… replace the idea of the city as a territorial economic engine with an understanding of cities as sites in spatially stretched economic relations" (Amin and Thrift, 2002: 63).

Clearly, these dispersed and disconnected parts of the logistics system need to be re-connected. Adding to the layers of the immaterial flows of knowledge, information and finance that are bound together in urban economies, these material connections are taken over by transport and mobility, by logistics and freight distribution. Consequently, logistics organization needs "organization space" (Easterling, 1999). Easterling assumes that contemporary urban developments such as transport interchanges, ports, airports, malls, economic franchises can best be understood as dynamic sites for organizing logistical processes. The sites where these processes take place tend to resemble urban functions in terms of connecting economic processes and places. Again Amin and Thrift (2002) have exemplified this observation in the case of the five global DCs operated by Eastman Kodak. They are considered key nodes within a newly emerging, flow based pattern of creation of value. This, in turn, changes the position of the city in relation to the network:

> Increasingly, the role of cities, through the miles of distribution complexes located near major transport nodes, is to keep produce from around the world "on hold" for customers well beyond the city. These are sites neither of production nor consumption. (Amin and Thrift, 2002: 69)

As an outcome of the scattered arrangement of DCs across space, the authors consider a new geography of delivery emerging that is virtually disconnected from the original geography of production and the final geography of consumption (ibid.).

It is still controversially discussed whether these de- and re-connected infrastructure hubs do represent a broader trend in urban and economic development – the dissolution of materials handling and freight distribution from core urban areas – which could thus be generalized. However, complex interdependencies of the local and the global as a result of large-scale network architecture and embeddedness seem to be the norm rather than the exception in contemporary economic development (Cidell, 2011). Empirical evidence does not support the assumption of a general "footlooseness" of the economy. However, the freight sector reveals an astonishing degree of disconnection of logistics networks from traditional urban and economic network topologies (Hesse, 2010). Thus the city, once a prime marketplace and site of economic exchange, might become transformed to a mere terminal, providing the transshipment of commodities from A to B without earning a certain added value that traditionally emanated from doing trade.

REFERENCES

Amin, A. and Thrift, N. (2002) *Cities. Reimagining the Urban*, Cambridge: Polity Press.

Belmonte, L. (2004) "Implications for building demand, design and location", in Urban Land Institute (ed.), *Just-in-Time Real Estate. How Trends in Logistics Are Driving Industrial Development*, Washington, DC: ULI, pp. 55–80.

Bonachic, E. with Hardie, K. (2006) "Wal-Mart and the logistics revolution", in N. Lichtenstein (ed.), *Wal-Mart. The Face of Twenty-First-Century Capitalism*, New York, London: The New Press, pp. 163–88.

Bowen, J.T. (2008) "Moving places: the geography of warehousing in the US", *Journal of Transport Geography* Vol. 16, pp. 379–87.

Bowersox, D., Smykay, E., and LaLonde, B. (1968) *Physical Distribution Management. Logistics Problems of the Firm*, New York, London: Macmillan.

Chinitz, B. (1960) *Freight and the Metropolis. The Impact of America's Transport Revolutions on the New York Region*, Cambridge, MA: Harvard University Press.

Cidell, J. (2010) "Concentration and decentralization: the new geography of freight distribution in US metropolitan areas", *Journal of Transport Geography* Vol. 18, pp. 363–71.

Cidell, J. (2011) "Distribution centers among the rooftops: the global logistics network meets the suburban spatial imaginery", *International Journal of Urban and Regional Research*, Vol. 34, No. 5, pp. 832–51.

Cushman & Wakefield (2009) *European Distribution Report* 2008, London: C&W.

Daskin, M. and Owen, S. (1999) "Location models in transportation", in R.W. Hall (ed.), *Handbook of Transportation Science*, Boston/Dordrecht/London: Kluwer, pp. 311–60.

De Ligt, T. and Wever, E. (1998) "European distribution centres: location patterns", *Tijdschrift voor Economische en Sociale Geografie* Vol. 89, No. 2, pp. 217–23.

Easterling, K. (1999) *Organization Space: Landscapes, Highways, and Houses in America*, Cambridge, London: The MIT Press.

Gattorna, J. (1990) *The Gower Handbook of Logistics and Distribution Management*, 4th edn., Aldershot: Gower.

Graham, S. (2002) "Flow city: networked mobilities and the contemporary metropolis", *Journal of Urban Technology* Vol. 9, No. 1, pp. 1–20.

Hall, P. (2007) "Seaports, urban sustainability, and paradigm shift", *Journal of Urban Technology* Vol. 14, No. 2, pp. 87–101.

Handfield, R. and Nichols, E. (1999) *Introduction to Supply Chain Management*, New Jersey: Prentice Hall.

Hatton, G. (1990) "Designing a warehouse or distribution centre", in J. Gattorna (ed.), *The Gower Handbook of Logistics and Distribution Management*, Aldershot: Gower, pp. 175–93.

Hesse, M. (2004) "Land for logistics: locational dynamics and political regulation of distribution centres and freight agglomerations", *Tijdschrift voor Economische en Sociale Geografie* Vol. 95, No. 2, pp. 162–73.

Hesse, M. (2008) *The City as a Terminal: Logistics and freight transport in an urban context*, Aldershot: Ashgate.

Hesse, M. (2010) "Cities, material flows and the geography of spatial interaction. Urban places in the system of chains", *Global Networks* Vol. 10, No. 1, pp. 75–91.

JonesLangLaSalle (2008) *Logistikimmobilienreport Deutschland*, Frankfurt a.M.: JLLS.

Kia, M., Shayan, E. and Ghotb, F. (2003) "Positive impact of distribution centres on the environment", *Transport Reviews* Vol. 23, No. 1, pp. 105–22.

Kohn, C. and Brodin, M. (2008) "Centralised distribution systems and the environment: how increased transport work can decrease the environmental impact of logistics", *International Journal of Logistics: Research and Applications* Vol. 11, No. 3, pp. 229–45.

Lasserre, F. (2004) "Logistics and the Internet: transportation and location issues are crucial in the logistics chain", *Journal of Transport Geography* Vol. 12, No. 1, pp. 73–84.

Leitner, S. and Harrison, R. (2001) "The identification and classification of inland ports", Research Report Number 0–4083–1. Center for Transportation Research, The University of Texas at Austin.

Martin, R. and Sunley, P. (2003) "Deconstructing clusters: chaotic concept or policy panacea?", *Journal of Economic Geography* Vol. 3, No. 1, pp. 5–35.

Matthews, H. and Hendrickson, C. (2003) "The economic and environmental implications of centralized stock keeping", *Journal of Industrial Ecology* Vol. 6, No. 2, pp. 71–81.

Mayor of London (2007) *Supply and Demand of Land for Logistics*, London: Greater London Authority.

McKinnon, S. (2009) "The present and future land requirements of logistics activities", *Land Use Policy* Vol. 26S, pp.293–301.

McCalla, R., Slack, B. and Comtois, C. (2001) "Intermodal freight terminals: locality and industrial linkages", *The Canadien Geographer/Le Géographe Canadien* Vol. 45, No. 3, pp. 404–13.

Notteboom, T. and Rodrigue, J.-P. (2005) "Port regionalization: towards a new phase in port development", *Maritime Policy and Management* Vol. 32, No. 3, pp. 297–313.

Notteboom, T and Rodrigue, J.-P. (2009) "Inland terminals within North American and European supply chains", *Transport and Communications Bulletin for Asia and the Pacific*, United Nations Economic and Social Commission for Asia and the Pacific, No. 28, pp. 1–57.

Pochet, L., Rumley, P.-A. and de Tilière, G. (2000) "Plates-formes logistiques multimodal et multiservices", Rapports du PNR 41, *Transport et environnement*, rapport B 9. Berne: OFCL/EDMZ.

Ryan, S. (1999) "Property values and transportation facilities: finding the transportation-land use connection", *Journal of Planning Literature* Vol. 13, No. 4, pp. 412–27.

Sahling, L. (2010) *How Will Higher Fuel Costs Impact the U.S. Warehouse/Distribution Markets?*, Denver, CO: ProLogis Research Insights.

Senator für Wirtschaft und Häfen (2008) Gutachten Fischereihafen. Unpublished report. Bremen.

Strauss-Wieder, A. (2001) *Warehousing and Distribution Center Context.* NJPTA Brownfield Economic Redevelopment Project. Prepared for the New Jersey Institute of Technology and the North Jersey Transportation Planning Authority, February 2001. Westfield: ASW.

Tioga Group (2006) *Inland Port Feasibility Study*, prepared for SCAG. Los Angeles: Tioga Group.

Torbianelli, V.A. (2009) "Road congestion generated by distribution centres in European port regions: risks and opportunities of the development of hybrid logistics", *Pomorstvo, Journal of Maritime Studies* Vol. 23, No. 1, pp. 21–39.

Transportation Research Board/TRB (2003) *Integrating Freight Facilities and Operations with Community Goals. A Synthesis of Highway Practice.* NCHRP Synthesis 320, Washington, DC: TRB.

Twist, D. and Binkley, A. (2010) *AMB Infill strategy*, San Francisco, CA: AMB.

Wagner, T. (2010) "Regional traffic impacts of logistics-related land use", *Transport Policy* Vol. 17, No. 3, pp. 224–29.

Waldheim, C. and Berger, A. (2008) "Logistics landscape", *Landscape Journal* Vol. 27, No. 2, pp. 219–46.

Waters, D. (2010) *Global Logistics. New Directions in Supply Chain Management*, London: Kogan Page.

11

The Role of Inland Terminals in Intermodal Transport Development

Ekki Kreutzberger and Rob Konings

INTRODUCTION

This chapter gives an overview of the different types of *inland* freight nodes that handle *trains* and/or *barges* and of their characteristics. Within the inland nodes the chapter focuses on *intermodal* rail or barge *nodes*, in particular intermodal *terminals*. Inland nodes exist in *maritime* land networks (= the hinterland networks of seaports) and in *continental* networks. Maritime land or continental networks can be rail or barge, international or domestic networks. Transport nodes serve the transport and logistic networks. The functionality of any node is derived from needs of the transport and logistic network. The networks themselves are continuously evolving, due to changing performance requirements, flow sizes and factor costs. Therefore also the transport nodes are continuously being adjusted, leading to a large variety of transport node types. Given this background the chapter gives much attention to the relation between terminals and networks.

The structure of this chapter is as follows. It starts with a description of historical developments, challenges and other backgrounds in rail and barge transport during the last several decades, partly even since their very beginnings, and the corresponding innovations, which have been implemented or discussed in this period. First the rail and barge transport sectors as a whole are reviewed and then we focus on the *intermodal* transport sector. All three subsections explain the role and major features of exchange nodes in transport networks. *Terminal transshipment* is a specific type of *node exchange*. Following this section which largely has a conceptual nature, we continue with an overview of the state-of-the-art and current practice regarding intermodal rail and barge transport in Europe, also giving quantitative indications about the market and terminal structure, and describing the actors involved in terminals, and terminal policies of public authorities. Next, the notions developed in the earlier sections are used to present a structured overview of the different types of intermodal terminals. In view of the important role of the functioning of inland terminals for the performance of the intermodal transport chain, the chapter ends with an outlook on promising directions of terminal innovation to support intermodal transport development.

HISTORICAL BACKGROUND

Rail transport

In the 19th century rail transport was the new mode, faster than barge transport and capable of integrally accessing a country. It was to become the most important inland transport system, serving the upcoming industries and fast growing cities, partly substituting barge transport. Many factories, trade houses and urban areas had track attachments, allowing them to be served more effectively and efficiently than ever before. In addition, a network of freight stations was built, representing interfaces between the rail and the road (or barge) system.

More or less from the very beginning of rail transport flow sizes of most commodities were smaller than the train sizes, requiring complex bundling, that is the process of transporting goods of different types and for different lengths of time in the same train during their journey. The central configuration was the so-called wagonload system, in which a system of local trains, flat or gravity shunting yards, freight stations and track attachments to single customers served to collect goods and build up trainloads in the regions of origins, then to move full trainloads through the trunk network, and finally to distribute goods in the regions of destinations, by which the size of trainloads gradually declined again. The wagonload system could be carried out more line-wise, say sequentially (as described in Dobeschinsky and Bitter, 2004), or more fork-wise, say parallel (as described by Beisler, Kettler and Molle, 1995), partly dependent on the geographical circumstances. Bulk goods like coal and steel had such volumes that direct transport, e.g. between mines and factories, was common.

When road transport emerged, rail transport was exposed to increasing competition. This was especially the case in the post-war period, when road transport reached substantial proportions and increasing labour costs led to a critical rise of rail costs. In addition, the quality of rail transport did not need to be accepted anymore, in particular the time effects of bundling such as long waiting times for part of the goods.

Given this background, the railway companies accelerated operational and network innovation and streamlining, and also other actors initiated rail innovations. The most important types of measures are listed below:

- Network concentration: fewer connections and fewer local rail branches.
- Cutting out layers of the wagonload system (B–F in Figure 11.1): fewer shunting nodes on the route; the ultimate result would be the direct train (F).
- Abolishing local rail networks with less-than-full-trainload-trains (as in D and F of Figure 11.1): the result could be a hub-and-spoke rail network, especially cutting off the small rail branches and direct tracks to factories etc. and substituting these with local road transport: avoiding expensive rail operations.
- Splitting large networks into smaller independent ones: reducing costly dependencies and reducing complexity (B–F in Figure 11.1).
- Avoiding single wagon exchange at rail–rail nodes and instead focusing on the exchange of wagon groups. The smaller number of sorting activities and the fact that a flat shunting yard will suffice and a gravity shunting yard is not required, can reduce rail exchange costs substantially. In Europe, wagon group trains were the backbone of intermodal rail transport in the 1990s (Kombiconsult and K+P Transport Consultants, 2007; UIC, 2008).
- Starting to serve large nodes or node clusters with more priority and quality. Good examples are:
    - the differentiation of the trunk network (traffic intertriage) in France in the early

1950s by operating two sets of shunting yards, the régime ordinaire (RO) and the régime accéléré (RA). The RA system focused on special markets like small shipments, perishable goods, containers, and goods, which could easily choose road transport. Its trains were faster (100 km/h or more) and shorter. Therefore the RA shunting yards were smaller (number and length of tracks) (Blier, 1991);
  - the InterCargo-network erected in Germany in the 1980s, a quality wagonload system, connecting only so-called "economic centres". Each such centre consisted of terminals, other stations and other nodes accessed by a collection and distribution rail network (Figure 11.2).
- The introduction of intermodal rail transport. The terminals in this system would for certain markets, especially general freight, eventually replace the freight stations.
- The introduction of dedicated intermodal trains for containers, swap bodies and maybe semi-trailers, or for only semi-trailers. Examples for the latter are different Alps-crossing services, and the French Autoroute ferroviaire.
- The introduction of innovative terminals for rail–road or, rail–rail transshipment of intermodal load units, optionally having robotised transshipment, sorting and storage operations. The innovation refers to the layout of terminals and/or to the employed technical concepts, and is partly accompanied by the introduction of technically innovative train or truck types. The aim of such terminals is a high performance for larger volumes, or low costs for small volumes. Many large inland rail–road terminals have high performances, the result of years of crane development and operational optimisation. At seaports the applied innovation is even more ahead introducing innovative and robotised internal transport and stack systems (Maasvlakte Rotterdam) or terminals truly developed for rail–rail transshipment (Mainhub Antwerp). Comparable innovations at inland terminals have up to now not passed the pilot stage. The implementation of innovative technical concepts has so far been restricted to very small nodes, where vehicle devices substitute terminal cranes etc. Examples are the horizontal transshipment at domestic rail terminals in Switzerland, Austria or the Netherlands, and crane barges in the Netherlands.
- The introduction of so-called rail ports in certain markets. The rail ports function as interface between non-intermodal trains and the local pre- and post-haulage system by truck.

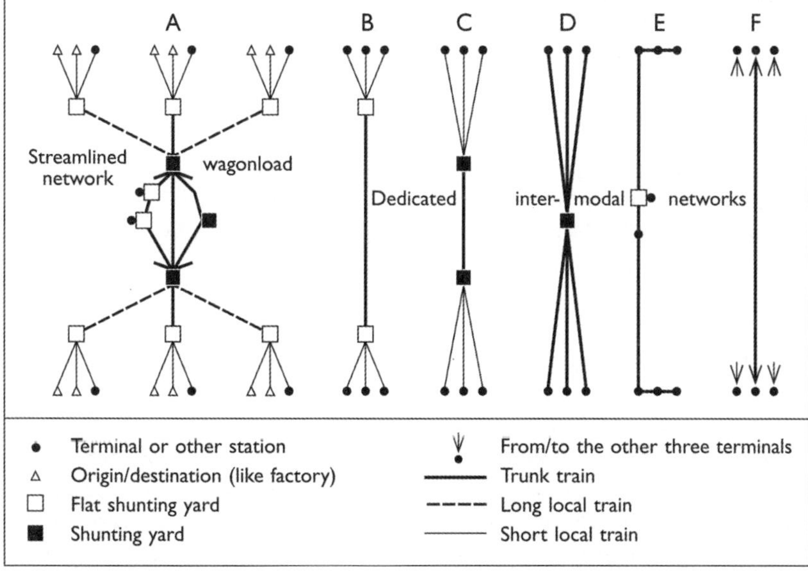

Figure 11.1 Streamlined and new rail networks

Source: Kreutzberger, 2008

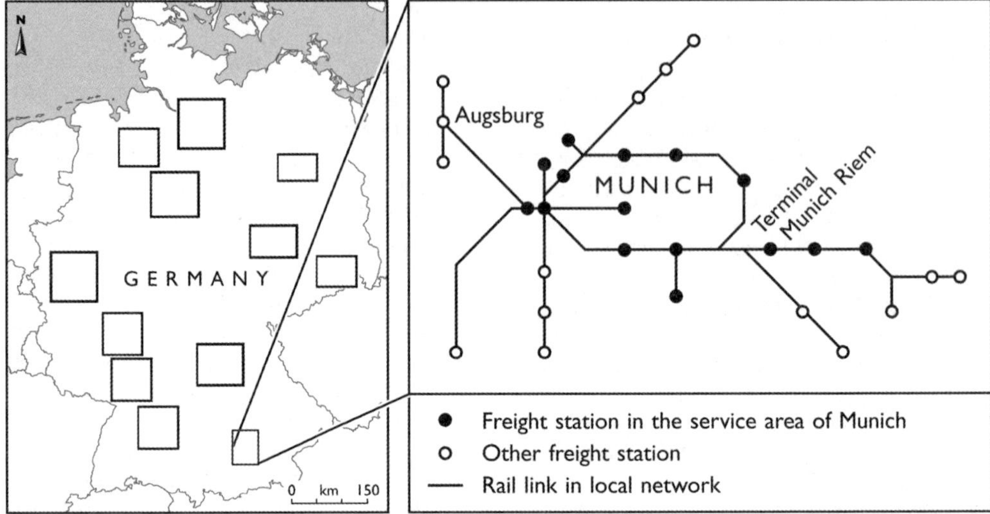

Figure 11.2 The economic centres in the InterCargo network (mixed intermodal and non-intermodal operations)

Source: Kreutzberger, 2008 (adapted from Deutsche Bahn, 1993)

- The introduction of the freight village concept in many countries (e.g. UK, the Italian interporti, French platforms logistiques, German Güterverkehrszentren, Dutch distriparks). A freight village is a spatial concentration of transport intensive activities around terminals and other rail stations. Its advantage is the reduction of distances and costs in pre- and post-haulage. At some freight villages, like Verona, several distribution halls are also directly accessed by rail.
- The development of specific rail concepts for the transport of less-than-container-load or less-than-truck-load flows. Special freight centres, road and rail bundling types and maybe small containers play a role in such concepts.

The results of these measures were improved wagonload networks and dedicated intermodal networks operating complete trains, block trains or shuttles. The innovation pattern and (intermediate) results in Europe differ largely by country, like the amount of shunting in intermodal networks (e.g. hardly any shunting in the UK, Netherlands and later also in Belgium), the applied complex bundling types (e.g. intermodal line networks in the Netherlands or hub-and-spoke networks in Belgium), or the policy of retaining small terminals (e.g. Switzerland, Austria and Belgium) next to concentrating networks.

Barge transport

Historically barge transport has been particularly important in transporting bulk goods (like ores, coal, sand, gravel and chemical products). Barge transport is a mode that combines high mass transport capacity with low operating costs, i.e. the line haul costs (per tonne-km) are low. Since transporting these products by road is relatively expensive, combined barge–road transport (that also requires additional handling) may easily override the costs savings of using barges in the transport chain. For this reason in many transport relations where barges are used, terminals also are the beginning and/or end point (begin-and-end) of the transport chain (= origin or destination), and intermediate exchange nodes are absent. In that case the terminal usually has a private status, i.e. is owned by the shipper or consignee.

In addition to bulk products barge transport also plays a role in the transport of neo-bulk (e.g. wood and cork) and so-called general cargo, which covers a wide range of finished and semi-finished products, such as steel products, transport equipment, machinery, engines and other apparatus. Because of the locations of their producers, barge transport depends on pre- and post-haulage by truck or other means. Therefore barge–road terminals were introduced. They serve many customers and have a public status. The higher value of these products has made combined barge–road transport an economically feasible option. A barge usually performs the long-distance transport and trucks the local collection and distribution of the products.

When the maritime container entered the market, this also affected inland navigation. But unlike in the rail sector, barge companies immediately started to run *dedicated* intermodal services, i.e. barges carrying containers only. Here the circumstances and conditions of general cargo apply: most customers have locations not directly next to the waterways; most terminals are not the origins and destinations of transport services. Many flows are too small for direct transport and therefore require complex bundling. Line bundling dominates the scene. Many barge–road inland terminals serve as begin-and-end and as line terminals.

As for many transport sectors, barge transport has also witnessed an increase of scale. In the early 1990s barges having about 200 TEU capacity were the largest barge-type, but the largest ones can now load about 300 or even 400 TEU. The increase of scale very much appears to be supply-driven: barge flows are growing, but barge sizes are increasing faster. The larger scale is noticeable at inland terminals and seaports in terms of longer handling times. At seaports there have also been big efforts made to collect and distribute containers at different terminals. At the same time, but on a limited scale, the opposite to scale increase has taken place. The so-called Neo-kempenaar type of barge was put into service. Its capacity is about 30 TEU, it misses scale advantages, but has relatively short handling, collection and distribution times. Smaller barges, however, have mainly been implemented to launch new services.

In general the features of a barge terminal depend strongly on the quay facilities and cargo type. In handling dry bulk the equipment can range from a fixed hoisting crane, mobile crane (with a bucket) to a belt conveyor or even a topple jetty from which a truck can unload. To unload light bulk (such as grains) pneumatic hoover installations are used. Pump installations are usually used to transship wet bulk products. This can also be direct transshipment between vessels (e.g. from sea vessel to barge). Ores and coal are transported using a limited number of transport relations and typically as hinterland transport, i.e. from seaports directly to the site of steel factories and power plants. Transport of chemical products, petroleum products in particular, shows a more or less identical pattern. Transports are often seaport-related and involve large consignments, predominantly between refineries and chemical industrial complexes or as intermediate deliveries between chemical companies. Sand and gravel are generally not transported over very long distances, origins and destinations are much more dispersed, volumes are smaller and are typically not seaport-related. Terminals are found both at the sites of extraction and processing (such as building materials factories).

In public barge terminals often many kinds of transshipment can take place such as bulk, general cargo and palletised goods. In some cases containers can also be transshipped. The typical barge transport market for general cargo has consisted mainly of large-sized or heavy units (e.g. rolls of paper or steel, machines). A very special category of general cargo is formed by rolling cargo, such as cars, tractors and military equipment. To enable transshipment of this type of cargo a ramp is needed at the terminal, and moreover adapted vessels are required. Some of the public barge terminals are acting as a logistics centre providing storage and transshipment services for local entrepreneurs. Except for adding additional services the traditional terminals for barge transport have not undergone significant changes.

Strategies to improve the performance of intermodal networks: implications for terminals

Dedicated intermodal networks are a result of innovation. For the operators they have turned into one of the most important options to grow and to increase their market shares. As rail and barge transport are relatively sustainable, there is also a public interest in successful intermodal transport. Yet, the market share of intermodal transport is limited, and the sector faces some serious obstacles. Intermodal rail transport often does not cover its costs (e.g. Trenitalia (Laguzzi, 2001); SNCF Fret (Hahn, 1998); CNC (Delavelle et al., 2003); Freightliner (ECMT, 2003); Railion Netherlands up to 2005 (Kennisinstituut voor Mobiliteitsbeleid, 2007); Inter Ferry Boats in the NARCON network in Belgium (Van Petegem according to Verberckmoes, 2007), ICF (Müller, 2005), and the quality of intermodal transport is good only in some heavy corridors, to and from large urban conglomerations, and in some other regions, in which transport is well organised (Cardebring et al., 2000). Intermodal barge transport has geographical restrictions, and – for the continental market – is not always fast enough, except for floating stock markets. Road transport remains having the largest absolute growth. To attract more transport and become more profitable, intermodal transport had to and still must become more attractive by performing better, meaning that costs should relatively decline, quality increase and the resources (infrastructure and land) should be used more efficiently. Therefore, the dedicated intermodal networks are continuously the subject of innovations. We observe the following innovation strategies:

1 Increase transport scale:
   - by appropriate bundling of flows. This is about the choice of bundling alternatives and about the choice of physical means. The terms are explained further on;
   - or by concentrating the service network, meaning to access a region by fewer rail connections and terminals.
2 Accelerate train or barge roundtrips by higher average link speed and/or shorter node dwell times.
3 Accelerate operations in order to reduce the door-to-door (DTD) time of load units and increase the service area. The acceleration can take place by increasing the average link speed and/or a better synchronisation of sequential and parallel transport operations.
4 Simplify networks.
5 Specialise network parts in a complementary way.
6 Design operations, which efficiently use a node's infrastructure and space.
7 Design appropriate terminal operations.

Some of these strategies can be contradictory.

Strategy 1 is about choosing one of the basic bundling types in Figure 11.3 or combinations of these and about choosing the physical means to carry out the bundling. A direct network (left network in Figure 11.3) has many vehicle (train or barge) routes through the network, requiring large network transport volumes. The complex bundling networks (the four network types on the right in Figure 11.3) have fewer routes and therefore smaller volume requirements: the hub-and-spoke network may be suitable for medium-sized volumes, the line, fork and mainline networks for small volumes. The potential scale advantages of choosing an appropriate bundling type are large vehicle loads, a high level of service in terms of network connectivity and service frequency, and derived from the size of vehicle loads, a

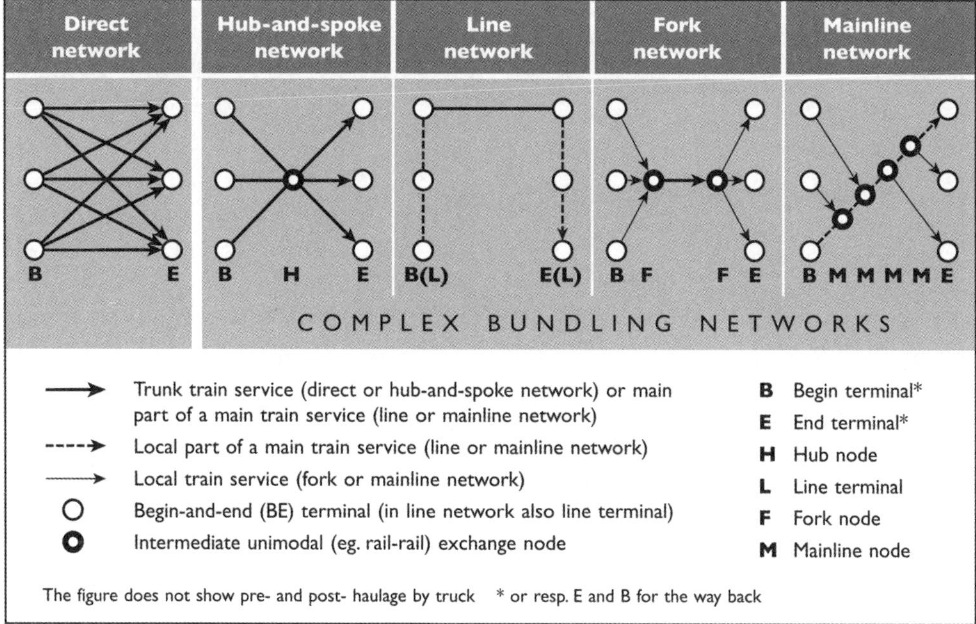

Figure 11.3 Types of bundling networks and their nodes

Source: Kreutzberger, 2008

high utilisation of infrastructure, of relevance especially in the rail sector (each train path is used by more load units).

Complex bundling networks have intermediate exchange nodes. In the hub-and-spoke network this is a hub, a unimodal node exchanging load units between trains or between barges. The line network has line nodes, which are multimodal nodes. The fork or mainline networks have unimodal exchange nodes. The unimodal nodes differ with regard to their position in the network, as a hub exchanges load units within the trunk network, while the fork or mainline nodes connect the trunk and the local network parts. The latter have smaller trains or barges or lower frequencies.

The choice of physical means refers to the type of nodes and vehicles involved. The same bundling type can be carried out by alternative physical means. For instance, the exchange at rail hubs can take place by shunting single wagons at a gravity yard, shunting wagon groups at a flat shunting yard or transshipping load units at a terminal. Load unit transshipment has better performances than single wagon shunting, while the costs and handling time of shunting wagon groups seem to be similar to terminal performances but not applicable for the less-than-wagon-group market. Therefore a *terminal* hub is the best solution for all intermodal rail hub-and-spoke markets.

In barge transport line and direct bundling are widespread. Motor vessels and terminal transshipment dominate the scene. Push barges are not common for intermodal transport. In rail transport all bundling types exist, the result of the process described in Figure 11.1. Shortcomings in the performance of node exchange and the sympathy of rail operators for network simplification (strategy 4) favoured direct bundling. However, many flows, also from and to large nodes like a large seaport (e.g. Rotterdam) or a megacity (e.g. Paris), were and still are too small for direct transport. Therefore often, except for large flow corridors (e.g. BLUE banana), direct bundling is introduced at the expense of transport scale, implying train lengths of

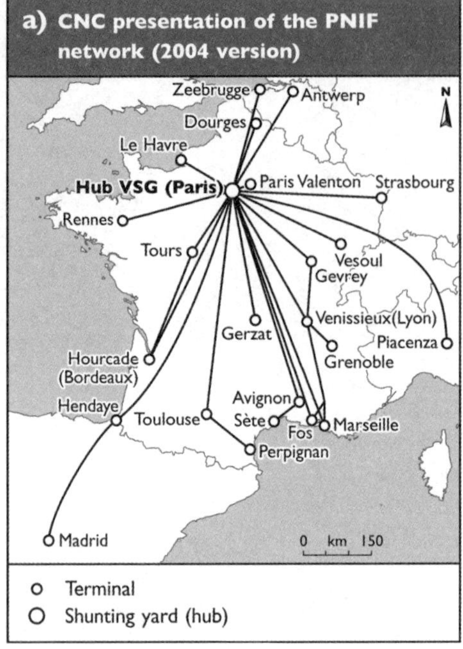

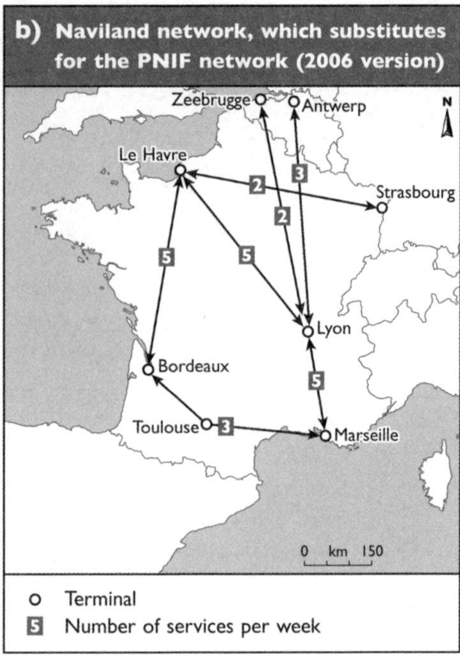

Figure 11.4 Substitution of the PNIF network (a) by the Naviland network (b)

Source: Kreutzberger, 2008 (adapted from (left) CNT, 2004 and (right) Naviland, 2006)

400–500 m instead of 600–700 m or less than five services per week per direction. The tension in this field is well illustrated by the French maritime rail network PNIF (Figure 11.4), a dedicated intermodal rail network implemented by SNCF-fret and the rail operator CNT in the early 1990s. Its hub was a gravity shunting yard near Paris. This was an explicit choice, after rejecting a technically innovative hub and train concept (Commutor; to be further discussed later on). The PNIF network connected about 25 domestic terminals with work-daily services. Due to its modest performances, in particular high costs, this network was substituted in 2005 by the Naviland network of direct train services, which focused mainly on a few heavy flow corridors. The Naviland network has much less exchange at intermediate nodes, and would intentionally be cost-covering. However, the network also has fewer connections, and lower frequencies. The switch to the new network meant, according to experts, a substantial loss of network volumes to the road sector (CNT, 2004).

Comparable with this innovation is the transformation of the InterContainers network with much hub-and-spoke bundling into a network with mainly direct bundling in 2005 (see Kreutzberger, 2008). It focused more strongly on the large flow corridors like the BLUE banana, while network connectivity was reduced.

Strategies 2 (roundtrip acceleration) and 3 (load unit acceleration) aim at enlarging the service area (market) of a (group of) operator(s). They otherwise have a slightly different focus, namely reducing respectively vehicle or shippers' other transport costs. The acceleration can take place by speeding up link operations (e.g. shortening dwell times at borders, or giving less priority to passenger trains, all maybe part of a Free-way measure), cutting out intermediate exchange nodes or by limiting the dwell time of vehicles or load units at intermediate nodes or begin-and-end terminals. Enlargement of

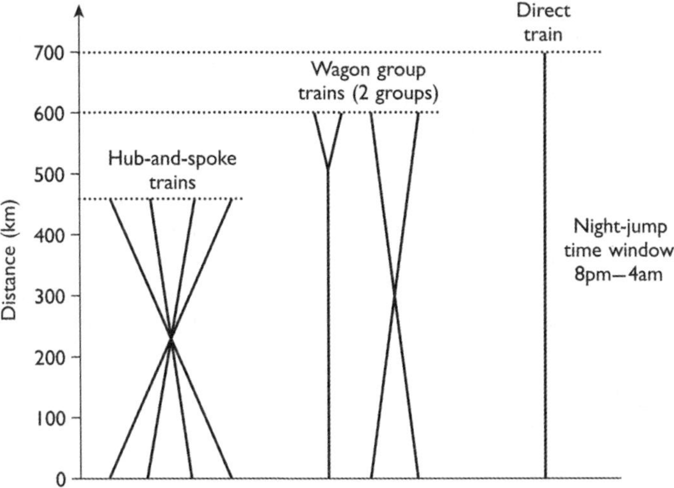

Figure 11.5 Distance covered by services in different bundling networks

Source: adapted from Beisler et al., 1995

the market area is at stake wherever there are critical time windows, like those of the night-jump in day-A/B connections of continental trains; or like day-A/C connections with night-jump departure and arrival times. The aim to cover a country in a night-jump may imply the need for faster intermediate exchange nodes, as Beisler showed in the 1990s in his comparison of different train operations (Figure 11.5). Direct trains score the best in this regard, however may lack transport scale.

Terminal dwell time has become a problem for large (e.g. 300 and 400 TEU) barges, as the unloading and loading at one side of the service takes 7 hours, increasing barge roundtrip times or limiting the distances which can be covered within a time window. The compromise between competing strategies, here 2 and 3 versus 4 (simplification), is faster intermediate and faster begin-and-end terminals. However, it deserves attention that not every operational acceleration leads to relevant performance improvements, for instance being cost-effective. Periodical departure and arrival times and the characteristics of the 8-hour economy of many shippers imply that some vehicle roundtrips or door-to-door transport services have time reserves, which only become larger, if operations are accelerated.

Strategy 4 (simplification) has already – with regard to networks and their nodes – been discussed above. Simplification may also directly address the choice of node types. An important example of a simple node solution is the so-called gateway terminal in rail networks, a rail–road terminal with small amounts of rail–rail transshipment. It is simple because no additional node infrastructure is needed like a real hub terminal or a shunting yard. Also, if own terminals are used – there are no dependencies at the node from other companies like node infrastructure providers.

For rail–rail load units the gateway terminal has inferior performances as it does not generate the scale advantages of true complex bundling networks and – for rail–rail containers – has long dwell times at the gateway. This is explained later on, in the section presenting a terminal typology. Therefore European rail experts conclude that this configuration is only competitive for long distances (KombiConsult and K+P, 2007).

Summarising, the simplification strategy is understandable in the historical context, but has often worsened instead of improved transport performances. There are important exceptions. One is to operate block trains or shuttles instead of complete or wagonload trains. The first two have a fixed wagon composition during respectively one or several sequential journeys, abolishing most shunting and saving time and costs. Block trains or shuttles can also be employed by complex bundling networks and again advocate terminals for intermediate exchange nodes.

Strategy 5 aims at improving total performances by using specialised physical means, each responding to specific network requirements. Typical results are the division between trunk network parts with trains or barges which are suitable for trunk transport, and local network parts with trucks or specific trains or barges which are suitable for the short haul and/or for visiting many exchange nodes. The interface is a specific terminal connecting different rail or barge networks, or connecting rail or barge networks with truck networks.

Another result is the complementary cooperation of two trunk modes, as in rail–barge networks. The interfaces are rail–barge nodes, being rail terminals next to barge inland terminals (as the PKV and DeCeTe terminals in Duisburg) or tracks on barge inland terminals (as the Renory terminal in Liège).

A further result is terminal-substituting exchange equipment on board of vehicles, like cranes on collection and distribution barges, to be found in some large seaports, or like advanced coupling devices for innovative vehicles (e.g. for modular trains or push barges). Only the crane barges have been introduced on a commercial level, mainly in seaports, and also only on a restricted scale. Examples of non-implemented concepts on the basis of strategy 5 are the container exchange barge (CUB) or the train coupling and sharing system (TCSS) of the German railways, for instance on the basis of the Cargo Sprinter.

Operations to use infrastructure and space more efficiently (strategy 6) is an increasingly important subject in large seaports, potentially with significant effects for inland nodes, and in some large inland nodes themselves. It can lead to the outplacement of port functions like train or barge buffering, decoupling points between port and hinterland parts of train or barge service networks, begin-and-end terminals of land modes, part of the maritime container stack,[1] sorting functions, supplementary transport functions (e.g. transferring goods between containers and trucks, empty container stacking and cleaning), distribution functions, empty depots, and other activities in the port (e.g. customs). These functions are outplaced to what we suggest calling *satellites*. To our knowledge the term was first used by Slack (1999) who observed the lack of space at terminals at large nodes while the terminals need to cope with ongoing and growing business. The author "explores ... the need for terminals to continue expanding sites that are often in zones of intense environmental and land use conflict. It goes on to consider an alternative comprising satellite facilities."

Dependent on the (main) function of what is outplaced, the location of outplacement, and the locations of the customers, a satellite may be a *transferium*, *bridgehead*, *extended gate-way* or an *(inland) hub*. A *transferium* is an inland terminal established when the begin-and-end terminals of land networks are pushed out of the port or other large node, and the new terminal location is near to the relieved large node (Figure 11.6): many hinterland vehicles no longer enter the port, and port transport employs specific modes or vehicles. This can be a barge (e.g. between Rotterdam and Ridderkerk in The Netherlands) or truck (e.g. between Dunkerque and Dourges in France). Locations for outplacements can be the landside of a port or an inland node located slightly further away, but having good access to all or many port hinterland corridors. Another barge example is the so-called Container Transferium (barge–truck terminal) that will be constructed 30 km eastwards of the port of Rotterdam and will have a similar function as Ridderkerk, but on a much larger scale. This

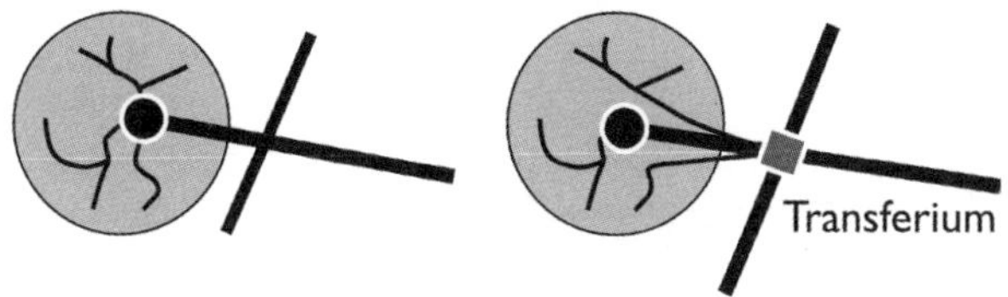

Figure 11.6 Outplacement of the interface between node and land transport to a transferium

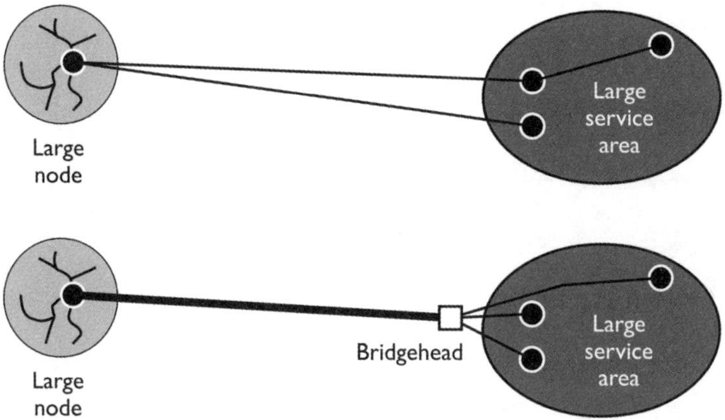

Figure 11.7 Increase of transport scale and service frequency by network concentration to a bridgehead

terminal will also have a major function as empty depot.

The *bridgehead* is an inland terminal designed to access a larger region from for instance a large node (Figure 11.7). The connection between the large node and the bridgehead has a rather large scale in terms of vehicle loads and service frequencies. From the bridgehead there may be all kinds of connections to the larger service area. The bridgehead and its connections are an alternative to complex bundling and come down to network concentration. The classic example is ECT rail terminal Venlo serving many relations between Rotterdam and the Eastern inland and also the result of network concentration: from here containers are distributed by truck to the Ruhrgebiet and to the freight villages in the region of Venlo. The main difference with a typical inland terminal is that the bridgehead serves a larger area which is located further away from the terminal, while the area of an inland terminal lies around and nearby the terminal.

From the viewpoint of the larger service area the bridgehead resembles a transferium as the trunk vehicles do not enter the larger service area. The difference between the two is the motive and the network configuration. The transferium is primarily designed to relieve the large node by outplacement of transport functions from that node to the transferium. Also, the transferium is the beginning and end of many trunk services. The bridgehead is developed to conquer a large market area by increasing transport scale and improving service quality by spatial concentration of services to one route and one node. The performance improvements take place between the large node and the bridgehead. The bridgehead, at least initially, is only connected to the initiating large node and not the begin-and-end of many trunk services. The differences between a transferium and bridgehead may be gradual, dependent

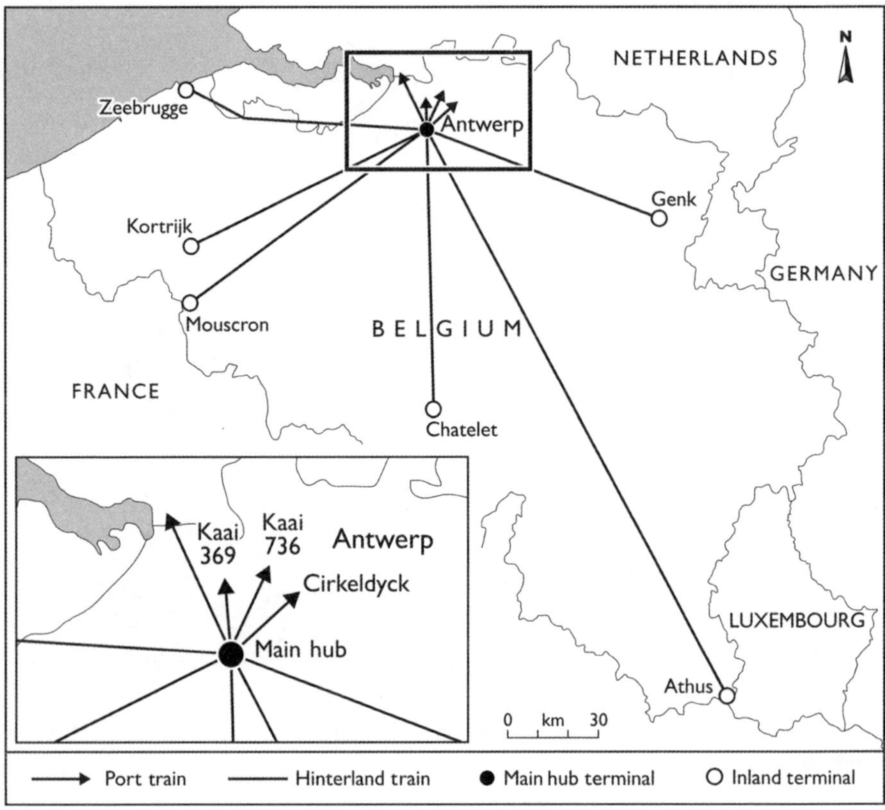

Figure 11.8 The NARCON network and the Mainhub terminal Antwerp in 2008

Source: adapted from Interferryboats, 2008

on the phase of development, the proportion of trunk and local transport services following the satellite. Also, the bridgehead may be the location of functions outplaced from the large node.

In the Belgian rail network NARCON that connects the seaports of Antwerp and Zeebrugge with inland terminals (Figure 11.8), some inland terminals seem to function as transferium and bridgehead. In this network the 'border' terminal Mouscron largely serves the northern part of France just as Athus mainly serves the industries of Luxemburg and of the region around Metz. One of the aims of the NARCON network is the decongestion of Belgian highways, for which reason the European Commission has sanctioned the Belgian subsidies to the network. In this regard the inland terminals of the NARCON network reflect the transferium idea.

The satellite approach also leads to results which are not a real transferium or bridgehead in the sense of the given definitions. An interesting example is the HUPAC terminal in Antwerp, which was also supported by the Swiss government, the thinking being that if the international containerloads have to go by train across the Alps, then start it right at the very beginning, where they are dropped from the deepsea vessels. In a similar approach Alps-crossing train services are extended to terminals further away from the Alps. Eventually the satellite approach can give birth to a new transport network. The best example is the Autoroute ferroviaire extending rail transport of semi-trailers from the Alps to the French inland.

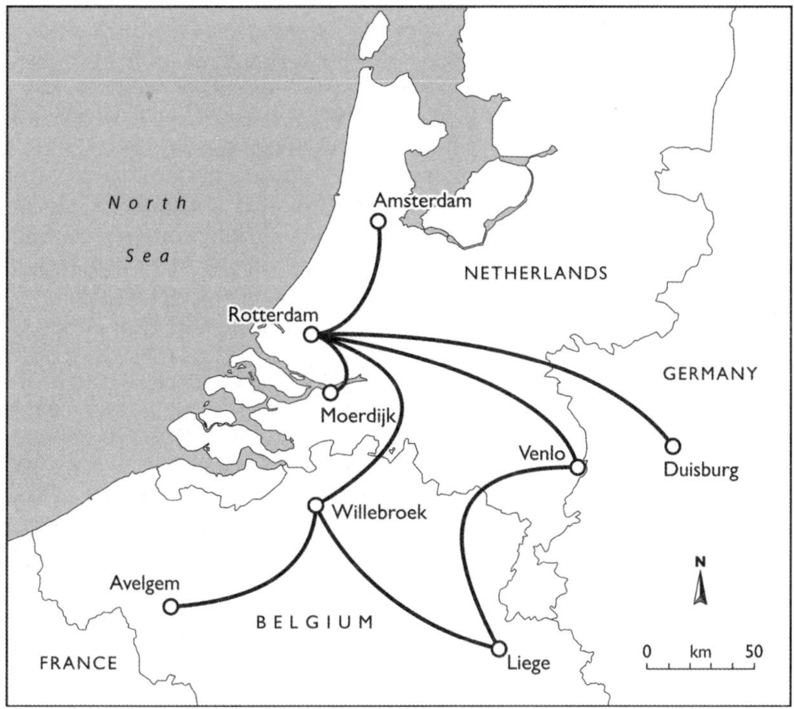

Figure 11.9 Extended gateway terminals of ECT in 2010

Source: ECT

The *extended gateway* is a satellite, typically a bridgehead, enriched with administrative functions, in particular customs. Container seaport terminal operator ECT in Rotterdam is strongly involved in developing hinterland services according to the extended gateway principle. By the end of 2010 its network of extended gateway terminals consisted of seven inland terminals (Figure 11.9).

Effective and efficient terminals or other transport nodes (strategy 7) support the above-mentioned strategies. As barge transport is relatively cheap, barge nodes are a large proportion in the door-to-door chain costs. In a typical hinterland transport chain it could easily amount to 30% (Macharis and Verbeke, 2004). In rail networks, node costs are less impressive (rather 10–20% in a continental chain and dependent on distances of the train service and pre- and post-haulage), but remain a point of attention, and in complex bundling networks can reach critical levels. Next to costs, handling time is an important node performance, at least wherever node handling instead of train roundtrips determine the dwell time of vehicle or load units at the node. For rail–road and barge–road transshipment, modern terminals have been developed, with equipment that is suitable to exchange and store load units of small to large flows. The terminals may be supported by advanced information systems, but handling typically takes place manually. Also shunting facilities have partly been modernised. Here part of the operations is even robotised, for instance the pushing together of wagons at gravity shunting yards by specific devices along the tracks or by robotised shunting locomotives. As far as terminal based complex bundling is concerned, rail–road or barge–road terminals dominate the scene. Numerous innovative terminal concepts, which in terms of layout or technical concept specialise on certain bundling functions, leading to a specific line terminal or hub terminal, or whose performances are improved by robotisation, have been developed and analysed plentifully, but hardly entered the market on a commercial basis. As indicated above, the inland terminal development in this regard is lagging behind the innovation of rail or barge terminals in seaports. The most relevant innovations at inland terminals are the concepts for horizontal transshipment at small flow terminals, like the Mobiler concept for rail–road transshipment in Austria or in the framework of the Swiss Cargo Domino network, or like the ACTS concept for rail–road transshipment in the Dutch rail network for reverse logistics. In barge transport there is a corresponding development, namely cranes on barges. In addition, there is the LoLo terminal concept of Modalohr in the framework of the French Autoroute ferroviair, a high-tech concept definitely improving transshipment performances for the transport of semi-trailers by rail.

INTERMODAL RAIL AND BARGE TERMINALS AND NETWORKS IN EUROPE: SOME FACTS AND FIGURES

Barge and rail transport represented a major market in European inland freight transport in the 1960s, but since then these modes have lost much business to the roads. In 2005 road transport accounted for 77% of the total transport performance (in tonne-km), while rail and barge had shares of 17% and 6% respectively (Eurostat, 2007). Structural changes in freight transport demand has lead towards a composition of cargo types of goods that have historically less affinity with rail and barge transport (semi-finished and consumer goods). In addition, new logistic concepts and changing customer demands have resulted in smaller and more frequent consignments of goods that strongly favoured and increased the role of road transport at the expense of rail and barge transport.

The introduction of cargo unitisation, as a solution to the time-consuming handling of goods, however, has opened up new perspectives for a revival of rail and barge transport, either in transport markets they were not involved in before or in the markets they lost to road transport (e.g. general cargo that was previously a major market for rail). Transporting cargo in load units made it possible to combine the benefits of barge and rail transport with the advantages of road transport, i.e. its high flexibility and accessibility to collect and distribute cargo. This way of freight transport, using load units and a combination of modes, has emerged into a new and promising transport market, which is known as intermodal freight transport.[2] Consequently this new way of transport caused the development of new types of terminals. Their development and characteristics are discussed further in the next sections.

Barge transport

Barge container transport in Europe still functions almost exclusively as a hinterland transport system. Its existence is a direct result of the containerisation of deep sea cargo and the opportunities this development created for barges to transport containers between the seaport and the hinterland when the container volumes to the hinterland increased.

Container barge transport has its roots in transport between Rotterdam, Antwerp and the Rhine river basin, serving the German hinterland. Volumes on the Rhine river have increased from 200,000 TEU in 1995 to some 1.8 million TEU in 2006 (Notteboom and Rodrigue, 2009).

Since the 1990s it has also developed strongly along the north–south axis between the Benelux and Northern France. In addition to these international services in this period domestic hinterland services in The Netherlands and Belgium have also emerged. The opening up of these domestic territories boosted volumes. In 2010 the barge container volume handled in Rotterdam was 2.4 million TEU and 2.3 million TEU in Antwerp. These volumes corresponded with a market share in hinterland transport of respectively 30% for Rotterdam and 33% for Antwerp.

In the meantime barge services have also been developed outside the Rhine–Scheldt–Meuse basins serving the hinterland of other ports. In France container barge transport is flourishing on the Rhone (59,000 TEU in 2010 accounting for 6% of total container hinterland transport of Marseille) and the Seine (170,000 TEU in 2010 which corresponds to a market share of 7% in the hinterland transport of Le Havre compared to 3% in 2000). In Hamburg the barge hinterland services via the Elbe river and the Elbe–Seite and Mittelland canal recorded a volume of 95,000 TEU in 2010 (1% market share in hinterland transport). Compared to the volumes of the other large container ports – Rotterdam and Antwerp – it is still very modest, but nevertheless growing (about 30,000 TEU in 2000). Initiatives are now also taking place to introduce small-scale barge services on the Mantova–Adriatic waterway in Northern Italy (Notteboom and Rodrigue, 2009). The estimated volume of containers transported on inland waterways in Europe amounted 4.5 million TEU in 2006 (Central Commission for Navigation on the Rhine and European Commission, 2008; Promotiebureau Binnenvaart Vlaanderen).

Characteristic of the Rhine river services are the combination of collection–distribution and line service features. In the port barges have to call at a large number of terminals (on average eight terminals) to collect and distribute their containers, while the number of terminals to visit in the hinterland is limited and the service has line bundling characteristics. The Rhine barge services call at three to five terminals per navigation area (Lower Rhine-, Middle Rhine-, Upper Rhine-basin). The inland vessels most commonly used for these Rhine services have capacities ranging from 150 to 208 TEU, but the trend is to bigger vessels, vessel–barge combinations and push convoys (up to 400 TEU and even more). Cost savings are a major stimulus for increasing the scale of operation.

The main driver for calling at a few terminals in the hinterland is to limit the transit time of a service, while on the other hand these multiple calls enable the achievement of a sufficiently high utilisation rate of barges as well as offering acceptable service frequencies.

The successful development of container barge transport on the Rhine has led to the establishment of many terminals. In 2010 about 25 Rhine terminals in Germany are operated. To some extent it is likely that the large number of terminals has resulted in different levels of competition between several of these terminals regarding their service areas. As a result the growth of the handling volumes of these terminals has dimmed, and hence, this line service network still remains very common. Moreover, the strong involvement of Rhine barge operators in the exploitation of inland terminals – and therefore linking their services to their own terminals only – reinforces the existence of this type of network. About two thirds of all terminals in the Rhine basin are operated by inland barge operators or the logistics mother companies of a barge operator. The remaining terminals are operated/owned by stevedoring companies of seaports, inland port authorities (e.g. port autonome de Strasbourg) or logistic service providers (Notteboom and Rodrigue, 2009).

Although container barge transport has reached a development phase of maturity only a few Rhine terminals generate sufficiently large volumes to enable a "one-stop" in the hinterland. The best example is the Duisburg Express, which is a service that only calls at ECT Maasvlakte and Waalhaven in Rotterdam and the DeCeTe-terminal in Duisburg.

Contrary to the Rhine river corridor, in the Dutch and Belgian hinterland calling at one inland terminal is the rule and calling at multiple terminals is the exception. This has much to do with the transit time. Since these barge services are on rather short distances (< 150 km) the transit time performance is more critical, because of heavier competition with road transport on shorter distances. Many of these inland terminals are set up by container trucking companies that exploit the terminal and possibly also the barge service, and execute the pre- and post-truck haulage themselves. The willingness of the container trucking companies to cooperate has been limited. This circumstance has also affected the presence of direct services. Nowadays some of these terminal operators have become owners of several inland terminals. For instance, in The Netherlands the four largest terminal operators own six terminals and have participations in two other terminals and as a result they control about 50% of the barge transport to Dutch inland terminals (Ecorys, 2008). It is interesting to note these holdings have their own geographical focus: Waalhaven Group is focused on South Netherlands (Born in Zuid-Limburg), Binnenland Container Terminals (BCTN) on the middle of East Netherlands (with Nijmegen and Den Bosch), HTS Group on West-Brabant (Oosterhout) en Holwerda with MCS terminals on North Netherlands with Meppel, Groningen en Lelystad. As a consequence these barge services are becoming better coordinated and it offers opportunities to bundle the flows of these terminals.

The characteristics of barge hinterland services in France and Germany are very similar to the services on the Rhine river. Both the limited volumes of inland terminals and the distance in the hinterland justify the multiple calling principle for the hinterland services. Since the French seaports (Le Havre and Marseille) are much smaller than Rotterdam and Antwerp the collection–distribution part of the services is less time-consuming.

The starting point for establishing an inland terminal and barge service is usually the presence of one or a few launching customers, which guarantee a minimum (threshold) transport volume to start operations and hence limit exploitation risks. In that initial phase, where volumes are still small, simple and inexpensive terminal equipment may be chosen, for instance a reach stacker (possibly second-hand) or a general-purpose crane that is mixed used for both container and general cargo transshipment. The accessibility of a location by barge is also a terminal location factor, as it influences the possible vessel size and hence the cost performance of the barge service. The presence of low bridges along the waterway that may limit the stacking height of containers on the vessel (i.e. three layers instead of four) or the presence of locks that can influence the transit time and the reliability of services are also considerations for the terminal location.

As Notteboom and Rodrigue (2009) explain, the size of a service area has a large impact on the competitiveness of an inland terminal (see Figure 11.10). In particular, on short distances from the seaport the threshold coverage of a service area is much smaller than far away from the seaport (see also Nierat, 1997). The larger pre- and post-haulage costs in larger service areas hamper the terminals' ability to attract new business, result in longer delivery times and increase the risk of competition with other inland terminals and this impedes the acquisition of new customers. Therefore the expected terminal profitability is highest for terminals with a high throughput and a small service area (Notteboom and Rodrigue, 2009).

The absence of an extra terminal handling and one pre- or post-haulage in the hinterland transport chain is a major explanation for the strong competitiveness of barge transport to road transport in hinterland transport, even on short distances (< 75 km). These additional cost factors are, among others, also a major reason why continental barge transport services have not really been developed yet (Konings, 2010). Government policies (at the local, regional, national and supranational level) that focused on a modal shift from road to barge transport had a strong influence on the establishment of barge terminals. Especially since the 1990s, the provision of subsidies for terminal investments and start-premiums for services has contributed to the rapid growth of the number of terminals, particularly in The Netherlands and in Belgium. Although the financial support has diminished now it still has an impact on the location to start new business.

Obviously expanding the terminal network may lead to a further fragmentation of

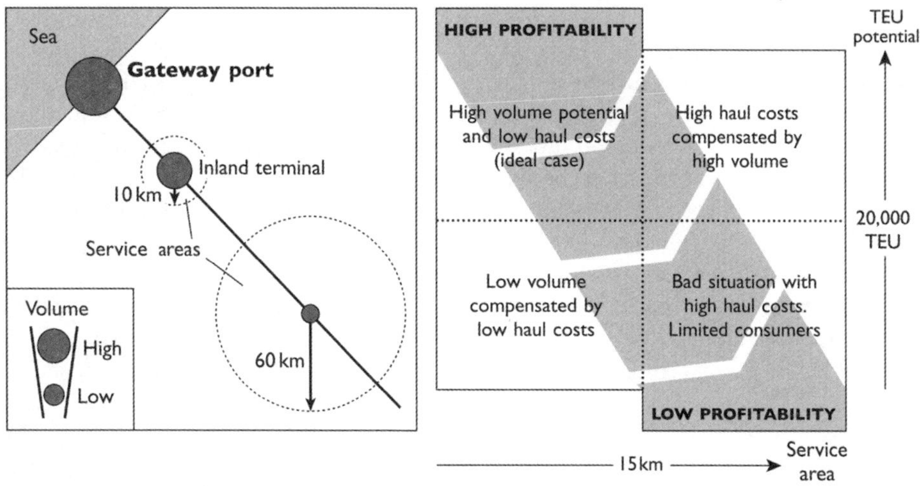

Figure 11.10 Relationship between the characteristics of the service area of inland barge terminals and terminal profitability (representative for the situation of Dutch inland terminals)

Source: Notteboom and Rodrigue, 2009

the hinterland flows, while there is actually a need for consolidation of flows at inland terminals. Consolidation of flows could substantially contribute to a more efficient handling of barges in the seaport, which could have a significant impact on the performance of hinterland transport. On the other hand, if the new terminal can achieve a high throughput based on a small service area it may create additional flows for intermodal barge transport without cannibalising the market of neighbouring terminals.

In reviewing the current location of inland barge terminals in Europe it is clear that their presence is to a large extent related to the quality and density of the inland waterway network. In 2009 The Netherlands accounted about 33 terminals in operation and many terminals still planned to be built, but also the terminal network in Germany (about 45 terminals along the Rhine and its tributaries) and Belgium (12 terminals) can be considered as rather dense. France recorded nine barge inland terminals.

Rail transport

Intermodal rail transport can take place in many forms. Following common definitions it may consist of unaccompanied transport, i.e. containers, swap bodies and trailers and accompanied transport, i.e. rail carriage of entire road vehicles. In addition, intermodal transport is applied both in hinterland transport and continental transport in the whole of Europe. Moreover, many operators are involved in the intermodal rail transport market. As a result it is a fragmented market, which hampers obtaining a comprehensive up-to-date overview of the transported volumes. In the market of unaccompanied transport the total volume in Europe (covering the 27 EU Member States as well as Norway and Switzerland) was estimated at 13.5 million TEU in 2005 (KombiConsult et al., 2006).

Although the history of intermodal rail transport started with continental transport shipments it seems that its development has been boosted by the emergence of hinterland (maritime land) transport by rail. About 56% of the total unaccompanied volume in 2005 was hinterland transport, while 44% consisted of continental transport. Within these market segments there is also a clear difference regarding the shares of domestic and international transport: domestic services accounted for 73% of hinterland shipments and only for 38% in continental transport. A major explanation is that in general the transport distance in continental services must be larger than in hinterland services in order to be competitive with road transport, because in the continental services both pre- and end-haulage is needed. Particularly in countries with a rather small territory, such as The Netherlands, Belgium or Denmark, domestic transport distances are usually too short for intermodal transport to compete with road transport.

Countries in which rail freight transport traditionally plays a relatively important role also show the strongest involvement in intermodal transport, i.e. Germany, Italy and France. In 2005 these countries performed more than 50% of all domestic unaccompanied intermodal rail transport (KombiConsult et al., 2006). The volumes of accompanied intermodal rail transport are much smaller (representing about 5% of the intermodal rail transport market) and are even more geographically concentrated: mainly in the corridors crossing the Alpine states of Austria and Switzerland. These intermodal flows are largely a result of the national transport policies of these countries pursuing a modal shift aiming at reducing the negative impacts of road transport especially cross-border and transit road traffic. In 2005 nine intermodal operators were offering these kinds of rail services and together they shipped more than 323,000 road vehicles.

Contrary to barge transport, launching a new intermodal rail service is much more complex and involves higher costs and risks. Finding the necessary critical mass in transport volume is a challenge. This is especially the case in continental transport relations where cargo flows tend to be more fragmented and dispersed.

The rail liberalisation has resulted in many new intermodal rail operators and consequently in the number of services offered. "Forwarders or shipping lines whose core business is to organise door-to-door or port-to-port logistics such as Ambrogio, CMA-CGM (Rail Link), DHL, Hangartner, Hellmann or Maersk (European Rail Shuttle), in the last decade have inaugurated intermodal services for own account" (UIC, 2008). In addition, the roles of old players are changing. For instance, alongside a classical railway company cooperating with one of its rail operators in a one-to-one relation, different one-to-many or many-to-many relations have emerged (Kreutzberger, 2008), especially in international networks. For instance, the rail operators HUPAC, CEMAT and KombiVerkehr together have organised a train service employing several traction providers in different countries (Kunz, 2004).

Another feature of changing roles is due to the scarcity of wagons, which has driven old and new rail operators to purchase their own wagons reducing the role of railway companies in intermodal transport to the provision of traction, contrary to the wagonload sector where the railway companies still provide whole trains. The rail liberalisation has also stimulated new traction providers to enter the market, and some rail operators to carry out their own traction (Kreutzberger, 2008). Or as UIC (2008) puts it: "Some of these new operators even push the inauguration further ahead by providing rail traction or terminal handling services of their own" (UIC, 2008). With regard to terminals, some rail operators have become involved in rail terminals while also seaports or their stevedores have started train services or become involved in terminals. For instance:

- the Swiss rail operator HUPAC exploits inland terminals and has recently opened a new terminal in the seaport of Antwerp;
- ECT operates the inland rail and barge terminal of Venlo.

Some of the seaport operators are developing intermodal rail and barge services which are under full own control (e.g. ECT in the port of Rotterdam). In addition to improving the hinterland transport service this is a way to bind customers in the hinterland, making them less footloose to switch to other seaport terminal operators or other ports. For instance, HHLA in Hamburg has participation in rail terminals (e.g. Melnik and Budapest) to support its rail products via Polzug, Metrans and HHCE (Notteboom and Rodrigue, 2009). The involvement of port authorities range from extending some of their traditional landlord tasks in the seaport to the hinterland to even participations in facilities. For example, the port of Rotterdam has provided the infrastructure of some inland terminals (i.e. Wansum, Alphen a/d Rijn and Alblasserdam) to support the terminal development at these locations. In Lyon the port authority of Marseille is one of the shareholders in the inland port of Lyon.

Rail terminals in Europe are often directly or indirectly built and operated by large railway undertakings. Before European rail liberalisation the respective national railway companies established national networks of rail terminals. The entry of new players due to the rail liberalisation process meant that major rail centres are now witnessing a multiplication in the number of rail terminal facilities, with each terminal being operated by a specific rail operator (Notteboom and Rodrigue, 2009). There is a trend towards splitting responsibilities regarding the management and ownership of terminals; however, most terminals operate on the basis of the principle of non-discriminatory access, at least for those terminals that have received public funding (European Intermodal Association, 2010).

The network of intermodal rail terminals is extensive. For instance, in Germany there are more than 100 terminals, many of them are trimodal (rail–barge–road) and a few have a major role in RoRo (roll-on roll-off) operations (i.e. Freiburg, Regensburg, Singen). In France the number of intermodal rail terminals is about 40. Austria has 15 rail terminals (among them four trimodal terminals), Belgium 13 inland rail terminals (among them six trimodal terminals) and The Netherlands 11 inland rail terminals (among them six trimodal terminals).

INTERMODAL INLAND TERMINALS: A TYPOLOGY

The evolution of rail and barge networks has led to a range of node types. This section gives an overview of the most important types, distinguishing between multimodal and unimodal nodes. The different types are classified, which leads to a typology. This typology is the result of field observations, literature study and the ideas from the previous sections.

Multimodal inland terminals in intermodal networks

Multimodal terminals like rail–road or barge–road terminals give access to the rail or barge network. They owe their existence to the labour division between trains and barges for trunk transport and trucks for local transport, or to the fact that inland the rail and especially the barge networks do not access all regions or locations. Pre- and post-haulage road networks connect these terminals with the origins and destinations, like factories, trade centres, or numerous activities in cities. The multimodal terminals can be begin-and-end terminals or line terminals. The latter are common in barge networks. Many barge–road terminals, in particular along the Rhine, are begin-and-end terminals for some services and line terminals for other services. Terminal layout and equipment are the same for both exchange functions.

Line bundling in the rail sector traditionally depended on shunting. The configuration is complicated, as each line terminal requires a flat shunting yard in its vicinity to (de)couple wagon(group)s from/to the passing freight trains. A local locomotive moves the wagons between this yard and the terminal. Terminal-based line bundling takes place in small amounts at regular rail–road terminals which – for other services – mainly serve as begin-and-end terminals.

Most rail terminals are LoLo (lift-on lift-off), mainly occupied with the transshipment of containers and swap bodies, and to some extent also semi-trailers. Networks with RoRo terminals serve niche markets, like Rollende Landstrasse (trucks) or semi-trailers, across the Alps or through the Channel Tunnel. Handling time at RoRo and LoLo terminals can be short. In practice, fast terminals have only been implemented for the transshipment of semi-trailers; these are LoLo terminals. Most inland terminals serve the continental and hinterland market, unlike seaports, which often have separate terminals for continental and hinterland flows.

In the second section of this chapter multimodal terminals were also categorised according to their function with regard to large nodes, like large megacities or seaports. Some inland terminals focus on their own service area, while others focus on the transfer function and resemble satellites of the large nodes: dependent on the motivation to perform this function, its role in the transport network as well as the kind of activities that take place in this inland node, this led to a distinction between, transferium, bridgehead and extended gateway terminals.

The types of equipment that are used at intermodal rail and barge LoLo terminals are rather similar although there are also differences. Rail and barge terminals have in common the use of cranes for large to medium flows, of mobile equipment, i.e. reach stackers and fork lifts for small terminals, and of specific equipment for very small terminals. The latter equipment must be suitable for train, truck or barge drivers to steer as there is no stable terminal staff. The differences between rail and barge terminals are the types of cranes or of specific equipment, and the situations when to choose one or the other. At rail terminals, cranes are used at a throughput of under 30,000 load units a year up to in excess of 200,000 units per year (Vrenken et al., 2005). These cranes span two to three, maximally, five tracks (exceptionally more, like the rail–road terminal in Basel) plus lanes for trucks, load unit positioning or even load unit stacking. For barges the span covers the quay, the storage area plus lanes for trucks.

A new development in intermodal barge handling technology is the emergence of self (un-)loading vessels, i.e. vessels that have a crane aboard. Such vessels offer a high level of flexibility regarding possible locations for loading and unloading containers, independent of the transport volumes. As such they can be considered as a promising solution to get small and dispersed container flows loaded and unloaded in a cost-effective way.

The utilisation rate of equipment very much determines the choice of type. With some utilisation rates, heavy equipment tends to have lower transshipment costs per load unit than light equipment. But for smaller flow sizes it is better to have well-utilised light equipment than badly used heavy equipment. This relation is – for barges – illustrated by Figure 11.11. The barge handler, which is a special type of reach stacker, has the lowest cost per unit for each transshipment volume. The capital costs of gantry cranes and mobile cranes are much higher and hence the handling costs are higher, particularly when the volumes are small. In establishing a new barge terminal facility mobile cranes or barge handlers may be used, but if handling volumes increase, besides costs, handling capacity and efficient land use at the terminal are gaining importance, and this makes the gantry crane the preferred facility at barge terminals. Nowadays most inland barge terminals in Europe, also

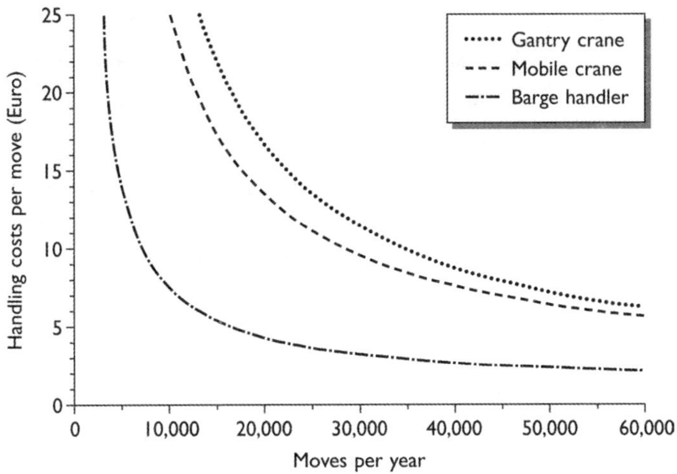

Figure 11.11 The relationship between transshipment volume and costs

Source: Konings, 2010

smaller ones, are equipped with a crane. Larger terminals may have two gantry cranes and ancillary equipment, i.e. reach stackers. Additionally empty handlers may be present to stack empty containers. Small terminals may have a mobile or gantry crane. Offering additional services such as container storage can generate additional revenue to cover part of the terminal operation costs.

Besides LoLo terminals there are the RoRo terminals:

- for trucks, typically serving dedicated RoRo trains. One can find them in the regions where trucks are forced to use trains, such as crossing the Alps or the Channel Tunnel.
- for semi-trailers, typically serving dedicated RoRo trains. The French railways have extended the concept to the most tangible result of any attempt to serve the road sector in a way, which it highly appreciates, not only for the Alps. The high-tech RoRo terminals of ModalOhr in the framework of Autoroute Ferroviaire for the unaccompanied transport of semi-trailers enable the loading or unloading of a whole train within 20 minutes if all trucks are present 45 minutes before the train's arrival and in the proper position (Chaumatte, 2004). Such performance favours fast train roundtrips and short door-to-door times (strategies 3 and 4).

Based on the characteristics of intermodal terminals as described here a classification of terminals can be made. This classification is presented in Table 11.1 and illustrated with some examples.

Unimodal inland terminals and unimodal exchange at other terminals in intermodal networks

Unimodal exchange of load units between trains takes place by shunting single wagons or wagon groups at gravity shunting yards, by shunting wagon groups at flat shunting yards or by transshipping load units at terminals. Unimodal exchange of load units between barges currently merely takes place, but where it does, it will always be transshipment at terminals. The exchange of pushed barges between push barge services does not exist. Most current rail–rail and all current barge–barge transshipment takes place at terminals

Table.11.1 Typology of implemented (including former) multimodal inland terminals*

	Regular inland terminal	Transferium	Bridgehead (with or without extended gateway functions)
LoLo terminal			
Large to medium volumes Gantry or portal cranes	Keulen Eifeltor (r, D), Duisburg (r + b, D)	Dourges (r, F), Ridderkerk (b, NL)	Venlo, (trimodal, NL) ↕
Smaller volumes Reach stackers, fork lifters. For barge mobile crane or barge handler	Bonneuil sur Marne (b, F)	Kortrijk LAR (NARCON, r, B) ↔	Avelgem (b, B)
Very small volumes, or irregular or niche market Transshipment equipment on board of vehicles. No steady terminal staff	Mobiler (r, AU and CH), ACTS (r, NL), Mercurius crane vessel (b, NL) ↔		
RoRo terminal			
RoRo trucks (mainly Alps)	Mannheim (Rhine RoRo services, b, D) ↕ ↕	Different Alp crossing rail services ↔	
RoRo for semi-trailers	Autoroute ferroviaire (F): terminals for turntable wagons ↔		

* The terminals are begin-and-end terminals. A few rail and many barge terminals, especially along the Rhine, also serve as line terminals. Also the Autoroute ferroviaire terminals can serve as line terminals
D = Germany, F = France, CH = Switzerland, AU = Austria, B = Belgium, NL = Netherlands
r = rail, b = barge

whose main function is multimodal transshipment (rail–road, rail–barge). In rail transport also the real rail–rail terminal exists (call it a true rail hub terminal).

The difference between both terminal types is that the true hub terminal is designed for rail–rail or barge–barge transshipment: it is capable of transshipping load units between trains or barges, which visit the terminal simultaneously. Its layout differs from that of a multimodal one. A true rail hub terminal is capable of dealing with larger amounts of rail–rail transshipment, therefore has more tracks under a crane than a rail–road terminal. In addition, the true rail hub terminal may have a terminal internal transport system, which is to connect crane segments, quickly move a container from the front position of one train to the end position of another train, and to substitute crane movements. In the layout of a true barge–barge terminal cranes cover several barges standing side-by-side in order to minimise crane distances. The unimodal terminals may also carry out multimodal transshipment, as this will most likely increase their utilisation rates.

The hub rail terminal was invented to improve the performance of rail-rail exchange and therefore of hub-and-spoke bundling (strategies 1, 2, 3 and 7). It has, as discussed before, acceptable costs and time performances for all rail hub-and-spoke markets including flows which are too small to fill wagon groups.

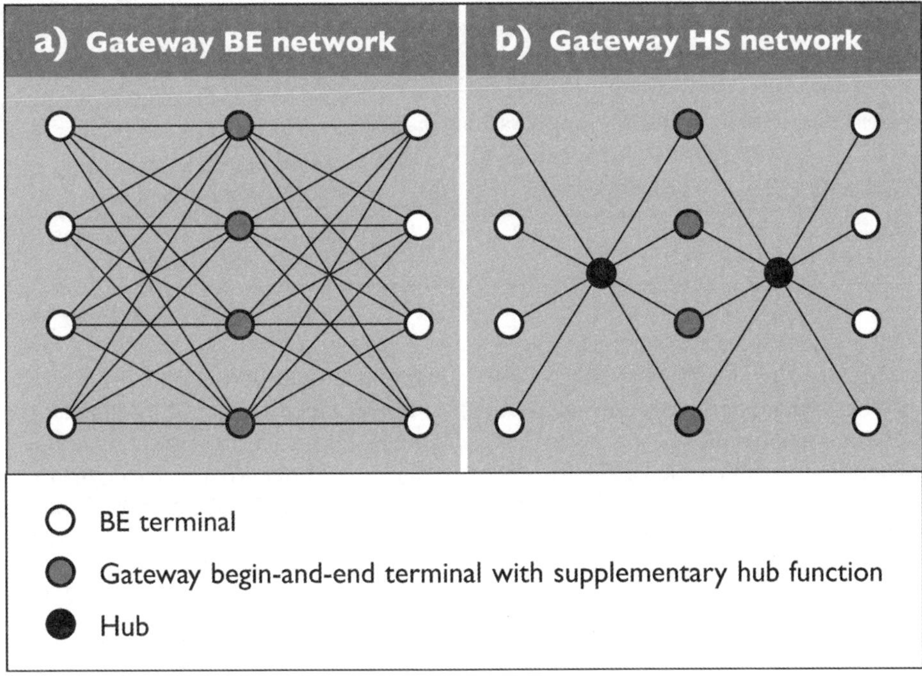

Figure 11.12 Gateway networks: interconnecting two direct (or other bundling) networks at their begin-and-end terminals

Source: Kreutzberger, 2008

Nevertheless, a network of true rail hub terminals is hardly implemented. The major example of an implemented true rail hub terminal is the Mainhub terminal Antwerp. Generally speaking, unimodal terminal transshipment at terminals is still exceptional, both in rail networks because most rail–rail exchange still takes place by shunting, and in barge networks because line bundling instead of hub-and-spoke or other bundling with barge–barge exchange dominates. In the rail sector the gateway terminal has become a mainstream configuration. It is applied by numerous rail operators, as it is much simpler to implement. Also, this solution makes the rail operator more independent from shunting yards and other node infrastructure of other companies.

The *gateway terminal*, not to be confused with the term *extended gateway*, is about organising rail–rail transshipment of load units between trains visiting at a begin-and-end-terminal. The rail–road terminal then has some rail–rail transshipment. HUPAC is the inventor of the concept and interconnects Italian service networks with north-European ones at its gateway terminals near Milan. The concept is also adopted by other operators with Italian services, such as CEMAT or SOGEMAR using the gateway terminals Verona, Melzo (Milan) and Padua, and by other operators on other European regions, or ERS using Czech rail–road terminals to interconnect train services. The gateway concept essentially pushes two direct networks together at their begin-and-end-terminals without generating scale effects (Figure 11.12). As most load units go from and to the region of the gateway terminals, most trains arrive in the late night to early morning and depart in the late afternoon to early night, meaning that the rail–rail load unit has a waiting time of for instance 12 hours. Such performance is the reason for, as already mentioned before, UIC recommending the gateway configuration only for long distances

Table 11.2 Existing unimodal terminals

	Large to medium amounts of unimodal transshipment	Small amounts of unimodal transshipment
Dedicated rail–rail terminals	Hub terminal: Mainhub Antwerp (B)	
Rail–road terminals with rail–rail transshipment		Gateway terminals like HUPAC and SOGEMAR terminals (I)
Barge–road terminals with barge–barge transshipment		Some barge-road terminals like DIT terminal in Duisburg (D)

(KombiConsult and K+P, 2007), for which the connection North-Europe/South Italy is a good example.

"A terminal is like a dance floor", says the CEO of Swissterminal (2010). The dancers decide how to use it. In this sense a gateway terminal could gradually evolve into a hub, as the share of rail–rail transshipment increases and more train services change to arrival and departure times, which are favourable for rail–rail transshipment. However, as a ballet floor may be unsuitable for a house party, so will the rail–road terminal be unsuitable for larger amounts of rail–rail transshipment. The terminal would very probably need to be "retrofitted" to a true hub terminal. Table 11.2 summarizes the different types of unimodal terminals.

FUTURE DEVELOPMENTS AND CHALLENGES

Intermodal rail and barge terminals derive their existence from the development of intermodal freight transport as a rather new and promising growth market for rail transport and inland shipping. On the other hand they are also an important facilitator to enable growth of intermodal freight transport: the functioning of terminals is crucial for the performance of the intermodal transport chain and the establishment of new terminals enables the extension of the geographical scope and coverage of the intermodal transport market. In view of the still very modest share of intermodal transport in Europe, which is estimated at less than 5% of the total surface traffic (in tonne-km) (Savy and Aubriot, 2005), and the need for more sustainable transport there remains a challenge to further improve the competitiveness of the intermodal transport in relation to road transport. This assumes an improvement in costs and quality of services in existing geographical markets that are already served, as well as establishing new services to capture new markets for intermodal transport. Inland terminals will have to play a major role to support these developments.

Some promising directions of terminal innovation at inland nodes that can support this intermodal transport development are:

1 a stronger market penetration of:
   a true rail hub terminals, optionally high performance ones;
   b specific line terminals;
   c innovative RoRo systems for semi-trailers for special geographic markets;
   d terminal concepts without or with hardly any terminal staff at inland nodes with very small, irregular or niche flows;
2 revised barge terminal operations to improve hinterland transport:
   e extended co-operation between inland terminals;
   f implementation of a barge hub terminal along the Rhine river;
3 the robotisation of operations for large inland terminals (rail, barge).

Hub terminals have been in discussion since the 1990s. Despite the superior performances of true hub terminals their market penetration is still very limited. In Germany, governments in 2012 have decided financing for the megahub Lehrte near Hannover. It is designed to be suitable for hinterland and continental flows. The terminal will allow batches of up to six trains with mutual load unit exchange to be handled simultaneously. Dwell times of trains and load units are planned to be relatively short. Next to rail–rail transshipment there will be rail–road transshipment. It will be the first hub terminal involving new technical concepts such as robotised sorting and internal transport and sorting. The terminal will have six tracks beneath the cranes plus truck lanes and a robotised internal transport and sorting system. The producer company for the transport and sorting system suggested a linear motor pallet system.

Less progressed is the preparation of SBB Cargo for a hub terminal in Limmatal which is to function as the interface between international train services and the domestic rail network. The transshipment will – according to project aims – consist of 80% rail–rail transshipment, mainly between international trains, and 20% rail–road transshipment (SBB Cargo, 2010). More recently, PCC has presented plans to integrate the flows of Gdynia, Gdansk and Sopot by means of a new hub terminal, the so-called intermodal container yard (ICY) Tczew. Here, load units can be transshipped between trains to and from the three nodes (PCC, 2012).

The megahub-Lehrte will be a high-performance hub terminal. The relevance of high-performance depends, as far as transport time is concerned, on the geographical situation. An example illustrating that the relevance can be high, is the Commutator network of SNCF fret, presented in the 1990s, which intentionally would have similar performances as a BE network (Jalard, 1993a and b). In other words, the majority of domestic services would be day A/B night-jump operations. The instruments were fast hub exchange by means of an NG terminal, and fast link transport. For different reasons the concept was rejected. Instead a national HS network with classical shunting was realised (shunting hub Paris, slower trains) only providing afternoon arrivals on day B or day A/C-connections for the majority of relations. This implied less quality and higher train costs. The negative performances urged the French actors to abolish this network in 2005, about ten years after its erection. We do not advocate the technical features of this ambitious concept, but emphasise the relevance of high performances for specific geographical settings.

For line bundling the central question for rail terminals is whether, as in barge transport, the handling of line trains should remain performed at begin-and-end terminals, or whether specific terminals should be developed that are better equipped for line train handling. These terminals should nevertheless still allow the handling of direct trains as well. Specific line terminals could sort a higher transport quality, and, if the improved operations lead to a higher roundtrip productivity, potentially also lower costs. Both, (fast) hub or line terminals face the challenge of how to combine electrical traction with load unit transshipment. Ideally the electrical locomotive is not decoupled from its wagons in order to reduce train handling and control time and costs at the nodes. Technical solutions in this field (like specific crane devices or switchable catenaries) have not been developed to maturity, perhaps a failure deserving an evaluation. The second best solution is electric trains entering a terminal by momentum, as practised in Germany. In the meantime, a concept with horizontal terminal transshipment and corresponding trains has also been proposed together with a network idea, namely the Italian MetroCargo (ILOG, 2006). The terminal having specific sliding techniques at the terminals (Figure 11.13b) has been tested in a pilot.

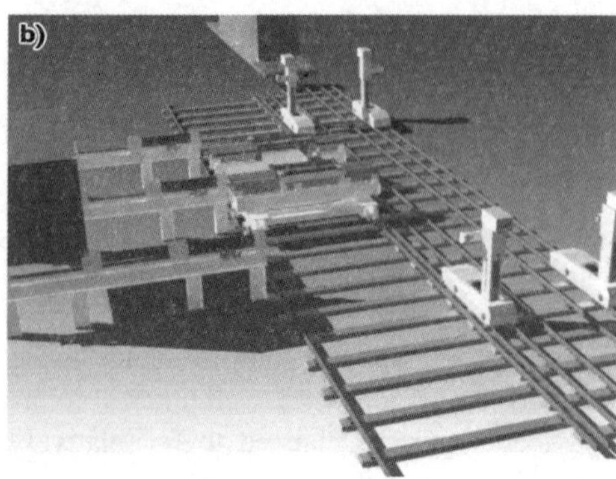

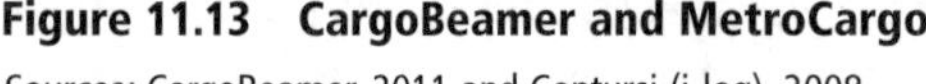

Figure 11.13 CargoBeamer and MetroCargo
Sources: CargoBeamer, 2011 and Contursi (i-log), 2008

Innovative RoRo concepts refer to the unaccompanied transport of semi-trailers between terminals with horizontal transshipment. They have better performances than concepts with vertical transshipment for semi-trailers and concepts for accompanied transport, according to the quick-scan of 81 concepts and analyses of six selected ones by Van Gorp and Van der Zandt (2003). There is a number of concepts with horizontal transshipment of semi-trailers, the Modalohr concept already being operated on a commercial basis. Another concept with horizontal transshipment of semi-trailers, namely CargoBeamer, is on its way to implementation. Cargo Beamer has announced (2012) to built a CargoBeamer terminal in Calais and develop CargoBeamer train services on two European corridors by 2014. Other concepts have hardly passed the pilot stage. In the Modalohr concept each wagon has a turntable. CargoBeamer employs sliding techniques mainly in the infrastructure (Figure 11.13a). Another difference is that (un)loading trains requires truck drivers in the Modalohr concept. In the CargoBeamer concept the truck and train operations are easier to decouple.

As regards the further development of intermodal barge transport in hinterland transport the major challenge for the ports of Antwerp and Rotterdam, where barge transport already has a strong position but also still has much room to grow, is to improve the efficiency of barge handling in these seaports. The solution for this problem can be found in the ports themselves or in the hinterland. The latter also assumes a different role of the inland terminals. The core of the problem is that barges have multiple terminal calls in the seaport and this makes the handling process time-consuming and causes unreliability of services due to waiting times of barges. Moreover, since barges visit multiple terminals also the average call size is small, leading to a relatively long handling time per terminal and hence lower terminal productivity. These effects are particularly pronounced for small barges visiting the port.

A possible solution to the problem of small call sizes and time losses in seaports is the bundling of barge container flows at a limited number of seaport terminals. This, however, increases inter-terminal transport and handling costs for the stevedore. Given the fact that handling costs take up a large share of the total port-to-door transport costs, particularly for short port-to-door distances, this would hamper the competitiveness of barge transport in relation to road transport (Notteboom and Rodrigue, 2009). A more promising solution would be to bundle the flows per sea container terminal at strategically located inland terminals, where bundling is performed either by trucks or barges. Some contours of developments in this direction

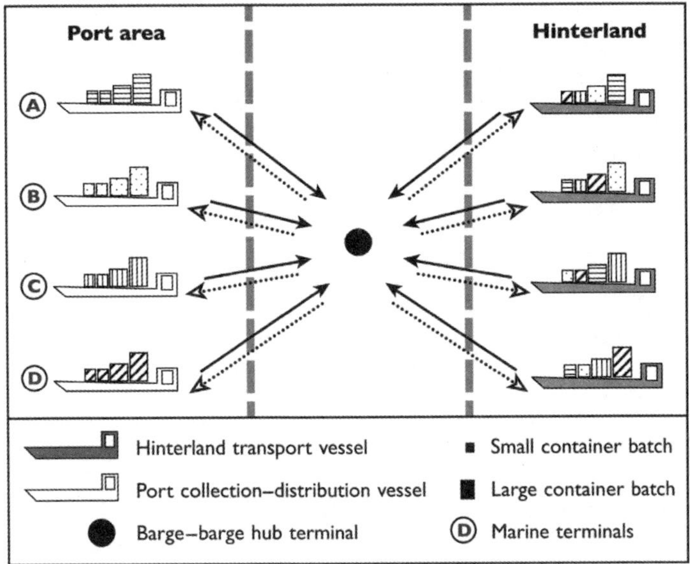

Figure 11.14 Visualisation of barge transport operations with a mega hub

have become noticeable. A group of four inland barge terminals in the southern part of The Netherlands, organised in Brabant Intermodal, has taken the initiative to pursue more efficiency, i.e. bundle their container flows to the port of Rotterdam. Containers that would lead to a small call size in the seaport are exchanged by truck between these terminals to have a smaller number of calls and larger call sizes of their vessels sailing between these terminals and Rotterdam.

Another direction to improve the handling process in the seaport would be the introduction of an inland hub terminal. After a decade of concept development and discussions in this field, there seems to be a serious attempt for implementation: Contargo, the largest container barge operator in Northwest Europe, is planning to build a mega-hub barge terminal in the German hinterland, which is scheduled for operation in 2015 or 2016. This terminal, having a projected annual handling capacity of 1 million TEU, will be a dedicated barge transshipment terminal: containers will be exchanged between inland vessels sailing dedicated to the terminals in the seaports of Rotterdam and Antwerp and inland vessels that only operate between the mega-hub and inland terminals upstream on the Rhine river (Figure 11.14). On the one hand such kinds of barge operations increase the call size of vessels in the seaport and hence improve the productivity of the seaport terminals. On the other hand it also improves the productivity of the inland terminals and results in a better utilisation of vessel capacity and a shorter turnaround time of vessels operating in the hinterland. The expectation is that the cost benefits that result from these revised services will more than offset the costs of additional handling in the hub.

The question arises whether high performance inland terminals, certainly hubs, will or should be (semi-)robotised in the future. As hub terminals are most likely developed to handle relatively large volumes in a cheap, fast and reliable way, robotised processes may be profitable. Moreover, continual increasing labour costs could also become an incentive for terminal robotisation, knowing that labour costs nowadays already have a significant share in terminal operation costs. The positive experiences with robotised processes at terminals in seaports (e.g. at ECT in Rotterdam and HHLA Altenwerder in Hamburg) could be a stimulus for robotised operations at large inland terminals.

NOTES

1 That part which does not equalise the rhythm differences between sea and land transport, but simply represents additional waiting.
2 Intermodal freight transport is generally defined as the movement of goods in one and the same loading unit or vehicle by successive modes of transport without handling of the goods themselves when changing modes (European Conference of Ministers of Transport et al., 1997). Loading units can be containers, swap bodies and trailers.
3 For instance, Rapp Infra (2007) comments that the width of a Modalohr terminal is too large for any potential location in northwest Switzerland.

REFERENCES

Beisler, L., J. Kettler and P. Molle (1995) "Rationalisierunbg bei der Zugbildung un Nahbereichsbedienung im Schienengüterverkehr", *Eisenbahntechnische Rundschau*, No. 4, pp. 225–231.

Blier, G. (1991) "Noevelle géographie ferroviaire de la France. Tome 1: Le réseau: structure et funtionnement", *La vie du rail*, Paris.

Cardebring, P.W., R. Fiedler, Ch. Reynauld and P. Weaver (2000) *Summary of the IQ project. Analysing intermodal quality; a key step towards enhancing intermodal performance and market share in Europe*, Hamburg and Paris: TFK and INRETS.

CargoBeamer (2011) "CargoBeamer Flyer", www.cargobeamer.com

Central Commission for Navigation on the Rhine and European Commission (2008) "Market observation 2007 for inland navigation in Europe", Strasbourg.

Chaumatte, M. (2004) "L'Autoroute ferroviaire Alpine: une solution originale pour le transit alpine des camions", *Revue Générale de Chemins de Fer* Octobre, pp. 5–16.

CNT (2004) "Restructuring of transport firms", *Transport/Europe. Bulletin of the Observatory on Transport Policies and Strategies in Europe*, May, Paris.

Contursi (2008) An innovative system for intermodal freight transport in villages and ports, *11th International Conference Cities and Ports*, Stockholm, i-log (MetroCargo), www.citiesandports2008.com

Delavelle, CH., V. Berest and J. Roger-Machart (2003) *Evaluation des politiques publiques en faveur du transport combiné rail-route*, TN Sofres Consulting in co-operation with Kereon, MDS Transmodal, Somea, PTV and ERRI, commissioned by the Comissiarat général du Plan, Paris.

Dobeschinsky, H. and S. Bitter (2004) "Untersuchung zum Güterbahnconcept an einer Hauptstrecke", *Eisenbahntechnische Rundschau*, No. 3, pp. 143–149.

ECMT (2003) *National Policies Towards Shifting Freight From Road to Rail. The Case Switzerland, the United Kingdom and France*, Paris.

Ecorys (2008) *Sectorstudie van zee- tot binnenhaven; Marktwerking in het goederenvervoer over water*, Rotterdam.

European Conference of Ministers of Transport, European Conference of Ministers of Transport, United Nations Economic Commission for Europe Statistical Division and European Union Eurostat (1997) *Glossary for Transport Statistics*, Paris.

European Intermodal Association (2010) *Intermodal yearbook 2010; Strategies, Statistics, Terminals and Players*, Brussels.

Eurostat (2007) *Panorama of Transport*, Luxembourg: Office for Official Publications of the European Communities.

Gorp, H.A. van, M.M. van der Zandt (2003) *Trailers-on-train, de praktische invulling, eindrapportage*, commissioned by the Ministerie van Verkeer en Waterstaat, The Hague.

Hahn, C. (1998) "L'Europe pour echiquier", *Fret Magazine*, No. 96, pp. 12–18.

ILOG (2006) "Metrocargo", www.ilog.it

Jalard, B. (1993a) "Le project Commutor de la SNCF", *TEC*, no. 116, January–February, pp. 20–23.

Jalard, B. (1993b) "The Commutor project", Cargo Systems, 1993, *Intermodal 93. Conference papers*, Hamburg.

Kennisinstituut voor Mobiliteitsbeleid (2007) *Marktontwikkelingen in het goederenvervoer per spoor 1996–2020* (concept), The Hague.

KombiConsult, UIC and K+P Transport Consultants (2006) *DIOMIS: Developing Infrastructure and Operating Models for Intermodal Shift, Final Report*, Work package A11: Report on Combined Transport in Europe 2005, Frankfurt am Main.

KombiConsult and K+P Transport Consultants (2007) *International Combined Transport Productions Systems including long and heavy trains*, Work package A7, commissioned by UIC in the framework of DIOMIS (Developing Infrastructure and Operating Models for Intermodal Shift), Paris.

Konings, R. (2010) *Intermodal Barge Transport: Network Design, Nodes and Competitiveness*, TRAIL Thesis series, Nr. T2009/11, Delft: TRAIL Research School.

Kreutzberger, E. (2008) *The innovation of intermodal rail freight bundling networks in Europe: Concepts, developments and performances*, TRAIL Thesis series, Nr. T2008/16, Delft: TRAIL Research School.

Kunz, B. (2004) "Mut wird belohnt", *Cargo, Das Logistikmagazin von SBB Cargo*, No. 2, p. 9.

Laguzzi, G. (2001) "The Italian gouvernment supports intermodal transport", *Fermerci* (Trenitalia), supplement no. 6, November/December.

Macharis, C. and A. Verbeke (2004) *Intermodaal binnenvaartvervoer. Economische en strategische asepcten van het intermodaal binnenvaartvervoer in Vlaanderen*, Antwerpen/Apeldoorn: Garant.

Müller, U. (2005) *ICF restructures its traffic after a difficult year in 2004 to focus on more promising routes*, ICF, Media release 06/05, www.icfonline.com

Nierat, P. (1997) "Market area of rail-truck terminals: pertinence of the spatial theory", *Transport Research Part A: Policy and Practice*, Vol. 31, No. 2, pp. 19–127.

Notteboom, T. and J.P. Rodrigue (2009) *Inland Terminals, Regions and Supply Chains, Dry Port Development in Asia and other Regions: Theory and Practice*, United Nations Economic and Social Commission for Asia and the Pacific, draft version, 28 March.

PCC (2012) *The network of intermodal connections*, www.pcc-intermodal.pl,

Rapp Infra (2007) *Raumplanerische und verkehrstechnische Machbarkeit von leistungsfähigen RoLa-Terminals im Raum Basel und Domodossola/Chiasso*, Basel.

Savy, M. and C. Aubriot (2005) Intermodal transport in Europe, *Bulletin of the Observatory on Transport Policies and Strategies in Europe*, issue 13–14, Paris.

SBB Cargo (2010) *Das Tor zur Welt im Limmattal, Cargo, Das Logistikmagazin von SBB Cargo* http://www.sbbcargo.com/index/cargomagazin/magazin_archiv-2/magazin_archiv0410-2/magazin_archiv0410–12.htm

Slack, B. (1999) "Satellite terminals: a local solution to hub congestion?", *Journal of Transport Geography*, Vol. 7, No. 4, pp. 241–246.

Verberckmoes, J. (2007) "Narcon breidt network uit. Spoor IFB verbindt Antwerpse haven met binnenland", *Nieuwsblad Transport*, 2 mei.

Vrenken, H., C. Macharis and P. Wolters (2005) *Intemodaal transport in Europe*, Brussels: European Intermodal Association.

UIC (2008) *Agenda 1015 for Combined Transport in Europe*, January, Paris.

SECTION 3

Transport, Economy and Society

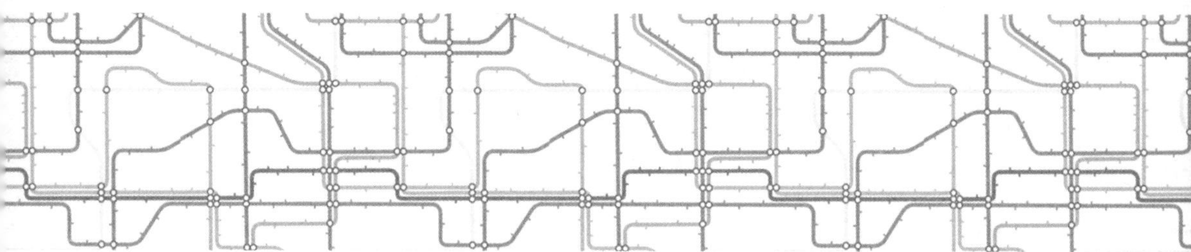

12

Transport Markets

Theo Notteboom

INTRODUCTION

How are transportation services brought to customers and how does the demand for passenger and freight transportation services respond to changes on the supply side of the market? These questions are at the core of many transport studies. A good insight into the functioning of transport markets is key to public policy decisions in the area of transport and mobility and the strategies and managerial decisions of companies providing transport services with respect to investments and service provision.

Well-functioning transport markets should allow transport supply to meet transport demand so that transport needs for mobility are satisfied. Transport in essence takes place to fulfill a need for moving people or freight. Button (2010) identified a range of reasons why passengers and goods are transported, such as the desire to obtain acceptable bundles of goods, to establish connections between production and consumption markets, to reach political and inter-cultural objectives (e.g. social cohesion and global sporting events), to have social interaction among geographically dispersed groups and to make it possible to separate residence and work place.

A distinction can be made between consumptive and productive transport needs. Productive transport needs have a clear economic focus. For example, the transport of semi-finished products from one production site to the final production or assembly site creates added value in the production process by benefiting from the locational advantages of each of the production sites. Consumptive transport needs generate less visible added value. For example, cruising on a Sunday afternoon does not really add value in a pure economic sense, but generates subjective utility and satisfaction to the driver and the passenger(s). A discussion on the functioning of transport markets is particularly relevant where it concerns the fulfillment of productive transport needs.

Transport demand that is met by a supply of transport services generates traffic (trucks, trains, ships, airplanes, buses, bicycles, etc.) on the corresponding transport infrastructure networks. The traffic capacity is generally larger than the actual transport demand since the average utilization degree of vehicles rarely reaches 100 percent: e.g. empty hauls of trucks, an underutilized container ship capacity sailing on a shipping route characterized by imbalanced container flows, an underutilized off-peak bus service and the "one person per car" situation in commuter traffic.

This chapter deals with the functioning of transport markets. We will discuss the economic significance of transport markets and their demand and supply sides. The chapter also provides a more holistic approach to transport service operations and their interaction with transport chain organization, transport infrastructure and locations.

THE ECONOMIC IMPACT OF TRANSPORT MARKETS

Transport markets create added value and employment to an economy. For example, the transport industry accounts for about 7 percent of the total GDP of the European Union and for close to 12 million jobs or 5 percent of total employment in the EU. Transport services alone are responsible for 8.9 million jobs while the remaining 3 million jobs are linked to transport equipment manufacturing (European Commission, 2009). The value-added and employment effects of transport services usually extend beyond the initial round of employment and value added generated by that activity; indirect effects are salient. For example, transportation companies purchase a part of their inputs from local suppliers. The production of these inputs generates additional value-added and employment in the local economy. The suppliers in turn purchase goods and services from other local firms. There are further rounds of local re-spending which generate additional value-added and employment. Similarly, households that receive income from employment in transport activities spend some of their income on local goods and services. These purchases result in additional local jobs and value-added. Some of the household income from these additional jobs is in turn spent on local goods and services, thereby creating further jobs and income for local households. As a result of these successive rounds of re-spending in the framework of local purchases, the overall impact on the economy exceeds the initial round of output, income and employment generated by passenger and freight transport activities. Thus, next to direct value-added and employment, transport firms and activities create impacts in three other ways:

- *Induced*: induced value-added and employment are created locally and throughout the wider national or supranational economy due to purchases of goods and services by those directly employed.
- *Indirect*: indirect value-added and jobs are the result of local purchases by companies directly dependent upon transport activity. Hence, transport activities are responsible for a wide range of indirect value-added and employment effects, through the linkages of transport with other economic sectors (e.g. office supply firms, equipment and parts suppliers, maintenance and repair services, insurance companies, consulting and other business services).
- *Related*: many economic activities and firms partly rely on efficient transport services for both passengers and freight. For instance, the steel industry requires cost-efficient import of iron ore and coal for the blast furnaces and export activities for finished products such as steel booms and coils. Manufacturers and retail outlets and distribution centers handling imported containerized cargo rely on efficient transport and seaport operations.

A poor transport service level can negatively affect the competitiveness of companies located in the region and thus have a negative impact on the value-added and employment generated by these companies. In November 2007, the World Bank published its first ever

Table 12.1 The Logistics Performance Index (LPI) ranking

	LPI rank	2010 LPI LPI score	% of highest performer	LPI rank	2007 LPI LPI Score	% of highest performer
Germany	1	4.11	100	3	4.10	97.9
Singapore	2	4.09	99.5	1	4.19	100.0
Sweden	3	4.08	99.3	4	4.08	97.4
The Netherlands	4	4.07	99.0	2	4.18	99.8
Luxembourg	5	3.98	96.8	23	3.54	84.5
Switzerland	6	3.97	96.6	7	4.02	95.9
Japan	7	3.97	96.6	6	4.02	95.9
United Kingdom	8	3.95	96.1	9	3.99	95.2
Belgium	9	3.94	95.9	12	3.89	92.8
Norway	10	3.93	95.6	16	3.81	90.9

Source: based on World Bank data

report which ranked nations according to their logistics performance based on the so-called Logistics Performance Index (LPI) (Table 12.1). These reports rank 150 countries according to their logistics performance. The LPI is a composite of a country's rating across seven criteria, some of which are strongly related to the performance of the freight transport market: customs clearance, logistics infrastructure, ease of international shipments, logistics competence/internal skills sets and service providers, tracking and tracing capabilities, domestic logistics costs and timeliness/consistency.

Not surprisingly, countries ranked high in terms of LPI are all among the wealthiest countries in the world. Efficient and sustainable transport markets and systems play a key role in regional development (see next chapter) although the direction of causality between transport and economic wealth is not always clear ("chicken and egg" problem). In quite a number of regions around the world, transport markets and related transport infrastructure networks are seen as key drivers in the promotion of a more balanced and sustainable development of the region or even the entire continent, particularly by improving accessibility and the situation of weaker regions and disadvantaged social groups. For example, the objective of enhancing social and economic cohesion among European Member States has always played a central role in the transport policy of the European Union, in particular at the level of the establishment of competitive transport markets and the creation of trans-European transport networks (TEN-T).

TRANSPORT SUPPLY

The supply side of the transport market relates to the transport services offered by private and public transport companies and other economic entities. This includes rail services, trucking, barge transport services, liner shipping, tramp shipping, public transport services, etc. using appropriate vehicles such as trains, ships, trucks, etc. Delivering transport services requires a fleet of vehicles and appropriate transport infrastructure to support a level of service. The vehicle stock for a number of countries and regions is depicted in Table 12.2. The market supply curve depicts the quantity of transport services supplied by the sum of all suppliers in the market. The Law of Supply states that the quantity of services offered increases when the price of the service increases. However,

Table 12.2 Vehicle stock in a number of world economic regions

		EU-27 2009	US 2008	Japan 2009	China 2009	Russia 2008
Passenger cars stock	million	236.1	238.3*	69.1**	31.4	30.3
Motorization	cars/1000	473	782	542	23	212
Commercial freight vehicles	million	33.84	9.01	6.36	14.8	5.35

*US includes all 2-axle 4-tyre vehicles (137 million passenger cars and 101 million other 2-axle 4-tyre vehicles)

**Figure includes 28.6 million light motor vehicles (engine capacity up to 660 cubic centimetres)

Source: Eurostat, 2011

transport supply does not always react strongly to price changes (weak elastic or inelastic supply) and in some cases transport companies might not be able to put more services in the market at higher prices due to capacity constraints in the infrastructure to be used.

The supply side of the transport market can be divided into two categories:

- Third-party transportation: professional transport companies offer transport services to users who require such services. Transport users pay for the services delivered. Examples include third-party trucking companies, container shipping lines, railway operators and bus companies.
- Own transportation: the transport user deploys his or her own transport means to move freight or to travel (e.g. motorists using private cars or large industrial companies owning a fleet of barges or rail wagons).

Freight transport services are increasingly being outsourced as many companies have acknowledged that transportation and warehousing are not part of their core business. Companies are reducing the number of transportation suppliers to reduce costs and improve services. The development of the logistics industry has enabled many transport companies to take control of larger segments of the supply chain. With an increasing level of functional integration many intermediate steps in the transport chain have been removed. Mergers and acquisitions have permitted the emergence of large logistics operators that control many segments of the supply chain: the megacarriers. Technology also has played a particular role in this process namely in terms of information technology (control of the process) and intermodal integration (control of the flows).

Table 12.3 Number of enterprises in the European Union and selected countries by mode of transport, 2008

	Road (freight)	Road (passenger)	Railways	Pipelines	Barge transport	Sea transport	Air transport	Warehousing and supporting activities
EU-27 of which	600,000	325,728	806	135	9,331	8,222	4,000	116,474
Belgium		2,259			263		199	2,863
Germany	36,442			46	1,428	1,895	521	15,605
France	40,058	37,599	26	26	1,096	697		8,804
Italy	89,466	27,402	28	12	824	639	240	21,544
Netherlands	8,996	4,257	19	8	3,636	685	251	4,345
Poland	87,241	50,769	91	5	635	161	111	8,567
United Kingdom	33,967	12,873	95	7	261	1,269	981	10,379

Source: author's own compilation based on Eurostat, 2011

Table 12.4 Transport infrastructure in a number of world economic regions

In 1000 km	EU-27 2008	US 2008	Japan* 2008	China 2008	Russia 2008
Road network (paved)	5,000	4,400	962	2,779	754
Motorway network	66.7	94.3**	7.6+	60.3	30
Railway network	212.9	202++	27.3	79.7	86
Electrified rail lines	110.5		15.2	25	43.2
Navigable inland waterways	40.9	40.7		122.8	102
Oil pipelines	37.7	272.9		50.8°	50°°

*Japan: data on the railway network and on the electrified rail lines are of 2007

**US: divided highways with 4 or more lanes (rural or urban interstate, freeways, expressways, arterial and collector) with full access control by the authorities

+Japan: national expressways

++US: a sum of partly overlapping networks

°China: both oil and gas pipelines

°°Russia: only crude oil pipelines. 16,000 km of oil products pipelines are not included

Source: Eurostat, 2011

The delivery of third-party transport services is often subject to intense competition from rival firms. Table 12.3 shows the situation in the European Union in terms of the number of companies active in specific segments of the transport market. The number of railway companies is rather low but rising due to the policy of the European Commission focused on European integration and rail deregulation. Since the mid-1990s the European rail freight sector has undergone major changes as a result of liberalization and with it the entry of new market players which made an end to a situation of national railway companies having a monopoly in their respective countries. At present, a wide array of rail operators make up the supply of rail service products. The largest players include DB Schenker Rail and SNCF but many smaller players are also offering services.

Transport services obviously need transport infrastructure. In comparison to vehicle operations, transport infrastructure is typically long lived, expensive to replace and has little alternative use. The management of such infrastructure is often in public hands or operated by private monopolies. Table 12.4 shows the basic transport infrastructure in a number of countries and regions in the world.

Transport supply is characterized by a series of new transport and logistics processes and technologies. Some examples:

- Mainporting: concentration of transport flows on a limited number of nodes (large airports, seaports or inland ports), serving ever larger areas by expanding their operations to the sub-regional and regional scales and beyond.
- Specialization: increased market segmentation and products variation call for tailor-made transport. The frequency of transshipment increases, the parcel-size decreases. This leads to further differentiation and segmentation in the transport market.
- Informatization: a decrease in costs, and an increase in reliability of, speed in and control over the supply chain is obtained by IT systems accompanying the transport flows. Modern IT systems are geared towards improving pipeline visibility in three core areas: (a) improved product flow visibility through real time information on flows with information presented based on user needs and the ability to re-plan, re-direct product flows; (b) event management in order to forecast events, to have real-time information on actual events and to generate proactive notifications of failures; and (c) performance management supported by quantitative carrier and asset performance data, performance accountability and continuous performance improvement opportunities. These advanced services are more and more aimed at

offering total pipeline/supply chain visibility to customers in terms of reliability performance through advanced tracking and tracing, environmental impact measurement (e.g. carbon footprint calculator), security risks and related event management.
- Focus on reliability: Transport service expectations of customers are moving towards a push for higher flexibility, reliability and precision. There is a growing demand from the customer for "make-to-order" or "customized" products, delivered at maximum speed, with supreme delivery reliability, at the lowest possible cost. The focus is on supply chain and transport excellence, with superior customer service and lowest cost to serve. As a result international supply chains have become complex and the pressure on the logistics industry and transport markets is increasing.

TRANSPORT DEMAND

The derived nature of transport demand

Transport demand has a "derived" nature, certainly when it concerns the satisfaction of productive transport needs. Transport, storage and transshipment of goods are in principle derived economic activities. If there is no extraction of raw materials, no production of intermediate and finished products or no consumption of these goods, there is no demand for cargo transportation, storage or handling. However, narrowing down the transport sector to just a derived activity of the basic economic activities does not give a complete picture. Transport increases the value of goods and services, not through changes in form or content, but basically through changes in place and time. Therefore one must not concentrate too much on that so-called service or passive role of transportation. In many cases transport is an independent industry, an active partner, not just a derived activity, in the global production system. Transport has been functionally integrated in the production chain. The logistics industry has evolved into a fully-fledged economic sector with its own dynamics. Major multimodal freight nodes in a transport system such as seaports and freight airports are increasingly functioning not as individual places that handle ships and airplanes respectively, but as turntables within global supply chains and global production networks.

Transport demand in figures

Since the industrial revolution and particularly with globalization, transport has been a growth industry. The main growth factors are:

- Changes in the structure of the manufacturing industry through shifts in production locations away from urban areas to new industrial sites. Economic integration (e.g. EU, NAFTA, ASEAN) has speeded up this kind of location shift;
- Changes in production methods, leading to stock reduction and a requirement for more flexible, varied and fast delivery systems. Shipment sizes are reduced but deliveries become more frequent;
- The growing importance of the service sector and its multi-site business activities has encouraged rapid growth in professional mobility;
- The rise in personal incomes and changing demographic patterns have led to a higher degree of car ownership and increased leisure and holiday travel.

Transport demand is usually expressed in number of passengers, tons of cargo, tonne-kilometers (tkm) or passenger-kilometers (pkm). The last two measurement units combine transport volumes with the distances travelled: a truck transporting 25 tons of freight over a distance of 400 km accounts for 10,000 tkm. Transport demand figures are ideally presented in an origin–destination matrix for each transport mode. The modal split can be determined by comparing the share of each transport mode in the total transport demand per origin–destination pair. Table 12.5 contains performance data by aggregating transport demand per mode at the level of entire countries or regions.

Table 12.5 Transport demand in a number of world economic regions

FREIGHT

In billion tkm	EU-27 2009	US 2008*	Japan 2009	China 2008	Russia 2009
Road	1,691.4	1,922.9	334.7	3,286.8	180
Rail	361.6	2,594.7**	20.6	2,510.6	1,865
Inland waterways	119.8	456.4		1,741.2	53
Oil pipelines	120.2	814.2		194.4+	2,246
Sea (domestic/intra EU-27)	1,336.0	303.5	167.3	3,285.1	97

*USA: data for road and oil pipelines are of 2007

**USA: Class I rail

+China: oil and gas pipelines

PASSENGER TRANSPORT

In billion pkm	EU-27 2009	US 2008	Japan 2009	China 2008	Russia 2009
Passenger car	4,781	7,201.8*	766.7**	1,345.1+	
Bus, trolley bus, coach	510.4	243	87.4		114.8
Railway	404.9	37.1	394	787.9	151.5
Tram and metro	88.8	21.1	++		49.8
Waterborne	40.0	0.6	4.9°	6.9	0.9
Air (domestic/intra EU-27)	522	977.8	75.2	337.5	112.5

*USA: including light trucks/vans

**Japan: including light motor vehicles and taxis

+China: including buses and coaches

++Japan: included in railway pkm

°Japan: 2008

Source: Eurostat, 2011

Table 12.6 EU freight transport: evolution of market shares of different transport modes (basis = tkm)

	Road	Rail	Inland waterways	Pipelines
1970	50.6%	27.8%	13.6%	8.0%
1980	60.6%	20.2%	10.8%	8.4%
1985	65.3%	18.6%	9.8%	6.3%
1990	69.9%	20.4%	9.2%	5.5%
1995	67.4%	20.2%	6.4%	6.0%
2000	69.6%	18.5%	6.1%	5.8%
2005	72.3%	16.7%	5.6%	5.5%
2009	73.8%	15.8%	5.2%	5.2%

Source: based on Eurostat data

Table 12.7 EU passenger transport: evolution of market shares of different transport modes, excluding bicycles, tram and metro and sea transport (basis = pkm)

	Private car	Rail	Buses and coaches	Air
1970	76.1%	10.0%	11.7%	2.2%
1980	77.8%	8.0%	10.6%	3.5%
1985	77.5%	7.7%	10.0%	4.9%
1990	79.0%	6.6%	8.9%	5.6%
1995	80.2%	6.2%	9.1%	4.5%
2000	80.0%	6.1%	8.8%	5.1%
2005	76.3%	6.3%	8.6%	8.8%
2009	76.9%	6.5%	8.2%	8.4%

Source: based on Eurostat data

The modal split figures in Table 12.6 demonstrates that growth in EU transport demand over the past decades has been borne unevenly by the different transport modes.

Transport by trucks accounts for the bulk of the increase in freight transport. Table 12.7 shows some figures on passenger traffic in the EU. Passenger traffic has increased significantly in recent decades, with most of the increase attributable to the use of private cars and airplanes. The volume of air traffic quadrupled in the past 20 years.

The uneven growth in the utilization of the different transport modes apparently creates some problems. Road transport systems are increasingly congested and often reach saturation levels in some regions of the European Union and elsewhere. Every year, about 3 percent of EU GDP is lost due to road congestion. Congestion moreover contributes to environmental problems. Concerns over the modal split evolution in the EU lie at the heart of the development of modal shift (later renamed "co-modal") policies of the European Commission.

A micro-economic perspective on transport demand

In line with micro-economic theory, the Law of Demand states that the demand for transport services decreases when the price of this service increases. This is reflected in the transport demand curve which plots the aggregate quantity of a transport service that consumers are willing to buy at different prices, holding constant other demand drivers such as prices of other transport services and goods, the budget or income and quality aspects such as reliability. Any change in another factor that affects the consumers' willingness to pay for the transport service results in a shift in the demand curve for the good. Exceptionally, there are possible cases where an increase in price leads to an increase in demand or, alternatively, where a price decrease leads to a decrease in demand, so the transport demand curve does not slope down with quantity (i.e. a perverse demand curve).

Transport demand is strongly influenced by a wide range of factors such as the industrial production in a region, the level of consumption, the land use and spatial planning characteristics, the level of international business activity, transport preferences of individuals and businesses, the price and quality of the available transportation options (i.e. transport modes and routing options), and demand management by public and private actors (e.g. parking policy in cities), etc. Three groups of determinants are of particular relevance: (a) the transport price, (b) the prices of other goods or services and (c) the income/budget of the transport user. We will discuss these three in more detail.

The transport price

The price of a transport service does not only include the direct out-of-the-pocket money costs to the user but also includes time costs and costs related to possible inefficiencies, discomfort and risk (e.g. unexpected delays). However, economic actors often base their choice of a transport mode or route on only part of the total transport price. For example, motorists are biased by short run marginal costs. They might narrow down the price of a specific trip by car to fuel costs only, thereby excluding fixed costs such as depreciation, insurance and vehicle tax. Many shippers or their representatives (like freight forwarders) are primarily guided by direct money costs when considering the price factor in modal choice. The narrow focus on direct money costs is to some extent attributable to the fact that time costs and costs related to possible inefficiencies are harder to calculate and often can only be fully assessed after the cargo has arrived. The same observation applies to motorists who will readily pay fuel prices as they drive, but will assume occasionally maintenance costs (e.g. an oil change or a flat tire) and will only realize depreciation costs if they sell their vehicle.

Price changes not only affect the level of transport demand, but can also lead to shifts of demand to other routes, alternative transport modes and or other time periods. In the medium or long term structural changes in the pricing of transport can affect location decisions of individuals and businesses.

The notion of price elasticity is at the core of transport demand. Several methods exist to determine price elasticity in transport markets. In its most basic form, the price elasticity of transport demand is the percentage change in transport quantity demanded brought about by a one percent change in the price of the transport service. In essence, elasticity is the ratio of relative (or percentage) changes in transport quantity Q and transport price P:

$$\varepsilon_{Q,P} = \frac{\Delta Q / Q}{\Delta P / P}$$

When a one-percent change in price leads to a greater than one-percent change in quantity demanded, the demand curve is said to be elastic ($\varepsilon_{Q,P} < -1$). When a one percent change in price leads to a less than one percent change in quantity demanded, the demand curve is said to be inelastic ($0 > \varepsilon_{Q,P} > -1$). When a one percent change in price leads to an exactly one percent change in quantity demanded, the demand curve is unitary elastic ($\varepsilon_{Q,P} = -1$).

A more advanced method for computing the price elasticity of transport demand is the arc elasticity which reflects the change in quantity Q resulting from each one percent change in the transport price P:

$$Q, P = \frac{\Delta \log Q}{\Delta \log P}$$

A large body of literature has analyzed the impact of price changes on transport activities (see e.g. Oum et al., 1992; Glaister and Graham, 2002; Arentze et al., 2004; Concas et al., 2005; Dargay, 2007; InterVISTAS, 2007; Barla et al., 2009). From this literature it can be observed that quite some differences exist among the obtained price elasticities, which raises questions about the transferability of the results to other locations and or other time periods. Hence, each case is characterized by a specific local environment in terms of modal choice options, budget/income of the transport user, spatial planning, price levels, etc. All these factors combined can make the behavior of transport users somewhat different across regions and settings.

The price elasticity of transport demand can influence the strategic behavior of economic actors. Container freight shipping serves as an example. Container shipping lines are faced with a highly inelastic demand due to the combined effect of a lack of close substitutes (i.e. the only alternative transport mode in the intercontinental transport of high value goods is air freight, but this market segment has a much lower cargo carrying capacity and prices are much higher) and the small impact of freight rates on total costs. For most shipments the total freight price only accounts for a very small portion of the shipment's total value; usually less than 5 percent. As container lines cannot influence the size of the final market, they try to increase their short run market share by reducing prices. As such, shipping lines may reduce freight rates without substantially affecting the underlying demand for container freight. The only additional demand can come from low value products which will only be shipped overseas if freight rates are very low (e.g. the market for waste paper and metal scrap). These "temporary" markets disappear again once the freight rate is above a threshold level no longer allowing a profit on trading these products overseas. The fairly inelastic nature of demand for shipping services constitutes the core problem for the poor financial performance of container shipping lines (Notteboom, 2012). Shipping lines have developed an intense concentration on costs and on negotiated long-term contracts with large shippers in view of securing cargo.

The prices of other alternative transport services or routes

The availability of cost-efficient and high quality similar alternatives or close substitutes affects the choice of a transport mode or route. The cross price elasticity shows the impact of a percentage change in the price

Table 12.8 Direct and cross-elasticities in urban passenger transport

	Train single fare	Train ten fare	Train pass	Single fare	Bus ten fare	Bus pass	Car
Train – single fare	–0.218	0.001	0.001	0.067	0.02	0.007	0.053
Train – ten fare	0.001	–0.093	0.001	0.001	0.004	0.036	0.042
Train – pass	0.001	0.001	–0.196	0.001	0.002	0.001	0.003
Bus – single fare	0.057	0.001	0.001	–0.357	0.001	0.001	0.066
Bus – ten fare	0.005	0.001	0.012	0.001	–0.16	0.001	0.016
Bus – pass	0.005	0.006	0.001	0.001	0.001	–0.098	0.003
Car	0.196	0.092	0.335	0.116	0.121	0.02	–0.197

Source: author's compilation based on Hensher, 1997

for a transport service on the percentage change in demand for another transport service. There is an abundant literature on cross-elasticities in transport. Table 12.8 provides an empirical example. It summarizes the results of a study by Hensher (1997) on elasticities and cross-elasticities between bus, train and car use. For example, a one percent increase in single fare train tickets will reduce rail demand (single fare) by 0.218 percent. However, the demand for buses (single fare) and car use increases by 0.057 percent and 0.196 percent respectively.

Another good example is the study by Abdelwahab (1998), which looks at elasticities of demand and modal choice in the intercity freight transport market in the US. The study concluded that the price elasticities of demand vary significantly across commodity groups and geographical areas. Among the 40 market segments considered, the truck price elasticity of demand ranged between –0.749 and –2.525; the rail price elasticity of demand was slightly larger, ranging between –0.956 and –2.489; and the rail–truck cross-price elasticity of demand ranged between 0.904 and 2.532.

While the transport price plays an important role in modal choice, firms using freight transport services are not always motivated by notions of cost minimization. They often show "satisficing behaviour" whereby the transport costs need to be below a certain threshold combined with specific requirements regarding reliability, frequency and other service attributes. Such complexities make it more difficult to clearly assess the role of transport price in the behavior of transport users.

The role of alternative transport modes and services can be illustrated by looking at the demand for car travel. In most studies the demand for car use in developed economies is found to be rather price inelastic. There are multiple reasons for this situation: an increasing preference for car travel when income levels rise, the development in the last 50 years of extensive highway networks combined with sprawled (sub)urban development, the perceived lower attractiveness of alternative modes such as public transport and the high share of fixed costs in total vehicle costs. Fixed costs such as depreciation, vehicle tax and insurance typically are weakly linked to the distance travelled, which implies these costs do not decline when the car owner would decide to reduce the use of his/her car. A full variabilization of car costs through road pricing schemes, city parking policies, fuel taxes and other distance-dependent costs might be a way forward to make automobilists more price elastic.

However, the success of the car and the associated road congestion between and in many cities in most wealthy countries have given incentive to public authorities to focus strongly on the supply and quality of alternative modes. For example, with the introduction of premium high speed train services in Europe (TGV, ICE, Thalys, Eurostar, etc.) the inter-city travel market welcomed a new high quality player successfully competing with air travel and car use, particularly in the distance range of 150 to 1,000 km. Many cities have developed mobility initiatives in the area of the upgrading of tramway systems, the development of inner-city bicycle lanes, the introduction of bike rental systems, etc. All these initiatives can help to increase the price elasticity of car travel: the more similar alternatives or close substitutes to car use are available to a motorist, the more the costs related to a specific transport mode choice are scrutinized. Still, empirical research seems to support the idea that car use is rather insensitive to the price of public transport. This would imply that subsidization of public transport has only a minor impact on the modal split, and should be more regarded as a social measure to guarantee an affordable mobility to the poorest or less mobile groups in the society.

The income or budget

People with a high income tend to be less sensitive to pricing and more sensitive to service quality than lower-income people. Thus income levels have an impact on modal choice. When the price of a specific transport service declines, all else kept constant, the purchasing power of individuals and companies rises (i.e. the so-called "income effect"). At the same time, the user is likely to adjust his/her consumption basket as the transport service becomes cheaper relative to other alternative transport services (i.e. the "substitution effect"). Public urban transport has often been tagged as an "inferior good": the higher the income and purchasing power, the less likely the consumer will end up using a bus, train or tram. For example, the rise of a middle class in China goes hand in hand with a fast increasing car orientation, even in large and congested cities like Beijing or Shanghai.

TRANSPORT MARKETS: MATCHING DEMAND AND SUPPLY

Balancing the demand for and supply of transport services

It is difficult to realize a perfect match between the demand for and supply of transport services at all times. First, transport demand shows fluctuations over time (i.e. hour of day, day of week, season, business cycles). Non-evenly distributed transport demand patterns challenge the supply side of the transport market (infrastructure and transport services) as it typically results in peaks and lows. As transport services cannot be stored like goods, users of passenger or freight transport services can influence the demand at a certain moment in time by postponing travel or the movement of freight until a more favorable price in the market and or a less congested transport system is reached. Freight and passenger transport that needs to take place within a certain timeframe might therefore pay a premium or peak price compared to flows which are more flexible in terms of the timing of the actual transport.

Second, the game of supply and demand works best in competitive transport markets where sellers and buyers are small and numerous enough so that they take the market price as given when they decide how much to buy and sell (price takers) and where fair competition within and between transport modes is achieved. This is done through a better alignment of charges with transport costs at the level of the individual transport user. However, transport markets hardly ever function as perfect competitive markets. Monopolistic or oligopolistic behavior of private or public transport operators is widespread, particularly when focused on specific relevant geographical markets and or product markets. Government intervention is often aimed at "helping" the market mechanism to work properly, avoiding market failure, preventing non-supply of services, containing external effects, preventing supply instability when demand is unstable and improving the openness (cf. remove barriers to entry) and efficiency of transport markets.

Third, the supply of transport services has difficulties in reacting effectively to strong upward or downward moves in demand. In the short term, transport operators can almost instantly react to a sudden increase in transport demand by maximizing the deployment and utilization degree of the existing vehicle capacity and transportation assets. Also when demand falls, operators can revise the allocation of existing assets. The container shipping industry provides a good example. In late 2008 at the start of the economic and financial crisis, a number of shipping lines started to postpone orders for new ships and older ships were put out of service in large numbers. Shipping lines also tried to absorb overcapacity by laying up vessels (12 percent of the world container fleet were laid-up in the fall of 2009) and by reducing the commercial vessel speed (the so-called slow steaming at 16 to 19 knots instead of the normal 21 to 25 knots).

However, such capacity utilization measures can only absorb smaller increases or decreases in demand. Transport operators are challenged to anticipate turning points in transport demand when planning asset investments. Such asset management decisions are particularly difficult in situations where the time gap between order and delivery of a transport means takes months or even years, as is the case for seagoing vessels, locomotives and barges. Capacity crises in transport markets are partly the result of exogenous factors such as an increase or fall in demand and partly the result of endogenous factors such as wrong asset investment decisions by transport operators. In other words, many of the under- or overcapacity problems in transport service provisions are linked to the failure by the key stakeholders – in the first place the transport operators and providers of finance (many without a transport-related background) – to correctly anticipate future market evolutions for different vehicle types and sizes. The transport community thus adds significantly to the volatility of the business environment and mismatches between supply and demand through investment and allocation decisions.

A multi-layered approach to the supply/demand balance

Transport involves the operation of transport services on links between places within a multimodal transport system. Transport service operations and the associated traffic flows do not take place in a vacuum but are strongly influenced by other functional layers (Figure 12.1). Thus, transport markets are not only about the supply of and demand for transport services. The interaction with locations (including intermediate locations), transport infrastructure and transport chain organization also deserves attention.

A first layer is the geographical location of origin and destination in economic space. Passenger and goods do not always follow the shortest path between origin and destination, but instead pass via intermediate nodes in the transport system in view of switching to another transport mode (e.g. transfer from rail to air in an airport) or to shift between small units to larger units of the same transport mode (e.g. transfer from a shorthaul intra-regional flight to a connecting longhaul flight or the transfer in a transshipment hub from a feeder vessel to a deepsea post-panamax container vessel). Thanks to an excellent location and economies of scale and density, many transport nodes such as airports, seaports, railway stations or intermodal terminals serve as important consolidation and bundling points in transport systems. By offering a good intermediate location, for example near the main maritime routes and/or near production and consumption centers, transport nodes can adopt an important turntable function in national or international transport service networks, thereby attracting not only destination traffic but also substantial transit flows.

The second layer involves the transport infrastructure. A favorable geographical location is meaningless if it is not valorized by means of the provision of efficient infrastructures. The infrastructural layer involves the provision and exploitation of basic infrastructure for both links and nodes in the transport system.

A last layer involves the transport chain organization layer. The transportation of passengers or freight between two places involves the use of a complex mix of transport infrastructures and transport services.

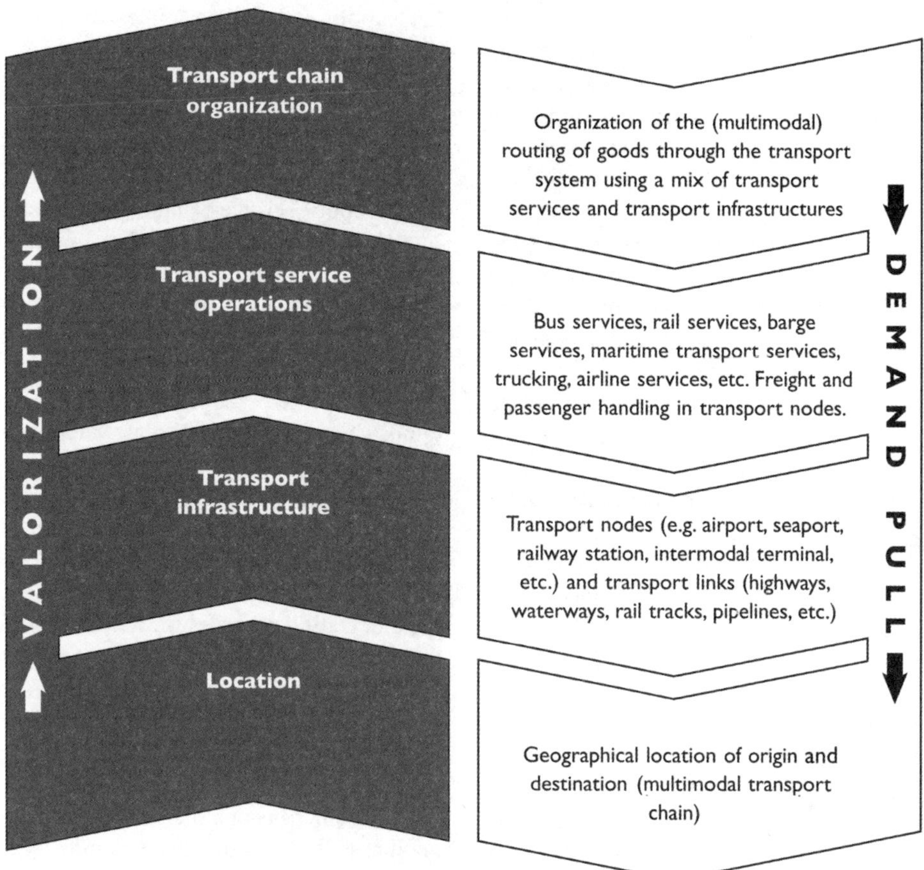

Figure 12.1 A multi-layer approach to transport
Source: after Notteboom and Rodrigue, 2007

The flow of passengers or freight through such a complex and multimodal transport system requires the involvement of actors who have the managerial capabilities to design a seamless and efficient transport chain. Logistics service providers and freight forwarders have developed a specialization in this area, supported by a good market knowledge and powerful information and communication systems. At the logistical layer shippers, freight forwarders, logistics service providers and other market parties design the routing solutions that best fit the requirements of the supply chains they are dealing with. The decision-making at the level of the logistics layers is mainly oriented towards the design of the distribution network and the choice of the transport route and associated transport modes and nodes.

The upward arrow in Figure 12.1 depicts that each layer valorizes the lower layers. The downward arrow represents the demand pull exerted from the higher levels towards more fundamental layers. In a demand-driven transport market environment the infrastructural layer serves the transport service and chain organization layers. The more fundamental the layer is, the lower the adaptability (expressed in time) in facing market changes. For instance, the planning and construction of major transport infrastructures (infrastructural level) typically takes many years. The duration of the planning and implementation of new transport services on specific transport corridors (transport level) usually varies between a few months up to one year. At the logistical level, freight forwarders and multimodal transport operators are able to respond almost instantly to variations in the market by modifying the commodity chain design, i.e. the routing of the goods through the transport system. As adaptable as they may be, they are still dependent on the existing capacity, but their decisions are often indications of the inefficiencies of the other layers and potential adjustments to be made.

The differences in responsiveness on the proposed levels leads to considerable time lags between proposed structural changes and demand fluctuations on the chain organization and the transport operation level and the necessary infrastructural adaptations needed to meet these changes adequately. This observation partly explains both the existing undercapacity (congestion) and/or overcapacity situations in transport systems around the world.

It is becoming increasingly common to see transport and logistics operators investing in the development of infrastructures such as terminals. Long delays in the realization of physical infrastructures could ultimately lead to a misallocation of resources. Hence, the market conditions might change considerably in the time-span between the planning phase and the actual realization of a piece of infrastructure. So, an infrastructure investment which at the time of its conception seemed feasible and market-driven, could end up as an investment in the wrong place, at the wrong time, for the wrong market and using the wrong technology. Such missteps can have serious impacts on transport markets in terms of rates, user costs and competition levels.

CONCLUSION

This chapter provided a holistic approach to transport markets by discussing their economic significance and the specific characteristics of and interaction between the supply and demand sides of transport markets. The transport industry cannot be narrowed down to a derived market. Given its role in economic development, the transport industry has always attracted strong government interest through self-provision of transport services and or far-reaching regulatory involvement in the functioning of private transport markets. Economies of scale and density and the need for integrated logistics services have facilitated consolidation and vertical integration along the transport and supply chain. Large container shipping lines (such as Maersk Line and MSC), global logistics companies (such as DHL, Kuhne and Nagel and DB Schenker) and global container terminal operators (such as PSA, Hutchison Ports Holding, DP World and APM Terminals) generate operating revenues of hundreds of millions or even billions of dollars. Despite the emergence of such large market players, the vast majority of the transport markets feature many providers ensuring a certain level of competition and choice to customers.

While micro-economic theory provides a good base for analyzing the dynamics of supply and demand, transport markets often do not function as perfect markets. Moreover, economic actors involved do not always show fully rational behavior (e.g. when choosing a routing option and transport modes/nodes) due to the existence of certain levels of inertia, bounded rationality and opportunistic behavior. The functioning of transport markets shows a high degree of complexity not the least because of the existence of a large number of geographical markets and product markets and because of the complexities associated with the balancing of demand and supply.

REFERENCES

Abdelwahab, W.M. (1998) "Elasticities of mode choice probabilities and market elasticities of demand: evidence from a simultaneous modechoice/shipment-size freight transport model",

Transportation Research Part E: Logistics, Vol. 34, No. 4, pp. 257–266.

Arentze, T., Hofman, F. and Timmermans, H. (2004) "Predicting multi-faceted activity-travel adjustment strategies in response to possible congestion pricing scenarios using an internet-based stated adaptation experiment", *Transport Policy*, Vol. 11, No. 1, pp. 31–41.

Barla, P., Lamonde, B., Miranda-Moreno, L. and Boucher, N. (2009) "Traveled distance, stock and fuel efficiency of private vehicles in Canada: price elasticities and rebound effect", *Transportation*, Vol. 22, pp. 389–402.

Button, K. (2010) *Transport economics*, Third Edition, London: Edward Elgar Publishing.

Concas, S., Winters, P. and Wambalaba, F. (2005) "Fare pricing elasticity, subsidies and the demand for vanpool services", *Transportation Research Record, 1924*, pp. 215–223.

Dargay, J. (2007) "Effect of prices and income on car travel in the UK", *Transportation Research Part A: Policy and Practice*, Vol. 41, No. 10, pp. 949–960.

European Commission (2009) "A sustainable future for transport – towards an integrated, technology-led and user-friendly system", Luxembourg: Publications Office of the European Union, 26 pp.

Eurostat (2011) *EU Transport in Figures: Statistical Pocketbook 2011*, Eurostat: Brussels.

Glaister, S. and D. Graham (2002) "The demand for automobile fuel: a survey of elasticities", *Journal of Transport Economics and Policy*, Vol. 36, No. 1, pp. 1–25.

Hensher, D. (1997) "Establishing a fare elasticity regime for urban passenger transport: non-concession commuters", Working Paper, ITS-WP-97-6, University of Sydney, Sydney.

InterVISTAS (2007) *Estimating Air Travel Demand Elasticities*, International Air Transport Association.

Notteboom, T. and Rodrigue, J.-P. (2007) "Re-assessing port–hinterland relationships in the context of global supply chains", in: Wang, J., Notteboom, T., Olivier, D. and Slack, B. (eds), *Ports, Cities, and Global Supply Chains*, Ashgate: Alderschot, pp. 51–68.

Notteboom, T. (2012) "Container shipping", in: Talley, W. (ed.), *The Blackwell Companion to Maritime Economics*, Wiley-Blackwell Publishing, pp. 230–262.

Oum, T.H., Waters, W.G. and Yong, J.-S. (1992) "Concepts of price elasticities of transport demand and recent empirical estimates", *Journal of Transport Economics*, pp. 139–154.

13

Transport and Economic Development

Iain Docherty and Danny MacKinnon

INTRODUCTION

There is generally a close and widely-accepted association between the quality of transport infrastructure and the level of economic development within a particular country or region (MacKinnon et al., 2008). Transport infrastructure and services are generally superior and more diverse in wealthy districts, countries and regions compared to less developed ones. Modes of transport are better connected, their geographical reach is greater, and fewer places are inaccessible. While such differences can be clearly identified, explaining how they have occurred is a more challenging task, requiring a sophisticated appreciation of 'the rich complexity of the transport-development interface' (Leinbach, 1995: 338). In particular, the question of the direction in which the linkage operates is crucial: 'does transport investment promote economic growth or does growth encourage more demand for transport, and thus further investment?' (Banister and Berechman, 2001: 214). The conventional view is that the relationship is two-way with transport both acting as an important facilitator of economic development and providing an important outlet for capital investment as economies grow (Hoyle and Smith, 1998; Simon, 1996; Vance, 1986). Recent research has emphasised the complexity of the relationship, indicating that the impacts of investment tend to be socially and spatially uneven, favouring some social groups and places over others (Hine, 2008).

This chapter aims to assess the relationship between transport investment and economic development, examining the dynamic linkages between the two. Our primary concern is with the secondary or additional effects of transport investment in altering economic conditions rather than its direct impact in terms of reduced journey times and increased accessibility *per se* (Banister and Berechman, 2001: 210; Lakshmanan, 2011). We view the relationship between transport and economic development as a two-way symbiosis; in a circular manner, each influences the other. In general terms, the expansion of economic development in a particular area will create demand for improved transport provision which will, in turn, support further economic growth. Such linkages are far from automatic, however, depending upon local circumstances and the development of the institutional and political capacity to prioritise appropriate forms of transport investment. And, just as the economic benefits of better transport will be unevenly distributed, so will the negative externalities of transport, such as local air pollution and traffic congestion. In many growing urban regions, processes of demographic and economic growth have tended to overwhelm the capacity of the existing transport infrastructure, generating significant diseconomies related to congestion and overcrowding.

The next section revisits some major theoretical frameworks that have been used to interpret and understand the nexus between transport and economic development. This is followed by a consideration of the relationship between transport and spatial development in developed countries, considering the role of transport in the shift to post-Fordist production systems and assessing the economic effects of investments in transport infrastructure. The second half of the chapter reviews recent research on the importance of transport to the economic performance and competitiveness of cities and urban regions, an issue that has become a major area of concern and enquiry as territorial competition between places has become more intense. A brief look to the future concludes the chapter.

THEORETICAL FRAMEWORKS

The principle that transport systems have determining effects on patterns of spatial economic organisation has been a key theme of location theory since von Thünen's seminal work in the mid-nineteenth century (MacKinnon et al., 2008). Traditional location theory is characterised by a deductive method of analysis, beginning with the assumption of a flat, featureless plain (an isotropic plain) on which economic activity is located. The focus is then on ascertaining the effects of distance on location with transportation costs viewed as a key expression of distance (Knox and Agnew, 1994: 66). According to von Thünen's theory of land use, the value of a location is determined by its access to the marketplace where consumption is assumed to take place, reflecting its geographical position, particularly in relation to major transportation routes. In his groundbreaking work on central places, Christaller also emphasised the spatially differentiating effect of transport infrastructure: 'Better transport connections result in a reduction of economic distance, a reduction not only in costs, but also in wasted time and the psychological inhibitions which impede frequent purchase of essential goods on uncomfortable, dangerous and sometimes impassable roads with bad traffic conditions' (Christaller, 1933: 53). Based on the assumption of economic rationality, central place theory offers an account of the size and distribution of settlements within an urban system. The need for shop owners to select central locations produces a hexagonal network of central places, organised into a distinct hierarchy of lower- and higher-order centres.

Whilst location theory generates neat models which real spatial patterns can be measured against, the assumptions upon which they are based are questionable (Massey, 1984). From a transport perspective, the notion that travel costs are equal in every direction is clearly at odds with the simple reality that transport networks and services sculpt landscapes of differential accessibility and land value (Knowles, 2006: 417). Motorway junctions are highly favoured by commercial property developers, for instance, for whom access trumps noise in manufacturing, wholesale and storage premises. Subway stations generate considerable passing traffic and nearby sites are prized by retailers seeking high volumes of consumer footfall. Concerted investment in new transport infrastructure has been a critical facilitator of urban regeneration in places such as London's Docklands, La Part Dieu in Lyon and Ørestad in Copenhagen (Book et al., 2010; Eddington, 2006b; Knowles, 2012; Thompson, 1995; Vickerman, 1997).

The 'new economic geography' (NEG), most closely associated with the work of economist Paul Krugman, seeks to explain the existence of agglomeration advantages and regional disparities, often taking a core–periphery form, within the system of economic equilibrium. One key assumption of the NEG is the 'iceberg' formulation of transport costs (Krugman, 1991), which states that a part of a good on its way from producer to consumer 'melts away' during transportation. This iceberg model is a mere analytical device, which clearly cannot be observed in reality, but which acts as a convenient way of accounting for the friction of distance whilst maintaining the overall properties of economic equilibrium. A key conclusion of the NEG is that reduced transport costs favour a concentration of manufacturing in a small number of centres rather than a more even dispersal across the economic landscape. This supports the earlier findings of the spatial polarisation theorists (e.g. Perroux), as economies of scale and scope, together with market-size effects, ensure that major agglomerations and growth poles gain certain competitive advantages over other locations. At the same time, countervailing forces such as immobile factors of production like land and labour and high rents and wages in central locations set limits on agglomeration and can, under certain conditions, encourage dispersal. Contrary to conventional assumptions regarding the benefits of transport improvements for peripheral regions, the NEG has shown that better and cheaper transport will promote the further concentration of economic activity in favoured locations (Eckey and Kosfeld, 2004): this is the 'two-way street' effect, so-called because the construction of a new (or improved) transport route can just as easily suck economic activity into the dominant centre as it can help disperse it.

As the influence of locational modelling and modernisation theory in human geography waned in the 1970s and 1980s, Marxian political economy became increasingly prominent. Whilst most of this work neglected the role of transport, Harvey (1982) built on Marx's resonant phrase about transport leading to the 'annihilation of space by time', relating this process to an underlying contradiction between the geographical fixity and motion of capital. Fixity of capital in one place for a sustained period – creating a built environment of factories, offices, houses, transport infrastructures and communication networks – is crucial in enabling production to take place. As economic conditions change, however, these infrastructures can themselves become a barrier to further expansion, growing increasingly obsolete in the face of more attractive investment opportunities elsewhere. In these circumstances, capital is likely to abandon existing centres of production and establish a new 'spatial fix' involving investment in different regions. The deindustrialisation of many established centres of production in the 'rustbelts' of North America and Western Europe since the late 1970s and the growth of new industry in 'sunbelt' regions and the newly-industrialising countries of East Asia can be understood in this light. Thus, while transport networks enable capital to 'annihilate space by time', linking distant sites of production, extraction and consumption, this can only be achieved through the production of fixed and immobile infrastructures which subsequently become vulnerable to devaluation as economic conditions change and other locations present more profitable opportunities for investment (Harvey, 1982).

A key development in human geography and the social sciences from the early 1990s was the cultural 'turn', which emphasises the importance of beliefs, identities and values in shaping social action and behaviour. From a transport perspective, the cultural turn suggests a focus on transport users, examining how their attitudes, identities and values shape transport behaviour, something that has been neglected by the dominant perspectives derived from economics and engineering. One of the key legacies of the cultural 'turn' for transport studies is the increased interest in travel across the social sciences, giving rise to 'the new mobilities paradigm', based on the notion that heightened mobility has become a defining characteristic of contemporary life (Sheller and Urry, 2006). Whilst 'the new mobilities paradigm' certainly defines a new interdisciplinary research agenda around questions of movement and transport, its exaggerated emphasis on the novelty of mobility risks a blindness to continuities between the past and present, whilst its rather one-sided celebration of the experiences of movement and of fluidity may be better recast in terms of the complex relationships between mobility and fixity, or 'flows' and 'places' (Harvey, 1982; cf. Castells, 1989).

TRANSPORT AND SPATIAL DEVELOPMENT IN DEVELOPED COUNTRIES

Industrialisation during the nineteenth and early twentieth centuries gave rise to a distinct pattern of regional sectoral specialisation, involving certain regions becoming specialised in particular industrial sectors (MacKinnon et al., 2008). Characteristically, all the main stages of production from resource extraction to final manufacture were carried out within the same region. As indicated by the new economic geography, new transport networks, based on canal systems and particularly railways, were important in facilitating increased concentration and specialisation, liberating factories from dependence on local resources and enabling them to serve larger markets. In shipbuilding, for instance, North East England and West Central Scotland accounted for 94 per cent of the sector's employment in Britain in 1911 (Slaven, 1986: 133). Similarly, the completion of a continental transport network based on railroads facilitated the growing concentration of industry in the US manufacturing belt in the North East and Mid West, resulting in the increased specialisation of individual cities (Lakshmanan, 2011).

The development of many industrial centres was linked to their position in relation to major transport networks, reflecting the wider tendency for important trading settlements to be located at highly accessible points such as the confluence of rivers, break-of-bulk points along coastlines, the end or mid-point of a rail line, or at the foot of mountain passes. In this way, some major towns owe their very existence to a so-called 'transport function'. The city of Chicago, for instance, owed its explosive growth from the 1840s to its role as the major transportation hub where the Western- and Eastern-orientated railroad lines and Great Lake shipping routes converged (Cronon, 1991). This enabled it to become a key agricultural market and processing centre, linking the resources of the vast American interior to the markets of the East coast and Europe. Grain, lumber and meat were channelled, processed and exported through Chicago and the city also operated as the key centre for the distribution of manufactured goods throughout the interior.

The pattern of regional sectoral specialisation began to break down from the 1920s, replaced by a new Fordist system involving the mass production of consumer durables. The growth of Fordism was closely associated with the emergence of new transport technologies based on the private car and investment in road networks. This facilitated mass consumption, by providing a market for industries such as automobiles and electronics and encouraging an increased spatial separation between home and work through the growth of suburbs, particularly in North America (Walker, 1981). Suburban lifestyles become closely associated with mass consumption, with every household requiring its car, washing machine and lawnmower (Goss, 2005).

By the late 1960s, a new phase of 'neo-Fordism' was apparent as mass production technologies became increasingly routine and standardised. This created a new 'spatial division of labour' as different parts of the production process were carried out in different regions, reflecting underlying geographical variations in the cost and qualities of labour (Massey, 1984). Companies were concentrating headquarters and research and development functions in core regions where there were large pools of highly educated and skilled workers, whilst routine assembly and production was located increasingly in peripheral regions and places where costs (especially wage rates) were lowest. This dispersal of routine production has also occurred on an international scale through the 'new international division of labour' as Multi-National Corporations (MNCs) based in Western countries have shifted assembly and processing operations to developing countries (Froebel et al., 1980).

International divisions of labour have become increasingly complex and intricate since the 1980s, involving an increased number of actors in different industries. In the semiconductor industry, for example, research and development functions might be based in Silicon Valley in California, skilled production carried out in the Central Belt of Scotland (the so-called 'Silicon Glen'), assembly and testing in the likes of Hong Kong and Singapore and routine assembly in low-cost locations in the Philippines, Malaysia and Indonesia (Knox et al., 2003: 235–6). Such arrangements are predicated on the existence of advanced transport networks that allow materials to be easily and rapidly moved between factories, although this is rarely considered in accounts of globalisation (Hall et al., 2006). These logistics chains require a large number of intermediate inputs and materials (as well as raw materials and finished goods) to be transported over long distances within global production networks, often controlled by large MNCs.

The increased globalisation of production systems over time has been facilitated by successive revolutions in transport and communications technologies (Leyshon, 1995). The concept of time–space convergence emphasises how 'places approach each other in time-space' 'as a result of transport innovation[s]' that reduce the travel time between them (Janelle, 1969: 357). It takes just over one hour to travel between London and Edinburgh by jet aircraft today, for example, compared to eight hours by train in the late nineteenth century and four (highly uncomfortable) days by stage-coach in 1776. The associated concept of time–space compression (Harvey, 1989) emphasises how the development of new technologies has dramatically reduced transport and communication costs, resulting in the 'annihilation of space by time'. As Knowles (2006) points out, the process of time–space convergence is socially and spatially uneven, occurring primarily between key nodes within the world economy and benefiting wealthy groups such as global business executives and middle-class tourists rather than those on low incomes. In many respects, the 'shrinking' of space between key centres such as the world cities of London, Paris, New York and Tokyo coincides with a 'widening of space' between economically marginal locations such as sub-Saharan Africa, much of Latin America and the former Soviet Union (Leyshon, 1995).

Since the 1980s, the parallel processes of globalisation and localisation have encouraged the rise of a 'new regionalism' in economic geography (MacKinnon et al., 2008). This emphasises the increased importance of regions as economic units within a globalised economy, compared to the post-war model of integrated national economies (Storper, 1997). In particular, the success of dynamic growth regions such as the City of London (financial and business services), Silicon Valley (advanced electronics), Southern Germany (vehicles and electronics) and North Eastern Italy (machine tools, textiles) is rooted in the specialised production systems that have flourished there. The new regionalism examines the effects of internal factors and conditions within regions – for example, skills, rates of knowledge transfer and innovation, entrepreneurship and institutions – in helping to promote or hinder economic growth (ibid). Transport systems play an important role in facilitating economic growth within such regions, not least in terms of enabling rapid movement of materials between suppliers and manufacturers or service providers, according to the dictates of 'just-in-time' systems. In addition, the devolution of political power from the national level means that regional authorities have gained direct control over transport investment, allowing this to be linked more directly to regional economic needs.

In some cases, high-technology clusters have grown along particular transport arteries, with examples including 'Route 128' near Boston and the 'M4 corridor' in Southern England. Good road links allow the rapid supply of both components to manufacturers and service providers and finished products to customers as required, reducing inventory costs. The locational pattern of inward investment is strongly influenced by transport networks with Japanese investment in the automobile industry in the American Mid-West concentrated along the I75 and I65 corridors, known as 'kanban' or 'just-in-time' highways (Hoyle and Smith, 1998: 35). The distinctive pattern of clustering along the major highways can be explained for the need for close contact and collaboration between manufacturers and suppliers, granting them the flexibility to serve an increasingly diverse and fragmented market by producing a range of niche products, necessitating the rapid supply of particular types and volumes of materials as required.

THE SPATIAL EFFECTS OF TRANSPORT INVESTMENT

It is generally accepted that improved transport systems are beneficial from a national economic perspective: better roads mean faster transport, better exchange of goods and services, the utilisation of comparative cost advantages and thus the enhancement of a highly specialised economy (MacKinnon et al., 2008). On the whole – without regarding the external costs of transport – a national economy will benefit from a good transport system. Far more ambiguous, however, are the incremental economic effects of the further provision of transport infrastructure in developed societies, which tend to already have high-capacity transport networks. In general, research suggests that the scope for substantial impacts on the economy is relatively limited in such cases, compared to earlier stages of development (Banister and Berechman, 2001: 217; Eddington, 2006b: 13). This reflects the diminishing benefits of transport investment in developed countries (Box 13.1). The tendency for additional transport investment to simply induce additional traffic by encouraging people to use their vehicles more is also well understood (Standing Committee on Trunk Road Assessment (SACTRA), 1994).

Focusing on the secondary effects of transport investment, statistical analyses have indicated that a 1 per cent increase in public investment can generate an increase in GDP of around 0.2 per cent, although such conclusions are subject to a host of important qualifications (Eddington, 2006b: 9–10). For instance, they do not disentangle transport from public investment more broadly or factor in the wider economic, social and environmental impacts of transport. Most importantly, the ambiguity about cause and effect remains unresolved by such research: do transport improvements generate economic growth or vice versa? As such, the difficulties of establishing any significant correlation between transport investment and regional growth have become increasingly apparent (SACTRA, 1999). In the 1980s in West Germany, a study found the long-standing assumption that the construction of national roads fostered spatial integration and economic development – upon which a key strand of transport policy had been based – to be untenable (Lutter, 1980). Positive regional economic development was discovered to be discernible only where peripheral, rural labour markets achieved improved internal accessibility and became larger and more independent from core regions due to tangential routing. A further development of radial long-distance road connections, linking large

Box 13.1 The diminishing impact of transport infrastructure improvement on regional development

In highly developed countries new transport infrastructure tends to have a diminishing impact on regional development as the economy matures. Reasons for this tendency are:

1. Regional accessibility is already high

In general, industrialised nations already have a well-developed transport network, meaning that the level of accessibility is high. Therefore, further improvements of the transport infrastructure will result in only minor reductions in travel time and will not open up new areas or markets.

2. Transport costs become less important

Due to economic changes such as the shift towards services, the relative importance of transport-intensive sectors is decreasing. In contrast to traditional activities such as manufacturing or mining, the growing service sector or the so-called 'new economy' does not rely as much on effective transport systems. Thus, transport costs become less important as a location factor, although the quality and efficiency of transport networks may become more important in line with the shift to just-in-time production systems, for instance.

3. Proximity is better than speed

Geographical proximity to major economic centres and clusters as a precondition of economic growth cannot be fully substituted by new transport facilities – thus peripheral regions tend to remain remote and do not substantially gain from improved accessibility. Indeed, in some cases, further transport improvements may result in externally-located firms penetrating local markets more effectively and in local residents spending more of their income externally.

4. Disparities may be deepened

Finally, an improvement in the connection of peripheral regions with central regions always works in both directions. According to the New Economic Geography, due to agglomeration effects – the advantages derived from the spatial concentration of large number of firms, suppliers, workers and consumers – central regions benefit most from such an improvement whereas peripheral regions are likely to be drained with regard to purchasing power or skilled labour. In particular, transport improvements may facilitate increased migration from peripheral to core regions.

Source: MacKinnon et al., 2008: 20

cities and clusters, tends only to intensify the draining effect in rural areas, enabling consumers, for instance, to spend more of their income outside the region.

In a review of surveys on transport infrastructure and regional economic development in Europe, Linneker (1997) distinguishes between the spheres of consumption and production. Improved accessibility relating to consumption definitely leads to an improvement in welfare for the population, with increased competition resulting in lower prices. For the sphere of production, however, after making allowances for regional disparities, the question remains open, allowing very different answers to be put forward. Here, recent academic discussion has perhaps become too dependent on analyses of large-scale infrastructural projects in growth regions, particularly the impact of the M25 in Greater London and the Channel Tunnel (Vickerman, 1991). Reflecting the essentially enabling role of transport, Linneker (1997: 60) concludes that 'Whether further development towards higher or lower levels of economic development potential are realised … is determined by a large number of other factors outside the transport sector.'

This point is developed by Banister and Berechman (2001) who identify a series of necessary conditions that must be in place for transport investment to stimulate regional economic development in developed countries. The three key conditions are (a) positive economic externalities, basically meaning a well-functioning local economy, particularly in terms of the links between firms and suppliers and the operation of the labour market; (b) investment factors referring to the availability of funds, the quality of the overall network and the timing of the investment; and (c) a favourable political environment, in terms of other supporting policies and a generally enabling policy framework. All three factors must be in place for transport investment to have a positive impact on the regional economy. If only one or two of these factors are present at the time of investment, certain effects such as an improvement of accessibility may occur – but not regional growth.

Rather than building new infrastructure to stimulate economic growth, one of the major transport issues requiring attention in developed countries is the reliability of transport networks (Eddington, 2006a). This represents the other side of the transport–economic development relationship in terms of the impact of rapid growth on infrastructure, creating problems when networks are unable to cope with increased demand, causing bottlenecks and congestion around key nodes and centres. These problems can constrain economic growth if left unchecked, impeding the movement of goods, information and labour and making an area less attractive to investors. Increased tendencies towards the geographical agglomeration or concentration of production in distinct clusters, coupled with the move to just-in-time supply systems, have compounded this problem.

As a result, enhancing the capacity and efficiency of transport networks through demand management measures has become a key preoccupation for policy-makers. Foremost among these is congestion charging, where the authorities charge users to travel on the roads within a particular area, allowing the funds to be spent on related measures such as public transport improvements. In the UK, for instance, the Eddington Report, commissioned by the Treasury and Department for Transport, recommended that policy should concentrate on enhancing reliability and efficiency. It identified three strategic priorities for action: congested and growing urban areas, key inter-city corridors and major international gateways such as the leading ports and airports (Eddington, 2006a: 7), rejecting the notion that the construction of large-scale new infrastructure is required. Congestion charging should form part of a suite of measures utilised to make better use of existing infrastructure and induce intelligent solutions for a sustainable transportation in line with market requirements (Deloitte Research 2003). The political difficulties of introducing such an ostensibly unpopular measure in a country when unrestricted private car travel has come to be regarded as a basic right remain substantial, however. The introduction of congestion charging in Central London by the former mayor, Ken Livingstone, remains exceptional within the UK, following its rejection or abandonment in Edinburgh, Manchester, the West Midlands and the East Midlands, while national government has shied away from road pricing since a 2007 Government petition which attached over 1.8 million signatures from opponents.

FUNDAMENTALS OF THE URBAN TRANSPORT DEBATE

The remainder of the chapter reviews the contemporary debate on the contribution of transport to urban economic development, since it is in cities, especially since the agenda of 'urban competitiveness' became widespread in the 1990s, where the debate about the role and value of transport in economic development has been most vibrant. This is in large part because as globalisation has developed, there has been an increasing realisation that transport is a critical determinant of both the performance of the urban economy, and the attractiveness of the city as a place to live, work and consume.

Transport and the production of cities

It is difficult to understate the extent to which transport has determined the shape of today's cities: look out of the window in any city in the world and what you will see is determined by the transport technologies available to the generation developing the city at any point in time. The links between transport and urban economic development, made most visible by settlement structure and the form of the built environment, reach far into the deepest layers of the urban economic, environmental and social systems, and can be usefully explored by applying the classic analytical dichotomy on the raison d'être of the city: it is both a *space* of production and exchange – that is the territory across which economic systems extend – and also a *place* of complex social interaction and cultural development (Hanson and Giuliano, 2004).

Focus on one or other of these perspectives has traditionally implied a quite different set of objectives and priorities for the development and management of the urban transport system. For much of the twentieth century, increasing the supply of physical mobility, first by the 'tracked' modes of the tram and railway but later and more profoundly by the revolution brought about by the mass adoption of the private car, was seen as a critical determinant of economic development potential. For several decades, the transport policy task of the state in most developed countries around the world was therefore defined as that of providing as much physical mobility as possible in the urban system so that industrial production, manufacturing and later the service sector could function as efficiently as possible through 'the compression of time–space' noted above (see also Glaeser, 2004; Laird et al., 2005).

In the contemporary urban economy, which for most developed world cities is substantially based on tertiary sector activity, these macro-policy concerns are translated into investment priorities aimed at maximising the capacity of urban road and rail networks, often through quite large investments such as the development of extensive metro or light rail networks, and/or urban expressways. The choice of particular modes notwithstanding, the policy objective of such investments is to supply sufficient mobility so that key functional markets, such as the housing and labour markets, operate as efficiently as possible (Krugman, 1991; 2011) since, in the simplest terms, transport 'links people to jobs; delivers products to markets; underpins supply chains and logistics networks; and is the lifeblood of domestic and international trade' (Eddington, 2006a: 11). Thus, if a major inward investor setting up business in a new city location can draw on the widest possible labour pool in order to maximise the skills base of its operation due to the enhancement of the transport network, then this should lead to positive economic returns.

Equally, the perceived importance of mitigating key transport 'problems' of under-supply of mobility, such as traffic congestion – the cost of which in terms of the lost productivity caused by people and goods being delayed in transit runs to a significant proportion of Gross Domestic Product if orthodox transport economics is to be believed – is such that many of the most politically bold transport policies of recent years have been based on attempting to more accurately price the value of the time spent travelling so that people and firms restructure their economic decisions accordingly. The introduction of congestion charging in London in an attempt to minimise delays and improve the capacity of the road network is one important example of this approach in practice. Its superficial rationale, to encourage the diversion of car trips to other modes, is only part of its strategic intent; the charge was also designed to improve travel conditions for the high value businesses and wealthy commuters in central

London prepared to pay significant sums to escape the delays caused by traffic congestion, but also to encourage low value economic activities to move out of central London altogether.

The alternative normative view of the purpose of urban transport, that is to facilitate the city's role as a place of social and cultural creativity, has an equal pedigree, much of it emerging from Jane Jacobs' (1961) seminal book *Death and Life of Great American Cities*. Although not ostensibly a transport text, *Death and Life* did powerfully and succinctly explain how a vicious circle of socio-economic decline could emerge if long-developed local systems and structures were disrupted by radical shifts in transport provision. Jacobs was, of course, writing about some of the negative impacts of the rise to dominance of the private car in meeting our mobility demands, specifically how the loss of pedestrian activity in local neighbourhoods can undermine the local economy, community interaction, social networks and public life more generally (see also Hass-Klau, 1993; Logan and Molotch, 2007). But it was not until decades later, when the problems caused by the degradation of the natural and human environment due to unrestricted growth in the use of the car had entered the political mainstream, that transport development was formally re-articulated towards wider policy objectives such as contributing to the economic diversity, cultural and social inclusivity of the city (Haywood and Hebbert, 2008; Shaftoe, 2008) – in other words, to improving the quality of the place in which people live and work.

Urban competitiveness

The emergence of a substantial literature addressing the seemingly simple – but in fact fiendishly complex – question of what factors make some urban economies perform better than others in the early 1990s led to the development of a new economic development policy paradigm based on the notion of 'urban competitiveness'. At its most straightforward, the concept of urban competitiveness attempts to distil a range of theoretical developments in the New Economic Geography and elsewhere to the core proposition that maximising the scale and quality of several complementary urban 'asset sets' – in most of which transport is a critical component – is the key to growth and prosperity (Begg, 2002; Lever, 1999). These 'asset sets' are the bundles of 'physical', 'human' and 'soft' resources ranging from land and property, critical infrastructures such as ports, airports and the energy supply grid, to the skills base, the legal, fiscal and regulatory environment, and quality of life factors such as the vibrancy of the creative industries.

The attractiveness of the competitiveness paradigm to many policy makers was that it rather elegantly brought together the two notions of the role of transport outlined above, which had often been in apparent conflict with one another in a practical policy sense (see Cahill, 2010). This is because, on the one hand, to improve competitiveness, transport had to operate as both a device to achieve greater direct economic returns through improving market efficiency, but it also had minimise the negative externalities of this mobility (pollution, noise, severance and so on) so as to play a positive role in generating sufficient 'quality of place' so that inward investors, visitors and especially the highly mobile knowledge workers on which high value, innovative sectors of the economy depend, would choose to locate in the city (Banister and Berechman, 2000; Kaufman et al., 2008; Lawless and Gore, 1999; Porter and Ketels, 2004).

The emergence of the competitiveness paradigm at the time when the negative impacts of car dependence were becoming a political hot topic, just as the economy emerged from the early 1990s recession and so more resources became available for public investment in new infrastructure, combined in many cities to produce a new policy approach based on the significant expansion of high capacity public transport networks. With more resources at their disposal, and the (probably self-fulfilling) belief that the race to secure economic competitiveness was gathering pace, cities around the world embarked on ambitious development projects such as new light rail (e.g. San Diego, Manchester, Strasbourg; see Figure 13.1) or full underground metros (e.g. Copenhagen, Warsaw, Taipei). At the same time, the importance of quality of life ideas for the rhetoric of city competitiveness focused new attention on the consumer experience of travelling around the city, and so considerable efforts were made to achieve the so-called 'seamless journey' through better physical integration between modes (i.e. through the construction of better bus/rail interchanges), through the applications of new technology to innovations such as smart ticketing, and between transport and other areas of public policy such as planning and the improvement of the public realm (Hull, 2005; Williams, 2005) and public health (Lopez and Hynes, 2006; Ming Wen and Rissel, 2008).

Such increasing complexity in the task of improving transport infrastructure and services for economic gain reflects the 'changing connections and inter-relations between social, political and cultural factors' (Painter, 1995: 276), which in turn often require more complex and flexible systems of governance if policy implementation is to be effective. At the city scale, those places that have most successfully transformed their transport systems in line with the model of the seamless journey – and thus offer a mobility system that genuinely improves quality of life – tend to have powerful special-purpose institutions and networks of transport governance (Marsden and May, 2006), plus strong political leaders

Figure 13.1 New tram development in Strasbourg, France

Note: Strasbourg, like other French cities, has witnessed significant investment in tram systems and associated public realm improvements in recent years

Source: photo I. Docherty

able to mobilise their mandates to introduce important innovations such as congestion charging and/or re-invigorating the urban realm. The radical greening and road space reduction of key radial roads in Paris (since copied in New York) and London's globally-significant Congestion Charge scheme are perhaps the best examples.

WHAT ECONOMIC DEVELOPMENT ROLE FOR TRANSPORT IN FUTURE?

Writing in the second half of 2012, the future for urban transport looks highly uncertain for many cities around the globe. In those countries most immediately and profoundly hit by the financial crisis, shortage of funds has led to the cancellation of many planned development projects, with additional financial difficulties apparent for existing networks given the fall-off in demand. In other places, however, the desire to keep the economy going through Keynesian intervention has been very good for transport, at least in the short term, although the oft-heard government mantra that transport investment is automatically good for the economy in terms of increasing growth is not especially well served by the evidence, as we have seen above.

Over the medium term, as the policy imperative moves from providing stimulus and avoiding unemployment to the – in some cases herculean – task of reducing debt levels and ongoing public expenditure requirements, the extent to which transport investment will be prioritised is uncertain. Given their capital intensity, transport projects can be easy political targets for cancellation at moments of economic crisis just as easily as they can be brought forward to try and stimulate growth. There is also uncertainty on the revenue side: although some public transport services are at risk as demand falls for commuting and leisure travel, others are benefiting from the combination of recession and continued high oil prices, with some early evidence that this is prompting some households to reduce their driving, and even their number of cars (Goodwin, 2011).

The nightmare scenario for many cities is that if the economy continues to shrink significantly, then both fares income to public transport operators, plus the overall tax revenues available to finance the public support needed to cover the costs of transport service subsidy, fall. Faced with such a revenue squeeze, a vicious circle can be created in which public transport declines, making it harder for newly unemployed people (who often do not have access to a car) to find alternative jobs, further depressing economic recovery. Over time, spatial differentiation effects (re)assert themselves, with public transport in more disadvantaged areas becoming (increasingly) residualised as private operators can no longer afford to operate services commercially and the state is increasingly unable to intervene given the general financial pressures upon it. The end result is the kind of impact on socio-economic disadvantage across space and between places that Jane Jacobs wrote about more than half a century ago.

In the longer term, the key policy question is how the imperative to reduce carbon emissions, plus other strategic uncertainties, such as the price of oil, security of energy supply and the development of new energy technologies, will impact on transport and its role in promoting economic development. At present, this debate is dominated by arguments over which of the alternative pathways to meet governments' targets for carbon reduction might be most successful (see, for example, Anable and Shaw, 2007). The implications for transport and its development contribution are important: many environment-led policy prescriptions envisage some really quite swift and sharp reductions in the amount of mobility we consume, which whilst perhaps entirely laudable and justifiable in environmental (and social) terms, would nonetheless probably generate some difficult economic dislocations in the short to medium term given the extent which current patterns (and costs) of mobility are built into important socio-economic practices such as logistics chains, commuting and household location choices.

Beyond this, the critical debate is about how the transport–economic development relationship will play out over the decades to come. Central here is the rhetorical (and normative) battle between proponents of 'conventional' notions of economic development and growth, which firmly places climate change and decarbonisation of transport as a challenge for technological development to overcome in order to stimulate the next wave of technical innovation, versus those who see the scale of the environmental crisis as a compelling reason to pose more fundamental questions about how society organises itself, and hence how transport facilitates socio-economic interaction. For those who might be termed the 'technologists', the so-called 'greening' of the car, i.e. the widespread adoption of electric vehicles, is the critical innovation process, since it will (arguably) 'solve' many of the environmental problems of the contemporary car-based 'mobility regime' (Geels et al., 2011). But for the opposing 'deep green' camp, the prospect of the wholesale substitution of the internal combustion engine for the electric motor offers little more than a dystopia of green congestion, in which the economic and social problems of highly polarised mobility and deeply unequal access to employment, educational and other opportunities are further entrenched.

Rather than 'just' greening the car therefore, many voices on the environmentalist side see the coming together of the climate change challenge with the great recession as an unparalleled opportunity to achieve a large-scale reorganisation of the transport system, so that a new model of socio-economic development fundamentally less reliant on physical mobility is achieved. But to manage such a transition would require the re-engineering of most of the contemporary economy, requiring firms and individuals to alter their established patterns of activity in the most profound manner. Whether this is actually possible in democratic societies is not at all certain: politicians (probably rightly) shy away from implementing genuinely radical policies in all but the moments of the most grave crises, judging that the impacts of such actions on people's lifestyles and (perceptions of) individual liberty as incompatible with the notion of a free society.

Although all of the above might suggest that transport's status as a 'wicked problem' is well deserved, the importance of quality of life to the urban competitiveness paradigm means that there are also substantial incentives to achieve this kind of change. The level of resources available for the largest public transport projects might turn out to be more limited in many cities in future than before. Many of the classic 'alternative' transport policies that emerged following the 'environmental turn' in the early 1990s in fact owed their existence to recession and lack of investment resources. But the prescription that motorised mobility and vehicles should be prioritised less, and 'active travel' and people on the move prioritised more, remains a compelling proposition. If the notion of 'peak car' – for whatever reason, be it climate change, oil prices or the technological revolution that means people would rather spend their time interacting with their smartphone than their automobile – turns out to be correct, then those cities that focus most on the ease of getting around without a car could turn out to be the winners in the decades to come.

REFERENCES

Anable, J. and Shaw, J. (2007) 'Priorities, policies and (time)scales: the delivery of emissions reductions in the UK transport sector', *Area* 39, 443–457.

Banister, D. and Berechman, J. (2000) *Transport Investment and Economic Development*. University College London.

Banister, D. and Berechman, J. (2001) 'Transport investment and the promotion of economic growth', *Journal of Transport Geography* 9, 209–218.

Begg, I (2002) (ed.) *Urban Competitiveness: Policies for Dynamic Cities*. The Policy Press, Bristol.

Book, K., Eskilsson, L. and Khan, J. (2010) 'Governing the balance between sustainability and competitiveness in urban planning: the case of the Orestad model', *Environmental Policy and Governance* 20(6), 382–396.

Cahill, M. (2010) *Transport, Environment and Society*. Open University Press, Maidenhead.

Castells, M. (1989) *The Informational City*. Blackwell, Oxford.

Christaller, W. (1933) *Die zentralen Orte in Süddeutschland*, Jena.

Cronon, W. (1991) *Nature's Metropolis: Chicago and the Great West*. W.W Norton, New York.

Deloitte Research (2003) *Combating Gridlock: How Pricing Road Use can Ease Congestion*. Deloitte Research, London.

Eckey, Hans-Friedrich and Kosfeld, Reinhold (2004) *New Economic Geography. Critical Reflections, Regional Policy Implications and Further Developments*. Volkswirtschaftiche Diskussionsbeiträge Nr. 65/04 des Fachbereiches Wirtschaftswissenschaften der Universität Kassel.

Eddington, R. (2006a) *Transport's Role in Sustaining the UK's Productivity and Competitiveness*. The Eddington Report, Main Report. HMSO, London.

Eddington, R. (2006b) *Understanding the Relationship: How Transport Can Contribute to Economic Success*. The Eddington Report, Volume I. HMSO, London.

Froebel, F., Heinrichs, J. and Kreye, O. (1980) *The New International Division of Labour*. Cambridge University Press, Cambridge.

Geels, F.W., Kemp, R., Dudley, G. and Lyons, G. (2011) *Automobility in Transition? A Socio-Technical Analysis of Sustainable Transport*. Routledge, London.

Glaeser, E. (2004) *Four Challenges for Scotland's Cities*. Allander Series. University of Strathclyde, Glasgow.

Goodwin, P. (2011). 'Three views on "peak car",' *World Transport Policy & Practice* 17(4) 8–17.

Goss, J. (2005) 'Consumption geographies', in Cloke, P., Crang, P. and Goodwin, M. (eds) *Introducing Human Geographies*, 2nd edition. Arnold, London, pp. 253–266.

Hall, P., Hesse, M. and Rodrigue, J.-P. (2006) 'Exploring the interface between economic and transport geography', *Environment and Planning A* 38, 1401–1408.

Hanson, S. and Giuliano, G. (2004) *The Geography of Urban Transportation*. Guilford Press, New York.

Harvey, D. (1982) *The Limits to Capital*. Blackwell, Oxford.

Harvey, D. (1989) *The Condition of Postmodernity*. Blackwell, Oxford.

Hass-Klau, C. (1993) 'Impact of pedestrianization and traffic calming on retailing. A review of the evidence from Germany and the UK', *Transport Policy* 1, 21–31.

Haywood, R. and Hebbert, M. (2008) 'Integrating rail and land use development', *Planning Practice and Research* 23(3), 281–284.

Hine, C. (2008) 'Transport and social justice', in Knowles, R., Shaw, J. and Docherty, I. (eds) *Transport Geographies: Mobilities, Flows and Spaces*. Blackwell, Oxford, pp. 49–61.

Hoyle, B.S. and Smith, J. (1998) 'Transport and development: conceptual frameworks', Hoyle, B.S. and Knowles, R. (eds), *Modern Transport Geography*. Wiley, Chichester, pp. 13–40.

Hull, A. (2005) 'Integrated transport planning in the UK: from concept to reality', *Journal of Transport Geography* 13, 318–328.

Jacobs, J. (1961) *The Death and Life of Great American Cities*. Random House, New York.

Janelle, D. (1969) 'Spatial reorganisation: a model and concept', *Annals of the Association of American Geographers* 59, 348–364.

Kaufman, V., Jemelin, C., Plfieger, G. and Pattaroni, L. (2008) 'Socio-political analysis of French transport policies: the state of the practices', *Transport Policy* 15, 12–22.

Knowles, R.D. (2006) 'Transport shaping space: differential collapse in time-space', *Journal of Transport Geography* 14, 407–425.

Knowles, R.D. (2012) 'Transit oriented development in Copenhagen, Denmark: from the Finger Plan to Ørestad', *Journal of Transport Geography* 22, 251–261.

Knox, P. and Agnew, J. (1994) *The Geography of the World Economy*, 2nd edition. Edward Arnold, London.

Knox, P., Agnew, J. and McCarthy, L. (2003) *The Geography of the World Economy*, 4th edition. Arnold, London.

Krugman, P. (1991) *Geography and Trade*. Cambridge, MA.

Krugman, P. (2011) 'The New Economic Geography, now middle-aged', *Regional Studies* 45(1) 1–7.

Lakshmanan, T.R. (2011) 'The broader economic consequences of transport infrastructure investments', *Journal of Transport Geography* 19(1), 1–12.

Laird, J., Nellthorp, J. and Mackie, P. (2005) 'Network effects and total economic impact in transport appraisal', *Transport Policy* 12(6), 537–544.

Lawless, P. and Gore, T. (1999) 'Urban regeneration and transport investment: a case study of Sheffield, 1992–1996', *Urban Studies* 36, 527–545.

Leinbach, T. (1995) 'Transportation and third world development: review, issues and prescription', *Transport Research* 20 A, 337–344.

Lever, W (1999) 'Competitive cities in Europe', *Urban Studies* 36, 1029–1044.

Leyshon, A (1995) 'Annihilating space? The speed-up of communications', in Allen, J. and Hamnett, C. (eds), *A Shrinking world? Global Unevenness and Inequality*. Oxford University Press, Oxford, pp. 11–54.

Linneker, B. (1997) *Transport Infrastructure and Regional Economic Development in Europe: A Review of Theoretical and Methodological Approaches*. TRP 133. Dept. of Town and Regional Planning. University of Sheffield.

Logan, J. and Molotch, H. (2007) *Urban Fortunes: The Political Economy of Place*, 2nd edition. University of California Press, Berkeley.

Lopez, R. and Hynes, P. (2006) 'Obesity, physical activity and the urban environment: public health research needs', *Environmental Health* 5, 5–25.

Lutter, H. (1980) *Raumwirksamkeit von Fernstraßen*. Eine Einschätzung des Fenrstraßenbaus als Instrument zur Raumentwicklung unter heutigen Bedingungen. Forschungen zur Raumentwicklung Bd.8. Bonn: Bundesforschungsanstalt für Landeskunde und Raumordnung.

MacKinnon, D., Pirie, G. and Gather, M. (2008) 'Transport and economic development', in Knowles, R., Shaw, J. and Docherty, I. (eds) *Transport Geographies: Mobilities, Flows and Spaces*. Blackwell, Oxford, pp. 10–28.

Marsden, G. and May, A.D. (2006) 'Do institutional arrangements make a difference to transport policy and implementation? Lessons for Great Britain', *Environment and Planning C: Government Policy* 24(5), 771–790.

Massey, D. (1984) *Spatial Divisions of Labour: Social Structures and the Geography of Production*. Macmillan, London.

Ming Wen, L. and Rissel, C. (2008) 'Inverse associations between cycling to work, public transport, and overweright and obesity: findings from a population based study in Australia', *Preventive Medicine* 46, 29–32.

Painter, J. (1995) *Politics, Geography and 'Political Geography': A Critical Perspective*. Arnold, London.

Porter, M. and Ketels, C. (2004) *UK Competitiveness: Moving to the Next Stage*. Framework paper to DTI and ESRC Cities Programme, www.isc.hbs.edu/econ-natlcomp.htm

SACTRA (1999) *Transport and the Economy: Full Report*. Report by the Standing Advisory Committee on Trunk Road Assessment.

Shaftoe, H. (2008) *Convivial Urban Spaces: Creating Effective Public Places*. Earthscan, London.

Sheller, M. and Urry, J. (2006) 'The new mobilities paradigm', *Environment and Planning A* 38, 207–226.

Simon, D. (1996) *Transport and Development in the Third World*. Routledge, London.

Slaven, A. (1986) 'Shipbuilding', in Langton, J. and Morris, R.J. (eds), *Atlas of Industrialising Britain 1780–1914*. Methuen, London and New York, pp. 136–39.

Storper, M. (1997) *The Regional World: Territorial Development in a Global Economy*. Guildford Press, London.

Thompson, I.B. (1995) 'High-speed transport hubs and Eurocity status: the case of Lyon', *Journal of Transport Geography* 3(1) 29–37.

Vance, J.E. (1986) *Capturing the Horizon: Historical Geography of Transportation*. Harper and Row, New York.

Vickerman, R.W. (1991) *Infrastructure and Regional Development*. London.

Vickerman, R.W. (1997) 'High-speed rail in Europe: experience and issues for future development', *The Annals of Regional Science* 31(1) 21–38.

Walker, R. (1981) 'A theory of suburbanisation: capitalism and the construction of urban space in the United States', in Dear, M. and Scott, A. (eds), *Urbanisation and Planning in Capitalist Societies*. Methuen, New York, pp.383–430.

Williams, K. (2005) *Spatial Planning, Urban Form and Sustainable Transport*. Ashgate, Aldershot.

14

Impacts of ICT on Travel Behavior: A Tapestry of Relationships

Patricia L. Mokhtarian and Gil Tal

INTRODUCTION

For most people in the developed world, information and communication technologies (ICTs) have permeated nearly every aspect of everyday life, affecting where and how we work, learn, shop, eat, play, reside – and travel. The travel impacts are myriad and complex, including direct effects on decisions about a given trip, as well as the collateral effects on travel arising from ICT impacts on primary activities, on the supply of travel, on medium-term decisions such as auto ownership, and on long-term lifestyle and location decisions. The goal of this chapter is to sketch the current state, and possible future directions, of knowledge with respect to the short- and medium-term impacts of ICT on travel behavior/demand. We focus primarily on the "new" ICTs involving mobile telephony and the internet, but we also consider older technologies such as television and even print media to be ICTs. We focus on personal travel (of all distances, modes, and purposes) rather than goods movement, and neglect the indirect impacts of ICT on travel demand through its impact on supply – an extensive topic in its own right which is covered elsewhere in this handbook. Thus, for example, we include the impacts of pre-trip or real-time route guidance on individual trip decisions, but exclude discussion of the aggregate effects of these and other intelligent transportation system (ITS) applications on traffic operations and effective network capacity.

This chapter takes the customary set of travel-related decisions addressed by regional demand forecasting models as its organizational framework. Our principal focus is on the short-term decisions of interest, namely trip and activity generation, destination, mode, and route choices, and the choices of execution time and duration. In looking to the medium term, we focus on automobile ownership. Space does not permit discussion of long-term decisions such as lifestyle and the locations of home and work, but we do consider some implications of how current trends might play out in the future and relate these to suggested directions for future research.

SHORT-TERM DECISIONS

Trip/activity generation

To travel, or not to travel? Before the advent of modern ICTs, an individual's choice could generally be characterized as "traveling in order to conduct an activity", or "not conducting it at all" (with "sending a letter and/or package" serving as a usually-inferior third option in only a very limited number of cases). With the inventions of the telegraph, telephone, and later technologies, "conducting the activity remotely, connected to others (as needed) via ICT" became an increasingly attractive alternative in a growing number of instances.

There is a natural tendency to think first of new technology as offering new ways to do (old) things, and only over time to realize that it also offers ways to do new things. At the same time, the age-old congestion and resource consumption challenges that transportation poses continue to beg for solutions. Putting those two conditions together, it is not surprising that specific ICTs have often been touted as the modern way to "travel". Expressions such as "virtual mobility", "information superhighway", and "tele-*x*" (where *x* = working, shopping, learning, medicine, and so on) stress the analogy (Salomon and Mokhtarian 2008) and channel the mind toward characterizing ICTs as alternative means of travel. From there, it is but a short step to suggest that ICTs will *replace* travel – not all of it, of course, but "a lot". A number of special interests are arrayed in the service of promoting ICTs as a trip substitution strategy (Salomon 1998; Mokhtarian et al. 2005): policymakers find it attractive because it appears to be a low-cost, low-pain, high-tech solution (not only to urban congestion, dependence on non-renewable energy sources, air pollution, and greenhouse gas emissions, but to rural underdevelopment, reduced economic opportunity for the mobility-limited, some labor market shortages, and the struggle to balance job and family responsibilities); equipment manufacturers, service providers, and associated consultants naturally see it as a business opportunity; and the popular media are drawn to the "gee whiz" anecdotes illustrating extreme applications.

The reality (as usual) is considerably more complicated. ICTs certainly do replace "a lot" of travel, so the anecdotes are genuine and the attraction is logical. At the same time, however, until the recent recession the aggregate indicators of transportation demand showed no apparent declining trend – more than 15 years into the "internet era" and the launch of modern mobile telephony, not to mention previous advances in ICT (fax machines and personal computers for example, but think back even farther to the impact of the printing press on travel, and before that the invention of the alphabet). Evidently, something else is happening besides *substitution*.

The literature (Salomon 1985, 1986) has identified several other possibilities: ICTs can *generate* new travel (*complementarity*, or *stimulation*), *modify* travel that would have occurred anyway, or *have no* (*net*) *impact on travel* (*neutrality*). Mokhtarian (2009) reviews the conceptual and empirical evidence to date and concludes that it strongly favors complementarity as the *dominant* impact. She points to *five reasons why ICT does not always reduce travel*: (1) not all activities have an ICT counterpart; (2) even when an ICT alternative exists in theory, it may not be practically feasible; (3) even when feasible, ICT is not always a desirable substitute; (4) travel carries a positive utility in its own right, not just as a means of accessing specific locations; and (5) not all uses of ICT constitute a replacement of travel.

She then describes *seven* (*overlapping*) *reasons why ICT actually increases travel*: (6) ICT saves time and/or money for other activities; (7) it permits travel to be sold more cheaply; (8) it increases the efficiency (and thus the effective capacity) of the transportation system, making travel less costly and therefore more attractive; (9) personal ICT use can increase the productivity and/or enjoyment of travel time, thereby also increasing the attractiveness and/or decreasing the disutility of travel; (10) ICT directly stimulates additional travel; (11) it is an engine driving the increasing globalization of commerce; and (12) it facilitates shifts to more decentralized and lower-density land use patterns.

However, she also identifies *four (now five) ways in which ICT does reduce travel*: (1) sometimes, ICT does directly substitute for making a trip; (2) ICT consumes time (and/or money) that might otherwise have been spent traveling; (3) when travel becomes more costly, difficult, or dangerous, ICT substitution will increase; and (4) ICT can be deployed to make shared means of transportation more attractive (reducing drive-alone trips); to which could be added (5) ICT can reduce unnecessary travel (as when GPS offers a shorter path than the one known to the driver, or a well-timed phone call for directions prevents getting too lost, or "letting your fingers do the walking" prevents driving to several stores to look for an item, or the timely notification of a cancelled lecture averts a needless trip to campus; Line et al. 2011).

Viewed another way, ICT impacts can be organized in terms of the mechanism by which they operate. The column heads of Table 14.1 present those mechanisms, crosstabulated against examples of each kind of impact for four activity types of major interest: commuting/working, business travel, shopping, and social/leisure. These examples serve to illustrate the intricate tapestry of interrelationships involved. With these kinds of impacts in mind, we turn now to a discussion of each of the four specific activity types ("trip purposes", in the parlance of regional travel demand forecasting). Because several recent reviews of the travel impacts of ICT have previously examined these activity types (Krizec and Johnson 2007; Salomon and Mokhtarian 2008; Andreev et al. 2010), we treat them only briefly, so as to permit an exploration

Table 14.1 Types and examples of ICT impacts on activities (generation choices)

	1. Choice between ICT-based and traditional activity (*replacement*)	**2. Generation of new ICT activities (*displacement* – ICTs *take* time or money from other activities)**	**3. Overlay of ICT activities onto other activities (*multitasking*)**	**4. ICT-enabled reallocation of resources to other activities (ICTs *give* time or money that permits other activities to occur)**	**5. ICTs as enablers/ facilitators/ modifiers of activities**
	Direct (own-activity) substitution: activity X is now done by ICTs instead of the traditional way	*Cross-activity substitution*: activity(ies) X affect(s) activity(ies) Y	*Directly, neutrality; indirectly, may be substitution, generation, or modification*	*Cross-activity substitution*: activity(ies) X affect(s) activity(ies) Y	*Activity generation or modification*: activity X either would not have occurred without ICT, or is materially changed by it
	ICTs are the end – the basis of conducting the new activity itself		*ICTs are the "end" for the overlaid activity, which can be the "means"* of saving time and/or money for other activities	*ICTs are the means* (of saving time or money, of obtaining information) – can affect non-ICT as well as ICT activities	
	Probably reduces travel	*May reduce travel*	*May have no impact on, reduce, or generate travel*	*May generate travel*	*Probably generates travel*

(Continued)

Table 14.1 (Continued)

	1. Choice between ICT-based and traditional activity (*replacement*)	2. Generation of new ICT activities (*displacement* – ICTs *take* time or money from other activities)	3. Overlay of ICT activities onto other activities (*multitasking*)	4. ICT-enabled reallocation of resources to other activities (ICTs *give* time or money that permits other activities to occur)	5. ICTs as enablers/ facilitators/ modifiers of activities
Commuting/ working	Telecommuting instead of commuting (*reduction*) Phoning nearby colleague instead of going to see her (*reduction*) Researching online instead of in physical locations (*reduction*)	Growing e-mail load displaces going out for lunch (*reduction*) Online activities displace coffee break in employee lounge (*neutrality*)	Streaming internet radio at work (*neutrality*) Texting a friend to set up lunch while in a meeting (*generation*) Reading an e-mail cancelling lunch while listening to a phone caller (*reduction*)	Going shopping with time saved by telecommuting (*generation*) Spending more time cooking dinner with time saved (*neutrality*)	Telecommuting makes working possible for mobility-limited people who would otherwise be un- or under-employed, increasing their income and therefore travel opportunities (*generation*)
Business travel	Teleconferencing instead of traveling to a meeting (*reduction*) Taking a professional development course online instead of in person (*reduction*)	Maintaining e-mail contact while away displaces in-person social activities (*reduction*) Maintaining e-mail contact while away displaces sleep (*neutrality*) Taking a course in person was not a feasible option; taking it online displaces time with family (*neutrality*)	Ability to work productively and remain in contact while traveling permits more travel to occur (*generation*) Using MP3 player on trips (*neutrality*)	Making more business trips with the time & money saved by teleconferencing (*generation*) Using the time saved by teleconferencing to spend more time with on-site staff (*neutrality*)	ICT makes distributed teamwork possible, which requires intermittent co-presence or temporary geographical proximity (*generation*) ICT undergirds the globalization of manufacturing and retailing operations, which require travel to maintain (*generation*)
Shopping	Shopping online instead of going to a store (*generates* a delivery trip; *may not save* passenger vehicle travel)	Shopping online displaces watching TV (*neutrality*) Shopping online displaces meeting a friend for coffee (*reduction*)	Ordering online while traveling (*impacts uncertain*)	Using the time saved by online shopping to spend more time with family (*neutrality*) Using the money saved by online shopping to eat out with family (*generation*)	Online retailers can attract customers from all over the world (*generation of goods movement*) Online searching or location-based marketing reveals hitherto-unknown stores, which are then visited in person (*generation*)
Social/leisure activities	Playing Wii online instead of meeting face to face to play (*reduction*) Watching a DVD instead of going to the theater (*reduction*)	Online games and chatting displace time at the gym (*reduction*) Time on social networking sites displaces reading for pleasure (*neutrality*)	Streaming online radio in the background (*neutrality*) Calling a friend for last-kilometer directions to the destination saves driving around lost (*reduction*)	Efficiencies of managing a community service group online leave more time for actual community service (*generation*) Online travel bargains prompt new trips, and/or permit traveling farther for the same amount of money (*generation*)	Online dating services turn up matches who are met in person (*generation*) Online information about places and activities stimulates the desire to go there and makes it easier to arrange (*generation*)

Source: adapted and expanded from Mokhtarian et al. 2006; also see Salomon and Mokhtarian 2008 of impacts beyond those conventionally considered.

Commuting

The adoption of telecommuting has apparently grown in the US, but efforts to monitor adoption and impact are still plagued with a lack of definitional clarity (Mokhtarian et al. 2005). For example, according to the US Census, the share of working at home as the usual "means of transportation to work" has grown from 3.3% in 2000 to a 4.0% average for 2006–2008, a non-trivial increase (http://www.census.gov/population/www/cen2000/briefs/phc-t35/tables/tab01–1.pdf and factfinder.census.gov, Table S0801 of the 2006–2008 American Community Survey 3-Year Estimates, both accessed August 12, 2010). However, these numbers both *include* home-based businesses (for whom the transportation impact is ambiguous, depending on whether their alternative is working full- or part-time at a job requiring commuting, or not working at all), and *exclude* less-frequent telecommuters. A better measure of the intensity (not just adoption) of telecommuting is obtained from the 2009 American Time Use Survey, which shows that among the *wage and salary* workers who worked on a given day, 12.7% (11.71 million) worked only at home (computed from http://www.bls.gov/news.release/atus.t07.htm, accessed August 13, 2010). However, this number includes self-employed workers whose businesses are incorporated, and overtime work at home on weekends (with little benefit to congestion) – the average amount of time worked at home by this group is less than 3 hours.

These statistics illustrate some of the issues involved in using a single term such as "telework" to include a variety of distinct arrangements: substituters (the classic "telecommuters", salaried employees substituting working at home for commuting), supplementers (those who bring work home to do on overtime), telecenter-based workers, remote back office workers, home-based business workers, field workers, mobile workers, long-distance telecommuters, and distributed team members, among others. Although it may suit some purposes to group these arrangements together, their travel impacts will be dramatically different, from reductions in travel (substituters) to no impact (supplementers, several others), to increases in travel (mobile workers and others). Certainly it is the travel-reducing forms of telework that attract attention as desirable public policy, yet it is precisely those forms that appear to be growing slowly at best or stagnating at worst, even while most of the other forms are flourishing and adapting to an ever-changing array of institutional and technological enablers (Bergum 2007).

It is no coincidence, then, that most empirical studies of the transportation impacts of telework have focused on classic telecommuting. This is not only because it is the "good" form of teleworking, which policymakers want to encourage; it is also because it is the form whose transportation impacts are easiest to assess. Telecommuting (in most cases) *does* replace travel with ICT, quite directly. Even the indirect and long-term effects are positive on the whole: based on the (somewhat limited) evidence to date, increases in non-work travel (Mokhtarian 1998) and negative impacts on residential relocation (Ory and Mokhtarian 2006) appear to be negligible. For other forms of teleworking however, even the direct transportation impacts are more ambiguous, let alone those which are indirect, longer-term, and contingent.

With respect to classic telecommuting, most studies of the travel impacts are disaggregate and based on relatively small samples. While it is useful to develop data on average reductions in travel by individual telecommuters, to assess the aggregate impacts of telecommuting it is imperative to adjust those reductions for the proportion of people telecommuting on any given day. We are aware of only two empirical studies of the aggregate impacts of telecommuting: a time-series analysis of US telecommuting through 1998 (Choo et al. 2005) found a reduction in nationwide vehicle-miles traveled of about 0.8% that could be attributed to telecommuting after controlling for other standard influences; and a cross-sectional analysis of commuting in Finland in the year 2000 (Helminen and Ristimäki 2007) found a reduction of 0.7% in *commute* kilometers traveled, due to teleworking. It would be of value to update those studies, although consistency of measurement would be a problem for the time series analysis. Combined with the disaggregate results, however, the evidence indicates that the impact of *telecommuting* on travel is benign, even if small in the aggregate (Mokhtarian 1998).

Business travel

The expectation that ICT would substitute for business travel dates back at least to the invention of the telephone. Indeed, de Sola Pool (1979) notes that the modern skyscraper would not be possible without the telephone, since the concentration of human messengers otherwise required to carry business communications would be untenable. More recently, videoconferencing systems ranging from full-room installations to laptop webcams have been touted for their time- and cost-saving advantages due to eliminating trips. They have also been highlighted as a solution when travel becomes dangerous, difficult, or impossible, whether from an ordinary blizzard, a volcanic eruption in Iceland, or in the fearful aftermath of the September 11, 2001 attacks on the United States (Denstadli 2004).

But like travel in general, business travel in particular has shown a dominant rising trend during the period of time coincident with the growth in modern ICTs (Beaverstock et al. 2009). The reasons are undoubtedly interwoven with the increasing globalization of commerce during the same time, itself enabled by ICT. The effects are both *direct* (through its ubiquity and superiority as a marketing tool, ICT generates the demand for more goods and services) and *indirect* (production efficiencies brought about by ICT conserve resources that can be redeployed to cultivate new products, processes, and markets). Some consequences are that:

> staff travel ever farther and more frequently to develop new clients and serve existing ones, employees are exchanged among global sites to enhance knowledge transfer and travel to professional meetings all over the world, inter-firm collaborations and geographically dispersed project teams have increased over time, cheaper labor and raw materials make it cost-effective to transport them from farther away, and the worldwide customer base created through internet-based marketing as well as more conventional channels generates greater travel in the transport of finished products to the consumer. (Mokhtarian 2009, pp. 8–9)

Accordingly, a number of scholars (Torre 2008; Lassen 2009) have commented on the continued need for face-to-face interaction (the "intermittent co-presence" of Urry 2003) despite the increasing effectiveness of ICT as a substitute.

Shopping

Online shopping continues the steady growth in adoption it has displayed since data began to be collected around 1999. In the US, it has risen from 1.1% of total retail sales in 2001, to 3.6% ($142 billion) in 2008 (http://www.census.gov/compendia/statab/cats/wholesale_retail_trade/online_retail_sales.html, Table 1054, accessed January 6, 2011). Although that *share* is far from overwhelming, the *dollar amount* is non-negligible, and both are likely to continue to increase relative to the economy as a whole. Nearly 75% of US internet users have bought products online (Table 1120 of the *2010 Statistical Abstract*, http://www.census.gov/compendia/statab/cats/information_communications.html, accessed August 13, 2010), and no large retailers and few small ones are without an internet presence today. Indeed, the internet has made possible the creation of thousands of small businesses (some of them growing quite large), offering a global reach with little incremental investment (at least initially) beyond that required for a local reach.

E-shopping may present urban planners with a dilemma. On one hand, it is tempting to hope for/expect travel reduction impacts as e-shopping substitutes for store shopping, and it is common to presume that it is the "green" way to go. On the other hand, under current US law, cities lose sales tax revenues on purchases made from virtual stores located elsewhere, and if e-shopping contributes to sapping the vitality of downtown retail districts, it is acting at cross-purposes to other planning goals. Accordingly, addressing the opportunities and challenges posed by this particular ICT application is not straightforward.

For that matter, the transportation impacts are not straightforward either. In a conceptual review of the possible impacts, Mokhtarian (2004) identifies a number of ways in which travel could increase, decrease, or remain unaffected by e-shopping. For example, the ease of finding online, and purchasing, handcrafts made by remote villagers may stimulate the demand for those items, requiring their transport over very long distances.

The empirical evidence to date is reviewed by Cao (2009), noting that the evidence is mixed (finding substitution as well as generation effects) and plagued with a number of methodological and data limitations. For example, some studies make little distinction between browsing and purchasing uses of the internet, even though travel impacts are likely to differ between the two. Other studies ask what the shopper would have done if the internet had not been available for a specific purchase, but if the answer is "gone to a store", there is no way of knowing whether the store would have been visited anyway, whether it was chained to another trip and had very little incremental impact, whether it would have been visited by car, transit, or walking/cycling, nor how far away it was. No studies have yet combined the shopper-side impacts (perhaps reducing travel) with the retailer-side impacts (perhaps increasing travel), to assess the net effects on transportation. Clearly, this is an area calling for further research.

Social/leisure activities

The nexus of ICT, social networks, and travel is an active frontier of research (Kwan 2007; Carrasco et al. 2008). Some early studies (Nie 2001) suggested that ICTs may contribute to greater social isolation, as people replace physical contact with solitary computer pursuits (the "time displacement" mechanism of the #2 column in Table 14.1). However, the preponderance of recent research appears to support the opposite – a complementarity between ICT use and social activity (Robinson and Martin 2010).

In an extended conceptual discussion of the impacts of ICT on leisure activities and travel, Mokhtarian et al. (2006) suggest that the dominant nature of its role is to expand an individual's choice set, making more leisure options available through the mechanisms forming the columns of Table 14.1. However, the extent to which those options are chosen, and thus the actual impact of ICT on activity engagement and travel, depends on a variety of situational and individual factors.

Schwanen and Kwan (2008) examine the relationship of ICT to activity in general, and social activities in particular, through the lens of Hägerstrand's (1970) classic three constraints (capability, coupling, and authority)[1] and other restrictions such as human indivisibility and limitations on multi-tasking. They highlight the paradox that although ICT relaxes those constraints in some ways, it also imposes constraints of its own. For example, even mobile ICTs are hostage to a variety of physical objects (phone, charger, electrical outlet, transmission tower, satellite), which must be spatio-temporally coupled in order to relax the coupling constraint of bodily co-location with fellow employees. Thus, again, the role of ICT defies a simple explanation.

Destination choice

In the preceding section, the choice between the ICT-based and traditional forms of an activity was characterized as a *trip/activity generation* decision. However, it can also be viewed as a *destination* choice: work at home versus in the regular office; attend the meeting (via teleconference) in the regular office versus traveling to its physical location; and so on. Doing so adds the important elements of travel cost and destination attractiveness to the decision context – elements not usually considered in conventional trip generation models.

There are a number of other ways in which ICT can affect destination choice, however. First, we must not overlook the role of ICT in *disseminating information* about specific destinations. O'Reilly (2006, p. 1008), for example, refers to the role of "mediascapes" (mass media) and "technoscapes" (personal ICTs) in stimulating the imagination, which "is central to all forms of agency including travel – the creation of places and people as objects of desire, the means to fulfill that desire, and the self-identity that develops out of the practice of travel". Such a process has been in play from time immemorial, as hunters returned home and communicated the novelties they had seen to those left behind, as youngsters dreamed about the unknown world beyond their small neighborhood and vowed to explore it someday. Travel writings (and maps, art, photography, videography) have inspired countless travelers to follow in another's footsteps and/or venture out in other ways. Multiply the intensity and reach of that phenomenon many-fold with internet-based marketing, social networks, instantly-transmitted photography, global positioning system (GPS) technology, and location-aware mobile services, and it is easy to see the possibilities for generating considerable new travel. Last-minute travel bargains may generate an impulsive trip whose destination was not even planned in advance.

Sometimes, as just described, ICT plants a seed with respect to a particular destination, but sometimes it is used to assist the *evaluation of an array of destinations.* The internet permits the rapid assembly of information about a variety of candidate destinations (and the associated travel) for a given activity (e.g. a vacation, or eating out, or shopping for a certain item). Locations without an internet marketing interface, or with a less-sophisticated one, may be disadvantaged.

At the same time, the availability of ICT infrastructure and services may be one *decision factor* in the choice of location, as when one chooses a hotel based in part on the availability of (free) internet access, or, alternatively, may choose a remote vacation spot *because* it has little contact with "the outside world".

In a destination choice context, ICTs are used not only for pre-trip planning, but for *real-time trip modifications*. Mobile telephony permits micro-coordination of meeting times and places, with destination adjustments a frequent outcome. Thus, already-engaged cab drivers convey information about waiting passengers to available colleagues (Elaluf-Calderwood 2009); Indian fishermen decide in which coastal village to sell their catch on the basis of real-time market information (and in so doing increase the average distance they travel; Foss and Couclelis 2009); and flash mobs materialize at a certain location, seemingly at random (Srivastava 2005).

To summarize, with respect to destination choice alone, ICT can serve as idea generator, data collection instrument (for the traveler), explanatory variable, real-time information channel, and/or the destination itself (Table 14.2). Little wonder that its impacts on travel are complex! Consideration of destination decisions in particular makes it clear that distance is hardly "dead", as some ICT enthusiasts proclaimed a few years ago (Cairncross 1997). ICTs vividly confront us with appealing destinations that are *not* the same as where we are, find a bargain price for us, facilitate the planning of the trip, and provide us with an indispensable tool throughout the trip itself. In so doing, they indisputably reduce the friction or impedance of travel, so to speak, but that only makes travel *more* attractive, not less. To be sure, on occasion ICTs provide the "destination" itself, when an ICT-based substitute is chosen to conduct an activity. Even then, however, distance is rarely invisible – the experience is never "the same as being there", even if sometimes it might be *preferable* to being there (Hilty 2008).

Table 14.2 Types and examples of ICT roles with respect to destination, mode, and route choices

	Destination	Mode	Route
Pre-decision roles of ICT			
Inspiration (disseminates information)	E-mail generated by web-based travel sites advertises bargain travel packages to a desirable location Online search for a collector's item identifies a seller within driving distance	E-mail advertises bargain airfares TV advertises the romance of intercity train travel; internet provides specific route and schedule information Transportation agencies offer online bicycle and bus trip planning tools, lowering the uncertainty barrier	TV travelogue on an appealing itinerary inspires emulation
Information provider (facilitates evaluation)	Internet searches gather information on prices, locations, amenities of alternative destinations Google Earth and Google Street View are used to view alternatives Sign approaching a destination announces waiting time, vacancies, and/or alternatives	Internet tools allow comparison of travel times, costs for a given urban trip by various modes Near-real-time rideshare matching capabilities may stimulate more carpooling; information sites such as http://www.slug-lines.com/ support casual carpooling Participation in carsharing may prompt greater use of walking and transit, as well as "right-sizing" the vehicle to the occasion when driving is chosen	GPS compares the distance and time of several alternative routes Google Earth and Google Street View are used to virtually traverse the route Sign approaching the entrance to a toll route announces congestion-based toll, and compares real-time travel times on toll and free routes
Explanatory variable (constitutes one decision factor)	A destination that is not in the GPS database may be avoided Hotel is rejected from the choice set if it does not offer free internet access Free Wi-Fi influences the choice of café	Real-time information on the arrival of the next bus reduces the disutility of uncertainty ICT-based games decrease the disutility of waiting Ability to work on buses, trains and flights increases their utility compared to driving Need for privacy of phone conversations while traveling increases the utility of driving compared to transit	Routes with mobile phone or data network "dead zones" are avoided Routes with variable message signs (VMS) stating real-time travel times are preferred
One of the alternatives	Home is an alternative destination for conducting the work activity, or shopping, or seeing a movie The corporate videoconference facility (or one's personal office, with a webcam) is an alternative destination for conducting the business meeting	ICT is a virtual mode of travel	ICT and non-ICT choices can be represented as alternative paths through an integrated physical/ virtual network

(Continued)

Table 14.2 (Continued)

	Destination	Mode	Route
Post-decision roles of ICT			
Changes the chosen alternative	A friend calls or tweets in mid-trip to say the party has moved to another location	When the connecting flight is delayed several hours, a car is rented by mobile phone to enable reaching the wedding on time Emerging and prospective applications use reputation monitoring, taste matching, and location awareness to help a traveler decide whether to join an instant carpool while a trip is in progress (Resnick 2004; Mitchell and Casalegno 2008)	VMS announces congestion ahead and advises alternative route A friend calls to advise of a large highway accident and suggests alternative route Your location-aware mobile phone calls you to suggest a short diversion to buy an item on sale at a nearby store (destination *addition*, route change)
Modifies the trip experience	Real-time coordination of meeting point reduces anxiety	ICT-based activities reduce boredom, increase the pleasure of the trip The ability to work productively while traveling means travel is no longer "lost time" Other people's use of ICT degrades the trip experience	ICT-based in-vehicle entertainment *decreases* attention to the route Location-aware information provision/interaction *increases* attention to the route

Mode choice

So far, we have seen that the choice between the ICT-based and traditional forms of an activity can be viewed as a trip/activity generation decision or a destination choice. We now note that it can also be considered a mode choice (Mokhtarian 1991). Indeed, ICT is often characterized as an alternative, virtual, mode of travel. Just as with destination choice, however, there are a number of ways in which ICTs can influence the choices among means of physical travel. In fact, we begin to see a pattern as we realize that the same types of roles of ICT generally apply across destination, mode, and route choices (Table 14.2).

ICT can offer mode-specific *inspiration* to travel, through the ease and low cost of widespread dissemination of promotional or affective messages built around a particular mode such as trains, cruise ships, or bicycles. In some cases the advertisement of slashed fares on a given mode can inspire a trip: the mode is decided first, and the destination afterward. The ready availability of information to "demystify" a mode such as transit (fare, route, and schedule information, station/stop site maps and street-view photos) or cycling (regional bike path maps) may generate trips via those modes.

ICT can provide pre-trip *information* facilitating the evaluation of alternative modes for taking a trip. Thus, for example, entering origin and destination addresses into an internet-based service such as Google Maps allows the traveler to obtain directions and travel times by driving, transit, walking, and biking. ICT further offers a practical platform for rideshare matching (Buliung et al. 2010), whether ad hoc or longer-term. Such services are offered both by transportation agencies and by private companies and organizations (see, for example, erideshare.com, which offers local rideshare matching along with cross-country trip matching, airport rides, and other options).

ICT also lies at the heart of the carsharing concept, in which subscribers can reserve and then drive a vehicle drawn from a diverse pool of options, choosing a different vehicle for each trip as needed or desired. On the supply side, carsharing companies use modern ICTs to manage fleet distribution, usage and maintenance (Kek et al. 2009), while on the demand side, customers use an ICT interface to view options and make reservations and payments. Although carsharing obviously still involves cars, it is commonly speculated that participation in such a program, by confronting the traveler with an out-of-pocket cost for each trip (rather than the large sunk cost of owning an automobile), can cause him/her to assess mode choices for each trip in a more considered rather than habitual way, resulting in making some trips by transit or non-motorized modes for which a personally-owned car would otherwise have been used (Shaheen et al. 2009). Thus, the ease of obtaining information about alternatives to driving a personally-owned vehicle may lead some people to "break the driving habit" for some trips, but to our knowledge no rigorous studies have been conducted of this impact of ICT on mode choice.

Most people find uncertainty uncomfortable, and accordingly the reduction of uncertainty can be an important factor in transportation decisions. For example, many studies have shown that people prefer a route with travel times that are longer on average but with lower variability, to a route that has a shorter average time but which may substantially exceed that time on any given day (e.g. Bogers et al. 2006). One factor making transit a less desirable mode choice for many people is precisely that uncertainty: When is the next bus coming? Do I catch it on the near side or far side of the intersection? Do I pay the driver or must I have a ticket in advance? Is exact change required? Will I be able to sit down? Will I have to wait in the rain? Driving a car may seem much more familiar in comparison, and apparently leaving the traveler much more in control of his/her circumstances. Accordingly, the more ICT can reduce that uncertainty, the more attractive transit will be. As mentioned above, ICT can facilitate information gathering about a *prospective* trip, which is one form of reducing uncertainty. But ICT also offers information (e.g. on time of next arrival) when a trip is *in progress*. That information not only affects the trip experience itself once a mode has been selected (e.g. reduces tension caused by uncertainty), but the *availability* of that information may be one factor in the mode choice decision in the first place.

Similarly, another important role of ICT in mode choice lies in the provision of activities to undertake while traveling. Of course, non-ICT activities (talking, scenery gazing, reading, sleeping) have always been available while traveling as well, but the modern proliferation of multi-featured portable communication and entertainment devices (mobile phone/text messager/ music-and-video player/ book reader/navigation device/internet browser/ game player/cameras, not to mention "ordinary" laptop computers) has multiplied the options available for keeping busy while traveling.

Like the uncertainty-reduction function just discussed, the work/entertainment capabilities of ICT play two roles in mode choice. First, they *affect the trip experience itself* once a mode has been selected. For example, they may simply reduce the boredom or tension of waiting for the next bus (by filling the time and distracting attention from the suspension of the journey), or redeem the time otherwise viewed as wasted in commuting – i.e., *reduce the disutility* of the trip. Alternatively, they may actively contribute to the pleasure of an otherwise desirable trip (e.g. by adding favorite music; or by interleaving scenery-gazing with the satisfying productivity boost obtained by reading and answering work-related e-mail during the commute; or by sharing photos, voice, or text with distant friends while en route) – i.e., *increase the positive utility* of the journey. Complex combinations are possible, such as when ICT indirectly reduces the negative utility of driving by increasing the positive utility of one's passengers. For example, the availability of back-seat DVD players along with portable video games allows parents to travel longer distances before their children get restless. Furthermore, modern car edutainment systems allow the front-seat passengers to listen to different music than their back-seat companions. In any of these ways, ICT can contribute to increasing the "experienced utility" or "remembered utility" of the trip (Ettema et al. 2010). Of course, it can also *decrease* utility, as when travelers are bothered by others talking on mobile phones – or when they are scolded for themselves bothering others with their own talking (Bissell 2010).

Second, therefore, the availability of that entertainment capability may be a *factor in the mode choice decision in the first place*. Ettema and Verschuren (2007) found, in a stated response study, that listening to music while traveling and the propensity to engage in multiple activities at once reduced an individual's value of time, meaning that the trip was considered less burdensome. The implication is that modes that support multitasking more will have greater utility for those who value that capability. Thus, a number of scholars (see references in this section) have commented that some travelers may prefer a longer commute on public transit if they are able to use the time productively, over a shorter one by driving where the time is largely wasted. Certainly, however, the ICT capabilities of automobiles are also continually improving, even while the current policy campaigns against distracted driving (see, e.g., http://www.distraction.gov/, accessed August 5, 2010) are narrowing the range of activities considered safe to undertake while driving.

There is a sizable and growing literature on activities conducted while traveling, including the enabling role played by ICT. In addition to several recent descriptive empirical studies (e.g. Ohmori and Harata 2008), the issue has received some thoughtful conceptual development. For example, Lyons and Urry (2005) note that travel time can be counterproductive, partially or fully productive, or even "ultraproductive", and that the prevalence of these conditions differs by mode. Jain and Lyons (2008) continue the discussion by observing that travel time can sometimes be a gift (either *of*, or *to*, the traveler), not just a disutility. As Metz (2008) and others have pointed out, the ability to use travel time productively calls into question the extent to which saving such time should be viewed as a benefit of a proposed transportation improvement (generally identified as by far the largest component of that benefit).

Route choice

Just as conducting an activity via ICT can be viewed as a generation, destination, or mode choice, it can also be considered a route choice. Nagurney has been instrumental in the conception of the ICT-versus-travel choice as a path-optimization problem through a network that integrates both the physical transportation network and the virtual ICT paths for "accessing" a destination (e.g., Nagurney et al. 2002; also see Shaw and Yu 2009). The other roles of ICT also apply to route choice as well as to the choices previously discussed. With respect to *inspiration*, the centerpiece of travel writing, mapmaking, photography, or video might just as well be a *route* as a region or *destination*. Whether of scenic, historic, cultural, or spiritual interest, numerous routes around the world have attracted attention, such as the Appalachian Trail (Bryson 1998), Natchez Trace, the Trail of Tears, the route of the Lewis and Clark Expedition, and the iconic Route 66 (Wallis 1990) in the US; the Great Wall of China (Gray 2006) and the Silk Road (Wilson 2010) of Asia; the English-countryside walking tours of William Wordsworth; or pilgrimage routes such as the Via Dolorosa in Jerusalem, the roads leading to Santiago de Compostela in Spain (Gitlitz and Davidson 2000), and the Hajj to Mecca.

As with the previous choices, ICT also enables the rapid collection of *information* on alternative routes, facilitating a selection among them. GPS devices and Google Earth can assist in pre-trip planning (Table 14.2), while variable message signs (VMSs) and GPS combined with real-time information may influence the choice between toll and free routes (Al-Deek et al. 2009). Beyond the travel information it provides, the availability of ICT itself for the *traveler's* communication needs may constitute one *factor in the choice* among routes, as when a driver (or transit passenger) avoids a route that does not provide complete mobile phone coverage.

Once a route has been chosen, ICTs can continue to play either of two roles. First, Advanced Traveler Information Systems (ATIS) including traditional radio, variable message signs (VMS), web pages, and onboard traffic data can *prompt a change to the route mid-trip*, for example by warning of congestion ahead and advising travelers to take an alternate route. A number of studies (e.g. Dia and Panwai 2007; Richards and McDonald 2007; Paz and Peeta 2009) have examined driver behavior with respect to willingness to accept such advice, and the impacts on traffic flow of various degrees of compliance.

Second, ICTs can *affect the trip experience* with respect to the route, much as they can for mode and destination. On the one hand, in-vehicle entertainment systems (back-seat video screens), together with personal entertainment/communication devices (MP3 players, enhanced mobile phones), may focus passengers inward and draw attention *away* from the passing scenery. Of course, this could be viewed positively or negatively, depending on whether the passing scenery is unappealing (with ICT reducing the unpleasantness of a long boring journey) or interesting (with artificially-mediated experiences diluting or even replacing the exposure to real-world beauty or experience). And, of course, "unappealing" versus "interesting" is in the eye of the beholder. On the other hand, however, currently-developing location-aware interactive technologies offer opportunities to engage travelers *more* with their passing surroundings, by prompting them to contribute to a common dataset as well as to use it (Gandy and Meitner 2007; Goodchild 2008; Chen et al. 2009).

Timing and duration of activity execution

It should already be clear that the impact of ICTs on activity patterns is far more intricate than simply offering a choice between conducting an activity "the old-fashioned way" or doing it via ICT. An important way in which the situation becomes more complicated is the contribution of ICTs to the increased fragmentation of activities in time and space. As Couclelis (2000) notes, whereas a few decades ago "work" and "shopping" and "entertainment" were largely confined to well-defined time periods and locations, it is now commonplace to interleave them almost at will, with "anywhere, anytime" being only a small exaggeration. She further perceptively speculates (pp. 346–348) that "this interweaving and mutual dependence of physical mobility and electronic communication, not merely the spreading use of ICTs, … is one of the reasons for the widely observed increases in travel demand in the industrialized world".

Several scholars have undertaken to empirically operationalize this concept of activity fragmentation. Lenz and Nobis (2007) cluster-analyzed a sample of 1,612 German workers on the basis of seven travel and ICT-related variables, and identified four clusters with distinct levels and types of fragmentation. Hubers et al. (2008) proposed several metrics (number of fragments, distribution of sizes of the fragments, and the degree of clustering of the fragments) that can be applied to standard travel diary data to quantify the degree of fragmentation in an individual's set of activities. Their empirical application to 826 residents of the Netherlands found evidence supporting the expectation that greater use of ICT is associated with greater temporal fragmentation (although ordinary sociodemographic variables appeared to contribute to it even more). For example, those with a higher frequency of internet use tended to have more work episodes, while those whose primary internet use was neither at home nor at work (connoting mobile workers and/or students) tended to have more, and shorter, daily shopping episodes. Similar metrics were applied to quantify the fragmentation of work activity (Alexander et al. 2010), again finding a positive association between ICT use and fragmentation, albeit with considerable variation among different representative work patterns, and with the direction of causality unclear.

One type of spatial fragmentation that warrants particular attention is that of "mediated co-presence", referring to the use of ICT to achieve the "virtual presence" of others. Conventional teleconferencing is one example, but we focus here on personal communications. Ito (2005), for example, refers to frequent text message exchanges between close friends or relatives as "ambient virtual co-presence", and the similar exchange of photos as "intimate visual co-presence". As she notes, such exchanges often do not convey "newsworthy" information, but rather the banalities of everyday life which nevertheless contribute to maintaining a relationship during physical absence. Greschke (2008) describes the role of the online community Cibervalle in bonding together Paraguayans all over the world, a phenomenon replicated in many other ways through social networking sites of all kinds.

What does this have to do with travel? For one thing, *it facilitates travel by reducing the pain of absence* (a current TV commercial illustrates this idea, featuring a businessman in a hotel room somewhere in Asia sharing a bedtime cookie-eating ritual with his young son at home, via webcams and laptops). From "nanny-cams" to medical-alert systems to daily blogs to frequent tweets, technology helps reassure the traveler that all is well at home and conversely (White and White 2007) – at the margin supporting travel that might otherwise have been suppressed in favor of staying home (interestingly, de Sola Pool 1979 attributes a similar reassurance role to the landline telephone, in contributing to the suburbanization of residences in the post-WWII era).

Furthermore (as discussed above for ICTs in general), *mediated co-presence can, in itself, generate travel*. Greschke (2008, p. 286) notes that "the virtually formed relationships seem to stimulate the need for face-to-face encounters", drawing on Urry's (2003) concept of the necessity of "intermittent co-presence" for maintaining heavily-mediated relationships. And Mascheroni (2007, pp. 527–528) echoes O'Reilly's (2006) reference to the importance of technoscapes in stimulating the imagination, and considers "the consistent use of new media while on the move" as an "incitement to travel".

While fragmentation generally implies shorter durations of the "fragments", it is also of interest to investigate how ICT may be changing the *total* amount of travel for various kinds of activities (whether measured in time or number of trips). Several studies have explored relationships between ICT and the duration of travel, using some form of simultaneous equations modeling of time use or travel/activity diary data. For example, analyzing data collected from 4935 Hong Kong residents in 2002, Wang and Law (2007) found that ICT use tended to generate more trips and more time for out-of-home recreation and travel. Using 2002–2003 data from 334 residents of Quebec, Canada, Lee-Gosselin and Miranda-Moreno (2009) found a negative association between internet access and trip frequency, but a positive association between mobile phone use and trips. And based on 2003–2004 data from 392 internet users in the Columbus, Ohio metropolitan area, Ren and Kwan (2009) found that the time spent on internet-based maintenance and leisure activities had complex and gender-differentiated impacts (both positive and negative) on the time spent on physical maintenance and leisure.

MEDIUM-TERM DECISIONS: AUTOMOBILE OWNERSHIP

With respect to medium-term decisions regarding automobile ownership, we see several of the same kinds of roles for ICT that have appeared earlier. Certainly the traditional broadcast and print media still promote the *inspiration* to buy a particular car, but recent research (e.g. Axsen and Kurani 2011) has also highlighted the role of social networks in providing both inspiration and information about new automotive technologies.

Most vehicles are still purchased in a dealership, though some new vehicles are purchased online and some used cars are purchased on eBay and other electronic auction sites. Nevertheless, obtaining online pre-purchase *information* is now an important part of the process for many buyers (Ratchford et al. 2007; Zettelmeyer et al. 2006). Used cars are now advertised online with more details, photos, and information than ever before. Unlike paper-based information, the online information is not restricted to experts' opinions, but rather includes users' and owners' experiences and opinions.

Even aside from the role of computers in vehicle operation and system optimization, an increasing number of occupant-interfaced automobile features are ICT-based, whether for entertainment (audio/video players), navigation (GPS), telephony (Bluetooth interfaces), computing (USB ports), diagnosis (warning messages), or safety/security (back-up camera, breathalyzers, recognition devices). These are evaluated together with other features when a buyer chooses among alternatives, hence ICT furnishes a number of potential *explanatory variables* to vehicle purchase decisions. Although hedonic price models of automobile choice are commonplace (e.g., Baltas and Saridakis 2009), they tend to include features such as horsepower, trunk size, and fuel economy; a focus on vehicle-user ICTs is not yet evident in the open literature.

Finally, carsharing was mentioned earlier as an ICT-enabled strategy with potential impacts on mode choice. But it is also commonly expected to reduce car ownership; indeed, that is largely the point of the strategy. Although studies report car disposal by 15–32% of participants and the postponement or complete avoidance of a car purchase by another 25–71% (Shaheen et al. 2009), carsharing so far remains a small niche market, and early adopters may not be typical of later entrants. For example, although early adopters tend to be higher-income (Burkhardt and Millard-Bell 2006), carsharing could over time be adopted by people who could not otherwise have afforded a (second) car, and to the extent it succeeds in providing a lower-cost alternative to personal vehicle ownership, the result may be more vehicle travel generated rather than less.

CONCLUSION

Tables 14.1 and 14.2 and the accompanying text illustrate a varied and complex set of relationships between ICT and travel. It should also be noted that the concomitant effects on congestion, fuel consumption, air quality, and greenhouse gas emissions are not straightforward either, since those are intricate functions of all the other decisions involved: trip generation, destination, mode, route, and vehicle. To date, only a fraction of the relationships discussed in this chapter have been studied specifically with respect to their travel-related impacts. The use of ICT to conduct certain activity/trip purposes (commuting, and to a lesser extent business travel and shopping) has been studied extensively, and the impact of the ability to conduct ICT-based activities while traveling has attracted a fair amount of attention of late. The decision to follow navigation advice has also been the subject of considerable study. Beyond those areas, however, our knowledge drops off dramatically, highlighting the need for additional study of the other cells in the tables.

Of course, the research needed is not a matter of closing the gaps in a static picture. Rather, in the meantime, the ICT landscape is constantly changing, creating ever-new and shifting gaps in knowledge. Although future technologies have the potential for inducing dramatic changes in travel behavior (for example, technologies that replace the driver and automate the roads, or technologies that make point-to-point air travel feasible and affordable to a mass market), for the near term we can identify several less dramatic technological and behavioral trends.

The most notable overarching trend is the growing use of more ICTs, by larger segments of the population. Three factors have facilitated this trend: greater availability of new technology as a result of technology improvement and cost reduction (supply); social changes and diffusion of innovations as they progress from early adopters to larger markets (demand); and public policies that facilitate ICT implementation both directly for transportation and for other uses.

In particular, these factors are paving the way for two-way communication technologies that not only provide "outbound" data tailored to individual needs (such as data on traffic conditions, available parking, or the next bus arrival), but also communicate "inbound" from the recipient back to the transportation system, both passively (permitting the assessment of real-time traffic conditions) and actively (reserving a spot in the parking facility or on the bus, for example, or paying for road use). Technology and policy can work together to combine data sources and improve accessibility to these data by the user. For example, an electric vehicle driver, having entered his/her destination into the in-vehicle navigation system, may be advised en route by the vehicle computer to stop at a certain charging facility coming up, as the computer calculates that the battery may be depleted before the end of the trip. The computer then can reserve a time slot at the charger and also recommend and reserve a restaurant nearby based on the driver's preferences. Similar scenarios can be constructed for public transit use and other circumstances. Such trends in the use of ICT reveal at least two major challenges in maximizing the potential transportation benefits: privacy and equity. Privacy issues may be the main barrier in using multi-database technologies, two-way communications, location-aware applications and devices, and other technologies that may expose sensitive information about the user. It is most often the role of policymakers, and not the technology developers, to find the balance between privacy requirements and efficient ICT usage and to prevent abuses that may result in public mistrust and slower adoption of new technologies. This is made more difficult by the fact that policymakers are generally playing "catch-up", with technological advances outrunning their abilities to assess and respond to the negative impacts of those advances.

Equity is the second challenge that policymakers must acknowledge and scientists must explore. Indeed, ICT may improve accessibility for some disadvantaged groups, such as people with mobility limitations, vision impairment, and other functional challenges, but whenever large segments of the population adopt a new technology, the segments not using it can be left behind and the equity gap can grow larger. For example, low-income groups, who are often captive transit users, may be the last to adopt smart phone applications for navigating the transit system and may be the last to know about service changes, price options, and so on. Future ICT policy must balance equity and cost when using public funds. For example, investing in web-based timetables is useful only to internet users, whereas printed timetables may be useful to everyone but more resource-intensive over the long run. Policy interventions such as subsidizing computers and/or smart phones, and installing multi-language electronic boards, can address these inequities for low-income, immigrants and other disadvantaged groups, but at a cost to the public.

Given the accelerated appearance of new ICTs and applications, attempts to study and address their impacts clearly involve grasping for a moving target. The alternative (ignorance, failure to anticipate and mitigate negative consequences) is even less desirable, however, and the challenges are intellectually invigorating. We can also summon to our aid the very technology we study, as ICTs are making it feasible to collect richer and more complete data on travel behavior than ever before (e.g. Clark and Doherty 2010). For example, the impact of ICTs and related transportation policies can be evaluated by utilizing Hägerstrand's (1970) accessibility prism to measure the effect of ICT on the cost and availability of activities such as higher education, shopping, and so on (Kwan 2000; Ren and Kwan 2007). ICT can change accessibility both by reducing the cost of traveling and by substituting activities, and may have differential effects on different populations.

There may be a limit, however, to what can be learned about impacts on travel from the micro-scale study of single mechanisms at a time. While disaggregate studies offer unparalleled insight into behavioral processes and causal levers, they may miss the "big picture" that only aggregate studies can provide. There have been several studies of aggregate relationships between communications and travel, including monetary relationships for industry (Lee and Mokhtarian 2008) and consumers (Choo et al. 2007), and activity-based relationships across all sectors (Choo and Mokhtarian 2007). These studies' collective findings echo the complexity of the conceptual picture drawn here, but their dominant theme appears to be that of complementarity. Even these studies, however, are plagued by small sample sizes and/or short time series, especially during the modern era of mobile phones and the internet. It will be critical to replicate such studies as more years of data are collected.

NOTE

1 "'Capability constraints' are those which limit the activities of the individual because of his biological construction and/or the tools he can command"; coupling constraints "define where, when, and for how long, the individual has to join other individuals, tools, and materials in order to produce, consume, and transact"; and authority constraints refer to domains "within which things and events are under the control of a given individual or a given group" (Hägerstrand 1970, pp. 12, 14, and 16, respectively).

REFERENCES

Al-Deek, H., S. R. C. C. Venkata, and J. Flick (2009) "Impact of Dynamic Message Signs on Satisfaction and Diversion of Toll Road Travelers", *Transportation Research Record*, No. 2099, pp. 1–13.

Alexander, B., D. Ettema, and M. Dijst (2010) "Fragmentation of Work Activity as a Multi-dimensional Construct and its Association with ICT, Employment and Sociodemographic Characteristics", *Journal of Transport Geography*, Vol. 18, pp. 55–64.

Andreev, P., I. Salomon, and N. Pliskin (2010) "Review: State of Teleactivities", *Transportation Research Part C*, Vol. 18, No. 1, pp. 3–20.

Axsen, J. and K. S. Kurani (2011) "Interpersonal Influence in the Early Plug-In Hybrid Market: Observing Social Interactions with an Exploratory Multi-Method Approach", *Transportation Research Part D*, Vol. 16., No. 2, pp. 150–159.

Baltas, G. and C. Saridakis (2009) "Brand-Name Effects, Segment Differences, and Product Characteristics: An Integrated Model of the Car Market", *Journal of Product & Brand Management*, Vol. 18, No. 2, pp. 143–151.

Beaverstock, J. V., B. Derudder, J. R. Faulconbridge, and F. Witlox (2009) "International Business Travel: Some Explorations", *Geografiska Annaler Series B, Human Geography*, Vol. 91, No. 3, pp. 193–202.

Bergum, S. (2007) "What Has Happened to Telework? Failure, Diffusion or Modification?", *The Journal of E-Working*, Vol. 1, pp. 13–44.

Bissell, D. (2010) "Passenger Mobilities: Affective Atmospheres and the Sociality of Public Transport", *Environment and Planning D*, Vol. 28, pp. 270–289.

Bogers, E. A. I., F. Viti, S. P. Hoogendoorn, and H. J. Van Zuylen (2006) "Valuation of Different Types of Travel Time Reliability in Route Choice: Large-Scale Laboratory Experiment", *Transportation Research Record*, No. 1985, pp. 162–170.

Bryson, B. (1998) *A Walk in the Woods: Rediscovering America on the Appalachian Trail*, New York: Broadway.

Buliung, R. N., K. Soltys, R. Bui, C. Habel, and R. Lanyon (2010) "Catching a Ride on the Information Super-highway: Toward an Understanding of

Internet-based Carpool Formation and Use", *Transportation*, Vol. 37, No. 6, pp. 849–873.

Burkhardt, J. E. and A. Millard-Bell (2006) "Who is Attracted to Carsharing?", *Transportation Research Record*, No. 1986, pp. 98–105.

Cairncross, F. (1997) *The Death of Distance*, Boston: Harvard Business School Press.

Cao, X. J. (2009) "E-shopping, Spatial Attributes, and Personal Travel: A Review of Empirical Studies", *Transportation Research Record*, No. 2135, pp. 160–169.

Carrasco, J. A., E. J. Miller, and B. Wellman (2008) "How Far and with Whom Do People Socialize? Empirical Evidence about Distance between Social Network Members", *Transportation Research Record*, No. 2076, pp. 114–122.

Chen, Y., S. Chen, Y. Gu, M. Hui, F. Li, C. Liu, L. Liu, B. C. Ooi, X. Yang, D. Zhang, and Y. Zhou (2009) "MarcoPolo: A Community System for Sharing and Integrating Travel Information on Maps", in *Proceedings of the 12th International Conference on Extending Database Technology: Advances in Database Technology* – EDBT 09, pp. 1148–1151. Available from http://portal.acm.org/citation.cfm?doid=1516360.1516500, accessed August 25, 2010.

Choo, S. and P. L. Mokhtarian (2007) "Telecommunications and Travel Demand and Supply: Aggregate Structural Equation Models for the U.S.", *Transportation Research A*, Vol. 41, No. 1, pp. 4–18.

Choo, S., T. Lee, and P. L. Mokhtarian (2007) "Do Transportation and Communications Tend to be Substitutes, Complements, or Neither? The U.S. Consumer Expenditures Perspective, 1984–2002", *Transportation Research Record*, No. 2010, pp. 121–132.

Choo, S., P. L. Mokhtarian, and I. Salomon (2005) "Does Telecommuting Reduce Vehicle-miles Traveled? An Aggregate Time Series Analysis for the U.S.", *Transportation*, Vol. 32, pp. 37–64.

Clark, A. F. and S. T. Doherty (2010) "A Multi-Instrumented Approach to Observing the Activity Rescheduling Decision Process", *Transportation*, Vol. 37, pp. 165–181.

Couclelis, H. (2000) "From Sustainable Transportation to Sustainable Accessibility: Can We Avoid a New 'Tragedy of the Commons'?", in D. Janelle and D. Hodge (eds), *Information, Place, and Cyberspace: Issues in Accessibility*, Berlin: Springer-Verlag, pp. 341–356.

de Sola Pool, I. (1979) "The Communications/Transportation Tradeoff", in A. Altschuler (ed), *Current Issues in Transportation Policy*, Lexington, MA: Lexington Books, pp. 181–192.

Denstadli, J. M. (2004) "Impacts of Video Conferencing on Business Travel: The Norwegian Experience", *Journal of Air Transport Management*, Vol. 10, pp. 371–376.

Dia, H. and S. Panwai (2007) "Modelling Drivers' Compliance and Route Choice Behaviour in Response to Travel Information", *Nonlinear Dynamics*, Vol. 49, No. 4, pp. 493–509.

Elaluf-Calderwood, S. (2009) "Organizing Self-Referential Taxi-Work with mICT: The Case of the London Black Cab Drivers", PhD Dissertation, London School of Economics.

Ettema, D. and L. Verschuren (2007) "Multitasking and Value of Travel Time Savings", *Transportation Research Record*, No. 2010, pp. 19–25.

Ettema, D., T. Garling, L. E. Olsson, and M. Friman (2010) "Out-of-home activities, daily travel, and subjective well-being", *Transportation Research Part A*, Vol. 44, pp. 723–732.

Foss, S. and H. Couclelis (2009) "Throwing Space Back In: A Tale of Indian Fishermen, ICT and Travel Behavior", *Journal of Transport Geography*, Vol. 17, pp. 134–140.

Gandy, R. and M. J. Meitner (2007) "The Effects of an Advanced Traveler Information System on Scenic Beauty Ratings and the Enjoyment of a Recreational Drive", *Landscape and Urban Planning*, Vol. 82, pp. 85–93.

Gitlitz, D. M. and L. K. Davidson (2000) *The Pilgrimage Road to Santiago: The Complete Cultural Handbook*, New York: St. Martin's Press.

Goodchild, M. F. (2008) "Commentary: Whither VGI?", *Geojournal*, Vol. 72, pp. 239–244.

Gray, N. H. (2006) *First Pass under Heaven: A 4,000 Kilometre Walk along the Great Wall of China*, New York: Penguin Books.

Greschke, H. M. (2008) "Does It Matter Where You Are? – Transnational Migration, Internet Usage and the Emergence of Global Togetherness", in R. G. Anghel, E. Gerharz, G. Rescher, and M. Salzbrunn (eds), *The Making of World Society: Perspectives from Transnational Research*, Piscataway, NJ: Transaction Publishers (Bielefeld), pp. 275–289.

Hägerstrand, T. (1970) "What about People in Regional Science?", *Regional Science Association Papers*, Vol. 24, No. 1, pp. 7–21.

Helminen, V. and M. Ristimäki (2007) "Relationships between commuting distance, frequency and telework in Finland", *Journal of Transport Geography*, Vol. 15, pp. 331–342.

Hilty, L. M. (2008) *Information Technology and Sustainability: Essays on the Relationship between*

ICT and Sustainable Development. Herstellung und Verlag: Books on Demand GmbH, Norderstedt. ISBN 9783837019704.

Hubers, C., T. Schwanen, and M. Dijst (2008) "ICT and Temporal Fragmentation of Activities: An Analytical Framework and Initial Empirical Findings", *Tijdschrift voor Economische en Sociale Geografie*, Vol. 99, No. 5, 528–546.

Ito, M. (2005) "Intimate Visual Co-Presence", position paper for the Seventh International Conference on Ubiquitous Computing, Tokyo, Japan, September 11–14, http://www.itofisher.com/mito/publications/intimate_visual.html, accessed August 11, 2010.

Jain, J. and G. Lyons (2008) "The Gift of Travel Time", *Journal of Transport Geography*, Vol. 16, pp. 81–89.

Kek, A., R. Cheu, Q. Meng, and C. Fung (2009) "A Decision Support System for Vehicle Relocation Operations in Carsharing Systems", *Transportation Research Part E*, Vol. 45, No. 1, pp. 149–158.

Krizec, K. J. and A. Johnson (2007) "Mapping the Terrain of Information and Communications Technology (ICT) and Household Travel", *Essays on Transport Economics*, New York: Springer Business+Economics, pp. 363–381.

Kwan, M.-P. (2000) "Interactive Geovisualization of Activity-Travel Patterns using Three-Dimensional Geographical Information Systems: A Methodological Exploration with a Large Data Set", *Transportation Research Part C*, Vol. 8, pp. 185–203.

Kwan, M.-P. (2007) "Mobile Communications, Social Networks, and Urban Travel: Hypertext as a New Metaphor for Conceptualizing Spatial Interaction", *Professional Geographer*, Vol. 59, No. 4, pp. 434–446.

Lassen, C. (2009) "Networking, Knowledge Organizations and Aeromobility", *Geografiska Annaler Series B, Human Geography*, Vol. 91, No. 3, pp. 229–243.

Lee, T. and P. L. Mokhtarian (2008) "Correlations between Industrial Demands (Direct and Total) for Communications and Transportation in the U.S. Economy 1947–1997", *Transportation*, Vol. 35, No. 1, pp. 1–22.

Lee-Gosselin, M. and L. F. Miranda-Moreno (2009) "What is Different about Urban Activities of Those with Access to ICTs? Some Early Evidence from Quebec, Canada", *Journal of Transport Geography*, Vol. 17, pp. 104–114.

Lenz, B. and C. Nobis (2007) "The Changing Allocation of Activities in Space and Time by the Use of ICT – 'Fragmentation' as a New Concept and Empirical Results", *Transportation Research Part A*, Vol. 41, pp. 190–204.

Line, T., J. Jain, and G. Lyons (2011) "The Role of ICTs in Everyday Mobile Lives", *Journal of Transport Geography*, Vol. 19, No. 6, pp. 1490–1499.

Lyons, G. and J. Urry (2005) "Travel Time in the Information Age", *Transportation Research A*, Vol. 39, Nos. 2–3, 257–276.

Mascheroni, G. (2007) "Global Nomads' Network and Mobile Sociality: Exploring New Media Uses on the Move", *Information, Communication & Society*, Vol. 10, No. 4, pp. 527–546.

Metz, D. (2008) "The Myth of Travel Time Saving", *Transport Reviews*, Vol. 28, No. 3, pp. 321–336.

Mitchell, W. J. and F. Casalegno (2008) "Moving around the City", Chapter 2 of Connected Sustainable Cities, MIT Mobile Experience Lab Publishing, available at: http://www.connectedsustainablecities.org/downloads/connected_sustainable_cities_chapter2.pdf (accessed August 18, 2010).

Mokhtarian, P. L. (1991) "Telecommuting and Travel: State of the Practice, State of the Art", *Transportation*, Vol. 18, No. 4, 319–342.

Mokhtarian, P. L. (1998) "A Synthetic Approach to Estimating the Impacts of Telecommuting on Travel", *Urban Studies*, Vol. 35, No. 2, pp. 215–241.

Mokhtarian, P. L. (2004) "A Conceptual Analysis of the Transportation Impacts of B2C E-Commerce", *Transportation*, Vol. 31, No. 3, pp. 257–284.

Mokhtarian, P. L. (2009) "If Telecommunication is Such a Good Substitute for Travel, Why Does Congestion Continue to Get Worse?", *Transportation Letters*, Vol. 1, No. 1, pp. 1–17.

Mokhtarian, P. L., I. Salomon, and S. Choo (2005) "Measuring the Measurable: Why Can't We Agree on the Number of Telecommuters in the US?", *Quality and Quantity*, Vol. 39, pp. 423–452.

Mokhtarian, P. L., I. Salomon, and S. L. Handy (2006) "The Impacts of ICT on Leisure Activities and Travel: A Conceptual Exploration", *Transportation*, Vol. 33, No. 3, pp. 263–289.

Nagurney, A., J. Dong, and P. L. Mokhtarian (2002) "Multicriteria Network Equilibrium Modeling with Variable Weights for Decision-Making in the Information Age, with Applications to Telecommuting and Teleshopping", *Journal of Economic Dynamics and Control*, Vol. 26, Nos. 9–10, pp.1629–1650.

Nie, N. H. (2001) "Sociability, Interpersonal Relations, and the Internet: Reconciling Conflicting Findings", *American Behavioral Scientist*, Vol. 45, No. 3, pp. 420–435.

O'Reilly, C. C. (2006) "From Drifter to Gap Year Tourist: Mainstreaming Backpacker Travel", *Annals of Tourism Research*, Vol. 33, No. 4, pp. 998–1017.

Ohmori, N. and N. Harata (2008) "How Different are Activities while Commuting by Train? A Case in Tokyo", *Tijdschrift voor Economische en Sociale Geografie*, Vol. 99, No. 5, pp. 547–561.

Ory, D. T. and P. L. Mokhtarian (2006) "Which Came First, the Telecommuting or the Residential Location? An Empirical Analysis of Causality", *Urban Geography*, Vol. 27, No. 7, pp. 590–609.

Paz, A. and S. Peeta (2009) "Behavior-Consistent Real-Time Traffic Routing under Information Provision", *Transportation Research Part C*, Vol. 17, pp. 642–661.

Ratchford, B. T., D. Talukdar and M. S. Lee (2007) "The Impact of the Internet on Consumers' Use of Information Sources for Automobiles: A Re-inquiry", *Journal of Consumer Research*, Vol. 34, No. 1, pp. 111–119.

Ren, F. and M.-P. Kwan (2007) "Geovisualization of Human Hybrid Activity-Travel Patterns", *Transactions in GIS*, Vol. 11, No. 5, pp. 721–744.

Ren, F. and M.-P. Kwan (2009) "The Impact of the Internet on Human Activity-Travel Patterns: Analysis of Gender Differences Using Multi-Group Structural Equation Models", *Journal of Transport Geography*, Vol. 17, pp. 440–450.

Resnick, P. (2004) "Impersonal Sociotechnical Capital, ICTs, and Collective Action among Strangers", in W. Dutton, B. Kahin, R. O'Callaghan, and A. Wyckoff (eds), *Transforming Enterprise*, Cambridge, MA: MIT Press.

Richards, A. and M. McDonald (2007) "Investigating Limits of Benefits Provided by Variable Message Signs in Urban Network", *Transportation Research Record*, No. 2000, pp. 25–34.

Robinson, J. P. and S. Martin (2010) "IT Use and Declining Social Capital? More Cold Water from the General Social Survey (GSS) and the American Time-Use Survey (ATUS)", *Social Science Computer Review*, Vol. 28, No. 1, pp. 45–63.

Salomon, I. (1985) "Telecommunications and Travel: Substitution or Modified Behavior?", *Journal of Transport Economics and Policy*, Vol. 19, No. 3, pp. 219–235.

Salomon, I. (1986) "Telecommunications and Travel Relationships: A Review", *Transportation Research Part A*, Vol. 20, No. 3, pp. 223–238.

Salomon, I. (1998) "Technological Change and Social Forecasting: The Case of Telecommuting as a Travel Substitute", *Transportation Research Part C*, Vol. 6, pp. 17–45.

Salomon, I. and P. L. Mokhtarian (2008) "Can Telecommunications Help Solve Transportation Problems? A Decade Later: Are the Prospects Any Better?", in D. A. Hensher and K. J. Button (eds), *The Handbook of Transport Modelling*, 2nd edition, Amsterdam: Pergamon, pp. 519–540.

Schwanen, T. and M.-P. Kwan (2008) "The Internet, Mobile Phone and Space-Time Constraints", *Geoforum*, Vol. 39, No. 3, pp. 1362–1377.

Shaheen, S. A., Cohen A. P., and M. S. Chung (2009) "North American Carsharing: 10-Year Retrospective", *Transportation Research Record*, No. 2110, pp. 35–44.

Shaw, S.-L. and H. Yu (2009) "A GIS-based Time-geographic Approach of Studying Individual Activities and Interactions in a Hybrid Physical-Virtual Space", *Journal of Transport Geography*, Vol. 17, pp. 141–149.

Srivastava, L. (2005) "Mobile Phones and the Evolution of Social Behaviour", *Behaviour and Information Technology*, Vol. 24, No. 2, pp. 111–129.

Torre, A. (2008) "On the Role Played by Geographical Proximity in Knowledge Transmission", *Regional Studies*, Vol. 42, No. 6, pp. 869–889.

Urry, J. (2003) "Social Networks, Travel and Talk", *British Journal of Sociology*, Vol. 54, No. 2, pp. 155–175.

Wallis, M. (1990) *Route 66: The Mother Road*, New York: St. Martin's Press.

Wang, D. and F. Y. T. Law (2007) "Impacts of Information and Communication Technologies (ICT) on Time Use and Travel Behavior: A Structural Equations Analysis", *Transportation*, Vol. 34, No. 4, pp. 513–527.

White, N. R. and P. B. White (2007) "Home and Away: Tourists in a Connected World", *Annals of Tourism Research*, Vol. 34, No. 1, pp. 88–104.

Wilson, P. (2010) *The Silk Roads: A Route and Planning Guide*, 3rd edition, Surrey, UK: Trailblazer Publications.

Zettelmeyer, F., F. S. Morton, and J. Silva-Risso (2006) "How the Internet Lowers Prices: Evidence from Matched Survey and Auto Transaction Data", *Journal of Marketing Research*, Vol. 43, pp. 168–184.

15

Transport and Social Exclusion

Karen Lucas

INTRODUCTION

Transport and social exclusion largely emerged as a research topic in the UK with the 1997 election of the New Labour government and its manifesto for social welfare reform (Social Exclusion Unit, 1998). Studies have most usually focused on the accessibility and time–space dimensions of the social exclusion problem and in particular the 'friction of distance' (Miller, 2007) which arises from spatial mismatches between the housing locations of low-income populations and the location of employment and other key service destinations (Cervero, 2004). However, there is also increasing recognition that transport-related exclusion is about much more than problems with physical access to services (Social Exclusion Unit, 2003). Studies with the people who are experiencing social exclusion have identified a number of specific transport-related problems such as the non-affordability of private and public transport, poorly routed or scheduled transport services, inadequate waiting and interchange facilities, limited pedestrian infrastructure and lack of public transport service information (Lucas et al., 2001), as well as other less tangible issues such as fears for personal safety, second-language and low-literacy barriers and lack of control over transport policy and planning decision process (Hodgson and Turner, 2003). Many economically and socially disadvantaged populations do not have much of an aspiration to travel and would prefer to undertake most of their activities within their own local neighbourhoods and are often reluctant to move outside of this 'comfort zone' (Green and Owen, 2006). This despite the evidence of significantly lower employment opportunity and poorer local service provisions within many deprived areas (Social Exclusion Unit, 1998, 2003).

In the light of the recognised importance of these issues to the economic and social participation of citizens across the developed and developing world, this chapter presents an overview of the theories and evidence for assessing transport-related exclusion, as well as offering some possible solutions for addressing this problem, as these have been identified through the practical experiences. The chapter demonstrates that the problem of transport-related exclusion is a highly geographically, spatially, demographically and culturally contextualised and specific phenomenon, as well as being a dynamic problem in that it changes over both time and space and at different stages of a person's life. Transport-related exclusion is also relational in that the level of mobility a person requires is in direct relation to the social norms of the society in which they live; the more mobile the society the more mobility a person generally needs to be socially included within it.

CONCEPTUALISING TRANSPORT-RELATED EXCLUSION

In this section of the chapter, I outline some of the core theoretical concepts which underpin our academic understandings of transport-related exclusion. I first offer some basic definitions of social exclusion as these have emerged from the social policy literature. I then transcribe these broad and generalised concepts in terms of the transport experiences of socially excluded population groups, as these have been identified through a range of case studies in the UK and elsewhere.

Defining social exclusion

The concept of social exclusion is most usually identified as originating from French social policy of the 1970s (Mandanipour et al., 1998). Definitions of social exclusion abound and are often contradictory in terms of who, how, when and where the different population groups are affected. This is largely because of the nature of the concept itself, which most commentators agree is complex and multi-faceted (Hills et al., 2002). The term has been broadly used within the policy literature to describe a *social process* within affluent societies arising from their economic restructuring, whereby certain individuals are seen to have 'fallen through the safety net' of the social welfare system (Mandanipour et al., 1998).

Those particularly 'affected' or 'at risk' include young adults, lone parents, disabled people, migrants and the uninsured unemployed, most of whom will be concentrated on social housing estates and other areas of deprivation on the outskirts of major cities or in areas of de-industrialisation. The exclusion of these groups is manifest in a multiplicity of social problems, including income insecurity, low levels of economic, social and political participation, family breakdown, housing insecurity, ill-health and low educational achievement (Social Exclusion Unit, 1998). More radical interpreters of the phenomenon (e.g. Walker and Walker, 1997) refer to a purposeful and systematic process of complete or partial 'lock out' by powerful financial and political elites of economically redundant populations from the mainstream economic, social, political and cultural processes which would facilitate their social integration.

Importantly, social theorists emphasise the multi-layered, multi-dimensional, dynamic and relational nature of the concept, as partially illustrated in Figure 15.1. The diagram particularly serves to emphasise that social exclusion is systematically, mutually reinforced at every level of activity, i.e. individual, family, community, local, national and even global. It also demonstrates that social exclusion is influenced by the outcomes of a person's past as well as present activities. It can also often be passed on between generations and/or can change in its nature and intensity over a person's lifetime. Many of the problems which are associated with social exclusion can be cumulative and become intensified over both time and space. For example, in their analysis of socially excluded neighbourhoods, Lupton and Power (2001: 135) identify that: '[A]s social organisation, participation and confidence diminish [within a neighbourhood], so does social control .... The process of diminishing social capital is

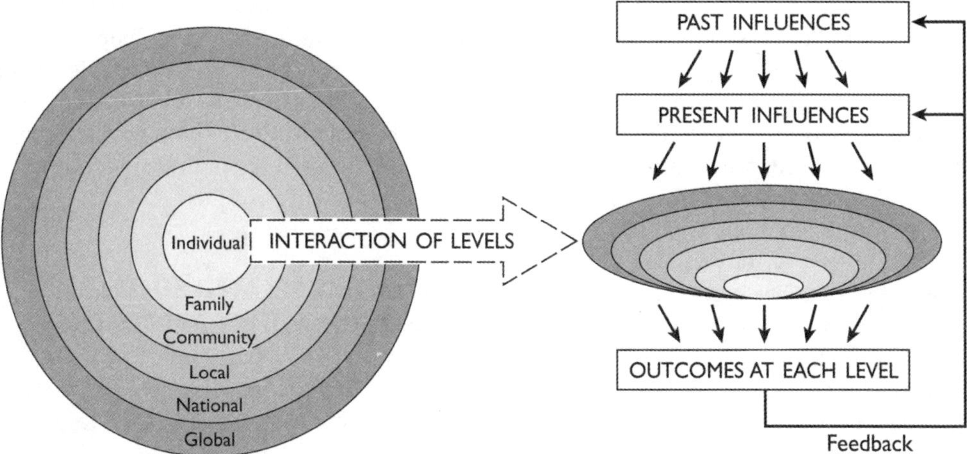

Figure 15.1 Diagram to demonstrate the inter-relational layers and dynamics of the exclusionary process

Source: after Burchardt et al., 2002

connected to a process of diminishing human capital.' Finally, it is important to recognise that the concept of social exclusion is relational, in that the activities of excluded individuals need to be considered in direct relation to the wider activities, norms and social expectations of the society in which they live (Atkinson, 1998).

Although numerous definitions of social exclusion refer to lack of access and non-participation in activities as a central factor in the exclusionary process (e.g. Mandanipour et al., 1998; Burchardt et al., 2002; Byrne, 2005), transport and mobility was not formally identified as a significant causal factor within the early social policy literature.

Understanding the role of transport in social exclusion and inclusion

Transport researchers in the UK have been identifying inequalities in the supply of transport in the UK since the mid-1970s (Banister and Hall, 1981), as well as highlighting the mobility disadvantages of particular social groups, such as women (e.g. Grieco et al., 1989; Hamilton et al., 1991), children (e.g. Hillman, 1993; Cahill et al., 1996; Mackett et al., 2003), young people (e.g. Pilling and Turner, 1998), older people (e.g. Gilhooly et al., 2002; Banister and Bowling, 2004), people with disabilities (e.g. Oxley and Richards, 1995) and certain minority ethnic groups (e.g. Institute for Employment Research, 1999).

It was not until the late 1990s, however, that the research began to emphasise direct causal relationships between transport inequality and the wider outcome of social exclusion (e.g. Church et al., 2000; TRaC, 2000; Lucas et al., 2001; Hine and Mitchell, 2003). The research made a number of important departures from past studies in this respect. First, it directly identified the social consequences of a lack of transport provision in terms of individuals' inability to participate in key life-enhancing opportunities, such as reduced job search activities, job losses, missed health appointments, school truancies, lower post-16 educational participation and increased physical isolation in later life. In this way it firmly established transport and mobility, or rather the lack of it, as a social policy problem.

Second, it differentiated between constraints which predominantly rest with the affected *individuals* themselves, such as their personal abilities, skills, resources and capacities to access the transport system and those which are predominantly externally determined by the *system of provision*, such as the location of local services, the levels and quality of public transport provision, travel information and so forth. The intention here was transformative, in that the research would lead to a set of practical policy and programme solutions across the appropriate areas of transport and land use service delivery. Third, it 'gave a voice' to the lived experiences of affected groups and individuals with the aim of articulating their concerns about the transport system to planners, policy makers and other decision-makers. To maintain this advocacy role, the research needed to be methodologically inclusive and transparent but also to retain a degree of impartiality in the presentation of its results.

Church et al. (2000) helped to identify the complexity of the issues involved, denoting seven specific features of the transport system which could contribute to and/or exacerbate the exclusion of certain population groups, including physical, geographical, exclusion from facilities, economic, time-based, fear-based and space-based. This early research served to establish that transport-related exclusion is highly contextually specific, both in relation to the affected social groups and their personal and familial circumstances and in terms of the systems of provision in local and wider geographical area in which they are located. The research also established that different social groups in different physical circumstances and locations are likely to be affected to a lesser or greater degree by these different exclusionary factors. Table 15.1 describes the specific transport concerns of different social groups which have emerged from my own studies in relation to an adapted list of these different exclusionary attributes of the widely diverse and multi-dimensional nature of transport-related exclusion (see also Lucas, 2004a: 45–46).

It is understandable, given the multiplicity of issues involved and complexity and multi-layered nature of the problem for even one of the affected population groups, that there has been greater success with understanding and analysing the issues than with the practical resolution of such problems on the ground, as the next section of this chapter will describe.

TRANSPORT-RELATED SOCIAL EXCLUSION: POLICY APPROACHES

The UK was the first country to formally recognise transport as a *social exclusion* policy problem and to develop a policy agenda to directly address this. A number of other countries have since followed the UK lead, largely following a similar approach. For this reason, it is first appropriate to consider the UK approach in some detail, in order to gain an understanding of its main strengths and weaknesses. Later in the chapter, I will present examples of some distinctly alternative policy approaches to transport and social exclusion that have been developed and applied outside of the UK and so offer new perspectives on both the nature of the problem and how it can best be resolved.

The Social Exclusion Unit report

In 2003, the Social Exclusion Unit published its now internationally recognised report on transport and social exclusion. This helped to firmly establish the negative social consequences of a lack of transport for identified low-income population groups in terms of their inability to participate in the key activities of employment, education and training, health care, food shops, and leisure and cultural pursuits. Most importantly, it identified that lack of transport had direct and indirect impacts on unemployment and job-uptake, low educational attainment, health inequalities and quality of life outcomes for recognised socially disadvantaged groups, and could serve to undermine key government targets in these policy areas. The report also set the framework for a cross-departmental

Table 15.1 Mapping core dimensions of social exclusion with transport-related effects for different social groups

	Children	Young people	Older people	Disabled people	Ethnic minorities	Women	Unemployed	Low-paid workers	Lone parents
Personal	Need to be escorted or driven	Semi-independent but with some restrictions	Very mixed picture in terms of abilities. Can be frail and confused in later life	Can be frail and may experience mobility and cognitive difficulties	May have language difficulties	Usually main carers within households and main escort person	May have low travel horizons and be unfamiliar with public transport outside the local area	May have low literacy and numeracy skills	Multiple work, caring and household responsibilities
Geographic Urban/ Peripheral/ Rural	Greater exposure to traffic in urban areas	More excluded from activities in rural areas	Problem of retirees moving to remote locations. Longer-term resident of social housing estates	More likely to be located in urban centres	More likely to be located in urban centres	Many low-income women work in call centres and out-of-town shopping centres in urban periphery	Issues of structural unemployment in ex-industrial and old mining areas	Often need to access dispersed jobs in urban periphery	Often need to access dispersed jobs in urban periphery
Spatial	Mostly localised activities	More distant activity destinations over age 14 years	Mostly localised activities but with longer journeys to hospital and visiting relatives	Can have long journey distances to specialist centres and meeting places	Can have long journey distances to specialist centres and meeting places	Most likely to make multiple destination journeys	Job centres mostly located in town centres. May have journeys to unfamiliar destinations for job search	May have long journey distances to work in de-industrialised areas	Many concentrated on low-income estates in urban periphery
Temporal	Slower walking times	Still in formative experimental years. Peak hour journeys to school. Time rich at evening and weekends when travel is important for leisure and social activities	Generally time rich. May be slower walking and boarding public transport. Less likely to travel after dark. Weekend travel important	May be slower generally. May have long journey times to specialist centres. Weekend and evening travel important	Can have long journey times to specialist centres	Usually time poor from meeting multiple demands and responsibilities. Often working part-time and evening or late night shifts	Generally time rich. May have issue with time-keeping and scheduling activities if long-term unemployed	Often working part-time and evening or late night shifts	Usually time poor from meeting multiple demands and responsibilities. Often working part-time and evening or late night shifts

(Continued)

Table 15.1 (Continued)

	Children	Young people	Older people	Disabled people	Ethnic minorities	Women	Unemployed	Low-paid workers	Lone parents
Economic	No independent income	Very little independent income	Most rely only on state pensions. Travel is free on public transport	Most rely only on benefits. Travel is free on public transport	Some ethnic groups are more economically stable than others	Lack of finance may not be a problem	Rely solely on state benefits. Few travel subsidies	Often earning only slightly more than benefit claimants	Often rely solely on state benefits or earning only slightly more than benefit claimants
Social	Mostly in terms of socialisation and assimilation. Early cognitive experiences can dictate later behaviours	Early social support networks are formed	Social support networks increase in importance	Carer support highly important. At risk of social stigmatisation	Can be socially isolated and at risk of social segregation	Need to maintain wide social networks for child care and family support	Need to maintain strong social networks for child care and family support	At risk of reduced social networks from non-employment activity	Need to maintain strong social networks for child care and family support
Cultural	'Stranger danger' suppresses childhood independence	Social stigmas attached to teenagers. Access to cultural activities can enhance social development	Ageism can lead to a socially constructed notion of the transport needs of older people which is not borne out in reality	Massive stigma still associated with disability, particularly for people experiencing mental ill-health	At risk of racial harassment when using public transport	Some women (e.g. Muslim) culturally excluded from using public transport or undertaking any unaccompanied travel	Social stigmas attached to unemployment	Ideas of 'good parenting' and the role of private transport in supporting or undermining this	Social stigmas attached to lone parenthood means that they are seen as undeserving of transport subsidy by politicians
Political	Some child poverty advocacy groups but little direct engagement	Often alienated from formal participative processes. Rarely engage in formal consultations	Often over-represented in engagement and participation activities, which can skew the outcome of these exercises	Have strong and organised political lobby groups to represent their needs, but are still highly marginalised by transport providers	Many recent migrant groups marginalised from political processes for cultural and language reasons. Some very powerful minority activists e.g. Asian business community	Gender equality can still be an issue and women are often under-represented within decision-making circles	Often characterised as undeserving by politicians and so their transport needs are under-valued	Often characterised as undeserving by politicians and so their transport needs are under-valued	May not be in unionised jobs and so poorly protected from job loss due to lateness, unreliability which can be the outcome of inadequate transport provision

Source: adapted from Church and Frost, 2000: 198–200 and Lucas, 2004a: 45–46 policy delivery agenda to address these problems, not all of which were identified as directly transport-system related. As such, this became known as the 'accessibility planning' approach.

The accessibility planning policy approach

Responsibility for implementation of the transport and social exclusion agenda was passed to the Department for Transport in 2004, which first undertook a series of pilot studies to test the approach (DHC and University of Westminster, 2004). It subsequently released a set of policy guidances to all local transport authorities in England[1] to undertake its delivery, which required them to implement what is now commonly referred to as accessibility planning as a core function of their local transport planning (Department for Transport, 2006).

The accessibility planning approach is interesting from a transport geography perspective because it specifically aims to draw policy attention (perhaps for the first time) to the nexus between the socio-economic conditions of populations, the physical location of essential services and the connectivity of the public transport system. The method is extensively described elsewhere (Lucas, 2006), but briefly it involves:

1 Strategic spatial assessment of socio-economic, demographic data and other deprivation indices (e.g. unemployment, housing tenure, health, crime, etc.) to identify where low-income and other 'at risk' populations are located;
2 Local accessibility assessments of identified 'at risk' neighbourhoods in terms of their public transport accessibility (based on door-to-door journey times) to key employment opportunities and other essential activities – ideally these analyses should also include assessment of temporal compatibility (with work shifts and opening times, etc.), journey affordability and cost dimensions, vehicle and facility accessibility and timetable information and should involve local communities to better understand their local needs and to garner their views on potential solutions;
3 Option appraisal and multi-stakeholder partnership working to identify a set of optimal practicable solutions over the short, medium and long term (including land use planning, relocation of services and housing, improvements to and reorganisation of public and specialist transport services, home and virtual delivery of services), and to determine how to fund and deliver these interventions across the different partner organisations;
4 Opportunities for local stakeholder feedback and ongoing monitoring and evaluation processes against nationally and locally devised performance indicators (Department for Transport website, 2010).

The approach is also quite far-reaching in its recognition that improvements in public transport services are not on their own sufficient for addressing the problem of transport-related social exclusion in many instances. It also recognises that socially excluded individuals may need other types of support such as travel training, financial assistance and individualised travel information to encourage them to be more mobile so that they are able to access opportunities in the wider area.

Local implementation of accessibility planning

In practice, many local authorities have found it extremely difficult to deliver accessibility as part of their transport planning. This is in part because it requires multi-stakeholder buy-in to achieve fundamental changes in accessibility on the ground. While the case for including consideration of social equity issues within transport policy is increasingly accepted by local transport professionals, many authorities have found it difficult to secure the interest of other key stakeholders locally, as the providers of these services do not recognise providing physical access to their services as being a part of their responsibility (Centre for the Research of Social Policy (CRSP), 2009). Many authorities have failed to get further than the assessment stage due to a lack of commitment to the process in some instances and/or the difficulties they have experienced in securing any additional funding for new initiatives in others (Preston, 2009).

Nevertheless, some local transport authorities have 'championed' the agenda and have successfully set up multi-stakeholder partnerships which have helped them to secure the necessary funding to implement a range of new initiatives to help socially excluded populations to secure new employment, education and training opportunities and to connect them to other essential services. The Merseyside case is probably the most comprehensive, long-running example of success in this respect and it is to this example that we now turn for some insights as to why this is so.

The Merseyside good practice example

Merseyside is a large metropolitan region in the North West of England and includes the city of Liverpool, which is its main administrative and commercial centre. In addition to the city, there are four local authorities: Knowsley, Sefton, St Helens and the Wirral. The region was historically associated with docking, ship building and other manufacturing industries, but has suffered from severe economic decline for many years. It is officially recognised as lagging well behind the European average in terms of economic performance and as such has been eligible to receive 'Objective One'[2] funding for three successive terms (1994–2000, 2000–2006 and 2006–2010), with the key aim of increasing economic prosperity and employment and reduce social disparities across the region.

As part of its regeneration strategy, 38 'pathway neighbourhoods' were identified as suffering from particularly high levels of structural unemployment, multiple forms of deprivation and social exclusion, and a key policy objective was to reduce the economic and social disparities between these areas and the rest of the Merseyside population. From the outset, the Merseyside Objective One Programme recognised that public transport played a vital role in the regeneration strategy, particularly in ensuring that residents in pathways neighbourhoods would be able to access the new employment, education, training and other opportunities in the seven Strategy Investment Areas for the programme. Although car ownership has been steadily growing in Merseyside over the last ten years (in line with trends for the rest of the UK), the majority (59%) of households in the pathway areas do not own a car and a further third (31%) only have regular access to one car, which is much lower than the UK average (Department for Transport (DfT), 2010). This means that most people in these areas are reliant on public transport services to connect them with employment and other activities in the City region.

Merseytravel (the Passenger Transport Authority for the region) has therefore been a key partner in the Merseyside regeneration strategy from its inception and therefore has a long history of experience in partnership working and delivering transport as part of a much wider social inclusion agenda. Indeed, in many ways Merseytravel can be said to have acted as the exemplar for the SEU's policy recommendations and was also heavily involved in the DfT's pilot studies and development of its policy guidance. Merseytravel considers that the main criteria for the successful delivery of its transport and social inclusion programme have been: (i) the level of financial resource they have received, (ii) strategic planning, (iii) partnership working with other key delivery agencies, (iv) strong links with community and voluntary sector, (v) a wide range of local initiatives, and (vi) a person-centred approach to tackling the transport needs of local people (Grant, 2004; Green, 2008).

Financial resources

Public transport was recognised as an essential requirement for the delivery of the 2000–2006 Objective One programme and approximately

£35 million was made available for improving transport services. This was matched with increased funding from the DfT for complementary measures in support of the programme. In addition, Merseytravel has also been able to secure additional funding for various local projects from other competitive funding sources, including Single Regeneration Budget, Urban Bus Challenge, Neighbourhood Renewal Fund, KickStart Programme, European Regeneration and Development Fund (ERDF) and the European Social Fund (ESF). The total funding resource for transport and social exclusion initiatives in the Merseyside region over the last ten years is estimated to be in excess of £100 million.

Strategic planning

The Merseyside transport approach has always relied on extensive research and analysis. In 2003, Regeneris undertook a detailed transport and accessibility study, which led to the development of an action plan for the pathway neighbourhoods. The action plan identified six target groups (young adults aged 16–19 years, adult jobseekers (especially the long-term unemployed), lone parents, minority ethnic groups, people with physical or learning difficulties, poor short-term health or chronic health problems and older people) and detailed the key transport issues which needed to be addressed. Further detailed GIS mapping exercises were then undertaken to assess existing public transport provision in the 38 pathway areas and their degree of connectivity to new employment and training opportunities across the city region. A series of practical initiatives were then identified on the basis of this combined evidence.

Partnership working

Merseytravel has consistently engaged with a range of external partners through the period of this programme and partnership working lies at the heart of its delivery strategies. At the strategic level it works in partnership with the North West Development Agency, the Public Health Authority, Jobcentre Plus,[3] the Learning and Skills Council, Connexions[4] Liverpool Housing Trust and Merseyside Community Transport. It is also a member of all Local Strategic Partnerships,[5] as well as supporting a number of smaller agencies in their delivery of local initiatives (see below). Merseytravel has also appointed a dedicated partnership officer to coordinate these various activities.

Voluntary and Community links

At the onset of the Objective One programme in 1994, Merseytravel established a Community Links Team with a specific aim of working with the residents of pathway communities to ensure that their transport needs were being met. The team identified with these communities the need for local community transport provision which could be owned and operated at the local level and would itself provide a source of employment and training for local people. Merseytravel and Liverpool Housing Trust, together with some of the smaller transport providers created Mersey Community Transport to promote and lobby for additional resources for the sector to develop and introduced a £5 million scheme to support local transport initiatives. Community Transport Forums for residents and key interest groups have also been established to provide Merseytravel with continuous feedback on the performance of the public transport system and to articulate their emergent needs.

Local initiatives

Merseytravel has consistently worked to create new journey opportunities for work, training and other essential activities through a range of practical local initiatives, including the provision of dedicated *Joblink* buses, which provide transport for referred JobCentre Plus clients and operate along fixed routes to designated employment sites and are timetabled to meet specific shift patterns at these sites, but are also flexibly-routed at other times of the day to take jobseekers to interviews and training.

A 'people-centred' focus

The *Workwise* initiative is designed to assist local people with travel information about their initial travel costs to work for the first month after they have secured a job and, in some cases, assist with a low-cost loan of a motor scooter or a free bicycle. *Neighbourhood Travel Teams* have also been established within each of the five Merseyside local authorities to provide travel advice and assistance in local job centres in the form of a personalised travel plan and information, a free bus pass and travel training. Both these projects have been instigated from the recognition that poor confidence, lack of experience of the transport system and unfamiliarity with other areas outside of their local neighbourhood can be just as significant a barrier to travel for many young people who are just entering the jobs market or for those who have been long-term unemployed or are returning to work after caring for young children or elderly relatives.

Key delivery challenges of the UK approach

Since the publication of the SEU report in 2003 there have been numerous academic studies which have further explored the various issues of mobility, accessibility and transport disadvantage in different geographical contexts in the UK. These have been invaluable in helping to identify the highly context- and person-specific nature of transport-related exclusion, which clearly not only differs in terms of the experiences of low-income rural and urban populations (e.g. McDonagh, 2006; Farrington, 2007; Wright et al., 2009), but has also been demonstrated to vary for different socially excluded population groups within the same local contexts (e.g. Rajé, 2004; Preston and Rajé, 2007; Jones and Wixey, 2008; Mackett et al., 2008). These are both hugely important considerations for any policy makers wishing to assess the potential for transferability of the UK's transport and social exclusion policy agenda to their own national context (Lucas and Currie, 2011). Other UK studies have aimed to evaluate the effectiveness of different interventions to reduce transport-related exclusion, such as the Urban Bus Challenge initiative (Lucas et al., 2008) and the KickStart projects (Bristow et al., 2008). In particular, these studies highlight absence of robust and commonly accepted methodology for evaluation of the social benefits of public transport (including walking and cycling). This presents a continued obstacle to the development of a socially inclusive approach to transport delivery in the UK.

Even in a best practice authority such as Merseytravel, officers report continuing difficulties with the delivery of their social inclusion agenda. First and foremost is their inability to adequately effect necessary changes in the commercially operated public transport system which exists in the UK outside of London. This leaves local transport authorities with little control in terms of planning the network, timetabling and fare levies. Second are the problems experienced with finding continuing subsidies necessary for operating socially necessary, non-profitable services once the initial 'pump-priming' period of a project has ended. Third is the need to get more non-transport stakeholders to recognise the value of transport in the delivery of their own policy agendas and to embed accessibility assessments within the decision-making frameworks of other of delivery sector providers. Finally, better evaluation metrics are needed in order to communicate the wider social benefit of small scale transport initiatives to political decision-makers at the national level of government, so that the importance of local public transport services to economic vitality and inclusion of low-income communities can be more fully recognised within future national policies

International research

In addition to work on transport and social exclusion in the UK, there has been growing international research interest, including in Germany (Schonfelder and Axhausen, 2003), Spain (Cebollada, 2009) and Norway (Priya and Uteng, 2009; Uteng, 2010), and further afield in Australia (Hurni, 2006; Battelino, 2009; Loader and Stanley, 2009; Currie, 2010; Currie and Delbosc, 2010; Stanley and Stanley, 2010), Canada (Páez et al., 2009), New Zealand (e.g. Rose et al., 2009) and South Africa (Lucas, 2011). In the United States, the environmental justice perspective has also long served to offer similar analyses of the social impacts of transport disadvantage on low-income individuals and communities (e.g. Lucas, 2004a). In parallel, studies of the interactions between transport and social inequalities have emerged from other disciplinary perspectives including social theory (e.g. Urry, 2000, 2007; Kauffman et al., 2004; Ohnmacht et al., 2009), sociology (e.g. Cass et al., 2005); psychology (e.g. Anable, 2005; Stanley and Vella-Broderick, 2009), time geography (e.g. Dijst and Kwan, 2005; Neutens et al., 2011), social network theory (e.g. Carrasco et al., 2008) and theories of social capital (e.g. Stanley and Stanley, 2010). These add further dimensions and complexities to discussion of what constitutes 'transport and social exclusion' but have also helped to enrich and enliven these debates.

Other international studies have concentrated on developing new and hybrid methodology for the identification and measurement of transport disadvantage and social exclusion. For example, Schonfelder and Axhausen (2003) and Páez et al. (2009) use the comparison of the different 'activity spaces' of population segments to identify whether these segments have significant differences in access to key destinations within the city, whilst Carrasco et al. (2008) use social network analysis for a similar purpose. Mackett et al. (2008) have used micro-level GIS-modelling of the pedestrian environment to assess its physical accessibility and Jones and Wixey (2008) have also applied adapted GIS-based tools to assess the relative accessibility of the public transport environment for different population sectors. In a more recent Australian study, Currie and Delbosc (2010) have employed structural equation models (SEMs) to explore relationships between transport disadvantage, social exclusion and well-being.

It is not within the scope of this chapter to offer a complete review of these studies (see Lucas, 2012 for a more comprehensive review). In summary they offer innovative ways to think about processes of transport-related social exclusion in different geographical contexts, as well as some useful new and hybrid methodological approaches. In addition, while they serve to demonstrate the strong transferability of transport and social exclusion as a theoretical concept, they provide a reminder of its far-from-consensual interpretation across the transport discipline. Furthermore, there are still numerous gaps in our theoretical understandings and methodological abilities in this field. How to practically design and implement a socially inclusive transport policy agenda is even less well understood, as is how to measure and evaluate the policy interventions which have been put in place. The final sections of this chapter will now look at some examples of the practical policies and transport initiatives which have been attempted outside the UK.

Transport and social exclusion policy delivery outside the UK

A 2002/3 comparative study of the Group of Seven (G7) nations (Lucas, 2004b), which was undertaken in direct collaboration with researchers in each of these countries, identified that, in addition to the UK, only France and the United States were actively pursuing transport policies which specifically aimed to reduce the transport barriers associated with social exclusion, although Germany, Italy, Japan and Canada were all providing more generic provision for older and disabled groups. More recently, Australian states (most notably the States of New South Wales (Battelino, 2009) and Victoria (Loader and Stanley, 2009) have been actively introducing new policies and local transport projects to address transport-related social exclusion). There is now evidence of the stirrings of similar policy activity in Canada (Páez et al., 2009), New Zealand (Rose et al., 2009), Barcelona (Cebollada, 2009), South Africa (Lucas, 2011).

Here I will discuss two examples with which I am familiar: the Californian Job Access and Reverse Commute (JARC) programme and the City of Paris Régie Autonome des Transports Parisiens (RATP) flexible transit model.[6] They are particularly of interest here because they offer some fundamental departures from the UK 'accessibility planning' approach, and thus can offer some new perspectives on possible policy responses to transport-related social exclusion.

Job Access and Reverse Commute (JARC) California

This programme is perhaps the longest standing attempt to address the issue of transport and social inequality, dating back to the US Civil Rights movement and Title VI of the 1964 Civil Rights Act: Non-discrimination in federally assisted programmes. A full description of this Act, how it relates to the provision of transportation in the US and the specific programmes which have been put in place to deliver the transportation and environmental agenda can be found in chapters 9–13 of Lucas (2004a). In summary, there are a number of ways in which the social transport agenda is implemented in practice within the US model, of these the Job Access and Reverse Commute (JARC) grant program is probably the most well recognised for delivering transport initiatives (Cervero, 2004).

As its emphasis is helping people to make the transition from welfare into work, the main focus of JARC is on providing transport to employment and as such the approach is less comprehensive than 'accessibility planning', which also includes access to non-work destinations. On the other hand, the JARC program is more comprehensive in the types of transport interventions that can be provided including modification of public transit routes and new feeder services, extended scheduling of services, bespoke fixed- and flexibly-routed bus services, door-to-door minivan services, child transportation, guarantee-ride home allowances, car-pool and van-pool schemes and low-interest loan assistance for the purchase or maintenance of a private vehicle.

In his longitudinal evaluation study of five Californian initiatives Cervero (2006) demonstrated that patronage on specialised job-access bus routes generally increased with larger concentrations of low-income, transit-dependent households at the origin end combined with either a single employment location or a concentration of entry-level and low-to-moderate skilled jobs at the destination end of the trip. It was also the case that the more sustained the funding for the intervention, the greater the patronage levels. Cervero further identified that a strategic approach to job access which aimed to place jobseekers in the most cost-effective and transport accessible locations helped to support the longer term sustainability of the programme, as well as to improve job uptake and retention. He concluded that the success of such interventions is highly dependent on the institutional capacity of operators to engage in multi-stakeholder cooperation and partnership working, but that lack of institutional capacity and professional skills at the local level of administration combined with short-term funding cycles can significantly undermine this.

Somewhat controversially, the study identified that the successful intentions in terms of job take-up and retention rates were associated with the most expensive transport solutions (door-to-door and child transport services). He also noted that the need to keep transit fares affordable for low-paid workers can often serve to undermine service quality and reliability, with severe consequences for the people who rely on these services as their only means of getting to work. However, in a similar study Blumenberg and Smart (2011) have concluded that making private vehicle ownership more affordable for low-income and immigrant populations is often the only reliable means of ensuring that people can fully participate within US society. To a large degree, this is because many of the people who are being actively targeted by the JARC programme are women (and often single parents) with parenting and home care responsibilities. This means that the commute constitutes only a small part of their overall travel needs and they must usually undertake complex multi-purpose trips in order to fulfil their multiple home/work responsibilities. Many of the jobs they secure are also undertaken at times of the day and locations which the women consider to be unsafe, which also accounts for the higher success rates and client popularity of door-to-door services and private transport interventions. The study helps to emphasise the highly individualised and situational nature of transport-related social exclusion in practice and the need for locally tailored, rather than blanket interventions.

Parisian Régie Autonome des Transports Parisiens (RATP) flexible transit model

As the originator of social exclusion policy (Mandanipour et al, 1998), it is hardly surprising that Paris also offers leadership on policies for transport and social exclusion. These operate in the context of an entirely different transport and social policy culture to the UK or USA. First, egalitarianism, fairness and justice are built into the French constitution and are, therefore, the fundamental guiding principles for all its public policy-making. Second, the 1982 law on domestic transport states that each citizen has the right to transport access: most transport operators have developed special transport services and special fare tariffs for the unemployed and those on low incomes as part of their standard operating policy. Third, employers and businesses are expected to contribute to both the provision of the transport system and the travel costs of employees through the French Transport Tax (*Versement Transport*). This means that access to public transport in the City of Paris as well as its affordability for most Parisians is already fairly high. Under these background conditions, both the need to address transport-related exclusion and the means to do so are policy 'givens' and are seen as part of mainstream transport policy.

This is not to say that transport-related exclusion does not exist in the French context – it clearly does (Fontanes et al., 2006). However, the policy approach for its resolution is quite different to the others that we have previously explored. Policies addressing transport-related exclusion apply to the whole country and are in three categories: (i) financial assistance is provided for job searching and home relocation on the uptake of a new job if this is necessary; (ii) public transport initiatives are delivered alongside other housing, education and business creation programmes in deprived areas; (iii) intermediate welfare associations whose task is to help socially excluded people towards economic social integration offer individualised mobility programmes for this purpose. It is this third intervention that is probably the most innovative approach in terms of addressing transport-related social exclusion. More than one hundred intermediate welfare associations of this kind had mobility programmes of this nature at the time of the study. Some examples of these are: *Abellie Aide Entraide a la demande*, which operates a van service that provides odd jobs to clients and escorts them to their place of work; *Auto-Insertion Loitoise* (*AIL*), which rents old cars and mopeds to its members for 2–3 months on the take-up of employment, the cost of which is partly paid by unemployment institutions when people are regularly registered as jobseekers; and *Cidf Baie* in Nancy, whose aim is the social integration of women, assists its members to obtain their driving licence.

These programmes are particularly noteworthy in the context of this chapter because they explicitly recognise that people who experience social exclusion suffer from specific barriers to travel which prevent them from using conventional public transport services, in particular: (i) issues of *social isolation and distrust*, which makes it difficult for them to communicate their specialist transport needs to mainstream public transport providers; (ii) *low levels of spatial knowledge* and a reduced ability to form mental maps of the city; (iii) the *loss of 'temporal markers'*, making it difficult for them to manage and master timing and scheduling activities; (iv) *lack of confidence and anxiety* in going places and interacting with other people, which undermines their ability to ask for help or directions whilst on route; (v) poor understanding and acceptance of the codes which are commonly accepted by the public sphere, which can result in inappropriate or unacceptable behaviours. It is possible to add to this list low literacy and numeracy skills, second language difficulties, mental or physical ill-health and other social problems which the average traveller does not generally experience or need to overcome. The French study serves to highlight the complexity of the transport and social exclusion problem, and that it is about much more than lack of transport services or the issue of affordability, although these are also important considerations in the whole picture. It is these 'softer' barriers to transport that policy makers most often struggle to embrace because they are highly individualised and so respond poorly to blanket policy solutions.

CONCLUSION

This chapter has presented an overview of research, policy and practice in the area of transport and social exclusion. This has only fairly recently emerged as a topic of interest within the transport discipline, but has nevertheless engendered a high level of interest within the academic and policy community. It would appear from the literature that whilst theoretical and empirical studies are identifying and increasing complexities between the physical, social, time–space and intra- and inter-personal aspects of transport-related social exclusion, many policy makers, local delivery agencies and transport operators are not.

Returning to the UK example, this is in part because there has been an over-emphasis within the UK on addressing the physical access to transport and spatial aspects of transport disadvantaged. There has also been a failure to adequately recognise the issue of transport poverty in direct relation to the needs and circumstances of the people who are experiencing or at risk of social exclusion. This calls for far greater appreciation of the myriad other problems they may encounter. Issues of structural unemployment, debt and financial insecurity, persistently low wage levels, high levels of crime and anti-social behaviour and the flight of local shops and services all conspire to undermine the full economic, social and political participation in society of people in particular areas. Lack of transport makes this worse but, actually, the most effective solutions may not necessarily be transport orientated. Affordability, the willingness and ability to travel given other family and household responsibilities, long travel times to destinations, knowledge of the transport system and the capacity to navigate non-integrated public transport 'networks', fragmented fares and ticketing policies and inaccessible and incomprehensible travel information are clearly all factors in the exclusionary process. But the housing, land use and public service delivery policies which segregate low-income populations from employment, education, healthcare, leisure and other opportunities are equally, if not more powerful contributors to transport-related exclusion.

Greater success tends to be achieved in addressing the transport-related social exclusion of populations where a more holistic, person-centred and evidence-based approach has been adopted, such as in the Merseyside, Californian and Parisian examples. Nevertheless, even here there are a number of important points that need to be borne in mind. First, transport-related exclusion is a *dynamic* process and is *relational* to transport trends in the rest of society. This means that the more car reliant we become as a society, the more those people who cannot afford or are unable to drive because of age or disability become excluded from the transport system.

Second, outside of the main urban centres, buses represent the main motorised form of transport for most non-car owning households. Many of the bus services in low income areas require subsidies for at least part of the day if they are to fully meet their social inclusion function (i.e. to connect people with essential activities easily, reliably and safely and at a reasonable cost). Where these subsidies are under serious threat within the present financial and political climate, and where the focus for public transport provision is largely on private sector run services, profit rather than social responsibility will all too quickly assert itself as the core operating principle. However, national and local policy makers outside of the transport sector appear to still be largely unaware of the full social consequences of their loss to the people who use them and to the impact this will have on wider society should it lead to their economic inactivity and the downward spiral of the areas in which they live. This suggests that we need better policy appraisal mechanisms to articulate the social equity implications of transport policy spending decisions.

Third, the need to address 'transport poverty' and related social exclusion is likely to become greater rather than lessened over time. In times of economic recession jobs become less available, public services get cut back and so people need to travel further to access them. The age structure of the population is also changing with many countries soon to reach populations with 25–30% over the age of 65, many of whom will be unable to drive over the longer term. 'Peak oil' is likely to mean that travel in general will become more expensive and even with a move to electric vehicle fleets, many of the people who currently rely on private forms of transportation will be unable to afford this in the future. This points to the need for a greater collaborative effort not only between policy makers across different sectors of government but also by public transport operators, employers and service providers to consider the social consequences of their transport decisions.

Finally, in order to be sustainable in the longer term, policies to improve the 'transport poverty' of already economically and socially excluded population groups need to include wider land use planning solutions, such as the re-introduction of more local employment opportunities, services and amenities and/or the relocation of social housing to more economically active areas. Policies which continue to promote the dispersal and segregation of home/work/leisure activities will ultimately lead to encouraging low income households who are able to buy and use cars as a solution to their mobility difficulties, which is not only likely to put further pressure on their already stretched financial resources, but is also in direct conflict with the environment and climate change agenda of most developed and developing societies.

ACKNOWLEDGEMENTS

I would like to thank John Smith, Paulette Lappin and the Merseytravel Community Links Team for their support in providing information for the Merseyside case study.

NOTES

1 Under the devolved governmental arrangements that were put in place by central government in 1998, Scotland, Wales, Northern Ireland and Greater London are responsible for developing their own transport policies and local authority guidances, while England continues to be governed and legislated for by the UK Government and UK Parliament. Throughout this chapter, therefore, when looking at the policies that were developed for transport and social exclusion I refer to those that were developed by central government but which are only implemented by local authorities in England (outside of Greater London). In practice, however, similar policy approaches have been adopted by all the other devolved administrations.

2 A European Union funding scheme designed to reduce differences in socio-economic conditions within the EU.

3 The delivery agency responsible for helping to get unemployed people back into work.
4 The agency which helps young people with decisions about education, training and employment.
5 These are non-statutory, multi-agency local partnerships which usually match local authority boundaries and are designed to bring together different stakeholders in the public, private, voluntary and community sector in order to deliver mutually reinforcing cross-sector initiatives.
6 In doing so, I draw heavily on the work of Professor Robert Cervero and his study team at the Institute of Urban and Regional Development, University of California, Berkeley and the work of Professor Jean-Pierre Orfeuil and his team at La Ville en Movement Institute (Cities on the Move Institute), Paris. The research was Phase 2 of an international comparison study of Transport and Social Exclusion in the UK, USA and France funded by the FIA Foundation.

REFERENCES

Anable, J. (2005) '"Complacent Car Addicts" or "Aspiring Environmentalists"? Identifying travel behavior segments using attitude theory', *Transport Policy* 12: 1: 65–78.

Atkinson, A.B. (1998) 'Social Exclusion, Poverty and Unemployment', in Atkinson, A.B. and Hills, J. (eds) *Exclusion, Employment and Opportunity* CASE paper 4 London: London School of Economics.

Banister, D. and Bowling, A. (2004) 'Quality of life for the elderly: the transport dimension', *Transport Policy* 11: 2: 105–115.

Banister, D. and Hall, P. (1981) *Transport and Public Policy Planning*. London: Maxwell.

Battellino, H. (2009) 'Transport for the transport disadvantaged: A review of service delivery models in New South Wales', *Transport Policy* (Special Issue: International Perspectives on Transport and Social Exclusion) 16: 3: 90–96.

Blumenberg, E. and Smart, M. (2011) 'Migrating to Driving: Exploring the Multiple Dimensions of Immigrants' Automobile Use', in Lucas, K., Blumenberg, E. and Weinberger, R. *Auto Motives: Understanding Car Use Behaviours*. Bradford, Emerald.

Bristow, A., Enoch, M.P., Zhang, L., Greensmith, C., James, N. and Potter, S. (2008) 'Kickstarting growth in bus patronage: Targeting support at the margins', *Journal of Transport Geography* 16: 408–418.

Burchardt, T., Le Grand, J. and Piachaud, D. (2002) 'Introduction' in Hills, J., Le Grand, J. and Piachaud, D. (2002) *Understanding Social Exclusion*. Oxford, United Kingdom: Oxford University Press.

Byrne, D. (2005) *Social Exclusion*. Berkshire: Open University Press.

Cahill, M., Ruben, T. and Winn, S. (1996) *Children and Transport: Travel Patterns, Attitudes and Leisure Activities of Children in the Brighton Area*. Brighton: University of Brighton, Health and Social Policy Research Centre.

Carrasco, J.A., Hogan, B., Wellman, B. and Miller, E.J. (2008) 'Agency in Social activity Interactions: The Role of Social Networks in Time and Space', *Dutch Royal Geographical Society KNAG*.

Cass, N., Shove, E. and Urry, J. (2005) 'Social exclusion, mobility and access', *Sociological Review*: 539–555.

Cebollada, A. (2009) 'Mobility and labour market exclusion in the Barcelona Metropolitan Region', *Journal of Transport Geography* 17: 226–233.

Centre for the Research of Social Policy (CRSP) (2009) *Presentation of interim findings from evaluation of accessibility planning in the UK*, 20 November. Department of Transport Offices, Marsham Street, London WC1.

Cervero, R. (2004) 'Job isolation in the US: narrowing the gap through job access and reverse commute programmes', in Lucas, K. (2004) *Running on Empty: transport social exclusion and environmental justice*. Bristol, United Kingdom: Policy Press.

Cervero, R. (2006) *Transport and Social Exclusion Phase 2: Evaluating the Contribution of Transport Projects to Welfare to Work – An International Study. US National Report*, http://www.fiafoundation.org/publications/Documents/se_us.pdf

Church, A., Frost, M. and Sullivan, K. (2000) 'Transport and social Exclusion in London', *Transport Policy* 7: 195–205.

Currie, G. (2010) 'Quantifying spatial gaps in public transport supply based on social needs', *Journal of Transport Geography* 18: 1: 31–41.

Currie, G. and Delbosc, A. (2010) 'Modelling the social and psychological impacts of transport disadvantage', *Transportation* 37: 953–966.

Department for Transport (2006) *Full Guidance on Accessibility Planning*, http://www.dft.gov.uk/pgr/regional/ltp/accessibility/guidance/gap/nicalguidanceonaccessibi3641.pdf (last accessed 30.11.09).

Department for Transport (2010) *Transport Trends 2009 Edition*, http://www.dft.gov.uk/pgr/statistics/datatablespublications/trends/current/ (last accessed 29.10.10).

Department for Transport (2010) 'Main stages of the accessibility planning process', http://www.dft.gov.uk/pgr/regional/ltp/accessibility/guidance/gap/accessibilityplanningguidanc3633?page=5#a1006 (last accessed 29.10.10).

DHC and the University of Westminster (2004) *Developing and Piloting Approaches to Accessibility*

Planning in Eight Case Study Authorities – Final Report to Department for Transport, http://www.dft.gov.uk/pgr/regional/ltp/accessibility/developing/research/ssibility planningdevelop3614.pdf (last accessed 30.11.09).

Dijst, M. and Kwan, M.P. (2005) 'Accessibility and Quality of Life: Time Geographic Perspectives', in Donaghy, K., Poppelreuter, S. and Rudinger G. (eds) *Social Dimensions of Sustainable Transport: Transatlantic Perspectives*. Aldershot, United Kingdom: Ashgate.

Farrington, J. (2007) 'The new narrative of accessibility: its potential contribution to discourses in (transport geography)', *Journal of Transport Geography* 15: 319–330.

Fontanes, M., Laousse, D., Lebreton, E. and Orfeuil, J.P. (2006) *Transport and Social Exclusion Phase 2: Evaluating the Contribution of Transport Projects to Welfare to Work – An International Study. US National Report*, http://www.fiafoundation.org/publications/Documents/se_fr.pdf

Gilhooly, M., Hamilton, K., O'Neill, M., Gow, J., Webster, N. and Pike, F. (2002) *Transport and Ageing: Extending Quality of Life via Public and Private Transport*, http://v-scheiner.brunel.ac.uk/bitstream/2438/1312/1/PDF%20ESRC%20Transport%20Final%20Report.pdf (last accessed 21.10.10).

Grant, M. (2004) 'Ensuring access and participation in the Liverpool city region', in Lucas, K. (ed.) *Running on Empty: transport social exclusion and environmental justice*. Bristol: Policy Press.

Green A.E. (2008) *Let's Get Moving Initiative (United Kingdom)*. Warwick: Institute for Employment Research.

Green A.E. and Owen, D. (2006) *The Geography of Poor Skills and Access*. York: Joseph Rowntree Foundation.

Grieco, M., Pickup, L. and Whipp, J. (1989) *Gender, Transport and Employment*. Aldershot: Gower.

Hamilton, K., Jenkins, L. and Gregory, A. (1991) *Women and Transport: Bus Deregulation in West Yorkshire*. Bradford, University of Bradford.

Hillman, M. (1993) *Children, Transport and the Quality of Urban Life*. London: Policy Studies Institute.

Hills, J., Le Grand, J. and Piachaud, D. (2002) *Understanding Social Exclusion*. Oxford, United Kingdom: Oxford University Press.

Hine, J. and Mitchell, F. (2003) *Transport Disadvantage and Social Exclusion: Exclusionary Mechanisms in Transport in Urban Scotland*. Aldershot, United Kingdom: Ashgate.

Hodgson, F. and Turner, J. (2003) 'Participation not consumption: the need for new participatory practices to address transport and social exclusion', *Transport Policy* 10: 265–272.

Hurni, A. (2006) *Transport and Social Exclusion in Western Sydney*. University of Western Sydney and Western Sydney Community Forum, Australia.

Institute for Employment Research (1999) 'Minority ethnic groups and access to jobs', *Bulletin No 51* Warwick, University of Warwick.

Jones, P. and Wixey, S. *Measuring Accessibility as Experienced by Different Social Groups: Final Report*, http://home.wmin.ac.uk/transport/download/SAMP_WP8_Final_Summary_Report.pdf (last accessed 25.10.10).

Kaufmann, V., Bergman, M.M. and Joye, D. (2004) 'Motility: Mobility as Capital', *International Journal of Urban and Regional Research* 28: 4: 745–765.

Loader, C. and Stanley, J. (2009) 'Growing bus patronage and addressing transport disadvantage – The Melbourne experience', *Transport Policy* (Special Issue: International Perspectives on Transport and Social Exclusion) 16: 3: 90–9.

Lucas, K. (ed.) (2004a) *Running on Empty: Transport, social exclusion and environmental justice*. Bristol: Policy Press.

Lucas, K. (2004b) *Transport and Social Exclusion: A survey of the Group of Seven Nations*. London: FIA Foundation http://www.fiafoundation.org/publications/Documents/social_exclusion.pdf

Lucas, K. (2006) 'Providing transport for social inclusion within a framework for environmental justice in the UK', *Transportation Research Part A* 40: 801–809.

Lucas, K. (2011) 'Making the connections between transport disadvantage and the social exclusion of low income populations in the Tshwane Region of South Africa', *Journal of Transport Geography* 19:6: 1320–1334.

Lucas, K. (2012) 'Transport and social exclusion: Where are we now?', *Transport Policy* (2012) 20: 105–113.

Lucas, K., Grosvenor T. and Simpson, R. (2001) *Transport, the Environment and Social Exclusion*. York: Joseph Rowntree Foundation/ York Publishing Ltd.

Lucas, K., Tyler S. and Christodolou, G. (2008) *The Value of New Transport in Deprived Areas: Who benefits, how and why?* Joseph Rowntree Foundation, http://www.jrf.org.uk/sites/files/jrf/2228-transport-regeneration-deprivation.pdf

Lupton, R. and Power, A. (2001) 'Social Exclusion and Neighbourhoods', in Hills, J., Le Grand, J. and Piachaud, D. (2002) *Understanding Social Exclusion* Oxford, United Kingdom: Oxford University Press.

McDonagh, J. (2006) 'Transport policy instruments and transport-related social exclusion in rural Republic of Ireland', *Journal of Transport Geography* 14: 355–366.

Mackett, R., Achuthan, K. and Titheridge, H. (2008) 'AMELIA: A tool to make transport policies more socially inclusive', *Transport Policy* 15: 372–378.

Mackett, R.L., Lucas, L., Paskins, J. and Turbin, J. (2003) 'A methodology for evaluating walking buses as an instrument of urban transport policy', *Transport Policy* 10: 179–186.

Mandanipour, A., Cars, G. and Allen, J. (1998) *Social Exclusion in European Cities: Processes, Experiences and Responses.* London: Jessica Kingsley Publishers.

Miller, H. (2007) 'Place-based versus people-based information science', *Geography Compass* 1: 3: 503–535.

Neutens, T., Schwanen, T. and Witlox, F. (2011) 'The prism of everyday life: Towards a new agenda for time geography', *Transport Reviews* 31: 1: 25–47.

Ohnmacht, T., Maksim, H. and Bergman, M.M. (2009) *Mobilities and Inequalities.* Surrey, United Kingdom: Ashgate.

Oxley, P.R. and Richards, M.J. (1995) 'Disability and transport: A review of the personal costs of disability in relation to transport', *Transport Policy* 2: 1: 57–65.

Páez, A., Mercado, R.G., Farber, S., Morency, C. and Roorda, M. (2009) *Mobility and Social Exclusion in Canadian Communities: An Empirical Investigation of Opportunity Access and Deprivation from the Perspective of Vulnerable Groups.* Toronto, Canada: Policy Research Directorate Strategic Policy and Research.

Pilling, A. and Turner, J. (1998) 'Catching Them Young: attitudes of young people to travel in Greater Manchester', *Proceedings of Universities Transport Study Groups (UTSG) Annual Conference*, Dublin, January.

Preston, J. (2009) 'Editorial', *Transport Policy Special Issue,* 16: 3: 140–142 (Guest editors Lucas, K. and Stanley, J.).

Preston, J. and Rajé, F (2007) 'Accessibility, mobility and transport-related social exclusion', *Journal of Transport Geography* 15: 3: 151–160.

Priya, T. and Uteng, A. (2009) 'Dynamic of transport and social exclusion: effects of expensive driver's license', *Transport Policy Special Issue International Perspectives on Transport and Social Exclusion* 16: 3: 90–96.

Rajé, F., (2004) *Transport Demand Management and Social Inclusion: The Need for Ethnic Perspectives.* Aldershot: Ashgate.

Regeneris (2003) Transport & Accessibility Improvement Study: Employment & Skills Issues, *Internal report for the Mersey-Dee Alliance.*

Rose, E., Whitten, K. and McCreanor, T. (2009) 'Transport Related Social Exclusion in New Zealand: Evidence and Challenges', *New Zealand Journal Of Social Sciences Online, http://www.royalsociety.org.nz/site/publish/journals/kotuitui/2009/028.aspx*

Schonfelder, S. and Axhausen, K.W. (2003) 'Activity spaces: measures of social exclusion?', *Transport Policy* 10: 273–286.

Social Exclusion Unit (1998) *Bringing Britain Together.* London: Stationery Office.

Social Exclusion Unit (2003) *Making the Connections: Final report on Transport and Social Exclusion.* London: Office of the Deputy Prime Minister.

Stanley, J. and Stanley, J. (2010) 'Investigating the links between social capital and public transport', *Transport Reviews* 28: 4: 529–547.

Stanley, J. and Vella-Broderick, D. (2009) 'The usefulness of social exclusion to inform social policy in transport', *Transport Policy: Special Issue International Perspectives on Transport and Social Exclusion* 16: 3: 90–96.

TRaC (2000) *Social Exclusion and the Provision of Public Transport.* London: Department of Environment Transport and the Regions.

Urry, J. (2000) *Sociologies beyond Societies: Mobilities for the Twenty-First Century.* New York: Routledge.

Urry, J. (2007) *Mobilities* Cambridge, UK: Polity Press.

Uteng, T. (2009) 'Gender, ethnicity and constrained mobility: insights into the resultant exclusion', *Environment and Planning A* 41: 1055–1071.

Walker, A. and Walker, C. (eds) (1997) *Britain Divided.* London: CPAG.

Wright, S., Nelson, J.D., Cooper, J.M. and Murphy, S. (2009) 'An evaluation of the transport to employment (T2E) scheme in Highland Scotland using social return on investment (SROI)', *Journal of Transport Geography* 17: 6: 457–467.

SECTION 4

Transport Policy

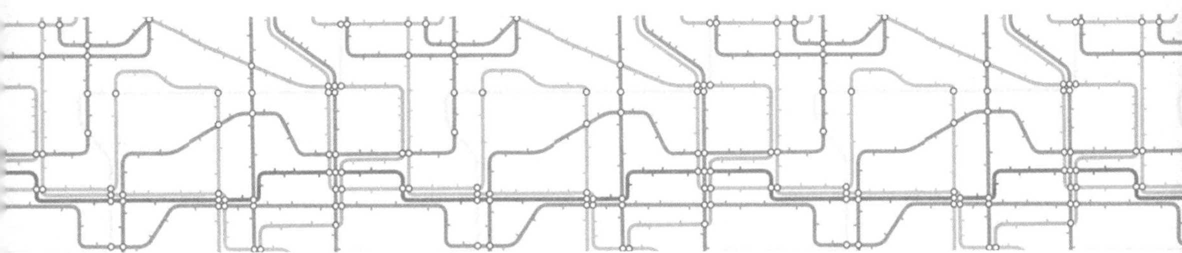

16

Transport Policy Instruments

Theo Notteboom

INTRODUCTION

The role of government in society has always attracted a lot of attention in policy and academic circles. The belief in liberal markets with little public interference was seriously reconsidered after the crash of 1929 and the economic downturn of the early 1930s. From that moment on governments were incited to extend the scope of their responsibilities. The public sector was an important trigger for the reconstruction of Europe in the aftermath of World War II (e.g. the Marshall plan in Europe), for the modernization of the industrial structure and for economic growth. Economic and social measures were directed towards the creation of the welfare state. The period from the 1940s to the 1970s were characterized by nationalization when socialist ideology was put into practice throughout the world. For example, the European transport industry saw the emergence of large national companies in public transport, freight rail, ferry services, deepsea shipping and the airline industry. These large nationalized companies could mobilize new sources and technologies, thereby contributing to the national objectives of economic growth and full employment. While the planned economic system in the Soviet Union involved a complete control by the public sector, governments in Western Europe and North America were also major players in the market through market control systems up to the full nationalization of industries considered to be of strategic importance to economic development and external trade.

The pendulum started to shift in the other direction in the 1980s with a return to a modified version of the laissez-faire philosophy and to market economics. The UK pioneered denationalization and privatization in 1979. Prime Minister Margaret Thatcher became the symbol of a political philosophy and economic policies focused on deregulation, flexible labour markets, the privatization of state-owned companies, and a reduction of the power and influence of public trade unions. Soon deregulation and a retreat of government in economic life became an international phenomenon, often promoted as being the cure for serious inefficiencies borne with state-owned enterprises. In this new environment, governments around the world are in an ongoing process of reassessing their role in transport markets. At the same time they are looking for a mix of transport policy instruments that will help to achieve the creation of open and efficient transport markets, mainly serviced by private companies.

This chapter discusses the role of government in deregulated transport markets. We analyze the reasons why some level of government intervention is still required, even if private companies are the main actors for the provision of transport services. Furthermore, an overview is given of transport policy instruments at the disposal of public authorities to facilitate the dynamics in transport markets. Throughout this chapter, the transport policy of the European Commission serves as a case study.

THE RETREAT OF THE PUBLIC SECTOR IN TRANSPORT SERVICE PROVISION

To a great extent, the transport industry has historically been the prerogative of the public sector, as (international) transportation was considered as being of great strategic value for both trade, energy supply, industrial development and national security. The same applied to public transit systems that were considered essential to the well-being of urban populations. The growth of world trade, structural changes in logistics and the increasing mobility of people have created a competitive market environment that has forced transport companies to become more market-oriented.

The public sector can alter its involvement in the transport industry in many ways. One of the common ways is to shift attention from the provision of transport services to the development of a transport policy that creates more open and efficient transport markets through private sector participation. Such a retreat of government takes place in the belief that an enterprise-based economy would allow for greater flexibility and efficiency in the market (e.g. through higher competition) and a better response to consumers' demands. Efficiency has a static/allocative dimension and a dynamic side (Wolf, 1987). Allocative efficiency refers to the capability of markets and organizations to achieve the highest possible output or benefits with a given level of inputs or costs. Dynamic efficiency relates to the capability of markets and/or organizations to gradually lower costs and raise productivity through organizational restructuring, technological innovation, human resource management and so on.

Transport service providers in rail, shipping and air transportation were often run like government departments, but later on witnessed the infusion of private money with the expectation of greater competition, higher productivity and eventually lower costs which will be passed on to the transport users. The entry of private economic actors in the provision of transport services typically involves the transfer of public assets (i.e. the transfer of ownership of state assets from the public to the private sector), the transfer of the provision of services from public bodies to private enterprises or letting new transport developments be assumed by the private sector. Some of the most commonly used methods of privatisation are public offering of shares, private sale of shares, new private investment in State Owned Enterprise (SOE), sale of government or SOE assets, management/employee buy-out, increased use of private sector financing of new activities (e.g. BOT – Build, Operate and Transfer) and concession or lease arrangements of publicly owned infrastructure or land. Privatisation schemes can encompass a segment of the market (e.g. the privatization of one ferry service between a Greek island and the mainland) or the entire transport market (e.g. the opening up of passenger rail transport in the UK in the 1990s).

Often cited reasons to opt for the privatization of transport services such as rail transport, ports, airports and airlines include:

- To improve efficiency and performance;
- To find new financial resources for development and maintenance;

- To strengthen entrepreneurial and managerial capacity;
- To relieve government's financial and administrative burden;
- To eliminate and/or minimize bureaucratic and political influence over management and operation;
- To reduce the power of public sector unions.

Often cited reasons not to privatize transport activities include:

- Loss of "public service" or social functions of transport;
- Public monopoly turned into a private one;
- Poorer coordination of investments and operations;
- Discriminatory treatment of transport users;
- Loss of public intervention needed when there is "market failure" (see later in this chapter);
- Need for expensive improvement of transport service assets prior to privatization in order to reach "a good deal";
- Property rights on e.g. land are a public task.

Empirical evidence shows that the objectives envisaged through private market entry are not always achieved. For example, Haubrich (2001) evaluated the results of the UK government's policy with regard to the privatization of British railways by reviewing the first five years of the privatized regime (from 1994/95 to 1999/2000). Out of nine policy objectives put forward by the government at the start of the privatization scheme only one has actually been achieved. In other words, it is risky to consider privatization schemes as a panacea for all the problems associated with publicly led transport organizations.

WHY DO WE STILL NEED SOME LEVEL OF GOVERNMENT INTERVENTION IN TRANSPORT MARKETS?

Governments are or should be concerned with efficient and well-functioning transport markets as transport activities produce significant benefits for society. Regardless of whether public or private companies are responsible for the provision of transport services, efficient and well-functioning transport markets require a number of key components to be in place.

First, governments are instrumental in avoiding *significant monopoly power*. The presence of significant monopoly power in a market typically reduces competition and the pressure for efficiency and innovation, resulting in reduced levels of choice and price protection. Monopolies can have a detrimental effect on the supply side of the market as they are eager to choose supply levels that maximize profits. They like to avoid the price-reducing effect of increased supply and technological innovations. As a monopolist has less incentive to increase supply than the perfect competitor, scarcity on the transport market can emerge leading to higher prices and unsatisfied/latent transport needs. However, monopolies cannot always be avoided. If a liberalized market is characterized by increasing returns to scale, so-called "natural monopolies" can emerge which have been thought to induce profit maximizing prices above marginal costs. There are many examples of transport markets where large economies of scale and density are pushing market players towards more consolidation and horizontal integration, ultimately resulting in oligopolistic or even monopolistic behavior. Cartels could be formed whereby a group of firms collusively determines the prices and output in a market. In other words, a cartel acts as a single monopoly firm that maximizes total industry profit. In such cases, government typically intervenes by regulating prices and or market behavior (for example, anti-cartel regulation or strict rules on mergers and acquisitions).

Second, in a market economy, the assumption is conventionally made that competitive forces will generate a pattern of the efficient use of resources. A rationale for central authority intervention emerges when, in certain circumstances, the competitive *market mechanism "fails"*. Three important circumstances in which the market will fail are when increasing returns to scale exist in the production of goods and services leading to a *natural monopoly* (see previous paragraph) and when *externalities* and *public goods* exist. Public goods are defined as those goods and services that could probably never be supplied sufficiently or satisfactorily by a competitive industry, or might not be supplied by them at all. [...] It concerns communal or non-rival consumption where it is impossible to exclude anyone on the basis of non-payment" (Suykens and Van de Voorde, 1998). As the market fails to offer public goods, it is up to the government to supply them. An example are the traffic management systems in seaports: all ships use them, but still in most cases these services are supplied by public bodies as no private party is willing to invest in radar chains and other equipment to monitor ship movements in and out the port.

Externalities emerge when an individual's utility contains real variables, whose values are chosen by others, without regard for the effect on the individual (Baumol and Oates, 1988). In a transport context, externalities relate to effects which are not or only partly included in the transport price. For example, externalities in road transport include congestion, pollution and accidents. The focus in research on externalities has largely shifted from congestion to air emissions and safety. When externalities exist, transport users will make sub-optimal modal choices leading to inefficiencies in the transport market. Governments have a role to play in designing policies to reduce externalities so that all of the costs and benefits of transport services provided are fully captured within the market. This can be done by taking a wide range of measures to reduce congestion and emissions and to improve safety, including pricing instruments (e.g. road pricing), investments (e.g. capacity increase in road system to reduce congestion) or restrictive measures (e.g. minimum standards on clean cars and trucks). The reduction of externalities is often a balancing game as it may lead to a negative impact on growth or income distribution.

Third, governments have a clear role to play in keeping *barriers to entry and exit* to transport markets low, thereby enabling transport markets to function efficiently, while barriers to entry reduce competition and efficiency. Governments can take measures to remove entry restrictions into the market and allow private sector firms to enter public sector markets. However, an open market does not necessarily result in fair competition, particularly if there is no equal level playing field among the market players. Baumol (1982) suggests that the removal of entry barriers will ensure efficient behavior even in cases of natural monopolies, provided it can be shown that the market is "perfectly contestable". This assumes that market entry is free, absolute and perfectly reversible. Under the conditions of contestability, all market dominating companies would hold their prices strictly down to costs as they fear "hit and run" entries of new players in the market. So, contestability theory suggests it would be possible to get the benefits of competition without the requirement of a large number of competing firms. Many authors (e.g. Shepherd, 1995) suggest that contestability theory is difficult to relate to reality, as markets are rarely fully contestable (see e.g. Brewer, 1996, for the contestability in UK rail freight markets). Very low entry and exit barriers can lead to opportunistic behavior of market players who enter and exit the market in view of realizing short-term gains. Such behavior is often associated with cut-throat competition and a negative price spiral initiated by "cowboys" in the business who are not always strictly following social and other stringent regulations. The trucking industry in some countries has suffered from such practices. The avoidance of excessive competition is often seen as a task for government.

Fourth, transparency is a key factor for well-functioning transport markets. Transport users can only make the right modal choices if they have access to information about prices, travel/transit times, service levels and other key attributes such as macroeconomic information. Government has a role to play to ensuring the *widespread availability of information* so that all parties in the market (businesses and users) are well informed if they are to make transport-related decisions.

For example, timely and accurate price information enables appropriate supply responses from businesses and demand responses from transport users, leading to better-quality services at the lowest possible prices.

Other arguments for having public sector involvement in efficiency-oriented transport markets include:

- The need to integrate transport into wider economic policies (macroeconomic or industrial policies);
- The need for integrated transport planning and for transport co-ordination in order to realize coherent, interoperable and interconnected transport systems without wasteful duplication;
- The issue of property rights and eminent domain (e.g. in case of expropriation of sites for transport infrastructure development);
- The financing of large scale transport infrastructure. In the past, most governments have predominantly funded the majority of large infrastructure works in transport systems. As many governments in the western world are now confronted with a public debt issue, they want to curb their financial participation in infrastructure projects through public private partnerships (PPP) and other forms of risk and cost sharing;
- The focus on the social dimension of transport, such as guaranteeing a minimum level of mobility to all citizens through affordable public transport services and other forms of assistance for groups in "need" of adequate transport;
- The design of policies which make transport users more aware of the genuine resource cost of non-renewable inputs (e.g. mineral fuel) and which facilitate a transfer from fossil fuels to alternative energy sources.

TRANSPORT POLICY INSTRUMENTS AVAILABLE TO GOVERNMENTS AND PUBLIC AUTHORITIES: THE EU CASE

Public bodies have a range of instruments and tools at their disposal to facilitate and influence transport markets. Further in this section we will discuss the main instruments of government intervention. Each of these instruments will be illustrated by looking at the transport policy of the European Commission. Before doing so, the following paragraphs provide a general outline on the EU transport policy.

EU Transport Policy development

The importance of an integrated European transport structure was already recognized by the authors of the Community's founding Treaty of Rome (1957). They set a Common Transport Policy as one of the Community's priority tasks. For many years progress towards the realization of a Common Transport Policy was slow, especially when measured against the importance of transport in the EU economy as a whole. The Court of Justice had to intervene several times on basic questions of interpretation of the transport provisions of the Treaty of Rome in order to make progress possible. This process reached its climax in 1985 when on May 22 the Court of Justice of the European Communities delivered a very important decision regarding the common transport policy. This decision was the result of an appeal lodged against the Council of European Communities by the European Parliament which reproached the Council for not having applied the common transport policy as laid down in the Treaty of Rome.

The bearing of the decision covered the Council's obligation to apply free movement of transport services, i.e. the inland transport of goods and passengers should be open to all community firms, without discrimination as to nationality or place of establishment. The decision also defined the extent of the Council's discretionary powers and its power of appreciation in transport matters.

Since then, all modes of transport have been forced to loosen, if not eliminate, national restrictions against operators from other EU countries. The result has been the creation of a more open European market reinforced by the creation of the internal market which formally came into force in January 1993. But some restrictions remain and a lot of work in other fields still needs to be done. With the ratification and the entering into force of the Treaty of Maastricht in November 1993, a further crucial milestone was reached on the way to European integration. This treaty gave a new impulse to the evolution of the Common Transport Policy. Measures to improve transport safety and the environment received full attention. The provisions on the creation of Trans-European Networks (TENs) and economic and social cohesion provided a new basis for the Community to contribute to the establishment and development of transport infrastructure.

In the framework of the Single Market concept the European Commission has worked to develop a common transport policy, through which several economic and social needs are fulfilled, such as improving infrastructure and using it in a more rational way, enhancing the safety of users, achieving more equitable working conditions and affording better protection of the environment. In following such a comprehensive approach the Commission clearly aims for sustainable mobility.

The aim of EU transport policy in the 1990s was set out in the so-called White Paper published by the European Commission at the end of 1992 entitled "The future development of the common transport policy: a global approach to the construction of a Community framework for sustainable mobility" (COM(92) 494 def). In short the common transport policy aimed at achieving a double integration:

- The integration of transport modes (road transport, railway transport, inland navigation, maritime transport) so that they form integrated systems, combining the use of different modes, where appropriate on the same journey (i.e. multimodal transport) and with special attention to the use of environmentally friendly transport modes;
- The integration of national transport networks into a coherent European network structure (the so-called Trans-European Transport Network or TEN-T). This network should help to raise economic and social cohesion among Member States.

Through this double integration process the need was stressed for environmentally friendly and safe transport services. In addition the White Paper laid down several social priorities. These concern access to the profession and job training, employment protection and the improvement of living and working conditions.

In 2001, almost ten years after the first White Paper, the European Commission launched a new White Paper entitled "European Transport Policy for 2010: Time to Decide", which proposed 60 measures for restructuring the EU's transport policy, with the intent of creating a more sustainable and less polluting and congested system. One of the key ideas was to decouple economic growth from transport growth to make transport more dynamic and less dependent on market factors. Also the ideas of establishing a modal shift from road transport to other transport modes, transport safety and the internalization of external costs were high on the agenda. The 2001 White Paper resulted in several policy initiatives, such as a European Road Safety Action Programme, the launching of the Marco Polo program to support a modal shift in freight transport, the development of Motorways of the Sea focusing on the role of shortsea shipping in intra-European transport, a further development of the TEN-T and the continued liberalization and harmonization of rail transport.

In June 2006 the EC published a "Mid-Term Review" of the 2001 White Paper on Transport. This review contained some interesting developments such as the observation that the objective of "decoupling" economic growth and transport is very hard to achieve. Also, the EC introduced the term "co-modality" instead of "modal shift" to reflect a stronger focus on interconnectivity and cooperation among transport modes. Nash and Matthews (2009) concluded that European policy makers largely failed to deliver the political targets set out in the European Commission's Transport White Paper of 2001. Progress has been particularly slow in terms of revitalizing the rail sector, introducing fair intermodal competition and fair and efficient pricing mechanisms and greening transport.

In March 2011, the European Commission presented a new Transport White Paper entitled

"Roadmap to a Single European Transport Area – Towards a competitive and resource efficient transport system". It consists of 40 concrete initiatives for the next decade to build a competitive transport system that will increase mobility, remove major barriers in key areas and stimulate growth and employment. The document contains ambitious targets such as a 60% reduction in CO_2 emissions within the transport sector by 2050 compared to 1990 levels. This is expected to be achieved by a series of measures such as introducing a 40% use of low-carbon fuels in the aviation and maritime sectors, phasing out conventionally fuelled cars in cities and increasing the share of medium-distance passenger and freight travel from road and air to rail and waterborne transport. The Commission expects that 30% of road freight over 300 km should shift to other modes such as rail or waterborne transport by 2030, and more than 50% by 2050. Another key objective is the establishment of a true single European transport area as an efficient, seamless and integrated transport area is seen as important in relation to Europe's competitiveness and economic growth. The 2011 White Paper also focuses on the TEN-T consisting of a core network and a comprehensive network. More and efficient entry points into the European markets are needed supported by efficient Motorways of the Sea. In general, the Commission expects that the multimodal TEN-T core network will be fully functional by 2030, with a high quality and capacity network by 2050 and a corresponding set of information services. In the coming years, the above goals will be translated into concrete actionable steps and commitments.

The distribution of responsibilities between EU and individual Member States regarding transport policy development and implementation has always been a major concern, certainly when considering the EU already consists of 27 Member States and the future potential of additional members. The Treaty of Maastricht emphasized that in accordance with the principle of subsidiarity the Common Transport Policy must consist of actions which cannot be realized adequately by the Member States individually and therefore, by reason of their dimensions or effects, are better realized by the EU. As such, EU actions must be analyzed in terms of this subsidiarity principle. This means: (a) the EU actions should relate to a shared competence between Member States and the EU; (b) the actions should relate to a problem in which many Member States are involved; (c) the solution based on the EU actions should be more efficient than the solution based on measures of the individual Member States; and (d) the actions should generate value added for the EU. The cost of no action must be high or at least exist.

The use of transport policy instruments in EU transport policy

Access to the profession and access to the market

A first important transport policy domain relates to *access to the profession* and *access to the market*. Through a set of laws and regulations government can influence the entry of newcomers in the market and the quality of the transport services delivered. There are many examples to be found in EU Transport Policy. The following paragraphs discuss the situation in the European road transport sector.

Already in 1974, Directive 74/561 laid down conditions for admission to the occupation, or profession, of road haulier for hire or reward. These conditions included professional competence, financial standing and a good repute. Professional competence was to be tested either by examination or by the holding of higher qualifications or experience. In 1989, the criteria on access to the profession were more specified. For example, anyone wishing to set up a road haulage business in the EU must put up a financial guarantee. Today, admission to the occupation of road haulage operator and road passenger transport operator in the European Union is governed by a 1996 directive (96/26/EC). This was amended in 1998 by stricter rules applicable after 1 October 1999 to new operators entering the market. These impose more rigorous criteria as regards good repute, professional competence and financial standing, in an attempt to halt the proliferation of unscrupulous "cowboy" firms which seek to corner a market share by skimping on safety.

The access to the road transport market was very restrictive for a long time. In 1968, regulation 1018/68 established a "Community Quota" of authorizations for unlimited international transport. The restricted number of holders of such an authorization could carry out unlimited international transport between any pair of Member States. It also included the so-called triangular traffic, i.e. transport between two other Member States than the country in which the haulier was based. However, in the existing bilateral agreements (agreement between two states), this type of operation was forbidden or severely restricted. Over the years, further liberalization was accomplished by increasing the size of the Community Quota. But even in 1986 the Community Quota still only covered about 5% of total intra-Community road haulage. The rest was covered by quotas contained in bilateral agreements between Member States. Several Member States like Germany argued that further liberalization was dependent on harmonization of the conditions of competition.

In 1985, the Court of Justice made it clear that common rules for international haulage could not await harmonization. From January 1993, all quota restrictions, both bilateral and Community, on non-national firms were lifted and replaced by a system of Community licences issued on the basis of qualitative criteria (Regulation 1841/88). Since January 1993 any road operator wishing to carry goods or passengers internationally – that is to say between at least two Member States – must hold a Community driving license issued by the Member State in which he or she resides. This document gives the driver unlimited access to the whole of the single market. To obtain it drivers must meet a number of conditions set in part by the Member States themselves. One condition, however, is binding on all 15 Member States: they must enforce the requirements of the EU directive on admission to the occupation of road haulage operator or road passenger transport operator.

The transport of goods inside another Member State, known as "cabotage", was still restricted. In July 1998, road cabotage in the movement of freight became in principle fully liberalized. However, as more Member States joined the EU in the early 2000s, many West-European countries started to have major concerns over a too liberal approach of cabotage. Years of debate resulted in Regulation 1072/2009 implemented in May 2010. Article 8 of the Regulation provides that every haulier is entitled to perform up to three cabotage operations within a seven day period starting the day after the unloading of the international transport. A haulier may decide to carry out one, two or all three cabotage operations in different Member States and not necessarily the Member State in which the international transport was delivered. For some of the new Member States, such as Romania, transitional periods still apply and hauliers from these countries are excluded from performing cabotage in certain other Member States.

Technical harmonization

A lack of technical harmonization for vehicles and infrastructures hampers the competitiveness of a transport mode and creates major problems in the area of interoperability and interconnectivity within transport systems. Therefore, it is no surprise that governments seek to set and implement supranational and even international standards in this area.

Many examples can be found in the European transport industry. For a long time, maximum lorry weights and dimensions varied from country to country, according to geography (mountainous countries tending to have low weight limits) and transport policies. The basis for harmonization of maximum weights and dimensions was laid by a 1985 Directive 85/3. This directive and the subsequent amendments led, for example, to a maximum length of 16.5 m for articulated vehicles, a maximum weight of 10 tonnes for a carrying axle and 11.5 tonnes for a drive axle. In July 1996 the Council of Ministers adopted Directive 96/53/EC which amended the maximum authorized dimensions. A more recent discussion relates to the cross-border use of megatrucks of up 25.25 m. As of today, the use of long modular trucks was allowed in Finland and Sweden, and being trialed in Denmark, the Netherlands and some German States. Based on local circumstances and concerns, each Member State can still decide to allow or not allow the use of longer vehicles in their territory. The Commission is planning to propose limited amendments to other aspects of Directive 96/53/EC on weights and dimensions in late 2012 (e.g. to improve cabin design and the aerodynamics of the truck).

Technical harmonization has always been a key issue in European rail transport. Historically, each country developed its own railway infrastructure and entrusted the management of rail operations and infrastructure to a public national railway company. The gradual liberalization of the rail freight sector since Directive 91/440 of 1991 meant that the existing technical differences in signaling and electric power systems among Member States formed major obstacles towards trans-European rail operations. Directive 2008/57 on the interoperability of the rail system within the EU set an agenda for the harmonization of technical standards in the area of structural components (i.e. energy, control-command and signaling, rolling stock) and functional components (i.e. operation and traffic management, maintenance and telematics applications).

Pricing, taxes and subsidies

Governments seeking to achieve efficient and well-functioning transport markets tend to develop a great interest in financial and fiscal arrangements in these markets. Government's involvement is especially felt at the level of pricing, taxes and subsidies. Below are some European examples.

The inland waterway market in the EU has been completely liberalized since 1 January 2000 following Council Directive 96/75 of 19 November 1996. Before that time, systems of "chartering by rotation" (tour-de-rôle) were operational in certain segments of the EU-waterway market (mainly in Belgium, the Netherlands and Northern France). The main part of the international waterway market, in particular the Rhine market, was already subject to a free regime. The "tour-de-rôle" system was a sort of alternate chartering system linked to specific *price fixing arrangements*. All shippers were listed at a kind of freight exchange. The first on the list could choose first whether he/she liked to take a freight consignment or not at a predetermined and fixed price. Once a consignment was accepted, he/she was placed at the bottom of the list. The system was installed in order to ensure that all shippers would have the same opportunities of getting a consignment in a recession period. The European Commission never expressed much sympathy for such systems as they are not in line with the general orientation of the Common Transport Policy. For instance, prices were not fixed based on the interaction between demand and supply, but based on the objective to make sure all listed barge operators could generate enough revenue, even though the number of trips per month were low. The liberalization of the inland waterway sector boosted the use of barges in domestic transport in Belgium and the Netherlands and on the north–south waterway axis (the Netherlands, Belgium and Northern France).

When it comes to *taxes*, the EU transport markets are confronted with a lack of fiscal harmonization. For instance, fiscal matters are probably the most important and obvious example of the unequal conditions of competition between trucking companies from various countries. Wide variations exist in: (1) the purchase price of vehicles; (2) the annual tax for putting a vehicle on the road; (3) the duty on diesel fuel; and (4) the practice of some countries like Italy and France in charging tolls for the use of motorways. The yield of factors (2), (3) and (4) is normally used to pay for the infrastructure. However harmonization in this field is very difficult and the question remains if it will ever be achieved. The yield of the second factor remains with the country in which the vehicle is registered (the so-called "nationality principle"). The fourth, where it exists, remains with the country in which the vehicles operate (the so-called "territoriality principle"). The fuel tax falls somewhere between the two. The problem of harmonizing fuel taxes is a complex one: fuel taxes are an important source of income for the Member States. The matter can therefore not be separated from the wider question of general fiscal harmonization in the EU.

Vehicle tax is even more complicated, because each country has not only different tax rates but also totally different tax structures. Moreover the level of vehicle tax is also influenced by the existence of road tolls and refund mechanisms. So far, every attempt by the Commission to harmonize vehicle taxes has failed. Road tolls are charged in France, Greece, Italy, Portugal and Spain. The Commission decided that those tolls can continue to be charged, but without direct or indirect discrimination on grounds of nationality, or the origin and destination of the traffic. In reaction to the existence of road tolls in other Member States and supported by the Commission, Germany, Belgium, Denmark, the Netherlands and Luxembourg jointly created the Eurovignet, a board paper which became obligatory for all road hauliers active in those countries on 1 January 1995. Germany introduced the LKW-Maut system for trucks on its highways in 2005. The levy is based on the distance driven, the number of axles and the emission category of the vehicle.

Limiting the tax discussion to just three cost elements – vehicle tax, fuel tax and road tolls – in isolation is risky as the whole range of costs, including wages and other social costs should be included. The Commission's Green paper of 20 December 1995, "Towards fair and efficient pricing in transport" (COM(95)691), was the first attempt to set out the details of a *fiscal policy on transport*. It analyzed the external factors and included taxation as one of the ways in which the State can have an impact on this sector. The Commission White Paper of 2 July 1998, "Fair payment for infrastructure use: a phased approach to a common transport infrastructure charging framework in the EU" (COM(98)466), adopted subsequently, set out a phased approach to run until 2004 for internalizing infrastructure costs. The aim was to replace the variety of charging systems in force in the various Member States and transport modes with a harmonized EU approach to transport charging. The charging principle the Commission still adopts today is that of marginal social costs. These are variable costs reflecting the cost of an additional vehicle or transport unit using the infrastructure. Marginal costs can include operating costs, the cost of wear and tear on infrastructure, environmental costs, the costs of congestion and scarcity and costs relating to accidents.

The European Commission argues that *internalization of external costs* in the total transport price should aim not to make transport more expensive but to ensure that existing costs are apportioned rationally, and that external costs must be apportioned among all modes of transport at the same time to avoid distortions of competition. The EC believes internalization should be based on marginal social cost, but that consideration should be given to the possibility of supplementing the marginal cost charging system by a multi-tier pricing system incorporating in particular taxes on emissions, energy and CO_2.

The European Union has never been very keen on the use of *subsidies in transport markets*. However, it has allowed some forms of subsidies to promote intermodal transport and public transport, and to reach objectives of social and economic cohesion. For example, under a 1996 regulation (2255/96/EC) Member States were allowed to grant aid, on a temporary basis, for investment in the infrastructure of inland waterway terminals or the fixed and mobile equipment needed for loading and unloading on to and from inland waterways. This scheme allowed Member States to subsidize up to 50% of the investment cost.

Social regulation

Government's involvement in transport markets includes rules to create good working conditions. Social regulation can be found in many segments of the transport market, often based on social dialogue between industry representatives, government officials and labor unions. For example, social harmonization in the road transport market includes rules on the maximum hours lorry drivers may spend at the wheel, and the minimum rest periods they must take. The applicable rules on driving and rest periods in the EU are contained in Regulation 561/06 which came into effect in April 2007. It includes very detailed rules on travelling time and daily and weekly rest periods with special arrangements for double manned vehicles and transport by ferryboat or piggyback train. Although the road sector now has social regulation on a European level, the Member States have varying interpretations and a category of hauliers deliberately misunderstand or distort the rules in order to profit from excessive hours driving with minimum rest. Closely associated with this regulation is the tachograph, a digital instrument in the lorry which records drivers' activities (speed, rest period, etc.). This instrument is compulsory in all Member States.

Competition policy and consumer protection

As most governments have retreated from service provision in the transport sector, the emphasis shifted to supervising fair and efficient competition in the transport markets. Public authorities are expected to act against price fixing, market sharing or other kinds of anticompetitive behavior. Consequently, competition authorities have acquired a more visible role than before. They can influence the market structure by imposing rules on the number of players in the market or by restricting further consolidation through mergers and acquisitions. The role of competition authorities is especially important when newly competitive markets are emerging as a result of either liberalization (e.g. European rail), the extension of the number of Member States, or repeal of specific antitrust rules (e.g. the repeal of the exemption from EC Treaty competition rules for liner shipping conferences, as laid down in Council Regulation 4056/86). In the structures of the EU public bodies, Directorate-General Market is the competent authority when it comes to safeguarding competition.

Measures are also needed to protect transport users' interests. A good example in a European context is EC Regulation 261/2004 which protects the rights of airline passengers. This piece of legislation applies to all passengers and all flights departing from an airport located in the EU, and to all passengers departing from an airport located in a third country to an EU airport in cases where the airline is registered in a European country. The legislation is built around a set of basic rights in events of denied boarding, flight cancellation and if the flight is delayed: the right to reimbursement, compensation or rerouting and the right to refreshments, meals, communications (such as a free phone call), and, if necessary, an overnight stay.

Research and development

The public sector typically adopts a key role in stimulating and funding research aimed at improving the technical, economic and environmental performance of transport systems and markets. Research budgets are made available at the local, regional, national and international level to allow multi-disciplinary and international teams to advance knowledge in these areas and to come up with results that can be implemented in practice.

The European Union is no exception. Via a system of framework programs (the latest one is FP7) the European Commission launches a series of 'calls for proposals' on specific research topics relevant to the European transport system. The central objective of transport research under FP7 is to develop safer, greener and smarter transport systems for Europe that will benefit citizens, respect the environment, and increase the competitiveness of European industries in the global market. The emphasis lies on research activities in the field of aeronautics and air transport; reduction of emissions; alternative fuels; sustainable surface transport; intermodal regional and national transport; and infrastructure construction and maintenance. A total of EUR 4.16 billion has been earmarked for funding this theme over the duration of FP7.

Provision of information and promotion

The public and the private sector have a joint responsibility in promoting the use of environment-friendly and efficient transport modes and in providing users and the general public with correct information on the routing and modal options available. Such actions also help to improve the image, general awareness and knowledge of the real potential of a specific transport mode or intermodal solution in terms of quality and reliability. As many stakeholders are involved, the coordination of promotion activities by all the actors concerned is key. For example, in quite a number of Member States, inland waterway promotion and development organizations have been set up by local or national governments or by industry (e.g. Promotie Binnenvaart Vlaanderen in the region of Flanders in Belgium, Bureau Voorlichting Binnenvaart in the Netherlands, etc.) while Inland Navigation Europe tries to bundle these initiatives at a European-wide level. The dissemination of information via these organizations is essential for businesses, economic and political decision-makers and the authorities in anticipating market trends. The tasks of government in facilitating information provision and promotion stretches to moral suasion in view of influencing the behavior of transport users. This category of initiatives includes all sorts of campaigns aimed at e.g. responsible driving and the wearing of seat belts in cars, social behavior when using public transport, etc.

CONCLUSION

Since the 1980s, deregulation, liberalization and privatization have played a decisive role in restructuring transport markets around the world. In Europe, these processes took place hand in hand with an increased economic integration between EU Member States. In this chapter we demonstrated that government has an important role to play in deregulated and increasingly competitive and international transport markets. We identified ten reasons favoring some level of government intervention. The instruments and tools at the disposal of public authorities to facilitate market dynamics and free and fair competition in the transport industry are diverse and often far-reaching. Next to basic tasks such as infrastructure provision, the relevant instruments and tools to influence and facilitate transport markets relate to the access to the profession; access to the market; technical harmonization; prices, taxes and subsidies; social regulation; competition policy and consumer protection; research and development; and the provision of information and promotion.

REFERENCES

Baumol, W.J. (1982) "Contestable markets: an uprising in the theory of industry structure", *American Economic Review*, Vol. 72, pp. 1–15.

Baumol, W. and Oates, W. (1988) *The Theory of Environmental Policy*, Cambridge: Cambridge University Press.

Brewer, P.R. (1996) "Contestability in UK rail freight markets: the economics of open access", *Transport Policy*, Vol. 3, pp. 91–98.

Haubrich, D. (2001) "UK rail privatisation five years down the line: an evaluation of nine policy objectives", *Policy & Politics*, Vol. 29, No. 3, pp. 317–336.

Nash, C. and Matthews, B. (2009) *European Transport Policy: Progress and Prospects*, Brussels: Community of European Railway and Infrastructure Companies (CER).

Shepherd, W.G. (1995) "Contestability versus competition: once more", *Land Economics*, Vol. 71, pp. 299–309.

Suykens, F. and Van De Voorde, E. (1998) "A quarter of a century of port management in Europe: objectives and tools", *Maritime Policy and Management*, Vol. 25, pp. 251–261.

Wolf, C. (1987) "Market and non-market failures: comparison and assessment", *Journal of Public Policy*, Vol. 7, pp. 43–70.

17

Transport Pricing and Subsidy

Chris Nash and Bryan Matthews

INTRODUCTION

In the early days of the development of the modern transport system, both infrastructure and operations were often paid for totally from user charges; for instance the turnpikes in Britain and the US and the British rail network. But during the twentieth century, governments commonly took on responsibility for transport infrastructure, and increasingly public transport operations were subsidised. The result has been increasing government involvement in transport pricing decisions, and in many cases the introduction of explicit transport subsidies.

Today, there is a diverse patchwork of approaches to pricing and subsidy throughout the sector, and varying calls for reform. For roads, direct user charges are the exception. This said, tolls, in one form or another, do continue to be used on some major highways in some countries, whilst road-related taxes, e.g. on car ownership and on fuel, are commonplace and a major source of tax revenue. Furthermore, there are a number of specific urban road user-charging initiatives that have been introduced as a means of rationing demand and raising revenue.

On the other hand, direct user charges for public transport – in the guise of fares – have and continue to be the norm. However, these charges have generally been subject to a mix of explicit and implicit subsidy. Governments have tended to maintain a significant role in relation to financing investment and, in some places, to the reimbursement of public transport operators in return for them providing specific services and/or for them holding down fares or even cutting them to zero, for particular groups such as older and disabled people.

In the rest of this chapter we seek to set out the key developments in relation to efficient pricing and subsidy regimes. First, we examine the literature on transport pricing principles. We then examine in turn road pricing, rail infrastructure charges, pricing air and sea infrastructure and the pricing of transport services. Finally, we attempt to summarise and point the way forward.

THE PRINCIPLES OF TRANSPORT PRICING

At the outset, we should address some definitional issues. Firstly, when referring to pricing, we generally mean charges to users, be they individuals or operating companies, that are related to their level of usage, independent of whether it is government or the private sector that set the prices and collect the revenue. This is as distinct from taxes, which are generally not related to the level of usage and are always set and collected by government. However, the two may overlap, as for instance when governments use fuel tax to charge for the use of the road system. Secondly, whilst subsidy is commonly viewed as government support to plug the gap between costs and revenues, this is not the only interpretation. Even within this interpretation though, there is the issue of whether to only consider money costs within the equation or to consider social costs, which we would argue gives a more complete picture. Furthermore, it is useful, when following this interpretation, to distinguish between explicit and implicit subsidy. That is, explicit subsidy refers to where governments decide to pay grants for the provision of particular activities, such as to provide unprofitable but 'socially necessary' services, to hold down fares or to support unprofitable investments in recognition of the social benefits they offer. In contrast, implicit subsidy is said to arise in three sets of circumstances:

a where transport infrastructure is provided and paid for by the government, and charges for its use do not cover the total cost of its provision;
b where transport is accorded favourable tax treatment (e.g., passenger transport is typically exempt from value added tax, or charged at a lower rate than in the rest of the economy); and
c where transport gives rise to substantial external costs, for which there is no corresponding revenue stream.

However, an alternative interpretation is to regard subsidy as arising wherever price fails to cover marginal social cost. Hence, rather than considering the balance of total social cost with total revenues, this interpretation requires the consideration of the relationship between marginal social cost and price. The first interpretation is often seen as important politically and in the consideration of equity issues, but it is the second that is appropriate in the consideration of economic efficiency. In transport, where both infrastructure and operations are typically characterised by major economies of scale, and where many externalities, such as congestion and noise, are important and strongly non-linear, these two interpretations are likely to produce quite different findings, evidence of which is provided in Nash et al. (2002).

Another important distinction to make is between the pricing of infrastructure and the pricing of services. One can view the transport system as being made up of the infrastructure and the services that are provided on that infrastructure, and one can identify the transport user (i.e. the traveller), the infrastructure provider and the transport operator (i.e. companies offering services over the infrastructure). In the case of private motoring, the user deals directly with the infrastructure provider, but in most other cases, the user deals with the operator and the operator deals with the infrastructure provider. In some cases, for instance vertically integrated railways, a single organisation provides both, but in road, air and water transport vertical separation is the norm and it is becoming more common in the rail sector, especially in Europe.

As noted above, traditionally transport pricing has been based, as has pricing in other sectors of the economy, on full cost recovery. Since the time of Dupuit (1844) it has been recognised that transport infrastructure is characterised by indivisibilities and economies of scale such that there is a conflict between marginal cost pricing and full cost recovery; Hotelling (1938) provides a formal argument for setting railway rates based on marginal cost, even though this will require provision of government subsidy. More recently, Mohring and Turvey (1975) pointed to a similar cost characteristic in the case of scheduled transport services, arising from the fact that when traffic rises, either larger vehicles or longer trains (which themselves enjoy economies of scale) are operated, or more frequent services result. But these more frequent services mean that existing users enjoy reduced waiting times or reduced schedule delay (i.e. the ability to get a service closer to the desired departure time). Jansson (1984) showed how the widespread nature of this feature of transport systems affects optimal pricing and leads to a widespread first best case for subsidy.

But it has also long been recognised that provision of subsidy has costs as well. Firstly, it may lead to reduced efficiency by leading to perverse incentives if managers believe that increased costs will always result in increased subsidy. The risk of this may be minimised by awarding contracts for subsidised services by means of competitive tendering, as first proposed by Chadwick (1859). But secondly, the raising of government revenue through taxes involves deadweight losses due to the distorting effect of taxes on the economy (Dodgson and Topham, 1986).

Thus there has been a longstanding interest in how to achieve full cost recovery, or at least a higher level of cost recovery than implied by pure marginal social cost pricing, at least cost in terms of distortions to demand. Dupuit (1844) argued for price discrimination according to willingness to pay, but where the most that can be done is to identify different products with different cost and demand characteristics, this gives way to Ramsey pricing (Ramsey, 1927). That is the argument that the percentage deviation between price and marginal cost should be inversely related to the price elasticity of demand, with greater excesses of price over marginal cost the lower the elasticity and therefore the less the impact on demand. This principle was rehabilitated in a famous paper by Baumol and Bradford (1970).

More recently, the case for reforming transport pricing has, in general, been grounded in the perceived potential for the price mechanism to serve as a tool for tackling the increasingly visible problems of congestion and environmental pollution. Congestion is perhaps the most significant transport problem of our time, resulting in journey-time delays and unreliability, over-crowding and scheduling problems. For example, it is estimated that, in Europe, costs associated with road congestion – roads being the most congested of the transport modes – amount to €70 billion, approximately 1% of its overall GDP (Nash, 2003a). In the top 85 US urban areas the estimate is some $63 billion – comprising 3.7 billion hours of travel delay and 2.3 billion gallons of wasted fuel (TTI, 2007). Furthermore, the environmental pollution costs, taken together with external accident costs, of road transport in Europe were found to be €122 billion, approximately 1.6% of Europe's GDP (Nash, 2003a).

The argument that road congestion forms an externality, whereby an additional road user slows the traffic and thus imposes costs on all other road users, and that this could be corrected through the pricing system, goes right back to the writing of Pigou (1920) and Knight (1924) in the 1920s. It was formalised in a classic article by Walters (1961). Interest in Pigovian pricing as a solution to pollution externalities is generally more recent, but was suggested as the basis of transport infrastructure pricing in the European Union in a Green Paper in 1995 (Commission of European Communities (CEC), 1995) and formally adopted in a subsequent White Paper (CEC, 1998).

The argument is essentially this. When car users, rail operators or the operators of other vehicles, aircraft or vessels decide to travel additional kilometres or to make additional trips they impose additional costs on themselves, on the infrastructure provider, on other users and on the rest of society. The costs to themselves are referred to as private costs, whereas the costs to other users and to the rest of society are referred to as 'external' costs. External costs are said to arise when the social or economic activities of one agent have an impact on the welfare of another agent, without that impact having been taken into account by the first agent.

The theory provides, at first glance, some clear principles that might be applied in order to bring together these private and external costs, a process referred to by economists as the internalisation of external costs. Essentially setting prices equal to short run marginal costs (that is, the additional costs to society associated with an additional kilometre travelled or an additional trip made, given that the capacity of the transport network is held constant). By placing monetary values upon externalities then they can be incorporated into the pricing mechanism by means of direct charges or subsidies; in this way they will then be taken into account by all economic agents.

Three components of cost, associated with the addition of extra traffic to the existing infrastructure, must be measured for the principle of short run marginal social cost pricing to be taken forward in the context of transport infrastructure (Nash and Matthews, 2005). The first is the cost imposed by additional use on the infrastructure provider. This comprises additional maintenance and renewals costs plus any additional operating costs. The second component is the marginal cost imposed on other infrastructure users, in terms of delays, congestion, accidents and opportunity costs (perhaps more commonly referred to as scarcity costs), on those modes where there is a physical limit and once all the slots are taken no one else can get one. The third element is the cost imposed outside the transport system and that is mainly environmental cost, but some elements of other costs such as accidents, for instance where these are borne in part by the police or health service and not recovered from users. Note that it is only environmental costs related to vehicle use that are relevant in this context; environmental costs related to infrastructure provision are relevant for investment decisions but not (directly) for pricing policy. (There is an indirect effect. If environmental costs limit infrastructure provision, for instance in cities or in environmentally sensitive areas, this will raise congestion and scarcity costs and thus raise price.)

Prices which reflect the additional infrastructure and external costs will act as signals to travellers about the 'social' costs associated with their additional travel. They will then base their demand decisions – whether, where, when, how and how far to travel – upon these price signals. In fact, prices fulfil several functions in parallel. In addition to acting as cost signals, the price mechanism is the best way to ensure that a limited supply of a good is made accessible to those who value it most. By raising prices until the total demand equals the available quantity, the consumers with the highest willingness to pay for the good receive the good. Also, in competitive markets firms will only succeed if their prices are kept as low as possible; otherwise their competitors will take their markets. In this way the price mechanism provides all producers with incentives to develop cost-reducing production techniques.

In recent years, the response of governments to the above problems has increasingly been to place greater weight on economic instruments as a way to tackle them, by giving transport users appropriate incentives to modify their behaviour. There are, however, numerous reasons why the simple 'textbook' approach to marginal cost pricing, as applied to transport, may not be optimal in practice. These reasons are comprehensively identified by Rothengatter (2003), but may be summarised as follows:

a measurement is complex;
b equity is ignored;
c dynamic effects, including investment decisions and technology choice, are ignored;
d financing issues are ignored;
e institutional issues are ignored;
f price distortions elsewhere in the economy are ignored;
g the administrative costs associated with implementation may not always be justified by the benefits.

All of these criticisms are well established in the literature and are, in a sense, undeniable. For some authors, the conclusion is that they render a policy based on the application of marginal social cost pricing unimplementable, whilst for others – the current authors included – they simply represent a series of issues that must be taken into account when taking forward the implementation of the theory. Our responses to these criticisms are outlined below, but a more detailed exposition is set out in Nash (2003b).

Firstly, it is undeniable that measurement of short run marginal social cost is complex. The nature of most external costs is that they are situation-specific. That is, the external cost associated with a particular vehicle, on a particular piece of infrastructure, in a particular place at a particular time is likely to be specific to that set of circumstances. The same vehicle, on the same infrastructure, in the same place but at a different time is likely to give rise to a different level of external cost. Similarly, the same vehicle at the same time, in the same place but on a different piece of infrastructure is again likely to give rise to a different level of external cost. This makes the accurate estimation of external cost a very case-specific task. In theory, a policy to internalise external costs would require cost estimates to be derived for every set of circumstances that exists, but a proposal to undertake such an enormous exercise would almost certainly lead policy-makers to abandon the policy itself. Instead, it is likely to be more fruitful to undertake case-specific cost estimation exercises wherever possible, and then to use those estimates to form an understanding of the ways in which costs vary from one set of circumstances to another. With this understanding, it should become possible to make reasonable approximations of costs in circumstances where detailed cost estimates are not available and where it is not possible, for whatever reason, for them to be undertaken. A great deal of research has been undertaken, much of it sponsored by the European Commission in recent years (see, for example, Nash and Matthews, 2005; and CE Delft, 2008).

In other words there is no reason for measurement problems to hold up moves towards marginal social cost pricing. In any event it is hard to argue that, were marginal social cost the right concept to use in pricing, measuring something else instead of using the best estimate possible would be a sensible approach.

Equity is an issue with any pricing system. The general approach in economics is to examine the impact of a policy decision on different income groups, using distributional weights reflecting the marginal social utility of changes in welfare for each group. But the more popular view of equity in this context is that individuals should pay for the benefits they receive. In practice, this might encourage price discrimination as a way of boosting cost recovery, but there is invariably a degree of averaging.

The issue of dynamic impacts is sometimes taken to justify long run marginal cost pricing rather than short. This may give better incentives to users regarding decisions which will have lagged impacts on demand (such as home or work location, sourcing of inputs, location of distribution depots etc.), and also on producers, who will be directly compensated for any investments they undertake. On the other hand, indivisibilities make the estimation of meaningful estimates of long run marginal cost difficult in the transport sector and time lags may mean that pricing according to long run marginal cost leads to under or over use of assets for prolonged periods of time. An alternative is to charge short run marginal cost but to smooth out fluctuations caused by foreseen changes in capacity.

The financing and institutional issues reflect the most common objection to marginal cost pricing – that it does not recover total cost. However, this conclusion may depend on the level of aggregation at which the comparison of costs and revenue is made. At the aggregate level, pricing to recover total cost typically implies big increases in rail and other public transport charges, together with reductions in road taxation, whereas marginal cost pricing often implies the reverse. Most transport infrastructure is subject to increasing returns to scale, which means if capacity is anything like optimal, then marginal cost pricing will not recover the total cost of the system. On the other hand, the cost of land and property acquisition limit expansion, particularly in urban areas, so efficient supply of capacity in urban areas will typically still involve significant congestion and consequently high charges for the use of infrastructure. So the likelihood is that marginal cost pricing will imply substantial surpluses of revenue over costs on urban roads, whereas on rural roads and much public transport, there will be deficits. Nevertheless, there remain two important questions. One is whether the whole package of effects satisfies government budget constraints. Does it provide enough finance, or are there other means of supplementing it if necessary? There is some evidence that typically surpluses in urban areas are so big that budget constraints are not a problem (Roy, 2002). But then there is a second issue, and that is whether a system whereby urban road users greatly cross-subsidise rural road users and public transport users is perceived as acceptable, both in terms of equity and in terms of influence on locational choice.

If for any of these reasons the budgetary outcome of marginal social cost pricing is seen as unacceptable, then of course we have to depart from marginal cost pricing, but as noted above there are well established principles governing the most efficient ways of meeting budget constraints.

Next we note the important requirement that prices equal marginal social costs elsewhere in the economy. Whilst the failure of this assumption might lead to some general adjustment to prices in the transport sector, it is most critical in the case of products with high cross elasticities of demand with that in question. Thus when considering the pricing of a particular mode of transport, it is divergences of price from marginal social cost on competing or complementary modes that will be most critical. The most common issue raised in the literature is the failure to charge road transport its external cost, leading to a case for reducing the price of rail and other public transport below marginal cost (Glaister and Lewis, 1978). Again there are well-recognised principles as to how to allow for this in so-called second best pricing and we return to this issue in the section on public transport below.

Finally we note the issue of complexity and administration costs. As noted above, accurate marginal social cost pricing would require prices which varied in time and space. Whilst this is the norm on some modes, such as air transport and long distance rail services, it is less common for urban public transport (where simplicity is attractive to the public and reduces the costs of collecting fares), and, particularly, use of roads, where relatively sophisticated technology is required to vary charges in this way and there are considerable costs as well as great public opposition to its introduction. Again, we return to this issue in the section on roads.

In conclusion, then, it is the view of the current authors that whilst considerations such as budget constraints, equity, institutional issues, simplicity and price distortions elsewhere in the economy lead to a need to depart from pure marginal social cost pricing, they do not change the position that the measurement of marginal social cost is the correct starting point in the development of any efficient pricing policy. For this reason, the phrase 'marginal social cost-based pricing' has entered the lexicon, to summarise the philosophy being proposed (Verhoef, 2001). It seems clear from a range of modelling exercises (Proost and Van Dender, 1999; Tavasszy et al., 2004; Kohler et al., 2008) that, provided that the revenues generated were efficiently used, the economic impacts of efficient pricing would overall be positive.

ROAD PRICING

Experience with road pricing may be divided into urban and inter-urban initiatives. Urban road pricing involves charging road users for their use of road space within defined parts of specific urban areas and/or during a particular time period, and there are a limited number of examples across the world. Inter-urban pricing involves charging road users for their use of inter-urban roads, typically highways of a strategic or trunk nature. Inter-urban road pricing includes the traditional tolling of privately-owned and operated roads, where tolls are principally associated with highway financing, as well as user charges for the publicly-owned parts of the inter-urban road network imposed by government.

Urban road pricing may take a number of different forms. *Point pricing* involves the levying of a price to pass a point on a road, not unlike conventional *toll systems*. However, a price on a single road is likely to encourage traffic to divert to avoid it and so most point pricing systems involve *cordon charging* (or toll rings) in which a series of charging points are established at all entries to a given area. This concept can be extended to a series of concentric cordons, or cells, or a cordon combined with radial screen lines. *Area charging* (or area licensing) is another variant of cordon charging, in which the price is levied to use a vehicle within a defined area, rather than just to enter it. This will also control vehicle journeys wholly within the cordon, which are unaffected by cordon charging (and might as a result increase).

The first such scheme in the world was introduced in Singapore in 1975. Initially, this was an Area Licensing Scheme to reduce congestion in the city centre. Drivers had to purchase licences for a day or a month to allow them to enter the defined area between 0730 and 1015. The initial charge was S$3; this was raised to S$4 in 1976. Vehicles with four or more occupants were exempt. Enforcement was by manual inspection. Subsequent modifications involved extensions to the evening peak, the working day and Saturdays, to a set of charging points on expressways, and to all cars however many occupants they had. Different charges were levied for different types of vehicle. In 1998 the Area Licensing Scheme was replaced by an Electronic Road Pricing Scheme: 97% of the 700,000 vehicles in Singapore were fitted with on board units, in which smart cards were inserted. Gantries at the *Area Licensing Scheme* entry points and expressway charging points were equipped to identify, interrogate, charge and, if necessary for enforcement, photograph, all vehicles passing. Charges are now levied per crossing rather than per day, and vary by time of day and vehicle type. Charges are revised quarterly to maintain speeds at between 20 km/h and 30 km/h in the city centre, and 45 km/h and 60 km/h on expressways. As a result charges are lower than with the Area Licensing Scheme for much of the day and have been waived on Saturdays. A more detailed assessment of the scheme and its impacts is set out in Chin (2009).

In 1986 Bergen, Norway's second largest city, was the first city in Europe to introduce a toll ring (or cordon) charging system. It was introduced with the objective of raising the finances required to accelerate the implementation of a wide-ranging programme of transport investment. The system charges all vehicles (other than buses in regular service) a flat fee for entering the city's central business district and operates between 6.00am and 10.00pm Monday–Friday. Toll rings were subsequently also introduced in Oslo and Trondheim. As in Bergen, the main objective is to raise revenue so charges are set according to revenue goals, though both Oslo and Trondheim use electronic toll collection and in Trondheim tolls are differentiated by time of day. A more detailed assessment of the schemes and their impacts is given in Ieromonacho et al. (2006).

In 2003, London introduced an area licensing scheme known as the London Congestion Charge. At first this covered an 8-square-mile area of Central London. Subsequently, in 2007, the charging zone was approximately doubled by including an area west of the original zone but that western extension was removed from operation in 2011. Drivers wishing to enter the zone between 7:00am and 6:00pm, Monday to Friday are required to pay the Congestion Charge. The charge was £5 per day when first implemented but has since risen to £10. However, there are a number of exemptions which apply to motorbikes, mopeds, taxis, buses, emergency vehicles, vehicles using alternative fuels and vehicles whose drivers are disabled, whilst residents of the zone receive a 90% discount. It is possible to pay the charge in advance on a daily, weekly, monthly or annual basis, either by phone, mail, internet or at retail outlets. Entry into the charging zone is indicated by a mix of street signs and pavement markings and enforcement is via automatic number plate recognition (ANPR), facilitated by a network of fixed and mobile cameras. A fine is levied in cases of non-payment, though this is reduced if paid within 14 days. Implementation costs in the first two years were £190 million – more than twice the amount expected – and annual operating expenses are approximately £130 million. The system has covered its capital and operating expenses every year since its inception, revenues amounting to some £268 million in the year ending June 2008 for example. All proceeds are ring-fenced for spending on improving transport within Greater London. For a review see Santos and Fraser (2006).

The most recent large international city to introduce congestion charging was Stockholm. A system of cordon-based variable pricing was deployed first on a trial basis from January 2006 to July 2006, before it was made permanent in August 2007 following a close-run public referendum in September 2006. The system charges vehicles registered in Sweden when they pass one of 18 'control points' entering or exiting the cordon (based on the CBD) between 6:30am and 6:30pm, Monday–Friday. The rates vary from 10 SEK (US$1.50) to 15 SEK (US$2.25) depending on the time of day for crossing a control point, up to a maximum charge per vehicle per day of 60 SEK (US$9). Exemptions from the charge are awarded to motorcycles, buses, taxis, certain alternative fuel vehicles (ECO-cars, LPG, and electric), emergency vehicles, those with disabled drivers and foreign-registered vehicles. There are no resident discounts, except for residents of one land-locked island, from which mainland Sweden is accessible only via the cordoned area. Enforcement is via ANPR, using digital imaging cameras mounted on overhead gantries. The costs of implementation included a 1.3 billion SEK (US $180 million) investment for the tolling system plus a massive 2 billion SEK (US $280 million) investment in related public transport improvements. A more detailed assessment of the scheme and its impacts is provided in Eliasson (2009).

At the level of the European Union, policy regarding infrastructure pricing for road transport largely concerns road freight traffic; the issue of pricing for the use of roads by the private car being an issue left to individual member states. Policy was initially, in the mid-1990s, aimed at limiting competitive problems within the road freight sector caused by the existence of very different methods and levels of pricing for infrastructure use in different member states. For example, vehicles licensed in a country with low annual licence duty plus supplementary tolls may have an unfair competitive advantage when competing with a vehicle licensed in a country with high licence duty and no supplementary tolls. Thus kilometre charges were permitted to be levied in a non-discriminatory way on heavy goods vehicles wherever they were registered.

Directive 2006/38/EC, revises the Eurovignette regime and represents the current legal position on European road goods vehicle pricing (CEC, 2006). The 2006 Directive allows the toll to be applied to all HGVs (vehicles weighing over 3.5 tonnes) as from 2012, replacing the 12 tonnes limit applicable until then. It is applied to the trans-European network (TEN) but permits application of pricing to other roads as well. It is also recommended that 'revenues from tolls or user charges should be used for the maintenance of the infrastructure concerned and for the transport sector as a whole, in the interest of the balanced and sustainable development of transport networks' (European Parliament, 2006).

In terms of differentiation, the 2006 Directive provides for variations according to a number of factors such as distance travelled, infrastructure type and location vehicle type and time of day. Thus prices can be differentiated to reflect the key variables determining marginal social cost. However, the legislation still ties the average charge to the average cost of building and maintaining the infrastructure, excluding externalities (except in the case of sensitive areas such as the Alps, where a mark-up can be applied and used to finance alternative transport infrastructure). Although proposals have been brought forward to permit charging for externalities in the level as well as the structure of prices, and a handbook produced on how to measure the relevant external costs (CE Delft, 2008), it has been impossible so far to get agreement on their implementation.

In parallel with these developments in EU-wide transport infrastructure pricing policy, a number of EU member states have been examining proposals for national schemes for the pricing of heavy goods vehicles. Indeed, Austria in 2004, Germany in 2005 and the Czech Republic in 2007 have introduced their own distance-based road pricing systems for heavy goods vehicles using their national motorway networks. However, these are somewhat removed from the thrust of European policy with regard to the internalisation of external cost. Instead, they are based on infrastructure capital, maintenance and operational costs and might be seen as an alternative means of roads finance, though they do incorporate some price differentiation according to environmental factors. Ironically, the one European country to have introduced charges for HGVs on all roads which explicitly include environmental costs is Switzerland. Part of these charges is earmarked for investment in new rail infrastructure (Nash, Menaz and Matthews, 2008).

In the US a number of road pricing initiatives aimed at tackling congestion and raising revenue have been implemented over the past two decades. Legislation in California to attract private capital to investments in new or previously programmed highway improvement projects led, in 1995, to the State Route 91 (SR 91) Express Lanes operating company implementing a variable toll schedule, which they labeled as 'Value Pricing'. At approximately the same time, the Federal government initiated funding for a number of demonstration projects focused on using pricing to tackle road congestion, which, in 1998, it renamed as the 'Value Pricing Pilot Program'. Under these initiatives, the US has – in particular – led the way in the variable pricing of lanes, whereby variable prices are charged on separated lanes within a highway, such as express-toll lanes or high-occupancy toll (HOT) lanes.

On SR91, the variable tolls on the express lanes range from $1.25 during off-peak times to as much as $9.80 on Friday afternoons. Adjustments are made to the tolls every 3 months based on traffic observed over the previous 3-month period. It is reported that speeds on the express lanes are 60–65 mph, as compared with speeds on the free lanes of 15–20 mph, and that, in the peak periods, the express lanes can carry almost twice the number of vehicles as the free lanes.

The San Diego HOT lanes, which operate on an 8-mile stretch of I-15 north of San Diego, are typical of HOT lanes elsewhere. They allow high-occupancy vehicles (public transport vehicles and cars containing two or more persons) to travel free, whilst single-occupant vehicles may access the lanes if they pay a variable toll ($0.50–$8.00). When it was opened in 1998, the San Diego scheme became the world's first fully dynamic variable-pricing operation. The toll varies based on the congestion level, which is analysed every 6 minutes, with tolls being modified as necessary. The scheme is seen as having been a clear success, and is being extended to a length of 20 miles, planned to open in 2012. HOT lanes have also been introduced in Houston and Minneapolis, and express lanes in Denver, though with less-clear cut success than appears to have been the case in San Diego. Also, variation in the pricing of existing tolled facilities has been introduced under the auspices of Value Pricing, such as for bridges in the New York/New Jersey area and in Fort Meyers, Florida. For a comprehensive assessment of the range of US experience, see Jackson et al. (2008).

RAIL INFRASTRUCTURE CHARGES

In the very early days of the rail industry in Britain, a variety of operators was allowed on the same track, but this was found to be unsafe, and from then on, vertically integrated rail companies providing both infrastructure and train operations became the norm. In some cases, for instance in North America, operators have received limited rights to run over their neighbours' tracks. But the issue of rail infrastructure charges only came to the fore with the policy of separating infrastructure from operations, devised as part of an attempt to introduce competition in rail operations in Europe, and certain other countries such as Australia.

In Europe, policy on railway infrastructure charging is enshrined in Directive 2001/14, on allocation of railway infrastructure capacity and levying of charges. In summary, the directive determines that charges must be based on 'costs directly incurred as a result of operating the train service'. They may include:

1 Scarcity, although where a section of track is defined as having a scarcity problem, the infrastructure manager must examine proposals to relieve that scarcity, and undertake them unless they are shown, on the basis of cost benefit analysis, not to be worthwhile;
2 Environmental costs, but these must not lead to a rise in the average level of charge unless they are levied on other modes;
3 Recovery of the costs of specific investments where these are worthwhile and could not otherwise be funded;
4 Discounts but only where justified by costs; large operators may not use their market power to get discounts;
5 Reservation charges for scarce capacity, which must be paid whether the capacity is used or not;
6 Non-discriminatory mark-ups, but these must not exclude segments of traffic which could cover direct cost.
7 Specific time-limited subsidy schemes are permitted to offset the effects of a failure to charge appropriately on other modes.

It seems from the list of elements that may be included in the charges that 'the direct cost of operating the service' is to be interpreted as short run marginal social cost.

In recent empirical studies of wear and tear costs it was calculated that charges based on marginal cost would cover only 20–30% of the total maintenance and renewal costs (Wheat et al., 2009). Most other costs of the infrastructure manager appear to be largely fixed, and although charges for congestion and scarcity might significantly increase cost recovery, it appears likely that pure marginal cost pricing will fall far short of covering total cost.

As noted above, where a higher level of cost recovery is required, the standard economic argument would justify mark-ups above marginal cost targeted more on markets where demand is less responsive to changes in price, such that the price elasticity of demand is low, as it is in these markets that the mark-ups will have less impact on demand. However, such mark-ups still give operators an incentive to cut services below what would exist with pure marginal cost pricing. The generally advocated alternative is two part tariffs, comprising a variable part equal to (or based on) marginal cost and a fixed part needed to achieve the cost recovery target. The attraction of two part tariffs is that the fixed part may be related to ability to pay, but leave the operator free to raise the necessary cash in the way that loses them the least traffic, whilst the variable part may be equal to marginal cost. The difficulty is that, if the fixed part is the result of a tariff, rather than negotiated on the basis of ability to pay, it almost inevitably favours large operators against small. This is not a problem with franchised services, provided that whoever wins the franchise pays the same fixed charge.

Nash and Matthews (2005) – partly updated in ITF (2008) – shows the wide range of practices in rail infrastructure charging within Europe regarding which cost elements are covered by the charge and the form of the charge, which ranges from a simple charge per gross tonne kilometre in Finland, to a mix of reservation charges and charges per train kilometre differentiated by type of infrastructure

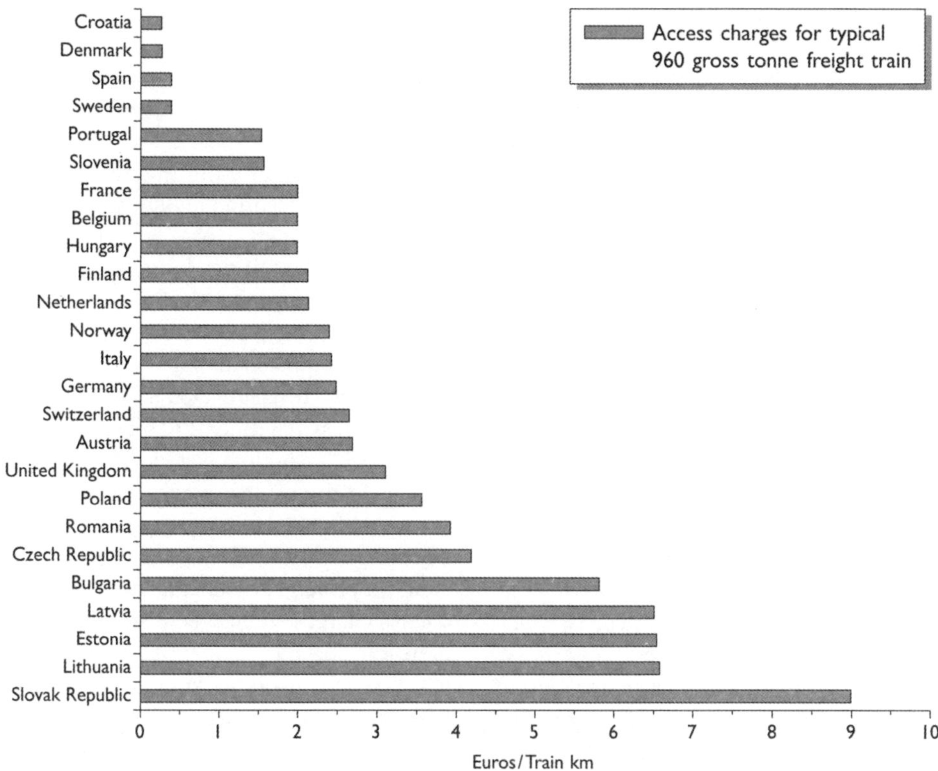

Figure 17.1 Typical freight access charges, € per train km in 2008

Source: ITF, 2008

and time of day in France. It appears that a wide range of approaches to this issue persist, which may lead to confusing and contradictory price signals for operators of international trains.

Figure 17.1 illustrates the variety of average levels of charge found for a typical freight train. It will be seen that these vary enormously from a fraction of a euro per train kilometre in Greece, Denmark, Spain and Sweden, to over €6 in Estonia, Latvia and Lithuania and €9 in Slovakia. There is a clear pattern of high charges for freight traffic in Central and Eastern Europe, and there are concerns that these may even exceed the 'stand alone' cost of the necessary infrastructure for freight operations in order to subsidise infrastructure needed for passenger services. Importantly, Directive 2001/14 is vague in relation to maximum charges, and whether it is permissible for them to exceed even stand alone costs. It should be noted also that further changes to the charges have already been announced for future years, including substantial increases in France.

Typical charges for different types of passenger train exhibit as much variety as in freight, but the pattern is rather different, with some of the Central and Eastern European countries that have high freight charges having very low passenger charges which implies cross subsidies of passenger businesses by freight ones. The other point not revealed in average figures is the very high charges that may apply for new infrastructure, such as high-speed lines (UIC, 2007), bridges or tunnels. These are up to €16 per kilometre for the busiest high-speed lines in France, and much more than that for the Channel Tunnel and the first high speed line in Britain. It is well understood that governments will want to recoup much of the cost of such projects from users and this is unproblematic if it does not greatly impact on rail market share, but there is evidence that on routes where the rail market position is less strong, high charges can damage rail market share so much as to destroy the case for the investment. Adler et al. (2008) find that the social benefits of high-speed rail are much greater if marginal cost pricing is used to promote efficient mode split than if very high charges are levied, leading to poorer utilisation of new infrastructure capacity. Moreover, at low infrastructure charges, a franchised operator can afford to pay a substantial lump sum towards infrastructure costs (or as a premium for the franchise, which can then be used to help pay for the infrastructure). This is a more efficient way of achieving this result than by high variable charges which discourage provision of high levels of service. But it is highly problematic when open access entry is permitted, as it may be judged discriminatory, and open access entry will in any case reduce the profitability of existing services and therefore the ability of the train operator to pay for a franchise.

Thus there is a real dilemma as to how to reconcile open access entry with recovering a high proportion of infrastructure costs from users. The same issue of course applied to the high charges for freight trains in some countries noted above. Vertical separation with open access competition makes it far more difficult to recover infrastructure costs by carefully differentiating prices to reflect willingness to pay in the final transport market; the ability of the infrastructure manager to differentiate according to willingness to pay is much less than that of the train operator who deals direct with the ultimate customer. The difficulty in reconciling open access competition, efficient infrastructure pricing and high infrastructure cost recovery is at the heart of the problem with EU rail policy in countries where governments cannot or will not make a significant contribution towards rail infrastructure costs.

CHARGES FOR AIR AND WATER

Pricing for infrastructure use in aviation is comprised of charges for air traffic control (or en route charges) and charges for airport use. Charges for air traffic control are generally organised according to the principle of a 'club', whereby the air traffic service companies allocate the full cost of the service to the airlines which use the service, according to accounting principles set by ICAO. Prices reflect the estimated average costs, including capital costs, disaggregated according to the type of aircraft and the flight distance. They are strictly bound to a cost ceiling, with any financial surplus being reimbursed. It has been speculated that 'pricing to take account of environmental pollution at high altitudes could in principle be integrated in air traffic control charges – however, institutional relationships and transactional costs may mean that kerosene taxation would achieve internalisation of these externalities more effectively' (Nash et al., 2001).

The most important aspect of airport use at major airports is runway capacity, as it dominates the determination of overall airport capacity. Airport slots are defined as time units of runway capacity which allow for one aircraft to either land or take-off. The allocation and management of these slots is, therefore, extremely important. The present system tends to be governed by a mix of administrative and pricing measures.

Firstly, the allocation of slots is based on a process developed under the auspices of the International Air Transport Association (IATA), founded on the highly controversial principle of 'Grandfather Rights'. This principle of historic precedence bestows rights upon incumbent airlines to be granted slots in the next timetable on the basis of them having had those slots in the previous period. It was designed in an era when there were few if any capacity constraints on airports but has survived, with much criticism but only relatively minor modification, to the present day.

Secondly, pricing of airport use is comprised of a range of fees and charges:

- landing fees – according to maximum take-off weight of aircraft;
- transfer and non-transfer passenger departing fees;
- parking fees;
- freight loading/unloading charges;
- security and control charges for passengers and freight;
- night charges – some airports charge higher tariffs for night-time movements and others lower tariffs, whilst other airports shut down at night;
- noise fees – at some airports, such as Schiphol Amsterdam, Belgium, Charles de Gaulle Paris, many of the German airports, Fumicino Rome, Arlanda Stockholm, Zurich, Heathrow and Gatwick;
- peak fees – at some airports, such as Heathrow and Gatwick, Schiphol Amsterdam, Dublin, Hamburg, Athens and Madrid, but tend to be very low;
- aircraft engine emission charges – at some airports, such as in Switzerland and Sweden.

Calculation of these various charges and fees is thought to be based on the allocation of fixed and variable airport costs and, hence, on the principle of average cost. This is the case even where noise or emission-related charges have been introduced, with these charge components serving as environmental-based indicators on which to base part of the allocation of airport costs; as distinct from charges that are based on an estimate of the marginal external environmental cost.

As with rail infrastructure, pricing is therefore not generally used to try to achieve an efficient allocation of scarce capacity. It is useful to make a clear distinction between the two problems arising from shortages in capacity – congestion and scarcity (National Economic Research Associates, 2004). Congestion at airports represents the expected delays resulting from the transmission of delays from one aircraft to another. The use of an additional slot at an airport reduces the airport manager's ability to recover from an incident and increases the probability of delays. This becomes worse at high levels of capacity utilisation, since there is a lack of spare capacity to recover from any delays. Congestion costs are the costs associated with these expected delays. In this way, the consumption of additional capacity and the resulting congestion at the airport imposes delay costs on airlines and, ultimately, passengers.

Scarcity at airports, on the other hand, represents the inability of an airline to obtain the slot they want in order to operate a particular service. The inability of the airline to provide the service it estimates will best meet its customers' demands represents a cost to society equal to the social value of that service, where social value comprises profit to the airline, consumer surplus to the passengers and net benefits to third parties – so-called 'externalities' – which may be positive or negative and which, for instance, include changes in pollution levels.

A number of proposals to reform the process for allocating slots and the weight-based approach to pricing airport use, so that they address the increasing problems of scarcity and congestion at airports, have been examined. Slots could be priced to better reflect their value and opportunity cost, auctioned in a way that allocates them to the optimum bidder who can best utilise the resource, or traded on a secondary market following either an administrative or market-based primary allocation. Alternatively, some combination of administrative and pricing mechanisms might be used. Yet few of these alternatives have been tested in real-world conditions, despite research and investigation into the subject dating back 40 years. In their seminal paper, Carlin and Park (1970) computed marginal congestion costs for New York LaGuardia airport. Even ignoring all other externalities, they reasoned that it was unlikely that airlines would be willing or able to pay the implied marginal cost-based landing fees. The indivisible nature of airport capacity means that marginal cost pricing may not lead to full cost recovery, so a number of authors have explored the application of Ramsey Pricing, with a financial break-even constraint, as a means of setting landing fees (Morrison, 1987; and Oum and Zhang, 1990). Daniel (1995) examined first-best peak-load congestion pricing in the context of large hub airports – using Minneapolis-St Paul airport as his case study – and found that congestion pricing would improve capacity utilisation by spreading the arrival and departure schedules over a longer peak thus reducing delays and future capacity requirements. Specifically, he concluded that existing capacity could serve 30% more traffic under congestion pricing, at the same average social cost per aircraft as applies today. However, the spreading of traffic would clearly have network wide effects, which would need to be considered. Furthermore, Brueckner (2001) argued that Daniel's work may have overestimated the appropriate congestion fees, as airlines might in fact internalise some delay, particularly at airports where one or two major carriers dominate.

Differentiation of slot prices may be a good way to reallocate the demand for slots from peak to off-peak periods, hence reducing scarcity at peak periods. It would, in all likelihood, lead to some prioritisation amongst different air services, but an optimal allocation of slots would require prices to be estimated with a high degree of accuracy. In actuality, it would be difficult to calculate what prices to charge. One proposal is for the airport authority to attempt to calculate directly the opportunity cost involved, though the scale and complexity of this calculation would be overwhelming. Alternatively, a process of iteration towards equilibrating prices may be a pragmatic means of arriving at appropriate price levels, but the time it might take to arrive at these prices, and the implied distortions along the way, are causes for serious concern.

Alternatively, there is a sizeable body of literature relating to the use of auctions for allocating slots (e.g., Grether et al., 1989; DotEcon, 2002; Nilsson, 2003). There are many different types of auctions to choose amongst. Nilsson argues that the sealed bid, one price auction – a sealed process where the highest bid is accepted at the lowest bid price – is the most efficient method of allocation as it allowed bidders to reveal their true valuation of the slots, and did not destroy their profits as the lowest bid determined the price. However, there is considerable concern regarding the practicability of designing an auction for airport slots, given the different complexities that most agree would have to be allowed for. Probably as a result of this concern, there is little actual experience of auctions in this setting.

The use to which the revenue generated from differential pricing and/or auctions would be put to, is a very important issue. This depends on who receives the funds, which in turn depends on who is judged to 'own' the slots – governments, airports or airlines. Using the price mechanism as a means of rationing demand would involve the transfer of economic rent from the airlines to the airports (or, in the case of a tax, to the government). In an environment where many airlines are already less profitable than airports, a further transfer in this direction is likely to be strongly resisted.

There is a strong case for a secondary market in slot allocation. After the primary allocation of slots via administrative forms such as grandfathering, slots could then be redistributed among airlines in a secondary market through barter trade or monetary trading, as has been the case at four of the busiest US airports (Starkie, 1994). This may ensure that all slots are efficiently allocated to the appropriate users; however, the market needs to be regulated to ensure against market concentration concerns.

Pricing in the maritime sector has received relatively little attention in terms of public policy and research. Current pricing practices appear to have been based on empirical intuition and past trends. In fact, Meersman et al. (2002) argue that outlining a typology of current port pricing schemes is not possible due to the complex, non-transparent and archaic systems in existence at present. In general it is understood that tariff levels do not reflect actual costs incurred by port operations and do not recover costs, Furthermore, the varying ownership and investment arrangements of individual ports contribute to some ports experiencing significant overcapacity and others, lacking in infrastructure, experiencing significant congestion.

Inland shipping charges, paid by inland vessels, are generally based on harbour and lock dues. The extent to which these reflect and/or cover construction or maintenance costs is unclear, but evidence suggests that the charges are often below cost (see, for example, Psaraftis, 1998). Some research into the possible benefits of pricing reform in the maritime sector does exist (e.g. Heggie, 1974; Haralambides, 2001), and some efforts have been made at the policy level (e.g. CEC, 1997; Swahn, 2002), but the process is at a much earlier stage of development than for the other modes.

PRICING TRANSPORT SERVICES

For freight transport services, pricing has typically been in the hands of commercial organisations, with the exception in some cases of rail freight services, and government intervention has been limited to dealing with two specific issues – controlling monopoly power and providing services to more remote areas at a price which did not disadvantage them. The trend in recent years has been to remove regulation of freight prices, following the deregulation brought about by the Staggers Act in the US in 1980, which has generally been regarded as a great success (Winston, 2006).

Public transport fares have been the subject of much more policy concern. The starting point for the determination of optimal public transport fares is, as with infrastructure pricing, the identification of marginal social cost. If we took a very short run view, we might estimate marginal social cost given the services currently running. In this case we would estimate marginal social cost as any increase in operating costs, for instance due to delays on boarding, plus the impact of additional crowding on other passengers. But, unlike infrastructure, services may be quickly adjusted, so it seems more sensible to base pricing on a somewhat longer run version of marginal social cost pricing, which allows for the marginal social cost of operating a larger vehicle or longer train, or the marginal social cost of increasing service frequency less the benefit of this to existing passengers. If services are optimally adjusted to demand, then of course all three concepts lead to the same results (Jansson, 1984).

In the case of private transport, if the infrastructure prices are right, essentially, the problem of efficient use of the system is solved. But with scheduled public transport services and with freight transport services that is not so. As already indicated, there are various cost characteristics – of scheduled transport in particular – which make that unlikely. This means that there is very often an a priori case for subsidising scheduled transport services in order to implement pricing policies which do not cover full cost. In the absence of efficient provision of the scheduled transport services themselves there is no guarantee that simply getting the infrastructure pricing right will even improve resource allocation let alone solve the problem.

Furthermore, as also noted above, public transport often competes with underpriced road transport (Glaister and Lewis, 1978). In this case, there is an argument for reducing public transport prices below marginal social cost. In simple terms this divergence should be equal to the difference between price and marginal cost on the competing mode, multiplied by the proportion of additional demand that is attracted from that mode. Thus if all demand attracted to public transport came from the alternative mode, then the divergence between price and marginal social cost should be the same for both modes. But the more additional demand is generated, or attracted from correctly prices modes, the less the optimal divergence of public transport fares below marginal social cost.

A further major argument for subsidies has been to provide adequate access to work, education, health services and shops for poorer members of the community. Such subsidies may be general or may apply to specific sectors of the community such as the pensioners or the disabled.

In practice, there is a strong distinction to be made between urban and local public transport and long distance. Urban public transport is typically publicly owned, or run on monopoly franchises awarded by the public sector, and with public sector control over prices (the major exception to this is the British bus sector, where most services are provided on a commercial basis, with no public control on pricing except for concessionary fares for the elderly and disabled, for which the government compensates operators on the basis of achieving an estimated neutral impact on revenue). Long distance public transport is typically provided on a more commercial basis, even where the operator is publicly owned. Where the aim of pricing is simply to maximise profits, Ramsey pricing is still relevant, but in this case prices will be raised for each product until the price elasticity of demand is minus one.

In the urban sector, passengers are making relatively short trips and often paying at machines or on the vehicle. Therefore there is a strong presumption in favour of a simple pricing structure where tickets may be quickly issued (although the growing use of smartcards makes this less critical). For this reason simple flat fares or zonal systems are common. Where fares do vary with distance, they are typically tapered, so that fare per passenger kilometre is less for longer journeys. Fares which vary with the distance for which the vehicle is full of course make sense in terms of the above suggestion as to how to measure marginal social cost, But a taper with distance most likely reflects a belief that price elasticities of demand rise with distance and with absolute fare level, and are a crude attempt at Ramsey pricing. Both in cost grounds and in terms of varying price elasticities of demand, there is a strong case for higher peak than off-peak fares – capacity is more likely to be stretched in the peak, but also the fact that a higher proportion of trips are discretionary off-peak contributes to a higher price elasticity of demand.

For longer distance trips, tickets are more likely to be researched and bought in advance, so simplicity is not so important. Again there is an argument for having higher prices the more heavily the service is loaded, and modern yield management approaches to pricing rely on tracking bookings and raising price for a particular service as the number of seats booked rises. There is much more scope for price discrimination. Generally business travel and commuting are less sensitive to price than leisure travel, so fares are likely to be higher at peak times and on routes with a higher proportion of business and commuting traffic. There is also some use of two part tariffs, in the form of railcards which may be purchased by particular categories of user, such as pensioners or the unemployed, giving discounts.

CONCLUSION

The transport sector remains characterised by a high degree of diversity in pricing policies and a high level of explicit or implicit subsidies. Whilst differing circumstances may justify diversity, and there are good arguments for transport subsidy, it is not clear that what is happening in practice always makes use of the best theoretical argument and evidence to achieve the desired goals in the most efficient way.

Moves towards more efficient transport pricing are apparent in a number of places around the world. These generally involve the more efficient use of subsidies in the face of economies of scale and better internalisation of external costs Whilst implementation of marginal social cost-based pricing requires a number of deviations from the 'pure' theory, it is clear – to the authors at least – that the theory still forms a useful basis for policy and that the required deviations can be achieved in a way that minimises any efficiency-loss. That said, initial plans for implementing pricing reforms have tended to be held up by a range of issues, in particular the difficulty in reaching agreement amongst the necessary stakeholders.

REFERENCES

Adler, N., Kroes, E. and Nash C.A. (2008) High-speed rail and air transport competition: game engineering as tool for cost-benefit analysis, *Transportation Research Part B*, 44, pp. 812–833.

Baumol, W.J. and Bradford, D.F. (1970) Optimal; departures from marginal cost pricing, *American Economic Review*, pp. 265–283.

Brueckner, J.K. (2001) *Airport Congestion When Carriers Have Market Power*, Working Paper, University of Illinois at Urbana-Champaign, United States.

Carlin, A. and Park, R.E. (1970) Marginal cost pricing of airport runway capacity, *American Economic Review*, 60, pp. 310–319.

CE Delft (2008) *Handbook on Estimation of External Costs in the Transport Sector*, Deliverable 1 of the Impact project prepared for the European Commission (DG TREN) in association with INFRAS, Fraunhofer Gesellschaft, ISI and University of Gdansk, Delft.

Chadwick, E. (1859) Results of different principles of legislation and administration in Europe; of competition for the field, as compared with competition within the field of service, *Journal of the Royal Statistical Society*, 22, pp. 381–420.

Chin, K.K. (2009) The Singapore Experience: the evolution of technologies, costs and benefits, and lessons learnt, discussion paper prepared for the ITF/OECD roundtable of 4–5 February 2010 on Implementing Congestion Charging, Paris.

Commission of the European Communities (1995) *Towards Fair and Efficient Pricing in Transport*, Brussels.

Commission of the European Communities (1997) Green Paper on Sea ports and maritime infrastructure, COM(97)678, Brussels.

Commission of the European Communities (1998) *Fair Payment for Infrastructure Use: A Phased Approach to a Common Transport Infrastructure Charging Framework in the EU*, Brussels.

Commission of the European Communities (2006) *Keep Europe Moving – Sustainable Mobility for our Continent: Mid-term Review of the European Commission's 2001 Transport White Paper*, COM(2006)314, Brussels.

Daniel, J.I. (1995) Congestion pricing and capacity of large hub airports: a bottleneck model with stochastic queues, *Econometrica*, 63(2), pp. 327–370.

Dodgson, J.S. and Topham, N. (1986) Cost-benefit criteria for urban public transport subsidies, *Environment and Planning C: Government and Policy*, 4, pp. 177–185.

DotEcon (2002) *Auctioning Airport Slots*, a report for the HM Treasury and the Department of the Environment, Transport and the Regions. Available online at www.dotecon.com.

Dupuit, Arsène Jules Étienne Juvénal (1844) De la mesure de l'utilité des travaux publics, *Annales des ponts et chaussées*, Second series, 8. Translated by R.H. Barback as On the measurement of the utility of public works, *International Economic Papers*, 1952, 2, pp. 83–110.

Eliasson, J. (2009) A cost–benefit analysis of the Stockholm congestion charging system, *Transportation Research Part A*, 43, pp. 468–480.

European Parliament (2006) Directive 2006/38/EC of the European Parliament of the Council of 17 May 2006 amending Directive 1999/62/EC on the charging of heavy goods vehicles for the use of certain infrastructures, Brussels.

Glaister, S. and Lewis, D. (1978) An integrated fares policy for transport in London, *Journal of Public Economics*, pp. 341–355.

Grether, D., Isaac, M. and Plott, C. (1989) The allocation of scarce resources: experimental economics and the problem of allocating airport slots, *Underground Classics in Economics*, Westview Press, Boulder, CO.

Haralambides, H.E., Verbeke, A., Musso, E. and Benacchio, M. (2001) Port financing and pricing in the European Union: theory, politics and reality, *International Journal of Maritime Economics*, 3, pp. 368–386.

Heggie, I.G. (1974) Charging for port facilities, *Journal of Transport Economics and Policy*, 8, pp. 3–25.

Hotelling, H (1938) The General Welfare in relation to problems of taxation and railway and utility rates, *Econometrica*, 6(3), July, pp. 242–269.

Ieromonacho, P., Potter, S. and Warren, J.P. (2006) Norway's urban toll rings: evolving towards congestion charging?, *Transport Policy*, 13 (5), pp. 367–378.

International Transport Forum (2008) *Charges for the Use of Rail Infrastructure*, Paris.

Jackson, D.W., Zirker, M., Peirce, S. and Baltes, M. (2008) Urban partnership proposals: review of domestic and international deployments and transit impacts from congestion pricing, paper presented at the 87th Annual Meeting of the Transportation Research Board, Washington, DC, 13–17 January, (No. 08–0820).

Jansson, J.O. (1984) *Transport System Optimization and Pricing*, Wiley, Chichester.

Knight, F.H. (1924) Some fallacies in the interpretation of social cost, *Quarterly Journal of Economics*, 38 (4), pp. 582–606.

Köhler, J., Jin, Y. and Barker, T. (2008) Integrated modelling of EU policy: assessing economic growth impacts from social marginal cost pricing and infrastructure investment, *Journal of Transport Economics and Policy*, 42(1), pp. 1–21.

Meersman, H., Van de Voorde, E. and Vanelslander, T. (2002) Port pricing issues: considerations on economic principles, competition and wishful thinking, paper presented at 2nd IMPRINT-EUROPE Thematic Network, Brussels.

Mohring, H. and Turvey, R. (1975) Optimal bus fares, *Journal of Transport Economics and Policy*, pp. 280–286.

Morrison, S. A. (1987) The equity and efficiency of runway pricing, *Journal of Public Economics*, 34(1), pp. 45–60.

Nash, C.A. (2003a) Final report for publication, UNITE (Unification of accounts and marginal costs for transport efficiency), funded by 5th Framework RTD programme, ITS, University of Leeds, Leeds.

Nash, C.A. (2003b) Marginal cost and other pricing principles for user charging transport: a comment, *Transport Policy*, 10 (4), pp. 345–348.

Nash, C.A. and Matthews, B. (2005) Transport pricing policy and the research agenda, in Nash and Matthews (eds), *Measuring the Marginal Social Cost of Transport*, Elsevier, Amsterdam.

Nash, C.A., Sansom, T. and Matthews, B. (2001) Final Report for Publication, CAPRI (Concerted Action on Pricing Research Integration), funded by 4th Framework RTD programme, ITS, University of Leeds, Leeds.

Nash, C., Bickel, P., Friedrich, R., Link, H. and Stewart, L. (2002) The environmental impact of transport subsidies, paper prepared for the OECD workshop on Environmental Harmful Subsidies, November 2002, Paris.

Nash, C.A., Menaz, B. and Matthews, B. (2008) Inter-urban road goods vehicle pricing in Europe, in Harry Richardson and Chang-Hee Christine Bae (eds), *Road Congestion and Pricing in Europe: Implications for the United States*, Edward Elgar, Cheltenham, pp. 233–251.

National Economic Research Associates (2004) Study to assess the effects of different slot allocation schemes, NERA, London.

Nilsson, J. (2003) Marginal cost pricing of airport use: the case for using market mechanisms for slot pricing, Swedish National Road and Transport Research Institute, VTI notat 2A-2003.

Oum, T.H. and Zhang, Y. (1990) Airport pricing: congestion tolls, lumpy investment and cost recovery, *Journal of Transport Economics and Policy*, 22, pp. 307–317.

Pigou, A.C. (1920) *The Economics of Welfare*, Macmillan, London.

Proost, S. and Van Dender, K. (1999) *TRENEN II STRAN: Final Report for Publication*, Centre for Economic Studies, Katholieke Universiteit, Leuven.

Psaraftis, H. (1998) When a port calls … an operations researcher answers, *OR/MS Today*, April, pp. 38–41.

Ramsey, F. (1927) A contribution to the theory of taxation, *Economic Journal* 37(1).

Rothengatter, W. (2003) How good is first best? Marginal cost and other pricing principles for user charging transport, *Transport Policy*, 10, pp 121–130.

Roy, R. (2002) The fiscal impact of marginal cost pricing: the spectre of deficits or an embarrassment of riches, paper presented at the second IMPRINT-EUROPE seminar, Brusssels.

Santos, G. and Fraser, G. (2006) Road pricing: lessons from London, *Economic Policy*, 21(46), pp. 264–310.

Starkie, D. (1994) Developments in transport policy: the US market in airport slots, *Journal of Transport Economics and Policy*, 28(3), pp. 325–329.

Swahn, H. (2002) Marginal cost pricing in the maritime sector: cost calculation, acceptance and Swedish infrastructure charging practice, paper presented at 3rd IMPRINT-EUROPE Thematic Network Seminar, Brussels.

Tavasszy, L., Renes, G. and Burgess, A. (2004). Final report for publication: conclusions and recommendations for the assessment of economic impacts of transport projects and policies, Deliverable 10, IASON (Integrated Appraisal of Spatial economic and Network effects of transport investments and policies), funded by 5th Framework RTD Programme, TNO Inro, Delft, Netherlands,

Texas Transportation Institute (2007) Urban Mobility Report, available at http://mobility.tamu.edu/ums.

UIC (2007) *Update of Study on Infrastructure Charges of High Speed Services in Europe*, ParisInternational Transport Forum (2008).

Verhoef, E. (2001) Marginal cost based pricing in transport: key implementation issues from the economic perspective, paper presented at the first Imprint-Europe seminar, Brussels

Walters, A.A. (1961) The theory and measurement of private and social cost of highway congestion, *Econometrica*, 29 (4), pp. 676–697.

Wheat, P.E., Smith, A.J.S. and Nash, C. (2009) *Rail Cost Allocation for Europe, Deliverable D8, CATRIN (Cost Allocation of TRansport INfrastructure cost)*, funded by Sixth Framework RTD Programme. VTI, Stockholm.

Winston, Clifford. (2006) The United States: private and deregulated, in J. Gomez-Ibanez and G. de Rus (eds), *Competition in the Railway Industry: An International Comparative Analysis*, Edward Elgar, Cheltenham.

18

Transport, Travel and Health in Public Policy: A Journey Begun

Adrian Davis and Hugh Annett

INTRODUCTION

This chapter is written as an account of a 'live' workstream to address transport, travel and health in the UK. This itself forms part of a broader public health approach seeking to address a range of health determinants situated beyond the heath care system. It is written from two perspectives: that of the Joint Director of Public Health for NHS Bristol and Bristol City Council (Annett), and a public health and transport specialist funded by NHS Bristol but embedded into the transport department of Bristol City Council (Davis). Bristol is the eighth largest city in England and economic capital of the south west. The City Council administers an area of 18 square miles and serves a resident population of over 421,000. The city is also home to over 17,000 businesses and is the national headquarters for more than 160 companies. Bristol's gross domestic product per head is higher than that of any city in England except London; overall, then, Bristol is both prosperous and ambitious. By 2020 it aims to be in the top 20 cities in Europe (Bristol Partnership, 2010).

But despite the south west being the healthiest English region as reflected by many health indicators including length of life, Bristol itself does not fare so well. Most health indicators for Bristol are worse than for England as a whole. This includes the facts that over 28% of Bristol children live in benefit dependent households, and on average, both men and women in Bristol live shorter lives than the England average (Association of Public Health Observatories/ Department of Health, 2010). Levels of physical activity among Bristol's population are also in decline and as inactivity increases the risks to health from a range of diseases and conditions – not least coronary heart disease, diabetes, osteoarthritis, some cancers, obesity and mental health problems – these are a significant public health concern.

We contextualise what follows with a brief discussion of the rise of a new public health agenda and some relevant transport policy history. We then move on to discuss our experiences of a workstream addressing wider determinants of health situated around planning, and provide a case study of work on transport and health within Bristol. Specific projects are highlighted where public health advocacy has helped to advance transport policy and practice in the city. We conclude with thoughts about the future both at the local and international level.

THE INTERNATIONAL AND NATIONAL TRANSPORT CONTEXT

Health and transport

The calls for action on transport from within public health from the mid 1990s arose out of renewed interest in public health in the 1980s. The Lalonde Report (1974) and the work of McKeown (1976) were catalysts for the re-emergence of public health in both the UK and elsewhere. They helped raise awareness about the part that social and environmental factors play as determinants of ill health, so that health problems are seen as being influenced by factors beyond as well as under the control of the individual.

The renewed interest in public health has not been without major challenges, however. Not the least of these has been that much of the focus within health services has remained orientated around a narrow biomedical model of health – not the promotion of health. In England, as Hunter noted in the 1990s, treatment of the sick has been the central function of the National Health Service: 'Despite the rhetoric and good intentions stretching back decades, the NHS is not a health service. Its whole ethos and bias is towards caring for the sick' (Hunter, 1995, p. 1589). Moreover, to place the NHS in a western European context, despite efforts to increase the focus on social and environmental determinants of health, most of the emphasis in many European countries also remained on medical services and containment of the costs of these services – so-called 'traditional items' (Dekker, 1994).

Specifically regarding transport and health, until the mid 1990s the disciplines of transport and health were almost wholly unconnected with each other beyond the acute injuries resulting from road traffic violence.[1] In order to appreciate the slow progress made to 2011 to forge stronger links between transport and public health it is helpful to draw on the literature around collaboration, especially inter-sectoral collaboration. Grey states that collaboration is the result of mutual understanding between stake holders of the value of joint work to achieve common goals and overcome problems that may be encountered: 'by collaboration we mean: the pooling of appreciations or tangible resources ... by two or more stake holders, to solve a set of problems which neither can solve individually' (Grey, 1985, p. 912).

There are many barriers, such as cultural difference in ways of working, and lack of trust. An indication of the degree of difficulty likely to be encountered when developing collaborative initiatives is that even between policy areas which recognise their close links, such as between health and social services, the barriers to collaboration are many (Booth, 1981; Blackman, 1995). This does not augur well for areas of public policy where the need for collaboration is less well understood as is the case with transport and health. One review of the literature on inter-sectoral collaboration for action on health by O'Neil et al. (1997) concluded that 'what the authors generally concede, in fact, is that this type of work fails more often that it succeeds' (O'Neil et al., 1997, p. 80).

Transport, as with other policy areas, has concentrated on a narrow set of policy objectives. By focusing on a narrow set of objectives, planners tend to under-value solutions that provide additional benefits. Reductionist decision-making often causes transport planners to overlook indirect health impacts (Litman, 2003). Consequently, there were few specific examples of inter-sectoral collaboration on transport and health issues beyond the traditional areas of concern such as traffic injuries and pollution by the mid 1990s. A conclusion to the period from the 1960s to the 1990s might be that health in itself did not have intrinsic value for transport policy makers at the national nor local level. Indeed, the word 'health' carried with it connotations of hospitals, medical services and the treatment of ill health (Davis, 2003).

One notable exception and example of collaboration in England is to be found in the growing acceptance of the value of walking and cycling in meeting access needs while providing regular, moderate aerobic physical activity necessary to provide health gains (Davis, 1997). This approach was supported by the World Health Organisation through the 3rd Ministerial Conference on Environment and Health, held in London, which adopted a Charter on Transport, Environment and Health (WHO, 1999). The importance of walking and cycling as a means of achieving greater environmental sustainability and health goals from transport was strongly promoted. At this time the British Medical Association had published its policy statement on transport and health, clearly setting out transport as a major determinant of health (BMA, 1998). Submitted as a consultation response ahead of the 1998 Transport White Paper it influenced the White Paper in making the wider health impacts of road transport a legitimate area of concern within transport policy for the first time.

Optimistically, the end of the 20th century might be reflected on as the start of the end of a conveniently narrow perspective on the relationship between transport and health. The first decade of the 21st century may be viewed as a period in which funding for the study of health impacts grew as did the international evidence base for the disparate range of health impacts from road transport. That is not to say that the health impacts of road transport are widely understood, or accepted, or that there has been any significant change in transport policies and practices. A 2010 statement from the American Public Health Association (2010, Executive Summary) could arguably have been drafted to address the situation in the UK:

> Our dependence on automobiles and roadways has profound negative impacts on human health: decreased opportunities for physical activity, and increased exposure to air pollution and the number of traffic crashes … Health impacts and costs have typically not been considered in the transportation policy, planning and funding decisions-making process.

Transport and health

On a parallel track, within transport planning across the developed world, the recognised negative impacts of road transport on health post 1950s were limited and often summed up as casualties, and air and noise pollution. In England, the early 1960s onwards was characterised by the maxim 'predict and provide' (what might be termed the 'old realism'), with the corollary that cities would need to be re-planned, reshaped and rebuilt to accommodate the car. A large proportion of transport budgets had already been committed to urban motorway projects although many had not been fully economically evaluated (Banister, 1994; *The Times*, 1963). The Buchanan Report on urban road transport, *Traffic in Towns* (Ministry of Transport, 1963), recognised that severe congestion would ensue unless road space was increased significantly and that as such the government had a stark choice – build sufficient road space to accommodate the new traffic or find alternative means of catering for mass mobility. Its introductory chapter concluded presciently, by noting that:

> The overriding context in which the problems of urban traffic have to be considered is the need to create or recreate towns which in the broadest sense of the term are worth living in, and this means much more than freedom to use motor vehicles. (Ministry of Transport, 1963, p. 32)

Nevertheless, little attention was paid to the implications of seeking to accommodate full motorisation on other modes (Hamilton and Potter, 1985) nor how this would lead to selective distribution of access among certain sectors of society (Studnicki-Gizbert, 1982). So, increasing car-based mobility became a key transport goal.

Unfortunately for longer term public health there was consequently minimal recognition of the potential scale of negative health impacts beyond traffic casualties. Indeed, in the 1990s transport was described as a hidden health issue (Jones, 1994). Thus while public health was becoming increasingly interested from the 1980s in transport impacts on health, there were no parallel stimuli influencing transport planning to consider health impacts beyond casualties, and air and noise pollution. This absence of awareness and account of health impacts has been reflected in the positive interpretation of expanding road network provision for motorised transport as evidence of human progress. 'Progress' has been and arguably remains a key value among politicians, transport planners and engineers in England. The assumption that the car should be the dominant and normative mode of travel was built on this value.

Growing interest in modes other than the car arose particularly during the 1990s and for reasons almost wholly concerned with the inability to supply road network capacity in response to motor traffic growth forecasts. It became recognised within highway authorities and among transport planners generally that it would be impossible to accommodate the projected growth in road traffic of between 83% and 142% by 2025. It was a matter of arithmetic, not politics (Goodwin, 1994). This recognition has been termed the 'new realism'. The outcome of this was increasing agreement across major political parties for demand management as part of urban transport policy. By the mid 1990s the rhetoric of demand management and reducing the need to travel had become policy goals (Department of Transport and Department of Environment, 1994):

> This means that demand will have to be moderated to meet supply. This is the core transport planning axiom of our time, and it will effect *everything* else in the transport sector of the economy. (Goodwin, 1994, p. 5)

With this portrayal of the health and transport policy 'landscapes' as a backdrop the Director of Public Health now describes the development of a public health capability within Bristol City Council.

THE JOINT DIRECTOR OF PUBLIC HEALTH'S PERSPECTIVE (ANNETT)

The July 2010 Health White Paper *Equity and Excellence: Liberating the NHS* (HM Government, 2010) commits the government to the creation by 2012 of a new national Public Health Service, with responsibility for health improvement transferring from the NHS to local government, who will employ the Directors of Public Health. In some respects this policy shift reverses those in 1974 when a range of public health responsibilities were removed from local government in England. Thereafter, Health Authorities (more recently Primary Care Trusts (PCTs)) were given certain public health duties and required to appoint Directors of Public Health as an executive member of the PCT board. As such, local government and public health in the NHS trod relatively separate, occasionally intertwining paths.

This bureaucratic arrangement did not, however, best serve the interests of improving the health of the public and reducing health inequalities, as this is a goal that requires local government, the NHS and other agencies to work closely together. Progressively since the 1990s partnership working between public and other agencies began to bridge the public health divide and eventually PCTs and some local authorities were encouraged to jointly appoint Directors of Public Health (DPH). By 2006 Bristol City Council and the PCT[2] had an established pattern of partnership working in a number of areas, a notable example being in promoting smoke-free public places, a campaign given public profile by the then Leader of the City Council. So, on taking up my appointment as the joint DPH for Bristol in late 2006 I had a good foundation of partnership working to address health inequalities in the city on which to build.

Public health strategy

Health and health inequalities are influenced more by the circumstances in which people live and by the way they live than they are by the provision of health services, though the latter are also important. This is reflected in the definition of health contained in the Constitution of the World Health Organisation, where it is defined as 'a state of complete physical, mental and social well-being and not merely the absence of disease or infirmity'. In pursuit of this goal, public health is concerned with the determinants of health, the patterns of distribution of those determinants in a population and also about how those determinants and their distribution might be modified through the organised efforts of society (Faculty of Public Health, 2010). From a public health perspective, how people live in a city and how healthy and happy they are depends to a considerable extent on their urban environment, their access to employment, to services, to travel and transport, to green space and on the community around them.

This understanding of the determinants of health and well being is strongly reflected in the Bristol Local Strategic Partnership's 'Sustainable City Strategy', known as the 'Bristol 20:20 Plan', and in the 'Bristol Development Framework' which underpins the City Council's approach to city design and planning. It is also captured and evidenced in *Fair Society, Healthy Lives: The Marmot Review*, which calls for action on six policy objectives, one of which is to 'create and develop healthy and sustainable places and communities'. In relation to transport and health inequalities the *Marmot Review* states:

> Transport accounts for approximately 29 per cent of the UK's carbon dioxide emissions and contributes significantly to some of today's greatest challenges to public health in England, including road traffic injuries, physical inactivity, the adverse effect of traffic on social cohesiveness and the impact of outdoor air and noise pollution. However, the relationships between transport and health are multiple, complex, and socio-economically patterned. (Department of Health, 2010, p. 81)

The final sentence in the preceding quote had not been written in 2007 when Bristol City Council agreed that promoting and enabling physical activity in everyday life should be one of my top priorities as DPH. So while there was cross-party endorsement for an 'Active Bristol' initiative it soon became evident that if it was too narrowly focused on individual behaviours it could not deliver the health and well-being objectives that the city council and the PCT aspired to for the people of Bristol. By an informal iterative process involving the strategic directors of the city council and especially the strategic director responsible for transport and city planning and the strategic director then responsible for neighbourhoods, green space, culture and leisure, it became evident that for public health to achieve its mission within the city council it had to actively engage with and bring added value to those parts of the council primarily responsible for place shaping, including transport.

In terms of road transport there was recognition that public health ambitions could not be developed and delivered without engagement from and ownership by those responsible for transport in the council. The decision was consequently taken to place a public health expert in transport within the transport department in order to act as a policy advocate, a change catalyst and an expert resource. This was in an environment where public health was already active in providing support to the transport officers, as exemplified in spring 2008. An opportunistic occasion had occurred in the spring of 2008. The invitation from Cycling England for bids for a Cycling Demonstration City enabled Bristol PCT to demonstrate that it was already working in close collaboration with the city Council on an Active Bristol programme (launched that April), which focused on everyday walking and cycling. The public health and transport specialist was able to draft a strong section in the bid document on the rationale for unequivocal support from the PCT from a population health perspective. Supporting the cycling city bid, including participation

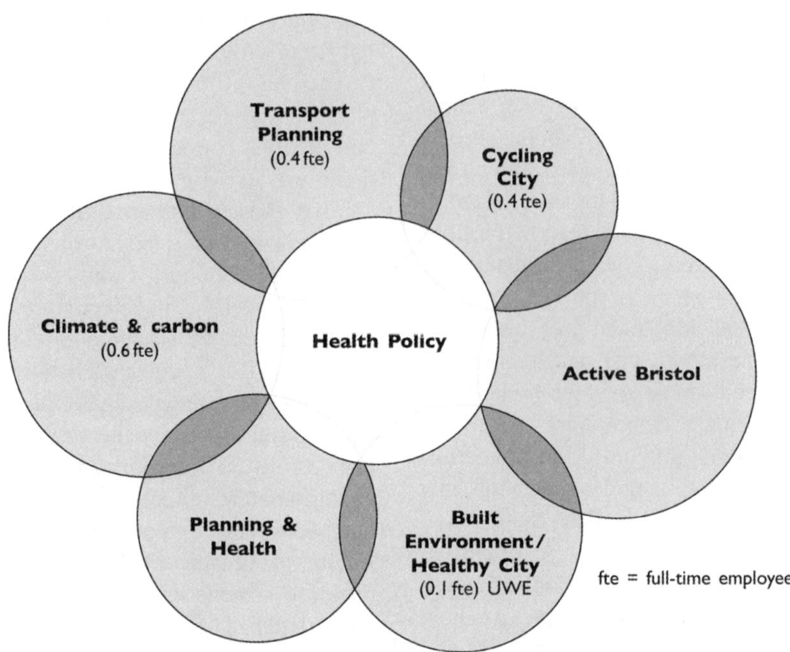

Figure 18.1 Public health staff appointed to posts within Bristol City Council

in the interviews by the Director of Public Health, and a letter of support from the PCT Chief Executive gave more credibility and political support for the role of a public health expert in the transport department. The announcement in June 2008 that Bristol had been selected to become Cycling Demonstration City occurred just as a nascent 'Healthy Urban Team' was being established.

The logic behind the Healthy Urban Team was the recognition that the role of the DPH alone is insufficient to address the range of wider health determinants. But by bringing together the spectrum of inputs through specialist 'experts' and developing the influencing skills at different levels of the system of local government change can be effected (albeit, as seen later in the chapter, influencing officers alone is insufficient and so the 'experts' must also be skilled at developing political support). Consequently, a number of Public Health specialist staff have been appointed to posts working inside Bristol City Council (Figure 18.1). All but the Health Policy Officer of the Public Health Partners 'hot-desk' at the Public Health team room at Bristol City Council's Council House, as well as having an office base or a hot-desk within another Council Department, or in NHS Bristol, or at a local academic institution. With the exception of the Health Policy Officer, all the Partner posts are funded by the NHS. Thus, while working on transport planning it is apparent that the transport and health specialist post is supported by colleagues working in allied and complementary fields of activity.

Indeed, building on initial process success of embedding a public health specialist in transport, the public health directorate was also looking at other closely allied areas. This includes the planning system. The public health directorate sought ways of engaging with the city planning function. Initially the public health directorate offered to provide an iterative Health Impact Assessment of the Council's Local Development Framework by placing a senior public health specialist trainee in the Planning section for a period within his training. This work helped to create trust and some greater understanding of the importance of health among planning officers. This post then paved the way for a full-time planner to influence planning from a health perspective, funded by public health. Additional support for this planning focused work has been bolstered through funding for some input from the WHO Healthy Cities Collaborating Centre at the University of the West of England. These initiatives were significant in helping to place public health more centrally within the framework of town and spatial planning within the Council.

Moreover, these local initiatives have been situated within a regional public health approach on transport and planning to win greater understanding and acceptance as to the importance of health across South West England. (We return to the regional initiatives of transport towards the end of this chapter.) A specific example of this has been regional public health funding for the WHO Healthy Cities Collaborating Centre to establish a study-tour visit to Freiburg in Germany of top tier transport and planning officers and their counter-part Directors of Public Health. Freiburg has an enviable reputation for its planning over more than 30 years to achieve a relatively highly environmentally sustainable transport system in which integrated public transport forms the backbone to enable walking and cycling to flourish. Freiburg has a 35 km length tram network which is within 300 m of 80% of the city's population. To carry people on public transport requires only about 10% of the road space compared to private cars with sole occupancy. This approach helps to ensure room is made for cyclists and pedestrians.

The importance of the first Freiburg Visit for Bristol has been in securing ownership and leadership of the agenda by the Strategic Director for City Development within the Council. Indeed, as Bristol strives to secure a reputation as England's green capital, the need to refocus its transport system becomes more pressing (despite its reliance on the car Bristol has challenged other cities for the title of Green Capital of Europe). The existence of many organisations and activists within the city representing a plethora of environmental organisations, has long helped to engender greater efforts within the city to put into practice a greener way of living and working. A long-standing Sustainable City team within Bristol City Council together with the Green Capital Momentum Group was central to the production of the first local authority report on a future after Peak Oil (Green Momentum Group and Bristol City Council, 2009).

This report has helped to create further opportunities for public health to provide policy and strategy support in relation to the dangers of climate change, environmental pollution from transport, the risks to food security and other population health hazards. It exemplifies how a public health analysis and interventions, such as food distribution and health care, can help move the city to an overarching sustainable development strategy that goes beyond the paradigm of economic growth to a paradigm of equity and well being. Since January 2010 the PCT has funded a senior public health consultant post focused on the twin agendas of climate change and building resilience for Bristol post peak oil.

'Active Bristol' ambitions

Work on transport and health commenced with a concern to address low levels of physical activity. Low levels of physical activity have become a major public health problem in most western societies. The evidence shows that the health impact of inactivity in terms of coronary heart disease, for example, is comparable to that of smoking, and almost as great as high cholesterol levels (Department of Health, 2004). In order to address the consequent disease burden in 2008 Bristol PCT and Bristol City Council launched an Active Bristol programme (Bristol City Council,

2010a). An ambitious five-year (2008–2013) programme, it aimed to:

- Reverse the decline in the physical activity of Bristol people
- Bring about a significant and sustainable increase in the number of Bristol people who are physically active.

It has sought to encourage individuals to be physically active, and also to promote environmental changes through which the healthy travel choices become the natural choices. It is predicated on the need to increase population physical activity levels from their current low base (according to the Bristol Quality of Life Survey, 65% of adults do not achieve a minimum of 30 minutes of moderate physical activity at least 5 days a week). It has not been the main goal of Active Bristol to get people who are already sufficiently physically active (i.e. achieve a minimum of 5 × 30 minutes of moderate physical activity on most days each week) to do more physical activity. People can become physically active in many ways. The international evidence base has identified that moderate activities (e.g. walking, cycling, gardening) are the most appropriate and effective for inactive people to engage in.

The five key areas for Active Bristol that are judged as being critical to the success or otherwise of the programme are:

- Reducing speeds driven in residential streets, i.e. widespread implementation of 20 mph speed limits
- Led walks targeting those aged 50+
- Bike It in schools (a Sustrans[3] programme)
- Attachment of a health and transport specialist to the highways department (0.4 full-time employee (fte))
- A Social Marketing programme targeted towards deprived communities.

The Active Bristol model (Figure 18.2) takes the built and natural environment as key determinants of behaviour. This is because the peer reviewed evidence strongly supports the view that environmental changes are likely to be more effective in changing long-term physical activity patterns than interventions centred on structured activities such as formal exercise programmes (Leslie et al., 2005; Transportation Research Board/Institute of Medicine, 2005; Urban Task Force, 2005). Importantly, research also suggests that the direction of causality is that increased opportunities afforded by the built environment for physical activity play a greater part than decisions of physically active people to live in certain residential areas (Heath et al., 2006).

Among the Active Bristol key areas ensuring that health is and remains a significant driver within transport planning policy and practice through embedding a health and transport specialist into the City's transport

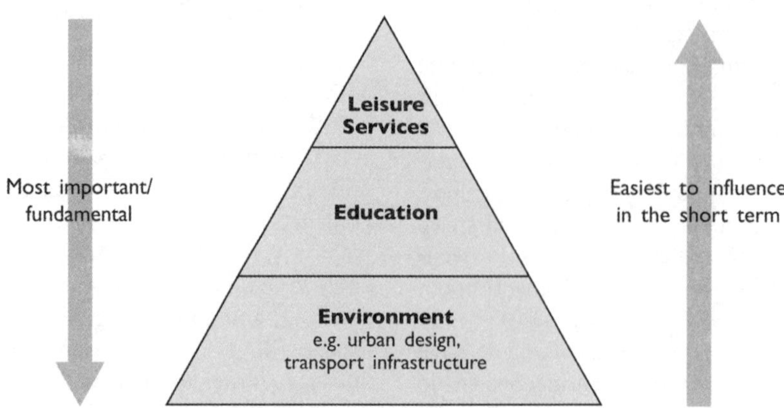

Figure 18.2 The Active Bristol model

department is the focus of the remainder of this chapter. A second key area is to reduce speeds driven in residential streets.

THE HEALTH AND TRANSPORT SPECIALIST'S PERSPECTIVE (DAVIS)

The following is an account of the work of the public health and transport specialist. From June 2008 I have been the embedded public health and transport specialist within the Transport Planning Team of the Bristol City Council's City Development Department. In previous work scoping the Active Bristol programme I had contributed to a bid to Cycling England for Bristol to become England's Cycle Demonstration City. In June 2008 Cycling England announced that Bristol had been successful (including part of the neighbouring South Gloucestershire local authority area). This brought £11.3 million over 3 years matched by the Councils and partners. As a result a desk was made available adjacent to this team which was being led by staff within the Traffic Management section.

The location and daily interactions with specific Council officers has had an influence on the focus of work, especially when I have been asked for support for such a major new and media attention-grabbing initiative as the Cycling Demonstration City. There has been a need to balance public health directorate objectives with pragmatism as to the requests from my 'host team' as well as the need to consider the development of trust and relationship building required to be effective over the longer term.

Before moving on to discuss the specific programmes I am engaged in, it is worth briefly reflecting on some of the barriers for those who might seek to take a similar approach to transport and health at the local authority level. The literature on inter-sectoral working, noted earlier in this chapter provides little grounds for optimism. Ways of working within different sectors are generally hierarchical in structure, often defensive, conservative in outlook, and sectorally exclusive. Having specifically studied barriers to inter-sectoral collaboration on transport and health (Davis, 2001), with a background in both transport planning and public health, I may be at some advantage compared with those public health staff without such transport experience who are similarly embedded. That warning given, it is absolutely not my intention to discourage other public health teams seeking to influence their local transport planning teams through this route – quite the reverse.

In seeking to have maximum effect, I had to be able to have influence among both officers and elected Members. Developing rapport and active involvement with senior management is a priority. Likewise, is the need to be able to communicate openly with Elected Members, not least the Member leading on transport issues. Being a representative of the PCT rather than a local government officer has given me much greater freedom and less timidity than that of officers. They are more constrained by their position in the local authority hierarchy than a 'partner'. A model of the potential range of Director of Public Health roles within local government has been described by Elston (2009) (Figure 18.3). I have also drawn on this to help inform my role which can be viewed as being 'a critical friend', 'catalyst' and 'independent adviser' within Bristol City Council's transport department. Thus I perceive that I am working within a Council represented by the top half of the sphere. Below I describe some of the main initiatives undertaken to date.

The Joint Local Transport Plan 3

Although the success of gaining the Cycling Demonstration City designation was a significant boost to the objectives of increasing population physical activity the main challenge has been preparation for the Joint Local Transport Plan 3 (JLTP3). This is not least because the most effective interventions to promote cycling and walking are largely not cycling and walking specific interventions but rather measures such as car parking control including price and spaces, road space

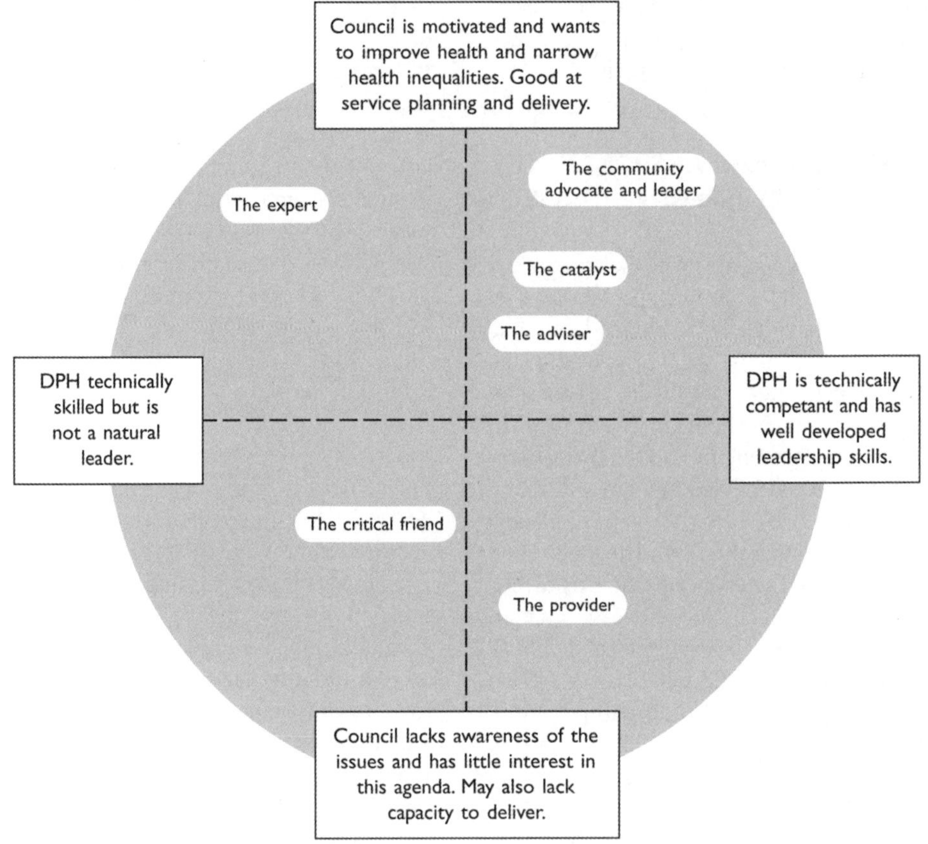

Figure 18.3 A model of the potential range of Director of Public Health roles within local government

re-allocation, and speed management. By 2009 the Department for Transport (DfT, 2009a) had issued guidance stating that unlike its predecessor which operated as a five-year plan (2006–2011) LTP3s were to span at least 15 years from 2011 to 2026. The Plan for Bristol is 'Joint' in that since 2006 the DfT had required there to be just one joint plan spanning the four local highway authorities in the west of England.[4] Spatially, this makes sense but bureaucratically it also poses challenges of coordination by a fifth party, the West of England Partnership, across authorities with differing political visions and organisational cultures.

The clear ambition for public health has been to have a significant input and influence on the drafting and outcome of the JLTP3. Specifically public health has sought to ensure that:

- health is not an afterthought but embedded throughout the document
- effective interventions to address population physical activity are identified and the evidence stated
- the major health impacts of road transport not be assessed as being of limited consequence by transport planners
- evidence is peer reviewed wherever possible and fully referenced.
- the JLTP3 process itself is part of developing a long-term relationship with officers from Bristol City Council as well as helping to enhance a public health relationship with those of neighbouring local authorities and the West of England Partnership.

Preparation for the JLTP3 began under the previous Labour Government (1997–2010), which had set out its objectives for transport policy in its *Delivering a Sustainable Transport System* (DaSTS) document (DfT, 2009b). At the strategic level, the policy had five goals:

- **support** national **economic** competitiveness and **growth**, by delivering reliable and efficient transport networks
- reduce transport's emissions of carbon dioxide and other greenhouse gases, with the desired outcome of **tackling climate change**
- **contribute to better safety security and health** and longer life-expectancy by reducing the risk of death, injury or illness arising from transport and by promoting travel modes that are beneficial to health
- **promote** greater **equality of opportunity** for all citizens, with the desired outcome of achieving a fairer society
- **improve quality of life** for transport users and non-transport users, and to promote a **healthy natural environment**.

Regarding the third goal, this objective alone has provided a strong entry point for public health as it begs the question, 'what is the illness or disease burden arising from transport?' Public health is arguably not only best placed to describe this disease burden but also to identify interventions and changes to current policy and practice that can ameliorate negative health impacts while enhancing the positives. In addition, LTP3 guidance states that '[U]ndertaking a Health Impact Assessment (HIA) should provide an evidence base to help the decision-making process in developing an effective LTP, and to mitigate the negative effects on health and well-being (whether physical and/or mental health)' (DfT, 2009a, point 40).

Yet the challenge for HIA practitioners working in transport is at least twofold. Firstly, despite reference to HIA in the DfT's LTP3 guidance, it is not a statutory requirement. This is in contrast to Strategic Environmental Assessment (SEA), which is. Consultants undertaking SEA for the development of LTP3s are usually also asked to conduct the HIA, but experience to date across the south west of England is that none of the consultancy companies undertaking the SEA for the LTP3s employ HIA trained specialists. Thus for our JLTP3 we have a short descriptive 'Health Impact' statement which does not adhere to the intentions of the LTP3 Guidance for HIA. Part of the blame for this situation, likely to be repeated across LTP3s can be laid at the Department of Health for failure to engage sufficiently with the DfT either to set out what minimum HIA process is acceptable, or to potentially contribute to the costs of this additional task. At the same time, the DfT's decision to request an additional process as part of an already process-heavy task was always likely to meet with little enthusiasm and often some resistance.

Thus, secondly, the lack of a detailed HIA has resulted in a failure to pull together in the JTLP3 a health-related evidence base that could help in formulating the document. This is especially unfortunate since there remains very much the need to integrate wider considerations of the relationship between transport and health into transport policy making. Indeed, reflecting the need to move beyond the narrow view of health impacts of road transport it remains a challenge to emphasise enough that it is sedentary lifestyles resulting from car use which is the biggest health impact of road transport. There is still resistance to this position from within transport planning. Figure 18.4 has been used to illustrate the premature mortality burden of inactive lifestyles from just three major conditions and to contrast this with the total number of fatalities due to road traffic violence. This is not to belittle the importance of efforts to address road traffic fatalities but simply to contextualise it within a wider set of causes of premature mortality.

While road transport cannot be responsible for all premature deaths from inactive lifestyles, there is robust evidence that transport is a key means by which people can routinely gain significant amounts of moderate to vigorous physical activity and that this has declined sharply with rising car ownership. The evidence is also that those that have substituted an active mode, including public transport (given there is often a walked element), for private motorised travel gain weight over and above those who have not changed to a sedentary mode (Bell et al., 2002). Research now shows that commuting by car to work is associated with overweight and obesity compared to active travel modes and use of public transport (Wen et al., 2006). Such evidence should help to gain greater understanding within transport planning as to the true impact of transport on heath. It is the intention that referenced information at least challenges any misconceptions that the health impacts are minor. Yet even if successful in persuading transport officers that the impacts are real does not guarantee a belief among the officers that actions to ameliorate the impacts are within their remits or that they are mandated to act.

Evidence-based practice is grounded in all public health work. However, today anyone faced with making a decision about the effectiveness of a road transport intervention, such as traffic restraint or cycling promotion behaviour change programme, faces a formidable task. The research findings to help answer the question may exist, but locating the research (Wenz et al., 2001), assessing its evidential 'weight' and relevance, and incorporating it with other information is often difficult (Petticrew and Roberts, 2003). Part of this difficulty refers back to the issue of sectors. One of the properties of sectors is a knowledge-base largely codified and maintained within a discipline and by default largely inaccessible to those outside of the discipline. Such a charge of 'sectoring' may readily be applied to public health (as with all scientific disciplines). Yet it remains that there is often evidence of interventions and other research which while being published within one discipline in codified language, and thus to all intents hidden, is wholly apposite for other disciplines if the other disciplines knew it existed, it were de-codified (de-jargonised) and it were made available in an accessible form.

Having worked previously to provide evidence-based research targeted particularly towards transport planners (Sustrans, 2010), I have since sought to provide, with greater brevity, accessible summaries of peer reviewed studies. These one page summaries

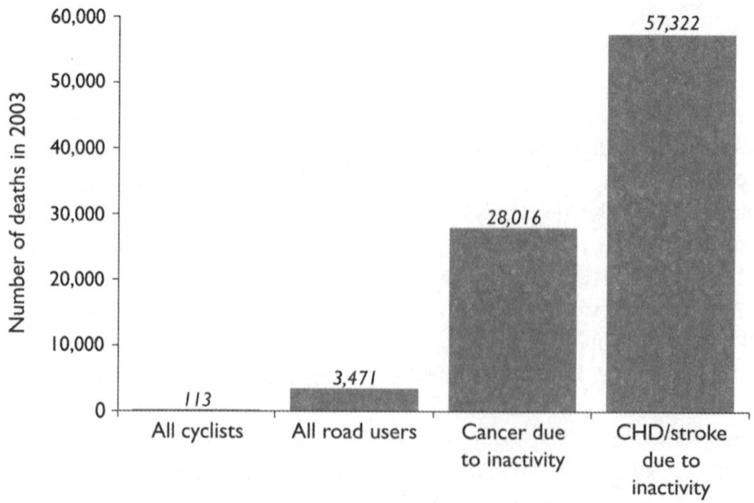

Figure 18.4 The premature mortality burden of inactive lifestyles compared with road traffic fatalities

Figure 18.5 Essential evidence on a page
Source: Bristol City Council, 2010b

have been issued on a bi-weekly basis as 'Essential Evidence on a Page' (Bristol City Council, 2010b) (Figure 18.5). Largely providing evidence on aspects of active travel and health, road danger reduction, habits and mode choice, the series started out as a set of summaries of pertinent information leaflets for the Cycling Demonstration City team. As of July 2010, Essential Evidence on a Page is issued to approximately 800 e-mail addresses, half of which are not within Bristol City Council nor based in Bristol. This dissemination programme is part of a continual and incremental approach which also includes an on-going series of topic research papers and reviews.

Value for money

Related to concerns about 'hidden' evidence is the status of economic assessments of the health benefits of active travel. The current Liberal Democrat-Conservative Coalition government is seeking to steer the UK out of economic difficulties. Particularly since the 2010 general election the test of value for money has become central to funding for a myriad of programmes previously funded through public policy programmes. Consequently Cost Benefit Analysis (CBA) is arguably now more important in giving support for funding programmes. In order to strengthen the case locally for walking and cycling (active travel) I undertook a desk-top review of the evidence for the cost effectiveness of active travel interventions.

From a DfT perspective, cost-benefit ratios play a central function in determining a proposed scheme's viability. Although all schemes with a benefit-cost ratio (BCR) greater than 1 (i.e. for every pound invested another pound is gained through investment e.g. in health care savings) might be worth pursuing, financial constraints mean that it is necessary to prioritise schemes, at least in terms of value for money. DfT guidance categories on value for money underline that schemes with a BCR over 2 are those most worth pursuing.

My review found that the volume of peer reviewed literature on CBA/BCR of interventions to promote routine walking and cycling had grown in recent years. It revealed that the economic justification for investments to facilitate cycling and walking has been undervalued or not even considered in public policy decision-making. Yet, almost all of the studies (UK and international) reported economic benefits which are highly significant, with BCRs averaging 11.5:1. Such high benefit to cost ratios are rare in transport planning. The resulting message was that environmental and other interventions to facilitate increased population physical activity through cycling and walking are likely to be a 'best buy' for public health, the NHS at large in terms of cost savings, as well as for the road transport sector. The evidence from the review was submitted as part of the public health contributions to the JLTP3, and subsequently some of the value for money evidence was included in the document.

Cycling Demonstration City (2008–2011)

One of the limitations of a two and a half year programme to double cycle use is the challenge to seek to do in a short timeframe what continental cities have sought to achieve over decades. Rather than developing an 'exit strategy' from the programme as the funding ends there is a need for a vision for the future. Thus at the half-way stage of the programme a self-imposed task was to draft a public health vision of what a 10-year cycling strategy for Bristol might contain (especially given the favourable cost-benefit ratios mentioned above). The consequent document highlighted the main policy drivers that will affect Bristol's public health in the coming decade – climate change, decarbonising the economy, energy security including peak oil, and obesity.

I proposed that a between 10–15% modal share for cycling in Bristol by 2020 would be a realistic but also cautious target to set in 2010 having compared the city to other comparable European cities which had taken up cycling investment and promotion (indicated by annual budgets) only in the past two decades (Rea and Davis, 2009). Presented to the Cycling City Board in November 2009 the production of the document sought to stimulate action to produce a 10-year strategy. While not the only actors promoting this ambition, the public health pressure is likely to have helped this become a reality by autumn 2010. This 10-year cycling strategy was then input to the JLTP3 planning.

20 mph residential streets speed limits

With regard to other aspects of my work, a benefit of being located initially within the traffic management section was in developing rapport with officers dealing with speed limits at a time when public health was pressing for 20 mph residential speed limits. In scoping the Active Bristol programme I had been the first visitor to assess the early impact of Portsmouth City Council's city-wide 20 mph residential streets speed limit. Members of Bristol's Liberal Democrat ruling group were supportive of exploration of the application of these sign-only interventions. When they agreed in 2009 to pilot two large areas I advised on the locations in order to best address health inequalities, not least because of the steep social class gradient in mortality rates from traffic crashes between children from higher and lower social classes. Being on-hand also enabled me to help shape the pre and post household interviews as well as provide grey literature evidence of previous signs-only interventions (notably a Scottish trial).

The ambition within the Liberal Democrat ruling group, re-elected in May 2010, is for a city-wide 20 mph residential streets speed limit. The public health directorate and

Communications teams within NHS Bristol and staff within the City Council are developing a communications programme to increase understanding and support across the city for residential 20 mph speed limits, providing evidence as to the benefits in order to influence social norms around 20mph as well as address as many as possible of the likely objections.

Road Danger Reduction

Finally, as part of on-going collaboration with local University public health colleagues, a nine-month Knowledge Transfer Partnership[5] project between Bristol City Council, Bristol NHS and University of the West of England was established in November 2009. Sixty per cent of local funding came from the public health directorate and the remainder from the traffic management budget of Bristol City Council. The aim of the project was to explore an alternative approach to road safety, Road Danger Reduction (RDR), and to examine the existing Casualty Reduction approach in Bristol City Council's road safety teams. The project assessed how a RDR approach could help align road safety practice with wider transport objectives. It is useful to briefly explain the essence of the project and its outcomes as part of public health work within the transport department.

Road Danger Reduction (RDR) is based on several fundamental concepts. One of these is that at present there is an inequity in our road system: at the moment it is often perceived to be more dangerous and more difficult for pedestrians and cyclists to get to where they want to go than it is for motorised vehicle users. A second defining concept is that RDR is based on a concern for social justice. A specific element of this is that the level of responsibility and liability taken on by road users should reflect the potential for harm posed by the means of transport that they use.

Thus RDR is concerned that a Casualty Reduction approach is reactive rather than proactive in that crashes have to occur before remedial action is taken. Moreover, the wider impacts of road danger and the prohibitive fear of road danger should be accounted for in road safety. These include negative and chronic health impacts including poor mental health, air and noise pollution, community severance as well as the suppression of walking and cycling. By contrast, RDR seeks to achieve a reduction in danger at source. It has a lower tolerance for any instance of road danger, even if the instance hasn't so far led to casualties. It also differs from Casualty Reduction in that it focuses more 'road safety' attention and action on reducing the source of road danger, fast moving motor vehicles and their drivers, rather than adjusting the behaviour or attitudes of the frequent receivers of that danger i.e. pedestrians and cyclists (Bristol City Council, 2010c).

RDR states that the surest way to improve road safety is to reduce the volume and speed of motorised traffic on the one hand, and to promote walking and cycling as means of transport on the other. It draws on the health benefits of active travel modes to justify its promotion of non-motorised modes. RDR points to the 'safety in numbers' theory in support of its strategy of encouraging more walking and cycling. In sum, this theory suggests that the more people walking and cycling, the safer each individual walking or cycling trip becomes (Jacobson, 2003; Robinson, 2005). An explanation for the processes at work that lead to safety in numbers is that motorists can only take into account a limited number of factors when they are driving. They select these factors according to the frequency with which they experience them. When they encounter cyclists and pedestrians frequently they will take them into account in their driving behaviour. When motorists encounter cyclists infrequently they do not register them at a conscious level (Walker, 2007).

Recommendations include that:

- all traffic management interventions need to be assessed as to whether they promote walking and cycling and if not, why not
- crash statistics should be regularly evaluated for the causes of crashes as research for the project

found that many were caused by careless driving such as 'failed to look' by drivers

- a historic emphasis on training children to cope and adapt to road traffic situations should be balanced through greater emphasis on adults, not least parents, and the everyday and 'normal' danger that driving a motor vehicle imposes on others including children.

SUCCESS SO FAR?

Having a clear and measurable influence on JLTP3 has been a key task. The experience to date has been mixed. The approved draft has notably more health emphasis than that of the previous JLTP2 and the first draft for JLTP3. Yet there remains still significant resistance to the public health evidence as to the importance of health. This is in spite of the evidence base supplied and the development of trust and rapport with some officers and councillors from the five main transport organisations involved in JLTP3.

While the importance of robust evidence is central to the work of public health it is on its own not sufficient to steer policy. While work to promote the active travel modes is underpinned by robust peer reviewed evidence decision-making is influenced by a range of factors. The parallel is often made with the long struggle for the control of smoking in public places. There are vested interests in the status quo, inertia, and those 'silo' barriers that beset all inter-sectoral endeavours. We might be so bold as to suggest that we have some noteworthy process successes in terms of establishing an embedded public health post within the transport department and a range of programmes. Yet, as the title of this chapter indicates, this is a journey begun.

In 2010 all areas of public policy in England are in transition with major financial cutbacks in state services. At the same time the announcement by the Coalition government that public health's future home will be back within local government (after a 40-year gap) means that Bristol is relatively well placed to ensure that the transition is a comparatively pain-free affair. Specifically in terms of transport work there is every intention to continue this programme – we have from the outset made it clear to our partners that collaboration on transport and health, like the changes that are required within road transport, is a long term programme and that we are here for the long term.

In July 2010 the government announced that its Offices for the Regions will be removed, and this places further emphasis on local government to work to support greater public participation in decision-making. This is likely to proffer both opportunities and challenges as decision-making moves to the neighbourhood level. Residents want safer streets but equally habitual car use has lead to psychological attachments and meanings which run counter to the need to reduce the role of the car in society and increase population physical activity. Our ability to win sufficient hearts and minds in the ambition for a truly high quality and prosperous but low carbon economy is likely to keep public health engagement with the transport sector high on our agenda. The political support for a city-wide residential streets 20 mph limit gives us grounds for optimism that positive change is achievable and that health inequalities are not immutable.

As a coda, on an international level there are clearly equally if not more challenging futures ahead. The most pressing is that many developing nations' economic leaders wish to replicate the health damaging car dominated societies of many developed nations. Across the globe the challenge for public health is at least three-fold. Firstly, it must draw together the evidence base of the health impacts, positive and negative and use this as a reason for at least being 'at the table' in the development of transport planning policies in order influence potential health impacts. Secondly, public health advocacy must become stronger in order to counter the influence of the motor lobby. Thirdly, but not least we must send a clear message that prosperity and health go together and this can *only* be achieved through a low carbon, and health promoting transport system.

NOTES

1 Violence is used here to de-codify the terminology which obscures the reality that most deaths and injuries on the highway results from violence inflicted by particular road users on others. The Swedish Government has used the term violence since 1996 when it established its successful Vision Zero national programme to cut road deaths on Swedish Roads and we follow their lead here.
2 In 2009 Bristol PCT was renamed NHS Bristol but both terms are still commonly used.
3 Sustrans is a British cycling and walking charity.
4 Bristol City Council, Bath and North East Somerset Council, North Somerset Council, South Gloucestershire Council.
5 A government-funded programme (40% of a nine-month project) to stimulate knowledge transfer between universities, business and the public sector.

REFERENCES

American Public Health Association, 2010. *The Hidden Health Costs of Transportation*, Washington, DC: APHA.

APHO/Department of Health, 2010. *Bristol Health Profile 2010.*

Banister, D. 1994. *Transport Planning in the UK, USA and Europe*, London: Spon.

Bell, C., Ge, K. and Popkin, B. 2002. The road to obesity or the path to prevention: motorised transportation and obesity in China, *Obesity Research*, 10(4), pp. 277–283.

Blackman, T. 1995. Recent developments in British national health policy: an emerging role for local government, *Policy and Politics*, 23(1), pp. 31–48.

Booth, T. 1981. Collaboration between health and social services, *Policy and Politics*, 9(1), pp. 23–49.

Bristol Partnership, 2010. *20:20 plan*. www.bristolpartnership.org (accessed 3 August 2010).

Bristol City Council, 2010a. Bristol Quality of Life Survey. Quality of life in your neighbourhood survey results 2009.

Bristol City Council, 2010b. www.bristol.gov.uk/tpevidencebase (accessed 21 July 2010).

Bristol City Council, 2010c. www.bristol.gov.uk/ccm/content/Transport-Streets/Road-Safety/road-danger-reduction-in-bristol.en (accessed 23 December 2010).

British Medical Association, 1998. *Road Transport and Health*, London: BMA Publishing.

Davis, A. 1997. An 'insider' looking out: the politics of physical activity in England, in Sidell, M., Jones, L., Katz, J. and Peberdy, A. (eds) *Debates and Dilemmas in Promoting Health: A Reader*, Basingstoke: Macmillan, 284–293.

Davis, A. 2001. *Transport Planning for Health: Explaining and Evaluating Barriers and Opportunities to Intersectoral Collaboration*, unpublished Doctoral thesis, Open University.

Davis, A. 2003. Can the health sector influence transport planning for better health?, in Sidell, M., Jones, L., Katz, J. and Peberdy, A., Douglas, J. (eds) *Debates and Dilemmas in Promoting Health: A Reader*, 2nd Edition, Basingstoke: Macmillan.

Dekker, E. 1994. Health care reforms and public health, *European Journal of Public Health*, 4, pp. 281–286.

DfT, 2009a. *Statutory Guidance to Support Local Transport Authorities in Producing Local Transport Plans*, London: DfT.

DfT, 2009b. *Delivering a Sustainable Transport System*, London: DfT.

Department of Health, 2004. *At Least Five a Week. Evidence on the Impact of Physical Activity and its Relationship to Health*, London: DoH.

Department of Health, 2010. *Fair Society, Healthy Lives. The Marmot Review. Strategic Review of Health Inequalities post-2010*, www.marmot-review.org.uk/, p. 81 (accessed 27 July 2010).

Department of Transport and Department of the Environment, 1994. *Planning Policy Guidance Note 13: Transport*, London: HMSO.

Elston, T. 2009. Health Appointments – 6 models of practice, in Hunter, D. (ed) *Perspectives on Joint Director of Public Health appointments*, London: IDeA.

Faculty of Public Health, 2010. What is public health? www.fph.org.uk/what_is_public_health (accessed 27 July 2010).

Goodwin, P. 1994. Traffic growth and the dynamics of sustainable transport policies, *Linacre Lectures 1994–95*, Oxford: Transport Studies Unit.

Green Momentum Group and Bristol City Council, 2009. *Building a Positive Future after Peak Oil*, Bristol: GMG/BCC.

Grey, B. 1985. Conditions facilitating inter-organisational collaboration, *Human Relations*, 38, pp. 911–936.

Hamilton, K. and Potter, S. 1985. *Losing Track*, London: Routledge and Kegan Paul.

Heath, G., Brownson, R., Kruger, J., Miles, R., Powell, K. and Ramsey, L. 2006. The effectiveness of urban design and land use and transport policies and practices to increase physical activity: a systematic review, *Journal of Physical Activity and Health*, 3, Suppl 1, S55–S76.

HM. Government, 2010. *Equity and Excellence: Liberating the NHS*, London: TSO.

Hunter, D. 1995. The case for closer cooperation between local authorities and the NHS, *British Medical Journal*, 310, pp. 1587–1589.

Jacobsen, P.L. 2003. Safety in numbers: more walkers and bicyclists, safer walking and bicycling. *Injury Prevention*, 9, pp. 205–209.

Jones, L. 1994. *Transport and Health: The Next Move*, Policy Statement 2, London: Association for Public Health.

Lalonde, M. 1974. *A new perspective on the health of Canadians*, Ottawa: Ministry of Supply and Services.

Leslie, E., Saelens, B., Frank, L., Owen, N., Bauman, A., Coffee, N. and Hugo, G. 2005. Residents' perceptions of walkability attributes in objectively different neighbourhoods: a pilot study, *Health and Place*, 11, pp. 227–236.

Litman, T. 2003. Integrating public health objectives in transport decision-making, *American Journal of Health Promotion*, 18(1), pp. 103–108.

McKeown, T. 1976. *The Role of Medicine – Dream, Mirage, or Nemesis*, London: Nuffield Provincial Hospitals Trust.

Ministry of Transport, 1963. *Traffic in towns: A study of the long term problems of traffic in urban areas*, London: HMSO.

O'Neil, M, Lemieux, V., Groleau, G., Fortin, J. and Lamarche, P. 1997. Coalition theory as a framework for understanding and implementing intersectoral health-related interventions, *Health Promotion International*, 12(1), pp. 79–87.

Petticrew, M. and Roberts, H. 2003. Evidence, hierarchies, and typologies: horses for courses, *Journal of Epidemiology and Community Health*, 57, pp. 527–529.

Rea, S. and Davis, A. 2009. *2020 Vision: A Public Health Vision for Cycling in Bristol 2020*. Unpublished.

Robinson, D. 2005. Safety in numbers in Australia: more walkers and bicyclists, safer walking and bicycling, *Health Promotion Journal of Australia*, 16 (1), pp. 47–51.

Studnicki-Gizbert, K. 1982 Equity and distributional issues in transport policy, *Transport Policy Decision Making*, 2, pp. 69–80.

The Times, 1963 Traffic report accepted by Government, 28 November, p. 12.

Sustrans, 2010. Active Travel and Health Information Sheets. www.sustrans.org.uk/resources/publications/information-sheets (accessed 21 July 2010).

Transportation Research Board/Institute of Medicine, 2005. *Does the Built Environment Influence Physical Activity? Examining the Evidence*, Washington, DC: Transportation Research Board.

Urban Task Force, 2005. *Towards a Strong Urban Renaissance*, London.

Walker, I. 2007. Drivers overtaking bicyclists: objective data on the effects of riding position, helmet use, vehicle type and apparent gender, *Accident Analysis and Prevention*, 39, pp. 417–425.

Wen, L., Orr, N. and Rissel, C. 2006. Driving to work and overweight and obesity: findings from the 2003 New South Wales Health Survey, Australia, *International Journal of Obesity*, 30, pp. 782–786.

Wenz, R., Roberts, I., Bunn, F., Edwards, P., Kwan, I. and Lefebvre, C. 2001. Identifying controlled evaluation studies of road safety interventions. Searching for needles in a haystack, *Journal of Safety Research*, 32, pp. 267–276.

WHO (1999) Third Ministerial Conference on Environment and Health, London, UK, 18 June. www.euro.who.int/__data/assets/pdf_file/0007/88585/E6904.pdf.

SECTION 5

Transport Networks and Models

19

Transport Flow, Distribution and Allocation Models, Traffic Assignment and Forecasting

Lóránt A. Tavasszy and Michiel C.J. Bliemer

INTRODUCTION

Our chapter summarizes the state of practice in passenger and transport modeling methods and techniques for strategic, spatial planning applications. We discuss a broad range of modeling topics of interest with the objective of introducing the reader to the task of modeling transport flows. We do not go into many details of theoretical specification of models, econometrical estimation issues, data challenges or application of models. Where necessary we provide literature references for further reading. For more extensive reading on the topic of transport models we direct the reader to the textbooks of Ortúzar and Willumsen (2001) and Hensher and Button (2007).

Since transportation of passengers and freight is of high economical importance, it is critical for policy development and transport decisions that transport flows and traffic states can be forecasted. For this purpose, transport planning models can be applied. These models can assist in making decisions about for example infrastructure investments. Typical outputs are passenger and freight flows and vehicle movements on infrastructure elements, traffic states (free-flow, congestion), and travel times.

Transport related decisions can have a large impact on the traffic system and the economy, and infrastructure investments are usually very costly. In order to make good decisions, it is required to have knowledge of the likely impacts, costs and benefits. One can distinguish between short term and long term impacts. In the short term (within a day to a year), minor adjustments within the transportation system may occur, such as route shifts and modal shifts. In the longer term (e.g., in ten years' time), also other adjustments may occur, such as changes in the residential and work locations, or the relocation of a distribution center. Depending on the time horizon, some or all of these changes need to be modeled. In a transportation context, these changes reflect for example trip decisions, vehicle ownership, mode choice, destination choice, departure time choice, and route choice. Activities and freight demand influence all these choices and lead to actual movements of people and freight and result in traffic. Traffic in its turn influences the accessibility of certain locations. In a spatial context, this accessibility influences location decisions for residents and firms, and development of new real estate, which in turn affects the activities and freight demand. This interaction between passenger travel and freight demand on the one hand and accessibility on the other illustrates the short to long term changes that continuously affect the transportation system.

The focus in this section is on structural models of transport demand: models that are based on a theory of transport decision making, that explain causal relations between choices by decision makers (people, or firms) and their environment, estimated on real-life data. These structural models can be applied in different ways for the purpose of forecasting or predicting the effects of changes in policy variables. They can be applied directly by calculating transport flows in the changed circumstances. If the estimated models perform well, and they are able to reproduce observed behavior closely, this approach to forecasting is warranted. Also, structural models can be applied in an indirect fashion, by deriving elasticities for general use (predicting, say, a percentage change in transport if the percentage change in price is known) or growth factors for specific situations. In these cases, elasticities and growth factors will be applied on a statistical base-year of observed flows.

The chapter is built up as follows. The following section provides a taxonomy of transport planning models, providing a mental map for the reader across different methods and techniques of modeling. We continue the chapter with a description of passenger transport models and freight transport models. There then follows a section providing some practical guidance to the modeling processes in planning situations. The chapter concludes with a brief look forward towards innovative developments that we can expect in the near future.

TRANSPORT PLANNING MODELS: A TAXONOMY

Demand and supply

Transport planning models describe the interaction between (travel and freight) demand and infrastructure supply. Infrastructure consist of roads, rail, sea, air, walkways, etc. The infrastructure is usually represented by a network in which each element has certain characteristics. For example, a road network has links that represent road segments, with corresponding attributes of capacity, length, number of lanes, maximum speed, road type, traffic controls, etc. A public transport network, such as a train network, not only consists of available rail connections, but also includes the train services, for example the line frequencies or the schedule. Pedestrian infrastructure in dedicated pedestrian models is often represented as a continuous space for walking instead of discrete network links.

Travel demand is determined by activities of people, and freight movements are determined by the demand for goods. Travel demand is assumed between origin–destination (OD) pairs, in which an origin and destination zone is typically defined by a postal code area. For passenger transport, the travel demand is the number of trips being made between each OD pair with a certain mode of transport, for example car, public transport, bicycle and walking. These trips are typically distinguished by purpose, such as work and education trips (often mandatory) and leisure and shopping trips (mostly voluntary). For freight transport the demand is characterized by the amount of goods being transported from an origin to a destination, yielding movements of vehicles such as trucks, ships, trains and airplanes.

Travel demand and infrastructure supply lead to traffic generation. The travel demand, which is input per zone, and the infrastructure networks, given by links and nodes, yields traffic flows with certain speeds. The demand and supply can be seen in an economic context. If the demand for trips increases, the infrastructure becomes more heavily used and congestion and delays may occur, increasing the cost (mostly travel time) of a trip. On the other hand, if the cost of a trip increases, fewer people will make a trip and therefore the demand decreases. Transport planning models typically find a (long term) equilibrium in demand and supply. This equilibrium state is then used as a prognosis for a future year.

Classical four stage models

In traditional planning models, the classical four stages are used. The first stage describes the trip generation, in which the total travel and flow departing from each origin (called the trip production) and the total flow arriving at each destination (called the trip attraction) is determined. The second stage describes the trip distribution, in which the choice of movement is modeled, and origins and destinations are combined to form trips. The third stage describes the modal split, in which mode choice is analyzed. Finally, the fourth stage describes the traffic assignment in which the route choice and flow propagation is determined. In this final stage, the demand and supply interaction takes place, where the demand is put on the infrastructure network, resulting in traffic flows and travel times on the network elements. This architecture of choices still largely holds in practice for both passenger and freight models, although refinements have been suggested that challenge the traditional four step approach.

Static versus dynamic models of transportation

Sometimes a fifth stage is added in which departure time choice is modeled. Often, time-varying variables are completely left out of the model, when a single time period (such as a morning peak) is considered. We refer to this type of model as a static model, which assumes stationary and average travel and traffic conditions. In contrast to dynamic models that explicitly take time-varying travel demand and traffic conditions into account. Clearly, transport and traffic are dynamic by nature and dynamic models are therefore superior to static models. However, for more strategic long term studies in which a forecast for an average flow in the peak period on a certain road is enough information, a static model may suffice. For more detailed studies with respect to traffic conditions and queues building up, a dynamic model provides better predictions and more insight.

Aggregate versus disaggregate demand approaches

The demand models in the classical transport planning models considered average people in the travel demand, irrespective of their characteristics such as income, age, and gender. The underlying assumption in such an aggregate (macroscopic) approach is that travelers are homogeneous and all have the same travel preferences. Although this simplifies the model, this assumption is rather strict and is often relaxed in a disaggregate approach. In the latter case, travelers are considered heterogeneous and are either split up in the model into several homogeneous segments or classes (mesoscopic), or are all travelers or households considered separately (microscopic). These disaggregate models are able to more accurately describe the travel decisions made by individuals, for example specifically modeling the travel preferences of the elderly, students, etc.

Microscopic, mesoscopic, and macroscopic supply approaches

Similar to the macroscopic, mesoscopic, and microscopic approaches to demand modeling, also the supply model can be categorized with these types. Traditionally, macroscopic (and static) traffic assignment models have been used to forecast traffic conditions, in which traffic flow is considered a homogeneous and continuous stream (as in water flow) in which individual vehicles cannot be distinguished. Over the years, more disaggregate approaches have been proposed by considering packets of vehicles (mesoscopic) or even each vehicle individually (microscopic). In a microscopic model, which is almost always a dynamic model, it is relatively easy to consider different modes of transport on the same infrastructure, such as cars, trucks, and buses, as they are modeled separately. In a macroscopic model it is much more difficult to take multiple vehicle classes into account. The main advantage of macroscopic models is, that they can usually be employed on large regional networks, while microscopic models are often only feasible on smaller networks due to high computer memory and computational requirements. Furthermore, macroscopic models describe average flow conditions, while most micro-simulation models depend on random draws from probability distributions, yielding perhaps realistic but random traffic conditions. When comparing scenarios, this can become problematic.

Passenger transport and freight transport

The above model classifications can be used both for passenger transport and freight transport. The main difference is the subject that makes the travel decisions; travelers make their own decisions, while logistic planners make the decisions for the goods. Accurately predicting freight transport at the level of individual decision makers is often much more difficult than predicting passenger transport. A lot of data is available about people, for example where they live, and where people work. But data about freight transport is usually confidential data from manufacturers or service providers or not available at all, making it difficult to build disaggregate models for predictions. Here we are confined to using incidental national shipper surveys, aggregate statistics on trade and freight transport. Alternatively, tailor-made surveys can be held to develop a new model.

In the next two sections we will describe the four stages of transport planning for both passenger transport and freight transport, and will discuss the differences in modeling.

PASSENGER TRANSPORT MODELS

In this section we give an overview of commonly used formulations in transport planning models covering the four stages in transport planning. In these models, a specific time period (say, the morning peak period) is considered. Different time periods require different models (evening peak models, rest-day models, weekend models, etc.). Both aggregate and disaggregate approaches will be discussed.

Trip generation

Trip generation models describe the number of trips being produced or attracted by zones, and relate to trip (frequency) choice behavior. In order to determine the number of trips being made by travelers, different trip generation models can be applied. Aggregate regression models relate the number of inhabitants to the total number of trips departing from each origin zone (trip production). Disaggregate regression models predict the number of trips per household or individual based on income, car availability, age, gender, household composition, etc. Cross-classification models distinguish segments of homogeneous groups of travelers, and repeated binary logit models forecast the number of trips by repeatedly modeling the probability of making an additional trip.

Not only the number of departing trips from an origin are of interest; also the number of arriving trips in a certain destination zone (trip attraction) can be predicted. Variables such as the number of jobs in a zone, the size of schools and universities, and the number of shops, play an important role.

Trip distribution

Once the number of departing trips for each zone are known (and sometimes also the number of arriving trips), then we have to model the destination choice by determining for each origin zone the number of trips that depart towards a certain destination zone. We call this trip distribution. The result is an OD matrix with numbers of trips T_{ij} between origins i and destinations j, as illustrated in Figure 19.1. The diagonal of this matrix consists of so-called intrazonal trips (within a zone), while all other trips are interzonal trips (between zones). We first describe the aggregate approach to trip distribution, then a disaggregate approach. In the following we assume that the total production of origin zone i is denoted by P_i and the total attraction of destination zone j by A_j.

The most widely used aggregate approach is the so-called gravity model, referring to the gravitational force between two planets that is proportional to the masses of the

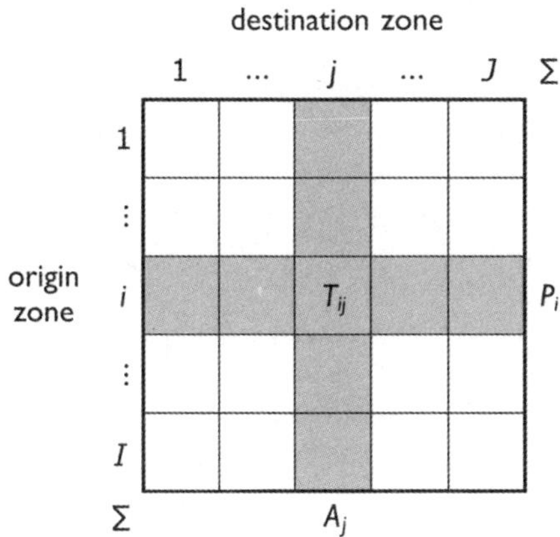

Figure 19.1 Trip matrix

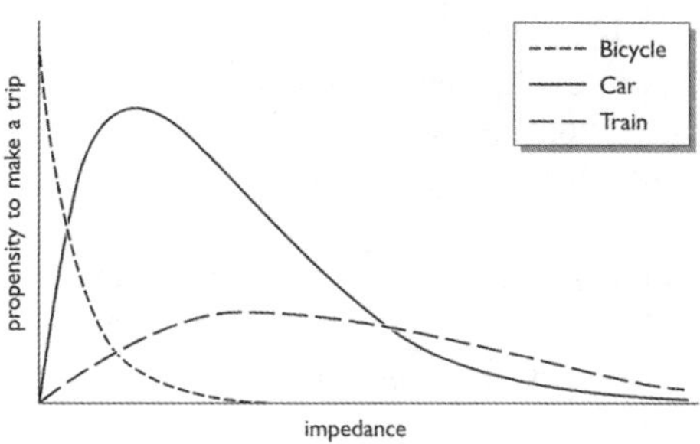

Figure 19.2 Trip distribution (deterrence) functions

planets and inversely related to the squared distance between the planets. The analogy to trips is, that the number of trips between an origin and destination zone is assumed to be proportional to some indicator of the mass of each zone (e.g. production and attraction), and inversely related to a function of the distance, travel time or travel costs:

$$T_{ij} = \mu_i \mu_j P_i A_j f(c_{ij}), \tag{19.1}$$

where c_{ij} denotes the impedance (distance, travel time, or generalized travel costs) from zone i to zone j, and $f(\cdot)$ is a (mostly decreasing) trip distribution function (also called deterrence function) describing the propensity to make a trip from i to j. Examples are the exponential function, $f(c_{ij}) = \alpha \cdot \exp(-\beta c_{ij})$ and the top-lognormal function, $f(c_{ij}) = \alpha \cdot \exp(-\beta \cdot \ln(c_{ij}/\gamma))$ (for some positive parameters α, β, and γ). Examples of trip distribution functions are given in Figure 19.2. Different modes have different impedances, hence the question is, which impedance to use? Often the minimum travel time over all modes is used. Alternatively, the so-called logsum of the impedances of the different modes is used, which is given by (omitting a possible scale parameter):

$$c_{ij} = -\log \textstyle\sum_m \exp(-c_{ijm}),$$

where c_{ijm} is the impedance of mode m. Since destination and mode choice are related, they are often combined, as will be discussed later in the model combinations section. Interestingly, this logsum value is smaller than or equal to the minimum impedance over all modes. The reason behind this is, that adding an alternative is always a 'good thing', and cannot make a traveler worse off, hence adding alternatives should lower the combined impedance.

The scale parameters μ_i and μ_j are determined such that the trips in the matrix satisfy the given productions and attractions, i.e., such that $\sum_j T_{ij} = P_i$, and $\sum_i T_{ij} = A_j$. When both productions and attractions are given, the resulting model is the so-called doubly constrained gravity model. In case only the productions or only the attractions are given, it is called a singly constrained model. In that case, the unknown productions or attractions are replaced with a potential or proxy, for example the number of inhabitants or the number of jobs. If neither is known, the direct demand model results, in which only such potentials are used. The term 'constrained' is somewhat confusing, as the productions and attractions do not necessarily act as real constraints, as the estimates are indifferent for their magnitude. The origin and destination specific parameters will act as regression parameters implicitly resulting in an additional local trip generation factor.

Instead of using the gravity model, often discrete choice models are used to model destination choice. We note, however, that gravity models can be derived from a discrete choice model for the choice of a trip on an origin/destination pair (see Erlander and Stewart, 1990). We return to this in the section on freight modeling. In the case of a discrete choice model, the number of trips from i to j is determined by computing the probability ξ_{ij} that destination j will be chosen:

$$T_{ij} = \xi_{ij} P_i, \; \xi_{ij} = \frac{\exp\left(\kappa_j - \lambda c_{ij}\right)}{\sum_{j^*} \exp\left(\kappa_{j^*} - \lambda c_{ij^*}\right)}.$$

The parameters κ_j denote the relative attractiveness of destination zone j. In case of given attractions (as in the doubly constrained model) these parameters have to be chosen such that $\sum_i T_{ij} = A_j$. Note that the trips always add up to the correct number of productions P_i, since by definition it holds that $\sum_j \xi_{ij} = 1$. The probability ξ_{ij} is derived from a multinomial logit model (see McFadden, 1974) with a utility function of $V_{ij} = K_j - \lambda c_{ij}$ for some positive parameters κ_j and λ. This formulation is often extended to include characteristics of households or individual travelers (e.g., income, age), such that different population segments s have a utility of V_{ijs}. Such a disaggregated approach is very flexible and describes choice behavior directly instead of indirectly using a trip distribution function in the gravity model that is derived from physics.

So far we just talked about trips from origin to destination. Several existing models consider tours instead of trips, where a tour consists of two trips, from origin to destination and back. In many cases, using tours is useful because trips are usually dependent and tours provide a natural way of restricting that people who leave home also return home again.

Modal split

Given the total number of trips T_{ij} made from zone i to j, we now have to compute how these trips are distributed over the different modes. In other words, we will model mode choice behavior. Obviously, for short distances, walking and bicycling will be the preferred modes, while for longer distances the car, train, or even airplane will be more preferred. In the disaggregate approach, the trips T_{ij} can be distributed over the different modes m by means of probabilities ψ_{ijm} that depend on the utility of each mode, consisting of for example travel times, travel costs, number of transfers, but also possibly aspects like the weather and segment variables (e.g., income, age). The number of trips by mode m can then be computed as (omitting the segment index s for simplicity reasons):

$$T_{ijm} = \psi_{ijm} T_{ij}, \; \psi_{ijm} = \frac{\exp\left(V_{ijm}\right)}{\sum_{m^*} \exp\left(V_{ijm^*}\right)}.$$

Traffic assignment

When the number of trips per mode are known, they can be assigned to the network. Assignment consists of route choice and flow propagation as will be discussed later. For modes that do not impede each other, for example because they are using different infrastructure, the assignments are typically done separately. For other modes that use the same infrastructure, such as cars and buses, the assignment has to be done simultaneously, often referred to as multiclass assignment. We will make a distinction between assignments for the modes walking, private transport modes (car, bicycle, motorcycle), and public transport modes (train, bus, metro, tram).

Since a pedestrian has a lot of freedom in movement on the available infrastructure, pedestrian assignment is often modeled with a space in which pedestrians can freely move towards their destination. They are possibly hindered by other pedestrians, especially in crowded areas, and may make slight detours instead of a straight line towards the destination. Such pedestrian assignment models have been developed for studies to simulate traffic in train stations, airports, other buildings and public spaces. When longer walking trips are considered, for example walking from home to the city center, such models with a free movement space are often infeasible. Instead, simple network links that represent footpaths and nodes that describe intersections are used. A certain fixed speed can be set on the links, corresponding to the average speed of a pedestrian. Alternatively, the speed can be an outcome depending on the number of pedestrians using the specific link.

Private transport modes are modeled on a network consisting of links and nodes. The links have properties such as the capacity (maximum number of vehicles per hour), number of lanes, maximum speed limit, length, etc. The nodes can have traffic light settings or priority rules. First of all, the number of trips T_{ijm} should first be translated into the number of vehicles, as people often for example share a car. A simple average car occupancy can be used for this conversion, or more elaborate models that distinguish drivers and passengers can be applied. Then we end up with a matrix consisting of vehicle movements, $\overline{T}_{ij}$. We first discuss the flow propagation, then the route choice. In the remainder we will omit the mode index m as we focus on a single mode.

The speed on each link and through each node is determined by the number of other vehicles on that link and through that node. If a large number of vehicles is present, congestion may occur and speeds may significantly drop, leading to increases in travel time. A well-known function for determining link travel times is the so-called BPR function (Bureau of Public Roads, 1964), which relates the number of vehicles flowing through a link and the capacity of the link to the link travel time:

$$\tau_a(q_a) = \frac{\ell_a}{v_a^{\max}}\left(1 + \alpha_a \left(\frac{q_a}{C_a}\right)\beta_a\right),$$

where τ_a is the travel time of link a, q_a is the link flow, l_a the link length, $v_a^{\max}$ the maximum speed, C_a the link capacity, and α_a and β_a some positive parameters depending on the link type (values of 0.15 and 4.0, respectively, are often used for motorways). For bicycles it is often assumed that they are not impeded by other traffic (much), such that $\alpha_a = 0$ and only free-flow travel times are used. The delays at intersections depend on the presence of traffic lights, priority rules, layout (e.g., roundabout), and the traffic flow from other directions. Several intersection models have been proposed in the literature. The above describes the flow propagation over links for static assignment models. In dynamic models with an explicit time dimension, the flow propagation is usually a (macro, meso or micro) simulation model that much more realistically describes the flow of traffic, including queues, spillback of traffic to upstream links, and shockwaves. These dynamic models are typically very complex and have high computational complexity, such that modeling a whole country with a dynamic model is usually not feasible, Rather, they are applied to smaller regions and cities. The most detailed flow propagation model, namely a microscopic simulation model, is often used for analyzing small parts of the network, such as forecasting effects of certain traffic light settings in a corridor. For larger areas, macroscopic models are applied.

Route choice for private modes is mostly based on the theory that travelers behave rationally and egoistically and choose the route that provides them with the highest utility or lowest cost (including travel time). Also, in transport planning in which we mostly aim for long term prognoses, it is assumed that travelers have perfect knowledge about the available routes and their characteristics. Hence, travelers have adjusted their routes to their individually optimal routes and cannot unilaterally switch to another route and be better off. This principle is called Wardrop's equilibrium law, formulated by Wardrop (1952). Let us define the minimum generalized route travel cost (which is a weighted summation of travel times, travel costs, and other factors that are important in their route choice) from zone i to zone j by π_{ij}, and let c_{ijp} denote the route travel cost on a certain path p. Furthermore, let h_{ijp} be the flow on path p. Then this so-called user equilibrium can be formulated as follows. If $h_{ijp} > 0$, i.e., path p is used, it must have minimum cost, π_{ij} (otherwise, travelers would switch). If $h_{ijp} = 0$, then $c_{ijp} \geq \pi_{ij}$ (by definition). In other words, for each OD pair, all used routes have equal travel costs, and are smaller than or equal to the costs on any unused route. This is known as Wardrop's first principle. Beckmann et al. (1956) established a mathematical non-linear programming problem that can be solved to find Wardrop's user equilibrium:

$$\min_{q_a} \sum_a \int_{w=0}^{q_a} \tau_a(w)\, dw,$$

subject to

$$\sum_p h_{ijp} = \bar{T}_{ij},$$

$$q_a = \sum_i \sum_j \sum_p \delta_{aijp}\, h_{ijp},$$

$$h_{ijp} \geq 0.$$

The three constraints consist of a flow conservation constraint (all route flows should add up to the travel demand), a definitional constraint (the link flow is defined by the summation of all route flows through that link), and non-negativity constraints (flows cannot be negative). The route-link incidence indicator δ_{aijp} equals one if link a is on path p from i to j, and zero otherwise. The objective function itself does not have a simple behavioral meaning, it merely solves the problem. Several algorithms have been proposed in the literature to solve this problem, initially the Frank-Wolfe algorithm and later on more efficient algorithms.

In the above formulation, all travelers are assumed to have perfect knowledge about the path travel times, which is a strong assumption. This can be relaxed by redefining Wardrop's first principle such that in equilibrium, the perceived (subjective) travel time is minimum. The route travel time is therefore assumed to be only known with some (random) error. The same multinomial logit formula (or more advanced logit models) can be applied again to compute the route flow proportions:

$$f_{ijp} = \phi_{ijp}\bar{T}_{ij}, \quad \phi_{ijp} = \frac{\exp(-\lambda c_{ijp})}{\sum_{p^*} \exp(-\lambda c_{ijp^*})}.$$

These logit models enable us again to also include characteristics of the traveler into the generalized cost or utility function, as different travelers may have different preferences, particularly in the weighting between costs and time. For example, for travelers with a high income, the weight on time relative to monetary costs may be higher than for students, expressed in a higher value-of-time (VOT) value, also referred to as a willingness-to-pay (WTP).

Assignment of public transport modes is very different from private modes. First of all, routes cannot be chosen by the travelers, but are dictated by the available service lines in the system. Hence, in public transport, travelers choose lines (including transfers) instead of routes. Second, delays due to congestion are usually not modeled for rail-based modes. The travel times are therefore determined by either the schedule of the mode, or approximated by using merely the frequencies of a line. Often, one or more transfers between public transport modes are required to reach the final destination, which need to be taken into account in the model as extra delay and nuisance to the traveler. Several models exist to perform public transport assignment; however, it is beyond the scope of this chapter to go into the details.

Combined model forms

Trip generation and distribution

We discussed trips and tours in trip generation models. However, these trip generation models usually do not allow for trip chains, such as trips from home to work, then to the supermarket, and then back home again. More detailed transport planning models have been developed, based on activity schedules of people, see e.g. Axhausen and Garling (1992). These so-called activity-based models consider activities such as working and shopping and forecast trip sequences in time, including the time spent at each location for each activity.

Trip distribution and modal split

In aggregate models, modal split is often computed simultaneously with the trip distribution. The gravity model can be adjusted such that it predicts the number of trips per mode m, T_{ijm}:

$$T_{ijm} = \mu_i \, \mu_j \, P_i A_j f_m(c_{ijm}),$$

where $f_m(\cdot)$ is now a mode-specific trip distribution function depending on the mode-specific travel impedance c_{ijm} (see Figure 19.2). The shape of these distribution functions now completely determine not only the destination choice, but also the mode choice.

Also in the disaggregated approach a simultaneous destination choice and mode choice model can be established. In that case, the mode-specific trips will be calculated by

$$T_{ijm} = \psi_{ijm} P_i, \;\; \psi_{ijm} = \frac{\exp(V_{ijm})}{\sum_{j^*} \sum_{m^*} \exp\,(V_{ij*m^*})}.$$

Modal split and traffic assignment

So far we have discussed trips that are made with a single mode (only walking, only car, only public transport). Clearly, in practice people make multi-modal trips in which these modes are combined, such as driving by car to the train station, take the train, and then from the train station walk to the final destination. Including such multi-modal trips yields somewhat more complex models (see Hoogendoorn-Lanser, 2005). One way of intuitively dealing with multi-modal trips is by employing what is referred to as supernetworks (or sometimes hypernetworks). Such a network is basically a layered network, with each layer representing a different mode, and virtual transfer links between the layers. A path in such a supernetwork then corresponds to a multi-modal path in which the links used per mode are indicated, supplemented with transfer links between the modes that can for example contain extra penalties or transfer delays. Although such a supernetwork is an elegant way of dealing with multi-modal trips, it quickly becomes intractable for real-size networks.

FREIGHT TRANSPORT MODELS

The basic architecture of freight transport models is similar to passenger transport models: the four step modeling approach is also the standard approach to modeling freight flows. There are, of course, some subtle differences; these relate e.g. to the number and position of decision makers in the system, the underlying theory of freight modeling and the definition of transport volumes and costs. As a result there is some debate whether these four steps are sufficient to address specific complexities of freight transport demand, in particular concerning its supply chains aspects (see Tavasszy et al., 2012; Liedtke et al., 2009). In this section we take the four step model as a starting point and discuss approaches that complement the traditional approach to four step modeling, taking into account specificities of the freight system. As with the passenger transport models, we limit ourselves to static (or: cross-sectional) freight models and do not go into the dynamic, or time series models.

Trip generation

These models describe the production and attraction of freight. We distinguish between the zonal trip rate models and Input/Output-based models.

Zonal trip rate models express the volume of in- or outbound freight to or from a spatially defined area. Aggregate models function at the level of regions and describe the daily volume of tons produced or received as a function of zonal aggregates such as the number of inhabitants and Gross Regional Product.

Input/Output (I/O) tables describe the relations between sectors of the economy in terms of their yearly exchanges measured in monetary terms. Each sector requires inputs from other sectors to produce goods and services. Households' consumption is noted as final demand in the table. Inputs and outputs are measured in monetary units; in order to transform these to physical quantities, functions relating values with weights or volumes must be constructed. The basic I/O model (Leontief, 1986) allows to calculate industry production **t** from final demand **y** using a matrix of technical coefficients **A**.

$$\mathbf{t} = \mathbf{y}(\mathbf{I}-\mathbf{A})^{-1},$$

where **I** denotes the identity matrix. Note that the matrix of coefficients is assumed to be constant. Changes in production technology or scale economies will not appear in forecasts of **t**.

In order to determine trip generation at the zonal level, the spatial dimension can be introduced by distributing the total activity of a sector within an area to different zones within this area.; of course, this procedure does not allow us to assess volume changes with zones. While the classical I/O model derives its coefficients directly from the I/O table and assumes that these remain fixed, this assumption can be relaxed by using production functions that describe the behavior of a sector in terms of its preferences for different types of input. These flexible coefficients, or production function models, are more sensitive to policy changes as they allow changes in the mix of products used by industries and changes in volume.

As Input/Output data are usually only available at the national level (its focus being on inter-industry interactions), the regional dimension needs to be added. Regional aggregates that are highly correlated with household consumption and industrial production (such as population, labor force, and GDP) are used to spatially disaggregate the data. As flows are noted in monetary units, a conversion needs to be made towards weight units. Usually, the commodity classification available in freight statistics (e.g. the NST/R classification in Europe) is a different one than the classification of trade sectors (e.g. SITC); also here, a translation of flow data is necessary.

Trip distribution

For freight, as for passenger transport, the gravity model has long been the basis for modeling the distribution of flows between regions. The spatial distribution of freight flows is first of all determined by decisions of producers and consumers about the sales and the sourcing of goods, in fact resulting in trade patterns. Second, warehouses en-route (i.e. not in the origin or destination region) may also influence the spatial patterns of transport. Theoretically, the gravity model can be interpreted as a discrete choice model for firms' choice of trading relations, albeit with a number of strong assumptions (see Erlander and Stewart, 1990). According to this derivation, the deterrence function $f(c_{ij})$ that appears in Equation 19.1 should be exponential and include all the costs incurred for the movement of the good, i.e. total logistics costs. In case the cost functions originate from underlying choice models (e.g. modal split models), costs should be aggregated using the correct composite measure (e.g. logsums in the case of the logit model, as explained earlier in this chapter).

The estimation of a gravity model for trade flows ideally requires observations of inter-regional trade. As trade statistics are not available for relations between regions of a country, however, gravity models are usually estimated on transport statistics. By estimating the gravity model on transport flows we miss one key mechanism of spatial distribution. Goods may pass through a warehouse, where items are stored after production, waiting to be picked from inventory and delivered on demand. Often these warehouses are not in the region of production or consumption, but at some location which lies central for several destinations. The spatial patterns of freight flows are also determined by the location of such intermediate inventories. In recent years we have seen a number of models where warehousing is specified as explanatory factor in addition to trade (see Tavasszy, 1996; Jin and Williams, 2005; Maurer, 2008; Friedrich, 2010). These models explain trade flows using a gravity model and take an additional step to re-arrange the transport flow matrix from production/consumption pairs (the P/C matrix) to transport origins and destinations (the O/D matrix).

Despite some theoretical limitations, gravity models are robust and tend to show a satisfactory fit to observed data of domestic and international transport flows, whether based on distance (Tavasszy, 1996), transport time (Hummels, 2001), or on total logistics costs (Hausman et al., 2004).

Modal split

The study of mode choice has a rich tradition in freight transportation modeling. Aggregate modal split models are most common, and generally based on statistical data on goods transport by mode, by country or region (see Burgess, 2001, for an overview of models used in Europe). Models used are the multinomial logit or nested logit model (e.g. Beuthe et al., 2001). The *generalized transport costs* function used most often in the logit model includes shipping rates and transport times and is as follows:

$$c_{ijgm} = r_{ijm} + \mathrm{VOT}_g \cdot T_{ijm} ,$$

where the subscripts i, j, m and g denote origin, destination, mode, and goods type, respectively, and where c, r, and T stand for costs, shipping rates, and time, respectively. The value of time (VOT) is used to convert time to monetary costs.

Note that VOT has the subscript g, which indicates that it is commodity specific. If we assume that the set of goods types carried is homogeneous within modes and sufficiently differentiated between modes, we can replace this with a subscript m, leading to a VOT that differs by mode. The benefit of this change in specification is that observations of the composition of goods within modes are not necessary to estimate a model. The drawback is that these models are less easy to use to study policies related to changes in modal split: it is not immediately clear which VOT we need to attach to those goods switching from one mode to another.

Disaggregate models are based on surveys following shipments of individual companies, or observations of shippers' real or stated (i.e. in experiments) choices. Disaggregate models come in different forms. Discrete choice models use logit (multinomial or nested) models based on stated or revealed preferences data (Vieira, 1992). A number of disaggregate models have been estimated with the primary purpose of obtaining indicators for VOT, to be used in cost-benefit analyses of transport projects (see Zamparini and Reggiani, 2007 for a review). The neoclassical models are based on cost and demand functions at the level of the firm, predicting the expenditure for different modes of transport (Friedlander et al., 1979). Inventory theoretic models assume that firms minimize total logistics costs (Blauwens et al., 2001), including inventory and handling costs. Some models of this latter group use shipment size as an additional endogeneous variable (see Abdelwahab, 1998; De Jong and Ben-Akiva, 2007; Liedtke et al., 2010).

A decision problem closely connected to the choice of transport mode and shipment size is the choice of vehicle type or vehicle size. All modes of transport allow considerable flexibility in choosing small or large units of transport, each with different characteristics in terms of fixed and variable costs. The default approach to model this choice is to assume fixed traffic conversion rates, to arrive from total transport demand volume (typically tonnes/year) to the number of trucks, wagons, ships etc. to assign to the freight network. Note that, theoretically, a non-linear relation between volume and number of trips would be more logical. Due to economies of scale in the logistics process, the efficient shipment size (the so-called Economic Order Quantity) will increase with growing demand, implying a less-than-proportional increase in the number of trips.

Traffic assignment

The default method to assign trucks to road networks is to assume that (1) trucks behave as passenger cars in terms of speed, availability of routes and routing preferences and (2) that the amount of space occupied by a truck can be expressed as a constant multiple of the number of cars – using an average *pcu* (passenger car unit) value. Recent research using a micro-simulation model shows that this value is quite stable and lies around 1.9 cars per truck (Minderhoud and Bovy, 2009). In practice, multiclass traffic assignment techniques can provide a means to specify differences between passenger and freight transport, as observed in the study area. There is relatively little empirical literature about the peculiarities of route choice for freight transport (see e.g. Russo et al., 2006, however, for a recent exception). Additional complexities for freight routing models are the following:

- Economies of scale: all freight modes of transport exhibit economies of scale, complicating network assignment due the fact that such non-convex cost functions do not allow to calculate a unique user equilibrium.
- Freight by road is often distributed by means of tours, where different destinations are served in consecutively linked trips. As data on tours are often lacking, simplified methods are needed to approximate the effect of tours on link flows (Wang and Holguín Veras, 2009).

Combined model forms

Trip generation and distribution

Regional freight generation models and I/O modeling can be integrated with models of spatial distribution such as the gravity model. Combined generation/distribution models can be based on various strands of theory in economic geography. The following families of models can be found, each with different assumptions, data demands and levels of practical applicability:

- Regression or elasticity models for land use/transport interaction (Wegener and Fürst, 1998), in their simplest form assume elasticities for zonal trip generation based on accessibility of regions.
- Regional production function models (Wegener and Bökemann, 1998) integrate these accessibility indicators in a function of regional economic aggregates, which can then be converted to freight flows.
- Multiregional I/O (MRIO) or spatial I/O models (for a recent review see Cascetta et al., 2008) with fixed or flexible technical coefficients take into account inter-industrial linkages.
- Linear programming-based interregional equilibrium (see Crainic and Laporte, 1994, for a review), predicting interregional equilibria in prices and demand.
- Interregional equilibrium models based on non-linear production functions (SCGE models, see Bröcker, 1998).

In general, the more complex the models become in terms of their theoretical framework (in the order as listed here), the more they lose in structural detail in terms of number of zones, sectors or commodities considered.

Trip generation and modal split – direct demand models

Where freight trip generation models are limited to one mode of transport, they are also classified as direct demand models. In this category also disaggregate models exist that predict trip production and attraction based on firm level attributes (e.g. number of employees or floor space, see Iding et al., 2002).

Note that the generation of empty trips, required to reposition vehicles, is a separate problem category. Empty running can account for up to about half of all vehicle trips. It requires an additional trip generation model, which relates empty movements to loaded trips and the repositioning distance (for details see Holguín Veras et al., 2010).

Trip distribution and modal split

As explained in the section on passenger transport models, gravity models can also be estimated simultaneously for transport flows of different modes, where the origin and destination parameters are the same for all modes of transport and the deterrence functions differ by mode. Estimations done for international freight flows by Tavasszy (1996) indicate that these models perform well empirically. Moreover, deterrence functions can be combined into one joint function, with only a minor loss in model performance, if differences between the generalized cost function of modes of transport are taken into account.

Modal split and assignment

Combined modal split and assignment models for freight transport were developed first in the 1980s. They model the network, close to reality, as connected links of different modes allowing transshipment at selected nodes. These multimodal assignment models, or supernetwork models, are particularly useful for evaluating investments in intermodal terminals (Figure 19.3).

Multimodal assignment models have recently been implemented in the US (see Crainic and Laporte, 1994), the Netherlands (Tavasszy and Ruijgrok, 1998), Belgium (Jourquin, 2005), and Sweden (Swahn, 2001; De Jong and Ben-Akiva, 2007). The calibration of these models may be difficult in the cases of a deterministic route choice method (a good fit with observed route will be difficult to achieve) or the use of simulation techniques to calculate route choice probabilities (long model run times allow only a few iterations). Probabilistic route choice models that are easy to evaluate in networks (e.g. modified forms of logit that operate well in networks, such as path size logit, see Ben-Akiva and Bierlaire, 1999, or C-Logit, see Cascetta et al., 1996) are recommended.

APPLICATION ISSUES

In the previous sections of this chapter we provided an overview of the specification of passenger and freight models for transport planning purposes. Once the parameters of the models have been estimated and the model has been validated using observed transport flows, the model can be applied to evaluate planning alternatives. By choosing the theoretical specification of the models we make sure that the underlying assumptions and principles are made explicit, and their performance can be judged against real-world observations. We cannot, however, ensure that the model will perform well in the specific context of its application. More so than the development activities, the application of the model takes place under scrutiny of the stakeholders, within the complex environment of the policy making process. The requirements placed by the stakeholders upon these transport models in terms of accuracy of outputs, speed of calculation, quality of visualization, etc., will depend on this context of the application, i.e. the design study in question, the specific transport policy case at hand and the process environment. We illustrate this by means of a number of cases. This list of cases is not meant to be exhaustive but should serve to demonstrate some typical application issues that modelers encounter.

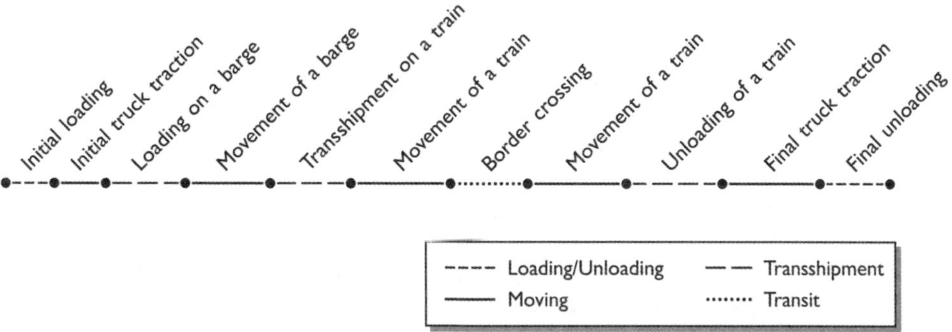

Figure 19.3 Illustration of the network architecture of the European multimodal network choice model NODUS

Source: www.fucam.ac.be

- In some planning situations a so-called sketch planning model will be sufficient, based on very crude default parameters, large zones and trend-based forecasting (see e.g. Cambridge Systematics, 2008, for freight transport). In other situations (e.g. a detailed network analysis to decide on the dimensions of a road), accurate outputs will be needed from a model calibrated on local data with predictions using scenario-based analysis. More complex models than the ones described here, for example, showing dynamics of traffic flows, may be needed here.
- The emphasis need not always be on reproducing the behavioral responses of travelers on transport policy, but rather on determining the fitness for use in interactive planning processes. In these cases aspects such as visualization and speed of calculation become much more critical (Te Brömmelstroet and Bertolini, 2008).
- Especially in design situations, a lack of data or a lack of funding may frustrate the development of models that are sufficiently accurate to apply directly to evaluate alternatives. In these cases, models can be applied to predict changes in flows instead of absolute values, using the so-called pivot point method (see Daly et al., 2005, for an overview).
- Applications for cost-benefit analysis (CBA) may require a proper inclusion of variables describing behavioral preferences. The magnitude of impacts (e.g. travel time gains) and their valuation (e.g. translating travel time gains into welfare gains in monetary terms) ideally originate directly from application of the model. In practice, however, values of travel are prescribed in CBA guidelines, and may not be consistent with the models used.

CONCLUSION

In this chapter on transport planning models we gave an overview of the state of art in passenger and freight model specification. We provided a taxonomy of the different model forms encountered in practice, and described the approaches used for developing four step transport models and more complex integrative models, derived from the basic four step architecture. We briefly illustrated the variety of planning situations in which transport models have to perform. Despite the fact that the four step architecture has been criticized for being rigid and incomplete, this approach still is the basis for all practical transport planning and forecasting models in use today. Modern transportation planning packages have integrated these models with advanced GIS functionalities providing powerful tools to support decision making in the public sector. We argue that with this basic framework, transport system behavior can be modeled in much detail.

Yet, new research and development efforts are underway that enrich and complement the four step framework. Research in logistics provides additional detail in freight models. Time series analysis, disequilibrium modeling, system dynamics, micro-simulation and dynamic traffic assignment are powerful methods to develop an insight into the time dependent behavior of the transport system. Agent-based modeling teaches us about the emergent properties of complex systems, where individual users of the transport system influence each other in unforeseen ways. Furthermore, there is a shift in focus from merely level of service indicators (e.g., travel times) to additional external effects, such as impacts on air pollution (PM_{10}, NO_x), climate (CO_2 emissions), safety, and noise. These external effects play an increasingly important role in policy making, and specific impact models exist in order to make forecasts.

The field of transport modeling has evolved gradually during the last half a century. In planning practice, we have seen models becoming increasingly rich in theory, and – slowly though – increasingly data hungry. As both models and their panning environments became more complex throughout the decades, their application became more sensitive to careful communication and quality assurance from modelers to policy makers, and vice versa. In the future we expect this trend to continue, perhaps even exacerbated by the growing data availability at the level of individual travelers and freight shipments. At the same time, as our transport behavior (of travelers and firms alike) is increasingly guided by automated travel assistants and advisory services, uncertainty in descriptive models due to unpredictability of human behavior may become less of an issue than it is now, allowing to use simple, normative models instead. Research on this topic is still in its infancy, however, and not likely to reach the stage of practical applicability within the next decade. Until then, the approaches described here will remain the basis for transport planning models.

REFERENCES

Abdelwahab, W.M. (1998) Elasticities of mode choice probabilities and market elasticities of demand: evidence from a simultaneous mode choice/shipment-size freight transport model, *Transportation Research Part E*, 34(4), 257–266.

Axhausen, K.W. and T. Garling (1992) Activity based approaches to travel analysis: conceptual frameworks, models, and research problems, *Transport Reviews*, 12(4), 323–341.

Beckmann, M., C. McGuire and C. Winsten (1956) *Studies in the Economics of Transportation*, Yale University Press.

Ben-Akiva, M. and M. Bierlaire (1999) Discrete choice methods and their applications to short term travel decisions. In: R. Hall (ed.) *Handbook of Transportation Science*, Kluwer, Dordrecht, pp. 5–34.

Beuthe, M.B.J., J.-F. Geerts, C. Koul and Ndjang Ha (2001) Freight transportation demand elasticities: a geographic multimodal transportation network analysis, *Transportation Research Part E*, 37, 253–266.

Blauwens, G., P. De Baere and E. Van de Voorde (2001) *Vervoerseconomie*, Standard Uitgeverij, Antwerp.

Bröcker, J. (1998) Operational spatial computable general equilibrium modeling. *Annals of Regional Science*, 32, 367–387.

Bureau of Public Roads (1964) *Traffic Assignment Manual*, US Department of Commerce, Urban Planning Division, Washington, DC.

Burgess, A. (2001) *The European transport Model Directory (MDir), Description of Modal Split Modeling in European Transport Models on the Basis of Mdir*. Paper presented at the THINK-UP Workshop 9, Rotterdam.

Cambridge Systematics (2008) *Forecasting Statewide Freight Toolkit*, National Cooperative Highway Research Program report 606, Transportation Research Board, Washington, DC.

Cascetta, E., A. Nuzzolo, F. Russo and A. Vitetta (1996) A modified logit route choice model overcoming path overlapping problems: specification and some calibration results for interurban networks. In: J.B. Lesort (ed.) *Proceedings of the International Symposium on Transportation and Traffic Theory*, Lyon, pp. 697–711.

Cascetta, E., V. Manzini and A. Papola (2008) Multi regional Input-Output models for freight demand simulation at a national level. In: M. Ben-Akiva, H. Meersman and E. van de Voorde (eds), *Recent Developments in Transport Modelling: Lessons for the Freight Sector*, Emerald, Bingley.

Crainic, T and F. Laporte (1994) Planning models for freight transportation, *European Journal of Operational Research*, 97, 409–438.

Daly, A., J. Fox and J.G. Tuinenga (2005) Pivot-point procedures in practical travel demand forecasting, *ERSA conference papers ersa05*, p.784, European Regional Science Association.

Erlander, S. and N.F. Stewart (1990) *The Gravity Model in Transportation Analysis – Theory and Extensions*. VSP Utrecht.

Friedlander, A.F. and R.H. Spady (1979) A derived demand function for freight transportation, *Journal of Economics and Statistics*, 1979, 430–438.

Friedrich, H. (2010) *Simulation of Logistics in Food Retailing for Freight Transportation Analysis*, PhD Thesis, University of Karlsruhe.

Hausman, W.H, H.L. Lee and U. Subramanian (2004) *Global Logistics Indicators, Supply Chain Metrics, and Bilateral Trade Patterns*, The World Bank, Policy Research Working Paper Series, no. 3773.

Hensher, D.A. and K.J. Button (2007) *Handbook of Transport Modelling*, 2nd edition, Emerald.

Holguín-Veras, J., E. Thorson and J.C. Zorrilla (2010) Commercial vehicle empty trip models with variable zero order empty trip probabilities, *Networks and Spatial Economics*, 10(2), 241–259.

Hoogendoorn-Lanser, S. (2005) *Modelling Travel Behaviour in Multi-modal Networks*. PhD thesis, Delft University of Technology, The Netherlands.

Hummels, D. (2001) *Time as a Trade Barrier*, GTAP Working Papers 1152, Center for Global Trade Analysis, Department of Agricultural Economics, Purdue University.

Iding, M.H.E., W.J. Meester and L.A. Tavasszy (2002) Freight trip generation by firms. 42nd European Congress of the Regional Science Association, Dortmund, Germany.

Jin. Y. and I. Williams, (2005) *The EUNET2.0 freight and logistics model – Final Report*. Regional Pilot for Economic/Logistic Methods, London: Department for Transport.

Jong, G. de and M. Ben-Akiva (2007) A micro-simulation model of shipment size and transport chain choice, *Transportation Research Part B*, 41, 950–965.

Jourquin, B. (2005) A multi-flow multi modal assignment procedure applied to the European freight transportation networks, *Studies in Regional Science*, 33, 929–945.

Leontief, Wassily W. (1986) *Input-Output Economics*, 2nd edition, Oxford University Press, New York.

Liedtke, G., H. Friedrich, P. Jochem, D. Keultjes and S. Schröder (2010) Estimation of the benefits of shippers from a multimodal transport network, *Proceedings of the 12th Annual WCTR meeting*, Lisbon.

Liedtke, G., L.A. Tavasszy and W. Wisetjindawata (2009) Comparative analysis of behavior-oriented commodity transport models, in *Proceedings 88th Annual Meeting of the Transportation Research Board*, January 11–15, Washington, DC. p. 21.

Maurer, H., (2008) *Development of an Integrated Model for Estimating Emissions from Freight Transport*, PhD Dissertation, Leeds: University of Leeds, Institute for Transport Studies.

McFadden, D. (1974) Conditional logit analysis of qualitative choice behaviour. In: P. Zarembka (ed.) *Frontiers of Econometrics*, Academic Press, New York, pp. 105–142.

Minderhoud, M. and Bovy, P. (2001) Extended time to collision measures for road traffic safety assessment, *Accident Analysis and Prevention*, 33, 89–97.

Ortúzar, J. de D. and L.G. Willumsen (2001) *Modelling Transport*, 3rd edition, Wiley and Sons.

Russo, F., A. Vitetta and A. Quattrone (2006) Route choice modelling for freight transport at national level, *European Transport Conference Proceedings*, Association for European Transport, London.

Swahn, H. (2001) *The Swedish National Model System for Goods Transport. A Brief Introductory Overview,* SIKA report, Stockholm.

Tavasszy, L.A. (1996) *Modelling European Freight Transport Flows*, PhD Thesis, Delft University of Technology, Delft.

Tavasszy, L.A., Ruijgrok, C.J. and I. Davydenko (2012) Incorporating logistics in freight transport demand models: state of the art and research opportunities, *Transport Reviews*, 32(2), 203–219.

Tavasszy, L.A. and C.J. Ruijgrok, (1998) A DSS for modelling logistic chains for freight transport policy analysis, *International Transactions in Operational Research*, 5(6), 447–459.

Te Brömmelstroet, M.C.G. and L. Bertolini (2008) Developing land use and transport PSS: meaningful information through a dialogue between modelers and planners, *Transport Policy*, 15(4), 251–259.

Vieira, L.F.M. (1992) *The Value of Service in Freight Transportation*, PhD thesis, Massachusetts Institute of Technology, Boston, MA.

Wang, Q. and J. Holguín Veras (2009) Tour-based entropy maximization formulations of urban freight demand, Paper presented at 88th Annual Transportation Research Board Conference, Washington.

Wardrop, J.G. (1952) Some theoretical aspects of road traffic research, *Proceedings of the Institute of Civil Engineers*, Part II, pp. 325–378.

Wegener, M. and D. Bökemann (1998) *The SASI Model: Model Structure. SASI Deliverable D8*. Report to the European Commission, Institute of Spatial Planning, University of Dortmund.

Wegener, M. and F. Fürst (1998) *Land-Use Transport Interaction: State of the Art. Deliverable D2a of TRANSLAND*, Report to the European Commission, Institute of Spatial Planning, University of Dortmund.

Zamparini, L. and A. Reggiani (2007) Freight transport and the value of travel time savings: a meta-analysis of empirical studies, *Transport Reviews*, 27(5), 621–636.

20

Structure and Dynamics of Transportation Networks: Models, Methods and Applications

César Ducruet and Igor Lugo

INTRODUCTION

The study of transport networks has long been at a crossroads between various scientific disciplines. Traditionally, transport networks are studied from a graph theory perspective, which is a branch of mathematics proposing concepts and measures about the topology of networks considered as sets of nodes (vertices) connected by links (edges). Limited computational power and the scarcity of relevant datasets restricted the analysis to relatively small networks, most of which are planar networks (i.e. with no crossings between edges) and accessibility problems based on pure topology. Decreasing interest for structural approaches in social sciences partly caused the stagnation of transport network analysis since the 1970s, notwithstanding progress brought in by Geographical Information Systems (GIS) and spatial economics from the 1980s onwards (Waters, 2006). Technology and information improvements as well as the wide popularization of the "network" concept contributed to the emergence of new analysis methods in the late 1990s. The research field of complex networks, mostly led by physicists eager to test their models and measures on real-world cases, provided many analyses of the structure and dynamics of large-scale networks of all kinds. Among them, transport networks have received much attention, thereby providing new ways of understanding their internal efficiencies and vulnerabilities.

However, most social scientists interested in transport networks, such as geographers, economists, and regional scientists, have long relied on classic graph theory and qualitative case studies. The integration of complex networks methods by transport specialists is very recent (Kuby et al., 2005) and comes as a complement to other approaches such as circulation routing and flow optimization which strongly focus on transport costs. So far, there remains little overlap and interaction between the different approaches. This state of affairs as well as the fast evolution of the field motivate this chapter, which proposes a review of existing studies of transport networks from a methodological point of view.

We propose distinguishing amongst the structure and the dynamics of transportation networks. The first section discusses the static dimension (structure) and reviews how transportation networks have been defined and analyzed with regard to their topology, geometry, morphology, and spatial structure. It presents a critical overview of main global (network level) and local (node level) measures and examines their usefulness for understanding transportation networks. The second section explores the dynamics of transportation networks, their evolution, and the properties underlying such evolutions. Each section provides a brief background of the relevant literature, concrete applications, and policy implications in various transport modes and industries, with an interdisciplinary focus. A discussion is provided evaluating the legacy of reviewed works and potential for further developments in transport studies in general.

STRUCTURE OF TRANSPORTATION NETWORKS

Transport networks are mostly studied in a static fashion. Research in this field is very voluminous and diverse, but one central goal is to highlight the overall characteristics of the network's structure based on its topology, geometry, morphology, and traffic flows. We divide the literature review between the global level, which is interested in describing the entire network, and the sub-levels, which look either at groups or individual nodes within the network.

Global level

Transport networks belong to a wider category of spatial networks, because their design and evolution are physically constrained (e.g. Euclidian distance) as opposed to non-spatial networks such as the Internet, scientific collaborations, multinational firms, social networks, and biological systems such as neuronal networks (Gastner and Newman, 2004; Boccaletti et al., 2006; Blumenfeld-Lieberthal, 2009). The physical grounding varies in relevance depending on the transport mode considered. Urban streets, roads, and railways are composed of track infrastructure, while maritime and air transports remain vaguely defined due to their higher spatial flexibility except for the location of terminals themselves (Rodrigue et al., 2009). Maritime networks remain more constrained than airline networks due to coastlines (Xu et al., 2007a). River networks typically form basins and can be classified as trees or dendrograms (Banavar et al., 1999).

Most research on transport networks has focused on planar networks (e.g. roads, railways) due to easier access to infrastructure data allowing topological measurements and because the planning and operation of such networks concern everyday mobility at the urban (e.g. street, bus, subway) or regional level (e.g. highway, interstate lanes). Other transport networks without track infrastructure (e.g. air, sea) necessitate the use of traffic data to build a graph of ephemeral links from either vehicle movements or scheduled service. Partly due to the absence of comparable data for urban studies, airline networks have become central in the analysis of systems of cities on various levels. Maritime transport has recently received more interest due to the use of newly available data on carrier services and vessel movements (see Ducruet and Notteboom, 2012).

In their review of the measures synthesizing the structure of communication networks, Béguin and Thomas (1997) introduce four different schools: graph theory, matrices of the shortest paths, geomorphometry (quantitative land surface analysis), and eigenvalues. Matrices of the shortest paths refer to the search for specific configurations in the network, such as the minimum cost tree, which is the part of the network in which all nodes remain connected by the lowest cost path. This approach can be at the global level to extract the optimal route from the network or at the local level to zoom to specific nodes using algorithms such as Kruskal, Floyd, or Dijkstra, among others (Ducruet,

2011). Geomorphometry mainly examines river networks based on several indicators such as the number of bifurcations and the length of the river, its number of junctions. There are two types of eigenvalues approaches: the application of multivariate statistical methods to adjacency matrices and the use of blockmodeling and structural equivalence to determine groups of nodes sharing similar connectivity patterns in the network (Beauguitte, 2011). Based on the simplification of real-world places and pathways into graphs, i.e. groups of nodes (vertices) connected by some links (edges), a wide set of concepts and measures have been proposed by graph theory since the seminal Seven Bridges of Koenigsberg problem proposed by Leonhard Euler in 1735. The main questions addressed are whether different transport networks share comparable properties and according to which criteria.

The integration of graph theoretical methods in geography and regional science with related applications to transport networks dates back to the works of Garrison (1960), Kansky (1963), Haggett and Chorley (1972), and Garrison and Marble (1974). The first set of studies was characterized by limited data, low computational power, and few modeling techniques (Xie and Levinson, 2009a) but is still used to analyze the structure of transport networks. Most common measures include the number of nodes and links (i.e. network size), the length and diameter of the network, its connexity (continuity of the network in terms of the number of connected components), connectivity (more or less optimal distribution of links among the nodes), and nodality. Notably, the three main indices Alpha, Beta, and Gamma[1] proposed by Kansky (1963) do not consider the real length, quality, and weight of the links; networks of equal size may exhibit contrasted topological forms (Béguin and Thomas, 1997; Kurant and Thiran, 2006). However, they remain useful for describing the changing structure of one given network (Scott et al., 2005; Xie and Levinson, 2009b). Using such indicators, Wang et al. (2009) demonstrate the phased development of the Chinese railway network from 1906 to 2000, highlighting its closeness with overall economic development and the formation of urban systems.

More recently, robust macroscopic measures have been proposed to refine those provided by graph theory (see Table 20.1). Barabasi and Albert (1999) define scale-free networks using a high exponent (over 1 and/or between 2 and 3) of the power–law slope drawn based on plotting the frequency of nodes versus the degree centrality distribution (i.e. the number of edges connecting direct neighbors). Many nodes have a poor number of connections, while only a few nodes multiply them, thus making the network highly heterogeneous or disassortative (Figure 20.1). In comparison, small-world networks (Watts and Strogatz, 1998) are defined by a high average clustering coefficient and a short diameter, which illustrates a high density of links and the existence of many cliques based on the probability that two randomly chosen neighbors of a node are also direct neighbors of each other. The average shortest path length is a measure of network efficiency (Barabasi and Albert, 2002). Considering actual account traffic, the rich-club index measures to what extent large degree nodes are strongly connected to each other. Scale-free and small-world networks tend to concentrate at a few high-order connections, whereas road networks are characterized by a large diameter (i.e. maximum path length). Other indices have been proposed, such as the assortativity coefficient, which highlights to what extent nodes of comparable connectivity are connected to each other in the network. Such properties imply dynamics and evolutionary paths that are specific to transport networks.

Several applications of complex networks have revealed interesting specificities and common grounds of different transport networks. Studies of the global maritime transport network (Hu and Zhu, 2009) and the global air transport network (Guimera et al., 2005) confirm their overall scale-free properties with regard to the existing literature on hub-and-spoke strategies of

Table 20.1 Most common measures used by complex networks

Global network measure	Basic definition	Formula
Hierarchy	Exponent of the slope for the power-law line drawn in a bi-log plot of node frequency over degree distribution	$y = ax^h$
Transitivity	Ratio between the observed number of closed triplets and the maximum possible number of closed triplets in the graph	$C_i = \frac{\lambda_G(v)}{\tau_G(v)}$
Average shortest path length	Average number of stops between two nodes in the graph	$l_G = \frac{1}{n^*(n-1)^* \sum_{i,j} d(v_i, v_j)}$
Assortativity coefficient	Pearson correlation between the degree of nodes at both ends of each link (edge) in the network	$r = \frac{M^{-1}\sum_i j_i k_i - \left[M^{-1}\sum_i \frac{1}{2}(j_i + k_i)\right]^2}{M^{-1}\sum_i \frac{1}{2}(j_i^2 + k_i^2) - \left[M^{-1}\sum_i \frac{1}{2}(j_i + k_i)\right]^2}$

Local network measure	Basic definition	Formula
Degree centrality	Number of adjacent nodes	$k_i = C_D(i) = \sum_j^N x_{ij}$
Eccentricity	Number of links needed to reach the most distant node in the graph	$e(x) = \max_{y \in X} d(x, y)$
Shimbel index	Sum of the length of all shortest paths connecting all other nodes in the graph	$A_i = \sum_{j=1}^N d_{ij}$
Betweenness centrality	Number of times a node is crossed by shortest paths in the graph	$C_B(i) = \frac{g_{jk}(i)}{g_{jk}}$
Average nearest neighbors degree	Average degree of adjacent nodes	$k_{nn,i} = \frac{1}{k_i}\sum_j a_{ij} k_j$

Source: compiled from various sources

carriers (see Fleming and Hayuth, 1994; O'Kelly, 1998). While a relatively high vulnerability of the network lays upon few large nodes, the truncated distribution reveals the costs of creating new links at large nodes facing congestion problems, as seen in other case studies of air transport networks (Li and Cai, 2004; Guida and Maria, 2007), public transportation networks (Latora and Marchiori, 2002; Sienkiewicz and Holyst, 2005; Von Ferber et al., 2005; Xu et al., 2007b), and railway networks (Sen et al., 2003).

Since most research focuses on one single network, there is a growing awareness that transport networks may be interdependent through issues of interconnectivity and the vulnerability of tightly coupled infrastructures regarding cascading failures, breakdowns, and attacks (Van Geenhuizen, 2000; Buldyrev et al., 2010; Vespignani, 2010). Notably, Zhang et al. (2005) argue that multi-layer infrastructure networks should be analyzed at various geographic levels with regard to the respective topology and function of individual networks and to potential inter-modal shifts and mutual influence. Examining the co-evolution of roads, canals, and ports during the English industrial revolution, Bogart (2009) reveals noticeable interdependencies among different nodes and networks over time based on spatial and

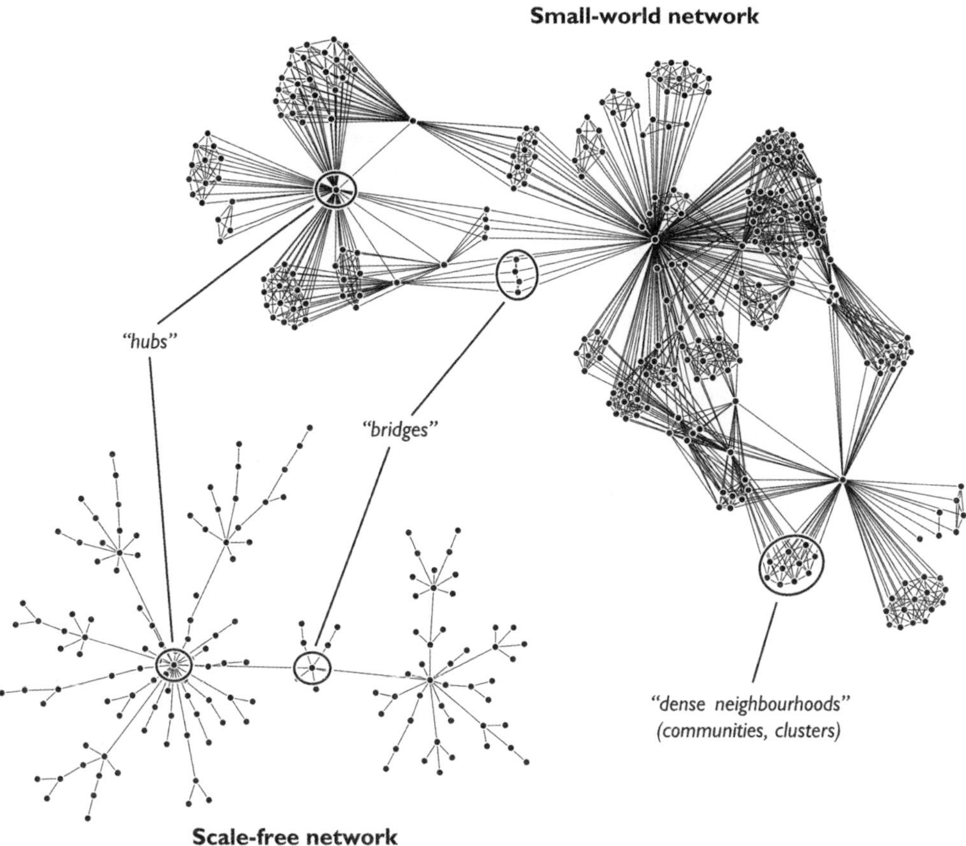

Figure 20.1 Two main network configurations

functional proximity. This underlines that initial network developments are often done to support and then compete with an existing network by expanding geographically and topologically in ways unavailable to the prior network. Ducruet et al. (2011) also highlights the complementarity between air and maritime networks in the formation of a global urban hierarchy. This is also apparent in the work of Parshani et al. (2010) on the inter-similarity between coupled maritime and air transport networks, which shows that well-connected airports tend to couple with well-connected seaports in general, based on their respective geographic locations and on their topological attributes. Finally, Jin et al. (2010) propose an indicator of transport dominance applied simultaneously to freeway, railway, and airline networks in China, stressing the importance of large urban concentrations and the role of distant cities serving as hubs for western areas.

Local level

Various local measures of networks have also been developed (Taafe and Gauthier, 1973; Cliff et al., 1979; Dupuy and Stransky, 1996; West, 1996; Degenne and Forse, 1999). The goal is to compare the relative position of nodes in the network and to highlight groups of nodes in the network. While a full list of measures would run beyond the scope of this chapter, it is possible to organize them by those indicating the situation of the node in the entire network and those focusing on the relations of the node with its adjacent neighbors.

The most common global measures of a given node include:

- betweenness centrality: number of possible positions on shortest paths;
- eccentricity (or associated number, Koenig number): number of links needed to reach the most distant node in the graph;
- Shimbel index (or Shimbel distance, nodal accessibility, nodality): sum of the length of all shortest paths connecting all other nodes in the graph. The inverse measure is also called closeness centrality or distance centrality.

Other local measures are those looking at the neighborhood of a given node:

- degree (or degree centrality): number of adjacent neighbors. The weighted degree is the sum of weights on adjacent links;
- hub dependence: share of the strongest traffic link in total traffic, a measure of vulnerability;
- average nearest neighbors degree: indicates to what extent the node is surrounded by large or small nodes;
- clustering coefficient: proportion of observed closed triplets in the sum of all possible closed triplets, a measure of tightness and density.

Plotting together some of the aforementioned measures may highlight specific features of transportation networks. For instance, nodes with low degree centrality and high betweenness centrality reveal their role as bridges between different subgroups, i.e. as a strategic position or intermediacy. Some hubs may also act as a redistribution platform within their adjacent regions, thus multiplying their links in addition to their bridge role (e.g. feeder links in liner shipping, air, or trucking). In maritime networks, Deng et al. (2009) underline the strong relation between actual throughput and degree centrality for container ports. The centrality of cities in air transport networks has received great attention in recent years. The relation between local measures and other local/regional indicators is also the focus of recent research on transportation networks. For instance, Wang et al. (2011) demonstrate the close relationship between the position of Chinese cities in airline networks (i.e. degree, closeness, and betweenness centralities) and their local socio-economic characteristics (i.e. total passenger traffic, urban population, and Gross Regional Product). Analyzing communication networks in the UK, Eagle et al. (2010) find strong interdependencies between the diversity of connections and the economic well-being of localities.

Local measures may or may not take into account the valuation of the edges concerned (i.e. weighted or non-weighted). This is of high relevance for transport studies, since transport networks are better understood by the usage level (e.g. number of passengers, tons, vehicles, capacity) than by their sole topology based on a binary state (i.e. presence or absence of links). The weighted degree centrality usually corresponds to the sum of edges' traffic, sometimes called node strength. The hub dependence index, which corresponds to the percentage of the strongest traffic edge in the total traffic of each node, is a measure of vulnerability, notably highlighting the contrast for Shenzhen port between its traffic growth and its maintained dependence upon the Hong Kong hub (Ducruet et al., 2010a). In their study of the worldwide air transport network, Barrat et al. (2004) demonstrated that the formation of cliques among major airports (also called rich-club phenomenon) is readable only using traffic weights. The inclusion of edge weight in the analysis can indeed reveal hidden patterns beyond the sole topology, such as the small-world structure of commuter flows in Italy (De Montis et al., 2010) and the identification of different city types through the relative efficiency of their urban street patterns and length compared to optimal configurations of greedy triangulation and minimum spanning tree (Cardillo et al., 2006).

Motivated by practical and policy implications, transport networks analysis has also benefited from further developments in accessibility studies. Various algorithms, such as the Koenig number and the Shimbel index, have been used to describe nodal accessibility in numerous empirical studies. The Shimbel index was used in several case studies to reveal nodal accessibility for European regions in the context of integration (Gutierrez and Urbano, 1996) and Belgian crossroads (De Lannoy and Van Oudheusden, 1991); the impact of deregulation and hub formation on air accessibility in China (Choua, 1993; Shaw, 1993) and in Southeast Asia (Bowen, 2000, 2002); and the impact of railway development on urban accessibility in Japan (Murayama, 1994). Examining the Indianapolis city road network, Gleyze (2007) refines topological measures of centrality and eccentricity by distinguishing between network and spatial effects. Chapelon (2005) applies the widely used Floyd algorithm of the shortest path, taking into account topological features and circulation constraints such as national regulations (e.g. speed limits), highway tolls, the types and capacities of main roads, and the travel time including loading/unloading delays at multi-modal junctions (e.g. ferry crossings). Based on such criteria, Chapelon (2005) calculated the topological accessibility of ports to population and regional wealth potentials within a 6-, 36-, and 72-hour drive (Figure 20.2). The results demonstrate clearly the privileged situation of North European Range ports regarding hinterland coverage and connectivity, while the correlation between road accessibility level and port throughput volume remains only moderately significant.

The search for subgroups of nodes or clusters in a network is another central issue in network analysis with related applications on transport networks. Sociologists "were the first to formalize the idea of communities, to devise mathematical measures of the number and cohesion of communities, and to develop methods to identify the subgroups of individuals within the network" (Boccaletti et al., 2006, p. 275). Such methods also allow for simplifying large datasets in order to make their structure more readable. In their general works on graph theory, Berge (1973) and Bollobas (1998) define subgraphs (or subgroups) as the union of a subset of nodes and the edges linking them. All methods seek to find relevant measures in order to bisect a given graph based on closeness within resulting groups (see Wasserman and Faust, 1994; Moody and White, 2003). Resulting subgroups exhibit various characteristics such as adhesion, with a centralization upon a leader node, cohesion, with more harmonized ties among nodes, cliquishness, exhaustiveness, reachability, and density (Gleyze, 2010). The identification of cut-sets allows the identification of the edges to be removed between subgroups, focusing on connections' existence, quality and robustness within and between subgroups, with reference to the concept of clique. The notion of modularity refers to the optimization of intra-group cohesiveness (measured by distance, structural similarity or dissimilarity among nodes) with regard to inter-group linkages.

One of the first methods introduced for delimitating coherent sub-regions was the Nystuen–Dacey or dominant flow algorithm (Nystuen and Dacey, 1961), first applied to telecommunication flows among Oregon cities. Its numerous applications on weighted transport networks have revealed barrier effects in air and rail transport flows (Cattan, 1995), which cities dominate the hierarchy of air flows (Grubesic et al., 2008), and which ports act as pivots in maritime systems (Ducruet and Notteboom, 2012). Retaining only the maximum flow link between each node simplifies the network's architecture and highlights the existence of so-called nodal regions. Independent nodes are those in which dominant flow connects a smaller node in terms of individual traffic size; subordinate nodes always connect a larger sized node. Notably, Cattan (2004) depicts the lowering integration level of the worldwide airline system, observing its growing polarization by fewer large hubs and the disappearance of sub-regional systems formerly well connected internally. Figure 20.3 gives a more concrete illustration with the evolution of the nodal region of Busan, South Korea based on interport container traffic flows, showing how the hub strategy has resulted in an extension of its

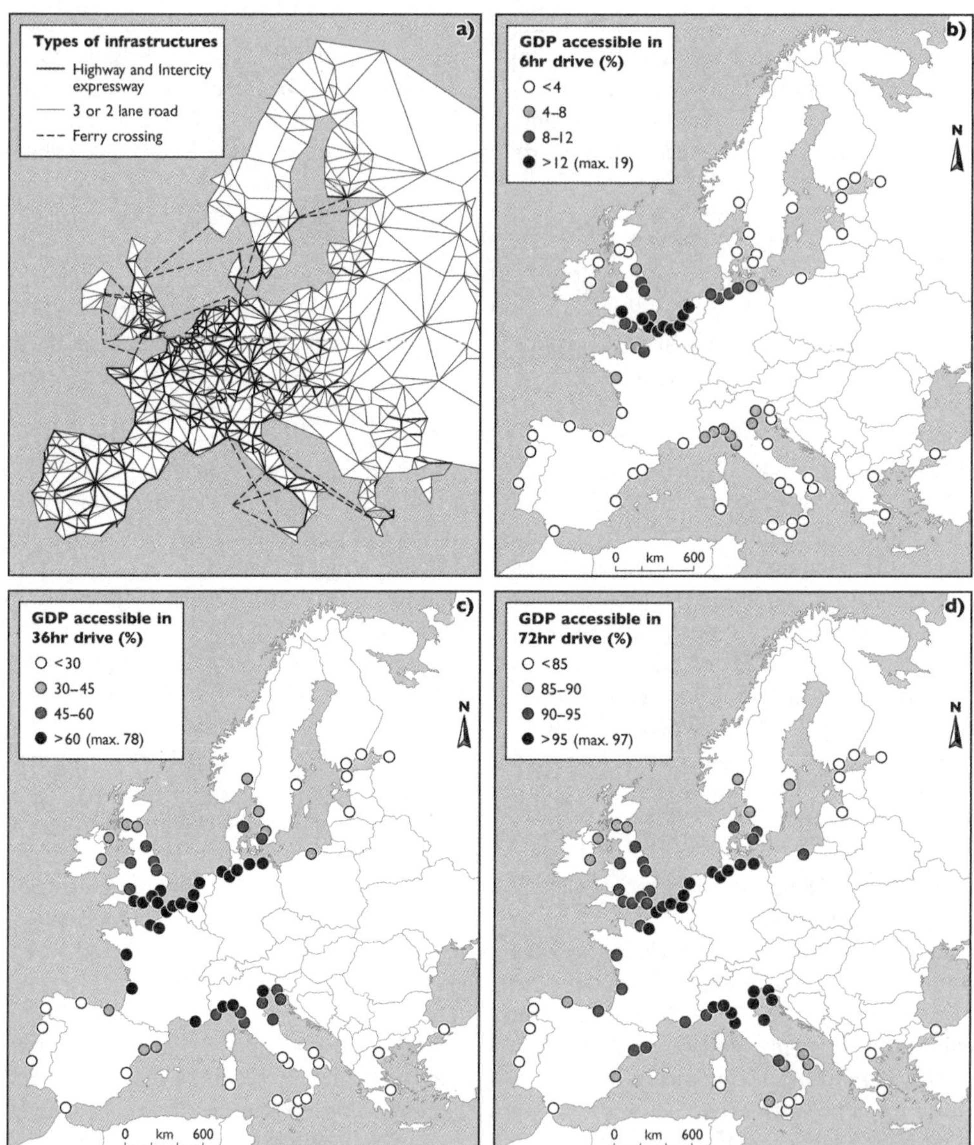

Figure 20.2 Example of accessibility measures, European ports in the road network

Source: after Chapelon, 2005

tributary area from mostly Japanese satellites to a number of Chinese secondary ports.

Because the Nystuen–Dacey algorithm neglects a large number of secondary links, other methods of graph clustering (or partitioning) have been preferred in order to take into account the complexity of the network (Gleyze, 2010) and its multi-level organization. For instance, the application of strength clustering on commuter flows in France reveals the polycentrism, cohesion and fragmentation of urban areas (Tissandier, 2011). It has also been applied to air passenger flows among cities worldwide (Amiel et al., 2005), showing the importance of geographic proximity in the formation of clusters and the multi-level

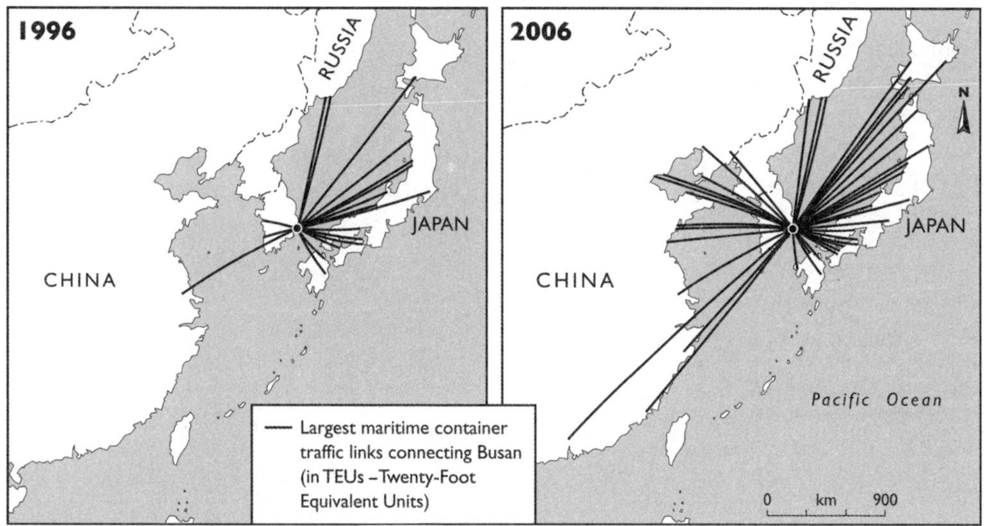

Figure 20.3 Example of a nodal region, the case of Busan, South Korea
Source: after Ducruet and Notteboom, 2012

relations among them. For instance, Asian cities tend to form dense neighborhoods, while some global hubs do not belong to a specific cluster due to their intermediate role between regions. Other measures include the z-score (share of the cluster in a node's connections) and the participation coefficient (connections to other clusters) applied to worldwide air traffic (Guimera et al., 2005). The availability of air traffic data on city pairs has helped foster a vast number of studies on the centrality of cities in such networks (see Shin and Timberlake, 2000). The bisecting K-means algorithm applied on all weighted maritime links among Atlantic ports verifies a strong interdependency within the Le Havre–Hamburg or North European range as well as strong ties among Iberian Peninsula ports and Brazilian ports. Other port groups are better defined by internal geographic proximity and peripherality from the whole system (Ducruet et al., 2010b). Overall, the only problem related to clustering methods is that there is no guarantee to reach the best result as it depends on the edge weight selected (e.g. traffic), and there is no indication about the right number of iterations needed unless it verifies valid hypotheses about the number, quality, and size of expected groups.[2] Simpler methods have been proposed, such as deleting edges with high betweenness centrality or removing the highest or lowest degree centrality nodes (Zaidi, 2011). Other approaches include clustering junctions on road networks (Mackechnie and Mackaness, 1999; Gleyze, 2008); the use of structural equivalence, blockmodeling, and lambda-set methods to study the regionalization of the US Internet backbone infrastructure network (Gorman and Kulkarni, 2004); and measures of node vulnerability in the Swedish road network (Jenelius, 2009).

DYNAMICS IN TRANSPORTATION NETWORKS

Understanding transport development requires analyzing complex and dynamic processes that produce temporal changes in the transport system. Two main issues are addressed in the literature: how the spatial structure of transportation networks evolves over time and the mechanisms modifying this structure. Several techniques have been developed to describe, compute, and simulate large-scale features of transport networks. Geographers describe topological transformations in the network based on intuitive mechanisms to replicate network geometries (Kansky, 1963; Taaffe et al., 1963; Garrison and Marble, 1962; Morrill, 1965); economists and urban planners compute and design statistical models for choosing the best design of the network from an explicit set of available variables and alternatives (Schweitzer et al., 1998; Leblanc, 1975; Yang and Bell, 1998; Gastner and Newman, 2006; Barthélemy and Flammini, 2006); and engineers and physicists simulate emergent attributes of networks applying the concept of self-organization and agent-based models (ABM) (Lam and Pochy, 1993; Helbing et al., 1997; Barabási, 2002; Newman, 2003; Yamins et al., 2003; Yerra and Levinson, 2005; Levinson and Yerra 2006; Fricker et al., 2009; Xie and Levinson, 2009a).[3]

In this section, we review briefly the application of Agent-Based Models (ABMs) to analyze the dynamics in transport networks. Although such an application is relatively new in the field of transportation networks, it provides important advantages over analytical models. For example, ABMs describe individual interrelationships and form emergent properties in the system. Therefore, ABMs are a class of computational models for simulating systems of autonomous components, called agents, and the relationships between them and their environment. Based on a set of simple behavioral rules, agents interact and produce unexpected collective behavior (Newman, 2003). From the perspective of complex systems, the self-organization process shows how global patterns or structures in a system appear without the influence of a central authority or planning entity (Vicsek, 2000). Therefore, ABMs are a good option to study the dynamics in transportation networks, because they are evolutive models and allow for flexible application to diverse theoretical approaches.

For the purpose of analysis, we present two different methods to conduct an ABM application: generative and degenerative processes. Then, we point out some important factors that analyze the change and growth in the spatial configuration of the network. Finally, we suggest some significant features to be considered when designing ABMs for transport networks.

Generative vs degenerative methods

When the goal of the analysis is to design, create, and compare a simulation model to empirical evidence in transportation networks, there are two general procedures to analyze dynamics. The first is a generative method of network formation, which explains how nodes connect by edges over time and which situations are considered rest-points in this process. Starting from an unconnected graph, the process begins to connect each node based on different mechanisms related to edges, for example, the cost of building or maintaining the link. Another process to connect nodes is based on their hierarchical attributes. For example, a link is created between two nodes based on their degree of connectivity. This process is known as "preferential attachment" and explains the dynamics of networks that generate a power law degree distribution in a system (Newman, 2003). Applying such a process to transportation systems may reveal some emergent behaviors in planar and non-planar networks, such as hub-and-spoke configurations (e.g. airlines and shipping lines) and the limitations imposed by the spatial structure of transport networks (e.g. number of connections per node for road and railway paths). Therefore, preferential attachment not only explains the dynamics of a system based on nodes' connectivity but also highlights the consideration of hierarchical attributes of nodes in order to explore the evolution of networks. The generative method has been used in various scientific fields, for example, in economics (Goyal and Joshi, 2002; Yamins et al., 2003; Kirman, 2011), geography (Jiang and Yao, 2010), and urban planning (Wilson and Nuzzolo, 2009).

On the other hand, the degenerative method proposes starting the analysis from a complete network, where all nodes are connected to each other. All edges represent possible paths

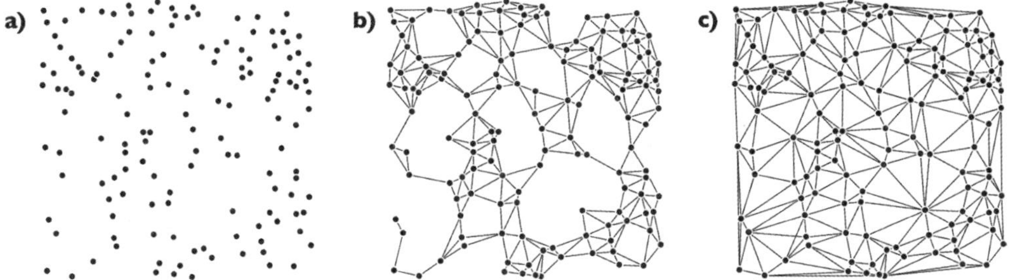

Figure 20.4 Generative vs degenerative methods: (a) generative method displays and unconnected graph; (b) a complex pattern resulting from connecting or deleting links with small and large distances, respectively; (c) degenerative method, shows a complete planar graph

that can be used in the system, but only the more valuable ones reinforce its existence and modify its attributes. For example, some local roads can reinforce their importance based on the number of users and the cost of maintenance as well as the hierarchy of nodes to which they are connected. Therefore, edges that are less valuable decrease in importance and in their probability to be considered part of a representative path. Civil engineering is the most common field of application for such a method (see Yerra and Levinson, 2005; Levinson and Yerra, 2006; Xie and Levinson, 2009b).

Both methods have the same purpose: explaining an endogenous change and growth that produces a particular network structure. For example, Figure 20.4 shows a planar network road system consisting of 150 nodes that are uniformly and randomly distributed in an array of 400 × 400 cells, where the initial configuration of the system in the generative method is shown in (a), and the degenerative method is displayed in (c). Phase (b) presents one possible outcome in the final structure of the network; the process behind this structure is a simple distance mechanism that connects shorter edges or deletes large edges to nodes.

Even though both methods start from different initial conditions and apply inverse distance mechanisms, they converge to explain the final configuration of the network. In other words, there are different stories to tell about a process that creates particular network configurations. With this in mind, pre-knowledge of the network structure, such as global/local measures, and its contextualization, such as social and economic conditions, make it possible to define a mechanism that well explains the dynamics behind such a configuration. Then, the dynamics can be related to local mechanisms particularly market areas, traffic flows, and socio-cultural characteristics (Christaller, 1933). Therefore, the next step in the process to make a simulation model is selecting those factors that guide the explanation of the evolution in the transportation network and specify them as parameters in the model.

Mechanisms for network change and growth

The evolution of the transportation network is closely related to the change and growth of central places. For example, Christaller (1933) explains the existence, characteristics, and evolution of such places. Transportation networks are one of the principal factors to describe the number, size, and pattern of spatial distribution of these places. The co-evolution process of central places and transport networks points out the strong connection between the dynamics of urban and transport systems, as seen in the works of Batty (2005, 2008) and Blumenfeld-Lieberthal and Portugali (2010).

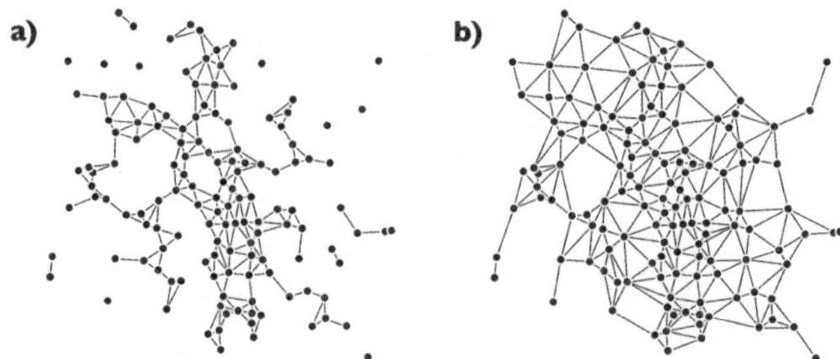

Figure 20.5 Variation in the transportation cost parameter and the emergent transportation network: (a) transportation network topology with high preference to have shorter links, in this case links under 0.15; (b) transportation network topology when larger links are desired, in this case links bigger than 0.25

The market factor applied to transport networks explains the importance of the transportation cost between places in order to maximize the trade-off between demand and supply of goods and services. The creation and maintenance of transportation systems depend on the distance between central places; the higher the distance between places, the more expensive it is to sustain the transportation system. In other words, short links in transportation are preferable. Therefore, the market area affects the transportation cost and shapes some emergent patterns in the structure of the network (Fujita et al., 1999).

In addition to the market factor, traffic is another important element that affects the structure of transportation systems. This explains the importance of the flow of individuals, goods, and services between central places. Components that describe this factor include the total travel time and speed on links (Xie and Levinson, 2009a). Large-scale properties of the network, such as the existence and hierarchy of links in the system, are analyzed by the traffic factor (de Dios et al., 2001; Levinson and Yerra, 2006).

The socio-cultural factor is a hierarchical order between central places showing the level of embedded systems across a particular geographical area, for example, an increased number of activities coordinated inside a city makes it more important compared to other cities. Economic and demographic variables, such as the Gross Domestic Product (GDP) and the urban population, valuate and describe the rank of a place in a system. Consequently, transportation links receive the effects of this factor, because more activities need to expand and distribute their influence to other places (Krugman, 1996; Batty, 2005; Pumain and Tannier, 2005).

As a result, depending on the spatial structure of the network, dynamics can be studied through the above factors and translated into parameters. Continuing with our example of a random planar network, links are classified into different levels according to the transportation cost. Each link has a specific cost associated to the distance between a node pair; the closer the nodes are, the easier it is to build and maintain their connection, and the less likely longer pairs are to exist. Defining a parameter beta, which provides a threshold value for selecting shorter links (distance of one link divided by the larger link), and modifying its value provides the results shown in Figure 20.5.

In the figure, (a) shows a topological structure when beta is defined as 0.15, meaning that links of bigger size (i.e. more than 15%), are not used to connect nodes or are deleted from the system. Conversely, (b) displays a dissimilar structure, because it includes larger links, where the threshold value is set at 25%. Hence, depending on the value of the parameter, different structures emerge in the system.

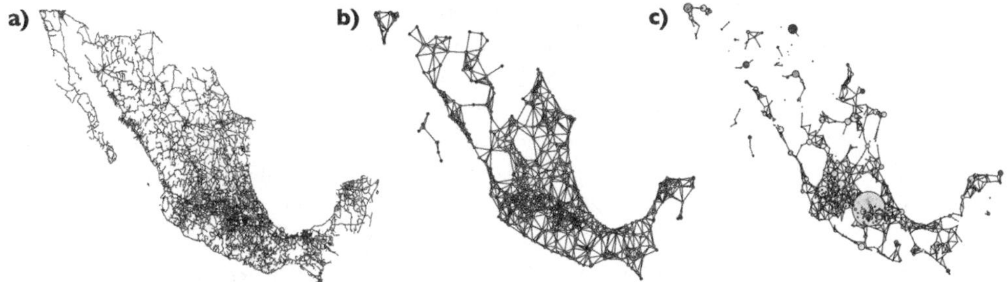

Figure 20.6 Application of ABMs to road networks – the case of the road system in Mexico: (a) road system of Mexico in 2005; (b) short roads based on a distance of under 10% of their maximum; (c) short roads based on a distance of under 6% of their maximum, and more than 10,000 inhabitants

Source: National Institute of Statistics and Geography of Mexico, 2005

Applications

Almost any transportation network shows properties of complex systems, and its structures can be explained by the self-organization process. Hence, ABMs are a natural method to search for explanations of the evolution of such systems, because they provide flexible and novel applications. For instance, Martens et al. (2010) simulate parking behaviors in a city, and Blumenfeld-Lieberthal and Portugali (2010) develop an urban simulation model to study the dynamics of a system of cities. After specifying the method and the relevant parameters of the analysis, the next step is to design and implement simulation experiments.

At a glance, ABMs are computational methods conforming to a collection of autonomous agents, each of which has specific attributes and behavioral rules; their interrelationships produce large-scale structures in the system. In order to apply ABMs to transportation networks, it is necessary to define the scale of the analysis and the type of agents in the system. The scale can be related to a region, a metropolitan area, or a city; the type of agents can be specified by nodes such as cities or terminals; and edges represent transportation links among them. The key point is to define an autonomous agent who has particular attributes and specific methods to interact with other agents and its surroundings. Attributes are intrinsic characteristics of the agent, such as its name, age, or location, and methods are mechanisms or behavioral rules that make possible the interaction with others and modify its attributes, for example, a method that changes the agent's location.

Applying such methods to the Mexican road system specifies two types of autonomous agents: cities as nodes and roads as edges. The former is defined as a central place with the attributes of location and population. The latter is defined as transportation links with the attributes of location and distance. The first method compares the distance between links and returns a group of the shortest ones; the second method compares the distance between links and the number of habitants between nodes in order to return short links to connect more populated cities. In Figure 20.6, (a) displays the road system of Mexico, (b) shows the simulation result based on short roads, and (c) exhibits a simulation output with regard to short roads and large cities.

Although this example is very simple, note that the process behind emergent patterns is an auto-organization between agents without a central authority or planner that can be applied to the analysis of the existence, geometry, or hierarchy in road networks.

In addition to the rigorous application of ABMs to transportation networks, the results must be communicated in a straightforward, structured, and scientific way. Simulation models are usually validated through comparison to empirical data. The simulation also needs to achieve other requirements, such as analyzing temporal changes in the topology of the network based on different network paths, measuring structural properties of the network, and making a sensitivity analysis where emergent patterns in the network are related to dissimilar initial conditions (Xie and Levinson, 2009a). Furthermore, there are some interesting proposals to create a basic framework for communicating ABMs results, the most useful of which is the ODD protocol (Overview, Design Concepts, and Details). Based on the work of Grimm et al. (2006), this protocol is applied to study large-scale system properties that emerge from the adaptive behavior of agents.

CONCLUSION

Transportation networks are at the center of network analysis in natural and social sciences. Recent trends show more interdisciplinary approaches and fast developments of new analytical methods explored by physicists. While transport network analysis still has a lot to gain from such advances, it maintains its specificity by bridging abstract measures and theories with knowledge of the transport industry and broader socio-economic and spatial issues. On the other hand, natural sciences give increasing importance to the spatial and social dimension of networks, thereby calling for further collaboration between natural and social sciences. One interesting research path lies in the field of intermodalism, which integrates local studies of planning and strategies with global-level approaches to multiple network topologies and interdependencies. Additionally, a closer look at meso-level measures would certainly foster understanding of how transportation networks are structured and how they evolve with regard to the combination of their local and global properties.

The study of dynamics in transport networks is improved through the application of ABMs. Although such models are relatively new in the field of transport networks, they help to understand endogenous mechanisms that produce unexpected collective behavior in the system. In order to apply ABMs to the analysis of network dynamics, it is important to define the method and mechanism of analysis based on theoretical and empirical evidence. In conclusion, applying complex systems to transport networks is preferred to complement theories and applications in different scientific fields.

NOTES

1 For a detailed explanation and illustration of graph theoretical measures and indices see http://people.hofstra.edu/geotrans/eng/ch1en/meth1en/ch1m3en.html.
2 See in-depth reviews of clustering methods by Fortunato (2010) and Schaeffer (2007).
3 For a complete review of the literature, see Xie and Levinson (2009a).

REFERENCES

Amiel, M., Mélançon, G., Rozenblat, C. (2005) "Multi-level networks: The example of worldwide air passenger flows", *Mappemonde*, Vol. 79, No. 3, http://mappemonde.mgm.fr/num7/index.html (in French, accessed July 2010).

Banavar, J.R., Maritan, A., Rinaldo, A. (1999) "Size and form in efficient transportation networks", *Nature*, Vol. 399, pp. 130–132.

Barabási, A.L. (2002) *Linked: The new science of networks*, Cambridge, MA: Perseus Publication.

Barabási, A.L., Albert, R. (1999) "Emergence of scaling in random networks", *Science*, Vol. 286, pp. 509–512.

Barabási, A.L., Albert, R. (2002) "Statistical mechanics of complex networks", *Review of Modern Physics*, Vol. 74, pp. 47–97.

Barrat, A., Barthélemy, M., Pastor-Satorras, R., Vespignani, A. (2004) "The architecture of complex weighted networks", *Proceedings of the National Academy of Sciences*, Vol. 101, No. 11, pp. 3747–3752.

Barthélemy, M., Flammini, A. (2006) "Optimal traffic networks", *Journal of Statistical Mechanics*, L07002.

Batty, M. (2005) *Cities and Complexity. Understanding cities with cellular automata, agent-based models, and fractals*, Cambridge MA: MIT Press.

Batty, M. (2008) "The size, scale, and shape of cities", *Science*, Vol. 319, No. 5864, pp. 681–860.

Beauguitte, L. (2011) "Blockmodeling and equivalence", FMR Working Paper, No. 5, http://halshs.

archives-ouvertes.fr/docs/00/56/64/74/PDF/fmr5_blockmodeling_equivalence.pdf (in French, accessed May 2011).

Béguin, H., Thomas, I. (1997) "The shape of the transportation network and the optimal location of facilities. How to measure the shape of a network?", *Cybergeo: European Journal of Geography*, No. 26, http://cybergeo.revues.org/index2189.html (in French) (accessed July 2010).

Berge, C. (1973) *Graphes*, Paris: Gauthier-Villars.

Blumenfeld-Lieberthal, E. (2009) "The topology of transportation networks: a comparison between different economies", *Networks and Spatial Economics*, Vol. 9, No. 3, pp. 427–458.

Blumenfeld-Lieberthal, E., Portugali, J. (2010) "Network cities: A complexity-network approach to urban dynamics and development", in B. Jiang and X. Yao (eds) *Geospatial Analysis and Modelling of Urban Structure and Dynamics*, New York: Springer Science + Business Media, pp. 77–90.

Boccaletti, S., Latora, V., Moreno, Y., Chavez, M., Hwang, D.U. (2006) "Complex networks: structure and dynamics", *Physics Reports*, Vol. 424, pp. 175–308.

Bogart, D. (2009) "Inter-modal network externalities and transport development: Evidence from roads, canals, and ports during the English industrial revolution", *Networks and Spatial Economics*, Vol. 9, No. 3, pp. 309–338.

Bollobas, B. (1998) *Modern Graph Theory*, New York: Springer-Verlag.

Bowen, J. (2000) "Airline hubs in Southeast Asia: National economic development and nodal accessibility", *Journal of Transport Geography*, Vol. 8, No. 1, pp. 25–41.

Bowen, J. (2002) "Network change, deregulation, and access in the global airline industry, Economic Geography", Vol. 78, No. 4, pp. 425–439.

Buldyrev, S.V., Parshani, R., Paul, G., Stanley, H.E., Havlin, S. (2010) "Catastrophic cascade of failures in interdependent networks", *Nature*, Vol. 464, pp. 1025–1028.

Cardillo, A., Scellato, S., Latora, V., Porta, S. (2006) "Structural properties of planar graphs of urban street patterns", *Physical Review. E, Statistical, Nonlinear, and Soft Matter Physics*, Vol. 73(2), No. 6, pp. 066107.1–066107.8.

Cattan, N. (1995) "Barrier effects: The case of air and rail flows", *International Political Science Review*, Vol. 16, No. 3, pp. 237–248.

Cattan, N. (2004) "Le monde au prisme des réseaux aériens", *Flux*, Vol. 58, pp. 32–43.

Chapelon, L. (2005) "Accessibility as a marker of disparities of influence among port cities in Europe", *Cybergeo: European Journal of Geography*, No. 345, http://cybergeo.revues.org/index2463.html (in French, accessed July 2010).

Choua, Y.H. (1993) "Airline deregulation and nodal accessibility", *Journal of Transport Geography*, Vol. 1, No. 1, pp. 36–46.

Christaller, W. (1933) *Die Zentralen Orte in Suddeutschland*, Jena: Gustav Fischer.

Cliff, A., Haggett, P., Ord, K. (1979) "Graph theory and geography", in R. Wilson and L. Beineke (eds) *Applications of Graph Theory*, London: Academic Press, pp. 293–326.

de Dios Ortuzar, J., Willumsen, L.G. (2001) *Modeling Transport*, Chichester: John Wiley and Sons.

De Lannoy, W., Van Oudheusden, D. (1991) "The accessibility of nodes in the Belgian road network", *Geojournal*, Vol. 2, No. 1, pp. 65–70.

Degenne, A., Forse, M. (1999) *Introducing Social Networks*, London: Sage Publications.

DeMontis, A., Chessa, A., Caschili, S., Campagna, M., Deplano, G. (2010) "Modeling computing systems through a complex network analysis: A study of the Italian islands of Sardinia and Sicily", *Journal of Transport Land Use*, Vol 2., Nos. 3–4, pp. 39–55.

Deng, W.B., Long, G., Wei, L., Xu, C. (2009) "Worldwide marine transportation network: Efficiency and container throughput", *Chinese Physics Letters*, Vol. 26, No. 11, 118901.

Ducruet, C. (2011) "Graph simplification and partitioning", FMR Working Paper, No. 6, http://halshs.archives-ouvertes.fr/docs/00/57/90/65/PDF/fmr6_partitionnement.pdf (in French, accessed May 2011).

Ducruet, C., Ietri, D., Rozenblat, C. (2011) "Cities in worldwide air and sea flows: A multiple networks analysis", *Cybergeo: European Journal of Geography*, No. 528, http://cybergeo.revues.org/23603 (accessed May 2011).

Ducruet, C., Lee, S.W., Ng, K.Y.A. (2010a) "Centrality and vulnerability in liner shipping networks: Revisiting the Northeast Asian port hierarchy", *Maritime Policy and Management*, Vol. 37, No. 1, pp. 17–36.

Ducruet, C., Notteboom, T. (2012) "The worldwide maritime network of container shipping: Spatial structure and regional dynamics", *Global Networks*, Vol. 12, No. 3, pp. 395–423.

Ducruet, C., Rozenblat, C., Zaidi, F. (2010b) "Ports in multi-level maritime networks: Evidence from the Atlantic (1996–2006)", *Journal of Transport Geography*, Vol. 18, No. 4, pp. 508–518.

Dupuy G., Stransky V. (1996) "Cities and highway networks in Europe", *Journal of Transport Geography*, Vol. 4, No. 2, pp. 107–119.

Eagle, N., Macy, M., Claxton, R. (2010) "Network diversity and economic development", *Science*, Vol. 328, pp. 1029–1031/

Fleming, D.K., Hayuth, Y. (1994) "Spatial characteristics of transportation hubs: Centrality and intermediacy", *Journal of Transport Geography*, Vol. 2, No. 1, pp. 3–18.

Fortunato, S. (2010) "Community detection in graphs", *Physics Reports*, No. 486, pp. 75–174.

Fricker, M.D., Boddy, L., Nakagaki, T., Bebber, D. (2009) "Adaptive biological networks", in S. Kelso (ed.), *Understanding Complex Systems*, Berlin: Springer, pp. 51–70.

Fujita, M., Krugman, P., Venables, A. (1999) *The Spatial Economy: Cities, regions, and international trade*, Cambridge: Cambridge University Press.

Garrison, W.L. (1960) "Connectivity of the interstate highway system", *Papers of the Regional Science Association*, Vol. 6, pp. 121–137.

Garrison, W.L., Marble, D.F. (1962) *The Structure of Transportation Networks*, Technical Report 62-II, U.S. Army Transportation Command.

Garrison, W.L., Marble, D.F. (1974) "Graph theoretic concepts", in M.E. Eliot Hurst (ed.) *Transportation Geography: Comments and readings*, New York: McGraw, pp.58–80.

Gastner, M.T., Newman, M.E.J. (2006) "The spatial structure of networks", *The European Physical Journal B*, Vol. 49, pp. 247–252.

Gleyze, J.F. (2007) "Making allowances for spatial and network effects when assessing indicators on infrastructure network nodes", *Cybergeo: European Journal of Geography*, No. 370, http://cybergeo.revues.org/index5532.html (in French) (accessed July 2010).

Gleyze, J.F. (2008) *Simplifying Geographical Networks: Assessment of relational dependences induced by the paths inside the network and nodes aggregation around transfer areas*, Working Paper, COGIT, IGN, Paris, France, http://halshs.archives-ouvertes.fr/docs/00/22/41/21/PDF/Plate-formes_relationnelles.pdf (in French, accessed July 2010).

Gleyze, J.F. (2013, in press) "Topological clustering tools on graphs: Which applications for networks geography?", in C. Rozenblat (ed.) *Multilevel Analysis and Visualization of Geographical Networks*, Springer Geography.

Gorman, S.P., Kulkarni, R. (2004) "Spatial small worlds: New geographic patterns for an information economy", *Environment Planning B*, Vol. 31, No. 2, pp. 273–296.

Goyal, S., Joshi, S. (2002) "Network of collaboration in oligopoly", *Games and Economic Behavior*, Vol. 43, pp. 57–85.

Grimm, V., Berger, U., Bastiansen, F., Eliassen, S., Ginot, V., Giske, J., Goss-Custard, J., Grand, T., Heinz, S.K., Huse, G., Huth, A., Jepsen, J.U., Jrgensen, C., Mooij, W.M., Mller, B., Pe'er, G., Piou, C., Railsback, S.F., Robbins, A.M., Robbins, M.M., Rossmanith, E., Rger, N., Strand, E., Souissi, S., Stillman, R.A., Vab, R., Visser, U., DeAngelis, D.L. (2006) "A standard protocol for describing individual-based and agent-based models", *Ecological Modelling*, Vol. 198, pp. 115–126.

Grubesic, T.H., Matisziw, T.C., Zook, M.A. (2008) "Global airline networks and nodal regions", *Geojournal*, Vol. 71, No. 1, pp. 53–66.

Guida, M., Maria, F. (2007) "Topology of the Italian airport network: A scale-free small-world network with a fractal structure?", *Chaos, Solitons and Fractals*, Vol. 31, No. 3, pp. 527–536.

Guimera, R., Mossa, S., Turtschi, A., Amaral, L.A.N. (2005) "The worldwide air transportation network: Anomalous centrality, community structure, and cities' global roles", *Proceedings of the National Academy of Sciences*, Vol. 102, No. 22, pp. 7794–7799.

Gutierrez, J., Urbano, P. (1996) "Accessibility in the European Union: The impact of the trans-European road network", *Journal of Transport Geography*, Vol. 4, pp. 1, pp. 15–25.

Haggett P., Chorley R. (1972) *Network Analysis in Geography*, London: Arnold.

Helbing, D., Keltsch, J., Molnr, P. (1997) "Modeling the evolution of human trail systems", *Nature*, Vol. 388, p. 47.

Hu, Y., Zhu, D. (2009) "Empirical analysis of the worldwide maritime transportation network", *Physica A*, Vol. 388, No. 10, pp. 2061–2071.

Jenelius, E. (2009) "Network structure and travel patterns: Explaining the geographical disparities of road network vulnerability", *Journal of Transport Geography*, Vol. 17, No. 3, pp. 234–244.

Jiang, B., Yao, X. (eds) (2010) *Geospatial Analysis and Modelling of Urban Structure and Dynamics*, New York: Springer Science + Business Media.

Jin, F., Wang, C., Li, X., Wang, J. (2010) "China's regional transport dominance: Density, proximity, and accessibility", *Journal of Geographical Sciences*, Vol. 20, No. 2, pp. 295–309.

Kansky, K. (1963) *The Structure of Transportation Networks: Relationships between network geography and regional characteristics*, Research Paper No. 84, Chicago: University of Chicago.

Kirman, A. (2011) *Complex Economics, Individual and Collective Rationality*, The Graz Schumpeter Lectures, London: Routledge.

Krugman, P. (1996) *The Self-Organizing Economy*, Oxford: Blackwell Publisher.

Kuby, M., Tierney, S., Roberts, T., Upchurch, C. (2005) *A Comparison of Geographic Information Systems, Complex Networks, and Other Models for Analyzing Transportation Network Topologies*, NASA Center for Aerospace Information (CASI), Contractor Report No. 2005-213522.

Kurant, M., Thiran, P. (2006) "Extraction and analysis of traffic and topologies of transportation networks", *Physical Review E*, Vol. 74, No. 3, 36114.

Lam, L., Pochy, R. (1993) "Active-walker models: Growth and form in nonequilibrium systems", *Computation Simulation*, Vol. 7, p. 534.

Latora, V., Marchiori, M. (2002) "Is the Boston subway a small-world network?", *Physica A: Statistical Mechanics and its Applications*, Vol. 314, No. 1(4), pp. 109–113.

Leblanc, L.J. (1975) "An algorithm for the discrete network design problem", *Transportation Science*, Vol. 9, No. 3, pp. 183–199.

Levinson, D., Yerra, B. (2006) "Self organization of surface transportation networks", *Transportation Science*, Vol. 40, No. 2, pp. 179–188.

Li, W., Cai, X. (2004) "Statistical analysis of airport network of China", *Physical Review E*, Vol. 69, No. 4, 46106.

Mackechnie, G., Mackaness, W.A. (1999) "Detection and simplification of road junctions in automated map generalization", *Geoinformatica*, Vol. 3, pp. 185–200.

Martens, K., Benenson, I., Levy, N. (2010) "The dilemma of on-street parking policy: Exploring cruising for parking using an agent-based model", in B. Jiang and X. Yao (eds) *Geospatial Analysis and Modelling of Urban Structure and Dynamics*, New York: Springer Science + Business Media, pp. 121–138.

Moody, J., White, D. (2003) "Social cohesion and embeddedness: A hierarchical conception of social groups", *American Sociological Review*, Vol. 68, No. 1, pp. 103–127.

Morrill, R.L. (1965) "Migration and the growth of urban settlement", *Lund Studies in Geography Series B Human Geography*, Vol. 26, pp. 65–82.

Murayama, Y. (1994) "The impact of railways on accessibility in the Japanese urban system", *Journal of Transport Geography*, Vol. 2, No. 2, pp. 87–100.

National Institute of Statistics and Geography of Mexico (2005), "Road vector map", INEGI Website, August 2010, http://mapserver.inegi.org.mx/data/inf_e1m/?s=geo&c=979.

Newman, M.E.J. (2003) "The structure and function of complex networks", *SIAM Review*, Vol. 45, No. 2, pp. 167–256.

Nystuen, J.D., Dacey, M.F. (1961) "A graph theory interpretation of nodal regions", *Papers in Regional Science*, Vol. 7, No. 1, pp. 29–42.

O'Kelly, M.E. (1998) "A geographer's analysis of hub-and-spoke networks", *Journal of Transport Geography*, Vol. 6, No. 3, pp. 171–186.

Parshani, R., Rozenblat, C., Ietri, D., Ducruet, C., Havlin, S. (2010) "Intersimilarity between coupled networks", *Europhysics Letters*, Vol. 92, p. 68002.

Pumain, D., Tannier, C. (2005) "Fractals in urban geography: A theoretical outline and an empirical example", *Cybergeo: European Journal of Geography*, No. 307, http://cybergeo.revues.org/index3275.html.

Rodrigue, J.P., Comtois, C., Slack, B. (eds) (2009) *The Geography of Transport Systems*, Second Edition, New York: Routledge.

Schaeffer, S.E. (2007) "Graph clustering", *Computer Science Review*, Vol. 1, No. 1., pp. 27–64.

Schweitzer, F., Ebeling, F., Rose, H., Weiss, O. (1998) "Optimization of road networks using evolutionary strategies", *Evolutionary Computation*, Vol. 41, pp. 419–438.

Scott, D.W., Novak, D., Aultman-Hall, M., Guo, F. (2005) *Network Robustness Index: A new method for identifying critical links and evaluating the performance of transportation networks*, Working Paper no. 9, Centre for Spatial Analysis, Hamilton, Canada, http://www.science.mcmaster.ca/cspa/papers/CSpA%20WP%20009.pdf (accessed July 2010).

Sen, P., Dasgupta, S., Chatterjee, A., Sreeram, P.A., Mukherjee, G., Manna, S.S. (2003) "Small-world properties of the Indian railway network", *Physical Review E*, Vol. 67, No. 3, 036106.

Shaw, S.L. (1993) "Hub structures of major US passenger airlines", *Journal of Transport Geography*, Vol. 1, No. 1, pp. 47–58.

Shin, K.H., Timberlake, M. (2000) "World cities in Asia: Cliques, centrality and connectedness", *Urban Studies*, Vol. 37, No. 12, pp. 2257–2285.

Sienkiewicz, J., Holyst, J.A. (2005) "Statistical analysis of 22 public transport networks in Poland", *Physical Review E*, Vol. 72, No. 4, 046127.

Taaffe, E.J., Gauthier, H.L. (1973) *Geography of Transportation*, New York: Prentice-Hall.

Taaffe, E.J., Morrill, R.L., Gould, P.R (1963) "Transportation expansion in underdeveloped countries: A comparative analysis", *Geographical Review*, Vol. 53, No. 4, pp. 503–529.

Tissandier, P. (2013, inpress) "Defining polycentric urban areas through commuting cohesion", in C. Rozenblat (ed.), *Multilevel Analysis and Visualization of Geographical Networks*, Berlin: Springer.

Van Geenhuizen, M. (2000) "Interconnectivity of transport networks: a conceptual and empirical exploration", *Transportation Planning and Technology*, Vol. 23, No. 3, pp. 199–213.

Vespignani, A. (2010) "Complex networks: The fragility of interdependency", *Nature*, Vol. 464, pp. 984–985.

Vicsek, T. (2000) "Complexity: The bigger picture", *Nature*, Vol. 418, p. 131.

Von Ferber, C., Holovatch, Y., Palchykov, V. (2005) "Scaling in public transport networks", *Condensed Matter Physics*, Vol. 8, pp. 225–234.

Wang, J., Jin, F., Mo, H., Wang, F. (2009) "Spatiotemporal evolution of China's railway network in the 20th century: An accessibility approach", *Transportation Research Part A*, Vol. 43, pp. 765–778.

Wang, J., Mo, H., Wang, F., Jin, F. (2011) "Exploring the network structure and nodal centrality of China's air transport network: A complex network approach", *Journal of Transport Geography*, Vo. 19, No. 4, pp. 712–721.

Wasserman, S., Faust, K. (1994) *Social Network Analysis: Methods and applications*, Cambridge MA: Cambridge University Press.

Waters, N.M. (2006) "Network and nodal indices: measures of complexity and redundancy: A review", in A. Reggiani and P. Nijkamp (eds), *Spatial Dynamics, Network and Modelling*, Cheltenham, UK and Northampton, MA: Edward Elgar.

Watts, D.J., Strogatz, S.H. (1998) "Collective dynamics of small-world networks", *Nature*, Vol. 393, pp. 440–442.

West, D.B. (1996) *Introduction to Graph Theory*, Second Edition, Upper Saddle River NJ: Prentice Hall.

Wilson, N.H.M., Nuzzolo, A. (eds) (2009) *Schedule-Based Modeling of Transportation Networks*, Volume 46, New York: Springer.

Xie, F., Levinson, D. (2009a) "Modeling the growth of transportation networks: A comprehensive review", *Networks and Spatial Economics*, Vol. 9, No. 3, pp. 291–307.

Xie, F., Levinson, D. (2009b) "Topological evolution of surface transportation networks", *Computers, Environment and Urban Systems*, Vol. 33, pp. 211–223.

Xu, X., Hu, J., Liu, F. (2007a) "Empirical analysis of the ship transport network of China", *Chaos*, Vol. 17, No. 2, 023129.

Xu, X., Hu, J., Liu, F., Liu, L. (2007b) "Scaling and correlations in three bus-transport networks of China", *Physica A: Statistical Mechanics and its Applications*, Vol. 374, No. 1, pp. 441–448.

Yamins, D., Rasmussen, S., Fogel, D. (2003) "Growing urban roads", *Networks and Spatial Economics*, Vol. 3, pp. 69–85.

Yang, H., Bell, M.G.H. (1998) "Models and algorithms for road network design: A review and some new developments", *Transport Reviews*, Vol. 18, pp. 257–278.

Yerra, B., Levinson, D. (2005) "The emergence of hierarchy in transportation networks", *Annals of Regional Science*, Vol. 39, No. 3, pp. 541–553.

Zaidi, F. (2011) *Analysis, Structure and Organization of Complex Networks*, Saarbrücken: LAP Lambert Academic Publishing.

Zhang, P.C., Peeta, S., Friesz, T. (2005) "Dynamic game theoretic model of multi-layer infrastructure networks", *Networks and Spatial Economics*, Vol. 5, pp. 147–178.

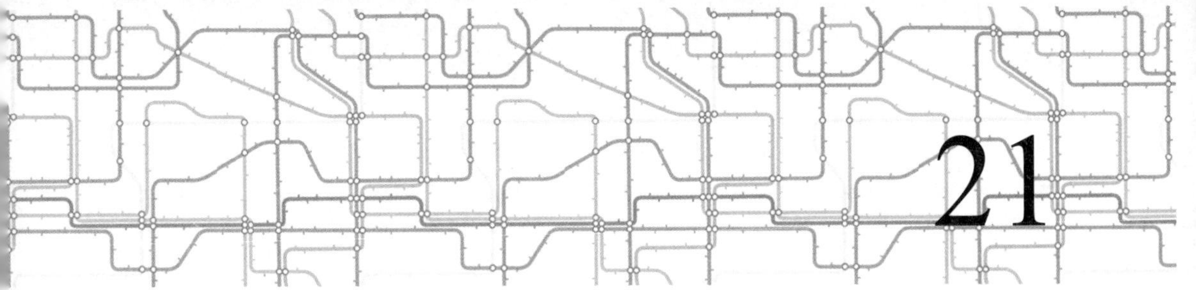

Locational Transport Models: Production and Attraction

Veronique Van Acker and Frank Witlox

INTRODUCTION

Despite virtual possibilities such as telecommuting, videoconferencing and e-shopping, people still travel from one place to another in physical space, which reminds us of the derived nature of travel. Although sometimes people travel just 'for fun' (Mokhtarian and Salomon, 2001; Ory and Mokhtarian, 2005), people mainly travel in order to access desired activities in different locations. After all, activities such as living, working, shopping and recreating are in most cases spatially separated and, thus, encourage the need to travel and induce a demand for transport. Changes in the spatial distribution of these activities can thus result in changes in transport demand. Consequently, the demand for transport has become a crucially important subject in transport planning and various models have been developed to forecast future transport demand.

The earliest transport models date back to the 1950s and 1960s, an era in which the fundamentals of transport modeling were mainly developed in the USA (e.g., Detroit and Chicago) and the UK (e.g., London). In these initial attempts, transport demand was reduced to four different components of travel: (i) trip generation (production and attraction) or the decision whether or not to travel, (ii) trip distribution or the choice of destination, (iii) modal split or the choice of transport mode, and (iv) route assignment or the choice of route. Although transport users might consider these four components simultaneously, most transport models are characterized by a clear sequence of trip generation, distribution and diversion. This resulted in the application of the four-step model that today remains one of the most extensively used transport models (Bates, 2000; McNally, 2000).

This chapter deals with the first step of the four-step model and describes how trip generation is modeled. The remainder of the chapter is structured as follows. First, some basic concepts of trip-based models such as the four-step model are presented. Second, the methodological framework of the four-step model and the position of trip generation within this framework are discussed. In the third section, regression analysis – one widely applied trip generation model – is discussed in detail. Finally, this chapter concludes with some important remarks on trip generation models as well as the discussion of some recent advances.

TRIP-BASED MODELS: SOME IMPORTANT CONCEPTS

We start by defining some basic concepts that are commonly used in trip-based models such as the four-step model. The central notion in the four-step model is a 'trip'. A 'trip' occurs if a person travels from one location where he/she performs a specific activity to another location where another activity will be performed (see Figure 21.1(a)). Trips are thus made for a specific purpose or 'motive' (e.g., working, shopping, recreating). The starting point is called the 'origin' or 'production', the end point 'destination' or 'attraction'. Trips starting from home are defined as 'home-based trips', whereas 'non-home-based trips' depart from other locations. One specific transport mode can be used along the trip, but also a combination of transport modes is possible. For example, somebody travels by train to work, but first cycles from home to the nearest railway station and takes the bus from the end railway station to the work address. In this example, bicycle and bus are used as access and egress modes respectively, and the home to work trip consists of three legs (b). Trips can also be linked to each other to form a trip-chain or a tour that starts and ends at home (c). For example, somebody goes shopping first on the way back home from work.

As the notion suggests, trip-based models usually estimate the number of trips and not the number of legs or tours as such. Such models can be refined by considering each trip motive separately instead of focusing on complete travel patterns. Working has been considered as one of the most important trip motives for a long time and, therefore, many trip-based models focus on working trips. However, recent travel surveys indicate that non-work trip motives such as shopping and leisure are equally important as working. Furthermore, some trip-based models also take into account time-of-day and distinguish between trips during and outside peak hour since this influences the share of different trip motives throughout a day. Mandatory trips such as work or school trips are restricted

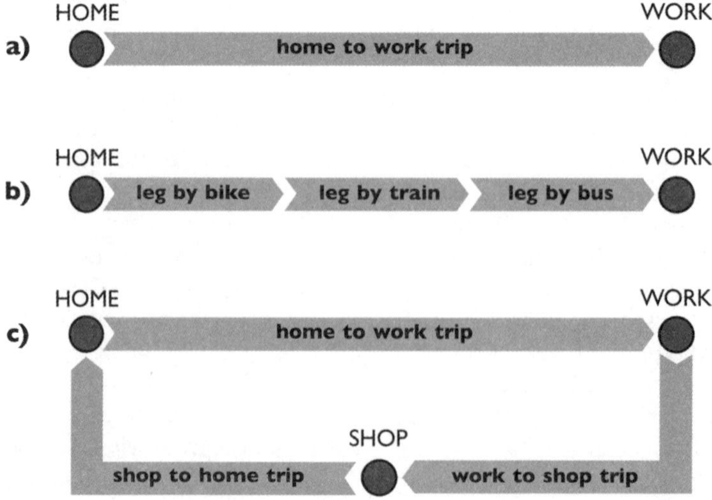

Figure 21.1 The difference between trips (a), legs (b) and tours (c)

by office and school hours and are, therefore, concentrated in peak hours. This is in contrast to optional trips such as shopping or recreational trips which are less bound by time restrictions.

METHODOLOGICAL FRAMEWORK OF THE FOUR-STEP MODEL

As already mentioned in the Introduction, the four-step model is a sequential demand model consisting of four consecutive steps, using a so-called trip matrix (Table 21.1).

Assume that the study area for which the model will be estimated is divided in I (or J) different zones. Each zone can be considered as an origin but also as a destination of a trip. In the trip matrix, x_{ij} represents the number of trips departing from zone i and arriving in zone j. R_i corresponds to the total number of trips departing from zone i, while C_j corresponds to the total number of trips arriving in zone j. R and C stand for R(ow) and C(olumn), but O(rigin) and D(estination) are also often used. Note that the resulting matrix is symmetrical, hence I and J are interchangeable.

$$R_i = \sum_{j=1}^{I} x_{ij}$$

$$C_j = \sum_{i=1}^{I} x_{ij}$$

The grand total X represents the total number of trips (e.g., number of passengers or tonnage) generated in the study area. This corresponds to the total of all row totals or the total of all column totals in the trip matrix:

$$X = \sum_i R_i = \sum_j C_j$$

In order to construct such a trip matrix, one can distinguish four steps (see Figure 21.2):

1 Trip generation: i.e. determination of the row and column totals R_i and C_j, or the number of trips 'produced' and 'attracted' by each zone, as well as the total volume of trips X in the study area.
2 Trip distribution: i.e. distribution of the row and column totals R_i and C_j over the separate flows x_{ij} between the zones.
3 Modal split: i.e. determination of the share of each transport modes (car, public transport, etc.) in the traffic flows x_{ij}.
4 Trip assignment: i.e. choice of route by each transport mode so that one can detect traffic congestion on the transport network. A feedback mechanism to prior steps might be included in the transport model so that in case of traffic congestion the number of trips will be re-distributed between the zones.

The four-step model thus starts with trip generation. In many cases, information on traffic flows is completely missing so that we have to estimate the number of trips departing from and arriving in each zone within the study area. The production submodel estimates the number of trips originated from each zone based on socio-economic characteristics of the traveler and spatial characteristics of these zones. Influencing factors affecting trip generation are, among others, income, car ownership, household structure and family size.

Table 21.1 Trip matrix

Destination Origin	1	2	3	…	I	Total traffic departing
1	X_{11}	X_{12}	X_{13}	…	X_{1i}	R_1
2	X_{21}	X_{22}	X_{23}	…	X_{2i}	R_2
3	X_{31}	X_{32}	X_{33}	…	X_{3i}	R_3
…	…	…	…	…	…	…
I	X_{i1}	X_{i1}	X_{i1}	…	X_{ii}	R_3
Total traffic arriving	C_1	C_2	C_3	…	C_i	X

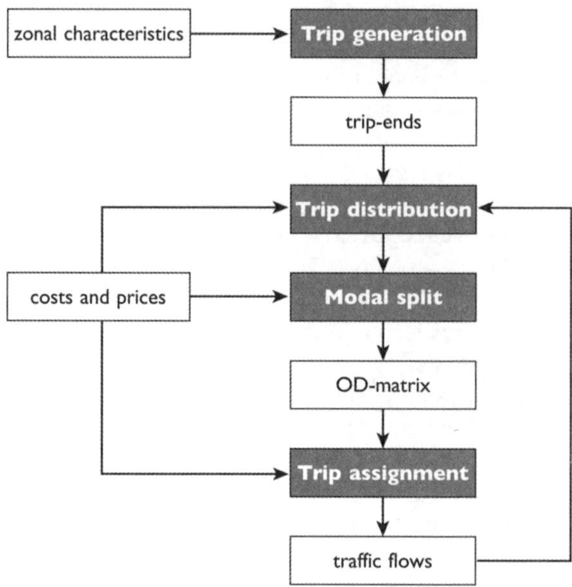

Figure 21.2 Structure of the four-step model

These four factors have been used in several trip generation studies that consider households as unit of analysis. Other trip generation studies use zonal data and therefore include value of land and residential density. Some zonal studies also use accessibility in order to study the consequences of changes in the transportation system and, consequently, elasticity of trip generation (Ortúzar and Willumsen, 2001).

It is important to note that, based on these influencing factors, the trip production submodel calculates the number of outgoing trips without taking into account the destination of these trips. However, each zone not only generates trips (and operates as an origin), but can also attracts trips (and operates as a destination). The attraction submodel therefore estimates the number of trips destined to each zone based on the attractiveness of these zones. Influencing attraction factors are employment, land use (industrial, commercial, services, etc.) and accessibility. Previously mentioned influencing factors all relate to trips of persons, but similar factors can be used to estimate the magnitude of freight transport. Production and attraction of freight is usually based on the number of employees and firm-related characteristics such as profit, built-up area, size, type and accessibility. These influencing factors are then used as input variables for estimation techniques of which regression analysis and category analysis are the two most widely used.

MODELS FOR TRIP GENERATION: REGRESSION ANALYSIS

Information on production and attraction factors can be used as input in a regression analysis that estimates the number of trips departing from and arriving in each zone of the study area.

The basics

A simple linear regression analysis estimates the effect of *one* independent variable X on one dependent variable Y. In a trip generation model this implies that the number of trips departing from or arriving in a specific zone is explained by one influencing factor such as income or employment density. For example,

Table 21.2 Example of household data for a simple linear regression

Household	Trip generation (average number of trips per household)	Income (average gross monthly household income in × €1000)
1	2	4
2	4	6
3	10	17
4	5	11
5	5	4
6	15	17
7	7	9
8	4	9
9	6	7
10	13	19
11	8	18
12	6	8
13	9	7
14	11	11
15	10	11
16	11	13
17	12	15
18	8	11
19	8	13
20	6	7

we can assume that high-income households generate more trips (Table 21.2) or that zones with higher employment densities will attract more trips.

A simple linear regression tries to fit a straight line to the scatter plot of the observations (Figure 21.3). This straight line, or the linear relationship between both variables, is mathematically represented by:

$$y_i = a + bx_i + \varepsilon_i \qquad (21.1)$$

where:

- y_i: observation i on the dependent variable Y (e.g., the number of trips per household);
- x_i: observation i on the independent variable X (e.g., household income);
- a: intercept of the regression line, or a parameter expressing the magnitude of trips if the independent variable X has value 0;
- b: slope of the regression line, or a parameter expressing the effect of a change in the independent variable X on the dependent variable Y;
- ε_i: residue, or a parameter expressing to which extent observations deviate from the estimated regression line.

The regression line is fitted to a set of observations, or in other words the parameters a and b are calculated in such a way that the magnitude of the residues is minimized. This approach is known as the 'ordinary least squares' (OLS) method since the estimation of the parameters a and b is based on the minimization of the squares of the residues ε_i:

$$\sum_{i=1}^{n} \varepsilon_i^2 = \sum_{i=1}^{n} (y_i - bx_i - a)^2 = min \qquad (21.2)$$

Deriving Equation 21.2 provides us with intercept a and slope b of the regression line:

$$\frac{\partial \sum_{i=1}^{n} \varepsilon_i^2}{\partial a} = 2\sum_{i=1}^{n} (y_i - bx_i - a) = 0$$

$$\frac{\partial \sum_{i=1}^{n} \varepsilon_i^2}{\partial b} = 2\sum_{i=1}^{n} \left[(y_i - bx_i - a)(x_i)\right] = 0 \qquad (21.3)$$

Elaborating the set of equations in Equation 21.3 results in:

$$b = \frac{\sum_{i=1}^{n} y_i \sum_{i=1}^{n} x_i - n\sum_{i=1}^{n} x_i y_i}{\left(\sum_{i=1}^{n} x_i\right)^2 - n\sum_{i=1}^{n} x_i^2}$$

$$a = \overline{y} - b\overline{x} \qquad (21.4)$$

Applied to our example of how income influences the number of generated trips per household:

$$b = \frac{(160 \times 217) - (20 \times 1963)}{(217)^2 - (20 \times 2751)} = 0.572$$

$$a = 8 - 0.572 \times 10.85 = 1.789$$

The regression equation can thus be written down as:

$$y = 1.789 + 0.572\ income$$

Or translated into human language: a marginal increase in income by 1,000 EUR (i.e. the basic unit in which income is expressed) results in 0.572 extra trips per household (Table 21.3).

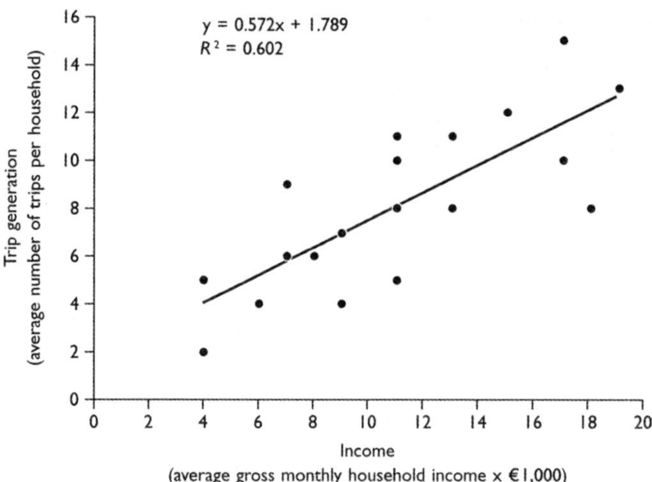

Figure 21.3 Simple linear regression line

Table 21.3 Example of how income influences the average number of trips per household

Household	y_i	x_i	$x_i y_i$	x_i^2	$\hat{y}$	$(y_i-\bar{y})^2$	$(y_i-\hat{y})^2$
1	2	4	8	16	4	36	4
2	4	6	24	36	5	16	1
3	10	17	170	289	12	4	2
4	5	11	55	121	8	9	10
5	5	4	20	16	4	9	1
6	15	17	255	289	12	49	12
7	7	9	63	81	7	1	0
8	4	9	36	81	7	16	9
9	6	7	42	49	6	4	0
10	13	19	247	361	13	25	0
11	8	18	144	324	12	0	17
12	6	8	48	64	6	4	0
13	9	7	63	49	6	1	10
14	11	11	121	121	8	9	8
15	10	11	110	121	8	4	4
16	11	13	143	169	9	9	3
17	12	15	180	225	10	16	3
18	8	11	88	121	8	0	0
19	8	13	104	169	9	0	2
20	6	7	42	49	6	4	0
$\sum$	**160**	**217**	**1963**	**2751**		**216**	**86**
average	**8**	**10.85**					

Figure 21.4 not only plots the regression line with its equation, it also mentions another parameter, R^2. Performing a regression analysis implies the estimation of the equation of the regression line that best fits the data points. A regression line that closely fits this scatter plot of data points explains more variance in the dependent variable than a regression

line that does not fit the scatter plot. The coefficient of determination R^2 illustrates the amount of observed variance in the dependent variable that is explained by the independent variable. In other words, R^2 describes the strength of the relationship between both variables. Figure 21.4 illustrates how the observed y_i for the dependent variable varies around its average value $\bar{y}$. This is the total variance S_Y^2 which we try to explain by performing a regression analysis. The total variance thus consists of (i) the explained variance R^2 predicted by the regression line, and (ii) the unexplained variance S_R^2 which remains unpredicted by the regression line. The coefficient of determination R^2 is then calculated by confronting the total variance $(S_Y^2 - S_R^2)$ with the unexplained variance S_R^2:

$$R^2 = \frac{S_Y^2 - S_R^2}{S_Y^2} = \frac{\sum_{i=1}^{n}(y_i - \bar{y})^2 - \sum_{i=1}^{n}(y_i - \hat{y})^2}{\sum_{i=1}^{n}(y_i - \bar{y}^2)} \qquad (21.5)$$

where $\hat{y} = a + bx_i$.

If all data points are situated along the regression line, the total variance S_Y^2 of the dependent variable is perfectly explained. In that case, the unexplained variance S_R^2 equals to zero and, consequently, the coefficient of determination R^2 is 1. If all data points are scattered around the regression line, the unexplained variance S_R^2 becomes larger and the coefficient of determination R^2 approaches zero.

In our example, 60.2% of the variance in the number of trips per household is explained by income:

$$R^2 = \frac{216 - 86}{216} = 60.2\%$$

This also means that 39.8% of the total variance in generated trips per household is not explained and is due to other influencing factors than income.

Parameters a, b and R^2 are calculated based on a sample of households and, therefore, does not necessarily hold for the total population of households. Consequently, we have to validate the statistical significance of these parameters. Assessment of the significance level of regression parameters a and b is based on the t-distribution, whereas the statistical evaluation of the coefficient of determination R^2 is based on the F-distribution.

Assessment of the regression parameters a and b is based on dividing these coefficients by their standard deviation:

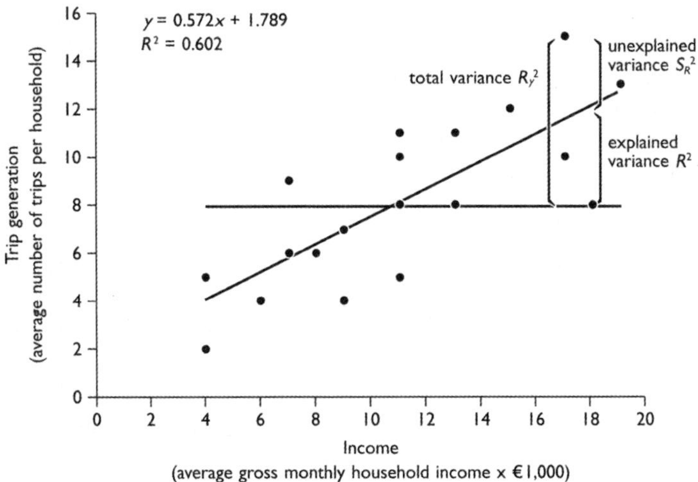

Figure 21.4 Coefficient of determination

$$t_b = \frac{b}{S_b}$$

with:

$$S_b^2 = \frac{\sum_{i=1}^{n}\left(y_i - \hat{y}_i\right)^2 / (n-k)}{\sum_{i=1}^{n}\left(x_i - \bar{x}\right)^2} \tag{21.6}$$

where n is the number of observations and k is the number of variables.

The null hypothesis H_0 assumes that the observed effect of the independent variable on the dependent variable is purely accidental, or $b = 0$. The calculated test statistic is then compared to the critical value in the t-distribution for a given significance level α and the appropriate number of degrees of freedom (i.e., $n - k$ degrees of freedom). The null hypothesis is rejected if the calculated t-value t_b is larger than the critical t-value $t_{\alpha,\, n\text{-}k}$.

Applied to our example, we can assume that any influence of income on trip generation must be positive (i.e., higher income groups travel more frequently). In this case, we should test H_0 against the unilateral positive alternative hypothesis H_a of $b > 0$:

$$t_{income} = \frac{0.572}{0.110} = 5.213$$

The critical t-value at $p \leq 0.01$ with 18 degrees of freedom and unilateral hypothesis testing is 2.552 so that statistical validity of the regression coefficient is supported at a significance level of 99%. Or in other words: it is unlikely that the observed effect of income on trip generation is purely due to chance. We can say that with 99% confidence the estimated parameter differs from zero; hence, the estimated parameter is be interpreted in a valid way.

The above-mentioned t-test is used to assess statistical significance of each regression coefficient individually. It means that, in our example, this t-test is applied to the regression coefficient b but also to the intercept a of the Equation 21.1. However, testing that each parameter is statistically different from zero individually is not the same as testing that both parameters are different from zero together. Assessing the complete model (a and b together) implies testing whether the coefficient of determination R^2 is statistically different from zero. It is thus based on comparing the ratio between the explained and total variance normalized by the degrees of freedom with the critical value in the F-distribution with k–1 degrees of freedom in the numerator and $n - k$ degrees of freedom in the denominator:

$$F_{k-1,n-k} = \frac{(S_Y^2 - S_R^2)/(k-1)}{S_R^2/(n-k)} \tag{21.7}$$

Similar to the testing of regression coefficients, a typical null hypothesis H_0 assumes that the explained amount of variance by the suggested regression model is purely accidental, or $R^2 = 0$. The calculated test statistic is then compared to the critical value in the F-distribution for a given significance level α and the appropriate number of degrees of freedom (i.e., k–1 degrees of freedom in the numerator and $n - k$ degrees of freedom in the denominator). The null hypothesis is rejected if the calculated F-value is larger than the critical F-value.

Applied to our example with $k = 2$ and $n = 20$:

$$F_{1,18} = \frac{(216-86)/(2-1)}{86/(20-2)} = 27.209$$

The critical F-value at $p \leq 0.01$ with 1 degree of freedom in the numerator and 18 degrees of freedom in the denominator is 8.29 so that statistical validity of the coefficient of determination is supported at a significance level of 99%. It is unlikely that the explained amount of variance in trip generation by the regression model is purely accidentally. Or in other words: at least one of the regression parameters (a and/or b) is statistically different from zero.

Multivariate linear regression

The previous section illustrated that one independent variable (i.e., average gross monthly household income) might be a good predictor of the observed variance in the dependent variable (i.e., generated average number of trips per household). Nevertheless, other influencing variables might also be important predictors. We could perform various simple linear regressions with each time another independent variable, but it is more appropriate to execute a multivariate linear regression in which the effects of all independent variables are estimated simultaneously. In this paragraph, we limit ourselves to the effect of two independent variables on the dependent variable, but the example can be expanded to n independent variables.

In the previous section, we explained the average number of generated trips per household by income solely, but it might also be influenced by car ownership (the average number of cars per household; see Table 21.4). The relationship between these two independent variables and the dependent variable is mathematically represented by:

$$y_i = a + b_1 x_{1i} + b_2 x_{2i} + \varepsilon_i \tag{21.8}$$

where:

- y_i: observation i on the dependent variable (i.e., the average number of trips per household);
- x_{1i} and x_{2i}: observation i on the independent variables x_1 (i.e., income) and x_2 (i.e., car ownership);

Table 21.4 Example of household data for a multivariate linear regression

Household	Trip generation (average number of trips per household)	Income (average gross monthly household income in × €1000)	Car ownership (average number of cars per household)
1	2	4	0
2	4	6	0
3	10	17	2
4	5	11	0
5	5	4	1
6	15	17	3
7	7	9	1
8	4	9	0
9	6	7	1
10	13	19	3
11	8	18	1
12	6	8	1
13	9	7	2
14	11	11	2
15	10	11	2
16	11	13	2
17	12	15	2
18	8	11	1
19	8	13	1
20	6	7	1

- *a*: intercept of the regression line, or a parameter expressing the magnitude of trips if income and car ownership is 0;
- b_1 and b_2: slope of the regression plane, or a parameter expressing the effect of a change in income and car ownership on the average number of trips per household;
- ε_i: residue, or a parameter expressing to what extent observations deviate from the estimated regression plane.

With two independent variables, the multivariate linear regression tries to fit a two-dimensional plane to the scatterplot of the observations (see Figure 21.5). Similar to a simple linear regression, estimation of the parameters of a multivariate regression is also based on the method of least squares. Results are presented in Table 21.5, and interpretation of these results is quite similar to that of a simple linear regression. The multivariate linear regression, accounting for the effect of income as well as car ownership, explains 97.3% of the total variance in trip generation per household so that only 2.7% of the observed variance remains unexplained. Furthermore, the effects of income and car ownership are both significant at a significance level of 99%. The regression equation looks like:

$$y_i = 2.047 + 0.216\ income + 2.779\ car\ ownership + \varepsilon_i$$

One extra car per household is likely to result in 2.8 extra trips per household, and an increase in income by €1,000 (i.e., one basic unit) is associated with an increase in trip generation with 0.2 extra trips per household. We now find a somewhat smaller income effect on trip generation compared to the results of the simple linear regression. This does not contradict each other. It is simply due to the fact that the simple linear regression did not consider the effect of car ownership in explaining trip generation. Also, income and car ownership are correlated with each other ($r = 0.635$) so that within the multivariate regression model part of the explanation by income is taken over by car ownership (and vice versa).

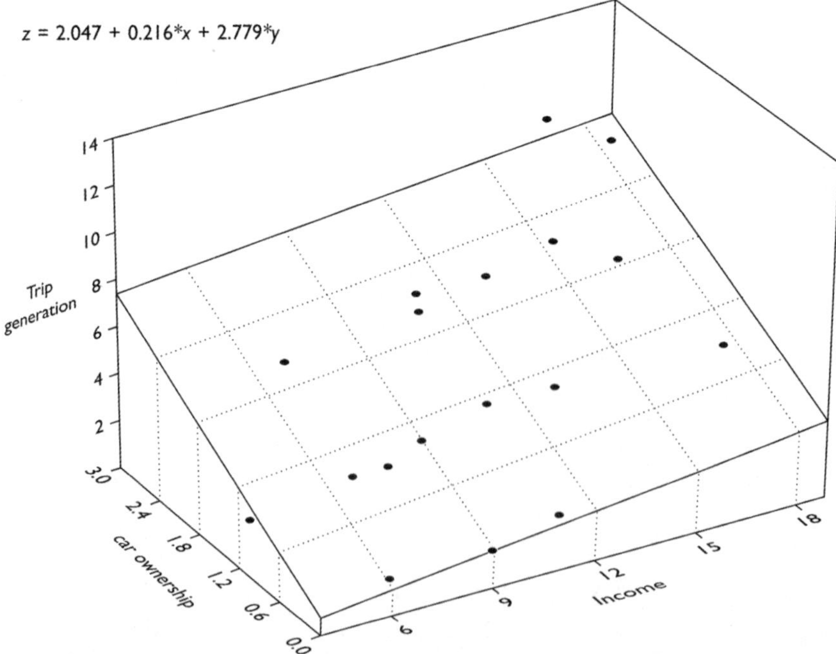

Figure 21.5 Multivariate linear regression plane

Table 21.5 Results of a multivariate linear regression

Model summary

Model	R	R Square	Adjusted R Square	Std. Error of the Estimate
1	0.973[a]	0.947	0.941	0.819

a. Predictors: (Constant), Cars, Income

ANOVA[b]

Model		Sum of Squares	df	Mean Square	F	Sig.
1	Regression	204,594	2	102,297	152,464	0.000[a]
	Residual	11,406	17	0.671		
	Total	216,000	19			

a. Predictors: (Constant), Cars, Income

b. Dependent Variable: Number of trips

Coefficients[a]

Model		Unstandardized Coefficients		Standardized Coefficients		
		B	Std. Error	Beta	t	Sig.
1	(Constant)	2,047	0.483		4,237	0.001
	Income	0.216	0.053	0.292	4,051	0.001
	Cars	2,779	0.263	0.761	10,548	0.000

a. Dependent Variable: Number of trips

By means of such a multivariate regression model, row and column totals of the trip matrix can be calculated. In a final step, the calculated totals for each row and column must be balanced by means of a correction coefficient.

A multivariate linear regression can also answer the question of which independent variable is more important in trip generation, income or car ownership? The effects of the independent variables are measured on different scales: '× €1,000' for income and 'number of cars' for car ownership. This has no consequences for the interpretation of the effects of these independent variables on trip generation, but comparing the size of the various coefficients in order to determine the most (of least) important influencing variable is impossible because of different scales. Or in other words: analyzing the absolute effect is based on the unstandardized coefficients b_1 and b_2, whereas we need standardized coefficients β_1 and β_2 to measure the relative effect of the independent variables. Regression coefficients are standardized by:

$$\beta_i = b_i \left(\frac{s_{xi}}{s_y} \right) \tag{21.9}$$

where:

- β_i: standardized coefficient of independent variable *i*;
- b_i: unstandardized coefficient of independent variable *i*;

- s_{xi}: standard deviation of the independent variable x_i;
- s_y: standard deviation of the dependent variable y.

This means that in our example trip generation is influenced by car ownership to a greater extent than by income.

A multivariate linear regression also reports an adjusted coefficient of determination R'^2. Using this adjusted R'^2 stems from a similar problem: the mutual incomparability of subsequent multivariate regression analyses. We recall that R^2 is calculated by dividing the explained variance $(S_Y^2 - S_R^2)$ (by the total variance S_Y^2 in the dependent variable. This means that each additional independent variable increases the size of the numerator (how small it may be) whereas the denominator remains constant. The addition of extra independent variables, even meaningless variables, will therefore always result in a higher R^2 often leading to misleading results. The adjusted R'^2 helps in detecting such problems by accounting for the degrees of freedom in the numerator and denominator:

$$R'^2 = 1 - \frac{(1-R^2)\,(n-1)}{(n-k-1)} \tag{21.10}$$

where n is the number of observations and k is the number of independent variables.

Unlike R'^2, a decrease in the adjusted R'^2 is possible when adding an additional independent variable. This occurs if the new independent variable has only limited explanatory power and, consequently, the decrease of the numerator is smaller than the decrease in the denominator of Equation 21.10. The adjusted R'^2 can therefore be used for comparison of subsequent regression analyses.

Preconditions of a linear regression analysis

Regression analysis is one of the most commonly used methods for calculating productions and attractions. However, several preconditions must be met before a regression analysis can be performed correctly. This section describes some of these preconditions but for more detailed information we refer to the specialized literature (e.g., Kutner et al., 2004; Montgomery et al., 2006; Kleinbaum et al., 2008).

Regression analysis is a dependency technique. It distinguishes independent variables from dependent variables. With this distinction between independent and dependent variables, we also assume the existence of unambiguous *causality*: independent variables x_1, x_2, ..., x_n explain the variance in y, and not vice versa. For example, in case of the interaction between attitudes and behavior, the direction of influence might be less clear. Perhaps the most commonly assumed hypothesis is that attitudes cause behavior. That is, people's decisions (and, thus, behavior) are based on their attitudes about their available alternatives. But once choices are made and someone gains experience about his/her alternatives, attitudes about the alternatives might change (Dobson et al., 1978; Lyon, 1984; Bohte et al., 2009). In our example of trip generation, it seems logical assuming that trip generation is influenced by income and car ownership, and not the opposite direction. Moreover, this assumption is also supported by a long-lasting research tradition dating back to the 1960s (e.g., Wootton and Pick, 1967; Golob, 1989; Kitamura, 2009). Nevertheless, we must remain cautious because of the existence of intermediary (latent) variables. For example, some recent studies point out that the effect of income on travel behavior is mainly because of the interaction with car ownership (Giuliano and Dargay, 2006; Van Acker and Witlox, 2010). An analysis involving reciprocal relationships and/or intermediary variables can be done by estimating a 'path model', or more generally, a 'structural equation model' (Raykov and Marcoulides, 2000; Byrne, 2001; Kline, 2005).

A second precondition is *linearity*. The type of regression analysis discussed in this chapter assumes a linear association between the independent and dependent variables. In reality, the association between variables is often described by other than mere linear mathematical functional relationships. For example, the alteration in the dependent variable might be exponential ($y = ab^x$) or polynomial ($y = a + b_1x + b_2x^2$) so that a linear regression analysis is no longer adequate. In practice, however, the use of a non-linear regression is not always that obvious. Rejecting the linear regression function in favor of a non-linear regression function must be underpinned with well-founded reasons. One way to detect non-linearity is by plotting the standardized residues against the observed values of the independent variable x. If this scatterplot illustrates 'pure chaos', no particular pattern can be observed which would indicate a dependency between residues and the independent variable (e.g., no U-shape in which small and large value of x would consistently result in an underestimation of y, and intermediate values of x in an overestimation of y). Moreover, the variation in standardized residues must be constant along the whole range of values of the independent variable x, referring to the precondition of *homoskedasticity*. In those cases, a linear relationship exists between the independent and dependent variable. In other cases of a non-linear relationship, the question remains of how to determine the correct function between the independent and dependent variables. If no a priori assumptions exist about the nature of the non-linear function, researchers fall back on a form of 'curve estimation'. Different functions are then examined on how well these functions describe the association between the variables. The function with the 'best' fit is then used in further analyses. However, this decision should not be based solely on statistics. It remains important to understand the underlying reasons why a particular function is better than another one.

As in other statistical techniques, linear regression analysis assumes a *normal distribution* of the variables and, in connection with this, the *absence of outliers* or extreme deviations from the estimated regression. Regression coefficients are estimated using the OLS-method which is based on the minimization of the squared residues. Extreme observations are thus blown up and have a disproportionately large influence. Each of these preconditions can be evaluated visually. For example, a histogram with the distribution of the variables can be compared with the normal distribution and outliers can be detected on the scatterplot. Such visual methods are, however, highly subjective and, thus, more formal evaluation methods are needed. Normality can be detected with the Kolmogorov–Smirnov test, which compares the distribution of the cumulative frequency of the observations with the theoretical expected normal distribution. If normality is not guaranteed, a popular solution is using the logarithm of the variable instead. By taking the logarithm of the variable, skewness of the distribution is reduced. However, one should remain aware that logarithms are used instead of the original variables when interpreting the regression results. Outliers can also be checked for in a more formal way. Outliers are extreme observations or typically points further than, e.g., three or four standard deviations from the mean. The simplest solution is omitting outliers from the data set. Although omitting extreme values results in a dataset which is more consistent with the preconditions of a regression analysis, it might also result in a loss of relevant and useful information. Consequently, outliers must only be omitted if these outliers are the result of measurement errors.

Another precondition applies only to multivariate linear regression. In the previous section on multivariate linear regression, we illustrated that the observed variation in trip generation could be explained better if the influence of car ownership was also included in addition to income. The coefficient of determination increased from 60% (in the simple linear regression with only income as independent variable) to 97% (in the multivariate linear regression with income and car ownership as independent variables). This increased coefficient of determination does not correspond to the simple combination of the variance explained by each of the two independent variables separately. Income and car ownership are also correlated to each other ($r = 0.635$) so that in a multivariate regression model part of the effect of income is taken over by car ownership, and vice versa. It is almost inevitable that such interactions occur, and the probability for this increases as more independent variables are included in the regression analysis. However, strong interactions among independent variables can exert a baleful influence on the estimation of the regression coefficients. The problem of such strong interactions between independent variables is also known as *multicollinearity*. Multicollinearity is detected by analyzing the correlations r between various independent variables. In many cases, a maximum value of $|r| = 0.50$ is tolerated. If correlations are higher than 0.50, then the regression analysis should be adapted. One solution, albeit rather drastic, is omitting one of the two highly correlated variables. After all, those two variables explain a common part of the variance in the dependent variable so that keeping both variables would add little additional information to the analysis. Another solution is to transform correlated variables into a new set of uncorrelated factors by factor analysis. These new factors can then be used as input for a multivariate regression analysis.

Multicollinearity refers to possible correlations among the independent variables, but correlations can also exist among observations within one independent variable which refers to the problem of *autocorrelation*. This interdependency among observations can be the result of various reasons (observations related to each other in time – temporal autocorrelation – or in space – spatial autocorrelation). Linear regression assumes, however, independent observations.

REMARKS AND SOME RECENT ADVANCES

The earliest forms of trip generation models used crude zonal characteristics such as total zonal population without correcting for zonal sizes (Bates, 2000) or used zonal averages without considering internal variation. Some other transport production and attraction models therefore use *category analysis* (or cross-classification analysis) instead of regression analysis. Category analysis was first proposed by Wootton and Pick (1967). Instead of assuming one average household profile per zone, category analysis identifies *different* household categories based on characteristics such as household income, car ownership and household size. The more characteristics, the more household categories are possible. Subsequently, trips are assigned to each household category based on observations in the base year. Forecasting the number of trips in a study area can then be made by multiplying the average number of trips per household category by the number of households in the category, and by summating over the categories considered. Category analysis thus assumes that households with equal characteristics travel an equal number of trips. However, this is also an important drawback since there is no test for analyzing this constant nature of the number of trips per household category (Blauwens et al., 2008).

Trip generation models as part of the four-step model are aggregated models. A frequently raised critique is that such aggregated models have no or insufficient behavioral grounding. As an alternative, more *disaggregated* approaches have been suggested such as a microeconomic approach and the activity-based approach. This shift emerged in the 1970s following changes in the transport policy environment. This is to say that in transport policy the emphasis shifted from long-term infrastructure expansion strategies to shorter-term infrastructure management strategies such as alternate work schedules, telecommuting and congestion pricing.

Understanding travelers' responses to such short-term transportation policies needed a more behavioral-oriented modeling approach which was lacking in the previously used trip-based models (Jones et al., 1990; Bhat and Koppelman, 1999; McNally, 2000).

The *micro-economic approach* to transport-choice behavior explicitly considers individuals or households rather than zones as units of analysis. The individual will make a discrete choice between *J* distinct alternatives in such a way that the individual's utility is maximized (Hammadou et al., 2008). Or in other words, the decision-maker will choose for that alternative offering the highest utility. Since this approach has mainly been applied in modal split studies and not to trip generation, interested readers are referred to the classic works by McFadden (1973, 1974) and Domencich and McFadden (1975).

The micro-economic approach might give the impression that transport choices are made rationally. Many transport researchers therefore feel the need to obtain a more realistic view of travel behavior by placing transport behavior in a broader, more holistic framework. Some argue that transport behavior must be studied in close relationship with activity behavior. After all, the spatial separation between activities (e.g., living, working, shopping and recreating) foster the need for transport. Consequently, activity behavior which refers to the spatial and temporal characteristics of the performed activities must be studied first in order to understand transport behavior (Pas, 1980; Jones et al., 1990; Axhausen and Gärling, 1992; McNally, 2000). The link between transport demand and the siting of activities was first articulated in 1954 by Mitchell and Rapkin, but today it remains highly researched. Since the 1970s, considerable progress has been made in activity-based travel research (for a recent review, see, e.g., Algers et al., 2005; Buliung and Kanarogloy, 2007). Nevertheless, some important problems remain. First and foremost, the activity-based approach has important data repercussions: insight is not only required into transport behavior but also activity patterns. Furthermore, a clear methodological orientation and a unified theoretical framework are still lacking. Such a theoretical framework would require the integration of concepts from various disciplines including psychology, sociology, geography and economics among others (Blauwens et al., 2008; Van Acker et al., 2010). Consequently, some issues still need to be addressed first before the new generation of activity-based models can replace the conventional four-step models.

REFERENCES

Algers, S., Eliasson, J., Mattsson, L.G. (2005) 'Is it time to use activity-based urban transport models? A discussion of planning needs and modelling possibilities', *Annals of Regional Science*, Vol. 39, No. 4, pp. 767–789.

Axhausen, K.W., Gärling, T. (1992) 'Activity-based approaches to travel analysis: Conceptual frameworks, models and research problems', *Transport Reviews*, Vol. 12, No. 4, pp. 324–341.

Bates, J. (2000) 'History of demand modelling', in D.A. Hensher and K.J. Button (eds) *Handbook of Transport Modelling*. Oxford: Elsevier, pp. 11–34.

Bhat, C.R., Koppelman, F.S. (1999) 'Activity-based modeling of travel demand', in R.W. Hall (ed.) *Handbook of Transportation Science*. Norwell: Kluwer Academic Publishers, pp. 39–65.

Blauwens, G., De Baere, P., Van de Voorde, E. (2008) *Transport Economics*. Antwerpen: Uitgeverij De Boeck.

Bohte, W., Maat, K., van Wee, B. (2009) 'Measuring attitudes in research on residential self-selection and travel behaviour: A review of theories and empirical research', *Transport Reviews*, Vol. 29, No. 3, pp. 325–357.

Buliung, R.N., Kanaroglou, P.S. (2007) 'Activity-travel behaviour research: Conceptual issues, state of the art, and emerging perspectives on behavioural analysis and simulation modelling', *Transport Reviews*, Vol. 27, pp. 151–187.

Byrne, B.M. (2001) *Structural Equation Modeling with AMOS. Basic Concepts, Applications, and Programming*. Mahwah: Lawrence Erlbaum Associates.

Dobson, R., Dunbar, F., Smith, C.J., Reibstein, D., Lovelock, C. (1978) 'Structural models for the analysis of traveller attitude-behavior relationships', *Transportation*, Vol. 7, No. 4, pp. 351–363.

Domencich, T.A., McFadden, D. (1975) *Urban Travel Demand*. New York: North Holland Publishing Company.

Golob, T.F. (1989) 'The causal influences of income and car ownership on trip generation by mode', *Journal of Transport Economics and Policy*, Vol. 23, No. 2, pp. 141–162.

Giuliano, G., Dargay, J. (2006) 'Car ownership, travel and land use: A comparison of the US and Great Britain', *Transportation Research A*, Vol. 40, No. 2, pp. 106–124.

Hammadou, H., Thomas, I., Verhetsel, A., Witlox, F. (2008) 'How to incorporate the spatial dimension in destination choice models: The case of Antwerpen (Belgium)', *Transportation Planning and Technology*, Vol. 31, No. 2, pp. 153–181.

Jones, P.M., Koppelman, F.S., Orfeuil, J.P. (1990) 'Activity analysis: state of the art and future directions', in P. Jones (ed.) *Developments in Dynamic and Activity-Based Approaches to Travel Analysis*. Aldershot: Gower, pp. 34–55.

Kitamura, R. (2009) 'A dynamic model system of household car ownership, trip generation, and modal split: Model development and simulation experiment', *Transportation*, Vol. 36, No. 6, pp. 711–732.

Kleinbaum, D.G., Kupper, L.L., Nizam, A., Muller, K.E. (2008) *Applied Regression Analysis and other Multivariate Methods*. Belmont: Thomson Brooks/Cole.

Kline, R.B. (2005) *Principles and Practice of Structural Equation Modeling*. New York: Guilford Press.

Kutner, M.H., Nachtsheim, C.J., Neter, J. (2004) *Applied Linear Regression Models*. Boston: McGraw-Hill/Irwin.

Lyon, P.K. (1984) 'Time-dependent structural equations modellng: A methodology for analyzing the dynamic attitude–behavior relationship', *Transportation Science*, Vol. 18, No. 4, pp. 395–414.

McFadden, D. (1973) 'Conditional logit analysis of qualitative choice behavior', in P. Zarembka (ed.) *Frontiers in Econometrics*. New York: Academic Press, pp. 105–142.

McFadden, D. (1974) 'The measurement of urban travel demand', *Journal of Public Economics*, Vol. 3, No. 4, pp. 303–328.

McNally, M.G. (2000) 'The activity-based approach', in D.A. Hensher and K.J. Button (eds) *Handbook of Transport Modeling*. Oxford: Pergamon, pp. 53–69.

Mitchell, R.B., Rapkin, C. (1954) *Urban Traffic: A Function of Land Use*. New York: Columbia University Press.

Mokhtarian, P.L., Salomon, I. (2001) 'How derived is the demand for travel? Some conceptual and measurement considerations', *Transportation Research A*, Vol. 35, No. 8, pp. 695–719.

Montgomery, D.C., Peck, E.A., Vining, G.G. (2006) *Introduction to Linear Regression Analysis*. New York: Wiley.

Ortúzar, J. de Dios, Willumsen, L.G. (2001) *Modelling Transport*. Chichester: John Wiley & Sons.

Ory, D.T., Mokhtarian, P.L. (2005) 'When getting there is half the fun? Modeling the liking for travel', *Transportation Research A*, Vol. 39, No. 2–3, pp. 97–123.

Pas, E.I. (1980) *Toward the Understanding of Urban Travel Behavior through the Classification of Daily Urban Travel/Activity Patterns*. Evanston: Northwestern University (PhD thesis).

Raykov, T., Marcoulides, G.A. (2000) *A First Course in Structural Equation Modeling*. Mahwah: Lawrence Erlbaum Associates.

Van Acker, V., Witlox, F. (2010) 'Car ownership as a mediating variable in car travel behaviour research using a structural equation modelling approach to identify its dual relationship', *Journal of Transport Geography*, Vol. 18, No. 1, pp. 65–74.

Van Acker, V., van Wee, B., Witlox, F. (2010) 'When transport geography meets social psychology. Toward a conceptual model of travel behaviour', *Transport Reviews*, Vol. 30, No. 2, pp. 219–240.

Wootton, H.J., Pick, G.W. (1967) 'A model for trips generated by households', *Journal of Transport Economics and Policy*, Vol. 1, No 2, pp. 137–153.

22

Incident and Emergency Management in Traffic

Pushkin Kachroo, Neveen Shlayan and Kaan Özbay

INTRODUCTION

As a growing share of the global population owns and/or operates a motor vehicle, accidents are increasing in absolute terms. According to the World Health Organization, there were more than 1.26 million road fatalities in 2007, in addition to about 30 million non-fatal injuries. Outside public health considerations, there is the issue of impacts that incidents and disabled vehicles have on road congestion. Incident Management is thus an integral part of freeway and arterial traffic operations and is designed to alleviate the problems associated with traffic incidents. Traffic incidents are non-recurring planned or accidental events that generally cause delay due to congestion as well as due to safety hazards. Planned events may be sports events, concerts, or else road maintenance or reconstruction projects. Accidental events include crashes, spills and disabled vehicles. The impacts of closures can be severe, particularly in societies having a high motorization level where delays have a substantial economic impact on the circulation of people (e.g. commuting) and freight (e.g. deliveries).

The issue of incident management is illustrated with reference to Las Vegas where two of the authors of this chapter live. Due to rapid growth in recent years, the 2 million metropolitan area is now experiencing considerable congestion even outside the normal peak periods. To this must be added close to 40 million annual visitors (20 times the local population) that are contributing to local circulation and thus road incidents. An estimate of user costs for a one-hour closure on highway I-15 in Las Vegas in the peak direction during the afternoon peak hour is approximately $240,000. This estimate does not include the traffic that would be caught in a queue that could propagate nearly 10 miles. The user cost of vehicles trapped at interchanges, including cross-street traffic, is not included nor is the cost of drivers who are rubber necking in the opposite direction. Finally, this user cost does not include the impact of the time needed for the traffic stream to recover once the closure is removed. This recovery time extends beyond the end of the peak period. The total cost could be three-quarters of a million dollars for a one-hour closure. Overall, incidents result in the reduction of the operational efficiency of the transportation network, which leads to costly delays for the travelers, increased risk of secondary incidents, and safety risks to the incident responders.

The aim of an incident management system is to minimize the total delay experienced by travelers and also to keep the whole operation safe. In order to achieve these two goals, the system should make optimal choices and use optimal designs. For the design of optimal solutions, appropriate mathematical models are needed for various tasks, and then mathematical techniques need to be developed. The mathematical models, their analyses and the creation of optimal solutions can help to create a framework for a decision support system for overall incident management. As an example, graph theoretic methods can be used with real-time traffic information to find out the best alternate route for traffic diversion after an incident. After an incident occurs, signal timings for signalized intersections or ramp meters also might have to be changed in order to respond to the transient traffic patterns and thus refocus traffic flows. Since these patterns are non-recurring, the signals would have to be able to respond to real-time traffic demands so that traffic can be brought back to pre-incident levels in the minimum time possible.

Incident-related traffic congestion including secondary impacts, highly affects public safety, the environment and the local economy. It was estimated that congestion cost the US public $75 billion in lost productivity and 8.4 billion gallons of wasted fuel in the year 2005 (US Department of Transportation (USDoT) and Federal Highway Administration (FHWA), 2012). Traffic incident related delays are estimated to cause 50–60% of the total congestion delay. These incidents pose a severe risk regarding the occurrence of secondary incidents, which account for 20% of all the incidents and 18% of total deaths (Carson, 2008). These secondary incidents further increase traveler delay, fuel consumption, reduce air quality and when combined with work zones, add delays and costs to construction projects. Figure 22.1 shows the causes of various congestions on highways (USDoT and FHWA, 2012).

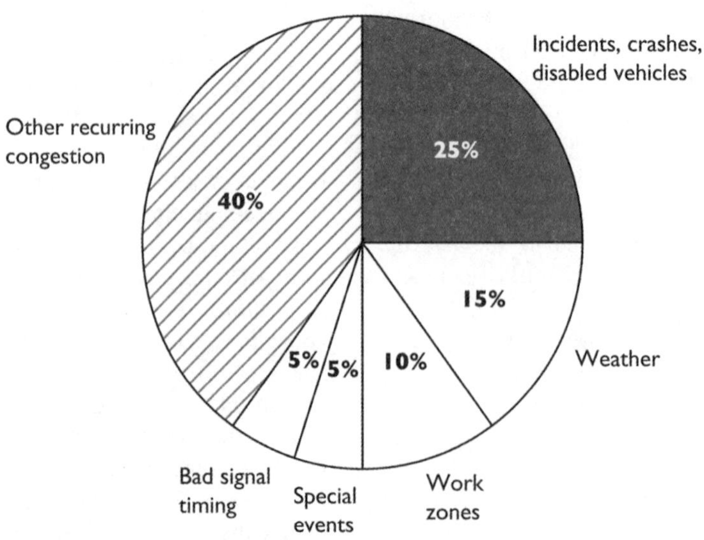

Figure 22.1 Congestion causes

Nevada, the state in which Las Vegas is located, is the seventh largest US state in size and 35th in population, with more than 2.4 million people residing in the state. From 1997 to 2006, Nevada's population increased by 47.8% while its annual total collisions increased by 5.5%. Although, Nevada's crash rate per 100 million vehicle-miles has been reduced in the past 10 years, it still ranks among the top ten states with the highest crash rates in the nation. During the year 2006, there was a total of 62,225 traffic collisions out of which 40,962 were property damage only (PDO), 20,876 were injury related and 387 were fatal. This reflects a 1.3% increase in overall collisions from the total 61,339 recorded in 2005. It is estimated that the total economic loss resulting from traffic collisions in Nevada for the year 2006 is $1.873 billion (Matinovich, 2006).

Nevada has in the past led the nation in population growth and the increase is projected to be approximately 60% between now and 2030. The rapid increase in population and the present statistics of crash rates indicates that proper management tools are needed to manage incidents and improve the safety of commuters on freeways. This is particularly salient because of the economic importance of tourism for the city. Incident management is a coordinated approach in managing incidents that occur on the highway (Özbay and Kachroo, 1999). It is the systematic, planned and coordinated use of human, institutional, mechanical and technical resources to reduce the duration and impact of incidents, and improve the safety of motorists, crash victims and incident responders. Effectively using these resources increases the operating efficiency, safety, and mobility of the highway (Neudorff et al., 2003). Incident management involves a series of activities, which can be carried out by personnel from a variety of response agencies and organizations.

The incident management process steps are summarized here:

1 Incident detection: a process by which an incident is brought to the attention of traffic incident management team. This can happen in many ways, such as calls from motorists, CCTV cameras, police patrols, automatic vehicle identification (AVI) combined with detection software, electronic traffic measuring devices (e.g., video imaging, loop or radar detectors) and algorithms that detect traffic abnormalities, department of transportation or public works crews reporting via two-way radio, aerial surveillance, traffic reporting services, fleet vehicles (transit and trucking), and roaming service patrols.
2 Incident verification: this is the process of confirming that the incident has taken place, getting the exact location and obtaining as many primary details as possible about the incident. Usually, arrival of the first responder on the scene confirms the incident. This can also be accomplished in many ways such as: CCTV cameras, dispatch field units (police or service patrols) to the incident site, communications with aircraft operated by the police, the media, or an information service provider, and calls from multiple motorists.
3 Motorist information: this involves creating public awareness about the incident that helps drivers to take the alternate routes. The following technologies are used to disseminate the information: commercial radio broadcasts, variable message signs (VMS), highway advisory radio (HAR), telephone information systems, in-vehicle or personal data assistant information or route guidance systems, commercial and public television traffic reports, and internet/on-line services available through mobile devices.
4 Response: this is the most important activity in the incident management process which involves dispatching appropriate equipment, personnel, and activating the required communication links. Effective response involves preparedness by a number of agencies (i.e., planned co-operatively) involved in the traffic incident management team.
5 Site management: this involves managing resources onsite in real-time following proper pre-determined protocols and policies. Site management ensures the safety of responders, incident victims and the oncoming traffic, particularly through lane closures. It usually involves following a formal command system known as incident command system (ICS). The ICS sets the guidelines for planned and organized approach to be followed by emergency responders at the incident.
6 Traffic management: this involves coming up with alternate routes, dispatching personnel at the incident for traffic management if necessary

and then managing traffic control devices to alleviate congestion on site.

7 Clearance: incident clearance is the process of removing wreckage, debris or any other element that disrupts the normal flow of traffic, or forces lane closures, and restoring the roadway capacity to its pre-incident condition.

The main incident management process decisions steps can generally be divided as shown in Figure 22.2.

BENEFITS AND COSTS OF INCIDENT MANAGEMENT

Incident management programs can provide enhanced customer satisfaction. These programs provide a heightened sense of safety and security for motorists on the highway system. The costs and benefits of incident management as evaluated in some American states are presented now.

In California, an incident management program was evaluated on Interstate 880 in Hayward in 1995; (Petty et al., 1995; Anderson et al., 2001; Nee and Hallenbeck, 2001). A 9.2-mile freeway was taken as a test site and 276 hours of incident and freeway data were collected (Anderson et al., 2001). This experiment was conducted during morning and afternoon peak periods on 24 weekdays prior to the implementation of the Bay Area Freeway Service Patrol (FSP) and 22 weekdays after implementation. The Bay Area FSP evaluation found that the mean incident duration dropped by 4%, the mean response times for breakdown incidents decreased from 33 to 18 minutes and that the overall program resulted in saving of 42 vehicle-hours per incident, resulting in an annual saving of

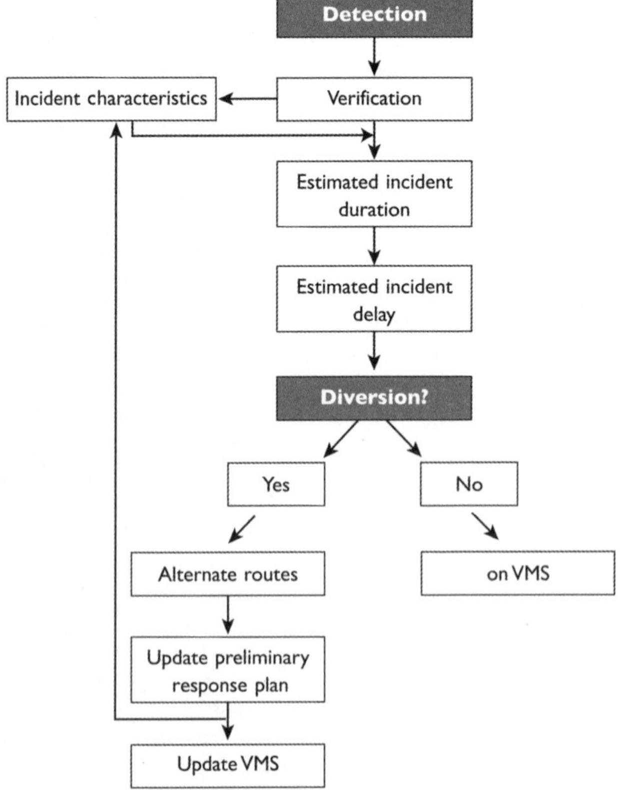

Figure 22.2 Process steps for incident management

more than 90,000 vehicle-hours. Similarly, improvements in fuel consumption and emissions were also documented. The Los Angeles FSP evaluation, performed after the implementation of an FSP program, focused on a 7.8-mile section of Interstate 10 in El Monte and Alhambra, California. The evaluation included a total of 192 hours' observation over 32 weekdays, with details on 1,560 incidents, 3,600 probe vehicle runs, and data from 240 loop detectors. The results of The Bay Area FSP and other state FSPs were analyzed to estimate the effectiveness of the program. The study found that the program was operating with a benefit-cost ratio between 3.8 and 5.6.

In Oregon, an evaluation of an Incident Response (IR) program used archived dispatch and traffic flow data collected after the program was initiated (Petty et al., 1995). Using statistical analysis of the incident data, reductions in fuel consumption and delay were estimated for more than 2,500 incidents logged in two 50-mile rural highway corridors. It was shown that the mean incident duration and thus delay per incident had decreased and that the benefits of the program far outweigh its cost. In Washington, the Puget Sound Region deployed its freeway service patrol in August 2000 (Nee and Hallenbeck, 2001). A study was conducted in which archived incident data from six months following implementation was compared to pre-implementation data from the same six-month period during the previous year. This study revealed a decrease in emergency response time from 9 minutes to 5.8 minutes. Faster response time was estimated to reduce annual vehicle-hour delay by 13,048 hours and it resulted in cost savings of nearly $200,000.

In Phoenix, a study into the effects of a Freeway Management System (FMS) on the safety of a freeway network was carried out by dividing the freeway into two sections, sections with and sections without an FMS (Olmstead, 2001). The data included crash records, traffic volumes and roadway characteristics for approximately 65 miles of urban freeways in the metropolitan Phoenix area between 1991 and 1998. The sections with an FMS showed reductions of 25% in crashes involving property damage only. There was also a reduction in the number of crashes involving possible injury and minor injury of 30% and 21% respectively. This study estimated an annual benefit in crash reduction to be between $4.8 and $13.2 million dollars from 1996 to 1998.

THE TRAFFIC INCIDENT MANAGEMENT COALITION GROUP

Against this background of costs and benefits, we now turn to discuss as a case study example the Traffic Incident Management (TIM) Coalition Group in Nevada. In 2003, there was a total of 63,582 traffic crashes in Nevada with an estimated loss of around $1.4 billion. With no specific incident management team, the local emergency management and transportation agencies cleared about 15,000 incidents every year on freeways. Such scale of incidents showed the need for an incident management program.

With the guidelines provided by FHWA almost every state now has a local traffic incident management group with different types of incident management programs. The TIM coalition is one such group formed in the Las Vegas region for efficient incident management. This team has worked on building a regional consensus for clearance time goals, HAZMAT (hazardous material) removal, TIM policies, best practices, technology improvements, communications, agreements and recommendations for a regional traffic incident management program that includes all first responding emergency and traffic agencies in the region. We present this example of an incident management coalition team to show incident management is performed at the state level.

For effective incident management, each and every agency participating in an incident clearance should have specific roles and responsibilities. The number of responders and their highly dependent roles and responsibilities underlined that the system is complex and relies upon collaboration. Any location will have a series of actors reflective of the governance structure of the region requiring cross-jurisdictional efforts that have to be undertaken to implement such schemes. Jurisdictions around the world will likely have a different mix of mandates and responsibilities, but the issue is that effecting incident management is a collective effort. Here is an exhaustive list of the existing roles and responsibilities of the emergency responders in the Las Vegas region:

1. Federal Highway Administration: the FHWA sets the standards, publishes best practices for traffic incident management, provides planning guides and training options for partners involved in traffic incident management and helps in operating highways.
2. Federal Emergency Management Administration: FEMA mainly manages national emergencies and hazards. It provides federal response and recovery efforts, trains first responders, and manages the National Flood Insurance Police and the US Fire Administration.
3. Department of Safety, Nevada Highway Patrol: the NHP is the primary first responding agency for incident management. It serves as incident command in most incidents on the freeway/highway for the Las Vegas region with the responsibility of managing the incident, traffic diversions, clearance of the roadway and investigation of crash scenes on state highways and interstate freeways. NHP serves as a Public Safety Answering Point (PSAP), taking 911 calls. It interacts with all emergency agencies including coroner's office in case of fatalities and public information media regarding incidents and maintains dispatcher availability 24/7. A Computer Aided Dispatch (CAD) system is used to locate and manage incident information, although this system cannot currently communicate directly with other agencies' systems and as such it primarily uses cell phones and radios for communication. NHP maintains a secure information system inaccessible by others and provides security oversight.
4. Nevada Department of Transportation District 1: NDOT provides staff assistants in providing traffic control, cleaning up debris, managing HAZMAT cleanup and repairing the roadways. It works with NHP and other regional emergency responders to provide 511 information about the region traffic status for the statewide 511 system feature. It uses newly provided hand held radios, cell phones and emails for communication. It operates and maintains four Highway Advisory Radios (HAR).
5. Nevada Department of Transportation HQ: staff in the HQ manage and fund Freeway Service Patrol (FSP) to assist drivers and NHP with traffic incident management. They manage 511 Statewide and Statewide Traffic Incident Management Team efforts, and review and make policy on traffic incident management and quick clearance, and make legislative recommendations for TIM development in the state of Nevada.
6. Freeway Service Patrol: the FSP offers roadside assistance to those who are in need. It assists in securing the safety of drivers and individuals at incident scenes. It provides assistance to the NHP with traffic control to prevent secondary incidents, and to ensure the rapid removal of vehicles and debris from travel lanes and paved shoulders.
7. Nevada Department of Transportation Communications Department: manages and oversees State NDOT radio systems, the statewide communications committee and helps in integration of communications systems whenever requested.
8. Las Vegas Metropolitan Police Department: the MPD serves as a Public Safety Answering Point and, along with NHP, manages incidents on county roads, traffic diversions and clearance of the roadway. It informs all emergency agencies and public information media regarding incidents via individual agency dispatchers. It owns and operates a 700-MHz radio system.
9. Law Enforcement: conducts traffic incident management on arterial and local (and some freeway) systems.
10. North Las Vegas Police Department: the NLVPD serves as a Public Safety Answering Point (PSAP) and operates a system for traffic incident management on corridors in the NLVPD area as well as managing traffic for the Las Vegas Speedway. NLVPD communicates with other first response agencies via individual dispatchers and attends traffic incident management calls.
11. Clark County Environmental and Risk Management: works with NHP during incidents that involve large commercial vehicles. It manages HAZMAT contract for clearance of HAZMAT spills and/or removal of commercial vehicles from the Clark County right-of-way.
12. Clark County Coroner's Office: along with NHP, the Coroner's Office participates in clearing and

investigating the incidents involving deaths. It assists in leadership efforts at the TIM to develop policies and support regional quick clearance agreement.

13 Clark County Office of Emergency Management and Homeland Security: this participates in emergency management, focusing on policy decision making, identification of resource capabilities (ingress/egress), public information and rumor control. It has no direct operational responsibilities in incident management and clearance.

14 Clark County Fire Department: the CCFD is the primary emergency responder or incident command agency for fire incidents, hazardous material spills, rescue, and extraction of trapped crash victims for Clark County. It helps the incident management team in clearing incidents and contacts a towing agency to tow the vehicle once the situation is stabilized. It keeps data records of past incidents.

15 Clark County Public Works (Maintenance): this department is responsible for managing incidents and the clearance of incidents on CC-215. It closes and reopens roadways for use whenever necessary and generates a report of incidents. Clark County traffic signals and roadside equipment on county rights-of-way are maintained by this department. It communicates with the MPD and the NLVPD using a dedicated radio channel during incidents.

16 Clark County Regional Flood Control District: the RFCD acts only when flash flood events occur. It collects data and shares with other agencies for analysis.

17 City of Henderson Police Department: the CHPD, like the MPD and NLVPD, serves as a Public Safety Answering Point, taking 911 calls for Henderson. It plays an important role in reporting incidents, preserving evidence, reopening roadways for use and generating reports of incidents in the Henderson area. It communicates with MPD and NLVPD using a dedicated radio channel and CAD technology to aid communication with NLVPD.

18 RTC Freeway Arterial Transportation System: operates RTC FAST center and performs traffic monitoring and control via CCTV systems, detectors, DMS, ramp meters and FMS software. RTC has full access to most signal controllers in the Valley which can alter the signal timings accordingly during incident clearance. It provides data and tools to identify incidents and assisting with remote monitoring of an incident scene. It provides trailblazer signs to assist diverted motorists with detour route information during incidents. It supports the TIM coalition by working with NDOT to support meetings and provide videotaping of incidents of a quality that can be utilized for debriefing.

19 Citizens' Area Transit: the CAT has contracts for vehicle removal, debris clean up, and HAZMAT cleanup for crashes involving a transit vehicle. It determines transit bus detour routes, and shares incident information with law enforcement agencies and Office of Homeland Security when requested.

20 American Medical Response Ambulance: the AMR is the primary source of providing first-aid at incident sites and thereafter transports patients to hospital. This service is requested by 911 or NHP.

21 Towing and recovery operators: these remove wrecked or disabled vehicles and debris from incident scenes. They work with TIM partners to accomplish regional quick clearance agreements.

22 HAZMAT Contractors: These help TIM in cleaning and disposing of toxic or hazardous materials at incident sites. Based on an incident's severity, the TIM coalition group set the timing goals in clearing the incident as follows: 30 minutes for fender-benders; 60 minutes for injury crashes; and 90 minutes for accidents involving fatalities.

MATHEMATICAL METHODS IN INCIDENT MANAGEMENT

To make the incident management process as efficient as possible, various mathematical modeling methods are used at various stages of the process. Some of those methods are summarized below. Further details can be obtained from Özbay and Kachroo (1999).

Incident detection and verification

As we have described, incident detection can happen in many ways. A person can alert the agency of an incident by making a phone call, or the traffic management center can be observing an incident as it happens on a monitor. There have been many algorithms developed for automatic incident detection over the years. The California algorithm (see Payne and Tignore, 1978) uses a pattern recognition method of decision trees with states based on the occupancy values of the section and the downstream. An incident is characterized by a high occupancy value at the section and a low value in the downstream area. The method developed by Willsky et al. (1980) uses macroscopic traffic model and employs multiple models with generalized likelihood ratio techniques. Many other methods for incident detection exist and use different pattern matching approaches (see Chang, 1994; Srinivasan et al., 2004; Wang et al., 2007). Reduction in the incident detection time can have a very serious effect on reduction of the overall incident duration, which reduces the probability of secondary congestion and incidents as well.

Incident duration and delay prediction

Incident duration estimation can be performed using computer simulations. However, the simulation model can require many site-specific parameters and calibration of these models can be difficult. Many real-time quick methods for incident duration have been developed. The duration of the incident depends on various stages, such as detection time, initial response, injury attention, emergency vehicle response, fatality, clean up and so on. Regression models (see Jones et al., 1991; Golob et al., 1987) have been built relating the duration time to various variables such as the number of lanes affected, number of vehicles involved, time of day, weather conditions, etc. A decision tree based method is developed and presented by Özbay and Kachroo (1999), and the same authors use a queuing model to estimate the delay due to an accident on traffic based on the estimated duration time.

Incident response

As we have mentioned, the incident management team prepares pre-planned incident response plans, and then uses the appropriate one depending on the type of incident that has occurred. A new method to streamline the incident response process has been developed using formal language methods (see Shlayan and Kachroo, 2012). This method uses finite state models for different agencies and models their processes and intercommunications so that they can be analyzed for inefficiencies or bugs in the operations. The methodology used utilizes the concept of shared actions in Labeled Transition Systems (LTS), which has the ability to model concurrent finite state processes. Software is used to code the models for the various processes representing various agencies, and then the software can be run to analyze the system. A sample code for an incident occurrence process is shown in Table 22.1.

Traffic diversion

The traffic diversion part of the incident management process follows a distinct logic. A diversion decision is based on the delay calculation after the duration estimation has been performed. The amount of delay is then compared with a threshold to make a decision on the diversion. If the diversion route(s) can reduce the travel time for travelers, then it can be established and motorists can be notified via dynamic message signs and other methods such as web sites, text notifications

Table 22.1 Program1: an FSP model for an incident occurrence process

PRE_ACCIDENT	= (accident->ACCIDENT),
ACCIDENT	= (call_911->CLRNSinPROCESS|callfailed->ACCIDENT),
CLRNSinPROCESS	= (congtn_clrd->PRE_ACCIDENT|stillcongested->CLRNSinPROCESS.

and so on. Once the decision to divert has been taken then the process of diversion can be started. There are many algorithms that can be used to generate the diversionary route (Özbay and Kachroo, 1999).

Real-time traffic control

Real-time control of traffic can be performed to optimize the dynamic performance of the traffic system. Feedback control methodology is the best way to achieve this since it uses the actual real-time data available from sensors to make control decisions. Some traffic control that can be performed using feedback includes ramp metering control, signalized intersection control and traffic diversion control (see Kachroo and Özbay, 1998 and 2003). We focus here on feedback ramp metering control that would be part of an incident management strategy. This design is based on the Godunov method, although many different ramp metering techniques have been used in the past (see Kachroo et al., 2011). Ramp meters are designed to control the inflow into freeways to reduce congestion on these roads. Ramp meters can be pre-timed, or can be operated in an actuated manner. Feedback control theory can be used to design real-time ramp meters so that the ramp flows can be made dependent on the current traffic conditions.

MODELING RAMP METERING AS AN INCIDENT MANAGEMENT STRATEGY

Ramp metering models that have been used for feedback control design using lumped parameter model have used dynamics that do not reproduce the rarefaction behavior of traffic. In those models, when the traffic is at jam density the outflow from a section becomes zero. However, this would mean that the traffic would never come out of the jam. By using a Godunov based model in the lumped setting we can reproduce rarefaction behavior and then present a feedback control design for ramp metering that provides asymptotic stable behavior for the closed loop system.

The Lighthill–Whitham–Richards model (LWR – see Lighthill and Whitham, 1955; Richards, 1956) is a macroscopic one-dimensional traffic model. The conservation law for traffic in one dimension is given by:

$$\frac{\partial}{\partial t}\rho(t,x) + \frac{\partial}{\partial x}f(t,x) = 0 \tag{22.1}$$

In this equation ρ is the traffic density and f is the flux, which is the product of traffic density and the traffic speed v, i.e. $f = \rho v$. There are many models researchers have proposed for how the flux should be dependent on traffic conditions. Greenshields' model (Greenshields, 1935) uses a linear relationship between traffic density and traffic speed:

$$v(\rho) = v_f\left(1 - \frac{\rho}{\rho_m}\right) \tag{22.2}$$

where v_f is the free flow speed and ρ_m is the maximum density. Free flow speed is the speed of traffic when the density is zero. This is the maximum speed. The maximum density is the density at which there is a traffic jam and the speed is equal to zero.

A space discretized model of Equation 22.1 for the ramp metering is presented in Figure 22.3. Here, $u(t)$ is the ramp inflow into the freeway. The ordinary differential equation (ODE) model from the figure for the ramp metering, assuming unit length for the section, is given by:

$$\frac{d\rho(t)}{dt} = f_{in}(t) + u(t) - f_{out}(t) \tag{22.3}$$

The outflow traffic using Greenshields' model is given by

$$f_{out}(t) = v_f\rho(t)\left(1 - \frac{\rho(t)}{\rho_m}\right) \tag{22.4}$$

Substituting Equation 22.4 for the outflow into the conservation Equation 22.3 shows that when the traffic density is equal to the

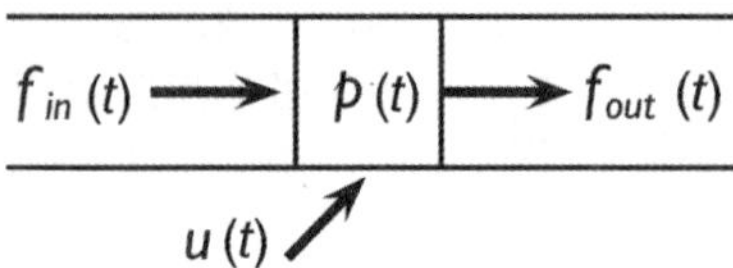

Figure 22.3 Discretized model

jam density, and the value of $u(t)$ is zero, the rate of increase in the traffic density is non-negative. In fact, for positive inflow, the density can increase according to the equation. Hence, there are two issues with this model that need to be fixed. When the traffic density is equal to jam density for the section, (1) the inflow from upstream can increase the density above the jam value, and (2) the outflow is zero from the section not allowing for the traffic to be dissipated to downstream.

The original distributed LWR model given by Equation 22.1 using the Greenshields' fundamental relationship (Equation 22.2) does not have these limitations. This can be seen by studying the characteristics emanating from an initial value problem for a Riemann's problem where the upstream traffic density is lower (Whitham, 1974; Haberman, 1987; Kachroo et al., 2009). Figure 22.4 shows the characteristics of traffic where the initial traffic data is shown on the x-axis, where the traffic density is piecewise constant. The middle section has the jam density ρ_m, the upstream has a lower density ρ_0 and the downstream has zero density. As time increases, as shown on the y-axis, the shockwave travels upstream and at the same time the jam dissipates as a rarefaction onto the downstream.

We can use Godunov's model to fix these two issues in the ODE model, and use the Godunov model as our nominal model for the control design. Note that we could also take the model given by Equation 22.3 as the nominal model for the feedback control design and let the closed loop system provide performance via its robustness for the real system. However, we chose the Godunov based nominal model so as to have better representation of the system in the nominal model.

The Godunov method is based on solving the Riemann problem where the initial condition is a piecewise constant function with two values ρ_ℓ and ρ_r for the upstream (left) and downstream (right) densities (Leveque, 2005). From the junction of the two densities either a shockwave or a rarefaction wave can emanate. A shockwave develops

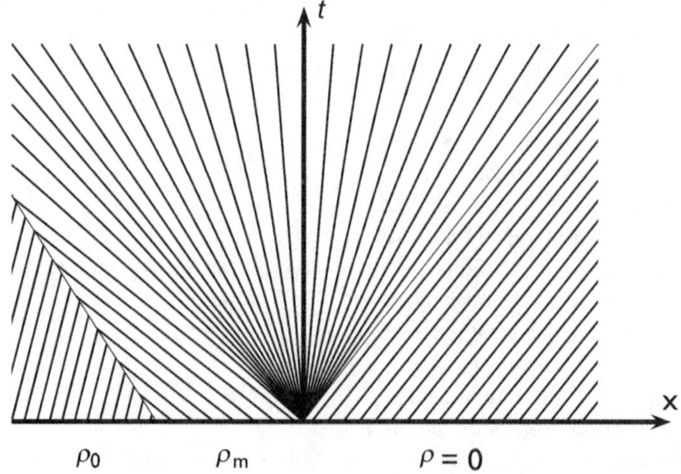

Figure 22.4 Traffic characteristics

if $f'(u_\ell) > f'(u_r)$ (Lax, 1987). The speed of the shockwave is given by Equation 22.5:

$$s = \frac{dx_s(t)}{dt} = \frac{[f(u_l) - f(u_r)]}{u_l - u_r} \tag{22.5}$$

In this equation, $x_s(t)$ is the position of the shockwave as a function of time. If the shock speed is positive then the inflow at junction between the two traffic densities will be a function of upstream traffic density, whereas if the shock speed is negative then the inflow at junction between the two traffic densities will be a function of downstream traffic density (Figure 22.5).

A rarefaction develops if $f'(u_\ell) < f'(u_r)$. The rarefaction can be entirely to the left, or to the right or in the middle (Figure 22.6). The analysis of the shockwave and rarefaction conditions gives us the Godunov based ODE model for traffic. The ODE for Godunov method is the same as the conservation law, and is given by Equation 22.6, where we have assumed unit length for the section:

$$\frac{d\rho(t)}{dt} = f_{in}(t) - f_{out}(t) + u(t) \tag{22.6}$$

To derive the rest of the model, see Figure 22.7. Now, the inflow $f_{in}(t)$ will be a function of upstream density $\rho\ell$ and downstream density ρr. Here upstream and downstream are with respect to the left junction.

Hence we have the relationship given by Equation 22.7 where we have used the function $F(.,.)$ that will be obtained from the Godunov method:

$$f_{in}(t) = F(\rho_l, \rho) \tag{22.7}$$

Similarly, for the right junction, the outflow $f_{out}(t)$ is given by Equation 22.8:

$$f_{out}(t) = F(\rho, \rho_r) \tag{22.8}$$

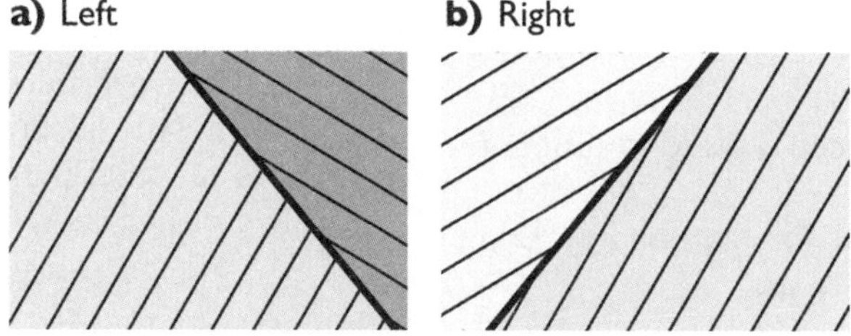

Figure 22.5 Shockwaves moving upstream (left) and downstream (right)

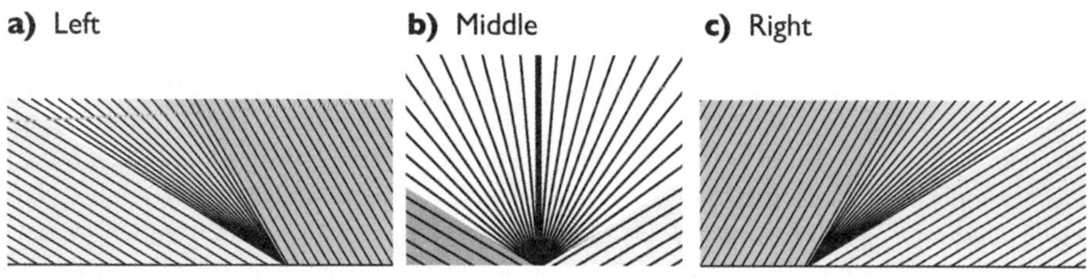

Figure 22.6 Rarefaction solution

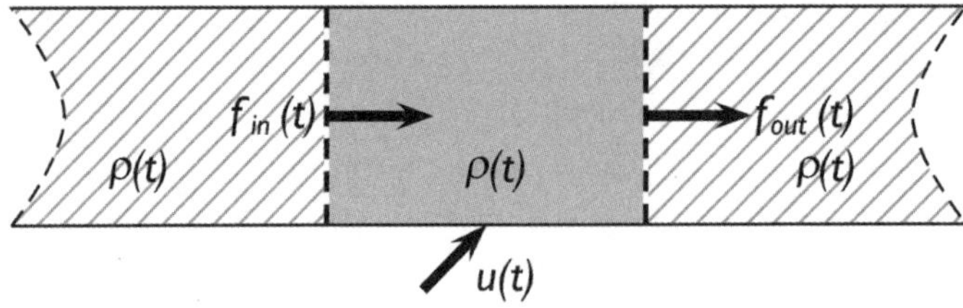

Figure 22.7 Godunov dynamics

The function $F(\rho_\ell, \rho_r)$ in terms of its arguments is given by the Godunov method as follows (Leveque, 2005):

$$F(\rho_\ell,\rho_r)=f\left(\rho^*(\rho_\ell,\rho_r)\right) \tag{22.9}$$

Here, the flow-dictating density ρ^* is obtained from the following (Leveque, 2005):

$$\begin{aligned}
&1.\ f'(\rho_\ell), f'(\rho_r)\geq 0 \Rightarrow \rho^* = \rho_\ell\\
&2.\ f'(\rho_\ell), f'(\rho_r)\leq 0 \Rightarrow \rho^* = \rho_r\\
&3.\ f'(\rho_\ell)\geq 0 \geq f'(\rho_r) \Rightarrow \rho^* = \rho_\ell\\
&\quad \text{if } s>0, \text{ otherwise } \rho^* = \rho_r\\
&4.\ f'(\rho_\ell)< 0 < f'(\rho_r) \Rightarrow \rho^* = \rho_s
\end{aligned}$$

Here, ρ_s is obtained as the solution to $f'(\rho_s) = 0$.

The ODE model for the ramp metering system can be written as:

$$\frac{d\rho(t)}{dt}=G_q(\rho_\ell,\rho,\rho_r)+u(t) \tag{22.10}$$

This is a switched hybrid system (van der Schaft and Schumacher, 1999), where the switching happens autonomously based on the values of ρ_ℓ, ρ and ρ_r. The function $F(\rho_\ell,\rho)$ can have three distinct values, (ρ_ℓ), $f(\rho)$, or $f(\rho_s)$. Similarly, $F(\rho, \rho_r)$ can have three distinct values. Hence, the dynamics can be written as:

$$\frac{d\rho(t)}{dt}=G_q(\rho_\ell,\rho,\rho_r)+u(t) \tag{22.11}$$

where $q \in \{1, 2, \ldots, 9\}$ and the different G_q functions can be obtained from Equations 22.9, 22.10 and 22.11. We propose the following feedback linearization based model for the ramp metering control that attempts to keep the mainline traffic density at ρ_c, which is taken to be the flow maximizing density. For the Greenshields' model this critical density is $\rho_m/2$.

$$e(t)=\left[\rho(t)-\rho_c\right]\to 0, \text{ as } t\to\infty \tag{22.12}$$

The closed loop dynamics obtained by using this control law (if the prevalent traffic conditions are enabling) provide an exponentially decaying error, i.e.

$$e(t)=\left[\rho(t)-\rho_c\right]\to 0, \text{ as } t\to\infty \tag{22.13}$$

The enabling conditions for the performance are obviously important, since if there are no vehicles at the ramp, then the control rate will not be achieved. Moreover, there is a maximum possible ramp inflow rate. In addition, vehicles cannot be taken out of the freeway using an entrance ramp. Hence, only those values of the ramp flow that are practically implemented are in the range of $[0, u_{max}]$.

CONCLUSION

With growing motorization across the world the number of road accidents is increasing, particularly in developing countries. This is in spite of lower levels of accidents per capita. Since road incidents are the source of substantial congestion, the need for effective management approaches is even more needed. Incident management involves several steps and the collaboration of numerous actors ranging from local police forces, departments of transportation and emergency response services (e.g. ambulances). As incidents have substantial impacts on traffic flows the need to model effectively incident management strategies is salient and some algorithms were presented, specifically those providing a feedback control design for traffic ramp metering. It was suggested that ramp metering is an important mitigation tool for incident management but requires proper timing and real-time adjustments. The case of Nevada is illustrative of the scale and complexity of incident management in a context of high automobile dependency. In societies that have a lower level of automobile dependency incident management takes a more complex dimension since other modes, such as buses, are much more likely to be involved.

REFERENCES

Anderson, E., Lindgren, R., Bertini, R., Tantiyanugulchai, S. and Leal, M. (2001) *Evaluation of Region 2 Incident Response Program Using Archived Data*. Transportation Research Group, Research Report.

Carson, J. (2008) "Traffic incident management and quick clearance laws". In: Texas Transportation Institute FHWA-HOP-09-005.

Chang, E. (1994) "Fuzzy systems based automatic freeway incident detection". In: Systems, Man, and Cybernetics (1994) *Humans, Information and Technology*. IEEE International Conference 1727–1733 vol. 2.

FHWA and USDOT (2000) *Incident Management Successful Practices: A Cross Cutting Study*. FHWA publications.

Golob, T. Recker, W. and Leonard, J. (1987) "An analysis of the severity and incident duration of truck-involved freeway accidents". *Accident Analysis & Prevention* 19.5, pp. 375–395.

Greenshields, B. (1935) "A Study in Highway Capacity". *Highway Research Board* 14, p. 458.

Haberman, R. (1987) *Mathematical Models: Mechanical Vibrations. Population Dynamics and Traffic Flow*. SIAM.

Jones, B., Janssen, L. and Mannering, F. (1991) "Analysis of the frequency and duration of freeway accidents in Seattle". *Accident Analysis & Prevention* 23.4, pp. 239–255.

Kachroo, P. and Özbay, K. (1998) *Feedback Control Theory for Dynamic Traffic Assignment*. Springer.

Kachroo, P. and Özbay, K. (2003) *Feedback ramp metering in intelligent transportation systems*. Springer.

Kachroo, P., Wadoo, S., Al-nasur, S., Shende, A., Singh, M.P. and Özbay, K. (2009) "Information technology requirements for intelligent evacuation systems". *World Review of Intermodal Transportation Research* 2.2–3, pp. 127–144.

Kachroo, P., Shlayan, N. and Wadoo, S. (2011) "Feedback ramp metering using Godunov method based hybrid model". *Intelligent Transportation Systems (ITSC) 14th International IEEE Conference on*. IEEE, pp. 1592–1597.

Lax, P. (1987) *Hyperbolic Systems of Conservation Laws and the Mathematical Theory of Shock Waves*. SIAM.

Leveque, R. (2005) *Numerical Methods for Conservation Laws*. Birkhauser.

Lighthill, M. and Whitham, G. (1955) "On kinematic waves. I: Flow movement in long rivers. II: A Theory of traffic on long crowded roods". *Proceedings of the Royal Society*. A229, pp. 281–345.

Matinovich, S. (2006) *Nevada Traffic Crashes 2006*. NDOT.

Nee, J. and Hallenbeck, M. (2001) "Evaluation of the Service Patrol Program in the Puget Sound Region." In: FHWA, US Department of Transportation WA-RD 518.1.

Neudorff, L.G., Randall, J.E., Reiss, R. and Gordon, R. (2003) "Freeway management and operations handbook". In: FHWA publications, p. 564.

Olmstead, T. (2001) "Freeway management systems and motor vehicle crashes: a case study of Phoenix, Arizona". *Accident Analysis and Prevention* 33.4, pp. 433–447.

Özbay, K. and Kachroo, P. (1999) *Incident Management in Intelligent Transportation Systems*. Artech House Intelligent Transportation Systems Library. Artech House.

Payne, H. and Tignor, S. (1978) "Freeway incident-detection algorithms based on decision trees with states". *Transportation Research Record* 682, pp. 30–37.

Petty, H., Rydzewski, K., Varaiya, D., Skabardonis, P., Noeimi, A. and Al-Deek, H. (1995) "Freeway service patrol evaluation." In: PATH Research Report UCB-ITS-PRR-95-5 (1995).

Richards, P. (1956) "Shockwaves on the highway". In: *Operations Research* 4, pp. 42–51.

Shlayan, N. and Kachroo, P. (2012) "Formal language modeling and simulations of incident management". In: *Intelligent Transportation Systems*, IEEE Transactions on PP.99, pp. 1 –9.

Srinivasan, D., Xin Jin and Cheu, R. (2004) "Evaluation of adaptive neural network models for freeway incident detection". In: *Intelligent Transportation Systems*, IEEE Transactions on 5.1, pp. 1–11.

USDoT and FHWA (2012) http://ops.fhwa.dot.gov/congsymp/sld004.htm (accessed 5 July 2012).

van der Schaft, A. and Schumacher, H. (1999) *An Introduction to Hybrid Dynamical Systems*. Springer.

Wang, W., Chen, S. and Qu, G. (2007) "Comparison between partial least squares regression and support vector machine for freeway incident detection". In: *Intelligent Transportation Systems Conference*, ITSC 2007. IEEE, pp.190 –195.

Whitham, G. (1974) *Linear and Nonlinear Waves*. John Wiley.

Willsky, A., Chow, E., Gershwin, S., Greene, C., Houpt, P. and Kurkjian, A. (1980) "Dynamic model-based techniques for the detection of incidents on freeways". In: *IEEE Transactions on Automatic Control* 25.3, pp. 347–360.

SECTION 6

Transport and the Environment

23

Transport and Energy Use

Stephen Potter, with Christopher Berridge, Matthew Cook and Per-Anders Langendahl

THE ENERGY CHALLENGE

Energy use in transport reflects a mix of core concerns that have varied over time and between countries. These could be represented as an interaction between three key groups of factors (Figure 23.1). In recent years our growing awareness of the environmental impacts of energy use has attracted considerable attention, but energy shortage and the related issue of the security of energy supplies have been powerful economic and geopolitical factors for hundreds of years. Recently this has been expressed in concerns around the role of high oil prices in triggering the 2008–10 recession, the implications for energy security in the wake of Russia's growing power through its oil and gas reserves and the uncertain political fallout of the 2011 democracy protest movements among Middle East oil producers. Transport energy strategies and policies are all part of this meta picture and, from the global to the local scale, approaches and measures need to address all these issues.

Recent transport energy policies strategies have sought to simultaneously achieve economic, political and environmental sustainability. But in practice, economic and political factors have tended to determine strategies, constraining approaches to address transport's environmental impacts. A distinction can be made between geographically specific impacts of transport's energy use (such as air pollution) and dispersed global impacts (in particular carbon emissions/climate change effects). However, this distinction is lessening as local air quality issues are tending to be subsumed within programmes focused on carbon reduction (e.g. policies seeking a transition to electric road vehicles). Existing forms of transport, with their high dependency on oil, are a major source of local air pollutants, including:

- Carbon Monoxide (CO) – a highly toxic gas that can impair brain function and, in sufficient concentrations, kill. Transport is the major source of CO, with some 90% coming from cars.
- Nitrogen Oxides (NO_x) – these cause respiratory problems and contribute to low level ozone

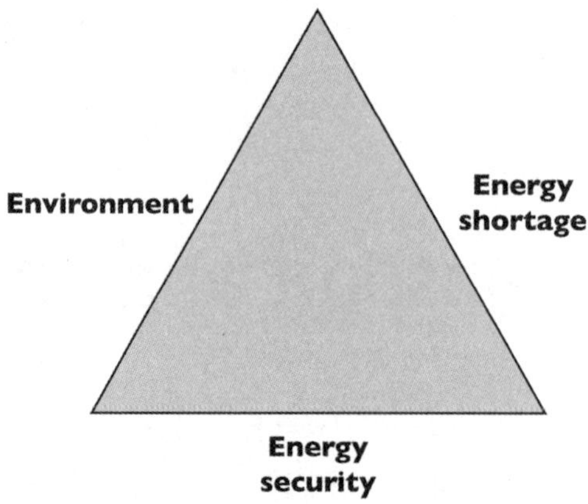

Environment	Energy shortages	Energy security
• Reduction in greenhouse gases (CO_2, NO_x, SO_x) • Reduction in local air pollutants • Desire to use renewable energy • Desire to meet emissions goals (Kyoto, Copenhagen, etc.)	• Peak oil constraints • Hydrocarbon gas supplies increasingly far from point of use • Emergence of rapidly developing economies greatly increasing World's energy requirement • Need for long-term energy solution	• Minimising reliance on imported energy • Changing political climate increases dependence on energy from unstable regimes • Non-geographic solutions sought

Figure 23.1 Transport's energy challenges
Source: after Berridge, 2010

formation and acid rain. Dinitrogen Oxide (N_2O) contributes to global warming. Transport produces about half of NO_x emissions. Diesel vehicles are an important source.

- Particulate Matter (PM) – responsible for respiratory problems and thought to be a carcinogen.
- Volatile Organic Compounds (VOCs) – Benzene and 1,3-butadiene are both carcinogens and are easily inhaled owing to their volatile nature. Other chemicals in this category are responsible for the production of ground-level ozone, which is toxic in low concentrations.

To date, the main response to address transport's air quality issues has been the use of technical measures to cut engine emissions coupled with cleaner fuel formulations (Lane and Warren, 2007). In developed countries, this approach has achieved a significant impact. For example, the UK Air Quality Pollutant Inventory Report (National Atmospheric Emissions Inventory, 2011) stated that 'overall air quality in the UK is currently estimated to be better than at any time since the industrial revolution'. It noted that CO emissions in 2009 were a 75% reduction on the emissions in 1990 and that the change in emissions between 1990 and 2009 'is dominated by the reduction in emissions from the road transport sector caused by the increased use of three-way catalysts in cars'. Furthermore, sulphur was cut by 89% as low sulphur fuels were introduced. Similarly tighter European vehicle emission standards in road transport were largely responsible for a 60% cut in NO_x over the same period and UK emissions of PM_{10} hydrocarbons declined by 58%.

But despite such improvements, NO_x and particulate emissions remain a source of serious concern, with measured levels of both levelling off in many UK cities above acceptable health levels. Some 60% of UK local authorities now have Air Quality Management Areas in an attempt to address this issue. In the USA, despite California's stringent emission standards for cars, air quality for the 14 million inhabitants of the Los Angeles basin currently fail to meet federal standards on around 130 days each year (albeit an improvement on the 226 days in 1988). In emerging economies, where emission standards are less developed, air pollution remains very severe. In Mexico City the summer smog can be so bad that industrial plants are ordered to cut production and schoolchildren are given the month off. For the 2008 Olympics, Beijing famously banned almost half the cities' cars for the duration of the games. In China as a whole, air pollution is estimated to cause around 750,000 deaths annually, although this is a very politically sensitive subject (McGregor, 2007). Even in Britain, the Parliamentary Office of Science and Technology (2002) noted that, looking to 2025, although mathematical models predict that most pollutant levels will continue to fall, targets for NO_x, PM_{10} and ozone may be breached in some areas. London is not expected to meet air quality standards until at least 2025. The technical improvements, although substantial, are not enough.

Attention is now moving towards the elimination of such pollutants not by cleaning existing transport fuels and their engines, but by moving to the use of fuels that produce few or no emissions at the point of use. This includes policies to promote electric and hydrogen vehicles, which allows pollutants to be either dealt with during manufacture (e.g. in generating electricity at power stations or producing hydrogen at refineries) or by using sources of energy that produce little pollution at all (e.g. electricity and hydrogen from wind or solar). The 2011 European Transport White Paper (Commission of the European Communities (CEC), 2011) envisaged that within 20 years internal combustion engine cars will simply not be permitted in cities. The move towards a fuel shift strategy very much brings together action to cut transport's local and global environmental impacts. It is also one that has the potential to link to the powerful political driver of energy security. But how viable is such a technical transition to a low carbon transport future?

The public policy aim of a transition to a low carbon future by the middle of this century is a particularly difficult challenge for the transport sector. This was highlighted in the 2006 UK Stern Report (Stern, 2006), where it was noted that, between 1990 and 2002, transport was the fastest growing source of carbon emissions in OECD countries (a growth of 25%) and the second fastest growing sector in non-OECD countries (36% growth). Rather than declining over the next 40 years, the trend is for transport CO_2 emissions to grow, particularly in non-OECD countries, where their share of global emissions is anticipated to increase from one third to one half by 2030.

Along with other countries, the UK Transport sector has failed to cut CO_2 emissions; indeed it was only the recession that meant that emissions in 2009 were the same as 1990 (previously they had risen above 1990 levels). With other sectors reducing their CO_2 emissions, the proportion coming from transport has grown from 15.6% in 1990 to 21.7% in 2009. Over 90% of the UK's transport CO_2 emissions come from road transport (Table 23.1). Passenger cars remain the biggest source of CO_2, but road freight emissions are significant and those for light vans have risen substantially. Rail produces only 1.7% of transport's CO_2 emissions, despite recent substantial rises in passenger-kilometres and freight carried.

Within this overall trend of little change in CO_2 emissions, it is notable that emissions from cars have dropped slightly, but there has been a strong rise in emissions from light duty vehicles (coinciding with the rise in internet shopping deliveries). Table 23.1 covers domestic emissions but excludes some sources, including international aviation. The 2009 UK report on climate change emissions (DECC, 2011) noted that, between 1990 and 2009, CO_2 emissions from UK-based aviation (this covers both domestic and UK-based

Table 23.1 UK CO_2 emissions by source (Mt CO_2), 1990 and 2009

		1990	2009
Aviation	Civil aviation (domestic)	1.4	2.0
Road	Passenger cars	73.1	70.9
	Light duty vehicles	9.4	15.3
	Buses	3.8	5.3
	HGVs	24.0	21.0
	Mopeds and motorcycles	0.6	0.6
	LPG emissions (all vehicles)	0.0	0.3
	Other (road vehicle engines)	0.3	0.1
Railways	Railways	2.1	2.1
Shipping	National navigation	1.8	1.5
Other mobile	Military aircraft and shipping	5.3	2.5
Other transport	Aircraft – support vehicles	0.3	0.5
Transport total		**122.1**	**122.2**
Transport as % of total		**15.6%**	**21.7%**
Total UK emissions		**781.6**	**563.6**

Source: Department of Energy and Climate Change, 2011

international flights) had more than doubled to 33 million tonnes carbon dioxide equivalent. It also noted that emissions at altitude have a greater global warming effect, and allowing for this means that they now represent 11% of the UK's total climate change impact. At currently predicted growth rates, the aviation sector will constitute about 33% of total UK climate change impact by 2050. So, even if all other sectors meet government CO_2 reduction targets, air travel is a key environmental issue for the 21st century (Bishop and Grayling, 2003).

Energy security and energy shortage were issues that attracted much attention in the 1970s, but came to be overshadowed as the environmental impacts of transport emerged as a major global concern. Until recently, energy supply has not been an immediate problem. According to BP, the ratio of world oil reserves to production have remained largely static in the 20 years to 2004, with there being around 40 years of reserves (BP, 2005). But reserves are only part of the issue. The concept of 'peak oil' is attracting increasing attention, with projections that global oil production will reach a resource-limited maximum (or 'peak') sometime between now and 2030 (for a review of projections, see Boyle and Bentley, 2008). Potentially, though, when production of oil actually reaches its peak is less relevant than when demand exceeds supply, which appears increasingly likely in the wake of the rapidly growing economies of China and India. The former Chairman of Shell, Lord Oxburgh, succinctly summed up the issue when he stated that 'There isn't any shortage of oil, but a real shortage of cheap oil that for too long we have taken for granted' (ITPOES, 2008).

This conclusion is reflected in the subsequent long-term rise in oil prices. In early 2007, the price of a barrel of Brent Crude was around $70. By mid 2008 the price had risen to $140, but rapidly dropped to around

$50 as the recession hit. Since then, the price has steadily risen again to stand, at the beginning of 2012, at around $110 a barrel. Short term economic factors produce price volatility, but there are all the signs of a long-term rise in price as globally demand approaches the limits of supply. Providing energy for transport is becoming expensive, involving difficult, costly and potentially riskier situations. The latter is illustrated by the 2010 Deepwater Horizon disaster in the Gulf of Mexico (at the time of writing, BP had spent $14bn in its spill response and cleanup operation and has set aside a further $20bn for damages claims).

Thus economic drivers are set to make energy an increasingly prominent factor in 21st century geo-politics. This is typified by the USA's 2007 Energy Independence and Security Act (GovTrack, 2009) with the stated aim to pass:

> an act to move the United States toward greater energy independence and security, to increase the production of clean renewable fuels, to protect consumers, to increase the efficiency of products, buildings, and vehicles, to promote research on and deploy greenhouse gas capture and storage options, and to improve the energy performance of the Federal Government, and for other purposes.

Although citing environmental factors as support issues, this policy's core desire is to reduce reliance by the USA on hydrocarbon fuels from politically unstable regions. This is what is emphasised in USA politics, epitomised by George W. Bush's preference to label hydrogen as the USA's 'freedom fuel' to symbolise its potential for energy security.

However, energy security and shortage can be less compatible with environmental requirements. The easiest and most secure way may not be to develop clean energy. This is typified by the burgeoning interest and development of oil shale reserves. In environmental terms, oil shale is an extremely 'dirty' fuel. Brandt et al. (2010) note that fuel-cycle carbon dioxide emissions from oil shale derived liquid fuels are likely to be 25–75% higher than those from conventional liquid fuels, and the processing also requires major water use. But oil shale is abundant and obtained from politically secure areas (with the USA and China having large domestic reserves). Oil shale (and also shale gas) can economically outcompete renewable energy. Thus it is difficult to see how environmental concerns will moderate such a powerful economic and political combination. Much the same can be concluded from China's extensive use of domestic and Australian coal for electricity generation.

For sustainable transport, the strategic energy challenge is to simultaneously achieve a low carbon transport future that also ensures adequate and secure supplies of energy. Although it is crucial to cut transport's CO_2 emissions, a sustainable transport energy approach is likely to be entirely sidelined unless it can also deliver economic, political and social sustainability.

Transport energy futures

The issues discussed above have led to a particular meaning emerging for the term 'sustainable transport'. This is not defined purely in terms of environmental sustainability, but has become a conceptual and ideological mantra moulded by the wider concept of 'sustainable development'. Sustainable development is the ideology that carbon reduction is not a constraint on growth but is an opportunity to be realised through 'green' economic growth. For transport, this philosophy is epitomised by successive CEC policy papers on transport. Stead (2006) reviewed the 2001 CEC White Paper on Transport (2001), and the subsequent mid-term review *Keep Europe Moving* (CEC, 2006), noting:

> The use of the term 'sustainable mobility' in the title of the mid-term review of the Transport White Paper serves to highlight a key dilemma of European transport policy, namely how to reconcile the free movement of people and goods, one of the basic pillars of the European Union, whilst at the same time protecting the environment and improving the health and safety of citizens.

The 2011 CEC Transport White Paper, *Roadmap to a Single European Transport*

Figure 23.2 A modern tram running through the car-free streets of central Strasbourg

Area (CEC, 2011), reiterated the same philosophy (and dilemma), seeking 'to build a competitive transport system that will increase mobility, remove major barriers in key areas and fuel growth and employment. At the same time, the proposals will dramatically reduce Europe's dependence on imported oil and cut carbon emissions in transport by 60% by 2050.' This viewpoint was also reflected in the 2011 UK White Paper, *Creating Growth, Cutting Carbon* (Department for Transport (DfT), 2011). Subtitled 'Making Sustainable Local Transport Happen', this policy White Paper sets out a vision 'for a transport system that is an engine for economic growth, but one that is also greener and safer and improves quality of life in our communities'. Thus transport planning, policy and management are increasingly responding and being moulded by the conceptual mantra of 'sustainable development'. But although we may be on the cusp of a transition to a very different type of transport energy future, quite what this future could be and how it will come about is a matter of great uncertainty. A number of scenarios are possible.

In terms of how it might look, one 'sustainable transport' future could be the widespread use of low carbon vehicles in the context of a continued rise in mobility amidst population dispersal – i.e. roughly business as usual but with clean technology vehicles. This sort of future was articulated over a decade ago by Tickell and Wright (1998) who envisaged a 2030 vision of green hyper mobility, on the basis that with car '*emissions cut to nearly nothing ... the main argument against roadbuilding has been swept aside*', so there is a massive rise in car use, further roadbuilding and suburbanisation, but congestion remains intense, being managed by advanced information technologies. Alternatively, there could be a sustainable transport future of active travel demand management with cities and towns reconfigured around high capacity electrified public transport systems, where walking and cycling dominates and car use restricted to a minority of trips (Figure 23.2). This is an approach perhaps epitomised in the seminal study by Newman and Kenworthy, (1999). Either end of this spectrum (and anything in between) could be claimed to represent 'sustainable transport'. This poses a key question: could 'sustainable transport' manifest itself in a series of different ways, or can only certain combinations of measures deliver a low carbon energy future?

This is a crucial question because we appear to be entering a new stage in the transport energy debate. Despite rearguard actions from those who benefit from fostering climate change denial, it is clear that we cannot continue transport's hydrocarbon intensive regime for much longer. Quite aside from climate change, energy economics, supply and security issues will require an alternative approach. We now need to explore questions around what sort of transport regime represents a viable energy future and how the transition to this future could be achieved. In terms of the magnitude of change, the 2011 EU Transport White Paper (CEC, 2011) envisages a 60% cut in transport's CO_2 emissions by 2050. An even greater 80% cut in all transport's CO_2 emissions by 2050 has emerged as the benchmark definition for a 2050 low carbon society as articulated in the UK Low Carbon Transition Plan (Department of Energy and Climate Change (DECC), 2009). Under the 2008 Climate Change Act, Britain has set legally binding 'carbon budgets', aiming to cut UK emissions by 34% by 2020 and at least 80% by 2050. This can be taken as a reasonable working definition of what kind of environmental improvement is needed within the wider concept of 'sustainable transport'.

Exploring transport energy futures

A list of greener transport initiatives is not difficult to compile, but how far they take us towards a low carbon and more energy secure future is debatable. The comprehensive E4tech report for the UK Department for Transport (E4tech, 2006), reviewed a range of vehicle technologies (including battery-electric, hybrid electric and fuel cells) and a range of related fuels (gasoline, diesel, bioethanol, biodiesel and hydrogen). This study concluded that, compared to conventional petrol and diesel-engined cars, hybrid cars can cut carbon emissions by around 20%. The use of low carbon fuels offers greater improvements; bioethanol can cut CO_2 emissions per vehicle kilometre by 25%, biodiesel by 45% and hydrogen by 40% or more. These fuels also have the potential to address fuel security concerns, although whether they can be produced in a sufficient volume is open to question. In addition, any carbon improvements very much depend on the production methods used. International studies (e.g. EUCAR et al., 2002) have produced similar results to those reported above, but almost all these technologies appear to fall short of the required 80% cut in all transport's CO_2 emissions.

In terms of fuel switch, in 2002 the UK Government set a target that low carbon cars should represent 10% of all car sales by 2012 and in 2005 announced the Renewable Transport Fuels Obligation, requiring suppliers to source 5% transport fuel sales from renewable sources by 2010/11, although in 2009 this target was cut to 3.5%[1] (the actual figure was 2.5% in 2009). This formed a major part of transport's contribution to the 2006 Energy Review (DTI, 2006). The promotion of electric road vehicles has achieved prominence in the last few years, and it is notable that the commitment to support low carbon battery-electric cars was the only transport policy measure to feature in the 2010 Conservative/ Liberal Democrat Coalition pact. A longer term transition path has now begun to emerge through the 2009 Low Carbon Transition Plan (ibid.) and the 2009 New Automotive Innovation and Growth Team (NAIGT) report on the future of the automotive industry, which anticipates cleaner internal combustion technologies being joined by an initial widespread uptake of battery-electric vehicles (including 'plug-in' hybrids) followed later by hydrogen fuel cell vehicles (NAIGT, 2009).

It is significant to note that the emphasis in all these recent reports and strategies is on switching to low carbon fuels. An alternative technical approach is to use fuel more efficiently. This is actually how hybrid cars cut carbon, but there is a greater potential than the 20–30% improvements that they achieve. Over a decade ago, Wemyss (1996) in his technological review considered that advances in vehicle technologies should allow cars to achieve a fuel consumption of 1.9 litres/100 km (150 mpg) within 10 years. That represents an 80% reduction in fuel use compared to the average fleet performance today. Yet, although there has been some progress in the fuel economy of new vehicles, there are still no cars on the market that achieve anywhere near this technically possible performance. It appears that, although car manufacturers had developed a number of energy efficiency technologies, these remained unapplied until the European Commission introduced, in 2009, its CO_2 emissions regulation (EC443/2009). This regulation sets a sales-weighted CO_2 target for new passenger cars; it specifies an average target of 130 g/km by 2015 (a 9.8% reduction on the 2010 level), proceeding to an average of 95 g/km in 2020.

The result of this regulatory action, which replaced a voluntary agreement with car manufacturers, can be seen in the sudden appearance of a range of 'eco' petrol and diesel cars incorporating a variety of fuel efficient technologies. Up until 2007, there had only been a gradual improvement in new car test CO_2 emissions[2] – in the ten years from 1997 to 2007 test CO_2 emissions were cut by 13%; yet in only three years to 2010, CO_2 emissions were cut by a further 13%. The change from a poorly enforced voluntary agreement of the 1990s to the 2009 EU regulations and prospective fines seems to have stimulated real action from the car industry.

Notwithstanding such improvements, these strategies essentially represent a supply-led approach envisaging a technical fix scenario of 'business as usual with clean vehicles'. There also exists a separate range of measures that involve a demand management approach, advocating modal shift from cars to more energy efficient forms of transport including light rail and innovative public transport systems, public shared bicycle schemes, car pooling, car clubs and teleworking/shopping. This is often coupled with proposals for planning controls to produce settlement patterns and conditions that will cut trip length, favour sustainable modes and disadvantage car use. Such an approach involves very different processes and understandings to that needed and used for a technical-fix based approach.

In his comprehensive review of this and other approaches, Banister (2005, Chapter 6) cites case studies of cities that have achieved a 10% drop in car use through approaches utilising planning controls and public transport development. The key thing about such an approach is that it seeks to 'lock-in' energy efficiency through travel patterns and behaviour rather than relying on massive technological and fuel system improvements. A further demand management approach is that of pricing mechanisms. Economists have long argued that the core problem is the under-pricing of the environmental costs of road and air transport and that marginal cost pricing should be adopted (Pearce, 1993; Maddison et al., 1996; Glaister and Graham, 2003), and *Green Budget Europe* (http://www.greenbudget.eu) has spearheaded the case for ecotaxation reform within the EU. The arguments and evidence for a tax neutral programme of green fiscal reform was presented by the 2009 report of the UK Green Fiscal Commission, including a detailed briefing paper on transport taxation (Green Fiscal Commission, 2009). Pricing mechanisms are seen as supporting changes in travel patterns and behaviours, but need to be applied with a political sensitivity that is difficult to represent in econometric models. In practice, fuel taxation protests and successful lobbying for fuel tax reductions indicate that pricing can be a difficult policy to pursue.

Overall, the sustainable transport energy debate is very much around the relative roles of technical measures to promote cleaner fuels and fuel economy as opposed to modal

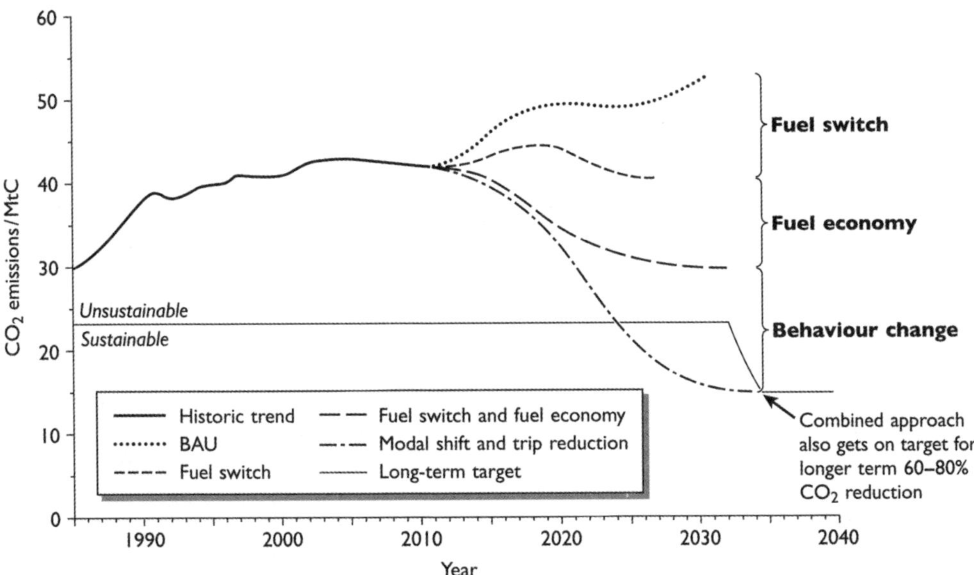

Figure 23.3 Ground transport CO_2 emissions and possible 'sustainable' projections, including a combined measures scenario

Source: Warren, 2007

shift and other demand management measures. What combination of factors is used involves a very different set of social and economic adjustments. This issue has been explored by a number of researchers (e.g. EPA, 1998; Kwon and Preston, 2005; Potter, 2007) who conclude broadly that there are substantial problems in seeking to achieve sustainable transport by using any one of these approaches in isolation. For example, using technical measures in isolation means that to even achieve a relatively modest 40% cut in CO_2 emissions from cars (while not addressing behavioural demand-generating factors), would require doubling fuel economy to around a fleet average of 5 litres/100 km and the widespread uptake of low carbon fuels that cut the carbon intensity of road fuels by 60%. This would require very substantial fiscal or regulatory actions to achieve such a substantial shift in vehicle purchase patterns. Politically this would be extremely difficult to achieve in the timescales required.

Equally, the studies show that, alone, even a substantial modal shift to public transport cannot attain a sufficient CO_2 reduction even assuming a politically 'heroic' reduction in car use. The need for a combined strategy is clear. If everything depends on one group of measures, then economic, social and ecologically sustainable transport becomes unattainable, even if improvements are pushed to technically and politically unrealistic extremes. At the very least, low carbon fuels must be introduced in conjunction with substantial improvements to fuel economy. Merely substituting petrol gas guzzlers by hydrogen guzzlers is no sustainable solution. The most viable combination is the integration of technical improvements with demand management that reduces trip lengths, promotes trip substitution and modal shift. This would counteract rises in transport costs and so help political, economic and social acceptance. Such a scenario is represented diagrammatically in Figure 23.3.

Despite the case for a combined approach, there is a real danger that it may be politically easier to develop some technical measures (e.g. fuel switch) more readily than demand management. Any success of technical measures could result in the neglect or abandoning of demand management policies, particularly as the latter are perceived as politically difficult. In reality the magnitude of the challenge is that while 'quick wins' are being implemented, the foundations of longer term and more tricky measures need to be put into place. Transport policies at the local, national and international level need to blend technical improvements to vehicles with modal shift and other aspects of travel behaviour, such as trip length, frequency and vehicle occupancy. Transport's energy challenge is of such a magnitude that, unless substantial progress is made on all these fronts, we will inevitably fail to achieve environmental, economic and social sustainability.

Towards an energy efficient transport system

The above analysis suggests that we should be seeking a transition to a transport system that is inherently energy efficient and one that is adaptable to future challenges. This could involve a variety of configurations that combine vehicle technical improvements with demand management. At the same time, the future may not necessarily be 'business as usual' plus low carbon cars; the transport energy future may be far more open than we think. New transport technologies and service systems are emerging, and developments in IT have already had a major impact on travel behaviour (e.g. the growth in web based shopping and home-based teleworking – see Chapter 14).

These developments are likely to affect different places in different ways. For major cities there may be an emphasis on high capacity public transport systems, roadspace reallocation to buses, cyclists and pedestrians, and demand management through road and parking pricing. Behavioural measures to reduce and manage travel needs, might include electronic substitution for commuting and business travel, distance access to services and education, workplace and leisure travel planning and a variety of new product-service systems such as car clubs and city electric car hire schemes (e.g. the Paris *Autolib*; see Willsher, 2011). For suburbs and smaller towns, some elements of such 'big city' formulations would be inappropriate. Here different sorts of clean, energy efficient transport systems will be needed rather than a lower-specification version of big city systems. Trams, metros and other high capacity public transport systems are inappropriate and unaffordable, but there are newer transport systems emerging that could work very well in such contexts. For example, advanced guided bus systems can provide the coverage and flexibility needed for cross-suburban travel or, as being applied in Cambridge, to provide a city link corridor serving a mix of established and new settlements.

There are also important emerging designs and technologies that have the potential to provide entirely new sorts of transport service. Demand Responsive Transport (DRT) is well suited to the dispersed pattern of transport demand found in suburbs, towns and rural areas. There are examples of successful systems in a number of countries and in some places in the UK. Several Canadian, Dutch, French and German suburban-style towns have entirely replaced their conventional bus routes by semi-scheduled DRT systems (Enoch et al., 2004). In the UK niche markets have emerged, including in Bicester where there is the Chiltern Railways shared taxi link to the station that has provided a popular alternative for car users. In the Netherlands shared 'Traintaxis' are available at most rail stations. Advances in IT now make it possible for a hybrid taxicab/minibus DRT service to provide a considerably better service than conventional bus or even light rail services, but the main barriers seem to be regulatory and financial, in that existing institutional structures do not recognise such a service system.

Personalised Rapid Transit (PRT) perhaps represents a vision of a long-term low carbon public transport system that has all the characteristics needed to provide a high quality low carbon service in suburbs and towns

Figure 23.4 A Heathrow PRT pod descending from the elevated guideway to a car park station

(Rogers, 2007). PRT offers a level of service that comes close to the convenience of the private car. The small automated battery-electric vehicles run on lightweight guideways that make up a network taking people directly from their origin stop to their final destination stop. The sort of service PRT provides can be thought of as akin to a driverless taxi service. The vehicles guide themselves automatically and, being automated, such PRT systems offer an on-demand 24/7 all-year service. People do not wait for a service to turn up, but the service is there when they arrive at a station. The first PRT system in the UK has been built at Heathrow Airport to link the car parks to Terminal 5 (ULTra PRT, 2011), and a number of systems are close to market application in several countries throughout the world (Figure 23.4).

Although systems like advanced DRT face institutional barriers and PRT has yet to be proven outside the sheltered confines of an airport operator, the potential is there for future transport systems to be very different to those of today. It is not just a matter of new technologies and designs substituting current vehicles, but of different business models for a new product-service system. For example, low carbon cars have a different cost structure compared to petrol and diesel cars. They are more expensive to buy and, for electric cars, battery packs are costly; however, this is counterbalanced by lower running costs. This cost structure is more suited to leasing packages rather than outright ownership. It is also suited to the development of new service models like public car schemes. This means that a possible future is one where many people may not buy one or two multi-purpose vehicles, but have a 'mobility package', whereby they have a lease car, plus the availability of specialist vehicles for specific uses coupled with 'add-ons' like discounted rail or public transport passes through integrated smart cards. If internal combustion-engined cars are to be phased out in cities, car access may be through schemes like Paris' *Autolib* city car hire scheme rather than individual car ownership. Much wider options are opening up to obtain car use, and the distinction between 'public' and 'private' transport could well become blurred.

These sort of technical and service system developments, together with behavioural measures that allow people to explore transport alternatives, suggest that customised packages of measures will need to vary by different types of settlements and patterns of travel demand. We could have a much more diversified transport future. However, the transition to a flexible and appropriate sustainable transport system requires more than developing a range of service and technical designs. There is a need to a change the process by which transport services and policies are implemented. As noted above, institutional, regulatory and assessment structures are built around the existing models of transport provision and make it difficult, if not impossible, for new design configurations to emerge. This is a largely unrecognised, but crucial part of the formula to deliver sustainable transport.

This institutional inertia is deeply rooted in the way transport policy is conceived and articulated. In almost all countries, both transport and energy policies have for long been supply-led processes. For example, energy policy has been about building increasingly centralised power stations and choosing the primary fuel used. It is about organising centralised production marketed to an exogenous dispersed demand. The technology may change (e.g. from coal generation to nuclear or renewables) but the process, the actors involved and the approach does not. Around this core logic has been built a professionally-oriented policy structure centred upon a small group of actors with civil engineering project management skills. This is how governments 'do' energy policy.

Equally, until recently, transport policy has evolved around a similar centralist logic and socio-technical regime structure. It has been about engineering skills to implement a supply-led solution of roadbuilding. As with energy policy, transport policy has been built around interactions with, and the management of, the specialist professions to deliver transport projects. Indeed, even when the need for transport demand management emerged in the early 1990s, this was done in a way that was compliant with the logic of the socio-technical regime. So instead of building roads, the civil engineering project approach shifted attention to building new metro and tram systems and upgrading the railways. It was used to build Britain's first high speed rail line (HS1) and is being used now as Crossrail in London and HS2 proceed. The supply-led technical approach has simply shifted onto different things to supply.

Even this relatively simple shift in focus has proved problematic. For example, the UK has not had the standardised processes to deliver cost-effective tram networks, particularly in the context of our privatised public transport systems. This has led to many schemes failing and tram systems falling from favour after only a handful were built in the largest cities. As noted by Hodgson (2011) the 2000 Ten Year Plan envisaged 25 new rapid transit lines to be delivered, but by the 2004 Future of Transport report, such light rail schemes were off the agenda. No new schemes have been authorised since Nottingham in 1994, with the exception of Edinburgh's politically motivated tram system, which is severely delayed, cut back and considerably over budget (Lowe, 2010). The main reaction to the difficulties in getting tram systems built in the UK has been to try instead for cheaper and lower performance guided bus schemes, but these too have suffered from similar problems of funding shortfalls and cost overruns. The Cambridge system (albeit now operating well and the longest guided busway in the world) was delivered two years late and at least a third over budget.

This highlights a key institutional issue that shifting the focus of a supply-led approach also requires a change in the regulatory and professional structures of transport policy. In the UK public transport privatisation and deregulation in the 1980s and 1990s produced an institutional context that makes major new public transport investments risky and expensive. Other countries, France in particular, have a policy context of state transport operations coupled with diverse funding mechanisms. Thus it has been much easier for France than for the UK to shift its supply-led approach to public transport systems. This institutional context also helps to explain why innovations, such as DRT services, struggle in the UK. Our system of deregulated bus operations is so structured around conventional 1980s style of registered services that it makes innovations (such as the taxi-bus fusion that works elsewhere) difficult to introduce other than for small niche markets.

Indeed, it is notable that, rather than addressing the key barrier of the institutional and regulatory structures, policymakers in the UK have sought to find projects that can be implemented within the existing structure. This probably means that many existing transport solutions (such as trams and DRT) will see little application in Britain and there is a real danger that retaining our old structures could also jeopardise the viability of many of the new innovative systems and technologies needed to radically decarbonise the transport system.

Such situations have been the subject of analysis in the literature around the transition process to sustainability. For example, Geels et al. (2008) argue that purely technical approaches are limited to incremental innovations and only slowly dismantle the unsustainable patterns of the production and consumption system. Such an approach typically seeks technical improvements that reduce environmental aspects without affecting the core production and consumption system. Even energy efficiency has also been done largely in a supply-led manner. There have been public information campaigns, but these are peripheral to the supply-side core approach of regulations and voluntary agreements with industry to improve vehicle fuel economy, backed up by central taxation 'nudges' to stimulate takeup. All these are essentially an adaptation of the centralist supply-led logic. It is what can be delivered within the approach of engaging only with the small core of actors who make up the supply system. Engagement with users is alien to the way the regime operates.

On moving towards transport demand management measures such as travel plans and new product-service packages, a real clash of practice and logics occurs. The management of travel demand is a process that requires engaging with end users and finding ways to work with them to accept responsibility for their travel behaviour. This requires a totally different set of skills to those in supply-led capital projects, and ones that are very undeveloped amidst transport professionals. It also requires a transport policy approach that recognises that, to deliver sustainable transport, transport policy processes and structures need to be reformed.

CONCLUSION

From this analysis, it can be concluded that a more comprehensive socio-technical approach is needed to address transformative change at a system levels (Geels, 2005). This comprehensive approach includes the emerging technologies as well as production processes and management/policy practices, which are entwined in relationships of technological innovations and socio-economic arrangements. Geels and Schot (2007) claim that transitions can be explained by using multi-dimensional levels. The key factors identified in this chapter suggest that such a multi-level approach needs to include actions that feed from the *product level* (new low carbon technologies) into the generation of *new service and mobility models*; these cannot succeed without a shift in the system's *institutional structures*. This last level is possibly the greatest and most neglected challenge; both institutional and regulatory structures are needed that facilitate (rather than hinder) innovative service and mobility models and transport policy and professional skills/organisations that understand and value such approaches. Only with such a multi-level systems understanding resulting in effective action at all levels can sustainable transport be a realistic proposition.

NOTES

1 For details see http://www.renewablefuelsagency.gov.uk/aboutthertfo.
2 In practice, on road fuel economy is around 20% poorer than under vehicle type tests.

REFERENCES

Banister, D. (2005) *Unsustainable Transport*, Taylor and Francis, London.

Berridge, C. (2010): *Hydrogen as a Fuel for Vehicles*, PhD Thesis, The Open University.

Bishop, S. and Grayling, T. (2003) *The Sky's the Limit – Policies for Sustainable Aviation*, IPPR, London.

Boyle, G. and Bentley, R. (2008) Global oil depletion: forecasts and methodologies, *Environment and Planning B*, 35(4), pp. 609–626.

BP (2005) *BP Statistical Review of World Energy*, British Petroleum, London.

Brandt, A. Boak, J. and Burnham, A. (2010) Carbon dioxide emissions from oil shale derived liquid fuels, Ch. 11 (pp. 219–248) of Olayinka, I., Hartstein, A. and Ogunsola, O. (eds), *Oil Shale: A Solution to the Liquid Fuel Dilemma Stanford*, American Chemical Society Symposium Series, Vol. 1032.

Commission of the European Communities (CEC) (2001) *White Paper. European Transport Policy for 2020: Time to Decide [COM(2001)370]* Office for Official Publications of the European Communities, Luxembourg (available from http://ec.europa.eu/transport/strategies/doc/2001_white_paper/lb_com_2001_0370_en.pdf).

Commission of the European Communities (CEC) (2006) *Communication from the Commission to the Council and the European Parliament. Keep Europe moving – Sustainable Mobility for our Continent. Mid-term Review of the European Commission's 2001 Transport White Paper [COM(2006)314]*, Office for Official Publications of the European Communities, Luxembourg.

Commission of the European Communities (CEC) (2011) White Paper *Roadmap to a Single European Transport Area – Towards a Competitive and Resource-Efficient Transport System*, Office for Official Publications of the European Communities, Luxembourg (available from http://ec.europa.eu/transport/strategies/2011_white_paper_en.htm).

Department for Transport (2011) *Creating Growth, Cutting Carbon: Making Sustainable Local Transport Happen*, Department for Transport, London, Cm 7996, January.

Department of Energy and Climate Change (2009) *The UK Low Carbon Transition Plan: A National Strategy for Climate and Energy*, DECC, London.

Department of Energy and Climate Change (2011) *2009 Final Greenhouse Gas Emissions* (available from http://www.decc.gov.uk/en/content/cms/statistics/climate_change/gg_emissions/uk_emissions/2009_final/2009_final.aspx).

Department of Trade and Industry (2006) *The Energy Challenge: Energy Review Report 2006*, DTI, London, CM 6887.

E4tech (2006) *Methodology and Guidance for Carbon Reporting under the Renewable Transport Fuel Obligation*, E4tech, London.

Enoch, M., Potter, S., Parkhurst, G. and Smith, M. (2004) *Intermode: Innovations in Demand Responsive Transport*, Department for Transport and Greater Manchester Passenger Transport Executive.

Environmental Protection Agency (EPA) (1998) *G-8 Environment and Transport Futures Forum*, EPA, Washington, DC (Report No. EPA 160-R-98–002).

EUCAR/CONCAWE/JRC (2002) *Well-to-wheels Analysis of Future Automotive Fuels and Powertrains in the European Context*, CEC, Brussels, December (available from http://ies.jrc.cec.eu.int/wtw.html).

Geels, F.W. (2005) *Technological Transitions and System Innovations: A Co-evolutionary and Sociotechnical Analysis*, Edward, Elgar, Cheltenham.

Geels, F. and Schot, J. (2007) Typology of socio-technical transition pathways, *Research Policy*, 36, pp. 399–417.

Geels, F.W., Hekkert, M.P. and Jacobsson, S. (2008) The dynamics of sustainable innovation journeys, *Technology Analysis and Strategic Management*, 20(5), pp. 521–536.

Glaister, S. and Graham, D. (2003) *Transport Pricing: Better for Travellers*, Independent Transport Commission, Southampton.

GovTrack US (2009) Energy Information and Security Act (2007), [online] (available from http://www.govtrack.us/congress/bill.xpd?bill=h110-6).

Green Fiscal Commission (2009) *Reducing Carbon Emissions Through Transport Taxation, Green Fiscal*

Commission Briefing Paper 6, Green Fiscal Commission, London (available from http://www.greenfiscalcommission.org.uk/images/uploads/gfcBriefing6_PDF_ISBN_v7.pdf).

Hodgson, P. (2011) *Modelling the Cost and Environmental Performance of Light Rail and an Equivalent Bus-Based System*, PhD Thesis, The Open University.

ITPOES (2008) *The Oil Crunch: Securing the UK's Energy Future*, Industry Taskforce on Peak Oil and Energy Security.

Kwon, T.H. and Preston, J. (2005) The driving force behind the growth of per capita car driving distances in Great Britain (1970–2000), *Transport Reviews*, 25(4), pp. 467–490.

Lane, B. and Warren, J. (2007) Sustainable road transport technologies, Ch. 2 of Warren, J. (ed.), *Managing Transport Energy*, Oxford University Press, Oxford.

Lowe, J.G. (2010) Edinburgh Trams: a case study of a complex project, *Proceedings of the 26th Annual ARCOM Conference*, University of Leeds, September.

McGregor, R. (2007) 750,000 a year killed by Chinese pollution, *Financial Times,* July 2 (available from http://www.ft.com/cms/s/0/8f40e248-28c7-11dc-af78-000b5df10621.html#axzz1lLGHiycH; accessed 3 February 2012).

Maddison, D., Pearce, D., Johansson, O., Calthorp, E., Litman, T. and Verhoef, E. (1996) *TheTrue Costs of Road Travel*, Blueprint 5, Earthscan, London.

National Atmospheric Emissions Inventory, AEA Group (2011) *Air Quality Pollutant Inventories for England, Scotland, Wales and Northern Ireland: 1990–2009*. DEFRA, London.

New Automotive Innovation and Growth Team (NAIGT) (2009) *An Independent Report on the Future of the Automotive Industry in the UK* (available from http://www.bis.gov.uk/files/file51139.pdf).

Newman, P. and Kenworthy, J.R. (1999) *Sustainability and Cities: Overcoming Automobile Dependence*, Island Press, Washington, DC.

Parliamentary Office of Science and Technology (2002) *Air Quality in the UK*, Postnote No 177, London, November.

Pearce, D. (1993) 'Foreword,' in Banister, D. and Button, K. (eds) *Transport, the Environment and Sustainable Development*: Chapman and Hall, London, pp. xiii–xiv.

Potter, S. (2007) Exploring approaches towards a sustainable transport system, *International Journal of Sustainable Transportation*, 1(2), pp. 115–131.

Rogers, L. (2007) Are driverless pods the future?, BBC News, Dec. 18 (available from http://news.bbc.co.uk/1/hi/uk/7148731.stm).

Stead, D, (2006) Mid-term review of the European Commission's 2001 Transport White Paper, *European Journal of Transport and Infrastructure*, 6(4), pp. 365–370.

Stern, N. (2006) *The Stern Review: The Economics of Climate Change*, HM Treasury and Cabinet Office, London.

Tickell, O. and Wright, M. (1998) 2030 Vision, *Green Futures*, Nov. Dec., pp. 34–37.

ULTra PRT (2011) ULTra at London Heathrow Airport (available from http://www.ultraprt.com/applications/existing-systems/heathrow).

Warren, J (ed.) (2007) *Managing Transport Energy: power for a sustainable future*, Oxford University Press, Oxford.

Wemyss, N. (1996) *Solving the Urban Transport Dilemma – The Motor Industry's Approach*, FT Newsletters and Management Reports, London.

Willsher, K. (2011) Autolib: the new car-sharing scheme that could put Paris streets ahead, *Guardian* online, 2 October (available from http://www.guardian.co.uk/world/2011/oct/02/le-bluecar-car-share-scheme-paris).

24

Transport, Climate Change and the Environment

Tim Ryley and Lee Chapman

INTRODUCTION

This chapter focuses on the links between transport and the environment, with a particular emphasis on climate change, and it incorporates discussion of both surface and air transport modes. It begins by examining the broad links between transport and environmental issues, over a range of spatial scales, from local noise problems to global sustainable development issues. The chapter then focuses on the relationship between transport and climate change. This relationship in considered in terms of climate change mitigation and adaptation, and geoengineering measures for transport applications. Although many of the examples in the chapter are from United Kingdom based material, the findings are applicable to other country contexts as discussed in the conclusions.

TRANSPORT AND THE ENVIRONMENT

The environmental impacts of transport

At the outset, it should be stated that there is a range of environmental impacts from the use of transport. The act of travelling produces pollutants (e.g. carbon monoxide, nitrogen oxides) that can have local air quality impacts, as well as global climate change implications. Noise from motor vehicles and aircraft is an environmental impact that can be a major concern for residents living near to major roads or airports. There are also impacts relating to the life cycle aspects of transport, from the construction of infrastructure, such as road and railway development, to the disposal of scrapped vehicles and associated waste oil and tyres. Furthermore, the environmental impacts have an ecological dimension, as transport can impact upon the biodiversity of a particular area, for instance affected animal habitats. Finally, there are health concerns associated with some of these environmental impacts, including casualties from transport accidents, local pollutant impacts and noise disturbance. The transport industry often has to trade-off between the various environmental impacts of transport. For instance, air traffic controllers have to decide whether aircraft take off along a path that minimises aircraft noise or one that lessens carbon emissions.

The role of sustainable development

The relationship between transport and the environment also needs to be set in the context of broader sustainable development. The starting point for this debate is the nature of sustainability. Implicit in this concept, "to provide the needs of the present without compromising the needs of the future" as outlined in the Brundtland Report (World Commission on Environment and Development, 1987), is that the way that humans behave today should not harm prospects for future generations. From this definition of sustainability, and through subsequent global UN Conferences on Environment and Development, such as the Rio Summit in 1992, sustainable development has evolved from a marginal environmental concern to the political mainstream.

Sustainable development has enabled many countries to get together and discuss progress, although a tension remains between developed countries, which have more of a concern for environmental protection alongside economic growth, in comparison with developing countries which naturally have a clear focus on economic development. Sustainable development is also a broader concept than environmental and economic aspects, incorporating other issues such as population increase, poverty, technology and social organisation.

However, sustainable development does have a core tension between economic and environmental goals: environmentalists claim that it is cover for continuing to destroy the natural world, whilst economists claim that there is excessive concern about depletion of the natural resources (Dresner, 2002: 2). Aviation, for instance, may be not environmentally sustainable, but it is economically and socially sustainable (Upham, 2003). The tensions between the economic and environmental tensions relating to aviation can be shown in the, albeit simplified, view of the for and against proposals for development of a third runway at Heathrow Airport, rejected when the current UK Government came into power, in May 2010. This also demonstrates an issue faced by some countries, such as the UK, that the lack of available land can provide environmental pressures in terms of where to locate transport-related development.

The UK Government's response in 1994 to the global stabilisation targets set at the Rio Summit, was to develop a UK Sustainable Development Strategy (Department of the Environment, 1994). The next strategy, in 1999 (Department of the Environment, Transport and the Regions, 1999) had four over-arching principles: economic growth, protection of the environment, social concerns and natural resources. It included fifteen measurable indicators of progress, but it can be argued that at the time more economic-based indicators were proving more of a success than the social-based indicators, which in turn were out-performing the environmental indicators.

The third, and most recent, UK Sustainable Development strategy (Department for Environment, Food and Rural Affairs, 2005) had a more explicit focus on environmental limits. Climate change has also had an increasing role within the concept of sustainable development, as shown by its more prominent role within this strategy, as one of the four agreed priorities. In terms of the role of transport within sustainable development, the most recent sustainable development indicator list (from Department for Environment, Food and Rural Affairs, 2010) has 68 indicators, of which the following eight indicators are directly transport-related (with indicator number in the list):

- 3. Aviation and shipping emissions (Greenhouse gas emissions from UK-based international aviation and shipping fuel bunkers at airports and ports)
- 7. Road transport (CO_2, NOx, PM10 emissions from all road transport)
- 8. Private cars (CO_2 emissions)
- 9. Road freight (Heavy Goods Vehicle (HGV) CO_2 emissions)
- 55. Mobility (Number of trips by walking/cycling and public transport/taxi)
- 56. Getting to school (Children walking/cycling to school)
- 57. Accessibility (Differences in access with and without car)
- 58. Road accidents (Number killed or seriously injured)

It should also be noted that transport appears indirectly in other indicators such as one of the sectors in CO_2 emissions by end user (indicator number 2). As with any attempt at monitoring, indicators included tend to be those that are easily measurable. For example, the road accident indicator (number killed or seriously injured) is taken from STATS19, a readily available data set compiled of Great Britain road accidents, in which the police record accidents involving casualties. That said, over time the number of indicators has increased to provide a more accurate picture of sustainable development trends. For instance, in the 1999 Sustainable Development Strategy there were only 15 indicators (Department of the Environment, Transport and the Regions, 1999). There does, however, remain a need to continue in the development of emissions measurement and monitoring, so that an accurate assessment of the transport situation can be provided.

There is, therefore, discussion of the attributes of what constitutes a sustainable transport system. Black (2000) states the following criteria: sufficient fuel for the future; minimal pollution from that fuel; minimal fatalities and injuries from motor vehicle accidents; and manageable congestion. In terms of moving towards a more sustainable transport system, there are requirements for minimal travel by methods with high carbon emissions, such as motorised and air travel, in contrast to greater travel by methods of travel with no or low carbon emissions, such as walking, cycling and public transport (which has lower pollution rates per passenger). These, though, are simplistic arguments as the emissions levels are also dependent on aspects such as the emissions levels from the vehicle or aircraft, and the number of passengers within the method of transport.

A background of increasing travel demand

There has been a dramatic increase in travel over the last few decades, and despite many developed countries such as the UK facing recession towards the end of the first decade in the 21st century, the mid-term and long-term trend is still for travel demand to increase. Road traffic has increased by 85% since 1980 (Department for Transport, 2009), although much of this rise was during the 1980s. Car use growth has been hand-in-hand with the rise in disposable incomes. In addition, although the real costs of motoring have remained at a similar rate, public transport costs have increased. The average time that people spend travelling has hardly changed over the last 50 years or so (around one hour per day), but nowadays individuals are travelling further. Air travel has experienced similar growth (Department for Transport, 2009): passengers flying to, from or between UK airports more than quadrupled between 1980 and 2008, from 50 million to 213 million.

An environmental segmentation study by the UK Department for Environment, Food and Rural Affairs (2008a) tested a range of actions to reduce carbon footprints as part of research aims at determining those most likely to reduce consumption. The twelve actions under consideration covered improvements to household efficiency, reductions in the impact of food consumption, and reductions in the emissions from travel. Three of the actions concern the final category: use more efficient vehicles, use cars less for short trips, and avoid unnecessary flights (short haul). When the twelve actions were plotted on a graph of actual behaviour versus carbon emissions impact, the three travel behaviour actions were the only ones in the quadrant for low levels of behaviour against high carbon emissions impact. Of the three transport actions, unnecessary flights had the greatest carbon emissions impact. Much of the problem relates to individual unwillingness to change travel behaviour. It has been shown (Davison and Ryley, 2010) that only a small segment of the population are trying to fly less for environmental reasons (8% in their survey of residents from the East Midlands region of the UK). Barr et al. (2010) have demonstrated that even the most committed environmentalists who behave sustainably in some areas of their life, such as with recycling, are unwilling to cut back on their low-cost air travel.

TRANSPORT AND CLIMATE CHANGE

There has always been a globally changing climate, but in recent times it has been possible to statistically link changes, associated to increased level of key greenhouse gas emissions, to human activity. This is causing an increase in the Earth's average temperature, the so-called "global warming" effect. In addition to meteorological evidence, the impacts of climate change can be demonstrated from physical geography consequences such as ice melt in the Arctic. Most climate scientists would agree that climate change is happening as a phenomenon, in that it is linked to human activity, but questions remain over the scale of the process. Much of the uncertainty relates to the difficulty with the prediction elements of climate models, due to the chaotic and dynamic nature of weather.

The Intergovernmental Panel on Climate Change (IPCC) has the role of assessing the scientific basis of risk of human-induced climate change, based on peer reviewed and published scientific literature. The IPCC Fourth Assessment Report (IPCC, 2007) stated that it is "very likely" that human activities are causing global warming, and that the probable temperature rise by the end of the 21st century will be between 1.8°C and 4°C, coupled with an increasing level of unpredictable and extreme weather patterns. For instance, the report states that it is very likely that parts of the world will witness an increase in the number of heat-waves and an increase in the intensity of tropical storms.

The issue in relation to the transport sector is that it is a major contributor to greenhouse gases and pollutant emissions; 39% of all energy in the UK is used for transport purposes (Department for Transport, 2010). This proportion is set to increase, as transport stubbornly appears to be one of the hardest sectors to achieve emissions reductions, especially when compared against other forms of energy such as industrial and domestic use. The levels of emissions from aviation growth means that the sector will take an increasingly significant proportion of any carbon budget (Anderson et al., 2007); the same could be stated for increases in surface transport demand. The impacts of aviation are particularly complex. Although there is clear scientific understanding of carbon dioxide emissions from aircraft, there is less certainty on the climate impact of other non-carbon aircraft emissions such as water vapour, the cause of condensation trails (or contrails), and methane (Bows et al., 2008).

The Kyoto Protocol, originally agreed in 1997 and subsequently ratified as the Kyoto Treaty, committed industrialised countries to an overall 5.2% reduction in emissions of main greenhouse gases from 1990 to 2008–2012. As part of the agreement, the UK had a

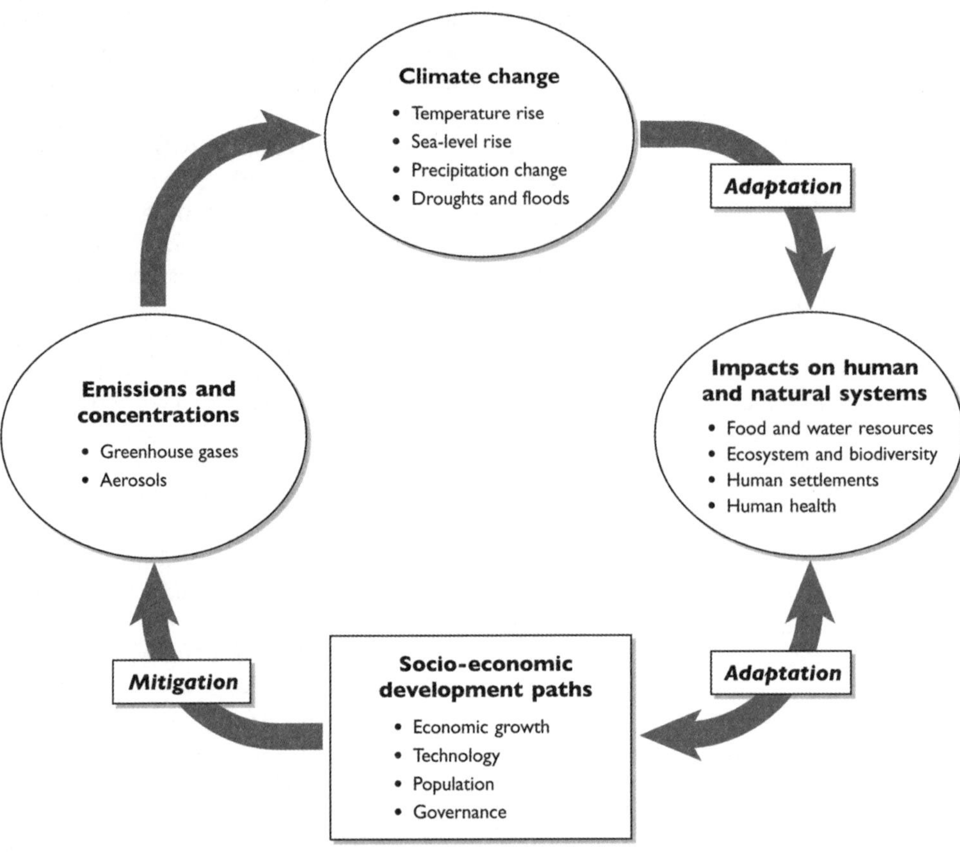

Figure 24.1 The climate change process
Source: IPCC, 2001

target to reduce greenhouse gas emissions to 12.5% below 1990 levels by 2008–2012 (Department for Environment, Food and Rural Affairs, 2005). The UK has been on course to meet this target, partly due to the manufacturing decline and changes in the energy sector "dash for gas", when many UK energy companies built new gas power stations, a cleaner and cheaper alternative to coal.

There was a major concern that CO_2 emissions from international aviation and shipping were not accounted for in the Kyoto Treaty, and that there has been an absence of an internationally agreed methodology for allocating these emissions at the national level. The UK policy response relating to the economics of climate change, through the Stern Review commissioned by the government (Stern et al., 2006), has called for the aviation industry and air passengers to cover their external costs of air travel (i.e. cost of climate change).

Looking further ahead, the Climate Change Bill (Department for Environment, Food and Rural Affairs, 2008b) has a commitment for a UK reduction of 80% in CO_2 emissions by 2050 based on 1990 levels, and an interim target of at least 34% by 2020. The UK has been the first country to make a legally binding commitment to cut greenhouse gases. Figure 24.1 puts climate change in the context of the socio-economic development paths, such as economic growth, technology, population and governance, that must be undertaken in terms of the (transport) emissions and concentrations caused by such development, and the two-way relationship with climate change (transport) impacts on human and natural systems. Climate change mitigation and adaptation, as shown within Figure 24.1, are defined and outlined in the next two sections of the chapter.

THE IMPACT OF TRANSPORT ON CLIMATE CHANGE: MITIGATION

Climate change mitigation refers to "anthropogenic (human activity) intervention to reduce sources or enhance the sinks (natural sources) of greenhouse gases" (IPCC, 2001). Table 24.1 summarises transport-related mitigation measures subdivided according to surface and air modes of transport. There are many types of mitigation measures that can be applied to reduce transport-related emissions.

Technological change

Chapman (2007) makes the argument that there is an increasing expectation that technological change will be what ultimately delivers the reduction in greenhouse gases in the sector. Indeed, there is evidence of continual technological improvement across all modes. For example, the aviation sector is now utilising lightweight engineering in both airframe and engine design, and making operational savings through improved air traffic management. These are small-scale improvements, some of which will be incorporated as new aircraft such as the Airbus A380 and Boeing Dreamliner come into full operation. Similar developments are evident in car manufacture. As well as lightweight design, low drag and improved aerodynamics, average engine sizes are now far smaller. The result is that a vehicle manufactured to today's standards has significantly reduced emissions when compared to a vehicle manufactured 10 years ago (Department for Transport, 2004). Indeed, since 1990, there has been a 20% increase in fuel efficiency in the freight sector and these improvements are continuing due to other developments in the industry (McKinnon, 1999).

However, it is the diversification of the fuels used by transport away from petroleum which provides the best example of technological change in the transport sector (Chapman, 2007). Indeed, it is this technology that has the greatest potential to enable transport to meet carbon reduction targets, although demand for travel will also need to be curtailed. Table 24.2 provides a summary of alternative fuels currently in development. A range of options is available, including biofuels, natural gas, hydrogen and electric motors, but there is clearly no perfect solution. Certainly none of the options are low cost, and many would require considerable investment in new

Table 24.1 A summary of the types of transport mitigation measures, split according to surface and air modes of transport

Surface transport mitigation measures	Air transport mitigation measures
Technological improvements	Technological improvements (e.g. aircraft design, alternative fuels)
Encouragement of a modal shift away from (sole occupancy) motorised transport	Encouragement of a modal shift away from air travel, including air freight (e.g. to inter-city rail travel)
"Carrot" and "stick" transport policy measures	EU Emission Trading Scheme
Driving improvements	Aviation tax
New fuel developments	Optimise existing air capacity (e.g. increase price of slots at airports) Air traffic management (e.g. finding optimal flight routings and altitudes)

Source: after Chapman, 2007

Table 24.2 Summary of alternative fuels and vehicles

Description	Advantages	Disadvantages
Internal Combustion Engine Vehicles can be modified to use **biofuels,** which are liquid transport fuels produced from recycled vegetable oils or starch and sugar plants. Most vehicles can run on a blend of petroleum with 5% biodiesel or bioethanol (the petrol equivalent) with little or no engine modification or specialist infrastructure.	• A sustainable fuel. As the plants grow, they take up CO_2, which is then released back into the atmosphere when the fuel is burned (Maclean, 2004).	• Additional energy input is required to process the fuel. • Energy yields vary with crop. • Increases in world population will place more demand on food production than biofuel from agricultural land (Black, 2001). • More expensive than conventional fuels.
Internal Combustion Engine Vehicles can alternatively be modified to use **gaseous fuels** such as Autogas or LPG (stored in compressed or liquefied form). These provide a 'clean-burning' alternative to traditional petroleum (Baert et al., 2004).	• Inexpensive. • CO_2 emissions can be reduced by around 30% (Lave et al., 2000). • Potential to extract the gas from landfill or water/sewage treatment.	• Most gaseous fuels are still derived from fossil fuels.
Fuel Cell Electric Vehicles make use of **hydrogen**, the most abundant element in the universe. Can be produced by the electrolysis of water, but is more commonly formed from the stream reformation of methane; a process by which the hydrogen atoms are separated from the carbon atoms along with emissions of CO_2 (Davidson, 2003). This can be done on the vehicle, but is more likely to be done at separate plants which will allow vehicles to refuel with pure hydrogen (Lovins, 2003). Once onboard the vehicle, the hydrogen is converted into electricity by reversing the electrolysis process using a stack of fuel cells.	• A high quality energy carrier which can be readily converted into electricity (Lovins, 2003). • The only emission is pure water. • Already proven popular with niche applications such as the urban bus market (Sperling, 2003).	• Does not occur naturally and needs to be liberated from chemical compounds. • Additional energy is required for electrolysis. As a result, Hydrogen would be more expensive to produce then diesel (Lovins, 2003). • Although hydrogen is light, it is bulky, making it expensive to transport, store and distribute. • Will require a specialist infrastructure.
Battery Powered Electric Vehicles were first built in the 19th century and originally outnumbered gasoline vehicles. Electric vehicles also use fuel cells to converts chemical energy into electrical energy, where the electricity producing reactants are supplied from an external source (Khare and Sharma, 2003).	• Zero emissions at source. • Electric motors increase efficiency by 20% by using a direct connection to the wheels and therefore use no power when the car is at rest or coasting (Khare and Sharma, 2003). • Additional energy production can be derived from regenerative breaking. • 90% efficient compared to 25% of traditional internal combustion engines (Sperling, 2003). • Fuel cell technology is continually improving.	• The size of the fuel cells adds to the weight of the vehicle and constrains the performance of the vehicle in terms of maximum speeds and the distance vehicles can travel before requiring recharging (Lave et al., 2000). • Driving ranges presently limited by technology. • The source of energy used for recharging is unlikely to be zero-carbon unless it is produced from renewables or nuclear.

Description	Advantages	Disadvantages
Hybrid Electric Vehicles provide an intermittent step between the internal combustion engine and the electric motor. An energy management system is used to optimise the fuel economy of both engines because electric and combustion engines work better under different driving situations.	• Provides the advantages of electric propulsion without the need for fuel cells (Lovins, 2003). Electricity is created with on-board generators or recover it from braking. • A middling technology (Sperling, 1995) and can take on many forms.	• Technology still reliant on the internal combustion engine. • Expensive, although grants are often available to help with the purchase but these rarely cover the higher costs involved (Lave et al., 2000).

Source: after Chapman, 2007

infrastructures, especially hydrogen. Furthermore, the implementation of such technological change needs strong governance.

Taxation policies are required to encourage a move away from fuels and vehicles with a large carbon footprint (Department for Transport, 2006), whereas incentives are needed to embrace the new cleaner technologies. Here, the biggest progress has probably been made with low carbon vehicles (electric or hybrid) in the form of government subsidies (Lave et al., 2000). However, such a move is only effective if the electricity used by the vehicle has been produced by clean (renewable) means. Overall, despite the large strides made in recent years towards cleaner fuels, alternatives are still mid-to-long term developments given the timescale required to make such fuels operational. Rapid changes are needed if society is to avoid the worst impacts of climate change.

There are broader technological change impacts that affect lifestyles and in turn environmental impacts from transport, through aspects such as internet shopping and working at home, although it can be questioned whether this will save on travel – if the individual does not travel, something else has to in order to deliver the goods. With working at home, it can be argued whether an individual will compensate for one journey (i.e. not travelling to work) with another trip at another point in time (Chapter 14).

Policy measures

Mitigation policy measures can be classified as "sticks" and "carrots" (Stradling et al., 2000). "Sticks" force individuals away from a mode (e.g. increasing cost and decreasing availability), whilst "carrots" encourage individuals in transport choices, enticing them towards a mode (e.g. public transport facilities). It is important to strike a balance between sticks and carrots measures. It is beneficial to sell the mitigation measures, promote the carrots ahead of sticks, but sticks are known to be more effective. For instance, transport marketing campaigns have tended to have limited impact. Individuals can see the hazards associated with the successful public information advertisement campaigns associated with cutting back on smoking and drink driving, but the environmental problems associated with unsustainable travel are not as evident. It has been suggested that there could be traffic reduction from "soft" transport policy measures (carrots) such as: travel plans (e.g. workplace, schools); personalised travel planning, travel awareness campaigns, public transport information and marketing; car clubs and car sharing schemes; and teleworking, teleconferencing and home shopping (Cairns et al., 2005). There has been an increase in the implementation of these measures in the UK in recent years, although they tend to be small scale.

A balanced approach is therefore required. With road user charging, for example, such that money from the sticks of congestion charges is "transparently" ring-fenced to the carrots of transport improvements. There has been an increasing trend for transport policy measures to be directly linked to the carbon emissions from vehicles. For instance, the level that vehicle owners pay in taxation has been applied to UK vehicle tax (vehicle excise duty) since 2009. Governments have to be careful in the way that they tax motorists. The UK Government gradually increased the tax on petrol during the 1990s as part of the "fuel duty escalator", but this resulted in fuel tax protests in the year 2000 and has proved an extremely unpopular policy.

Broader land use planning measures

There are broader mitigations measures in terms of land use planning. The principles of sustainable development are clear: "higher densities required and most new development should be in settlements of sufficient size to support full range of services & facilities, possibly with mixed land uses" (Banister, 2002: 110). Therefore, it is important to focus on land use planning in urban areas where there is a particular lack of space. Thomson (1977) identifies seven facets of the urban transport problem that need to be overcome: traffic movement, parking difficulties, environmental impact, pedestrian difficulties, accidents, peak-hour crowding of public transport, and off-peak inadequacy of public transport.

As cities develop, they tend to sprawl out, with associated land use trends such as an increase in out-of-town shopping centres, lower-density housing and suburbanisation. One study (Goudie, 2002) has shown that outer urban dwellers use about three times more fuel than their more central counterparts. The urban environment has been developed in a manner that is geared towards motor car travel, through the road network, petrol stations and location of car parks, reinforced by the construction of motorways and ring roads. Furthermore, without any policy interventions, motor vehicles can travel in any direction over any distance, compared with public transport that is confined to fixed routes, and walking and cycling that are confined to short trips. These aspects need to be overcome in order to develop a sustainable transport system with reduced travel-related carbon emissions.

Therefore, broader land use planning mitigation measures are required that concern the design of cities in a more sustainable, compact form, including promotion of the city centre, high-density buildings and surrounding greenbelt land. It would also be supportive of public transport and the non-motorised modes of walking and cycling. Such measures need to be complemented by restricted motor car access and parking. Various international examples of good urban sustainable transport practice are put forward. These include the development of high-density transit corridors such as in Curitiba, Brazil, and new town development that is focused on sustainable transport such as in Houten, the Netherlands, where the road design makes it difficult to drive through the town.

THE IMPACT OF CLIMATE CHANGE ON TRANSPORT: ADAPTATION

In terms of the scientific literature, and indeed climate change policies, the focus of discussion has very much been based on mitigation (e.g. Chapman, 2007). However, given the timescales involved with mitigation, there is now a general sense that the world is committed to some degree of climate change. As a result, there is increasing discussion of how existing infrastructure can be adapted to become more resilient to the changing climate. Hence, climate change adaptation refers to "adjustments in natural or human systems in response to actual or expected climatic stimuli or their effects" (IPCC, 2001).

The potential impacts of climate change on transport are numerous and are evident

Table 24.3 The effects of climate change on transport

Increased numbers of hot days	1 Increased thermal loading on road pavements: a Melting tarmac b Roadway buckling c Expansion/buckling of bridges d Increased numbers of tyre blow-outs 2 Increased railway buckling 3 Increased heat exhaustion of maintenance and operations staff 4 Effects of higher density altitudes on aviation: a Reduced engine combustion efficiency b Increased runway lengths required
Decreased numbers of cold days	1 Reduced winter maintenance costs for road and rail 2 Improved working conditions for personnel in cold environments 3 Permafrost problems: a Unable to rely on "frozen roads" b Infrastructure problems caused due to settlement when permafrost thaws c Increased subsidence and landslides on slopes & embankments 4 Positive effects on marine transportation: a Less de-icing required and freezing fog b Less icebreaking required c Potential opening of the new sea passages in polar regions
Increased heavy precipitation	1 Road submersion and underpass flooding 2 Increased landslides and undercutting 3 Poor visibility 4 Exceedance of existing 100-year flood
Seasonal changes	1 Longer summers/shorter winters will mean changes in timing of: a Leaf-fall for railways b Winter maintenance regimes c Shift in ice/snow belts 2 Reduction in frozen precipitation – significant improvements in road safety
Drought	1 Navigation problems on inland waterways
Sea-level change	1 Locations of ports maybe inappropriate 2 Other infrastructure – many airports are built <10 m of sea level 3 Localised problems, e.g. storm surges
Extreme events	1 Increased numbers of tropical storms? 2 Increased lightning effects of aviation NB: No clear projections are available for wind

Source: Jaroszweski et al., 2010

across numerous modes (Table 24.3). The transport sector has always been subject to meteorological hazards, but it is clear that a changing climate will present an increased number of threats and opportunities. With respect to impacts on vehicles and hard infrastructure, climate change will decrease some events, such as the amount of snow and ice, whilst others, such as higher temperatures, will become more frequent. The general consensus is that the weather is likely to be more severe with more frequent and erratic extremes. In terms of the road and rail network, they are affected by issues including flooding, landslides, rail buckling and user visibility. In terms of the aviation industry, airports will have to adapt to some of these weather-related aspects. This comparison with surface transport shows that at times air travel may be a viable option when travel by surface transport is difficult (and vice-versa).

Climate change impact assessment

The first step towards adaptation of the transport network is an appreciation of how the climate will actually change. This is achieved by consulting scenarios produced by organisations such as the United Kingdom Climate Change Impacts Programme (UKCIP). Such scenarios of the future climate form the cornerstone of climate change impact assessments required when adapting, or designing new, transport infrastructure. Relationships between disruption and impacts are derived for the current climate, before being extrapolated for future climates via scenarios (see Koetse and Rieveld, 2009, for a review of many case studies utilising this approach). Whilst in many cases this is a useful first step to assessing the future impact of climate change, this approach is fundamentally flawed (Jaroszweski et al., 2010). Climate change impacts on transport are not simply a function of meteorology because the vulnerability of the transport network is equally important. For example, fifty years ago, the UK did not even have a motorway network. Hence, how will the existing network evolve over the next 50 years? Given the speed of innovation and technological change in terms of hard infrastructure and vehicles (e.g. High Speed Rail and antilock braking systems as two examples), it is very difficult to make long-term generalisations regarding the vulnerability and the resilience of the transport network.

Furthermore, the incorporation of socioeconomic scenarios into the analysis is a further crucial step. It is clearly of importance to consider the broader question of how people will travel in the coming decades. Changes in working practices as discussed (i.e. home working and teleconferences) will at least in theory reduce the need for people to travel. Similarly, a change to regional production would significantly reduce continental freight movement (Jaroszweski et al., 2010). Consideration also needs to be given to how people will respond to a changing climate, and how their travel habits would change in response to climate change effects (e.g. not make the air travel journey or use an alternative transport mode). There would also be a change in background social and economic relationships as a consequence of climate change (e.g. health and social care with an ageing population; leisure and tourism; economic activity). For these reasons, an interdisciplinary approach is the only way forward to ensure best value from adaptation measures.

Adaptation measures

Given the likely impacts of climate change (Table 24.3), there are many actions which can be taken to improve the resilience of transport networks in light of climate change. The increased cost of climate proofing new infrastructure is perceived to be small (just 1–2% of overall build costs), but could yield a cost benefit of 4:1 (DEFRA, 2011). Under the Climate Change Act, major UK organisations responsible for key aspects of national infrastructure have to explain how they will cope if the climate alters as forecast. This includes transport organisations such as the Highways Agency, Network Rail and Transport for London, and, more importantly in an aviation context, large airports such as London Heathrow.

At this point, it is useful to make a distinction between the design of new infrastructure and adapting existing transport infrastructure. In the case of new hard infrastructure, once the socio-economic case has been made to justify development, engineering design codes can be simply modified to take into account the projected change in climate over the design life of the asset. Design life is very important, for example new railway signals with an estimated operating life of 20 years will require little adaptation compared to a new transport corridor such as High Speed

Rail which could be in operational use for over a century. In such a situation, the infrastructure would effectively need to be over engineered for the present climate. Examples of this would include strengthened embankments and bridges resistant to increased river flows and scour (DEFRA, 2011). Furthermore, dual use infrastructure is very much in vogue at the moment. A classic example is the Stormwater Management and Road Tunnel in Kuala Lumpur, which doubles both as a transport corridor and an emergency floodwater diversion facility (Royal Academy of Engineering, 2011). Similarly, road and rail embankments can double as emergency floodwater defences.

The argument holds for the adaptation of existing infrastructure. This falls under the general theme of "adaptive capacity", which in simple terms is a method of ongoing adaptation measures taken as and when required. This is often a preferred approach as it removes the element of economic risk posed by uncertainties in climate change scenarios (i.e. committing funds to something that might happen), but is unlikely to be the most cost effective approach in the long term. The approach is particularly well suited to maintenance regimes which operate over smaller timescales. For example, there has been a recent move by the UK Highways Agency to apply road surface specifications currently used in the south of France, to improve resilience to high temperatures on the road network (DEFRA, 2011). Similarly, changes could be made on the rail network to reduce the risk of buckling (Dobney et al., 2010).

A further complication when considering the resilience of transport is the growing interdependency of the network on other national networks. As discussed earlier, the electrification of transport networks is perceived as a key means of diversifying the fuels used for transportation and is therefore pivotal in meeting climate change mitigation targets in the sector. However, this also brings a new set of adaptation challenges as there is then a need to consider and incorporate adaptive capacity in both the energy and transport sectors. A significant failure on the electricity network could ultimately cascade onto the transport network with far reaching consequences (Royal Academy of Engineering, 2011). Hence, it is for this reason that there is now a growing desire to consider adaptation and resilience of all critical infrastructure networks at a national scale.

GEO-ENGINEERING

Geo-engineering sits midway between climate change mitigation and adaptation. Indeed, it could be viewed as an extreme mitigation measure. Numerous grand schemes have been proposed to offset the impact of climate change (see Royal Society, 2009, for a detailed review). These tend to fall into two distinct categories: solar radiation management (e.g. solar reflectors, stratospheric aerosols) and carbon cycle engineering (e.g. carbon capture and sequestration in the marine environment). The general view of such schemes is that they are risky and problematic due to the need to obtain multilateral agreement of several (if not all) nations to implement successfully. However, there is a growing sense that geo-engineering may be a quick answer to a global problem should other attempts to mitigate against climate change prove to be too slow to be effective (Fox and Chapman, 2011).

At a local scale, geo-engineering technology can be used to complement adaptation measures. For example, solar radiation management can be implemented in the form of local, terrestrial albedo management (IMechE, 2009). Changing blacktop road surfaces to lighter shades not only reduces pavement temperatures, but would also reduce ambient temperatures as less energy will be stored and emitted by the surface. However, perhaps the greatest potential for the transport sector is the use of artificial trees to collect carbon emissions. Greenhouse gases released from transport are non-stationary, which can make them difficult to capture. An artificial tree effectively removes CO_2 from the air in much the same way as a normal tree, but is far more efficient (Lackner, 2009). The CO_2 is then sequestered either deep underground or in the marine environment where it can no longer effect the global climate. Hence, the installation of such devices could prove to be very effective if located at strategic locations along transport corridors, or at emission hotspots such as airports, and would help the transport sector meet climate change targets during the transitional period to alternative fuels.

CONCLUSION

This chapter has shown that transport has a wide range of environmental impacts, across a range of spatial scales, incorporating noise, life cycle, ecological and health elements, as well as the increasingly important phenomenon of human-induced climate change. Although all transport elements have impacts, it is climate change and its damaging consequences that are cause for the greatest concern.

As a result, over the last 30 years or so, environmental issues have evolved from the margins to the mainstream in transport debate and policy. However, despite increased global discussions, particularly concerning sustainable development, environmental issues in transport are still often secondary to economic aspects. For instance, in the UK, although in some cases such as when the Heathrow third runway proposals were rejected largely on environmental grounds, it tends be the norm, particularly with the current recessionary pressures, that economic arguments take priority. The role of transport in the climate change debate has been discussed. As a major contributor to greenhouse gas emissions, the focus of debate over the last decade has been centred on how the transport sector could evolve to reduce emissions, and thus pull its weight in relation to other sectors. However, given the interdependencies between sectors, it is debatable how relevant it is to actually consider transport as a sector in its own right. Often transport is linked in to broader debates, such as how to plan and utilise land in urban areas, a key part of sustainable development. Whilst a number of policies have been implemented, including those to encourage behavioural and technological change, in many cases the timescales involved will lessen the impact of such measures. Set against this is the underlying and in some cases increasing demand for travel by both surface and air transport modes. As such, there is a pressing need to embrace climate change adaptation and maybe even local-scale geo-engineering to ensure a resilient transport infrastructure for the next century.

Whilst this chapter has presented evidence from the UK, the impacts of climate change – in terms of extreme weather patterns, such as an increase in the number and intensity of heat-waves and tropical storms – will be felt to varying degrees around the world. Developed countries, with more resources available, and in transport terms a more resilient infrastructure, will be able to deal with these issues better than developing countries. There are global implications associated with emissions from international travel modes such as aviation and shipping, for which it is hard to allocate emissions at a national level. In addition, it is difficult to link impacts from these transport emissions back to the source. As such, there is an aspect of fairness and equity when considering transport and climate change. It can also be argued that although some developed countries, such as the UK, appear to be progressing well in terms of meeting initial emissions targets, much of this can be attributed to the "dash for gas" and manufacturing decline, the latter effectively "exporting" emissions to other areas of the world such as China and the Far East where many goods are now made. Naturally, there are transport freight emissions implications in the transfer of these goods to markets in developed countries.

This chapter has also demonstrated a need to further develop methodologies to measure and model climate change emissions from the transport sector, and also improve the monitoring of the environmental impacts (and associated sustainable development indicators). As climate change concerns increase over time, and more of its environmental impacts are realised, there will be a need for stronger action both at a political and an individual level. The UK Government has produced much environmental rhetoric, through various sustainable development strategies, and subsequently through the Climate Change Act. It also currently has a two-pronged transport policy approach through low carbon vehicles and High Speed Rail. Although both are commendable, it would be preferable to have a wider range of mitigation approaches and more resources underpinning their delivery. There remain the twin issues of increasing demand for air and car-based travel, and the unwillingness amongst the general public to change travel behaviour. Perhaps there is a need to promote "sticks" over "carrots", forcing much-needed behavioural change towards more sustainable travel, and consequently reducing transport-related carbon emissions.

More widely, there is, and will become, a more urgent need for practical sustainable transport solutions in the developing world as well as in developed countries. Rapid changes are needed if society is to avoid the worst impacts of climate change, and this means that a wide range of solutions are required, incorporating climate change mitigation, adaptation and possibly geo-engineering.

REFERENCES

Anderson K., Bows A. and Footitt, A. (2007) Aviation in a low carbon EU. A research report by the Tyndall Centre, University of Manchester. Friends of the Earth (http://www.foe.co.uk/resource/reports/aviation_tyndall_07_main.pdf).

Baert, R.S.G., de Rojke, J. and Smokers, R.T.M. (2004) Natural gas on the road for lower CO_2, in Duret, P. and Montagne, X. (eds) *Which Fuels for Low CO_2 Engines*. International Conference on Which Fuels for Low CO_2 Engines, 22–23 September 2004, Rueil Malmaison, France, pp.109–121.

Banister, D. (2002) *Transport Planning*. Second Edition. London and New York: SPON Press.

Barr, S.W., Shaw, G., Coles, T. and Prillwitz, J. (2010) 'A holiday is a holiday': practicing sustainability, home and away, *Journal of Transport Geography*, Vol. 18, pp. 474–481.

Black, W.R. (2000) Socio-economic barriers to sustainable transport, *Journal of Transport Geography*, Vol. 8, pp. 141–147.

Black, W.R. (2001) An unpopular essay on transportation, *Journal of Transport Geography*, Vol. 9, pp. 1–11.

Bows, A., Anderson, K. and Upham, P. (2008) *Aviation and Climate Change: Lessons for European Policy*. London: Routledge.

Cairns, S., Sloman, L., Newson, C., Anable, J., Kirkbride, A. and Goodwin P. (2005) *Smarter Choices – Changing the Way We Travel. Department for Transport* (http://www.dft.gov.uk/pgr/sustainable/smarterchoices/). London: HMSO.

Chapman, L. (2007) Transport and climate change: a review, *Journal of Transport Geography*, Vol. 15, pp. 354–367.

Davidson, S. (2003) Towards the forever fuel, *ECOS*, Vol. 117, pp. 20–24.

Davison, L.J. and Ryley, T.J. (2010) Tourism destination preferences of low-cost airline users in the East Midlands, *Journal of Transport Geography*, Vol. 18 (3), pp. 458–465.

Department for Environment, Food and Rural Affairs (2005) *Securing the Future – UK Government Sustainable Development Strategy* (http://www.defra.gov.uk/sustainable/government/publications/uk-strategy/index.htm). London: HMSO.

Department for Environment, Food and Rural Affairs (2008a) *A framework for environmental behaviours: a report*, London: HMSO.

Department for Environment, Food and Rural Affairs (2008b) *Climate Change Bill*. London: HMSO.

Department for Environment, Food and Rural Affairs (2010) *Measuring Progress. Sustainable Development Indicators*. 2010 Edition (http://www.defra.gov.uk/sustainable/government/progress/data-resources/sdiyp.htm). London: HMSO.

Department for Environment, Food and Rural Affairs (2011) *Climate Resilient Infrastructure: Preparing for a Changing Climate*. London: HMSO.

Department for Transport (2004) *The Future of Transport, a Network for 2030*. UK Department for Transport, London: HMSO.

Department for Transport. (2006) *Visioning and Backcasting for UK Transport Policy (VIBAT)*. Stage 3 Report: Policy Packaging and Pathways. Department for Transport, London: HMSO.

Department for Transport (2009) *Transport Trends 2009*. 12th Edition (http://www.dft.gov.uk/pgr/statistics/datatablespublications/trends/current/). London: HMSO.

Department for Transport (2010) *Transport Statistics Great Britain 2010*. 36th Edition (http://www.dft.gov.uk/pgr/statistics/datatablespublications/tsgb/), London: HMSO.

Department of the Environment (1994) *Sustainable Development, The UK Strategy*. London: HMSO.

Department of the Environment, Transport and the Regions (1999) *The UK Strategy for Sustainable Development. A Better Quality of Life. A Strategy for Sustainable Development for the United Kingdom* (http://collections.europarchive.org/tna/20080530153425/http://www.sustainable-development.gov.uk/publications/uk-strategy99/index.htm). London: HMSO.

Dobney, K., Baker, C.J., Chapman, L. and Quinn, A.D. (2010) The future cost to the UK's railway network of heat related delays and buckles caused by the predicted increase in high summer temperatures due to climate change, *Proceedings of the Institution of Mechanical Engineers, Part F, Journal of Rail and Rapid Transit*, Vol. 224, pp. 25–34.

Dresner, S. (2002) *The Principles of Sustainability*. London: Earthscan Publications Ltd.

Fox, T. and Chapman, L. (2011) Engineering geo-engineering, *Meteorological Applications*, Vol. 18, pp. 1–8.

Goudie, D. (2002) Zonal method for urban travel surveys, *Journal of Transport Geography*, Vol. 10, pp. 287–301.

IMechE (2009) *Geo-engineering. Giving us the Time to Act?* London: Institution of Mechanical Engineers.

IPCC (2001) *Climate Change 2001, The Scientific Basis*. Intergovernmental Panel on Climate Change (http://www.grida.no/climate/ipcc_tar/index.htm).

IPCC (2007) *Climate Change 2007*, IPCC 4th Assessment Synthesis Report. Intergovernmental Panel on Climate Change (http://www.ipcc.ch/publications_and_data/publications_ipcc_fourth_assessment_report_synthesis_report.htm).

Jaroszweski, D., Chapman, L. and Petts, J. (2010) Assessing the potential impact of climate change on transportation: the need for an interdisciplinary approach, *Journal of Transport Geography*, Vol. 18, pp. 331–335.

Khare, M. and Sharma, P. (2003) Fuel options, in Hensher, D.A and Button, K.J. (eds) *Handbooks in Transport 4: Handbook of Transport and the Environment*, New York: Elsevier, pp.159–184.

Koetse, M.J. and Rieveld, P. (2009) The impact of climate change and weather on transport: an overview of empirical findings, *Transportation Research Part D*, Vol. 14, pp. 205–221.

Lackner, K.S. (2009) Capture of carbon dioxide from ambient air, *European Physics Journal Special Topics*, Vol. 176, pp. 93–106.

Lave, L., Maclean, H., Hendrickson, C. and Lankey, R. (2000) Life-cycle analysis of alternative automobile fuel/propulsion technologies, *Environmental Science & Technology*, Vol. 102, pp. 205–209.

Lovins, A.B. (2005) Twenty hydrogen myths, available at: http://www.rmi.org.

Maclean, H.L. (2004) Alternative transport fuels for the future, *International Journal of Vehicle Design*, Vol. 35, pp. 27–49.

McKinnon, A. (1999) A logistical perspective on the fuel efficiency of road freight transport. Report presented to the workshop "Improving Fuel Efficiency in Road Freight: The Role of Information Technologies", organised by the International Energy Agency and European Conference of Ministers of Transport, APRIS, 24 February 1999.

Royal Academy of Engineering (2011) Infrastructure, engineering and climate change adaptation – ensuring services in an uncertain future (www.raeng.org.uk/adaptation).

Royal Society (2009) *Geo-engineering the Climate; Science, Governance and Uncertainty*. London: The Royal Society.

Sperling, D. (1995) *Future Drive: Electric Vehicles and Sustainable Transportation*, Washington, DC: Island Press.

Sperling, D. (2003) Cleaner vehicles, in Hensher, D.A. and Button, K.J. (eds) *Handbooks in Transport 4: Handbook of Transport and the Environment*, New York: Elsevier, pp.185–202.

Stern, N., Peters, S., Bakhshi, V., Bowen, A., Cameron, C., Catovsky, S., Crane, D., Cruickshank, S., Dietz, S., Edmonson, N., Garbett, S.-L., Hamid, L., Hoffman, G., Ingram, D., Jones, B., Patmore, N., Radcliffe, H., Sathiyarajah, R., Stock, M., Taylor, C., Vernon, T., Wanjie, H. and Zenghelis, D. (2006) *Stern Review on the Economics of Climate Change*. London: HM Treasury.

Stradling, S.G., Meadows, M.L. and Beatty, S. (2000) Helping drivers out of their cars: integrating transport policy and social psychology for sustainable change, *Transport Policy*, Vol. 7(3), pp. 207–215.

Thomson J.M. (1977) *Great Cities and their Traffic*. London: Penguin.

Upham, P. (2003) *Towards Sustainable Aviation*. London: Earthscan Publications Ltd.

World Commission on Environment and Development. (1987) *Report of the World Commission on Environment and Development: Our Common Future* (The Bruntland Report) (http://www.un-documents.net/wced-ocf.htm).

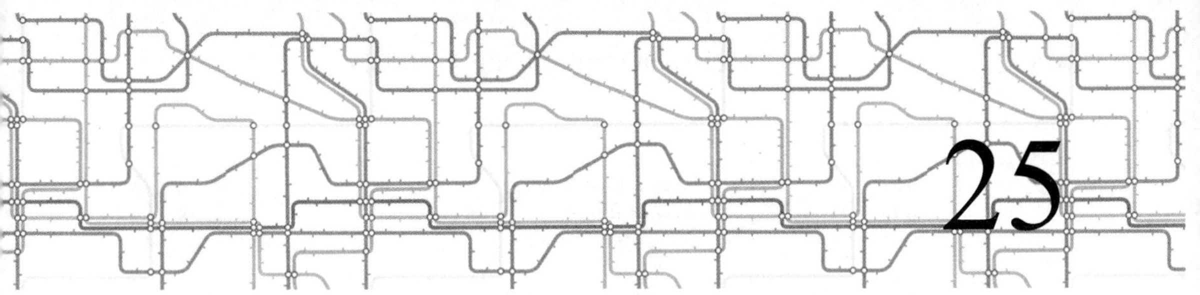

Green Supply Chain Management

Jean-Paul Rodrigue, Brian Slack
and Claude Comtois

INTRODUCTION: GREENNESS AND LOGISTICS

Logistics are at the heart of the operation of modern transport systems and implies a degree organization and control over freight movements that only modern technology could have brought into being. It has become one of the most important developments in the transportation industry. Greenness has become a code word for a range of environmental concerns, and is usually considered positively. It is employed to suggest compatibility with the environment, and thus, like logistics is something that is perceived as beneficial. When put together the two words suggest an environmentally friendly and efficient transport and distribution system. Green Logistics: supply chain management practices and strategies that reduce the environmental and energy footprint of freight distribution. It focuses on material handling, waste management, packaging and transport.

The loosely defined term covers several dimensions related to production planning, materials management and physical distribution, opening the door to a wide array of potential applications of environmentally friendly strategies along supply chains. This implies that different stakeholders could be applying different strategies, all of which being labeled as green logistics. One corporation could be focusing on product packaging while another on alternative fuel vehicles; both are undertaking green logistics. However, on taking a closer look at the concept and its applications, a great many paradoxes and inconsistencies arise, which suggest that its application may be more difficult than what might have been expected in the first place. Although there has been much debate about what green logistics truly entails, the transportation industry has developed very narrow and specific interests about the issue. If transportation costs are reduced and assets such as vehicles, terminals and distribution centers better utilized, the assumption is that green logistics strategies are being implemented.

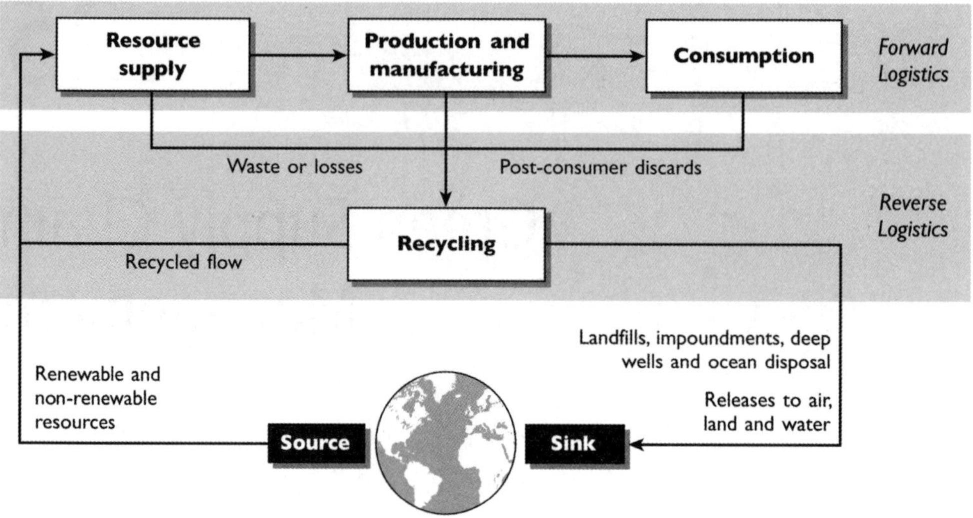

Figure 25.1 Material flows cycle
Source: after USGS Fact Sheet FS-068-98, June 1998

In common with many other areas of human endeavor, greenness became a catchword in the transportation industry. It grew out of the emerging awareness of environmental problems, and in particular with well-publicized issues such as acid rain, CFCs, waste disposal and climate change. Environmental concepts, such as material flows or the carbon cycle (see Figure 25.1), became readily applicable to supply chain management.

Supply chains are part of a complex material flows cycle that starts with the extractions of renewable and nonrenewable resources which then become part of the resource supply system. Through a forward logistics process, these resources are transformed by the manufacturing sector to become final consumption goods. All the processes of forward logistics are generating wastes and discards that enter the reverse logistics cycle. What can be recycled will reenter the resource supply cycle, while what remains will be put into a sink, most commonly a landfill.

The World Commission on Environment and Development Report (1987), with its establishment of environmental sustainability as a goal for international action, gave green issues a significant boost in political and economic arenas. The transportation industry was recognized as a major contributor to environmental issues through its modes, infrastructures and flows (Banister, 2008; Black 2010; Schiller et al., 2010). The developing field of logistics was seen as an opportunity for the transportation industry to present a more environmentally friendly face. Yet, environmental perspectives and transportation sustainability issues remain predominantly focused on passenger transportation.

Interest in the environment by the logistics industry manifested itself most clearly in terms of exploiting new market opportunities. While traditional logistics seeks to organize forward distribution, that is the transport, warehousing, packaging and inventory management from the producer to the consumer, environmental considerations opened up markets for recycling and disposal, and led to an entire new sub-sector: reverse logistics. This reverse distribution involves the transport of waste and the movement of used materials as well as activities related to recycling, take-back, repair and refurbishing (Hawks, 2006). Even if the term reverse logistics is widely used, other names have been applied, such as reverse distribution, reverse-flow logistics and even green logistics. Inserting logistics into recycling and the disposal of waste materials of all kinds, including toxic and hazardous goods, has become a major new market but it does not reflect the full extent of green logistic which is the greening of both the forward reserve segment of supply chains.

GREEN LOGISTICS AND ITS PARADOXES

An overview of the standard characteristics of logistical systems reveals several inconsistencies with regards to the mitigation of environmental externalities. They take the form of five basic paradoxes; costs, time, reliability, warehousing and e-commerce.

The cost paradox

The purpose of logistics is to reduce costs, notably transport costs. While the former remain the most salient logistics cost, inventory carrying costs come second. In addition, economies of time and improvements in service reliability, including flexibility, are further objectives. Corporations involved in the physical distribution of freight are highly supportive of strategies that enable them to cut transport costs in a competitive setting. Economies of scale in transportation as well as higher load densities are common cost-saving strategies that concomitantly lead to environmental benefits in terms of lower fuel consumption per tonne-km. On some occasions, the cost-saving strategies pursued by logistic operators can be at variance with environmental considerations that become externalized. This means that the benefits of logistics are realized by the users and eventually to the consumer if the benefits are shared along the supply chain. However, the environment assumes a wide variety of burdens and costs, which form a hierarchy ranging from costs internal to the supply chain to externalized costs. To produce and make goods available on the market a hierarchy of environmental costs is concerned, from internal costs that are easy to quantify to external costs that remain vague and complex to assess and even more to quantify. Although managers are keenly aware of the costs involved in the management of supply chains, there is commonly a lack of methodologies available to formally assess them. This makes environmental accounting a challenging process far from being an exact science. Still, this endeavor concerns five cost categories (US Environmental Protection Agency, 2000):

- Internal costs are well understood as they concern the inputs costs (materials, labor) related to what has been produced. Most firms have a good level of control for these costs as they directly disburse them.
- Compliance costs concern an array of expenses that do not contribute to the output but are related to the regulatory framework. Environmental issues, such as emission standards, are common and all come with costs assumed by firms to insure compliance. Compliance can also have some benefits, particularly if it implies subsidies, lower levels of taxation or lower insurance premiums.
- Contingent costs. Depending of the sector of activity and the part of the supply chain, there is always a risk of accidents or hazardous materials releases. Although it can almost be certain that such an event will eventually happen, its moment and its intensity remains only a probability. Contingent costs thus imply a form of supply chain risk management where a low level or a lack of compliance can be weighted in terms of the involved risks, such as being fined.
- Image and relationship costs. A firm or a product that is perceived negatively from an environmental standpoint can incur significant costs in terms of lower sales and litigation. Public relations on environmental matters are a complex and commonly costly endeavor. If skillfully done it can also lead to positive impacts in terms of better sales of products perceived as "environmentally friendly".
- External costs relate to an array of costs that are externalized, implying that they are assumed by the collectivity and not by the firm. Growth often results in a higher level of usage of transport infrastructures, more emissions of

Figure 25.2 The food-mile: yogurt supply chain, Germany

pollutants and higher risk for accidents. All these costs are commonly assumed by the wider economy and can therefore be considered to be outside the firm.

Society is becoming less willing to accept these costs, and pressure is increasingly being put on governments and corporations to include greater environmental considerations in their activities. A salient example concerns food supply chains that have been impacted by lower transport costs, enabling a diversification of the suppliers and longer transport chains. The concept of food miles has been developed as an attempt to capture the full costs of food distribution by using the distance food is carried as a proxy (Figure 25.2). It tries to capture the distances involved in all the stages and processes of food production, from the farm up to the consumer. It is assumed that more food miles are related to less environmentally efficient supply chains.

A classic example concerns a yogurt supply chain in south Germany (Böge, 1995). Although a simple product, a yogurt pot involves a wide variety of components ranging from milk, sugar and jam (product) to labels, jars and boxes (packaging). It may indicate that the supply chain is environmentally damaging because of the distances involved and that these distances should be shortened to achieve greener logistics. However, statements in the line that supply chains should be more locally and regionally focused can be misleading. The following nuances should be considered:

- Input weight factor (material index). Location theory has for long underlined that a location is often influenced by the weighting of the industrial inputs. The higher the material index of an input the more important it is as a location factor. A yogurt pot can be considered a bulky product with more than 85% of its weight (milk and sugar) and 90% of the package (glass jars) being sourced regionally. Other inputs play a small, if not negligible role. From an input weight factor perspective, the concerned food supply chain appears much more optimal.
- Different location factors. Suppliers within a supply chain may have different location factors which may appear to be far from optimal in relation to their customers, but can be optimal in relation to their suppliers. Changing their location to optimize one supply chain (or simply one segment) could lead at the aggregate level to diseconomies for other supply chains.
- Economies of scale and regional specialization. The extension of food miles is in part reflective of emerging regional specializations in food production, many in developing countries where agribusiness is a growing source of employment and income. The benefits derived in terms of lower input costs and economies of scale may outweigh higher transport costs.

Consequently, the example of the yogurt pot as an environmentally damaging supply chain is mostly inaccurate and misleading. Striving to shorten supply chains may appear at first glance to be imminently desirable but must be considered within a wider context, namely the nature of the inputs and the location factors of the suppliers.

The time paradox

In logistics, time is often of the essence. By reducing the time of flows, the velocity of the distribution system is increased, and consequently, its efficiency. This is mainly achieved in the main by using the most polluting and least energy efficient transportation modes. The significant increase of air freight and trucking is partially the result of time constraints imposed by logistical activities. The time constraints are themselves the result of an increasing flexibility of industrial production systems and of the retailing sector. Logistics offers door-to-door (DTD) services, mostly coupled with just-in-time (JIT) strategies. Other modes cannot satisfy the requirements such a situation creates as effectively. This leads to a vicious circle; the more DTD and JIT strategies are applied, the further the negative environmental consequences of the traffic it creates (Figure 25.3). The slow steaming strategy pursued by maritime shipping

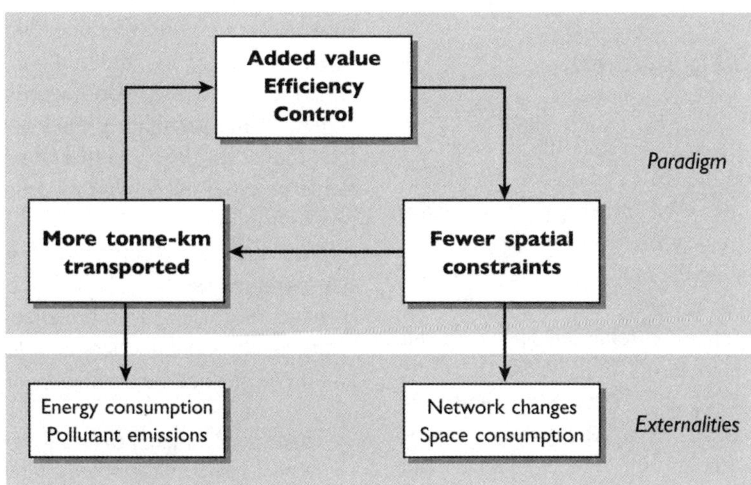

Figure 25.3 Environmental vicious circle of logistics

companies is further challenging time management within long distance supply chains.

Added value, efficiency and control are the main drivers of supply chain management. The search for added value enables to capture economic opportunities along the supply chain with activities related to consolidation, deconsolidation, transshipment and transloading. Efficiency drives the improvement of cost and performance attributes of the supply chain through better modal and intermodal options. Control insures reliability in terms of performance and costs along the supply chain undertaken through mergers and information technologies. The application of logistics involves a paradigm on freight distribution systems that results in two specific externalities:

- The first externality relates to spatial constraints. The more physical distribution is efficient, the less production, distribution and retailing activities are constrained by distance. This results in changes in the configuration of distribution networks and a higher level of space consumption by logistical activities.
- The second externality relates to the usage level of transportation. A less spatially constrained supply chain involves more ton-km of freight transported, both in terms of the number of trips and the average haul length. This is associated with higher level of energy consumption and correspondingly with more emissions.

The reliability paradox

At the heart of logistics is the overriding importance of service reliability. Its success is based upon the ability to deliver freight on time with the least breakage or damage. Logistics providers often realize these objectives by utilizing the modes that are perceived as being most reliable. The least polluting modes are generally regarded as being the least reliable in terms of on-time delivery, lack of breakage and safety. Ships and railways have inherited a reputation for poor customer satisfaction. For instance, the schedule reliability of container shipping is around 50%, implying that about half the time a container ship will not arrive at a port terminal at the scheduled day. Lower reliability levels are linked with lower levels of asset utilization and higher inventory levels, which is wasteful and indirectly damaging to the environment. The reliability of the logistics industry is built around air and truck shipments which are the two least environmentally-friendly modes.

The warehousing paradox

Logistics is an important factor promoting globalization and international flows of commerce. Modern logistics systems economies are based on the reduction of inventories, as the speed and reliability of deliveries removes the need to store and stockpile. Consequently, a reduction in warehousing demands is one of the advantages of logistics. This means, however, that inventories have been transferred to a certain degree to the transport system, especially to roads but also to terminals. Inventories are actually in transit, contributing still further to congestion and pollution. The environment and society, not the logistical operators, are assuming the external costs. Not all sectors exhibit this trend, however. In some industrial sectors, computers for example, there is a growing trend for vertical disintegration of the manufacturing process, in which extra links are added to the supply chain. Intermediate plants where some assembly is undertaken have been added between the manufacturer and consumer. While facilitating the customizing of the product for the consumer, it adds an additional external movement of products in the production line.

There has been a convergence in the use of transportation assets for logistical purposes, all of which are trying to rationalize scarce real estate assets. Containerization was an important driver in such flexibilities, which include:

- Inland ports. Facilities commonly designed in co-location with terminal infrastructures (particularly rail) and offering a wide array of logistical infrastructures and services.

- Inventory at terminal strategies. Consider using the storage capacity available at terminals as a temporary buffer within freight distribution systems as part of inventory management.
- Inventory in transit strategies. Consider using the storage capacity available while in the transport process. The mode thus becomes a mobile warehouse and part of inventory management strategies as long as the flows have a good level of reliability.

The information technologies paradox

Information technologies have led to new dimensions in retailing. One of the most dynamic markets is e-commerce. This is made possible by an integrated supply chain with data interchange between suppliers, assembly lines and freight forwarders. Even if for the online customers there is an appearance of a movement-free transaction, the distribution online transactions created may consume more energy than other retail activities. The distribution activities that have benefited the most from e-commerce are parcel-shipping companies, such as UPS, Federal Express or DHL, that rely solely on trucking and air transportation. Information technologies related to e-commerce applied to logistics can obviously have positive impacts. So once again, the situation may be seen as paradoxical.

It can be argued that the paradoxes of green logistics make it challenging for the logistics industry to become significantly greener. The internal inconsistencies between the goal of environmental sustainability and an industry that gives undue preference to road and air transport can be seen as being irreconcilable. Yet internal and external pressures promoting a more environmentally-friendly logistics industry appear to be inexorable. How the logistics industry has responded to the environmental imperatives is not unexpected, given its commercial and economic imperatives, particularly in view of the paradoxes it is facing.

A BLUEPRINT FOR GREEN LOGISTICS

Top-down approaches: Regulations

Pressures are mounting from a number of directions that are moving all actors and sectors in the economy in the direction of increasing regard for the environment. In some sectors this is already manifest, in others, such as the logistics industry, it is latent but quickly emerging (McKinnon et al., 2010). The issue is when and in what form it will be realized. Three scenarios are possible. While not mutually exclusive, they each present different approaches and implications:

- A top-down approach where 'greenness' is imposed on the logistic industry by government policies through regulations;
- A bottom-up approach where environmental improvements are coming from the industry itself through the adoption of best practices;
- A compromise between the government and industry, notably through certification schemes.

First is that government action will force a green agenda on the industry, in a top-down approach. Although this is the least desirable outcome for the logistics industry, it is already evident that government intervention and legislation are reaching ever more directly over environmental issues. In Europe there is a growing interest in charging for external costs, as the EU moves towards a "fair and efficient" pricing policy. A sharp increase in costs could have a more serious impact than a more gradual, phased-in tax. In North America there is a growing interest in road pricing, with the re-appearance of tolls on new highways and bridges built by the private sector, and by congestion pricing, especially in metropolitan areas.

Pricing is only one aspect of government intervention. Legislations controlling the movement of hazardous goods, reducing packaging waste, stipulating the recycled content of products, the mandatory collection and recycling of products are already evident in most jurisdictions. Indeed, it is such legislation that has given rise to the reverse logistics industry. Truck safety, driver education, limits on driver's time at the wheel, are among many types of government action with a potential to impact the logistics industry.

A difficulty with government intervention is that the outcomes are often unpredictable, and in an industry as complex as logistics, many could lead to unintended consequences. Environmentally-inspired policies may impact on freight and passenger traffic differentially, just as different modes may experience widely variable results of a common regulation. Issues concerning the greenness of logistics extend beyond transport regulations. The siting of terminals and warehouses are crucial to moving the industry towards the goal of sustainability, yet these are often under the land use and zoning control of lower levels of government whose environmental interests may be at variance with national and international bodies. A positive trend has been the joint planning and siting of logistics zones and intermodal terminals as co-located facilities.

Bottom-up approaches: reverse logistics

If a top-down approach appears inevitable, in some respects at least, a bottom-up solution would be the industry preference. Its leaders oppose leaving the future direction to be shaped by government action. There are several ways a bottom-up approach might come about. As with reverse logistics, these occur when the business interests of the industry match the imperatives of the environment. One such match is the concern of the logistics industry with empty movements, which ranges from empty trucking backhauls for regional freight distribution to the repositioning of empty containers across oceans. With the growing sophistication of fleet management and IT control over scheduling and routing, further gains are achievable. Another match involves fine tuning the routing and operations of freight transport systems with higher energy prices. The adoption of slow steaming strategies by maritime shipping companies is using the rationale of environmentalism to reduce the fuel consumption and improve the utilization of their ship assets.

Less predictable, but with a much greater potential impact on the greenness of the industry, are possible attitudinal changes within logistics and without. These changes are comparable of that which has already occurred in recycling. There has emerged striking public support for domestic recycling. This has been extended by some firms in successfully marketing their compliance and adoption of green strategies. Firms have found that by advertising their friendliness towards the environment and their compliance with environmental standards, they can obtain an edge in the marketplace over their competitors. Traditionally, price and quality characteristics formed the basis of choice, but because environment preservation is seen as desirable in general, greenness can become a competitive advantage. Ultimately, pressure from within the industry can lead to greater environmental awareness and respect. Companies that stand apart will lose out because purchasers will demand environmental compliance.

A middle-ground: certifications

Somewhere between the bottom-up and top-down approaches are the moves being implemented with environmental management systems. Although governments are involved in varying degrees, a number of voluntary systems are in place, notably ISO 14001 and EMAS (Environmental Management and Audit System). In these systems firms receive certification on the basis of establishing an environmental quality control tailored to that firm, and the setting up of environmental monitoring and accounting procedures. Obtaining certification is seen as evidence of the firm's commitment to the environment, and is frequently used as a public relations, marketing, and government relations advantage (Rondinelli and Vastag,

2000). This represents a fundamental commitment of the corporation to engage in environmental assessment and audit that represent a significant modification of traditional practices, in which efficiency, quality and cost evaluations prevailed.

Of the three possible directions by which a greener logistics industry may emerge, it is realistic to consider that they will concomitantly help shape the industry of the future. Although there is a clear trend in policy guidelines to make the users pay the full costs of using the infrastructures, logistical activities have largely escaped these initiatives. The focus of much environmental policy is on private cars (e.g. emission controls, gas mixtures and pricing). While there are increasingly strict regulations being applied to air transport (noise and emissions), the degree of control over trucking, rail and maritime modes is less. For example, diesel fuel is significantly cheaper than gasoline in many jurisdictions, despite the negative environmental implications of the diesel engine. Yet trucks contribute on average 7 times more per vehicle-km to nitrogen oxides emissions than cars and 17 times more for particulate matter. The trucking industry has been able to avoid the bulk of environmental externalities it creates, notably in North America.

APPLYING GREEN LOGISTICS TO SUPPLY CHAINS

Green strategies

Although in the past the environment was not a major preoccupation or priority in the industry itself, the last decades have shown a remarkable change as green logistics became increasingly part of the supply chain management discourse and practices. The standard themes of materials management and physical distribution can be expanded with an additional focus on strategies able to mitigate the paradoxical nature of green logistics:

- Product design and production planning. The conventional focus of product design and development is the improvement of its commercial and competitive attributes such as price, quality, features and performance. This process is common for electronic goods as each new generation of a product (computers, phones, televisions) is quantitatively and qualitatively better. Products are increasingly being considered from a supply chain perspective, namely their sourcing and distribution where the concern is about designing or redesigning supply chains that are more environmentally friendly. This can involve the physical characteristics of the product itself (lighter, alternative materials) or production processes that allow for a higher transport density of parts. Suppliers that are closer (near sourcing) may be considered even if they may be more expensive, so that transportation costs can be reduced. A decision can also be made to preferably contract suppliers that have demonstrated that the parts and resources they provide have been procured in a sustainable manner.
- Physical distribution. Concerns strategies to reduce the environmental impacts of physical distribution, namely the transportation and warehousing processes. It could involve the usage of facilities that have been certified as environmentally efficient (Leadership in Energy & Environmental Design – LEED® – is a globally recognized certification scheme) as well as carriers abiding to environmentally friendly principles. Preferences could also be placed on delaying shipments until a sufficient load factor is reached. The usage of alternative modes and fuels is increasingly applied, particularly for city logistics. For long distance travel a modal shift to rail and economies of scale on maritime shipping are considered strategies that may lead to greener supply chains.
- Materials management. Concerns reducing the environmental impacts related to the manufacturing of goods in all their stages of production along a supply chain. A salient strategy involves better packaging to increase the load density as well as to reduce materials consumption and waste. Low impact materials, particularly recycled resources, can be preferred as industrial inputs. As products, or their components, tend to be increasingly recyclable, waste management strategies are being pursued to insure that the end products are either discarded properly or, preferably, being recycled to other uses.

- Reverse distribution. Concerns activities and movements related to taking back consumed goods as well as waste to be recycled or discarded. It has opened up new market opportunities over specific aspects of materials management (mostly recycling and waste disposal) and physical distribution (collection channels). Here the environmental benefits are derived rather than direct. The transportation industry itself does not necessarily present a greener face; indeed, in a literal sense reverse logistics adds further to the traffic load and facilities required to handle them. The manufacturers and domestic waste producers are the ones achieving the environmental credit.

Specific logistical strategies

While costs have always been an important driver of supply chain management strategies, the rising cost of energy has been a strong incentive to rationalize supply chains and indirectly improve green supply chain management. Depending on the objective, there are several strategies that are being adopted to mitigate energy and environmental constraints:

- Shipping less. The setting of demand responsive systems where supply chains are tightly integrated so that the goods being delivered are the outcome of an expressed demand. A better level of order fulfillment tends to reduce returns.
- Changing suppliers. Reassessing sourcing both at the global and domestic levels. This is best done if a comprehensive array of logistics costs is considered, particularly in light of energy and environmental constraints. While a supplier may appear to offer the lowest cost, if factors such as higher transport costs, more inventory in transit, longer response times and a higher level of unreliability are considered, alternative, but closer, suppliers could be more advantageous.
- Shipping scheduling. Adapt the scheduling of flows to insure a greater level of utilization of existing transportation and warehousing assets. By allowing greater shipping time and outside rush periods the same assets can be used more rationally, which conveys energy and environmental benefits.
- Efficient packaging. Reduce the shipment volume of the same load by using less packaging or by changing how a good is packaged. This results in higher transport densities. For instance, the introduction of the second generation of iPads in 2011, a popular tablet computer, involved a reduction in its packaging dimensions with a box that is 10% lighter (mostly from lighter product design) and has 18% less volume (mostly from better packaging). This is an important consideration for air shipping since the final assembly of the product was taking place in Shenzhen, China.
- Modal shift. Use a mode or a route that is more energy and environmentally efficient, which can involve a change in the routing of cargo. Rail is the logical alternative to trucking over longer distances, but short sea shipping can be suitable for coastal regions (Mulligan and Lombardo, 2006).

The spatial footprint of freight distribution

Applying green logistics to supply chains must also consider the network and spatial footprint of freight distribution. The hub structures supporting many logistical systems result in a land take that is exceptional (McKinnon, 2009). Land requirements for freight distribution take two major dimensions:

- Transportation. Both modes and terminals consume space for the setting of their respective infrastructures. The land take of infrastructures such as roads and ports can be extensive, particularly in metropolitan areas that are points of convergence of global material flows. The true transportation land take for freight distribution is difficult to assess as many infrastructures, such as roads and airports are dominantly used for passenger movements and can be considered as shared facilities.
- Storage. Include various facilities to hold freight in inventory such as bulk storage facilities (e.g. oil reservoirs or grain silos) and warehousing facilities for break-bulk. Distribution centers are particularly space-consuming as a wide array of added value activities are performed, including consolidation and deconsolidation, cross-docking and storage. The latter can also require specialized facilities as for cold storage.

Airports, seaports and rail terminals are among the largest consumers of land in urban areas. For many airports and seaports the costs of development are so large that they require subsidies from local, regional and national governments. The dredging of channels in ports, the provision of sites, and operating expenses are rarely completely reflected in user costs. In the United States, for example, local dredging costs were nominally to come out of a harbor improvement tax but this has been ruled unconstitutional and channel maintenance remains under the authority of the US Corps of Army Engineers. In Europe, national and regional government subsidies are used to assist infrastructure and superstructure provision. The trend in logistics towards hub formation is clearly not green as it incites the convergence of traffic flows and their externalities within a well-defined area. On the positive side, this confers opportunities to mitigate these environmental externalities since they are focused and clearly identifiable.

Improvement of logistics flows and performance required the setting of new facilities in suburban areas, a trend that has been labeled as "logistics sprawl" (Dablanc, 2009). In turn, this process is related to additional land take and a level of disorganization of freight flows within a metropolitan area. The setting of logistics zones is an attempt at providing a more coherent setting for distribution centers, including shared facilities such as parking areas and intermodal terminals. They confer the advantage of being able to more effectively minimize the impacts of freight distribution on surrounding areas such as with direct access ramps to highways (less local intrusion) or the setting of buffers to mitigate noise and emissions. There is an array of rationale and settings for logistics zones and correspondingly environmental mitigation strategies. Still, the environmental impacts of distribution centers remain a daunting issue to mitigate.

CONCLUSION: GREENER LOGISTICS

There is growing evidence that green logistics results in increased supply chain performance, particularly since greenness favors an integrated perspective about supply chains (Rao and Holt, 2005). The actors involved in logistical operations have a strong bias to perceive green logistics as a means to internalize cost savings, while avoiding the issue of external costs. The top environmental priority is commonly reducing packaging and waste. The rise in energy prices is conferring additional incentives for supply chain managers to improve upon logistics and will correspondingly push energy and emissions to the forefront. These observations support the paradoxical relationship between logistics and the environment that reducing costs does not necessarily reduce environmental impacts. By overlooking significant environmental issues, such as pollution, congestion, resource depletion, means that the logistics industry is still not very green. Green logistics remains an indirect outcome of policies and strategies aimed at improving the cost, efficiency and reliability of supply chains.

While a decade ago we concluded that logistics was far from being green (Rodrigue et al., 2001), the situation has improved, implying that greener forms of logistics are being implemented. A key aspect of more environmentally friendly freight distribution systems concerns city logistics where the "last mile" in freight distribution takes place as well as a large share of reverse logistics activities. Still, even in this context the driving force is not directly environmental and sustainability issues, but factors linked with costs, time, reliability, warehousing and information technologies. This continues to underline that green logistics is the most effectively achieved when commercial and environmental interests are converging.

REFERENCES

Banister, D. (2008) "The sustainable mobility paradigm", *Transport Policy*, Vol. 15, No. 2, pp. 73–80.

Black, W.R. (2010) *Sustainable Transportation: Problems and Solutions*, New York: The Guilford Press.

Böge, S. (1995) "The well-travelled yogurt pot: lessons for new freight transport policies and regional production", *World Transport Policy & Practice*, Vol. 1, pp. 7–11.

Dablanc, L. (2009) *Freight Transport: a Key for the New Urban Economy*, World Bank, Freight Transport for Development: a Policy Toolkit.

Hawks, K. (2006) "What is reverse logistics?", *Reverse Logistics Magazine*, Winter/Spring.

McKinnon, A. (2009) "The present and future land requirements of logistical activities", *Land Use Policy*, Vol. 26S, pp. S293–S301.

McKinnon, A., S. Cullinane, M. Browne and A. Whiteing (eds) (2010) *Green Logistics: Improving the Environmental Sustainability of Logistics*, London: Kogan Page.

Mulligan, R.F. and G.A. Lombardo (2006) "Short sea shipping: alleviating the environmental impact of economic growth", *WMU Journal of Maritime Affairs*, Vol. 5, No. 2, pp. 181–194.

Rao, P. and D. Holt, (2005) "Do green supply chains lead to competitiveness and economic performance?", *International Journal of Operations & Production Management*, Vol. 25, No. 9, pp. 898–916.

Rodrigue, J.-P., B. Slack and C. Comtois (2001) "Green logistics", in A.M. Brewer, K.J. Button and D.A. Hensher (eds) *The Handbook of Logistics and Supply-Chain Management*, Handbooks in Transport #2, London: Pergamon/Elsevier, pp. 339–351.

Rondinelli, D. and G. Vastag (2000) "Panacea, common sense, or just a label? The value of ISO 14001 environmental management systems", *European Management Journal*, Vol. 18, No. 5, pp. 499–510.

Schiller, P.L., E.C. Bruun and J.R. Kenworthy (2010) *An Introduction to Sustainable Transportation*, London: Earthscan.

US Environmental Protection Agency (2000) *The Lean and Green Supply Chain: A Practical Guide for Materials Managers and Supply Chain Managers to Reduce Costs and Improve Environmental Performance*, Environmental Accounting Project, EPA 742-R-00–001.

World Commission on Environment and Development (1987) *Our Common Future*, Oxford: Oxford University Press.

Index